Hiking and Expl

Paria River

Including: The Story of John D. Lee and the
Mountain Meadows Massacre

5th Edition

Michael R. Kelsey

Kelsey Publishing

456 E. 100 N.
Provo, Utah, USA, 84606-3208
Tele. & Fax 801-373-3327
Email Addresses--one of these should work:
kelsey@canyoneering.com (Best)
kelsey@broadweave.net
(Identify yourself or your email with the name of a canyon or mountain)

For updated information about other guidebooks by Michael R. Kelsey,
please go to the website:
kelseyguidebooks.com

Other websites which may have updated information
on related canyons or hikes are:
climb-utah.com (Shane Burrows)
toddshikingguide.com (Todd & Stephanie Martin)
ajroadtrips.com (Ryan Cornia)
jonjasper.com (Jon Jasper)
adventure-geek.com (AJ Pastula)
http://groups.yahoo.com/group/canyons/

First Edition November 1987
Updated Edition September 1991
3rd Edition January 1998
4th Edition July 2004
5th Edition May 2010
Copyright © 1987, 1991, 1998, 2004 & **2010** Michael R. Kelsey All Rights Reserved
Library of Congress Catalog Card Number 2010900127
ISBN 0-944510-26-4; New 13 digit ISBN 978-944510-26-1

Primary Distributor
All of Michael R. Kelsey's books are sold by this distributor. A
list of his titles is in the back of this book.
Brigham Distribution, 110 South, 800 West, Brigham City, Utah, 84302, Tele. 435-723-6611, Fax 435-723-6644, Email brigdist@sisna.com.

Most of Kelsey's books are sold by these distributors.
Alpenbooks, 4206 Chennault Beach Road, Suite B1, Mukilteo, Washington, USA, 98275, Website alpenbooks.com, Email cserve@alpenbooks.com, Tele. 425-493-6380, or 800-290-9898.
Books West, 11111 East, 53rd Avenue, Suite A, Denver, Colorado, USA, 80239-2133, Tele. 303-449-5995, or 800-378-4188, Fax 303-449-5951, Website bookswest.net.
Liberty Mountain, 4375 West 1980 South, Suite 100, Salt Lake City, Utah, 84104, Tele. 800-578-2705 or 801-954-0741, Fax 801-954-0766, Website libertymountain.com, Email sales@libertymountain.com.
Treasure Chest Books, 451 North, Bonita Avenue, Tucson, Arizona, USA, 85745, Tele. 520-623-9558, or 800-969-9558, Website treasurechestbooks.com, Email info@rionuevo.com.

Some of Kelsey's books are sold by the following distributors.
Canyonlands Publications, 4860 North, Ken Morey Drive, Bellemont, Arizona, USA, 86015, Tele. 928-779-3888, or 800-283-1983, Fax 928-779-3778, Email info@clpbooks.net.
High Peak Books, Box 703, Wilson, Wyoming, USA, 83014, Tele. 307-739-0147.
Rincon Publishing, 1913 North Skyline Drive, Orem, Utah, 84097, Tele. 801-377-7657, Fax 801-356-2733, RinconPub@UtahTrails.com.
Recreational Equipment, Inc. (R.E.I.), 1700 45th Street East, Sumner, Washington, USA, 98390, Website rei.com, Mail Orders Tele. 800-426-4840 (or check at any of their local stores).
Online--Internet: amazon.com; adventuroustravelers.com; btol.com (Baker-Taylor); Ingrams.com; Bdaltons.com; borders.com (teamed with amazon.com).

For the **UK and Europe**, and the rest of the world contact: **Cordee,** 3a De Montfort Street, Leicester, England, UK, LE1 7HD, Website cordee.co.uk, Tele. Inter+44-116-254-3579, Fax Inter+44-116-247-1176.

All fotos by the author, unless otherwise stated.
All maps, charts, and cross sections drawn by the author.

Front Cover   Location of Fotos

1. Wahweap Toadstools
2. The Wave, Coyote Buttes
3. Middle Reservoir, Sand Hills
4. Buckskin Gulch

Back Cover   Location of Fotos

5. The Cockscomb Ridge & Valley, and Cottonwood Wash
6. Northwest Fork of Deer Creek
7. Rock Art--Best Panel, Coyote Buttes
8. White Pockets, Sand Hills
9. Bryce Canyon National Park
10. Yellow Rock, The Cockscomb

Printed by Press Media
1601 West 820 North
Provo, UT 84601
www.press-media.com

Printed on recycled paper

Table of Contents

Acknowledgments

Many people helped with information for this book, but special thanks should go to the following. The most important person, at least for the first 2 editions, was the late Rod Schipper (killed in a car wreck in September, 1997), more commonly known as "Skip". Until 1990, he was the BLM employee who lived and worked at the Paria Ranger Station. He began that job in 1980 and knew the lower Paria River Canyon better than anyone. Skip spent hours proofreading the hiking section of the first 2 editions of this book. See the small memorial to Skip in front of the Paria Ranger Station & Visitor Center.

Besides Skip, residents of Kanab the author interviewed were: Calvin C. Johnson, Jeff Johnson, Leola Scheonfeld, the late Merrill MacDonald, Mason Meeks, Merrill Johnson and Dunk Findlay; also, the late Mel Schoppman and Bill Leach of Page, Arizona, and George Fisher of Las Vegas. There was also Bryce Canyon ranger Nate Inouye, plus Gayle L. Pollock of the Natural History Association; St. George BLM employees Tom Folks, Mike Small & Jennifer Jack; also the head of the newly-created Vermilion Cliffs National Monument which is headquartered out of St. George, Becky Hammond; plus BLM employees in Kanab Pete Kilborne, Bill Booker, Mary Dewitz & Mary Cassidy. Mike Salamanca, the one who replaced Skip as the Paria Ranger, proofread and helped update the 3rd Edition.

In the Bryce Valley towns, the author interviewed Ken Goulding Sr., Layton Smith, Marian Clark, Joe Dunham, Kay Clark and Herm Pollock (all deceased), and Ralph & Jack Chynoweth, Bob Ott, George Thompson, and Wallace Ott. Nearly all of these people were in their 70's or older when interviewed, while Marian Clark & Wallace Ott, were in their 90's; therefore lots of good information was gathered about the canyons, trails & old roads, early-day ranchers and oil wells.

Others who contributed with information or fotographs for the 4th Edition were the late Ken Goulding, Jr., Don Mangum, Fred Syrett, Charley Francisco, Ferrell Brinkerhoff, Desmond Twitchell, Mae Pollock Chynoweth, Jim Ott, Thayne Smith, Twila Mangum Irwin, Dale Mangum, Darrell Blackwell, Joe Thompson, Don Chynoweth, Mary Jane Chynoweth Fuller, LaKay Clark Quilter, Merrilyn Johnson Cornell, Tom H. Morris, JR Jones, Lula Chynoweth Moore, Iris Smith Bushnell, Afton Pollock, Hobart Feltner, Rhoda Henderson Shafer and Kay Sturdevant.

Here's a list of those who contributed to the **5th Edition**, which includes a much more comprehensive history of the Sand Hills & Angora goats. Most of these people live in Fredonia, Arizona (just south of Kanab and the Utah-Arizona state line) or Kanab, Utah. The most important source of information was Trevor Leach of Kanab; he was the oldest man around who had knowledge about Angora goats in the Sand Hills. Also, the late Bessie Averett Ford Mackelprang, Bob Ford, Dixon Spendlove, Brent Robinson, Calvin C. Johnson again, & grandson Tyson Johnson, Charles D. Hepworth of Page, Christina Hamblin Fox, Danny & Melvin Mognett, Molly Mognett Houston, Dennis F. Judd, Dianna Glover, Grace Laws Jensen of St. George, Hollis Jones from Arizona, Ira M. Schoppman of Cedar City, Jackie Rife, Jay Findlay of Snellville, Georgia, John Rich, Ken Glover, Lanny Talbot, Lynn Findlay II of Salt Lake, Mark Hamblin, Richard Cothern, Richard & Marvin Rider, Ron Glover, Ron Henderson, Roy Mackelprang, Rosco (Rock) Burgoyne, JR Jones and son Justin Jones, Thayne & Georgia Smith, Jeff Frost, Harold R. Bowman III of Salt Lake, and Whit Bunting & John Herron of the St. George BLM.

The Author

The author, who was born in 1943, experienced his earliest years of life in eastern Utah's Uinta Basin, first on a farm east of Myton, then in or near Roosevelt. In 1954, the family moved to Provo and he attended Provo High School and later Brigham Young University, where he earned a B.S. degree in Sociology. Shortly thereafter, he discovered that was the wrong subject, so he attended the University of Utah, where he received his Master of Science degree in Geography (minoring in Geology), finishing classes in June, 1970.

It was then real life began, for on June 9, 1970, he put a pack on his back and started traveling for the first time. Since then he has seen 223 countries, republics, islands, or island groups. All this wandering has resulted in self-publishing 17 books, some of which are in their 4th & 5th editions. Here are his books as of 2010, listed in the order they were first published: *Climber's and Hiker's Guide to the World's Mountains & Volcanos (4th Edition); Utah Mountaineering Guide (3rd Edition); China on Your Own, and the Hiking Guide to China's Nine Sacred Mountains (3rd Edition) Out of Print; Non-Technical Canyon Hiking Guide to the Colorado Plateau (5th Edition); Hiking and Exploring Utah's San Rafael Swell (3rd Edition); Hiking and Exploring Utah's Henry Mountains and Robbers Roost (3rd Edition); Hiking and Exploring the Paria River (5th Edition); Hiking and Climbing in the Great Basin National Park (Wheeler Peak, Nevada) Out of Print; Boater's Guide to Lake Powell (5th Edition); Climbing and Exploring Utah's Mt. Timpanogos,* **Out of Print (but will be Reprinted someday);** *River Guide to Canyonlands National Park & Vicinity,* **Out of Print (but may be Reprinted someday);** *Hiking, Biking and Exploring Canyonlands National Park & Vicinity,* **Out of Print (but may be Reprinted someday);** *The Story of Black Rock, Utah; Hiking, Climbing and Exploring Western Utah's Jack Watson's Ibex Country; and the Technical Slot Canyon Guide to the Colorado Plateau, 2nd Edition.*

He also helped his mother Venetta Bond Kelsey write and publish a book about the one-horse town she was born & raised in, *Life on the Black Rock Desert--A History of Clear Lake, Utah,* **Out of Print (but at some time in the future will be Reprinted).**

Introduction: Hiking the Paria River

The Paria River begins at Bryce Canyon National Park and nearby high plateaus, and flows almost due south across the Utah-Arizona state line ending at the Colorado River and Lee's Ferry. After the Grand Canyon, Zion Narrows and the Escalante River system, this river basin has more visitors than any other canyon drainage on the Colorado Plateau. If you like narrow canyons, including the single best slot canyon in the world (the Buckskin Gulch), this is the place for you. You can take day-hikes in some of the shorter tributaries, or go on a week-long marathon walk in the lower end of the Paria Canyon. The northern half of the area covered by this book is now included in the western part of the Grand Staircase-Escalante National Monument (GSENM).

The Paria River drainage is located about halfway between Kanab, Utah, and Page, Arizona, and right in the middle of some of the best hiking parts of the Colorado Plateau. To the west is Kanab, St. George and Zion National Park; to the north is Richfield, Panguitch, and the Bryce Valley towns of Tropic, Cannonville, and Henrieville; to the northeast is Capitol Reef National Park, Torrey, Boulder and Escalante; to the south is Flagstaff, and to the southeast is Page and Lake Powell.

Local Towns and Facilities

In the last few years, since tourism has been so important to the local economies, better accommodations and roads have been built. Here's a rundown on what's where in the immediate area. Population figures are from **2000**.

Page, Arizona (population 6809) This town was created to house & accommodate the workers who built Glen Canyon Dam across the Colorado River creating Lake Powell. Today it's the southern gateway to Lake Powell and the local headquarters for the National Park Service, which administers Glen Canyon National Recreational Area. Page has 2 supermarkets, a good shopping center in the middle of town, and a new shopping mall south of town. Page is full of tourists, as well as Navajos from the reservation, and slows down only in about 3 months of winter. There are many motels and other facilities, and a pretty good place to shop for about everything.

Kanab (population 3564) Kanab is a little smaller than Page, and it's more quiet--mainly because the reservation and lake are farther away. Kanab has 2 supermarkets, plus numerous convenience stores. Its facilities are similar to those of Page, with many motels, gas stations and restaurants. Kanab is the Kane County seat, and has 2 book stores, an interesting museum, an airport, and golf course. Kanab has been the movie capital of southern Utah and is the jumping-off point to the north rim of the Grand Canyon, which is open from about mid-May until late October. Kanab has a BLM field office (north end of town), the headquarters for the newly created GSENM (in the center of Kanab), and a new GSENM visitor center just east of town next to the golf course.

Panguitch (population 1623) This town is located just northwest of Bryce Canyon National Park and is half the size of Kanab. Panguitch is the Garfield County seat and has moderately good facilities, including one small supermarket, and many motels and restaurants. Panguitch still depends on farming and ranching for support, but in the warmer half of the year it's busy with tourists.

Bryce Canyon Facilities Along the highway between Panguitch and Bryce Canyon National Park, are many motels, convenience stores, gas stations and independent campsites. On the Paunsaugunt Plateau, and just north downhill from the entrance to the park, is Ruby's Inn. This is a huge complex, with gas station & garage facilities, store (including curios and guidebooks), restaurant, laundry center, campground, horseback rides, a rodeo 3 nights a week in season, and helicopter rides into the park. The Bryce Canyon airport is just north of Ruby's Inn, and they have fixed-wing planes for tourist flights. Some of these facilities are now open year-round.

Inside the national park are 2 campgrounds, open in summers only. Bryce also has an historic old lodge and cabins for rent, and they're open from early April through October.

Tropic (population 508) This is the biggest town in Bryce Valley which is just east of Bryce Canyon N.P., and it's where the area's high school is located. Tropic has a gas station along with a small supermarket, several motels plus bed & breakfast establishments, a burger & malt shop (it's open from about Easter until after the deer hunt, at the end of October); and one garage, the only one in the valley. The burger stand, gas station and motels are open on Sundays, everything else is closed. As time goes on, Tropic is becoming more dependent on tourism--and less dependent on farming & ranching.

Cannonville (population 148) This small town in Bryce Valley is located at the junction of Highway 12 and the paved road running to Kodachrome Basin, and the Cottonwood Wash Road. Cannonville has one business complex called the Grand Staircase Inn. This is a motel, store, restaurant and gas station, all in one large building. One block west of that is a KOA Campground, and a block south is the GSENM Visitor Center which is right on the road to Kodachrome Basin. This visitor center was first opened in 2003; it's closed in winter--Mid-November to roughly Mid-March (?).

Kodachrome Basin State Park In 1987, Bob Ott and family from Cannonville, opened a small camper's store in the state park just south of the campground. They now have full-service cabins, a new camper's store, plus horseback & wagon rides, and cater to senior citizens and campers. The campground has showers and a dump station. There's now a paved road all the way from Cannonville to Kodachrome Basin, and throughout the park.

Henrieville (population 159) Henrieville, which is also in Bryce Valley, no longer has any retail businesses in town. About the only public buildings are the church & post office.

Escalante (population 818) A town full of ranchers, farmers, former sawmill workers, and a growing number of BLM, Forest Service and National Park Service personnel. It has at least 3 gas stations, several motels, 2 small supermarkets, several restaurants, and one burger stand, which does good business in the spring, summer and fall, with the hikers heading into the Escalante River country. There's

5

a new multiagency visitor center on the west end of town, plus nearby offices for the BLM, Forest Service and the National Park Service.

Road Report

For the most part, access to most of the canyons in this book is reasonably good. If you're going down the Lower Paria River Gorge, you're in luck; you only have to drive about 3 kms on a graveled, all-weather road, and you're at the White House Trailhead. At the bottom end of the river, which is Lee's Ferry, you'll be on pavement all the way. For the rest of the hikes, with the exception of those inside Bryce Canyon National Park, you'll have to do some driving on dirt or sandy roads, but as a general rule, most of the hikes featured in this book are fairly easy to get to with an ordinary car in dry weather.

Skutumpah Road This is a main link between the little community of Johnson or Johnson Valley, located about 16 kms (10 miles) due east of Kanab; and the Bryce Valley towns of Cannonville, Henrieville and Tropic. The Skutumpah Road itself begins at the head of Johnson Canyon, where the road divides and the pavement ends; at that point one road goes northwest to Alton, while the Skutumpah Road heads northeast to Cannonville. It's 99.5 kms (61.8 miles) from Kanab to Cannonville, first along Highway 89, then up Johnson Canyon, and finally along the Skutumpah Road.

The road up Johnson Canyon is paved up to the Alton--Skutumpah Junction, then it's graveled & well-maintained up to about the Deer Springs Ranch. After that it's maintained and graded, but made out of whatever material the road passes over. In places it's just ordinary dirt; other places it's gravely, and still other places it's made of clay. When it rains only lightly, it seldom affects the road. All you have to do is wait 'till the sun hits it a few minutes, and away you go. **When heavy rains soak the area, it may be a one or two-day wait in the warmer season before this road is passable; maybe a week's wait--or longer--during the winter season.**

For the most part, this road is closed in winter, but 4WD's sometimes do it, especially during dry spells, or in the morning hours when the road bed is frozen. However, on the dugway just south and above Willis Creek is a seep next to the road. This sometimes makes the road icy in winter, and 4WD's occasionally slide off. For the most part, the Skutumpah Road is open for all traffic from sometime in March or the first part of April through mid-November, but each year is different. Because there are a number of ranches (and in recent years summer homes) along this road, it's well-maintained, and carries up to 40-50 cars a day during the warm season when it's dry. Expect traffic to increase because of the newly created national monument.

Cottonwood Wash Road The Cottonwood Wash Road runs south out of Cannonville, to and past Kodachrome Basin State Park, to Grosvenor Arch, down the Cockscomb Valley (Cottonwood Wash or Canyon), and eventually to Highway 89, at a point between mile posts 17 & 18.

The Cottonwood Wash Road was built in 1957 by a cooperative effort organized by then 72-year-old **Sam Pollock** of Tropic, who wasn't paid a dime for his efforts. It included people from Bryce Valley, Escalante and Antimony. That group of people wanted a shortcut to the Lake Powell area to increase tourism in their own little area.

For the job, Pollock leased a bulldozer from the Soil Conservation Service and it was operated by Harvey Liston; a road grader was borrowed from Garfield Country, and it was driven by Loral Barton; Byron Davis donated a compressor and helped run it (it was used for only 9 days, and they blasted in only 2 places). Doyle Clark also helped on the operation. It took 100 days for planning, engineering and construction, but only 70 days to complete once they got rolling. The project was started on June 28, and completed in early October of 1957. A dedication ceremony was held at Rush Bed Spring.

The state of Utah had surveyed 2 routes for a road to Page and the Glen Canyon Dam. They chose the route east from Kanab because it was cheaper and less complicated to build. The other more direct route through Cannonville and Cottonwood Wash would have cost $9.5 million. The road Sam Pollock built cost $5500. They got the money to build it from Garfield County, and from donations & sales of various kinds. Today it's a maintained county road.

That part of the Cottonwood Wash Road running from Cannonville to Kodachrome Basin is now paved. East of the Kodachrome Basin Turnoff (KBT), the road is made of sand, dirt and/or clay and in good weather is used by maybe 200-300 cars daily. Expect traffic to increase because of the new GSENM.

2009 Road Update: Kane County and the Monument BLM have been squabbling over wilderness areas and what constitutes a road or cow trail, and other such nonsense (finances may have been a factor too?), so in the summer of 2009, roads all over the county were the worst this writer has ever seen. If traveling the Cottonwood Wash Road, first get a road report from any of the visitor centers.

For the most part, this is a warm weather, summertime road, as there are slick spots in places whenever it rains hard, making it impassable. When it's wet, not even 4WD's can make it! The spots that become extremely slick are made of the gray-colored clay beds of the Tropic Shale that are in the middle and lower end of the canyon. Whenever it rains hard, water flows across the road because there are few bridges or culverts, and no barrow pits or proper drainage. After floods, and after it dries a few days, a Kane County road crew out of Kanab (Tele. 435-644-5312) has to grade it again and again. Don't expect this road to be upgraded in the near future because it's in Kane County, and those people want tourists to drive through Kanab to reach Bryce Canyon National Park and Bryce Valley.

Nipple Ranch Road This is a maintained county road (except in 2009) to the Nipple Ranch just northwest of Mollies Nipple. It begins at Highway 89, just east of **mile post 37**, and runs north to an old oil well drill site north of Kitchen Canyon called Oil Well Hill. This is a graded road, but it gradually deteriorates the further north you drive. In its northern parts just west of Mollies Nipple, there are several big sand traps. If you don't have a 4WD, forget going over the pass and down to the Nipple Ranch. Beyond that pass, there can be deep sand for 2-3 kms across the bottom of upper Kitchen Canyon. Because of the sand, this is one of the few roads which will be easier and safer to drive if the surface is wet, because sand sets-up and becomes more firm when wet. This road will get you close to the middle part of the Upper Paria River Gorge, plus Deer Creek and surrounding canyons.

House Rock Valley Road This maintained county road runs from Highway 89 just west of The Cockscomb (between mile posts 25 & 26), south to Highway 89A (between mile posts 565 & 566) where an old ranch (formerly a store & gas station) called **House Rock**, is located. This is the approach road

6

to the Buckskin Gulch and Wire Pass Trailheads, and to the several entry points to Coyote Buttes and the Sand Hills or Paria Plateau. The road runs for 48.1 kms (29.9 miles), from highway to highway. Normally it's open almost year-round, but in winter, or right after heavy rains, it will be slick in places. In recent years the state of Arizona has improved its half of the road by hauling in gravel to cover the clay beds, most of which are near the Utah-Arizona line (Arizona has made a campground immediately south of the state line). Crews in Utah usually work this road over in April each year, or when there's a little moisture in the area. It's periodically closed during and right after flash floods. During the warmer half of the year it has moderately heavy traffic (including cars) for such an out-of-the-way road.

Pahreah Road The road to the Old Pahreah townsite and the Paria Movie Set leaves Highway 89 between mile posts 30 & 31 about halfway between Page & Kanab. This is a good 10 km (6 mile) road, which is well-used in the warmer half of the year. In winter it may be slick in spots, because most of it runs along the Moenkopi clay beds. It is definitely impassable during or just after heavy rains, but ordinarily it's a good road for all vehicles.

Cedar Mountain Road This road leaves Highway 89 between mile posts 17 & 18, right across the highway from the beginning of the Cottonwood Wash Road, but heads south, then east to the top of East Clark Bench, Flat Top and Cedar Mountain. This is the area north of the Lower Paria River Gorge, and this road gives access to the north rim of that canyon. This is a sandy road all the way, but it's graded occasionally up to the communications facility near where the road passes under the power lines. After that it gets even more sandy and you'll normally need a HCV & 4WD to successfully get through the sandier places along a loop on top of Cedar Mountain. Wet conditions makes this road better because it's made of mostly sand.

Roads in the Sand Hills For tips on how to drive on **SANDY ROADS** in the Paria River Country, especially the **SAND HILLS** (Paria Plateau), see the chapter, **Introduction: Driving, Touring & Fotography in the Sand Hills,** page 218. That part explains how to drive in very sandy conditions.

Emergency Provisions for your Car

Everyone reading this book should remember that once you leave the paved highways, some parts of the Paria River Country are very isolated. Special care should be taken in planning for a worse-case emergency situation. Perhaps the thing you need most is a **reliable vehicle**, one you can depend on. Besides that, here is a list of things everyone should have in their vehicle before venturing into remote areas. Take a **full tank of fuel**, and depending on where you're going and the size of your fuel tank, maybe extra fuel. Also, take a few simple **tools**, plus a **tow rope** or **chain, battery jumper cable, shovel, tire pump & gauge, extra oil, matches** or **cigarette lighters**, some kind of **first aid kit, tire chains for winter driving**, and a **good spare tire** (check the air pressure before leaving home).

Also, take more **food** than you think you'll need, and if you're heading to a far away place, especially in hot summer weather, take lots of **water and/or liquids**. This writer is usually alone and during hot weather and in remote places, he starts out with as much as 35-40 liters of water, fruit juice and soda pop. That's about 10 gallons. In summer heat you'll drink about 3-4 times more than in the cooler months. Also, consider taking more clothing than you think you'll need. In spring or fall, weather can turn from summer to winter in a matter of hours. Also, always let someone know exactly where you're going and when you expect to return. The main thing to remember is, **GO PREPARED** for any problem that might arise!

Off Road Vehicles

Perhaps the most contentious issue on public lands policy involves the use of **off road vehicles (ORV's)**. These come in all sizes & shapes, from **motorcycles** to all terrain vehicles (**ATV's**) to **4WD's** of all kinds (pickups & SUV's). They're now everywhere on our public lands and running around free as birds; and no one seems to know what to do about it. These people and their vehicles are not only using public lands, but **abusing** them as well. This is the heart of the problem and at the center of most arguments about the use of public lands today.

In the Grand Staircase-Escalante National Monument (GSENM), which is run by the BLM, the fight has escalated with Monument BLM crews erecting signs of road or ATV track closures, and the local sheriff pulling them down. This battle over the definition of what is, and what is not a road, has been going on for a long time in southern Utah and will likely go on for a while longer. It's in the court system as this book goes to press.

At some time in the future, it's hoped that some homemade ATV or 4WD tracks will be closed permanently. In the meantime, maybe we all need to think about the use of public lands, as opposed to the abuse of what little virgin country we have left. There's not a private landowner in this country or the world who would allow ORV enthusiasts to use his/her property like they've been using/abusing public lands for so many years! Before it's too late, **please keep your vehicle on an established and designated road.**

Best Time to Hike

For those heading into the Lower Paria River Gorge, the ideal time for hiking in the spring is from about late March through the end of May (but late May through June for the Buckskin Gulch). For some of the canyons higher in the drainage, April through mid-June is usually the best time. The biggest problem with going into the Lower Paria Canyon in cold weather is that you'll be wading in water much of the time, and in the early morning hours your feet will feel like blocks of ice!

In the fall season and in the lower gorge, mid or late September into late October is preferred, but higher in the drainage, early September through October is usually best, although snow can come during that time. For the high country hikes in Bryce Canyon and Table Cliff Plateau, the warmer months, or from about late May through October are usually the best, but early or late bad weather spells can shorten the season. If you're not wading, then late February and March, and November can be reasonably good times to hike in various parts of this canyon country.

The time of year when the flash flood danger in the narrow slot canyons is highest, is from about mid-July through August (the worst time) extending to mid or late September. Regardless of the time of year, one should always stay tuned to the local radio stations and have a generally good weather forecast before entering places like the Buckskin Gulch. The employee at the Paria Ranger Station & Visitor Center always has the latest weather forecast posted in front of the ranger station and **somewhere on the information board near the highway.** Always stop there and check things out before entering any narrow canyon in that region.

With increased visitor use, especially during April, May and October, consider going in the hotter summer months of June, July and August. There's a lot of good dry weather then, and if you're going into the slot canyons, the temperatures there are much cooler than out in the open.

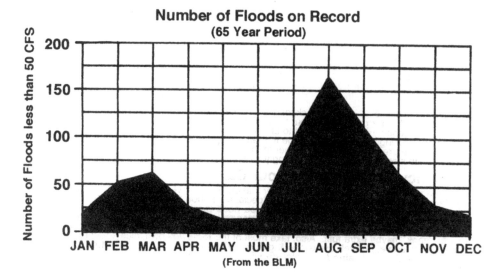

Number of Floods on Record
(65 Year Period)
(From the BLM)

Drinking Water

In recent years there seems to be great controversy over what is and what is not suitable drinking water in the backcountry. The US Public Health Service requires the National Park Service and the BLM to inform hikers to boil all surface water, including water coming directly from springs. This seems to leave little room for common sense. One reason they do it is to save themselves from possible lawsuits.

Here are some steps the author takes to prevent getting a bellyache while hiking in the Paria River country and elsewhere. On day hikes, he always carries a plastic bottle full of tap or culinary water. However, if he passes a good spring, which is obviously unpolluted, he normally drinks from it because it's often colder. An unpolluted spring is basically one which cattle or other animals cannot get into. If it is free-flowing, comes right out of the ground or a crack in a wall, and has no fresh signs of cattle nearby, then it should be at least reasonably safe to drink as-is (?).

When it comes to some of the small side-canyon streams, the thing you'll have to look for is any fresh sign of cattle. If there are cattle in the area, then you'd better purify or filter any running water. But if it's summer, and the cattle have been taken out of the canyons to higher summer ranges, and the water is free flowing, then the risks are lower. The Giardia cysts cannot swim; they can only float downstream. After a flash flood, most side-canyon streams have better water than before, because all the cow poop has been washed away.

The chief reason for taking precautions is to escape the intestinal disorder called **Giardiasis**. This is caused by the microscopic organism, Giardia Lamblia. Giardia are carried in the feces of humans and some domestic and wild animals. The cysts of Giardia may contaminate surface water supplies. The symptoms of this stomach problem include diarrhea, increased gas, loss of appetite, abdominal cramps and bloating. It is not life-threatening, but it can slow you down and make life miserable. If you take the precautions mentioned above and below, you'll surely miss out on this one.

If you're still not convinced, you can buy a water filter for $30-$40, and up. You can also buy small bottles of Iodine tablets for about $3-$4 (containing 50 tablets--one per liter). On all overnight hikes, the author carries a bottle of Iodine tablets, but rarely uses them.

Here's a tip for those who will spend several days in the Lower Paria Canyon Gorge camping. Take along one or more large water jugs--3.78 liters or one US gallon. This will enable you to carry water from a spring to your campsite, which may be a ways from a good water supply. Available water and possible hazards are discussed under each hike.

Insect Season

For the most part, insects are not a serious problem in the Paria River country. The insect season seems to begin in late May, and continues to about mid-July in most of the Paria River drainage. In the wider parts of the canyons above both Lee's Ferry and Old Pahreah, there are small **gnats** which get into your hair and bite. One remedy for this is to wear a hat of some kind. Sometimes insect repellent helps. In these same open areas there can be large gray **horse flies** which bite the back of bare legs. Wearing long pants takes care of this problem. These horse flies are always found around areas where there's water and tamaracks and other brush. For some reason they mostly disappear in about mid-July, or about when the first monsoon rains begin. In the fall there seems to be a general absence of these pests, especially from mid-September on.

The author can't remember any of these pesky insects in the narrow canyons, such as the Buckskin; nor can he remember any mosquitoes, except in swampy places (or in some narrow slots after floods have left pools of water), such as around Adair Lake. Nor can he remember any mosquitoes in the Lower Paria River Gorge. He has been there on at least 2 dozen trips over the years, and in all seasons.

Equipment for Day-Hikes

For those with less experience, here's a list of things the author normally takes on day-hikes. You may want to add to this list. A small-to-medium-sized day-pack, a one or 2-liter bottle of water (you'll drink up to 4 liters while hiking on hot summer days!), camera & lenses, extra digital memory card & batteries for digital cameras, a short piece of nylon rope or parachute cord, toilet paper, pen & small notebook, map, chapstick, compass, altimeter watch, pocket knife, a walking stick (in the Lower Paria River Gorge) for probing deep holes in the sometimes-murky water (perhaps a ski pole with a camera clamp on top which substitutes as a camera stand), sunscreen and a cap with a "sun shield" or "cancer curtain" sewn on around the back, a pair of long pants (for colder temperatures or possibly deer/horse flies or other insects) and a lunch for longer hikes.

In warmer weather, he wears shorts and a T-shirt; in cooler weather, long pants and a long-sleeved shirt, plus perhaps a jacket and gloves. In cooler weather and with more things to carry, a larger day-pack may be needed.

Equipment for Overnight Hikes

Here's a list of things the author normally takes on overnight hikes. You may add to this list as well. A large pack, sleeping bag, sleeping pad (Thermal Rest), tent with rain sheet, small kerosene (your choice) stove, several lighters (no more matches!), 10m or more of nylon cord or light rope, camera & lenses, extra memory card & batteries for digital cameras, sometimes a walking stick for the Lower Paria, one large water jug, a 1-2 liter water bottle, a stitching awl & waxed thread, small pliers, canister with odds and ends (bandaids, needle & thread, patching kit for sleeping pad, wire, pens, etc.), maps, small notebook, reading book, chapstick, compass, altimeter watch, toilet paper, pocket knife, rain cover for pack, small alarm clock, candles for light & reading (or better still an LED headlamp), tooth brush & toothpaste, face lotion, sunscreen and a cap with cancer curtain, soap, long pants and long-sleeved shirt, and maybe a lightweight coat and gloves. Also, a plastic bowl, cup, spoon, small cooking pot and extra fuel for the stove.

Food usually includes such items as oatmeal or cream of wheat cereal, coffee or chocolate drink, powdered milk, sugar, cookies, crackers, candy, oranges or apples, carrots, Ramen instant noodles, soups, macaroni, canned tuna fish or sardines, Vienna sausages, peanuts, instant puddings, bread, butter, peanut butter and salt & pepper.

Boots or Shoes

Because many of the canyons you'll be hiking in have running water, you'll want some kind of a boot or shoe which can be used when wet--some kind of a wading shoe. Most people just use an ordinary pair of running shoes, but here are some precautions: (1) If the shoes are too worn out, you may lose them before the hike ends, especially if taking in all of the Lower Paria Gorge. (2) If the running shoe is too old, it may lack proper support for the foot--a tip for older hikers. (3) A shoe made of canvas, rubber or nylon will last longer in a watery situation, than one with leather parts. (4) Leather shoes should be treated with oil after a trip with wading, such as through the Upper or Lower Paria Canyon. (5) You might consider starting with an older pair of shoes, but have an extra lightweight pair in your pack.

Also, while light weight running shoes are great for hiking, there is a downside. If you're in a sandy area, beware of shoes with a thin mesh around the toe. This is for ventilation and to keep shoes light weight, but it also allows sand in. In sandy areas, a shoe without the ventilating mesh is better.

Hiking Rules and Regulations

Bryce Canyon National Park

There are some rules to backpacking in Bryce Canyon, as there are in any of our national parks. If you're planning to camp overnight in the backcountry, then you'll need a **camping permit**. Pick this up at the park visitor center, along with any other last minute information. You must camp in designated campsites only, and use a stove of some kind--no camp fires allowed. Camping is limited to 3 days in any one site. **If day-hiking, no permit is needed**. No wheeled vehicles of any kind are allowed on the backcountry trails. Get all the latest information at the visitor center just as you enter the park and just west of the Fee Gate. Or see their website at **www.nps.gov/brca**.

There aren't many hikers camping in the backcountry of Bryce Canyon. One big reason is, there is very little live running water in the park. Largely because of this, most people do day-hikes only.

Paria Canyon & Buckskin Gulch--Vermilion Cliffs Wilderness Area

Here's a list of regulations pertaining to the **Lower Paria River Gorge** between the **White House Trailhead** and **Lee's Ferry.** This also includes the popular **Buckskin Gulch,** the main tributary to the lower Paria.

Day Hiking
1. No Reservations needed for day-hiking. The **$6 fee** per person/per day may be paid, and hiking information obtained, at kiosks located at each trailhead. Be sure to have the **correct change** upon arrival. You are asked to obtain an envelope at the trailhead, fill in the blanks, tear off the stub placing that in the windshield area of your car; then place the $6 in the envelope and drop that in the metal box provided.
2. There is no quota on the number of day-hikers in these canyons. Everyone who comes can hike.
3. Group size is limited to 10.

4. No overnight camping without a permit.
5. **Dogs are now allowed** in the Lower Paria and the Buckskin Gulch, but you must pay a fee for them which is the same fee as for you, $6 a day.
6. Children under the age of 12 hike free.

Overnight Hiking & Camping

1. Permits Required: Reservations are most likely required in the busy seasons of spring & fall.
2. For overnight camping anywhere in the canyon(s), $5 per person, per night.
3. Only 20 people are allowed to enter the canyons per/day for camping.
4. If you arrive at the Paria Ranger Station & Visitor Center (or the BLM offices in St. George or Kanab--see addresses below) and there are slots available, then you can get a permit on the spot without reservations. Midsummer sees fewer hikers, and in winter (roughly mid-November through early March) there are few, if any hikers, so you can often pickup a permit on the spot for these time periods. Call or go to their website.
5. Maximum group size 10.
6. Dogs are allowed in the canyon but you must pay the same fee for them as for yourself.
7. There are no refunds, but they will change a date for your permit--for $30.

How to get a permit--Online Reservation Method

To quickly view available hiking dates, secure a reservation, and pay fees (credit card only), please consult the Paria Canyon Project Website at **www.az.blm.gov/paria (or https://www.blm.gov/az/paria /index.cfm?usearea=PC).** If you do not have access to the Internet, or cannot obtain access at your local library, contact staff at the Arizona Strip Interpretive Association (ASIA) at 435-688-3246; or at the Kanab BLM Field Office at 435-644-4600, and they will access the website for you.

Or **Mail** your request and payment of fees to: ASIA, Paria Project, 345 East Riverside Drive, St. George, Utah, 84790; or the Kanab BLM Field Office, 318 North, 100 East, Kanab, Utah, 84741.

Or **Fax** your request and credit card payment to ASIA, Paria Permits, 435-688-3258; or Kanab BLM Field Office, 435-644-4620.

Once your hiking date is reserved, a permit & map will be mailed to you or you may choose to pick it up at one of the BLM offices listed above, or the Paria River Ranger Station & Visitor Center.

Other Information or Recommendations

1. Use existing campsites rather than creating new ones.
2. Trenching around tents is not needed in the canyons.
3. If camping in one of The Confluence campsites, please carry out your human waste in plastic bags. They may give you one at the Kanab BLM office, or at the Paria River Ranger Station & Visitor Center. For those going all the way downcanyon to Lee's Ferry, this isn't as critical--nobody will carry a bag of crap for 3 or 4 days anyway, so bury that waste in a cat hole and cover it. Try to defecate or urinate anywhere but near a regularly-used campsite.
4. Wash without soap to minimize water contamination or use a biodegradable soap away from water sources. Carry water away from the stream and wash dishes away from campsites.
5. Don't leave any food scraps (or any garbage of any kind) at campsites. It will only attract flies and make the next campers miserable.
6. There is no water at any trailhead so have some before you arrive, or get water at the well & tap 40m west of the Paria Ranger Station & Visitor Center.
7. If you plan to do the entire canyon hike from White House Trailhead (or walk through the Buckskin Gulch) to Lee's Ferry, call the BLM office in Kanab at 435-644-4600, and ask if they have a list of people who perform shuttle service between Whitehouse Trailhead and Lee's Ferry. Or better still, go to the website **www.az.blm.gov/paria,** and click on **Shuttles**. Here's what was listed on the internet in 1/2010 (these were the authorized shuttle services, but there may be others?): Circle Tours - Kyle Walker, PO Box 3681, Page, AZ 86040, (888) 854-7862; End of the Trail Shuttles - Betty Price, PO Box 6135, Marble Canyon, AZ 86036, (928) 355-2252; Paria Outpost - Susan and Stephen Dodson, PO Box 410075, Big Water, UT 84741, (928) 691-1047 (the Paria Outpost is immediately west of the Paria River & the ranger station).

Coyote Buttes Information

To get into Coyote Buttes, and more specifically to **The Wave**, the most popular destination around, you must get a permit and pay a $7 fee. Each day 20 permits are given out to the North Coyote Buttes & The Wave; 10 of which you have to make reservations for, 10 are given out as walk-ins (also 20 a day to the South Coyote Buttes, but these are normally easy to get and reservations are normally not needed). Read more about the Coyote Buttes Special Management Area in the Hiking Section, **Map 37A,** for all the rules & regulations.

Comments--This is your land, write letters--be heard

As this book goes to press, the BLM is in the never-ending process of retooling their management plan for the Paria River & Buckskin Gulch, as well as the Coyote Buttes & The Wave. If you have any disagreements with their policy and/or suggestions to offer on how they can improve the situation in this part of the Paria River drainage, you're urged to write to the **BLM--Paria River Project, 345 E. Riverside Drive, St. George, Utah. Tele. 435-688-3246; or BLM Field Office, 318 North 100 East, Kanab, Utah, 84741, Tele. 435-644-4600.**

This is your land, not theirs, and these people work for you & I. Generally speaking, the BLM is about as good as any government agency when it comes to listening to people's' concerns, which in the end, helps them set policy. The bean counters in St. George & Kanab do count letters, especially if the writer has legitimate and thoughtful proposals--not just complaints.

Here are some complaints this writer has regarding **Coyote Buttes & The Wave.** He has talked to no less than a dozen hikers in the last few years, and none have ever seen 20 permittees out there! One friend went there on December 26, 2002, and never saw a soul, even though the 10 reserved permits were filled. Some people think this may be the work of wilderness radicals just filling the slots with no intention of going there, just to keep others out. Or it may be professional photographers who reserve several days permits to ensure they have a fighting chance to be there on a sunny day. Because of this, the author believes more permits can & should be issued on the spot as walk-ins, and maybe fewer reserved. Why not issue 25 or 30 walk-ins (or more), and only 5 or 10 permits with reservations? One argument for giving out so few permits is, the powers-that-be in the BLM wants everybody to have a true wilderness experience! For that, there are a million other places in southern Utah you can be alone. Is going to some place with up to 19 other people a true wilderness experience?

Throughout the Coyote Buttes, it's nothing but sand & slickrock and the author has never seen any negative effects on the land due to hikers. With every rainstorm, or the passing of every cold front with subsequent winds, trails in the sand disappear in minutes. Nor can you see any effects on the slickrock.

Apparently in the past, some fotographers claimed to have seen a slight gray smudging in the middle of The Wave due to people walking right on what everybody wants to take pictures of, but this writer has never seen it. If that should ever be a problem, then hikers can be asked to take off their shoes at the beginning of The Wave. Besides, with every rainstorm, any sole mark gets washed off--that's how canyons are made, by naturally weathering away.

Another point. BLM rangers who go to The Wave, regularly kick over stone cairns (piles of stones) that hikers erect so that others can more easily find the way. This is not an easy place to find, especially right after a storm with lots of wind & rain. Since most people going there don't know how to read a map or use a compass, why not erect a line of cairns to lead the way? There would be much less impact on the area if there was a single marked trail or route, instead of a dozen. This has to be the only place in the world where land managers want to eliminate any semblance of a trail. In every other wilderness area this writer has seen, rangers want everyone to stay on one narrow path, leaving everywhere else pristine.

Visitor Use--Lower Paria River Gorge

The diagram below shows the number of visitors (those who volunteered to sign their names) to the Lower Paria River Gorge and the Buckskin Gulch during the 1994-1996 seasons. These figures should give you some idea of when to go to avoid the biggest crowds.

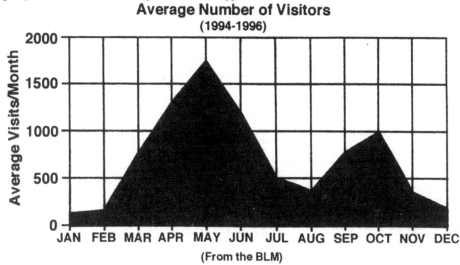

Average Number of Visitors
(1994-1996)

(From the BLM)

Hiking Maps for the Paria River Country

Shown on the next page is an index map showing most of the USGS topographic maps of the region. Any serious hiker should get one or several of the maps shown on this index.

There used to be 3 sets of maps for the area. They include: the USGS or BLM metric maps at **1:100,000 scale**; the mostly-new and highly detailed series at **1:24,000 scale (7 1/2' quads)**; and there used to be maps at **1:62,500 scale (15 minute)**, but they're no longer being printed. However, some may still be available.

For driving & orientation, the author prefers the newer metric maps, and uses these frequently. If you buy the 4 most important maps--**Kanab & Smoky Mountain** in Utah, and **Glen Canyon Dam & Fredonia** in Arizona, you can hike and tour the entire region. Other than these, you'll need the **Escalante** map for a couple of hikes, and the **Panguitch** map covers the northern end of the Skutumpah Road and Bryce Canyon. The **Fredonia** map covers the House Rock Valley Road and part of the Coyote Buttes. For those people who want to hike the Upper Paria River Gorge, Hackberry Canyon and The Cockscomb, then the **Kanab & Smoky Mountain** maps just about cover it all. Only one small corner of the Panguitch map might help with the Upper Paria River hike.

One reason the author likes the metric maps is they are relatively new, all dating after 1980, so nearly all present-day roads are shown. These maps are the best for driving. Some of the 1:24,000 scale maps date from the 1950's, and lack some of the newer roads, but if you want detail, these are the ones. The only disadvantage to these is that you may need several maps to cover one hike; whereas usually just one metric map covers several hikes. The metric maps also fold up and fit in your pocket.

For those who don't understand metrics, you can still get along with these maps because they're laid out in one square mile squares called **sections**. Since all land was surveyed in these section & townships grids, it seems we will never get away from this old system entirely.

For the Lower Paria River Gorge, you might find 3 USGS maps at 1:62,500 scale, **Paria, Paria**

Plateau and **Lee's Ferry.** These are no longer being printed, so if you see any, buy them quick! For this hike, these maps are the very best. Or you might buy the USGS publication titled **MF-1475-- Miscellaneous Field Studies.** In this series of 4 maps, A, B, C & D, Geochemical Data, Mines & Prospects, and Mineral Resource Potential are covered. Maps C or D might be the best for hiking the canyon. These maps are at 1:62,500 scale, and are based on the old USGS maps at the same scale. The great thing about these maps is, each one includes all the Lower Paria River Gorge, Lee's Ferry, the Sand Hills-Paria Plateau and the House Rock Valley Road--all on just one map.

Probably the single best map for those hiking from Whitehouse Trailhead to Lee's Ferry, if you can find it, is the old BLM publication, **Hiker's Guide to Paria Canyon.** This map is presently out of stock, but one BLM employee stated it will be reprinted again soon (fat chance!). It's based on the 1:62,500 scale maps, but concentrates on just the lower gorge with numbers indicating springs, abandoned meanders, campsites, etc., but omitting the Paria Plateau or Sand Hills. This map has been replaced by a newer plastic log-book-type booklet map titled, **Hiker's Guide to Paria Canyon.** It shows the entire canyon in 30 short segments. It has river miles, campsites, abandoned meanders and springs labeled. Its disadvantage is that it doesn't show the entire canyon on one map; that's the reason some would also like the return of the other BLM map mentioned above.

The last set of maps you'll want if you're a serious hiker are the USGS maps at **1:24,000 scale or the 7 1/2' quads.** The maps needed to cover the area from Old Pahreah down to Lee's Ferry are: **Eightmile Pass, Fivemile Valley, Pine Hollow Canyon, West Clark Bench, Bridger Point, Glen Canyon City, Coyote Buttes, Poverty Flat, Wrather Arch, Water Pockets** and **Ferry Swale.** The Index to Topographic Maps (next page) shows the ones you'll need for all hikes in this book. Most of these maps are fairly new and of course very detailed. The only problem with this scale is, they cover a small area and you may have to carry several maps to do just one hike.

Fotography in Slot Canyons (Updated May, 2010)

Here are some tips on cameras, carrying cases and how to come home with good pictures on your first trip down a deep, dark, slot-type canyon.

Film cameras are all but history now, so in this edition, it's **digital fotography only**. First thing to consider when buying a camera for hiking is the size. In today's world you can get really good pictures with a small camera--there's no need to buy something that weighs a ton or is dreadfully bulky. If you're a hiker, you'll want a small camera--period! Start with one that fits in your shirt pocket.

Next thing to look for in a camera is one that fits into a small, plastic carrying case. This writer now has **3 Canons, Power Shot A550 & A560 (and A1000IS)**, all of which shoot at **7.1 or 10 mega pixels (mp)**; almost all pictures in this book were taken with one of these. These cameras fit perfectly into a **Pelican #1010 plastic case** that can be carried on a second belt around the waist for easy and quick access. Remember, a camera in the pack does not take pictures! This is the smallest case Pelican makes, and it, and the cameras mentioned above are a perfect fit. Buy this case first, then find a camera to fit it. **Otter** also makes small plastic cases for cameras & cell fones. Maybe others?

The reason for a plastic case is to protect a very sensitive piece of electronic equipment. **Dust** and **water** are the 2 biggest enemies of all cameras, and the #1010 box is the best thing this writer has ever seen. He can swim through potholes worry-free with it attached to his belt, and it doesn't scratch the LCD screen. Plus, damage from dust is almost a thing of the past. The only negative thing about this way of carrying a camera, if you're not paying attention, you can drop it while taking it out of the case.

Something to look for in a camera is its ability to take good pictures in **low light situations**. For example, in darker slots, all cameras automatically go down to lower shutter speeds, but you also want one that raises or lowers the ISO (same as the old ASA) settings automatically to adjust to the low light.

Here's an example; when set on **automatic**, the Canon A560 goes down to 1/8 of a second in low light and with an ISO setting of perhaps 100 or 200. With a little less light, it automatically pushes the ISO up to as much as 400 or 800--but the shutter speed stays at 1/8. If you're careful, you can hold your hand & camera against a wall, and get sharp pictures at 1/8 of a second--but not less than that. If the shutter speed goes to 1/4 second or less, you'll need a tripod, or set it on a rock or pack.

If the A560 camera is in low light conditions and set on **auto**, it wants to push the ISO up to 800, 1200 or even 1600. This is fine, but although the picture might look good on the LCD screen, the quality isn't as good as pictures shot at low ISO's such as 80 or 100--same as with the old fashioned film cameras. The higher the ISO, the more **"noise"** there is in digital images, which translates to the *equivalency* of *graininess in film*, and a lower quality picture. **The lower the ISO, the better the foto quality.**

In very low light conditions, if your camera wants to automatically jack up the ISO to say 1600 (like the Canon 560), then switch to **Manual** mode. Then you can set the ISO at between 80 & 1600--best to set it at 100 or 200--or anything less than 1600! This also means your shutter speed will drop, perhaps making it necessary to use a tripod, or place the camera on a rock or pack.

Here's something few people think about when choosing a camera; the **battery**. The smallest & thinnest cameras come with a one-of-a-kind size battery that fits only one camera and can only be bought in specialty fotographic stores. They also cost a small fortune--about $30 in 2009. You must always carry one or more backup batteries, so it's best to have a camera that uses **AA's**. These can be purchased in any store, gas station, kiosk or supermarket in the world!

When it comes to AA batteries, best to spend a little extra in the beginning and get the **rechargables** which often come with a **recharging kit** that works at home or in your car. That way, you'll always have fresh batteries. Or you can buy new alkaline batteries anywhere as backups.

If you enjoy taking pictures with people in most scenes, then prior to your trip, inform everyone to wear **colorful clothing**. The author prefers red, something like the University of Utah's color. Others prefer bright yellow, orange or blue. This not only gives your fotos additional color, but it helps to separate the person from the background. If you're end product will be a B+W picture, sometimes you can't tell a person from a rock.

Squeeze the Trigger! When ever you're taking pictures, regardless of how bright or dark the scene is, press the **shutter release button slowly.** Otherwise your picture may be blurred. It's just like shooting a gun; if you jerk the trigger, you'll miss the target. Remember, your finger does not determine how fast the camera's lens opens & closes! This is the biggest difference between good & bad pictures, or between professionals & amateur fotographers. **Hold your breath, and in between heart beats, squeeze the trigger slowly!** This is especially true when shooting a dark scene.

When in any **slot canyon**, avoid taking a foto when there's direct sunlight in your subject area. If you

Index to Topographic Maps--Paria River Country

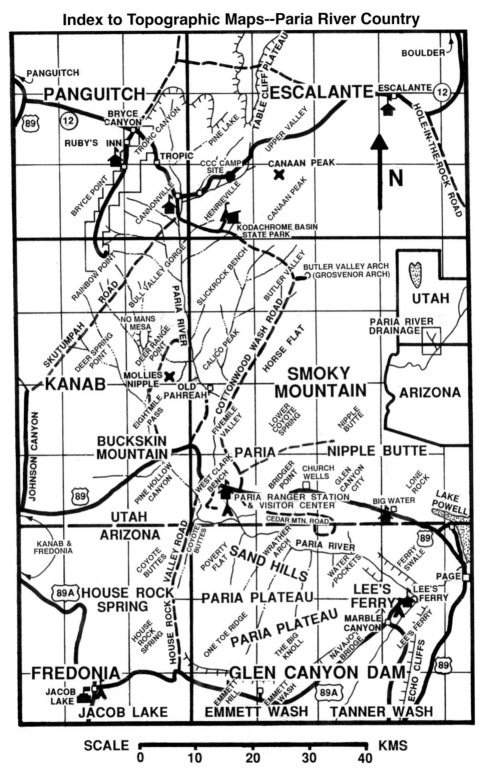

do, part of the picture will be washed out with too much light; the other part will be dark or totally black. Instead, take a picture where the sunlight is being bounced off an upper wall or from around a corner, and diffused down or back into the dark corners. One exception to this rule would be if you're after special effects. In the case of **Antelope Canyon** near Page, Arizona, there is one place **(The Crack)** where a shaft of sunlight reaches the bottom at around high noon in June. Some fotographers set their camera on a tripod, then throw sand in the air which creates dust in the shaft of light. This technique exaggerates the small sunny part adding a pleasing effect to the picture.

Another way to get a good foto with bright sun covering half the scene is to wait for a **cloud** to block the sun, then the light is diffused, eliminating the harsh difference or contrast between sun & shadow. The best time to take fotos in slot canyons is generally from **late morning to early afternoon**. At that time you'll have to find a place where the sun isn't shining directly into the slot, but instead is coming from around a corner, and the light from the strong mid-day sun is bounced into the darker recesses. The **lighter the subject area** (but not direct sunlight), the **brighter & richer the colors will be. Darker scenes in dark slots subdues colors** and you won't be as happy.

If you're in a slot at or near high noon, you can get really good light & colors, and no sun, if you back up or walk forward a little, or around a corner. If at all possible, move around just enough to keep that one streak of sunlight out of your picture. Or, if you do get a small bright sunny streak in a corner of the frame, you can sometimes clone-stamp-it-out at home on your computer using **Photoshop**. One more idea when shooting in slots and making vertical frames, aim the camera down a little so you don't include the sky in the image, otherwise that part will be totally washed out. Doing this also reduces the harsh contrast between the lighter sky above, and the darker slot below.

If you should slip while wading, or somehow drop your **camera in water**, here are the steps to take. Immediately take out the batteries. Open the camera (if possible) and shake and blow out any water. Allow it to sit in the hot sun to dry, turning it occasionally to help evaporate any water inside. If you're near your car, start the engine, turn on the heater, and hang the camera in front of a vent. The warmer the camera gets, the quicker the water evaporates. The quicker the water evaporates, the less corrosion there will be on the electrical system and less rust on metal parts.

If your camera is under water for just a nano second or so, there may not be any water deep inside. In this case, by following the above steps, you may be back in business again in half an hour, especially if the water is clear, no sand has gotten inside, and if the sun is warm. The author had several of these little accidents with each of his older mechanical Pentax K-1000's film cameras. The last several times, no repair work was needed because he did the right things to get the camera dry fast. But he has lost about 5 digitals since 2003. Fortunately, each camera had a no-questions-asked **extended warranty** (had he been using the **1010 Pelican case**, most of those cameras would still be alive!).

Regarding the author drowning several of the older Canon A60 digitals, the good thing about those accidents was, he never lost any images because **memory cards** are well sealed. With his extended warranty, the cameras were replaced without charge, but the pictures he had taken were saved.

Remember, if you drop a digital camera into water, it likely can't be repaired, so they throw it away. When buying a new camera, pay a little more and get an **extended warranty (plus a plastic case)**; that way if you drown a camera in the warranty period, they'll replace it free (read the small print!). Ritz or affiliated camera stores offer such extended warranties, but the cost of the warranty for digital cameras is almost double that of film cameras. At this stage in fotographic history, it seems fewer people know how to fix digitals.

The Grand Staircase-Escalante National Monument (GSENM)

The GSENM is one of our newest national monuments; it was established September 18, 1996 by President Clinton and Interior Secretary Babbit. It's one of only 15 national monuments in America administered by the BLM. Their website is **www.us.blm.gov/**

Here are the approximate boundaries of the GSENM which is entirely in southern Utah. On the west is Johnson Valley or Canyon; on the south it's roughly US Highway 89 or the Utah-Arizona line and Lake Powell; on the north & northwest it's the Skutumpah Road which is close to Bryce Canyon National Park, and Bryce Valley, Escalante & Boulder; while on the east it's Capitol Reef National Park and Glen Canyon National Recreation Area.

Commentary: In the time since this monument was created, the BLM has turned a quiet forgotten backwater into a bureaucratic nightmare. Management is now in the process of dreaming up reasons for you to come to one of their 5 visitor centers to pickup a camping permit! Even if you're just going to pull off the road--any road, including those for 4WD's only--and camp in places like the Rock Springs Bench, Cottonwood Wash, or in even more lonely outposts east of the Paria River drainage, they want you to come in and register--presumably for your own good!

In just the last few years, they've installed hiker's registers at some of the major trailheads. The stated reason is, they want to know how many people are going there. It's assumed that if an area is being visited a lot, that allows them to fill out a requisition form and demand more money--which to this point has gone into building 5 brand new visitor centers (east Kanab, Paria River, Big Water, Cannonville & Escalante). By building these visitor centers, the people in charge of this shootin' match are going out of their way to attract customers (people) who otherwise would have no interest at all in this region. And of course the staff & budget is 7-8 times, maybe 10 times bigger, than it was in 1996 before the place was put on the map!

Most land in the GSENM, including just that part covered in this book--the Paria River drainage--is wild & rugged and accessible only by seasonal dirt roads that may be graded once a year--others never touched by a bulldozer! Yet management is going about their business as if this was in the Appalachian Mountains and surrounded by 100 million people!

One big question; what's the need for this rush into the black hole of bureaucracy? Basically nothing's changed since 1996, except that a few people have gotten it into their heads that they now have to keep track of how many people have come, and that they--the BLM--now has to worry about preventing people from walking on their cryptogrammic soil, getting lost, or something (?). To you readers, this is your land, so if GSENM policies & policy makers burn your 3-letter A-word like they do this writers, write letters and be heard. Policy is based on letters & comments.

Vermilion Cliffs National Monument (VCNM)

America's newest national monument is the Vermilion Cliffs National Monument, created November

15, 2000 by President Clinton. Its boundaries are roughly Highway 89A on the south and southeast, Glen Canyon National Recreation Area on the east & southeast, the Utah-Arizona state line on the north, and the Coyote & House Rock Valleys on the west. Their website is **www.blm.gov/az/**.

As this book goes to press, this monument still has no visitor center and it gets very little publicity. Hopefully it will remain that way instead of turning into another bureaucratic nightmare like the GSENM mentioned above.

More will be explained about the VCNM in the chapters on the Sand Hills, but briefly: on September 28, 2005, all the grazing, water rights and private land in the Sand Hills, and parts of House Rock Valley was purchased by the North Rim Ranch, LLC. This acquisition for the most part paralleled the boundaries of the VCNM. North Rim was a conservation group of some kind. Then on January 29, 2009, it changed hands again. It's now owned and/or managed by the **Grand Canyon Trust**.

Important BLM Offices--Colorado Plateau

Before starting any hike in the Four Corners region, stop at one of these BLM offices and get the latest information on road, trail, water, flood or weather conditions. In some cases, the information in this book may be outdated the minute it goes to press! This is especially true in slot canyons where conditions can change dramatically with every flash flood. People at the BLM normally have good information on road conditions, and can go online to get the latest weather forecast. Here's a list of most of the offices on the Colorado Plateau.

Utah
Cedar City, 176 East, D. L. Sargent Drive, 84720, Tele. 435-586-2401.
St. George, 345 East, Riverside Drive, 84790, Tele. 435-688-3200. Visitor Center, Tele. 435-688-3246.
Escalante, Visitor Center, Tele. 435-826-5499; BLM & Grand Staircase-Escalante N.M. office, Tele. 435-826-5600; Glen Canyon National Recreation Area office, Tele. 435-826-5651. These offices are in the same building complex located on Highway 12 on the west side of Escalante, 84726.
Kanab, BLM Field Office is at 318 North, 100 East, 84741, Tele. 435-644-4600. Read below for the various visitor centers in the Grand Staircase-Escalante National Monument (GSENM).
Richfield, 150 East, 900 North, Tele. 435-896-1500.
Hanksville, southwest part of town, P.O. Box 99, 84734, Tele. 435-542-3461.
Moab, 82 East, Dogwood, 84532, Tele. 435-259-2100.
Multiagency Visitor Center, middle of Moab, Tele. 435-259-2468.
Price, 125 South, 600 West, 84501, Tele. 435-636-3600.
Monticello, 435 North, Main Street, 84535, Tele. 435-587-2141 or 1500.
Vernal, 170 South, 500 East, 84078, Tele. 435-781-4400.

Colorado
Grand Junction, 2815 H Road, 81506, Tele. 970-244-3000.
Montrose, 2505 South, Townsend Avenue, 81401, Tele. 970-249-5300.
Durango, 15 Burnett Court, 81301, Tele. 970-247-4874.
Dolores, 100 N. 6th Street, 81323, Tele. 970-882-7296.

New Mexico
Grants, 2001 E., Santa Fe Avenue, 87020, Tele. 505-285-5406. Or better still, stop at the new building nearby: **Northwest New Mexico Visitor Center,** 1900 E. Santa Fe Avenue, Tele. 505-876-2780.

Arizona
St. George, Utah (for the Arizona Strip District north of the Grand Canyon and Colorado River), 345 East, Riverside Drive, 84790, Tele. 435-688-3200. Visitor Center, Tele. 435-688-3246.
Kingman, 2475 Beverly Avenue, 86401, Tele. 928-692-4400.
Phoenix Field Office, 21605 N. 7th Avenue, 85027, Tele. 623-580-5500.

National Park/Monument Offices & Visitor Centers in Southern Utah

Arches National Park, Visitor Center, North of Moab, Tele. 435-719-2299, or website **nps.gov/arch**.
Canyonlands National Park, Headquarters at 2282 S.W., Resource Blvd., Moab, Tele. 435-719-2100; Visitor Information, Middle of Moab, Tele. 435-719-2313; Backcountry Reservations, Tele. 435-259-4351; Island in the Sky Visitor Center, Tele. 435-259-4712; Needles Visitor Center, Tele. 435-259-4711; Maze (Hans Flat) Visitor Center, Tele. 435-259-2652; or website **nps.gov/cany.**
Capitol Reef National Park, Visitor Center, Tele. 435-425-3791, or website **nps.gov/care**.
Grand Staircase-Escalante National Monument (run by the BLM), Escalante Interagency Visitor Center, West Side of Escalante, Utah, Tele. 435-826-5499; Kanab Visitor Center, 754 E, Highway 89, Kanab, Utah, Tele. 435-644-4680; GSENM Monument Headquarters, 190 East Center Street, Kanab, Tele. 435-644-4300; Cannonville Visitor Center, Cannonville, Utah, Tele. 435-679-8981; Big Water Visitor Center, 100 Upper Revolution Way (just south of Highway 89), Big Water, Utah, Tele. 435-675-5868, website **ut.blm.gov/monument.**
Natural Bridges National Monument, Mailing address HC-60, Box 1, Lake Powell, Utah, 84533, Visitor Center, Tele. 435-692-1234, Headquarters, Tele. 435-719-2100, website **nps.gov/nabr.**
Vermilion Cliffs National Monument, Interagency Information Center, 345 Riverside Drive, St. George, Utah, Tele. 435-688-3200, website **az.blm.gov** or **blm.gov/az/**
Zion National Park, Visitor Center, Tele. 435-772-3256; Backcountry Desk, Tele. 435-772-0170, website **nps.gov/zion**

Other Important Websites & Home Pages--US Government
Bureau of Land Management (BLM) -www.blm.gov
United State Forest Service (USFS) -www.fs.fed.us
National Park Service (NPS) -www.nps.gov

Warning: Don't Blame Me!

People should keep a few things in mind when it comes to hiking in the canyons of the Paria River drainage. This writer has done his best to collect information and present it to readers as accurately as possible. He has drawn maps as carefully as possible, and encourages everyone to buy the USGS topo maps suggested for each hike. He has tried to inform hikers that canyons change with every flash flood, and that many of the hikes in this book are in isolated wilderness regions. He's also tried to tell hikers that some canyons are for experienced and tough hikers or canyoneers only. Some hikes discussed here are easy, but others are definitely not a Sunday picnic in the park!

For the first time, this edition presents several canyons which involve serious downclimbing and/or rappelling to get all the way through. Some rappelling anchors are chokestones or trees, others are bolts in the canyon walls. If you choose to take on these challenges, it's your responsibility to check each anchor carefully, especially knots, slings, or webbing & bolts. Floods can alter, damage or wash away these sites, especially chokestones and webbing, so proper tools, equipment and supplies must be taken to ensure you get through alive! No matter what, always take extra ropes or webbing to meet any kind of new situation or emergency. So for those who will somehow get lost, stranded, or have to spend an extra night in a canyon and be rescued, all I can say is, I've done my best. The rest is up to you, so don't blame me or this book for your mistakes, lack of preparedness--and yes, even your stupidity!

Before doing any hike, always stop at the nearest BLM office or visitor center, and get the latest information on road, trail, water, flood or weather conditions & forecast. Also, tell someone exactly where you're going and when you expect to return. That way, friends can call for help if you don't return on time. One last thing; in some cases, the information in this book is different than in previous editions and can be outdated the minute it goes to press!

From the air and looking northeast, we see **Powell Point** at the end of the **Table Cliff Plateau**, one of the more dramatic scenes around. The **Under the Point Trail** contours around the base of Powell Point in the lower right-hand corner of the picture. Foto was taken December 9, 2003.

Metric Conversion Table

1 Centimeter = 0.39 Inch	1 Mile = 1.609 Kilometers	1 Ounce = 28.35 Grams
1 Inch = 2.54 Centimeters	100 Miles = 161 Kilometers	1 Pound = 453 Grams
1 Meter = 39.37 Inches	100 Kilometers = 62.1 Miles	1 Quart (US) = 0.946 Liter
1 Foot = 0.3048 Meter/30.5 Cms	1 Liter = 1.056 Quarts (US)	1 Gallon (US) = 3.785 Liters
1 Kilometer = 0.621 Mile	1 Kilogram = 2.205 Pounds	1 Acre = 0.405 Hectare
1 Nautical Mile = 1.852 Kms	1 Metric Ton = 1000 Kgs	1 Hectare = 2.471 Acres
1 Kilometer = 3281 Feet	1 Mile = 1609 Meters	0.1 Mile = 161 Meters
1 Cubic/Liter = 61 Cubic/Inches	50 C/L = 3050 C/I	100 C/L = 6100 C/I

Meters to Feet (Meters x 3.2808 = Feet)

100 m = 328 ft.	2500 m = 8202 ft.	5000 m = 16404 ft.	7500 m = 24606 ft.
500 m = 1640 ft.	3000 m = 9842 ft.	5500 m = 18044 ft.	8000 m = 26246 ft.
1000 m = 3281 ft.	3500 m = 11483 ft.	6000 m = 19686 ft.	8500 m = 27887 ft.
1500 m = 4921 ft.	4000 m = 13124 ft.	6500 m = 21325 ft.	9000 m = 29525 ft.
2000 m = 6562 ft.	4500 m = 14764 ft.	7000 m = 22966 ft.	8848 m = 20029 ft.

Feet to Meters (Feet ÷ 3.2808 = Meters)

1000 ft. = 305 m	9000 ft. = 2743 m	16000 ft. = 4877 m	23000 ft. = 7010 m
2000 ft. = 610 m	10000 ft. = 3048 m	17000 ft. = 5182 m	24000 ft. = 7315 m
3000 ft. = 914 m	11000 ft. = 3353 m	18000 ft. = 5486 m	25000 ft. = 7620 m
4000 ft. = 1219 m	12000 ft. = 3658 m	19000 ft. = 5791 m	26000 ft. = 7925 m
5000 ft. = 1524 m	13000 ft. = 3962 m	20000 ft. = 6096 m	27000 ft. = 8230 m
6000 ft. = 1829 m	14000 ft. = 4268 m	21000 ft. = 6401 m	28000 ft. = 8535 m
7000 ft. = 2134 m	15000 ft. = 4572 m	22000 ft. = 6706 m	29000 ft. = 8839 m
8000 ft. = 2438 m			30000 ft. = 9144 m

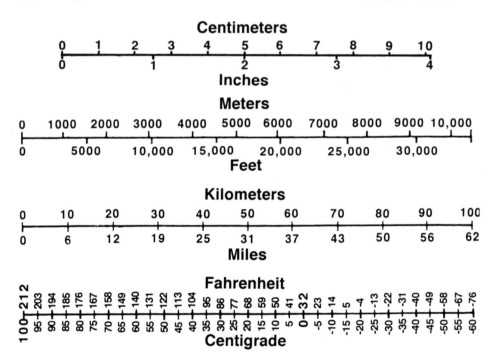

Converting Fahrenheit to Centigrade, or Centigrade to Fahrenheit

Centigrade Temperature x 1.8, + 32 = Fahrenheit (Example 10°C x 1.8, + 32 = 50°F)

Fahrenheit Temperature - 32, divide by 1.8 = Centigrade (Example 50°F - 32, divide by 1.8 = 10°C)

Map Symbols

Town or Community - - - - - - - - - - - -☐	Peak & Prominent Ridge - - - ━✗━
Building, Cabin or Home - - - - - - - - ◻	Stream or Creek, Desert - - - - - ∿
Backcountry Campsite - - - - - - - - - - ▲	Stream or Creek, Mountain - - - ∿
Campsite with Vehicle Access - - - - - ⬢	Well, Metal Tank or Trough - - - - - - - ● ●
Campground - - - - - - - - - - - - - - - 𝗔	Dry Creek Bed or Channel - - - - - ━⋯
Grave Site or High Point - - - - - - - - - ●	Narrow Canyon - - - - - - - - - - - - 𝗍𝗍𝗍𝗍𝗍
Ranger Station, Visitor Center - - 🚩🏠	Lake, Pond or Stock Pond - - - - -⬭ ⬮
Hotel, Motel or Lodge - - - - - - - - - - 🏨	Large Pothole - - - - - - - - - - - - - - ⟲o
Airport or Landing Strip - - - - -⊏▭⊐✚	Waterfall or Dryfall - - - - - - - - - - ━�┼━
U.S. Highway - - - - - - - - - -┿┿ ⑧⑨ / 20 21	Spring, Seep or Well - - - - - - - - - - - - o
Utah State Highway - - - - - - ━ ㉔	Canyon Rim, Escarpment - - - - ⬩⬩⬩⬩
Road--Maintained - - - - - - - - ═══	Natural Bridge or Arch, Corral - - ∩ ∩
Road--4 Wheel Drive (4WD) - - -═════	Mine, Quarry, Adit or Prospect - - - - ↖ ↗
Track--Seldom Used - - - - - - ━ ━ ━	Geology Cross Section - - - - - - ⌊ ⌉
Trail, Foot or Horse - - - - - - - - ▬ ▬ ▬	Pass or Divide - - - - - - - - - - - - - - ≍
Route, No Trail - - - - - - - - - - - - ●●●●●●	Rock Art--Pictograph - - - - - - - - - - (PIC)
Cowboy Signature (s) - - - - - - - - - -CS	Rock Art--Petroglyphs - - - - - - - - - - (PET)
Elevation in Meters - - - - - - - - - -1490	Mile Posts (mp) Markers - - - - -╱╱ / 30 31
600 Meters - - - - - - - - - - - - - - -600m	Car-Park or Trailhead - - - - - - - - - - Ⓟ

Abbreviations

Canyon - - - - - - - - - - - - - - - - - -C.	Campground - - - - - - - - - - - - - - -CG.
Lake -L.	Campsites or Cowboy Signatures - - - - -CS.
River -R.	Two Wheel Drive Vehicle or Road - - - - -2WD
Creek -Ck.	Four Wheel Drive Vehicle or Road - - - -4WD
Peak -Pk.	High Clearance Vehicle or Road - - - - -HCV
Waterfall, Dryfall, Formation - - - - - - - - -F.	Off Road Vehicle - - - - - - - - - - - - - -ORV
Kilometer(s) - - - - - - - - - - - - - - -km, kms	All Terrain Vehicle - - - - - - - - - - - - - -ATV
North, North East - - - - - - - - - - - - - -NNE	Spring -Sp.
South, West South - - - - - - - - - - - -SWS	Sandstone - - - - - - - - - - - - - - - - - -SS
Piñon/Juniper Forest - - - - - - - - - - - -P/J	July 24, 2010 - - - - - - - - - - - - - -7/24/2010

United States Geological Survey -USGS
National Park Service -NPS
Bureau of Land Management -BLM
Grand Staircase-Escalante National Monument -GSENM
Vermilion Cliffs National Monument -VCNM
Civilian Conservation Corps -CCC's
National Geographic Society -NGS

18

Reference--Index Map of Hikes

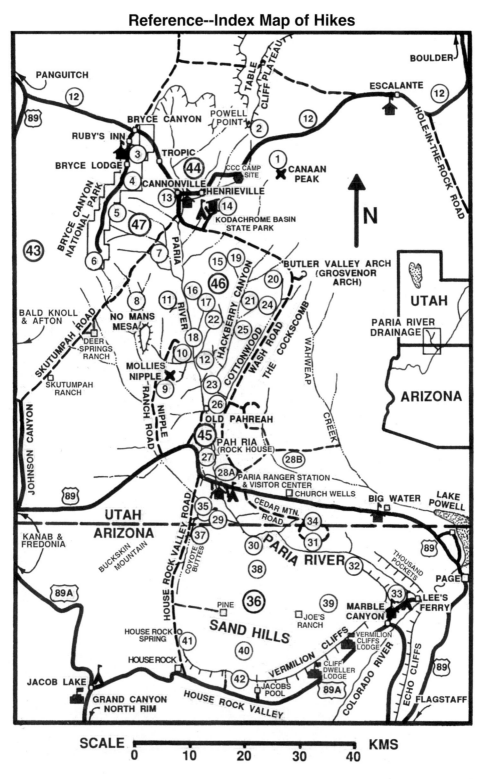

Canaan Peak

Location & Access **Canaan Peak** at 2833m, is located roughly halfway between Escalante and Bryce Valley (with the 3 towns of Tropic, Cannonville & Henrieville). It's also just south & southeast of **Highway 12** as you pass through the area. The original name for this was **Kaiparowits Peak** as shown on an 1884 map of Utah. The top part of Canaan is made of the same rock formations as in Bryce Canyon National Park and on Table Cliff Plateau, but its bright red limestone cap rock is almost eroded away. All other surrounding hills or mountains have lost this **Claron** (formerly known as the Wasatch) **Formation** cap except Table Cliff Plateau, which is located just to the northwest. See the next map.

To get to the trailhead, drive along Highway 12, the link between Bryce Canyon NP and Escalante. Between **new mile posts 44 & 45**, turn south at the sign stating, *South Hollow & Canaan Peak*. Drive south 7.6 kms (4.7 miles) on a good & well-maintained dirt road (#146). At that point you'll come to an **open meadow** and another sign on the right or south reading *Canaan Mtn. Loop Trail & Pole Spring*. Turn right from the main road and drive 30-40m and park. In that area is now a new sign and a new beginning of the trail to Canaan Peak (formerly you would drive off the main road for 300m to near Pole Spring, but the new trail keeps hikers away from where cattle drink out of troughs). Park and/or camp at the new trailhead which has lots of shade from big pine/spruce/fir trees.

Trail/Route From the **new trailhead**, first head west along the new trail which parallels the road for about 100m. It soon zig zags south up to the top of a minor ridge, then heads southeast and south. After about 1 km you'll come to a **little pass** where the **old trail & cattle trails cross the new trail** you're on. At that point, continue south and a little east staying on the minor ridge--don't veer to the southwest on the old trail which is used by cattle. Once on this new main trail and beyond the **little pass**, it's easy to follow, but you may have to jump over some downed trees occasionally. As you arrive on the west side of the main peak, and after you cross over another minor pass, the trail drops down to intersect a very old logging road, which is now unusable for vehicles. At about that point, you can walk eastward straight up the slope to the top-most ridge, then head south to the summit; or continue on the trail around to the southeast side of the mountain and summit from there. The south face of Canaan Peak is very rugged and a nice place to take pictures. That scene resembles Bryce Canyon National Park

Elevations The new trailhead, about 2590m; Canaan Peak, 2833m.

Time Needed To the top is only about 3 kms, but may take from 2-4 hours to climb, round-trip.

Water Take your own. Also at Pole Spring or a cattle watering trough (purify before using!), but none on the mountain above.

Maps USGS or BLM map Escalante (1:100,000) for driving & orientation; and Canaan Peak & Upper Valley (1:24,000--7 1/2' quads) for hiking; but neither of these maps show the road to the mountain.

Main Attractions A short half-day-hike in a cool and little-known mountain region, with many good, free campsites. A nice place to visit on a hot summer day.

Best Time to Hike From about mid-May until the end of October, but each year is a little different. Get there too early in the spring, or too late in the fall, and you'll find muddy roads.

Boots/Shoes Any dry weather boots or shoes.

Author's Experience The author had to hunt for the trailhead on his first trip, but after locating it, went quickly up the trail to the summit from the southeast side. He came down the west slope and returned to his car in less than 3 hours. He re-hiked roughly the same route in about 2 hours on a 2nd trip in 1997. In 2003, he did the hike again with a digital camera; 2 1/2 hours round-trip. In 8/2009, he did the hike again in just over 2 hours-- then discovered the new trailhead and checked out the new trail beginning.

Canaan Peak as seen from the southern base of the mountain.

Map 1, Canaan Peak

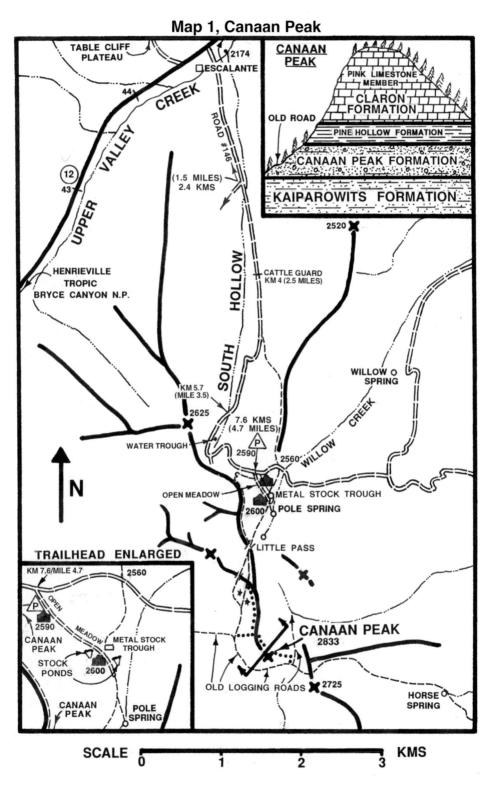

TABLE CLIFF PLATEAU

□ESCALANTE

2174

CANAAN PEAK

PINK LIMESTONE MEMBER

CLARON FORMATION

OLD ROAD

PINE HOLLOW FORMATION

CANAAN PEAK FORMATION

KAIPAROWITS FORMATION

CREEK

ROAD #146

44

12
43

UPPER VALLEY

(1.5 MILES) 2.4 KMS

HENRIEVILLE
TROPIC
BRYCE CANYON N.P.

SOUTH HOLLOW

2520

CATTLE GUARD
KM 4 (2.5 MILES)

KM 5.7
(MILE 3.5)
2625

WATER TROUGH

7.6 KMS
(4.7 MILES)
P
2590

WILLOW
SPRING

WILLOW CREEK

2560

N

OPEN MEADOW

METAL STOCK TROUGH

2600 P POLE SPRING

LITTLE PASS

TRAILHEAD ENLARGED

KM 7.6/MILE 4.7

2560

P
OPEN
2590

CANAAN PEAK

STOCK PONDS

2600

MEADOW

METAL STOCK TROUGH

CANAAN PEAK

POLE SPRING

CANAAN PEAK
2833

OLD LOGGING ROADS

2725

HORSE SPRING

SCALE

0   1   2   3   KMS

21

Table Cliff Plateau and Powell Point

Location & Access Table Cliff Plateau is located about halfway between Escalante, and the 3 Bryce Valley towns of Tropic, Cannonville & Henrieville. **Table Cliff Plateau,** or at least its very southern tip known as **Powell Point,** is one of the most prominent landmarks in southern Utah. On an 1874 map of Utah, this high country already had 2 names, **Summit of the Rim** and **Table Rock.** To get there, drive along **Highway 12** between Henrieville & Escalante. The shortest driving route to the trailhead in **Water Canyon** is to leave the highway between **mile posts 44 & 45** and head west, then northwest on **Forest Road #148**, as shown on the map. After **4.8 kms (3 miles)**, turn left at the sign & junction and drive a rougher track for 1.6 kms (1 mile) to the end of road and the **Water Canyon Tailhead**. 2WD vehicles can make it up the last section of this **old logging road #500** to the trailhead at 2485m.

Another way to reach the trailhead is to leave the highway right at **new mile posts 46** next to a corral and drive northwesterly **6.2 kms (3.8 miles)** on **Forest Road #144** to the **Garden Spring Junction** (this loop-road #148 & #144 is in good condition for all vehicles). At that junction is a sign pointing the way toward Water Canyon. From there, drive southwest another 300m (.2 mile) and turn right or northwest to reach the same Water Canyon Trailhead mentioned above. Park/camp in a meadow 160m below the actual beginning of the trail. This trailhead makes a nice campsite in the heat of summer.

Trail/Route From the trailhead, there's a well-marked path to the top of **Table Cliff Plateau**. Once on the trail, it's easy to follow as it first runs up the bottom of Water Canyon with several nearby springs (in summer there are cows around, so purify the water before drinking!). This trail has ax marks on trees shaped like the letter "i". Higher up, it zig zags up the steeper parts to the flat top. After about 5 1/2 kms, the Water Canyon Trail meets a rather good vehicle track running south to Powell Point. Once on this track, walk through white & douglas fir, limber & ponderosa pines and quaking aspen to where the road ends and a foot trail begins. Then it's a short walk through mostly-**bristlecone pines to Powell Point**. The west side of the Plateau is the most fotogenic, so arrive after midday for better pictures.

In this area is also an improved road running from near **Stump Spring** around to the southeast side of Table Cliff & Powell Point. See map. From Stump Spring, drive southwest and west 2.4 kms (1.5 miles) to a new trailhead for the **Under the Point Trail**. From that trailhead, you can walk west underneath Powell Point, and end up at Pine Lake or the Henderson Canyon Trailhead northeast of Tropic. Only problem with this setup is, you have to return to the same trailhead--or have another vehicle at the other end! Best to walk for 30-40 minutes, have some nice views of the cliffs and return the same way.

Elevations Trailheads, 2485m & 2621m; Table Cliff Plateau, 3125m; Powell Point, 3105m.

Time Needed One to 2 hours to reach the top of the Plateau, then the easy 3 km road-walk south to the end of the road, and another km to Powell Point. Round-trip should take from 4-7 hours.

Water There's running water in Water Canyon (year-round flow). There's no water on top or along the Under the Point Trail, so always take some in your car and in your pack.

Maps USGS or BLM map Escalante (1:100,000) for driving & orientation; and Upper Valley & Pine Lake (1:24,000--7 1/2' quads) for hiking.

Main Attractions Splendid views, a cool summer hike, and cool quiet campsites.

Best Time to Hike From mid or late May to late October, but each year is a little different.

Boots/Shoes Any light weight boots or shoes. Running-type shoes will work just fine.

Author's Experience On his first trip, the author walked up an off-trail route in Pine Hollow from his car near the highway, then came down Water Canyon and road-walked back to his car; all in 5 hours. In 2003, he car-camped at the Water Canyon Trailhead and did the normal hike the next morning in just over 4 hours, round-trip. In 2009, he did the same hike in the same time, plus walked the Under the Point trail for more than 45 minutes and returned.

Looking north along the western face of **Table Cliff Plateau** from the southern tip near **Powell Point**.

Map 2, Table Cliff Plateau and Powell Point

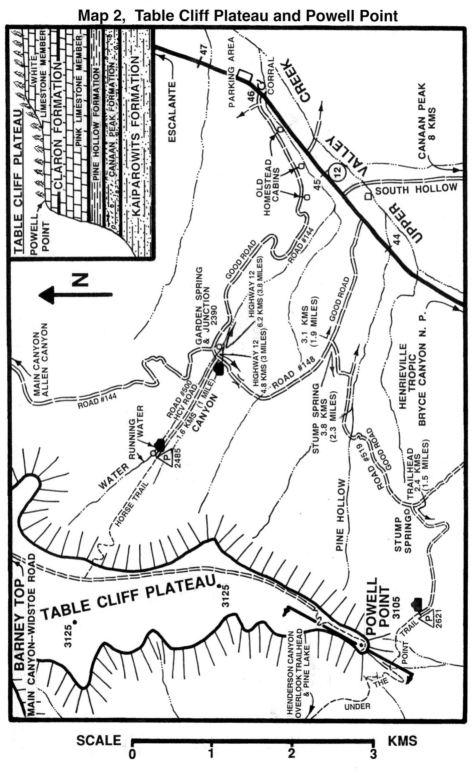

TABLE CLIFF PLATEAU

CLARON FORMATION

WHITE LIMESTONE MEMBER

PINK LIMESTONE MEMBER

PINE HOLLOW FORMATION

CANAAN PEAK FORMATION

KAIPAROWITS FORMATION

POWELL POINT

ESCALANTE

47

PARKING AREA

CORRAL

46

45

12

44

CREEK

UPPER VALLEY

OLD HOMESTEAD CABINS

SOUTH HOLLOW

CANAAN PEAK 8 KMS

N

GARDEN SPRING & JUNCTION 2390

GOOD ROAD

ROAD #144

HIGHWAY 12 6.2 KMS (3.8 MILES)

HIGHWAY 12 4.8 KMS (3 MILES)

GOOD ROAD

3.1 KMS (1.9 MILES)

ROAD #148

MAIN CANYON ALLEN CANYON

ROAD #144

ROAD #500 HCV ROAD

CANYON

2485 — 1.6 KMS (1 MILE)

WATER RUNNING WATER

P

HORSE TRAIL

STUMP SPRING 3.8 KMS

STUMP SPRING 2.3 KMS

ROAD #519

GOOD ROAD

STUMP SPRING TRAILHEAD 2.4 KMS (1.5 MILES)

HENRIEVILLE TROPIC BRYCE CANYON N. P.

PINE HOLLOW

BARNEY TOP

MAIN CANYON—WIDSTOE ROAD

TABLE CLIFF PLATEAU

3125

3125

HENDERSON CANYON OVERLOOK TRAILHEAD & PINE LAKE

UNDER

THE

POWELL POINT 3105

THE POINT TRAIL

P 2621

SCALE

0   1   2   3   KMS

Fairyland Trail, Bryce Canyon National Park

Location & Access Included in this book are 4 maps covering the trails in Bryce Canyon National Park. The **Fairyland Trail** is the most-northerly of the 4, and is the most-northerly of all footpaths in the park. This trail is located roughly due east of the park visitor center and North Campground. One place to begin hiking is at **Fairyland Point.** To get there, drive south from Ruby's Inn on the highway entering Bryce Canyon. From the national park boundary, which is well-marked by signs, continue south for .7 km (.4 mile) then turn east on the paved road signposted for **Fairyland Point**. Drive another 1.6 kms (1 mile) and park. A 2nd place to begin hiking this loop trail is at **Sunrise Point**. To get there, first pass through the fee gate which is next to the visitor center, then continue south for about 800m (.5 mile) and turn left or east at the road signposted for **Sunrise Point**. Or continue south another short distance to near mile post 2 and turn east again at a 2nd access road. Just follow the signs to Sunrise Point using this or the free map they'll give you as you enter the park. A 3rd starting point is anywhere within the confines of the North Campground.

Trail/Route The Fairyland Trail, as with all trails in this national park, is a well-maintained walking path. You can't get lost, and all trail junctions and points of interest are signposted. This trail is easy walking but it's an up & down hike all the way. The better known points of interest along the way are the **Chinese Wall** and the London or **Tower Bridge** (this is actually an arch, not a bridge). Depending on the time of day, you may have better light for fotographing this arch by walking around to the back side. At least from the south side you'll have lots more sun.

Elevations From a high point of about 2465m on the rim, down to about 2200m in Campbell Canyon.

Time Needed This hike is divided into 2 parts; the **Fairyland Trail,** running down into the canyons; and the **Rim Trail**. If you start at Sunrise Point and walk down along the Fairyland Trail, then it's just over 8 kms to Fairyland Point. From Fairyland Point back along the rim to Sunrise Point is just over 5 kms. So the length of the loop is about 13 kms. Some people can do this loop-hike in as little as 3 hours, but for others it's a 4-5 hour walk. You can shorten it just a bit, if you begin at the campground or Fairyland Point, thus eliminating the short walk to or from Sunrise Point. Or, you could eliminate the Rim Trail part between trailheads by using a mtn. bike on the paved roads. Or, start at Sunrise Point, walk down to Tower Bridge and return the same way, which is the best part of the hike.

Water There are no springs or running water anywhere along this trail, so if it's summer with hot weather, be sure to take some water--up to 2-3 liters for some on a hot summer day. In cooler weather, and if you're a fast & fit hiker, you can likely make it without water (or very little) or a lunch.

Maps Trails Illustrated/National Geographic map Paunsaugunt Plateau, Mount Dutton, Bryce Canyon (1:50,000); Bryce Canyon National Park (1:31,680); or the free map given to you upon entry to Bryce.

Main Attractions Easy access, a good & well-maintained trail, very little other foot traffic, and perhaps the second best area in the park to walk through and see the hoodoos. See the geology cross section.

Best Time to Hike May through October. Mid-summer can be a bit warm as the altitude is only moderately high. Winter hiking could be fun too, for the properly equipped, but it's not marked for winter use. Snow cover is generally light in this section of the park during winter, but in some years it can be up to 2m or more deep--like in the winter of 2009-'10.

Boots/Shoes Any comfortable light-weight boots or shoes. Running shoes are the best.

Author's Experience The author started at Sunrise Point and made the loop-hike in about 3 hours on a very cool May morning. On another trip from Sunrise Point, he went down to Tower Bridge and the Chinese Wall, waited a while for clouds to move, and returned in less than 2 hours.

One of the better scenes along the **Fairyland Trail** is **Tower Bridge**.

Map 3, Fairyland Trail, Bryce Canyon National Park

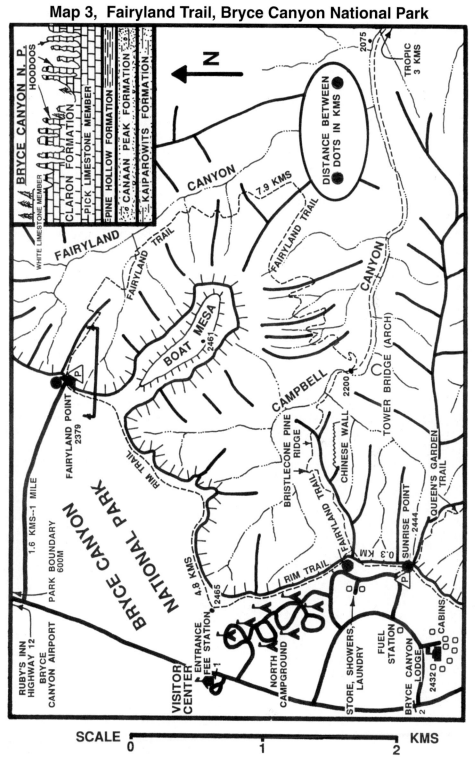

These are the type of **cabins** you can rent if you stay inside Bryce Canyon National Park. These rustic cabins are just south of the **Bryce Canyon Lodge**.

The lower part of **Wall Street**. This was closed in 2009, but hopefully it'll be open when you arrive.

Typical scene from the **Bryce Point** area. Notice the trail, tunnel and people in the lower right; that trail is part of the **Peekaboo Loop Trail**. See next map.

An aeriel view looking west in winter of the hoodoos making up the **Wall Street & Navajo Loop Trail** area of Bryce Canyon National Park. Sunset Point is in the upper right and on the rim.

Navajo, Peekaboo & Queen's Garden Trails, Bryce Canyon N.P.

Location & Access The trails on this map are near the center of Bryce Canyon National Park, and in that part which has the best scenery and most visitors. It's here you can walk right through the narrow canyons of **hoodoos**, the erosional features so prominent in this section of the park and for which Bryce Canyon is famous. About 1 1/2 kms (1 mile) after entering the national park, you'll come to the **fee station** (they will give you a small **map**) next to the **visitor center**. From there, continue south a ways and look for signs pointing out the access roads to **Sunrise Point** (& the historic **Bryce Canyon Lodge** just beyond mile post 2) & **Sunset Point** on the left or east. A little further (2.9 kms/1.8 miles from the visitor center/fee station) is the turnoff to **Inspiration, Bryce & Paria Points**. All the roads up to the turnoff to Bryce Point and the winter gate are kept open year-round.

Trail/Route There are 3 possible starting points for hikes from the rim: **Sunrise, Sunset** and **Bryce Points.** The first 2 are the most used, since they're near the historic Bryce Canyon Lodge & cabins, and campgrounds. All trails on this map are heavily-used and well-maintained. All junctions are signposted, and in some places you'll find benches to sit on and rest. Walking is very easy and enjoyable. Most people here are tourists, not necessarily hikers, and for the most part they walk down one trail a ways and return the same way. The best trail in the park for taking pictures is the **Navajo Loop Trail.** It's a one-way hike that zig zags down & through a narrow, fotogenic gorge called **Wall Street.** This part has a couple of tall pine trees trying to reach the sun. Then the trail loops back up passing another little canyon with **2 natural bridges** before returning to the rim. From the top of this trail looking northeast toward Powell Point in the distance, is the best place in the park for taking fotos of **hoodoos.**

Elevations Sunset Point, 2431m; Sunrise Point, 2444m; Bryce Point, 2529m; Inspiration Point, 2483m; and the lowest part of the Navajo Trail, about 2280m.

Time Needed On this map are some large dots with numbers in between. These numbers represent the kilometers between dots. None of the distances are very great. To walk down the Navajo, then along the Peekaboo Loop Trail, and finish the hike by walking up the Queen's Garden Trail to Sunrise Point, and finally back to the starting place at Sunset Point, is to walk about 10.5 kms. This can be done in as little as 2 hours by a fast hiker, but most would want about 4 hours, or about half a day for the trip. Some may want to take a lunch and spend more than half a day on this hike, especially if taking in some short side-trips, such as the walk into **Bridge Canyon.** A mtn. bike left at one trailhead would eliminate a tiresome road-walk, or take the rim trail back to your car, especially if you start or end at Bryce Point.

Water There is no running water anywhere in this area, so take your own.

Maps Trails Illustrated/National Geographic map Paunsaugunt Plateau, Mount Dutton, Bryce Canyon (1:50,000); or Bryce Canyon National Park (1:31,680); or just use the simple free map given to you as you pass through the fee station. The first 2 maps can be bought at the visitor center.

Main Attractions The trails on this map give hikers the best opportunity of any location in the park to see at close quarters the famous bright red/orange spires of Bryce Canyon called hoodoos.

Best Time to Hike May through October, but mid-summer can be a little warm at lower altitudes. Because of relatively light snowfall, it's also possible to hike these trails in winter. However, in some winters the snow can pile up to more than a meter deep. Each year is different.

Boots/Shoes Any light weight boots or shoes; simple running shoes are best.

Author's Experience The author worked at Bryce Canyon Lodge in the summer of 1965, so he has been on these trails many times. Later, he walked the Queen's Garden & Navajo Loop in a couple of hours. In 2003 & 2009, he re-hiked & fotographed the scenes along the Navajo Trail Loop Trail.

The historic **Bryce Canyon Lodge** is near the beginning of the Navajo Loop Trail

Map 4, Navajo, Peekaboo, Queen's Garden Trails, Bryce C.N.P.

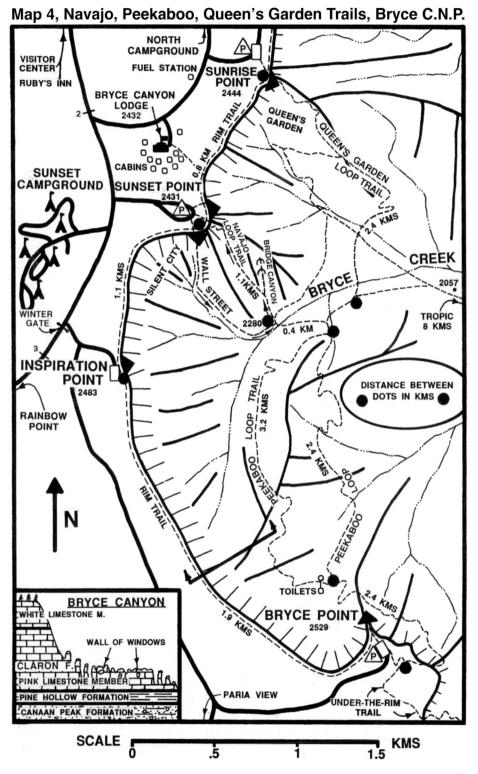

VISITOR
CENTER
RUBY'S INN

NORTH
CAMPGROUND

FUEL STATION

SUNRISE
POINT
2444

BRYCE CANYON
LODGE
2432

QUEEN'S
GARDEN

2

0.8 KM RIM TRAIL

QUEEN'S GARDEN
LOOP TRAIL

CABINS

SUNSET
CAMPGROUND

SUNSET POINT
2431

2.4 KMS

NAVAJO LOOP TRAIL

BRIDGE CANYON

CREEK

BRYCE

2057

1.1 KMS

1.1 KMS

WALL STREET

SILENT CITY

2280

0.4 KM

TROPIC
8 KMS

WINTER
GATE

3

INSPIRATION
POINT
2483

DISTANCE BETWEEN
DOTS IN KMS

RAINBOW
POINT

PEEKABOO LOOP TRAIL
3.2 KMS

2.4 KMS

PEEKABOO LOOP

RIM TRAIL

N

TOILETS

2.4 KMS

BRYCE CANYON
WHITE LIMESTONE M.

WALL OF WINDOWS

CLARON F.

PINK LIMESTONE MEMBER

PINE HOLLOW FORMATION

CANAAN PEAK FORMATION

1.9 KMS

BRYCE POINT
2529

PARIA VIEW

UNDER-THE-RIM
TRAIL

SCALE   KMS
0   .5   1   1.5

The **Tropic Ditch** as seen immediately south of Ruby's Inn and next to the campground. This is just west of the highway running south into Bryce Canyon National Park.

Powell Point at the very end of Table Cliff Plateau, as seen along the Under the Point Trail, #051.

Above From the beginning of the **Navajo Loop Trail** looking east, is one of the best scenes in Bryce Canyon National Park. Not seen here, but off in the distance is Powell Point and Table Cliff Plateau. Colors are at their best here.

Left From near the top of **Wall Street** looking at the trail zig zagging down and through the hoodoos for which Bryce Canyon is famous.

Under-the-Rim Trail, Bryce Canyon National Park

Location & Access The **Under-the-Rim Trail** runs from **Bryce Point** near the center of Bryce Canyon, south to **Rainbow Point**, at the southern end of the park. It runs north-south along the eastern base of the Pink Cliffs, and offers both day and overnight hikes. In recent years, roads in the park up to Bryce Point have been kept open year-round. And if snow isn't too deep, and if graders are available, the road is sometimes plowed all the way to Rainbow Point. Before going anywhere, stop at the visitor center (VC) next to the fee station or entry gate for current information, maps, rules & regulations for campers, and if you're planning an overnight trip, pick up a free camping permit. From the VC, head south and follow signs to the trailhead you wish to hike from. The turnoff to Bryce Point is 2.6 kms (1.6 miles) from the VC; Rainbow Point is 27.5 kms (17.1 miles) from the VC (right at mile post 18). Three connecting trails are in between.

Trail/Route The Under-the-Rim Trail is well-marked & maintained, so you can't get lost There are signs at all trail junctions, and at campsite locations. Because this hike is so long--if you want to do it in one trip--it's necessary for most people to camp one night and do it in 2 days. There are 7 campsites along the way, all in the shade of ponderosa pines. Campsites are shown on the map. These campsites are never crowded, as very few people camp along the way. Water is scarce, which discourages camping. For this reason, most people hike it in stages, by using one of the connecting trails. This eliminates the need to carry water for camping. The connecting paths are called: **Sheep Creek, Swamp Canyon, Whiteman,** and **Agua Canyon Trails.** On this map, distances between dots are in kilometers (kms).

Elevations Bryce Point, 2529m; low point on the trail, about 2050m, Rainbow Point, 2776m.

Time Needed From Bryce Point to Rainbow Point is about 35 kms. This means the average person will need 1 1/2, or 2 days, and carry a large backpack. However, a fast hiker could do it in one long day with an early start and 2 cars; or perhaps a car & mtn. bike. If using a bike as a shuttle, leave it at Rainbow Point for a fast ride downhill.

Water One major problem along this trail is lack of water. In the spring season, just after the snow melts, there's often some running water in most creek bottoms, but they dry up later on. Consult park rangers at the VC as to the whereabouts of water before hiking. Iron Spring has a good flow, but the water is undrinkable; Birch Spring has a small discharge and may be dry late in summer. Lack of good water is the reason this is not a popular place for backpacking.

Maps Trails Illustrated/National Geographic map Paunsaugunt Plateau, Mount Dutton, Bryce Canyon (1:50,000); Bryce Canyon National Park (1:31,680); or just use the little free map they give you upon entering the national park. Maps can be bought at the VC; also at Ruby's Inn where a better selection can be found.

Main Attractions A forested trail hike along the base of the Pink Cliffs.

BestTime to Hike May through October, but there will be more water available in May or June.

Boots/Shoes Any dry-weather boots or shoes. Running shoes work great on any trail in Bryce Canyon.

Author's Experience The author has hiked the entire trail, but in 4 stages, using all connecting trails. This took 2 days to complete. One stage from Bryce Point to Sheep Creek Trailhead, then the road-walk back to his car, took about 4 1/2 hours. A mtn. bike would eliminate a road-walk. All connecting trails were hiked a second time in 2003; half these trails were again hiked in 2009.

Looking north from the **Agua Canyon Viewpoint**. The **Under-the-Rim Trail** runs north-south along the eastern (right side) base of these Pink Cliffs in the pine trees.

Map 5, Under-the-Rim Trail, Bryce Canyon National Park

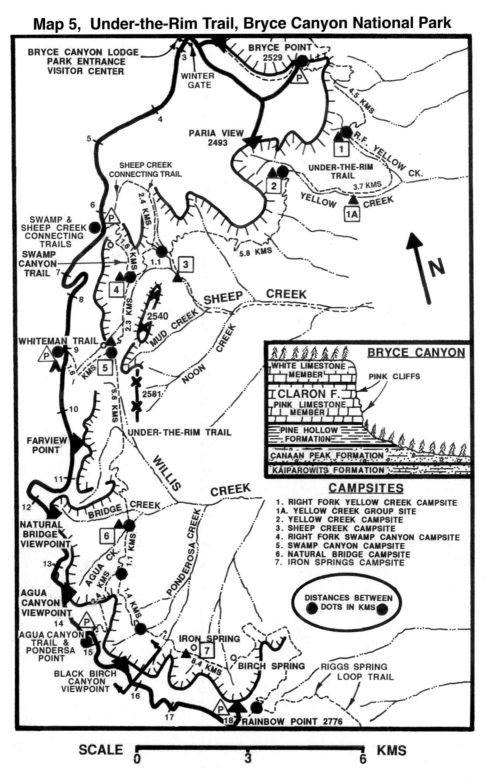

BRYCE CANYON LODGE
PARK ENTRANCE
VISITOR CENTER

BRYCE POINT
2529

WINTER
GATE

PARIA VIEW
2493

R.F. YELLOW CK.

4.5 KMS

UNDER-THE-RIM
TRAIL

SHEEP CREEK
CONNECTING TRAIL

3.7 KMS

YELLOW   CREEK

5.8 KMS

SWAMP &
SHEEP CREEK
CONNECTING
TRAILS

SWAMP
CANYON
TRAIL

WHITEMAN TRAIL

SHEEP   CREEK

2540

MUD CREEK

NOON   CREEK

2581

UNDER-THE-RIM TRAIL

FARVIEW
POINT

WILLIS   CREEK

BRIDGE   CREEK

NATURAL
BRIDGE
VIEWPOINT

AGUA CK.

PONDEROSA CREEK

AGUA
CANYON
VIEWPOINT

AGUA CANYON
TRAIL &
PONDERSA
POINT

BLACK BIRCH
CANYON
VIEWPOINT

IRON SPRING

BIRCH SPRING

RIGGS SPRING
LOOP TRAIL

RAINBOW POINT 2776

BRYCE CANYON

WHITE LIMESTONE
MEMBER

PINK CLIFFS

CLARON F.
PINK LIMESTONE
MEMBER

PINE HOLLOW
FORMATION

CANAAN PEAK FORMATION

KAIPAROWITS FORMATION

CAMPSITES

1. RIGHT FORK YELLOW CREEK CAMPSITE
1A. YELLOW CREEK GROUP SITE
2. YELLOW CREEK CAMPSITE
3. SHEEP CREEK CAMPSITE
4. RIGHT FORK SWAMP CANYON CAMPSITE
5. SWAMP CANYON CAMPSITE
6. NATURAL BRIDGE CAMPSITE
7. IRON SPRINGS CAMPSITE

DISTANCES BETWEEN
DOTS IN KMS

N

SCALE
0   3   6   KMS

Riggs Spring Loop Trail, Bryce Canyon National Park

Location & Access This is the last of 4 maps covering the trails of Bryce Canyon National Park. Shown here is the **Riggs Spring Loop Trail** at the extreme southern end of the plateau and the national park. The beginning & end of this hike is at **Rainbow Point,** which is at the end of the paved park road. In recent years, roads in Bryce Canyon up to **Bryce Point** have been kept open year-round; south of the winter gate it's normally closed (see Map 4). However, if the snow isn't too deep, the road to **Rainbow Point** is sometimes plowed, depending on availability of equipment. At Rainbow Point there are toilets and sometimes drinking water (their spring was dry in the summer of 2003). To get to the trailhead, drive south into the park from the Ruby's Inn area. It's best to stop at the visitor center located next to the fee station for any last minute information on road & trail openings--or closures--or maps. From there continue south for 27.5 kms (17.1 miles) and stop at the big parking lot next to mile post 18.

Trail/Route The Riggs Spring Loop Trail is well-maintained and because of the availability of water at 2 locations, it's one of the better hikes in the park, and certainly one of the better areas for backcountry camping. From Rainbow Point, you can do the loop-hike either clockwise or counter clockwise. From the parking lot look for any path heading south toward **Yovimpa Point** and the **Bristlecone Loop Trail**. At nearby trail junctions are signs pointing out the beginning of the Riggs Spring Trail. Once on it, head east or west. For this description, head west down toward **Yovimpa Pass**, a distance of about 2 1/2 kms. From there continue south on a good trail (actually an old road) to **Riggs Spring** and nearby campsite which is about 5 1/2 kms from your car. From there, head north, then east along the base of the escarpment. Along the way, you'll pass the **Corral Hollow Campsite** (which has no water). From there continue easterly a ways, and south a little, then north & northwest back to the parking lot. If you're interested in a short walk, some of the nicest views around can be had from Yovimpa Point and from along the Bristlecone Loop Trail.

Elevations Rainbow Point, 2776m; Yovimpa Pass, 2548m; Riggs Spring, 2269m.

Time Needed The total length of the Riggs Spring Loop Trail is about 14 kms. Fast walkers can do this hike in about 3 hours, but for others it can take 4-6 hours. However, of all the trails in the park, this one has some of the nicest campsites, so you might consider spending a night on the trail. Riggs Spring is the best campsite, with good water and lots of shade & grass.

Water Riggs Spring is fenced off to keep cattle or deer away from where the water comes out of the ground in a pipe. It has a good, year-round flow, but of course the NPS insists you purify it first! Yovimpa Pass has a spring and maybe a little running water, some of which is pumped up to the parking lot at Rainbow Point (except during times of drought, as was the case in 2003!). The Corral Hollow Campsite is normally dry; unless you arrive in spring, when some water is available for a short period of time in the creek bed.

Maps Trails Illustrated/National Geographic map Paunsaugunt Plateau, Mount Dutton, Bryce Canyon (1:50,000); or Bryce Canyon National Park (1:31,680). Both maps can be bought at the visitor center. Or just use the little free map they give you when you pass through the fee station.

Main Attractions The highest & coolest part of the park is at Rainbow Point, making it a nice cool hideout in summer. The walk to Yovimpa Point is a good place to see old bristlecone pine trees.

Best Time to Hike From about early to mid-May, until the end of October. Each year is a little different.

Boots/Shoes Any light weight boots or shoes; simple running shoes are best.

Author's Experience As usual, the author was in a hurry on this loop-hike, which usually included a short side-trip along the Bristlecone Loop Trail; round-trip was about 3 hours on 3 different hikes. His last trips in 2003 & 2009 took 2 3/4 hours.

This is **Riggs Spring** in 2009. The log enclosure is new so water should be safer now.

Map 6, Riggs Spring Loop Trail, Bryce Canyon National Park

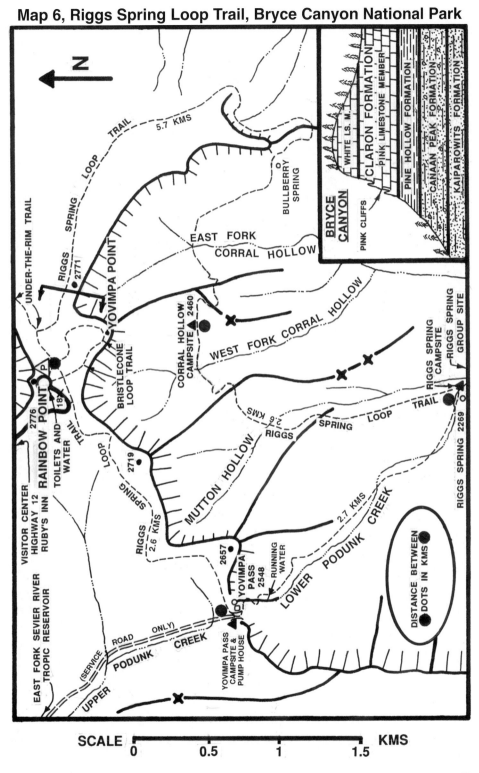

SCALE   KMS

0   0.5   1   1.5

Bull Valley Gorge, Willis Creek and Averett Canyon

Location & Access This map shows 4 canyons located southwest of the small town of Cannonville. Get there via the **Skutumpah Road,** which runs from the area just south of Cannonville in a south-westerly direction towards these canyons, and on past the Swallow, Deer Spring & Skutumpah Ranches. The Skutumpah Road ends (or begins) at the upper end of Johnson Canyon northeast of Kanab. This is the shortest link between Kanab and Cannonville.

The Skutumpah Road is generally open to all vehicles from around the first of April until sometime in November. But each year is different. During years with dry winters, it's possible to travel it all the time, except for a week or so right after a storm. Parts of this road just south of the Bull Valley Gorge Bridge are made of clay, which becomes very slick when wet. Also the steep dugway just south of the old Clark Ranch on Willis Creek is sometimes icy in the coldest part of the year. In the winter of 1986-87, two 4WD's slid off that part of the road and had to be pulled out. However, it's a better road now. In the warmer half of the year, the clay beds dry quickly after storms and it's a good road for all vehicles with a fair amount of spring, summer and fall traffic.

One way to get there is to drive east from Kanab on Highway 89. Between mile posts 54 & 55, turn left or north onto the paved Johnson Valley Road. At Km 26.6/Mile 16.5 is a junction at the head of Johnson Valley. Turn right or northeast onto the graveled & graded Skutumpah Road going toward Cannonville. You'll pass the Skutumpah, Deer Spring & Swallow Park Ranches, then at Km 67/Mile 41.6 (distance from Highway 89) will be the **Bull Valley Gorge Bridge.** Continue northeast to **Willis Creek** at Km 69.9/Mile 43.4; and to **Averett Canyon** at Km 72.4/Mile 44.9. If you continue northeast, you'll come to the paved Kodachrome Basin Road at Km 79.9/Mile 49.6. Cannonville is another 4.7 kms (2.9 miles) north.

If coming from Cannonville, head south on the **Kodachrome Basin Road** for 4.7 kms (2.9 miles) until you reach the Skutumpah Road then turn south. From there, drive 7.6 kms (4.7 miles) to Averett Canyon; or to Willis Creek at Km 10/Mile 6.2; or on to the Bull Valley Gorge Bridge at Km 12.9/Mile 8.
Trail/Route There are no trails in these canyons; you simply walk down the dry creek bed or along a very small stream flowing through Willis Creek Gorge. If you make the loop-hike of Bull Valley Gorge & Willis Creek, using the middle part of **Sheep Creek** as a link between the two, then you'll walk along a seldom used 4WD track in the bottom of the dry wash of Sheep Creek. About twice a year, the grazing permit holders, take in or bring out cattle from the middle part of the Upper Paria River Gorge via Sheep Creek but they are no longer allowed to take motor vehicles with them. But the ban on vehicles doesn't stop all ATV's--some still go down Sheep Creek anyway.

Averett Canyon & Monument To find the monument (read more about it below), walk from the Skutumpah Road down the dry creek bed a little less than 1 km; or 8 minutes at a fast walk. You'll know you're near the monument when you see an old trail running up the east side of the canyon. The monument is about 8m above and 30m back from the dry creek bed on a low bench on the right or west side. It's in a small clearing, facing east and surrounded by piñon-juniper trees (be there in the morning hours to take pictures). If you continue downcanyon another km, you'll come to 3 dropoffs in about 100m. Walk along the west side of the canyon and just below the 3rd dropoff, climb down a ramp to the bottom. From there you can walk up Willis Creek to the road.

Willis Creek Simply walk in or out of the canyon with no obstacles. About 800m into the hike is a small waterfall; walk around it. The best narrows are about 300m before or above the junction with Averett Canyon. Below that the canyon slowly opens up and gets deeper--but a little less interesting.

Bull Valley Gorge Park on the north side of the bridge next to the fence, or at another site about 200m east, then walk along the north side of the narrow slot canyon west of the bridge about 350m. At that point you simply walk into the dry creek bed. Just below that there used to be a big log jam, but that's gone now, washed away in a big flood. In about the same area are now 2 short dropoffs of about 2-3m each caused by chokestones. Most people can get up or down these OK, but take a short rope to help less-experienced hikers. Near the bridge could be another dropoff from a huge boulder; in 2009, this was an easy downclimb, but things change with each flood. The best narrows in the canyon are in this upper part before coming to the bridge. When you reach the bridge, look up and you'll see the remains of the pickup which slid into the upper slot and took 3 lives. Read more below.

There's a steep route out of the gorge located about 100m or so below the bridge. The author went up this route once, but those unaccustomed to rock climbing may feel uneasy using this entry/exit (E/E). On the map are other possible E/E routes to the gorge; the best one may be about 1 1/2 kms below the bridge. Or just retreat back upcanyon the same way you came. If you like longer hikes, walk down to Sheep Creek, turn north a ways, then head west up Willis Creek and back to the road.
Elevations Bull Valley Gorge Bridge, 1853m; trailhead on Willis Creek, 1847m; the junction of Bull Valley Gorge and Sheep Creek, the low point on a loop-hike, about 1643m.
Time Needed Most people just hike down each canyon about a km or so, see the best parts, and return the same way. Doing this takes a little 1-3 hours. Or for long distance hikers, the length of the walk down Bull Valley Gorge and up Sheep & Willis Creeks back to the Skutumpah Road, is about 20 kms. Combine that with the 2 1/2 km walk along the road between the trailheads and you have an all-day hike from 6-9 hours (a mtn. bike would eliminate the road-walk). It's also possible to do the hike in 2 days, making an overnight camp in the lower part of Sheep Creek, near where it enters the Upper Paria River Gorge. In that area you should find running water, presumably year-round (?), and good campsites. If taking in big packs, it'll be easier to go down Bull Valley Gorge, rather than up.
Water For day-hikes take your own from a culinary source, but there's year-round running water in much of Willis Creek. You could probably drink this water as-is in winter, as the land above the road is summer range for cattle. It's best to purify it first however. Bull Valley Gorge is dry, as is most of Sheep Creek. Water does begin to flow out of seeps in the lower part of Sheep Creek as the red-colored lower parts of the Navajo Sandstone begin to be exposed. This should be good water in summer, as the cattle at that time are out of the canyons and in the mountains.
Maps USGS or BLM map Kanab (1:100,000) for driving & orientation; and Bull Valley Gorge (1:24,000-7 1/2' quad) for hiking.
Main Attractions The upper one or 2 kms of each canyon have some nice fotogenic slots similar to the Buckskin Gulch. The scenery in the lower part of Bull Valley Gorge, with the huge Navajo Sandstone walls dotted with pine trees, is worth seeing too. Also interesting is the unusual bridge over the upper part of Bull Valley Gorge, and the 1954 accident scene where 3 men were killed. Also, the Averett Monument discussed below.
Best Time to Hike From April through October. This time period offers the best chance for the Sku-

Map 7, Bull Valley Gorge, Willis Creek and Averett Canyon

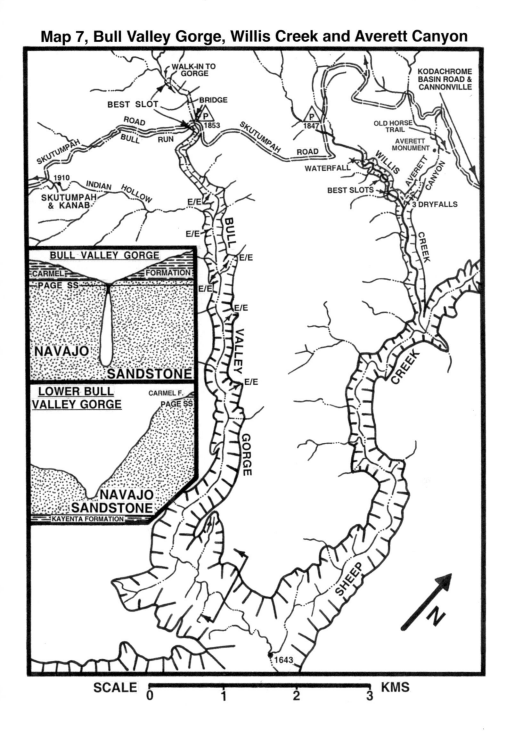

tumpah Road to be open & dry. May or June, and September or October, might be the ideal time.
Boots/Shoes Willis Creek is small and you can hop right across, but it's best to have wading-type shoes for that part of the hike. Bull Valley Gorge has no running water, but just up from the bridge, you may find pools which can hold water and mud for a few days or a week after each storm. For the entire loop-hike, wading-type shoes may be best.
Author's Experience The author first tried hiking Bull Valley Gorge on a very cold mid-April morning,

but found big pools of water & mud near the bridge. A month later it was dry and he made 2 more trips into the gorge at that time. Another time he went down Willis Creek on his way to Deer Creek in the middle part of the Upper Paria River Gorge. His last trips were in 2003 & 2009 with a digital camera.

History of the Bull Valley Gorge Bridge

One of the more spectacular and unusual bridges you'll ever see is the one spanning the upper part of Bull Valley Gorge. The top part of this extremely narrow slot is only about 1m wide. One reader, whose name has been lost, measured the depth of the slot from the top of the bridge to the bottom at 44m. The rock involved is the ever-present Navajo Sandstone, the most prominent slot canyon making formation on the Colorado Plateau.

This bridge was first built sometime in the mid-1940's by **Marian Clark, Ammon Davis and Herm Pollock**. The first stage of that operation involved using a winch to drag several large logs across the gap to serve as a foundation for the bridge. Then planks were laid across the logs, making a rather simple bridge which was first used by local cattlemen. This was the first time Bryce Valley and the Kanab & Johnson Canyon areas were linked. A later event forced the county to upgrade the bridge which is safe & sound today.

That event was the accident which occurred sometime on Thursday, **October 14, 1954**. Three men died as their pickup got out of control and slid off the bridge and wedged in the upper part of the gorge. The victims were **Max Henderson**, 33, and **Hart Johnson**, 37, both of Cannonville; and **Clark Smith**, 32, of Henrieville. The **Garfield County News** carried the story in the October 21 edition.

Quoting from the newspaper report; *They started out Thursday to set up a deer hunting camp on range land one of the men owned in Kane County. When they had not returned by Saturday, a search was started for them.*

A party led by Kendall Dutton of Cannonville, crossing the Bull Valley Gorge bridge, at 1 p.m. Sunday, sighted the pickup truck lodged in the narrow gorge about 50 feet [15m] below the bridge.

Bodies of two of the victims were still wedged into the truck, the third body had fallen clear and crashed to the Gorge floor almost 200 feet [60m] lower down.

The Highway Patrol and county Sheriff were called in and the rescue operation started. Garfield County Sheriff Deward Woodard was in charge of removing the bodies which was a hair-raising operation. His son, Paul Woodard, with a rope around his waist, worked for hours sawing away parts of the truck--including the steering column--in order to free the bodies [Herm Pollock recalls they also used an acetylene torch for a while]. He worked at the dizzy height above the canyon floor, with the swaying truck threatening to give [way] under him at any time [from the truck to the bottom of the gorge is about 30m]. When one of the bodies was released from the truck, the weight almost pulled 22 men over the edge as the slack in the rope was suddenly snapped up.

According to the Sheriff, in reconstructing the accident, the light pickup truck the men were riding, stalled on the south side of the bridge and rolled backwards and into the gorge, dropping 50 feet [15m] before the narrowing sides crushed the cab and the men inside it.

Hart Johnson was buried in the Georgetown Cemetery south of Cannonville; Max Henderson was buried in the Cannonville Cemetery north of Cannonville; and Clark Smith was buried in the Henrieville Cemetery. All tombstones are dated October 14, 1954.

Since the accident, the Bull Valley Gorge Bridge has been rebuilt. It appears workers simply pushed trees and large rocks down into the narrow chasm where they became lodged in the upper narrow part. Then a bulldozer must have pushed more rock and debris on top of that, making a very solid and much wider bridge than was first built.

When you stop there today, walk west from the bridge along the north side of the gorge and from there you can see the pickup still lodged in the narrow slot. As you walk along the bottom of the gorge you have an even better view of the truck from below. Or tie a rope onto trees and rappel down past it, something the author did in the summer of 2009. Some of the pictures here were taken as he jumarred back up. Because the pickup is sitting high & dry and protected from rain and snow by the bridge, it will be there in the same position for a long time.

Averett Monument

Another interesting thing to see in the immediate area is the **Averett Monument** (some people spell it Everett). First the story behind the grave.

In August of 1866, a Mormon cavalry company from the St. George area was ordered by Erastus Snow to go on an expedition to the Green River against the Indian Chief Black Hawk and his group. This company, under the command of James Andrus, left the southern Utah settlements and went east past Pipe Springs, Kanab, up Johnson Canyon, and northeast to the upper Paria River Valley. This was before there were any settlements in the area and traveling was rough.

By the time they reached the spot where Cannonville is today, many men were sick. It was decided to send these men back home. So 6 men and 14 head of disabled horses headed back. Along the way the small group was attacked by Indians. **Elijah Averett Jr.** was in the lead and he was shot and killed. The rest of the group escaped and managed to circle around and return to the main unit in the upper Paria. The Indians, presumably Navajos, were pursued, but escaped. Later, Averett was buried on August 27, 1866, where he died. This is in the bottom of what is now called **Averett Canyon**. The place is right on the old trail which was used by early-day stockmen and settlers before the present-day road was built.

Later in 1871, Frederick S. Dellenbaugh wrote about visiting the place in his diary. He stated he came across the grave marked by a sandstone slab with *EA 1866* cut on it, which the wolves had dug out, leaving the human bones scattered around. Later, local cowboys reburied the bones and erected a cedar post with Averetts name on it. Many years later, the Boy Scouts of Tropic put that cedar post in their little museum or scout hall in Tropic, and replaced it with a permanent stone marker that you see there today. According to Wallace Ott of Tropic, the new monument, the larger of the two, was dedicated in April, 1937. About 15 people showed up and James L. Hatch, the local Stake President of the Mormon Church, conducted the dedication ceremony.

Above Both the old and new **monuments** along **Averett Canyon**.

Left This is the old and apparently the original monument to **Elijah Averett** (Everett?).

IN MEMORY OF
ELIJAH EVERETT, JR.
KILLED HERE BY INDIANS IN 1866;
BURIED BY HIS COMRADES OF THE
CAPT. JAMES ANDREWS CO. U.S. CAVALRY.

Left The newer monument to **Elijah Averett**. One question here would be, was it the US Cavalry, or a Mormon Militia?

This is a closeup foto of the pickup truck that slipped off the bridge and fell into the **Bull Valley Gorge** on October 14, 1954. The only way to get a picture like is to tie a rope to a tree and rappel down next to it (roughly 10m). If you try this trick, it's best to rap all the way down, then using ascenders, jumar back up. This will allow you to let go with your hands at various places to take fotos. It's roughly 44m from the tree to the bottom.

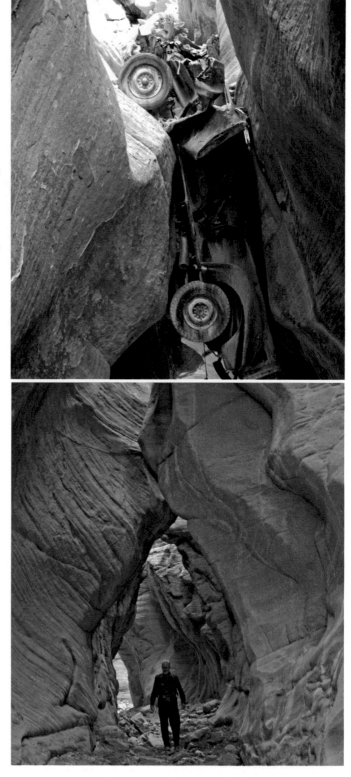

This is one of the better sections of the narrows in upper **Bull Valley Gorge**. This part is about halfway between where you enter, and the bridge on the Skutumpah Road.

Above The lower narrows of **Willis Creek**. There is running water here, but the stream is so small, you can step right over it most of the time. The Navajo Sandstone in this section has a yellow tint to it.

Left In the upper part of the **Bull Valley Gorge**, you'll always find something like this. It's a wide open canyon to this point, then it slots-up quick and the logs can only jam-up. Normally it's not a major problem, but things do change with every flood. Just in case, take a short rope or two to help each other down, or back up. This picture was taken in June, 2009.

Above This is the little waterfall in the middle part of **Willis Creek**. You can walk around this on the left (on your right side going downcanyon). Or you can downclimb it quite easily, but you may get your feet wet in the little pool.

Right New for 2009 is this boulder you have to walk under in about the middle of the **Bull Valley Gorge Narrows**. Expect boulders and other features in the bottom of every slot or narrow canyon on the Colorado Plateau to change with every flash flood.

From inside the **Bull Valley Gorge** and immediately above the bridge, you'll have a clear view of the **pickup truck** that became lodged in the slot on October 14, 1954. From the top of the bridge to the canyon floor is 44m.

Bullrush, Tank & Deer Range Canyons, Lick & Park Washes, and No Mans Mesa & the Jepson Goat Trail

Location & Access These canyons & mesas are located about halfway between Johnson Valley (which is 16 kms/10 miles east of Kanab) and Cannonville. Before going, have the **Kanab** metric 1:100,000 scale map in hand. One way to get there is to drive along Highway 89 east of Kanab. Between mile posts 54 & 55, turn north onto the paved Johnson Valley Road. At the head of Johnson Valley and at Km 26.6/Mile 16.5, is a junction. Turn right or northeast onto the graveled & graded **Skutumpah Road** heading towards Cannonville. You'll pass the Skutumpah and Deer Spring Ranches, then at Km 50.5/Mile 31.4 (distance from Highway 89) is **Lick Wash**. Just before the dry creek bed, turn south onto a side-road and drive 100m to the trailhead parking & trail register. This should now be considered the place to park if you're going down Lick Wash to **No Mans Mesa** & the **Jepson Goat Trail**. In the past, the route beginning just west of the Swallow Park Ranch was acceptable, but there is private land there and a gate has been erected just off the Skutumpah Road--so forget going in there.

Or continue north to Km 57/Mile 35.4 and park at or near **Bullrush Hollow** (the gorge part is downstream a ways). This is the best place to park if you're planning to make a loop hike of both **Bullrush** and **Deer Range Canyons** if you have a **2WD car**. Or if you have a HCV/4WD, continue northeast to a junction at Km 60.2/Mile 37.4, then turn south toward **Deer Range** and **Tank Canyons**. Drive 300m (.2 mile) to another junction. Left is the main road. If you turn right onto a seldom-used track, you can only drive another 1.5 kms (1 mile) or so before the track is washed out. If you use this route, park at the washout and walk one of the old ATV tracks to Tank Canyon.

Or follow the main road (**sandy** in places) to Km 3.6 (Mile 2.2) and park next to a **fence & gate** where 2 upper forks of Deer Range Canyon meet. By parking there, you can walk down Deer Range and up Tank Canyon. The scenery is much better in Tank & Deer Range Canyons than in Bullrush. Or if you want to visit **Deer Range Point** which has some interesting views down into upper Deer Creek to the east, or North Swagg to the south, then follow this map north a little, then south to about Km 9.8 (Mile 6.1). That road is pretty good, but **sandy**. But the foto ops aren't as good as this writer once thought.

If you continue northeast on the Skutumpah Road, you'll come to the paved **Kodachrome Basin Road** at Km 79.9/Mile 49.6. **Cannonville** is another 4.7 kms (2.9 miles) to the north. If coming from Cannonville, head south on the Kodachrome Basin Road for 4.7 kms (2.9 miles) until you reach the Skutumpah Road, then turn southwest. From there, drive 19.6 kms (12.2 miles) and turn south to the road junction near Deer Range Canyon mentioned above. Or for people with 2WD's, continue southwest to Bullrush Hollow at Km 22.9/Mile 14.2 (from the Kodachrome Basin Road) and park. Or continue southwest to Lick Wash at Km 29.3/Mile 18.2 and park at the trailhead 100m to the south.

Trail/Route Starting from the **Lick Wash Trailhead**, walk down the dry creek bed; soon you'll come to some short narrows in the upper part of the gorge, then still using the dry wash and old AVT track near the bottom end, make your way to the **LeFevre Cabin** (and the **Jepson Goat Trail,** read more below). This old cabin, according to Ferrell Brinkerhoff of Tropic, was brought into the canyon from Ruby's Inn in about 1967. It had been one of the Inn's original rustic cabins. It was placed on a corner of what used to be a Utah state section. That state section has been horse-traded away since the monument was created. Because of the private land in Swallow Park, using Lick Wash is the best way to reach the LeFevre Cabin and the Jepson Goat Trail.

To hike up to **No Mans Mesa** along the **Jepson Goat Trail,** first make your way to the LeFevre Cabin. From there, walk eastward on the old road coming down from Swallow Park. As you reach the north end of No Mans Mesa, notice the talus slope coming down from the top. This is where the Jepson Goat Trail is located. To get on it, walk to the east side of a little hill at the northern base of the talus slope, then head straight up. You may go up halfway before finding the actual trail. Once on it, it's easy to follow. The upper part, which zig zags around some minor cliffs, is very obvious and is still in reasonably good condition. At the very top is a wire gate and short fence which kept the goats on the mesa. About 100m from the top of the trail on the east side, is another steep route up or down.

If you want to see **Adair Lake**, drive to a point about 800m (.5 mile) north of the turnoff to Lick Wash Trailhead. There you'll find a home-made ATV track heading east. It climbs up on the mesa and goes down the other side just south of James D. Ott's private land at Swallow Park. This writer hasn't been on it, but has seen it from both sides. Using this ATV track will get you to Adair Lake.

Here's a loop-hike possibility. Walk down **Bullrush Hollow & Gorge,** then along the sandy road in Park Wash to very near the north end of No Mans Mesa, then turn northward into the dry wash coming out of **Deer Range Canyon.** Walk north up the dry creek until you reach **Tank Canyon;** then veer left and continue up to a very short slot & dryfall. To get around this, climb up an easy route on the left or west side, and exit Tank Canyon as shown. At about the road junction marked 2075m altitude, turn left, and with compass in hand, walk west cross-country back to the Skutumpah Road and your car.

However, a better plan for these latter 2 canyons would be to start in upper Deer Range Canyon. Simply walk downcanyon to where Tank comes in on the right, but continue down Deer Range for at least another 3 kms to see the best part of that drainage, then return and walk out of upper Tank Canyon. Upper Tank has some colorful rocks on its upper east wall & rim. From somewhere in upper Tank, road-walk back to your car. These 2 canyons with red & yellow streaked white Navajo Sandstone walls, plus blue skies & green ponderosa pines, offer some of the better foto ops around. If you make it out to **Deer Range Point,** walk east to view Deer Creek, or south to see North Swagg.

Elevations Trailheads; 1905m, 2025m, 2012m, 2073m & 2164m, and down to about 1835m at the LeFevre Cabin.

Time Needed If you park on Bullrush Hollow, walk downcanyon and up Deer Range & Tank Canyons, then due west cross-country back to your car, it will be a long day for some, somewhere near 7-11 hours round-trip. If driving to upper Deer Range and hiking down that drainage and up Tank Canyon, you'll likely need 5-8 hours round-trip, but it will depend on how far down Deer Range Canyon you walk.

To walk down Lick Wash and up to the top of the goat trail, it'll take most people all day, maybe 5-8 hours depending on how far you actually walk. Or for just Lick Wash, walk downcanyon 2-3 kms, see the best parts, and return the same way, all in a couple of hours.

Water These are all dry hikes so carry your own, and have plenty in your car. Nearby are springs in Swallow Park and in Bullrush Gorge, but with cattle there year-round, forget it! Cattlemen used to pipe water from Adams Spring down to around the LeFevre Cabin, but that isn't happening any more.

Maps USGS or BLM map Kanab (1:100,000) for driving & orientation; and Rainbow Point, Bull Valley Gorge, Deer Spring Point & Deer Range Point (1:24,000--7 1/2' quads) for hiking.

Map 8, Bullrush, Tank & Deer Range Canyons, Lick & Park Washes, and No Mans Mesa & the Jepson Goat Trail

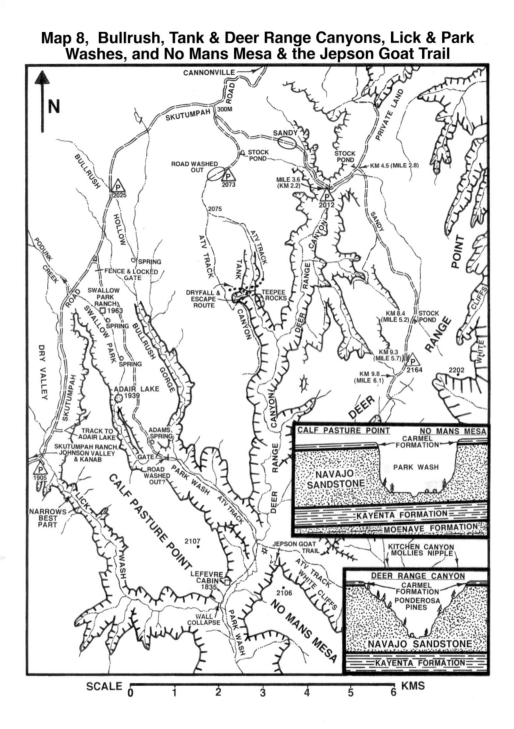

Main Attractions Lick Wash has some pretty good narrows in its upper end. Or for scenery, see Tank & Deer Range Canyons. Those canyon walls have cracks allowing ponderosa pines to grow, making a unique scene. In some places, the colors are similar in some ways to the Coyote Buttes country. Also, Adair Lake, an old ranch, historic trail and grand views of the nearby parklands and White Cliffs from the top of No Mans Mesa.

Best Time to Hike Spring or fall, but it's also possible in summer because of the higher altitudes.

Boots/Shoes Any comfortable boots or shoes; simple running shoes are likely the best.

Author's Experience Once the author parked on the road at Bullrush Hollow, walked down the gorge, then up Deer Range & Tank Canyons, and finally cross-country back to his car, all in 6 1/2 hours. A 2nd trip took 6 1/4 hours. He once walked down Lick Wash to the LeFevre Cabin, then around to the east side of No Mans Mesa, and climbed it along the route shown. He later came down the goat trail and re-turned via Park Wash and the Swallow Park Ranch. That took a little over 7 hours. Another time he parked at the corral & gate east of the ranch, walked down the road and up the goat trail, then checked out the LeFevre Cabin. After that he headed back, but climbed up the east side of Calf Pasture Point. That allowed some good views down on the LeFevre Cabin and No Mans Mesa. From there, it was back to his car, all in about 5 2/3 hours. In 2003, he actually drove his Tracker to the gate just beyond Adams Spring, rehiked the goat trail, saw the cabin, photographed lower Deer Range Canyon and returned, all in 3 3/4 hours. In 2009, he went down Lick, up the goat trail, and back in 4 1/2 hours. He wandered around on Deer Range Point for about 4 hours looking for something interesting, but it's not so good.

The History of Swallow Park Ranch

Swallow Park is a high valley just under 2000m elevation and located along the Skutumpah Road about halfway between the upper end of Johnson Valley and Cannonville. It's also just south of the southern end of Bryce Canyon National Park.

From the **Biography of John G. Kitchen,** it appears the first settler at Swallow Park was Frank Hamblin. This had to have been in the early 1870's because on an 1874 map of the state of Utah, Swal-low Park and Adair Lake are shown for the first time (also Molly's Nipple--but it's spelled Mollies on today's USGS maps). Hamblin's occupancy extended into the 1890's to beyond the turn of the century. For several years, Hamblin was the only neighbor John G. Kitchen had while he lived at the Nipple Ranch. Read more about Kitchen in the chapter on Kitchen Canyon and the Nipple Ranch.

If the memories of some of the old timers in Bryce Valley are correct, the second owner of the ranch was a man named **George Adams**. George married Minda, one of the daughters of Frank Hamblin, thus giving him a toehold on the ranch. George's name is on the spring located southeast of Adair Lake. Wal-lace Ott of Tropic believes Adams got there sometime in the early 1900's. Actually, it was November 23, 1917 when George first got the patent deed (first deed given to someone from the US Government) and official ownership under the homestead act. There are no other records of land ownership prior to that time, but most early settlers just squatted on the land without having a deed. It also took 5 full years of occupancy to gain official title. Frank Hamblin apparently never got the patent deed to the ranch.

Adams owned the ranch only a couple of years, then sold the lower part of the valley, around Adair Lake, to **Jackson Riggs** in December, 1919. Just prior to this sale, **William Sears Riggs**, settled and filed ownership on the northern part of the valley in November, 1919. In 1926, W. S. Riggs then bought more land from the federal government, which was an enlargement of his original 160 acres which is a quarter section. Sears Riggs is the one who built the first house at the ranch, which is still there today. His name is also on the good spring located near the head of Lower Podunk Creek, just south of the southern tip of Bryce Canyon and along the Riggs Spring Loop Trail.

Wallace Ott, who was born in 1911 (still alive in 2009), bought the entire spread on December 11, 1940. He lived there part time, using it as a summer ranch until 1955. During his stay at Swallow Park, part of the property was sold to **John H. Johnson** in March, 1945. Then Wallace Ott sold out entirely to one of his relatives, **Layton Ott**, in December, 1955. Less than a month later, John H. Johnson sold his part of the Park to **Calvin C. Johnson** of Kanab. Many transitions have taken place over the years, but as of recently, 3 Brinkerhoff brothers owned the land north of the Skutumpah Road, while **James D. Ott** of Kanab owned the lower part of the old Swallow Park Ranch which gets close to Adair Lake.

In the middle of Swallow Park today (south of the Skutumpah Road), you'll see the old shack, built by Sears Riggs, and a newer, larger house next to it. Regarding this home, and according to Ferrell Brinkerhoff of Tropic: *We tore down my Dad's old barn, and Les LeFevre constructed that house from the lumber. That would have been in about 1960.*

Also in this big pasture area are a couple of small dams and duck ponds which are nearly always full of water and are fed by several springs. Perhaps the most interesting thing to see is Adair Lake. It's been on early-day maps of the state of Utah as far back as 1874. It's at the southern end of the park, and right at the beginning of a little narrow section of upper Park Wash.

The lake is actually on a faultline, or just to the east of it. This faultline forms the cliffs you can see from upvalley. The west side has been raised, thus creating the lake just to the east. The lake and a swamp have always been there, but sometime prior to 1874, a very low dam was built, maybe a meter or less in height, to create a slightly larger and deeper lake.

One old-timer from Bryce Valley thought it was Frank Hamblin who built the dam, but a more likely scenario might be this. If you read the history of Pah Ria (Rock House), Pahreah and Adairville in the back of this book, it states that Jacob Hamblin and a small group of Mormons went to the Paria to set-tle in 1869 somewhere below The Box of the Paria. In the early 1870's they had floods & irrigation prob-lems and part of that group, including Thomas Adair, went south and formed a small community later known as Adairville. It's very likely that Jacob & Frank Hamblin (?) and Tom Adair were together at Swallow Park and used that as a summer range for their cattle. It's almost certain that Adair built the lake which still bares his name.

The lake is there year-round, throughout wet and dry years (but it was dry in the summer of 2003, and was a lake again in 2009). On 2 occasions Wallace Ott attempted to plant bass there, but appar-ently it was too shallow to sustain them throughout the winter. Presently in the lake, and for as long as anyone can remember, are salamanders, or what the locals call *water dogs*. The lake also has an abun-dant waterfowl population for much of the year.

Right on top of the low and almost invisible dam, is a corral. Wallace Ott used this corral for holding cattle, but others used it as a trap. They would herd cattle or horses up Park Wash from the area of No Mans Mesa. When they reached the corral, they were automatically trapped in one easy operation.

According to the *Kanab BLM metric map* which shows land ownership, **Adair Lake** is just south of the private land in Swallow Park, so if you come in from the west as suggested above, you'll be on the public domain all the way.

No Mans Mesa and the Jepson Goat Trail

No Mans Mesa is a remnant of the former plateau to the north. At one time it was part of Calf Pas-ture and Deer Range Points, but erosion has left it high & dry, and surrounded by unclimbable cliffs. It's 6-7 kms long and about 2 kms wide. The walls you see are white Navajo Sandstone, which are part of the prominent feature across southern Utah known as the **White Cliffs.** The capstone is the Carmel Formation, a more erosion or weather resistant rock than the Navajo. The top of the mesa is flat, except it tilts down slightly to the north and northwest, as shown on the geology cross-section. The height of the cliffs range from 200m in the north, to about 400m at the south end. The altitude of the mesa top ranges from about 2075m on the north end, to 2235m to the south.

The author has found 2 routes to the top. One is up the east side of the northernmost point; the other is the nearby **Jepson Goat Trail.** Here are 2 versions of the same story about the goats up on No Mans Mesa. First, in 1927, a local rancher by the name of **Lewis Jepson** built a trail up the extreme northern end of the mesa. He had 800 **Angora wether goats** (*wether* means a castrated goat) on the mesa in the spring and summer of the first year, and 1300 to 1500 (one source states 3000) in the spring of 1928. One story says the goats were taken to the mesa top to hide them from the bankers who had a lean on their owner (?). This seems to have been the Richfield Bank.

A 2nd version comes from **Charley Francisco** of Tropic: *I think the man who built that trail was Delbert Stocks, and he lived here in Cannonville. His boy's name was Bert Stocks. I don't know who he was working for but somebody hired him to build it. He was just a laborer.*

The goats were up there for 2 years, and when they went back up there to get 'um, there was only about 200 head there--out of 3000 or something (?). The rest of 'um had jump over the gate and dropped about 35 or 40 feet down there and got away from 'um--they was scattered all over the country. Now I'm more or less guessing, but at that time the banks was repossessing a lot of these sheep and goats and cattle, because the price dropped right out of 'um--they weren't worth nothing really!

The goats did fairly well for the short time they were there, but lack of water prevented it from becoming a good pasture, and has prevented any further grazing of livestock there since. For the most part, No Mans Mesa is untouched and is very pristine.

From the top of the **Jepson Goat Trail** and **No Mans Mesa** looking northwest toward Bryce Canyon National Park. This is the gate at the top of the trail. In the Park Wash Valley below, you can see an old 4WD road; now only ATV's use it. Also in the valley and to the left and out of sight is the LeFevre Cabin.

This is a scene from the walls of **Tank Canyon** as seen from the opposite side.

The **LeFevre Cabin** at the foot of the **Calf Pasture Point**. To the right 500m or so is No Mans Mesa.

Above The north end of **No Mans Mesa** as seen from Park Wash. The Jepson Goat Trail goes up the obvious triangular-shaped talus slope, then veers left and ends at the top.

Left From the cliffs above, looking down on **Adair Lake**. This lake is located in the south end **Swallow Park** and just off the Skutumpah Road. Notice the corral at the bottom of the picture. It sits on top of a low dam which makes it a reservoir.

Above A telefoto lens shot at the **Brinkerhoff House** in the middle of **Swallow Park**. In the far background are the pink cliffs of the southern end of Bryce Canyon National Park.

Right From Deer Range Point and from the elevation marked 2202m, looking southeast at big cliffs and spires of **Deer Range Point**. At the bottom of this foto is the beginning of Deer Creek.

Above The **Teepee Rocks** on the eastern rim of **Tank Canyon** as seen from the opposite side.

Left A typical scene as you walk down **Lick Wash**. The walls of all the canyons on this map are dotted with ponderosa pine, which coupled with blue skys and red rocks, make for fotogenic scenes. The route through Lick Wash is now the normal way to reach No Mans Mesa and the Jepson Goat Trail.

Mollies Nipple & Starlight Cave, Burch Ranch, the Kitchen Corral Point/Telegraph Flat CCC Spike Camp & Pottery Knoll

Location & Access Mollies Nipple is located just a few kms north of Highway 89, and about halfway between Page & Kanab. This peak is made of white Navajo Sandstone, but at the very summit is a brown and more erosion-resistant capstone. The author believes it could be the Carmel Formation; but it could also be a harder iron-rich layer within the upper Navajo. The name **Mollies Nipple,** supposedly comes from the wife of John G. Kitchen, whose name was Mollie. However, the name **Molly's Nipple** (it comes with 2 different spellings) was first shown on an 1874 map of the state of Utah, which seems to be a little earlier than when Kitchen first arrived in that part of the country (?). Read more about Kitchen and his ranch under the next map, **Kitchen Canyon** and the **Nipple Ranch.**

To get there, drive along Highway 89 between Page & Kanab. About 200m east of **new mile post 37,** turn north onto the **Nipple Ranch Road.** Drive 9.1 kms (5.6 miles) until you come to Kitchen Corral Point. There on the right or east side of the road will be a corral and **stone building** which was built by the **CCC's** who had a camp just up the road in the 1930's. If you want to visit the old **Burch Ranch,** park there. If you want to see where the old **Kitchen Corral Point/Telegraph Flat CCC Spike Camp** was situated, continue north on the Nipple Ranch Road to about Km 11.1/Mile 6.9, and park on the right side of the road. From there, you should see a **cement water tank** off to the east maybe 100m or so; and behind that a short canyon or indentation in the canyon wall with cottonwood trees. There's a spring located there, and the spike camp piped water down to the cement tank for their use. Due west of that and across the wash is **Pottery Knoll** and some big **Anasazi ruins (KM 10.3/Mile 6--cattle guard).**

To reach **Mollies Nipple** and perhaps the best route to **Starlight Canyon & Cave,** continue north on the Nipple Ranch Road. At a junction known in the early days as **Five Pines,** which is **16.4 kms (10.2 miles)** from the highway, veer right or northeast and drive through a gate (if it's closed when you arrive, close it behind you). Just beyond that gate is a shallow canyon and several pine trees, thus the name of the place below. At **Km 18.2/Mile 11.3,** turn right onto a **sandy track.** If you have a 2WD vehicle, drive about 100m and park next to 2 big round rocks & a juniper tree. If you have a 4WD, continue south-easterly on a very sandy track used mostly by ATV's. Most 4WD's can get up to a high point 1.9 kms (1.2 miles) from the Nipple Ranch Road. That place is marked **6152** (1875m) on the *Deer Range Point 7 1/2' quad.* Or go downhill a little then up to elevation **6355** (1937m) and park. From there, you go down a steeper sandy slope; so only those who have lots of confidence in their vehicle should continue. In winter, or whenever there's moisture in the sand, any 4WD can make it to the base of Mollies Nipple; otherwise, park at one of these 3 suggested places and walk from there.

The improved Nipple Ranch Road was originally built by Pan American Petroleum which drilled a test hole near the high point marked 1937m on the *Kanab metric map.* That place is north of Kitchen Canyon and on top of **Oil Well Hill.** This road is now periodically graded by the county.

Trail/Route With so many 4WD's & ATV's around these days, the normal route to **Mollies Nipple** is along the sandy track mentioned above. From wherever you start, just follow this track east to the base of The Nipple as shown on the map. As you walk along, observe closely and you may see in a couple of places, scattered **pottery fragments** which indicate old Indian campsites (?). Watch carefully, and you'll also see remnants of one of Kitchens old **rip gut** or **stake & rider fences.** This sandy track ends at the base of the peak with some ponderosa pines. Head straight up to the northeast. About halfway up you should see a faint hiker's trail emerging and after climbing a couple of steep pitches on the western side of the summit area, you'll be on top.

If you have a full day at your disposal, here is perhaps the easiest way to reach **Starlight Cave.** From the end of the sandy track at the base of the Nipple, contour eastward around the peak. Also observe **Map 10, Kitchen Canyon....,** and the *Deer Range Point 7 1/2' quad* carefully. On the east side of the peak, head northeast just to the right of one outcropping, down a minor ridge, cross a larger drainage not far east of another point with the elevation **6216** (1895m). From there, continue east down a ridge just north of a larger side-drainage of **Starlight Canyon.** Further along, you'll see cattle trails which will take you right down to the cave which is in a minor side-drainage of Starlight Canyon. The ceiling of this cave is black with soot, indicating it's seen lots of campfires. It also has a number of **pictographs** made with charcoal. Pot hunters, or archaeologists, have been digging there a lot too.

Elevations Mollies Nipple, 2216m; parking places, 1795m, 1875m, 1937m or 2011m.

Time Needed To climb only **Mollies Nipple** and return should take from 3-6 hours; depending mostly on where you park. It you decide to see **Starlight Cave** on the same hike, count on a full day, maybe 6-10 hours, depending on where you park.

Water There's none around, so carry all the water you'll need for camping & hiking.

Maps USGS or BLM map Kanab (1:100,000) for driving & orientation (also Eightmile Pass, 1:24,000- -7 1/2' quad for the drive from the highway); and Deer Range Point (1:24,000--7 1/2' quad) for hiking.

Main Attractions A fotogenic pyramid-shaped peak with excellent views, plus Starlight Cave, one of the more interesting places around. Also an old abandoned ranch, remains of a CCC camp, and the ruins on Pottery Knoll.

Best Time to Hike Spring or fall, but it can be climbed year-round.

Boots/Shoes Any comfortable light weight boots or shoes.

Author's Experience Years ago, and from the pass at 1825m, the author made it to Mollies Nipple in 1 1/4 hours. He then went north down into Kitchen Canyon to the Monkey House, Nipple Lake & Ranch, then road-walked back to his car. Round-trip took 4 1/4 hours. In November, 1997, he walked from the Nipple Ranch Road along the sandy track to Mollies Nipple and explored upper Starlight Canyon & Cave. He returned the same way, all in 8 1/4 hours. In the summer of 2003, he drove his 4WD Chevy Tracker to the high point marked 1875m (6152') and stopped there because the sand was very dry. He walked east along the sandy track and explored the peaks to the south along Pilot Ridge (some call this Starlight Ridge), then climbed Mollies for the 3rd time and returned, all in 5 1/4 hours. On 7/22/2009, he parked in the same place, and climbed The Nipple, then walked down and had lunch in Starlight Cave. He return in a total time of 6 3/4 hours.

The Burch Ranch

On your way to climb Mollies Nipple, you'll pass an abandoned ranch along the way. This is the **Burch Ranch,** one of the last to be built & occupied in the Paria River drainage. This old homestead is located in the northwestern corner of Section 33, T41S, R3W. Park beside the Nipple Ranch Road which is 9 kms (5.6 miles) from Highway 89 & mile post 37, and very near the old CCC stone building.

Map 9, Mollies Nipple & Starlight Cave, Burch Ranch, Kitchen Corral Point/Telegraph Flat CCC Spike Camp & Pottery Knoll

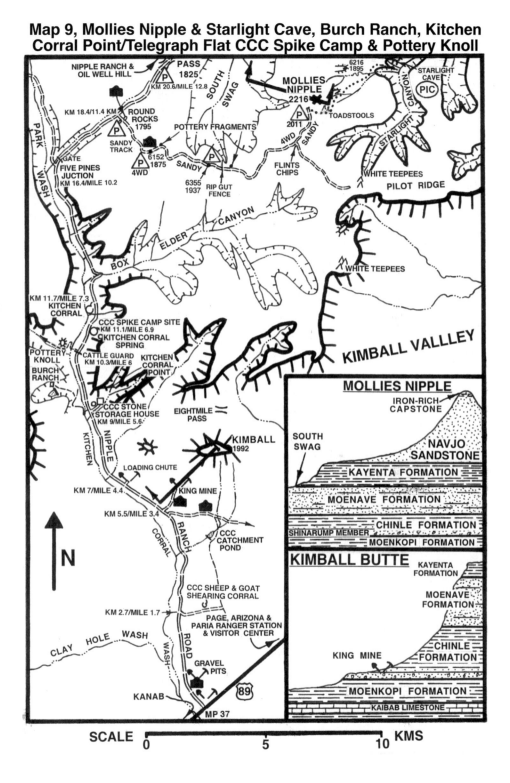

NIPPLE RANCH & OIL WELL HILL

PASS 1825
P KM 20.6/MILE 12.8

6216 1895

MOLLIES NIPPLE 2216

STARLIGHT CAVE
PIC

KM 18.4/11.4 KM
ROUND ROCKS 1795

SOUTH SWAG

P 2011

TOADSTOOLS

POTTERY FRAGMENTS

SANDY TRACK

P 6152 1875
4WD

SANDY

4WD

SANDY

STARLIGHT CANYON

FLINTS CHIPS

WHITE TEEPEES

PILOT RIDGE

GATE
FIVE PINES JUCTION
KM 16.4/MILE 10.2

6355 1937
RIP GUT FENCE

ELDER CANYON

BOX

PARK WASH

WHITE TEEPEES

KM 11.7/MILE 7.3
KITCHEN CORRAL

CCC SPIKE CAMP SITE
KM 11.1/MILE 6.9
KITCHEN CORRAL SPRING

CATTLE GUARD
KM 10.3/MILE 6

KITCHEN CORRAL POINT

KIMBALL VALLLEY

POTTERY KNOLL

BURCH RANCH

CCC STONE STORAGE HOUSE
KM 9/MILE 5.6

EIGHTMILE PASS

KITCHEN

NIPPLE

KIMBALL 1992

LOADING CHUTE

KM 7/MILE 4.4

KING MINE

KM 5.5/MILE 3.4

CORRAL

RANCH

CCC CATCHMENT POND

N

CCC SHEEP & GOAT SHEARING CORRAL

KM 2.7/MILE 1.7

ROAD

PAGE, ARIZONA & PARIA RANGER STATION & VISITOR CENTER

CLAY HOLE WASH

WASH

GRAVEL PITS

KANAB

89

MP 37

MOLLIES NIPPLE

IRON-RICH CAPSTONE

SOUTH SWAG

NAVJO SANDSTONE

KAYENTA FORMATION

MOENAVE FORMATION

CHINLE FORMATION

SHINARUMP MEMBER
MOENKOPI FORMATION

KIMBALL BUTTE

KAYENTA FORMATION

MOENAVE FORMATION

CHINLE FORMATION

KING MINE

MOENKOPI FORMATION

KAIBAB LIMESTONE

SCALE 0   5   10 KMS

Before going any further, remember part of the land you'll be walking over to see the Burch place is private and belongs to **Calvin C. Johnson** of Kanab. To rightfully explore the site, you should first telephon him and get permission. There's really nothing out there to disturb, but as a matter of respect, call him first at 435-644-2384. It was Calvin C. Johnson who the author interviewed for this Burch Ranch story. Or you might also walk over to the CCC-built stone storage building east of the corral and talk to one of Calvin's hired hands and ask him if it's OK to proceed. In 2009, that was Chuck Beu who lived there in a small trailer house.

With permission or acknowledgment, walk across the main road from the corral to an old track running due west along a fence. Follow this track about 75m to a gate just before the **Kitchen Corral Wash**. Open, then close the gate behind you, and first walk southwest along this old road, then enter the gully and turn north for 75m in the dry wash bottom. Soon this old track veers up to the left out of the wash and heads west along another fence. After walking about 250m along the fence, turn right, pass through a 2nd gate and continue north along still another old road & fence. After 100m, veer northwest onto a cattle trail and walk another 500m to an old **stock pond dam**. The remains of the old Burch Ranch house is northwest of the dam about another 100m. This place is roughly 1 1/2 kms WNW of the Kitchen Corral Point and the CCC stone house.

History of the Burch Ranch In the early 1930's, Dood Burch, his wife, and 2 young sons, Robert & Omer, migrated from Texas to the House Rock Valley area, which is just south of the Vermilion Cliffs and Sand Hills/Paria Plateau in northern Arizona. They lived there a couple of years, then homesteaded this ranch in about 1934 just below where Deer Spring Wash and Park Wash meet.

The first thing they did was build a small house out of lumber and a storage cellar behind the house. The cellar was dug out of the hillside and lined with rocks. It was likely a place for food storage, but they may have lived in it too (?). They built several corrals, a small dam to hold back flood waters, and a blacksmith shop. Their water came from a small spring on the hillside about 200m south of the home & cellar. At one time they had water piped to the house where they raised a small garden.

One interesting feature of their home was that Mrs. Burch built a special floor, like nothing the author has ever heard of. When she had collected enough old fruit jars, she turned them upside down and placed them in the floor of the cabin. They must have been packed together very tightly so they wouldn't break. On top of the bottles, she laid goat hides. This is according the Calvin C. Johnson who later bought the place. When the author visited the site, there were a number of old bottles around, but apparently at a later date they installed another floor made of wood (?).

The Burches were horse & rodeo people. They supplied some stock animals during the rodeo season in southern Utah and northern Arizona. They brought with them a number of quarter horses, and also ran Angora goats in the hills around the ranch.

Evidently the Burches had marital problems. They never officially got a divorce, but he took off for Texas not too long after they had settled at this ranch. Sometime later he was killed when his horse stepped in a gopher hole and stumbled. Mrs. Burch ended up raising the boys by herself.

County courthouse records show the patent deed for the land was first obtained officially from the government in January, 1945. It was listed in the name of Omer Burch, the youngest of the 2 boys. Robert got married to a local girl and drove the mail truck for several years in the Kanab area before moving to Provo, where he lived for the rest of his life.

Omer and his mother moved to Oregon in 1947 after they sold the land to Johnson. Omer ended up as a brand inspector and continued in the rodeo stock business. After their departure, Johnson used the place as a kind of line cabin for several years afterwards, until the house and facilities literally fell apart and decayed. Parts of the house, cellar, and corrals are still there today.

The Kitchen Corral Point/Telegraph Flat CCC Spike Camp

From where you park right on the Nipple Ranch Road, **11.1 kms (6.9 miles) from Highway 89**, look almost due east and you should see a cement structure about 100m away. This was a water storage tank for a Civilian Conservation Corps (CCC) spike camp. This was just one of hundreds of camps built throughout the west during the 1930's to do conservation projects of various kinds. If you walk over there, you'll see some old pipe running up the short drainage behind it. Up that drainage a ways and near the cottonwood trees is a pretty good spring which used to be piped down to the cement tank. About 50m or so northwest of the tank is a little depression which used to be a small pond. It looks like it was lined with rocks (?). Other than these things there's nothing left to see of what was known to Kanab residents as the **Kitchen Corral Point Spike Camp**. But at least one of the boys who worked at the camp knew it as the **Telegraph Flat Spike Camp**.

The term spike camp, refers to a temporary camp the CCC's set up near some project they were working on. Workers at spike camps lived in tents, whereas in their main camps they were housed in army-style barracks. It was largely the US Army which organized, built and ran the main CCC camps. When the young men left their main camps to go out on work projects, they were supervised by either civilians and/or employees of the Grazing Service, which was the forerunner of today's BLM.

Calvin C. Johnson of Kanab, who was born in 1923, remembered a few things about this place: *That was just a little spike camp where the cement tank is. They set up their tents there. They piped water from that spring up the canyon into the cement tank for their culinary supplies. They also honed out some logs for water troughs, and those troughs caught the overflow from the tank, then it would overflow into a little reservoir. They didn't have or use horses; they had convoy trucks, and they did all the work by hand. The guy who managed the spike camp was out of Tropic, which was my uncle John, a cousin to my grandad. John H. Johnson had a sheep permit out there and at one time owned the Nipple Ranch. Now in some way he organized that spike camp to do work in the Kitchen Point country.*

That rock building the CCC's built was a **sheep herder supply house**. *It was located in the center of the winter sheep range and the sheepmen would take their herds down there in the fall & winter. All those sheep wintered around there and down below to the south. That was a 4 room supply depot for the sheepmen to store stuff in during the winter. It was made of native rock that the CCC's gathered up, then the sheepmen contributed money to buy lumber and other materials for the building; anything they had to buy was purchased by the sheepmen, but the CCC boys did the work.*

Down south of there a couple of miles and to the east of the Nipple Ranch Road, they built quite a **large stock pond**, *and rocked-it-up. It's south & east of that* **King Manganese Mine** *about a mile [it's right on the line between Sections 11 &12, T42S, R3W]. They made a dike, then rocked-up the lower side of that, then they poured cement with rocks and made a spillway on the southeast side of that pond. At first it held water pretty good, but then it washed some of the sand away from the cement &*

54

rocks. The dike is still there but the spillway is partly washed out.

Hobart Feltner of Cannonville, who was one of the enrollees at the main Henrieville CCC camp just northeast of Henrieville, worked at this spike camp during the warmer half of 1937. He was a cook, and the cooks would rotate every 3 or 4 weeks with other cooks back at the main camp. Here's some of the things he remembered about the place, and an experience or two:

*I'd say there was around 20 men there at that camp, maybe a few more. It wasn't a big camp. It was called the **Telegraph Flat Spike Camp.** There was 3 or 4 tents that the boys slept in and a cook tent. All the tents had wooden floors, and were boarded up around the sides, then they were capped with canvas. We cooked and ate in one big tent. We ate home style.*

That cook stove burned coal. Them was great big long army cook stoves, and we had a little monkey stove in the back that you'd heat your water with, and we had an ice box to store food in. We could set our parishables in there and keep it cold. They'd bring ice in once a week. The supply truck came in once a week and it would bring supplies and we'd ship out laundry or whatever.

When the weather was good, the supply truck came right down the Pyree (Paria) Crik and we'd stop at Crack Spring and get a good cold drink of water. In bad weather they'd have to go around by Kanab. When they took me in, we went right down the crik, but when I left, they took me around by Kanab.

There wasn't any army guys at the spike camps, it was just Grazing Service men and the enrollees. No flag raisin' or reveille! I was a cook and me and a helper got up and got everything ready for the boys and they ate their breakfast and they'd take the sandwiches we made for 'um and go out for the day. Then we'd have a darn good dinner for 'um when they came back in.

*After we made lunches for the boys and they left to go to work for the day, then we'd have all this time to putter around, so we'd go over to **Pottery Knoll** and pick up broken pottery where they had dug them old boys up That spike camp was just across the wash from Pottery Knoll, an old Indian burial ground.*

We had a spring cemented-up into the side of the hill, then we had a cement tank that contained the water. Then there was a latrine tent where we could wash up and shower.

Chick Chidester was the head of the grazing end of the Henrieville camp, and he didn't like me and I didn't like him. So he was thinkin', I'll put him down at the spike camp and anchor him there! But of course I was workin' for the army and I didn't have to worry too much about ol' Chick Chidester! I didn't mind pullin' my time out there, at least something that was reasonable.

At that camp, a supply truck come in once a week and I told the driver, tell 'um to send a man out to replace me! But he didn't do it. So when the next truck come in, I said you tell them fella's up there-- tell ol' Chick and that bunch--if he doesn't want these guys a cookin' for themselves, he'd better send somebody down here to take my place because this boy is comin' in on the next truck. Well, they had somebody to replace me on the next truck!

In 2009, Calvin Johnson mentioned another project the CCC boys built near this spike camp. That was a stockade-type corral especially built for **shearing sheep & goats**. It shows up on the *Eightmile Pass, 1:24,000--7 1/2' quad*. To get there, drive north from Highway 89 on the **Nipple Ranch Road**. **After 2.7 kms (1.7 miles)**, turn east onto a pretty good track. After another 800m (.5 mile), you'll come to the corral. It was well-built, and even in 2009, was in good condition. It was made with cedar (juniper) posts set upright and wired tightly together. It has a number of compartments where shorn or unshorn sheep or goats could be placed for counting purposes.

For more information about other CCC camps in the area, read the chapter in the back of this book titled, **The Henrieville CCC Camp** on page 330.

The east side of **Mollies Nipple** and one of several toadstools on that part of the mountain. You'll see these if you walk from Mollies Nipple to Starlight Cave near the head of Starlight Canyon.

Mollies Nipple from the air looking at the southwest face. The north face is to the left in shadows.

Kitchen Corral Point and the sheepmen's **rock storage building** built by the **CCC's** during the summer of 1937 (right). The house to the left was built later. That's where Chuck Beu lives.

Above This is the cement water storage tank located at the **Kitchen Corral Point/Telegraph Flat CCC spike camp**. In the background left if the overflow pond. Beyond the little hill on the left is the Nipple Ranch Road.

Left Some of the junk left at the old **Burch Ranch** which is now long abandoned.

CCC boys lining up for chow at the mess tent at what appears to be the **Kitchen Corral Point/Telegraph Flat Spike Camp**. To the right and out of sight is the cement water storage tank. Above that in a minor canyon is the spring (Hasle Caudill foto).

Starlight Cave in the middle part of Starlight Canyon. Notice the black soot on the ceiling; this indicates there were lots of campfires here over the years. The pictographs are made with charcoal.

Pottery fragments from **Pottery Knoll** which is a short distance west of the CCC spike camp. There are ruins on top of this hill, and potsherds scattered everywhere.

This is the **rip gut or stake & rider fence** seen just east of the 4WD parking place at 6355 (1937m) and along the sandy track going to Mollies Nipple. **Mollies Nipple** is seen in the distance.

Kitchen Canyon, the Monkey House, the old Kitchen Ranch & Cabins, and the Nipple Ranch & Lake

Location & Access **Kitchen Canyon** is located in the area north of Highway 89 about halfway between Kanab & Page. Presently, the only way to Kitchen Canyon is to leave Highway 89 about 200m east of mile post 37, and drive north along the **Nipple Ranch Road.** At Km 9.1/Mile 5.6 you pass a stone building on the right at Kitchen Corral Point; at Km 16.4/Mile 10.2 is a road junction long known locally as **Five Pines**--turn right or northeast and close the gate behind you; at Km 20.6/Mile 12.8 is a pass marked 1825m on the map. 2WD's can make it up to that point, but that's where they must stop. Only 4WD's can go down the other side to the head of Kitchen Canyon and the Nipple Ranch--and get back out. This last part is **extremely sandy!**

In the past you could get to the old Kitchen Cabins from old Pahreah townsite via lower Kitchen Canyon, but sometime before 2009, floods undercut the old wagon road above and around Kitchen Falls. That route is now impassible. You could go up Starlight Canyon on a round-about route, but that's not a practical way.

If you have a 4WD, continue north from the pass down to another junction at Km 24.5/Mile 15.2. From there, turn right and head southeast to the **locked ranch gate** which is 25.1 kms (15.6 miles) from Highway 89. Now if you're planning to use this route to get to Nipple Lake, the Monkey House and the old Kitchen Ranch Cabins, you must pass through private property. To get permission to walk along the upper part of Kitchen Canyon or Valley, call Calvin C. Johnson of Kanab at 435-644-2384. A simple telefon call will ensure permission as he simply wants to know who is walking on his land.

Trail/Route From where you park somewhere near the Nipple Ranch, and with permission first, jump the fence at the locked gate, and walk along the sandy vehicle track on the north side of the big meadow which in wetter times, is **Nipple Lake.** Near the low dam, which used to make the lake bigger, you'll have a nice view of **Mollies Nipple** to the south. This old vehicle track ends at the **Monkey House** and another bigger dam Calvin C. Johnson bulldozed to stop further downcutting of the big meadow.

From the Monkey House, continue east down inside one of the recently-made erosional gullies with running water, then after less than 1 1/2 kms, look for a cow trail heading up the embankment to the south. You'll have to do some route-finding in this valley because of these recently-made gullies, but there are lots of cow trails up one side or another. If you want to checkout **Kitchen Falls** from the top, continue down the main stream & gully right to the top of the falls. From there and out in front of you on the left, is where the old wagon road used to be. To go beyond an old gate is a life-threatening proposition.

Elevations Kitchen Ranch Cabins,1642m; and Nipple Ranch & Lake, 1693m.

Time Needed With permission from Calvin C. Johnson, and a 4WD, you can see these historic sites in about half a day starting at or near the locked gate.

Water Take plenty in your car & pack. Lower Kitchen Valley & Canyon has running water, but there are cattle around throughout the year, so treat or purify all that water.

Maps USGS or BLM maps Kanab & Smoky Mountain (1:100,000) for driving & orientation; and Deer Range Point & Calico Peak (1:24,000--7 1/2' quads) for hiking.

Main Attractions Kitchen Falls, Nipple Lake, the stone Monkey House, and the ruins of the oldest ranch in the entire region, the John G. Kitchen Cabins, and the Nipple Ranch. Once there, observe the unusual *rip gut or stake & rider fence.*

Best Time to Hike Spring or fall. Or perhaps in winter warm spells. Summers are pretty hot, too hot for most people to enjoy hiking.

Boots/Shoes Any comfortable light weight shoes. Waders shouldn't be needed as the stream is small.

Author's Experience He first visited the canyon on his 1st Mollies Nipple hike and from the pass at 1825m, then made 2 more foto trips into the canyon from Old Pahreah. One trip to Starlight, lower Kitchen and lower Hogeye Canyon, took about 9 1/2 hours round-trip. Another trip from Old Pahreah to Seven Mile Flat and the Monkey House, took 8 1/2 hours round-trip--this was before the old wagon road around Kitchen Falls was washed out. In October, 1997, he parked at the pass marked 1825m, walked to the ruins below, to the Kitchen Ranch Cabins and Monkey House, and returned, all in 4 1/4 hours. In 2003, he parked at the locked gate at the head of Kitchen Valley, walked down to the historic cabins, past Kitchen Falls, up to the cave in Starlight Canyon, then back to the valley and car, all in 6 1/2 hours. In 2009, he parked at the locked ranch gate, and made 2 trips down the valley to as far as the waterfalls. The longest hike took 3 1/2 hours.

History of the Kitchen or Nipple Ranch

One of the very first ranches to be built in this entire area is what most people call the **Nipple Ranch.** In researching the history of this old homestead, the author obtained a copy of the **Biography of John G. Kitchen,** from Adrian Kitchen (a great grandson) presently of Kanab. This short history of the original founder of the Nipple Ranch was compiled by Nephi Johnson of Mesquite, Nevada, and Ramona Kitchen Johnson of Kanab. They got the information from John G. Kitchen, Jr. The following is the history of John G. Kitchen and the Nipple Ranch, which has been edited slightly for this book.

John G. Kitchen was born in Canada in 1830. Very little is known of his childhood or his early youth. The first anyone knows of him was during the gold rush days of California. There at the age of 19, his willingness to work and his determination to get along in the world began to assert itself. Money was plentiful at that time in California. A gold mine was to be had almost for the taking, but young Kitchen was not interested in a gold mine. His heart was set on a cattle ranch in the Rocky Mountains. So he worked at the job that paid the best and saved his $11.00 per day to make that cattle ranch dream come true.

In 1873 he arrived in Johnson, Utah [this is Johnson Valley east of Kanab], with a herd of heifer calves, which he had purchased in and around St. George. Sixtus Johnson was then running the Dairy Ranch, two miles [3 kms] north of Johnson, and he took the calves to manage while Kitchen went back to his job in California for the winter. This arrangement lasted for several years, with Kitchen returning each fall with more calves; or money to buy more.

In 1878, he took a herd of steers to Nephi, Utah, to sell. While there and waiting for the train to load his steers, he became acquainted with Martha or Mollie Grice. She was waiting tables at the Seely Hotel, and keeping house for her uncle, William Grice. John married Martha and brought her back to the Dairy Ranch, which he had leased. There the couple lived until their first baby, Rose, was born. The following spring [1879] with the assistance of Nephi Johnson, they moved their cattle into Mollies Nip-

Map 10, Kitchen Canyon, the Monkey House, the old Kitchen Ranch & Cabins, and the Nipple Ranch & Lake

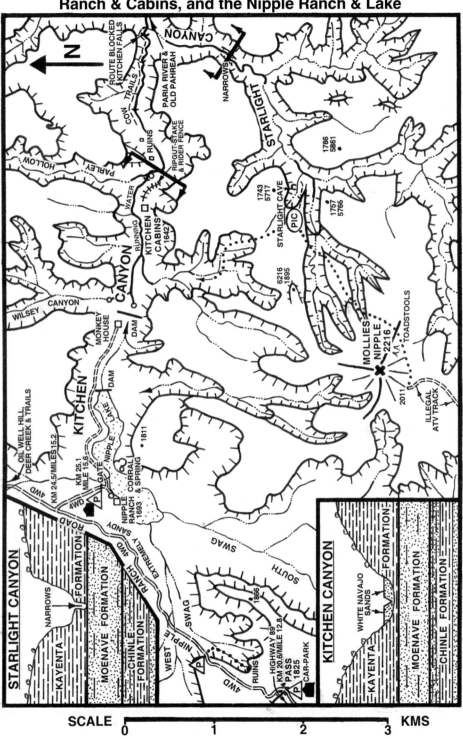

ple Ranch.

The ranch received its name because of the peculiar shape and coloring of a large knoll or peak located to the south of the ranch and Kitchen Valley. Martha's nickname was Mollie, because it's common knowledge around the country this peak was named after Kitchen's wife. This peak of course, is named Mollies Nipple. When you see it, you'll understand how it got the name.

[Let's stop for a moment. On an 1874 map of the state of Utah, it shows among other places, **Molley's Nipple** for the first time. This means that Kitchen was actually there earlier than suggested above; or that the peak was not named after Mollie Grice Kitchen. Also, there are at least 2 ways of spelling this name. All the latest USGS maps spell it **Mollies Nipple.**]

Their life at the Nipple Ranch, though filled with hardships and disappointments, was successful. They started with meager beginnings and built slowly as time and means would permit, while faced with drought years, crop failures, and menaces such as gophers, squirrels, and chipmunks. For several years, Kitchen did all of his own riding on an old mare, "Dolly", upon which he carried food and a quilt for a bed when he was forced to camp away from home for a night or two. In later years he brought back a few blooded horses each fall or spring when he shipped his steers and thus built up a fine band of horses, along with his cattle.

Those first few years at Mollies Nipple Ranch were never to be forgotten by the Kitchens. They had a new country to conquer, land to clear, buildings and fences to be built, and cattle to tend. The cattle were so well taken care of, that other cattle men said jokingly, that "Kitchen knew where every cow laid down each night." He knew his cattle so intimately that many of them were given names, such as Betsy, Posey, Kill Deer, Brin, Blue Neck, Red Rony, and Jennette.

Most of his cows were red Durham, branded with the box brand on the left ribs, and marked with a Kitchen Slit in each ear. The Kitchen Slit was a circular cut just above and following the vein in the lower part of the ear, and is so called because Kitchen was the first man in Southern Utah to use that mark.

To build up a better grade of cattle, he used to bring in blooded bulls each fall or spring when he returned from taking his steers to the railroad. One of these was a roan Durham named Paddy that cost him $500. The original cattle were Hereford stock.

A man named John Mangum helped the Kitchens with the buildings at Mollies Nipple Ranch. The corrals and fences were made of cedar logs and posts secured there in the valley and constructed in the stake & rider [sometimes called rip gut] style, which consisted of two posts set in the ground so as to form an X every 8 or 10 feet [2 or 3 meters] with a cedar pole rider placed in the saddle of the X to connect the pairs of posts. [Only those who have tried to chop down a cedar tree with an ax can appreciate the amount of work which went into this type of fence!]

The buildings were made of pine logs or native rocks laid up with mud. The roofs were of split pine logs. The split side was laid down, then covered with bark and about a foot [30 cms] of sand. It was on these roofs, warmed from the heat within, that the wild flowers first bloomed in the springtime.

The dwelling house, which consisted of two long rooms [actually two cabins and a store room placed next to each other], was constructed of hewed logs in the shape of a "T". One room served as a kitchen, living and dining room, and was heated by the cook stove and fireplace. The other room had a large fireplace and it served as a bedroom and a school room. The floors of both rooms were unplained lumber, but Mrs. Kitchen kept them scrubbed clean and white; "so clean you could eat off them", was a familiar family expression.

After their children became old enough, the Kitchens had a school teacher who boarded with the family every winter. These private tutors boarded with the family and assisted with the ranch labor when not teaching. Among these teachers were Robert Laws, Lydia Johnson, Jim Burrows, and a Mr. Ramsdale.

A little distance from, and at the back of the home, were the cellar and smoke house. These buildings were of much the same construction as the ranch house, except that the cellar was excavated about six feet [2 meters] in the ground. Here many bushels of fruit and vegetables were stored in winter, and milk and butter were kept cool in summer. The smoke house was constructed of rock, and here Kitchen cured beef, pork, and venison.

While their home was still being built, another child was born to them. For this occasion, Martha went to Pahreah, where she could have the assistance of other women during childbirth. The child was a boy and they named him John G. Kitchen, Jr. Their next two children were Rosena and Mattie, born at the Nipple Ranch. Their fifth child, Una, was born in Kanab.

In addition to stock raising, Kitchen farmed and always had a garden to keep his family alive. There were several large springs that boiled up at the foot of the mountains creating a meadow land for several miles up and down the valley. These springs he dammed up and used for irrigation purposes. He would store the water for several days, until the ponds were full, then run the water off onto his crops. It was on the hillside just above the ditches that he used to build his hot beds. Early in the spring he would level off a small space on the mountain side, where the sun shone early and late and was protected from the cold. Here he would plant some of his seeds.

Before he began irrigating each spring he would carry water to the young plants. After he began irrigating, the hot beds were so located that he could scoop water from the ditches onto the plants with a shovel. He raised cabbage, cauliflower, squash, turnips, carrots, potatoes, corn, watermelon, rye, and hay. One year he raised over 800 bushels of corn. He had a span of oxen, Ben and Brady, to assist him with the farming, and other heavy work such as hauling wood and securing rocks for building.

Because of the lack of roads and long distances to any settlement, there was practically no demand for his produce, except what his own family, hired help, and what the livestock consumed. He delighted in taking a pack load of vegetables to his Hamblin friends at Swallow Park some 7 or 8 miles [11 or 12 kms] to the northwest. And each fall he enjoyed taking part of a beef to Pahreah, and distributing it among his less fortunate friends.

As his cattle increased and financial conditions improved, Kitchen purchased the Meadows Ranch from Chet Patrick. [In Dunk Findlay's history of his family's ranch, he states that Alexander Duncan Findlay sold his squatters rights of the Meadows to Kitchen for 50 head of steers]. This ranch was northwest of the Nipple, not far below the Pink Cliffs on Meadow Creek. It's just to the northwest of the present-day Deer Springs Ranch. That place was used primarily as a summer ranch. There he added dairying to his ranching activities. Some summers he milked as many as 50 cows. From the milk, they made butter and cheese, which were packed and stored for winters use at the Nipple. [The late Dunk Findlay stated that a man by the name of Joe Honey lived in a dugout Kitchen had built as a shelter at the Meadows for one winter, to preserve Kitchen's claim to the land].

At the Meadows Ranch, with the assistance of Edwin and John Ford, and Thomas Greenhalgh,

This is the original **house** or cabin built by **John G. Kitchen**. It has twin chimneys, a large rock cellar and smoke house behind. At least some of these structures must date from the 1880's

This is part of the **rip gut or stake & ridge fence** still seen near the Kitchen cabins.

Kitchen built a dugout shelter [it's still at the upper end of the Meadows today] and large corrals and fences. One night the cowboys had five hundred head of three and four year old steers ready to drive to the railroad the next morning. About two o'clock in the morning something frightened them, and they stampeded. The cowboys were camped only a short distance from the corral and when they heard the cattle running and bellowing, they rushed to the scene. The corral was built on a sidehill, and on the downhill side, the cattle were piling up and being trampled. Fear seized the cowboys, lest so many would die, so they spent the rest of the night fighting the steers back from the downhill side of the corral. The next morning revealed one steer dead, and several lame and bruised.

Another interesting event happened just south of Kitchen's Ranch. One winter Ira Hatch of Panguitch, Utah, had his sheep camp in the high country close to Mollies Nipple. One afternoon it began to storm, and it snowed all night. The next morning the sheep bunched up beneath cedar trees, unwilling to brave the deep, newly fallen snow. Still the storm continued. For three days it snowed and when the storm finally broke, Hatch and his sheep were virtually prisoners in four or five feet [about 1 1/2m] of snow.

Hatch left his freezing, starving sheep and made his way to the Nipple Ranch for help. Kitchen took one team, Ned and Colonel, cut down a tree, and dragged it around to make trails for the sheep to follow into lower country where the snow wasn't so deep.

During the summer of 1895, Kitchen let Ebbin Brown dairy at the Meadows Ranch and paid him $1.00 per head for all the three and four year old steers he could roundup. He gathered 500 head. Then Kitchen and other cowboys gathered another 500 head and drove them to the railhead at Milford, Utah. There they were loaded on cattle cars and shipped to Kansas City, Missouri, and to Omaha, Nebraska. Young John Jr. accompanied his father on this trip, traveling with and tending the cattle until they reached their destination. It was on this trip, and while in Salt Lake City on their return journey, that his father gave him the gold watch which he still carries (1947) and treasures so much, and a bicycle, which was the first one ever owned in Kanab.

At the lower end of the canyon there were clumps of squawberry bushes. Every fall Piute Indians would come to the Nipple country to hunt deer and to gather squawberry brush to make baskets. Kitchen made it a practice to buy two baskets, two tanned deer hides, and several deer hams from them each fall. The baskets were used to haul laundry and for storing dried fruits and vegetables. The deer hides were used to make belts, saddle strings, harness parts and shoe laces. The deer hams were cured in the smoke house and eaten during the winter.

One interesting story is told about the "tally stick" method of keeping track of calves branded. Whenever Kitchen went out to brand calves, he would carry a short stick in his back pocket. When he branded a calf, he would whittle a notch in the stick. In the evenings after he had returned to the house, the notches were transferred to a much larger tally stick, which was 8 or 10 feet [2.5 or 3 meters] long and kept overhead on the rafters in the kitchen. Whenever he desired a count of the seasons branding, he would take down the tally stick and count the notches. One side represented the heifers; the other side the steers. It was when his branding count reached enormous figures that he became known as "The Cattle King of Southern Utah." It was estimated at one time that he owned about 5000 head of cattle, ranging from St. George on the west, Panguitch on the north, and to the Colorado River on the east and south. [When the late Dunk Findlay of Kanab heard about the 5000 head of cattle, he doubted very much the country could have sustained that many. Maybe 1000 could have been a closer figure, according to Dunk].

Kitchen was a great lover of knowledge, and so that the children might have an advantage of better schooling, and his family enjoy some of the finer things of life, he appointed George Adams foreman of his ranch, and moved the family to Kanab in the early 1890's. [It was during this time, 1894, that 18-year-old Will Chynoweth of Pahreah was hired to help with the cattle, which was reported to be 2000 head. He worked for Kitchen for 2 1/2 years, according to the Chynoweth family history compiled by Mary Jane Chynoweth Fuller] This move seemed to climax his career, and his star of success began waning. Liquor had always been his weakness, so while in Kanab and with plenty of leisure time and money, drinking got the upper hand. Trouble began brewing, which ended in the divorce courts.

The loss of his family was a great blow to Kitchen. Mollie ended up marrying Joe Honey, a man who once worked for Kitchen. Sorrowing, Kitchen made a liberal settlement both of alimony and for the education of his children, which Thomas Chamberlain faithfully administered. He sold his cattle to Scott Cutler and Hack Jolly, who moved them out of the country. The remnant of the box brand was sold to Johnny Findlay.

In 1898, Kitchen went to Lee's Ferry, where he lived only a short time. He died very suddenly, and under mysterious circumstances. A rider was dispatched to Kanab with the news. Young John rode in haste all night, but the body was already buried when he reached the Ferry.

Thus ended the career of a man with clouds of uncertainty hovering about the cause of his death as well as about the disposal of his property. In his will he bequeathed to each of his daughters $20,000, and to his sons $25,000, but through faulty administration, the fortune was dissipated. Although his family spent years in the inheritance courts, not a dollar was ever recovered.

In 1904, his children erected a monument to his memory at Lee's Ferry Cemetery. The monument which was there in 2010 read, "John G. Kitchen, Born in Canada, March 25,1830, Died July 13, 1898."

After the death of Kitchen, there seems to be a gap in history of the Nipple Ranch. Evidently, it was in the courts for some time. Some of the old timers in the area thought it may have gotten into the hands of 2 men named Hunter and Clark, then after a time it may have been taken over by Jim Henderson. However, the first recorded transfer of the property (Kane County Courthouse) was on July 2, 1908. The land, part of a grant of 100,000 acres, was given to the state of Utah by the Federal government, for the use of the "Institution for the Blind".

The next transfer of ownership was on March 11, 1912, when the Cross Bar Land & Cattle Co. purchased the ranch from the state of Utah. Later, on May 7, 1927, John H. Johnson bought the land from Kane County, apparently for back taxes owed by the cattle company. The last time the land officially changed hands was January 16, 1956, when Calvin C. Johnson bought it from John H. Johnson.

At the ranch today, Calvin has a small cabin & windmill which pumps well water to a trough. It's located west of Nipple Lake, along with several corrals. Hikers are asked to stay away from this part of the ranch. About 1 1/2 kms west or upcanyon from Kitchen Falls are the ruins of an old chimney in one location, and a rock wall in another, as shown on the map. Calvin thinks these were built by the early white inhabitants of the valley.

Less than 1 km west of these ruins, and south of the 2 big gullies, are the Kitchen Ranch houses or cabins. These are in ruins, but in fair condition considering their age. The roofs have collapsed, but parts of log walls and the 2 chimneys are still standing. When the author first saw the twin chimneys and rooms, he thought it was the home of an old Mormon polygamist. Instead the second room was for the school and school teacher. Nearby is an old corral and a log fence running southeast, both of which are made in the *"rip gut or stake & rider"* fashion. The holes you'll see in the corral gate posts, are said to have been made by Kitchen who used a hot iron poker to run through the posts. Also the ruins of the rock smoke house & rock cellar, and other structures.

From Kitchen's Ranch cabins, route-find west in & out of 2 big gullies. After about a km, you'll see some of Calvin C. Johnson's work in erosion control. Crossing the valley is an earthen dam, and just to the northwest of it is a rock cabin called the Monkey House.

The Monkey House and Nipple Lake

According to Calvin C. Johnson and others, the Monkey House was built in 1896 by Dick Woolsey, at the mouth of what the USGS maps call **Wilsey Hollow** (it apparently should be "Woolsey" Hollow). It's made of stones, and it sits up against a large boulder. Here's an old tale about how this place came to be known as the Monkey House. When Woolsey and his wife first settled in at this location, they had with them a monkey. The monkey was kept in a box or cage on top of a pole near the cabin. When someone approached the homestead, the monkey would chatter loudly. However, Cal Johnson later talked to a descendent of Peter Shirts who lives in Escalante. He told Johnson the name comes from the shape of the rock which forms the back wall of the rock cabin.

Inside the cabin and on the wooden doorway structure, are many names of early-day cowboys. At least one new roof has been added, and the ramada or porch has been taken off from the original structure, evidently in the years John H. Johnson owned the land. The Monkey House is in quite good condition today. Behind the cabin is a small pen or corral in a small opening of the cliff.

About 1 km west of the Monkey House is Nipple Lake. Evidently there has always been a small shallow pond in this swampy area, but today you'll see a low dam, maybe a meter high, which backs up the clear blue water to form the lake. However, the flash floods of 1997 filled in about half of this lake; and in August of 2003, the lake was completely dry. That was the 5th year in a row with below average precipitation in Utah. In the summer of 2009, it was still dry and could be that way for a long time to come. As you walk through this valley, you'll see to the south, the ever-present Mollies Nipple, towering above the landscape. This makes a nice picture.

Other Historic Sites

If you're coming into the area to climb Mollies Nipple from the west, there are several historic things to see along the way. Leave Highway 89 about 200m east of mile post 37, and drive north on the Nipple Ranch Road. See some of these historic sites under **Map 9** which includes the **CCC sheep & goat shearing corral, King Manganese Mine, a CCC-built catchment pond & rock storage building, the old Burch Ranch, and the Kitchen Point/Telegraph Flat CCC Spike Camp.**

Further along the Nipple Ranch Road at about Km 11.7/Mile 7.3, is an **old stockade-type corral** (with the poles standing upright and stuck in the ground). This is called the **Kitchen Corral,** but he didn't build it. According to Calvin C. Johnson: *It was the old stockmen who ran cattle in there who built that Kitchen Corral. There was Kitchen & Findleys, and Swapps, Hamblins, and the people who had cattle, then they* run a **rip gut or stake & rider fence,** *up there on the hill back of that corral. It goes from a natural ledge there on [a point next to] Box Elder Canyon, up to the natural ledge that drops into the Nipple Ranch.* If you take that sandy track to Mollies Nipple, you'll see part of that fence crossing the road. See **Map 9** for its location.

By parking at the pass marked 1825m, you can also include on your trip, a quick look at the only **cliff dwellings** in the immediate area. From the pass, walk or drive north down the very sandy road about 1000m (about Km 21.7/Mile 13.5 from from Highway 89). There you'll be in what is known as the West Swag. Once there, walk due south in this valley to the head of what could be called the south arm of

The **Monkey House** got its name because of the shape of the rock behind the stone cabin. Looking at it from the south, it strongly resembles a monkey's face.

the West Swag. Right at the southern end, and under the overhang, are 2 cliff dwellings. These rock & mud structures have been partially damaged by time and cattle.

The strange thing about these dwellings is, they're under an overhang and facing north--the first of its kind this author has seen. The Indians who inhabited this site were likely a part of what archaeologists call the Virgin Anasazi. But the site is very near the transition zone between the Sevier, Great Basin, or Fremont Culture area, and the Anasazi Cultures to the south. Just north of the ruins, and along the east-facing wall, are some minor petroglyphs. You'll have to look hard to find these.

Top Inside the Monkey House. On the wooden doorways are old signatures of cowboys. **Above Left** John G. Kitchen died in 1898 at age 68. This picture is from the late 1880's, or the 1890's. **Above Right** Mollie Grice Kitchen, perhaps from the 1890's. (Merrilyn Johnson Cornell foto)

An aerial view looking west at **Nipple Lake**, but it was dry on December 9, 2003. Near the bottom of the picture you can just make out a low dam which helps create a lake--when there's enough water.

Left Kitchen Falls as seen from the old wagon road/trail that used to run down to Old Pahreah. It's now impossible to go any further than where the author took this foto. Sometime before 2009, floods undercut the talus slope creating a cliff and totally cutting the trail. **Right** Fence posts at the **old Kitchen Ranch**. The holes in the posts were apparently made by drilling with a hot poker.

Mollies Nipple as seen from the north (looking south) and what is in wetter times **Nipple Lake**. Notice the low dam on the left. That helps create a lake in wetter times.

In a south branch of the **West Swag** of **Kitchen Canyon** are these **Anasazi ruins**. Time and the stomping of cattle have taken a toll, but there are still several metate grooves where corn was ground.

Inside **Starlight Cave**. There's been lots of digging here--either pot hunters or archaeologists (?). Notice all the black soot on the ceiling; this tells us there were lots of fires built here in the past.

Left Metate grooves on top of a large flat stone; there are several of these places near the ruins located in a south arm of the **West Swag** of upper **Kitchen Canyon**. **Right** Corn cobs and pottery fragments at the same Anasazi ruins in upper **Kitchen Canyon**.

Deer Creek (Including Main, Northwest, Left Hand & Little Forks), and Oak Canyon

Location & Access At least one canyon complex on this map requires **ropes & rappelling gear** to get all the way through; this is the **Main and Northwest Forks of Deer Creek**. For those with no experience in technical canyoneering, it's recommended you go with someone who has the experience, equipment & skills needed. Or if you've done some rappelling, read parts of this writer's other book, ***Technical Slot Canyon Guide to the Colorado Plateau, 2nd Edition***, for a description of equipment & techniques.

Featured here is the **Main and Northwest Forks of Deer Creek Canyon** and several tributaries including the **Left Hand Fork & Little Fork** (author's name), plus **Oak Canyon** which enters the middle part of the Upper Paria River Gorge just below Deer Creek and the CCC & Deer Trails Trails. Also of interest to fotographers are a multitude of hoodoo, mushroom or **toadstool-like rocks**. These are concentrated mostly along the Main Fork of Deer Creek. The author has found one with a pink pedestal.

To get there, drive along Highway 89 about halfway between Page & Kanab. Just east of **mile post 37**, turn north onto the **Nipple Ranch Road**; this is the road that runs to the Nipple Ranch, Mollies Nipple and Kitchen Canyon. Drive north past Kitchen Point and the CCC-built sheepman's rock storage building on the right (**Km 9.1/Mile 5.6**), then at **Five Pines Junction (Km 16.4/Mile 10.2)**, turn right or northeast and drive through a gate--closing it behind you. At **Km 20.5/Mile 12.7** is a pass between the Park Wash Drainage and Kitchen Canyon. From that point on **you must have a 4WD** with good clearance (if not, you'll have to park there and walk an extra 8 kms/5 miles). From the pass continue north downhill. In this area, you'll have pockets of **deep sand** for about 2 kms. At **Km 24.2/Mile 15.1** is a turnoff to the right which takes you to Calvin C. Johnson's **Nipple Ranch**; but continue north in **deep sand** across the head of upper Kitchen Canyon or Valley, then as you start to climb up toward **Oil Well Hill**, rocks are mixed with sand making driving easier. At **Km 28.7/Mile 17.8**, you'll be on top of a ridge where the road turns right and runs east to an old oil well drill site. Stop at that curve where you see the very sandy ATV track heading northwest. Park and/or camp there in some big cedar trees.

Rating Main Fork of Deer Creek, **3A (this can be a B) III** or **IV;** Northwest Fork of Deer Creek, **2 or 3A III** depending on which branch; Left Hand Fork, **3A III;** Little Fork, **3A II** or **III;** Oak Canyon, **3A III.**

Equipment For the **Main Fork of Deer Creek**, rappelling gear, one 60m rope, some webbing or old rope for slings, several Rapide/Quik Links (R/QL) and bolt kit & 1 bolt just in case. If you descend the northern branch of the **Northwest Fork of Deer Creek** with a small group, a short rope is all that's needed; for the south branch, take a 50m rope & webbing. If planning to rappel over all the dropoffs in the **Left Hand Fork** (read more below) **& Little Fork of Deer Creek**, and **Oak Canyon**, rappelling gear, one 60m rope, lots of webbing & one shorter rope, and several R/QL's will be needed.

Trail/Route Main Fork of Deer Creek From the 4WD parking on Oil Well Hill, walk northwest along a very sandy illegal ATV track. After 600m, and about 1 cm northeast of elevation **6139** (1871m) on the *Deer Range Point (DRP) 7 1/2' quad*, will be a cairn marking a cow trail heading due north downhill. This will be the end (or beginning) of the **Deer Trails Trail** you'll use to get back to your car. But don't use it now; instead continue northwesterly on the sandy track toward **Deer Range Point** (DRP). Directly beneath this prominent peak, you'll cross upper Little Fork, then veer right or northeast as the track fades. Finally as the track veers right or northeast, you veer left a little onto an emerging **hiker's trail** and continue north around the eastern base of DRP, then northwesterly. When you're due north of the mosteasterly peak on DRP, and at the head of Deer Creek's Left Hand Fork, you'll come to the first of many **toadstool-like rocks**. These features all have a piece of weather-resistant iron-rich caprock on top which shelters a softer layer of Navajo Sandstone below leaving something that looks like a giant toadstool. They're all over this region, but the best clusters seem to be north of DRP and at the head of, and on the west side, of the Main Fork of Deer Creek. Also at the head of Left Hand Fork.

From the head of **Left Hand Fork**, continue west or northwest over a low divide near elevation **6273** (1912m) and route-find down into the head of the **Main Fork**. Walk downcanyon. Soon you'll come to **Rappel 1**, a double drop of about 17m into a nice slot. Tie webbing around a nearby chokestone and rappel; just below that will be an interesting 7m downclimb in a vertical chute, then a short walk out of the **Upper Slot**. Below the upper slot are a couple of escape routes out to the east and several short narrows before coming to the **Lower Slot**. This is the good part. After about 400m of moderately cool dark slot, you'll come to **R2**, a drop of about 16m. There you should find 1 bolt & hanger (B&H) on the right (one report from 6/2009 stated that bolt was getting loose, so be prepared to replace it if necessary). Rap down into a deep hole, then continue east for another 30m to find a steep, tight 8m downclimb in the darkest part of the slot. Beginners may want to be belayed, but it's easier than it first appears. At the bottom is a pothole, possibly with water--no more than waist deep--and a 90° left turn, then a 2nd possible pool (could be a swimmer?; or it could be completely dry!), and a 90° right turn. After that, walk out through a 100m-long, 2-3m-wide slot, after which it opens up into a gorge.

Below R2, you'll walk along a sandy wash inside an open gorge. After 500m will be the **Northwest Fork** coming in on the left or west. Walk up this 200m to find another nice straight slot before coming to a 7m sloping dryfall. But let's stop here and discuss the **2 branches** of the Northwest Fork.

To reach the **northern branch**, it's likely best to head for **Rock Springs Bench** using **Map 15**, then switch to **Map 16** and walk from **Johnson Hole Saddle** down the **Johnson Hole Canyon Trail** to the **Paria** and **Lone Rock**, then upriver to the **Asay Bench Trail** and **Asay Bench**. From there, walk westward across a couple of minor drainages until you're in the northern branch. From there head downcanyon. Along the way you'll encounter about half a dozen easy downclimbs. One drop is about 3m which a tall person can stretch across and downclimb (he can belay others, then the others can help him from below if needed). In our case, we rapped from an Ibis hook set in a natural hole in the wall. At the end of the canyon is the 7m sloping dryfall. You can downclimb halfway, then slide 3m into soft sand.

To do the **south branch**, it's likely best to come in from Oil Well Hill. Use the same route discussed above, but you'll have to work your way from the head of the Main Fork to the west side, then head north. Along the way, and up on the slickrock aways, will be a **toadstool** with a **pink pedestal**. Continue north skirting several short side-canyons before dropping in as shown. Head downcanyon (no slot here) to eventually find a 20m, 2-stage rap right where the north & south branches meet. If just doing the Northwest Fork, you can climb out up the Main Fork by climbing back up to the **Asay Bench** to the north; or head south climbing onto **Cad Bench**, as shown on the map. Otherwise, let's continue downcanyon.

In the 2 kms between the Northwest Fork and Rappel 3, you'll find the 2 escapes just mentioned, then immediately above R3 will be a 40m-long slot which you can downclimb into. At the end, you could

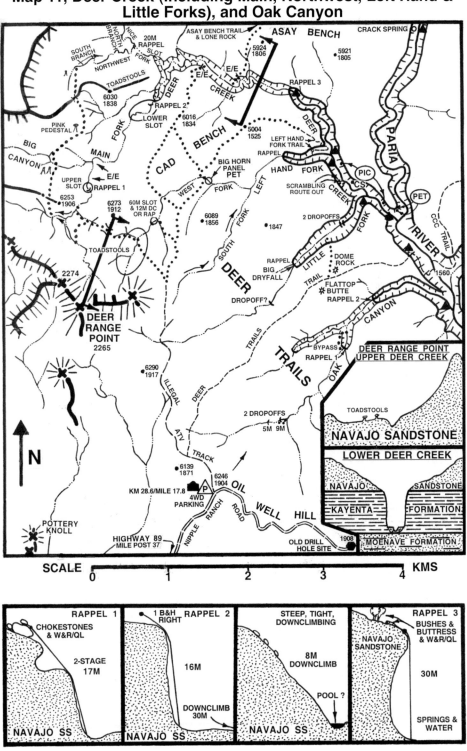

arrange a chokestone to rappel from, but it will likely be an awkward start for a 30m rappel (a report from 6/2009 states there is now a bolt & hanger there)

Or, climb on to the bench to the right or south side to find webbing around 2 bushes & a rock outcropping. There you'll have an easy start for the 30m rappel right off the nose of a larger buttress. At the bottom will be springs, running water & trees. Walk downcanyon in or beside the small creek. In the lower end of the canyon are many campsites, 2 panels of pictographs, and a long panel of petroglyphs, as shown on the map. There's also a deer & horse trail out of lower Deer Creek up to Cad Bench which you could use to return to your car. Read more about it under the **Left Hand Fork** below. Also, on his last trip, the author found a **scrambling route out** of lower Deer Creek on the west side.

Less than 1 km below where Deer Creek meets the Paria, pay close attention to the right side of the ATV track to find a cairn marking the bottom end of the constructed **Deer Trails Trail** zig zagging up the west side of the Paria River Gorge (this trail begins about 100m below the beginning of the **CCC Trail** on the east side of the canyon). After zig zagging up about 100m, it heads northwest along a bench, then cuts up through the final cliff band. From there this old cattle trail levels some and heads southwest up a sandy hogsback ridge between **Oak Canyon & Little Fork**. Soon it passes between a prominent little **dome rock** on the right, and a round, **flat-topped butte** on the left, as shown on this and the 7 1/2' quad. This trail eventually meets the sandy ATV track near the main road as described above. From there, it's 600m back to the main Nipple Ranch Road and your vehicle.

Left Hand Fork of Deer Creek This is the largest & longest of all the tributaries of Deer Creek except for the Main Fork. To get into it from the top, use the exact same route as if going to the Main Fork, but when you reach a point just east of DRP, follow that drainage (let's call it the **South Fork**) down to the north & northeast. Along the way are a number of dropoffs, all of which you can skirt around to the left or west. You could rappel these, but there seems to be no slots of consequence, so rappelling seems pointless. When you reach the confluence of the **South & West Forks**, head up the West Fork skirting around 2 dropoffs. About 600m up the West Fork is one of the best petroglyph panels around. Wallace Ott of Tropic alerted the author to this. Read his story below. This **Big Horn Panel** is along the south side of a 2m-wide straight-sided slot. Most of the art is of big horn sheep which are 2-3m above the dry wash; other markings are up as high as 5-6m. Those seem older than the lower ones.

You can also walk into the upper end of the **West Fork**, but after about 500m or so, you'll come to a **10-12m vertical dropoff**. There you'll find a large tree trunk & roots which you could loop a rope around for a rappel, but you can also downclimb the whole thing since it's about 1m wide all the way. Immediately below this drop is a nice tight 60m slot that's worth the effort. About 1 km below that will be the Big Horn Panel.

Below the confluence of the West and South Forks is one short slot a good climber can downclimb into, or skirt around it to the left and re-enter just below. Finally, about 650m above Deer Creek, will be a big **55m dropoff** which you could rappel by using chokestones & webbing. That would put you into the lower canyon with water & trees.

Or, instead of rappelling, get out of the canyon on the left or north, and route-find east toward the point between the Main Fork and Left Hand Fork of Deer Creek. As you approach the end of that point, be looking for signs of an old trail which was first used by deer. Let's call this the **Left Hand Fork Trail**. Look for some stone cairns. This trail zig zags southeast right off the point, then one bench above the floor of the main canyon, it turns west and follows the same bench into the Left Hand Fork for about 225m before heading down through oak brush to the creek below. Wallace Ott & Wallace Henderson modified this old deer trail--read Ott's story below.

Little Fork This is the short drainage between the Left Hand Fork and Oak Creek. To do this canyon from the top end, start from the 4WD parking on Oil Well Hill, and walk down the Deer Trails Trail in the direction of the Paria. About 1 km above the **dome rock** and **flat-topped butte**, turn left or north and work your way down into the upper end of the canyon. At the very beginning, you should come to at least one dropoff; you can either rig things up for a rappel--followed by some kind of slot or narrows-- or skirt around this part on the right or left. About 750m below the first dropoff will be a **big dryfall** of 30-35m or so. The author hasn't done this, but has seen it from below. You may need two 50m ropes, plus webbing & rappelling gear.

Below this big dryfall is an uninteresting V-shaped canyon. There are several possible exits as shown, one of which the author used to escape south. One km below the big dryfall are **2 dropoffs** of 7-8m each, one after the other. You can downclimb the first, but it'll be tricky with crumbly-looking rocks on the right--so help each other. Or rap/handline from boulders. Walk around the second drop on the left. From there, it's 800m along a small steam to the mouth of the canyon and Deer Creek.

If you're in Deer Creek, you can walk up this short side-canyon (Little Fork) and perhaps climb up the second dropoff on the left--it's tricky upclimbing too, as part of that rock wall looks like it's ready to fall! Once in the middle part of the drainage, there should be several escape routes out to the north, and at least one exit to the south up steep slickrock as shown. That's the one the author used.

Oak Creek To do this canyon from top to bottom, walk north and a little east from the 4WD parking at 1904m/6246. After about 1 km, you'll be in the main drainage. You'll soon come to a 5m drop; chimney 6m down a crack on the left side. About 300m below that will be a 9m dropoff; skirt around this on the right and scramble to the bottom. After about 1500m of easy walking, you'll come to a big dryfall of about 20m. If you wish to rappel, you can install webbing around some bushes or trees near the edge. If you don't want to rappel, then **bypass** the dropoff by walking 200m along the left (northwest) rim and re-enter the drainage just above a side-canyon. Below R1 is an easy walk of about 800m with at least one exit on the left or north, then comes R2, a drop of 25m. You can either exit and head down the Deer Trails Trail, and walk up the lower end of Oak Canyon from the bottom; or if rappelling, there are nearby trees or rocks you can attach webbing to. At the bottom of this drop are springs, trees & running water all the way down to the Paria. Along the way are old signs that beaver have been there, but nothing new as of 2003. If you see fresh signs of beaver, drink water from the spring source only; or purify it. Oak Canyon doesn't have any slot or real narrow parts, so most people won't be interested in rappelling through this drainage. The best part is the lower end with all the good water (?) and trees.

Elevations 4WD trailhead, 1904m; bottom of Deer Trails Trail along the Paria River, about 1560m.

Time Needed To hike and rappel through the **Main Fork** and return via the Deer Trails Trail, will take from 9-12 hours. For the **Northwest Fork** or Forks of Deer Creek, returning via Cad Bench, 8-10 hours. To do the **Left Hand Fork**, view the Big Horn Panel, then rappel into the bottom--or walk down along the Left Hand Fork Trail--and return via the Deer Trails Trail, will take 8-11 hours. The time it takes will depend on your fitness, route & side-trips. To explore **Little Fork or Oak Canyon** will take from 6-9 hours, depending on whether you actually rappel or skirt the dryfalls, or go on any side-trips.

Water Running water is found in the lower parts of each fork of Deer Creek & Oak Canyon, but take it directly from the spring source to avoid contamination from cattle or beaver. Or treat it. Cattle may be there during the winter grazing season--from about November 1 to May 1, depending on the ever-present drought conditions.
Maps USGS or BLM map Kanab (1:100,000) for driving & orientation; and Deer Range Point & Bull Valley Gorge (1:24,000--7 1/2' quads) for hiking.
Flash Flood Danger High in the lower slot (above R2) of the Main & Northwest Forks, low elsewhere.
Best Time to Hike Spring or fall, but you can hike year-round.
Boots/Shoes Normally, you can get by with dry-weather shoes in the upper canyons, waders in the lower end of each, and along the Paria River.
Author's Experience On one scouting trip, he went down the Main Fork as far as Rappel 2, then rim-walked other parts before going down Deer Trails Trail to the river, up Oak Canyon, up lower Deer Creek and back to his Chevy Tracker at the 4WD trailhead--all in 9 1/2 hours. Another scout trip took him down Johnson Hole Canyon Trail (see Map 16) to Lone Rock, up Asay Canyon, onto Asay Bench, down into the middle part of upper Deer Creek, then returned, all in 10 1/4 hours. Another trip was with Nat Smale. We went down the Main Fork (setting up all rappelling stations), out the bottom end, up Deer Trails Trail and back to the Tracker in 9 3/4 hours. Your trip will likely go faster now the canyon has been prepared, but check the bolts & webbing closely. Later, the author explored the Left Hand Fork including the West Fork slot, the Big Horn Panel & Left Hand Fork Trail, plus explored Little Fork & parts of Oak Canyon, on 2 trips of about 8 hours each. In 9/2009, and with Brian Olliver & Nick Smith, we started on Oil Well Hill, walked to and skirted the west side of the Main Fork, then dropped into the South Branch of Northwest Fork. We rapped 20m, then finished and escaped Main Fork to Cad Bench, visited the Big Horn Panel, then back to the trailhead in 7 1/2 hours total. You'll need more time than this because you'll surely get lost and have to back-track some!

History of the Left Hand Fork Trail & the Big Horn Panel

Here's the story of the building of the **Left Hand Fork Trail** and the discovery of the Big Horn Panel of petroglyphs as told by Wallace Ott of Tropic:

Wallace Henderson and I built that trail in the 1930's. We took some powder down and done some blasting. He was 20 years older than me, but we worked and run cattle together, and we built that trail and fixed that waterin' hole. I fixed it so cows or horses could come down to water in that Left Hand Fork, then they'd go back out there on Cad Bench. I had a big log at the bottom so the horses couldn't go down the creek. It didn't work as good for cows as we thought it would, so later I run some horses out there and raised some colts. I'd only have to go out there about 3 times in the whole summer. Wallace Henderson has been dead for about 57 years [as of 2003], and I don't know of anybody else who ever run livestock on that trail--but there's been a few deer hunters use it. Wallace Henderson was the younger brother of Jim Henderson, the one who owned the old Nipple Ranch at one time.

Here's Wallace's story of how he found the **Big Horn Panel**: *It was deer season, and we had camped just off the Paria a little ways up Deer Creek. I had one of my older brothers and one of my brother-in-laws with me. We had gone up that Left Hand Fork Trail to look for deer on Cad Bench. I run out of canteen water; it had been stormin' a little, and I was lookin' for a little tank [pothole]. And that's when I saw that panel. Joe Dunham, he lived there in Cannonville, is the only other guy I've talked to that's seen 'um, and he's been dead a long time. I saw that panel sometime between 1936 & 1940 after the CCC's was there. The CCC's was there at the mouth of Deer Creek Canyon in about 1935 & '36. That's when they built that CCC Trail out of the Paria on the east side.*

On the way to the upper end of Deer Creek, you'll pass this peak called **Deer Range Point**.

Left Downclimbing in the **Upper Slot** just below Rappel 1 in the **Main Fork** of **Deer Creek**. **Right** Downclimbing in the Upper Slot of Deer Creek. These fotos were taken a day after minor flooding

Nat Smale starts down the **16m Rappel 2** in the Lower Slot of the Main Fork of **Deer Creek**.

Left The bottom of Rappel 2 is into a dark hole. **Right** This picture was take a day after a minor flood went down **Deer Creek**. This pool is immediately before the slot opens up into a wider gorge.

The beginning of the **30m Rappel 3** into lower **Deer Creek**. At the bottom of this rap is running water, trees and campsites, and the lower gorge. If you're coming up this canyon from the bottom end and the Paria River, this is where your hike ends.

This toadstool is what the author calls the **Pink Pedestal**. It's located between the big White Cliffs and the middle part of Deer Creek. You'll pass by this one on your way to the Northwest Fork.

More toadstools at the head of the **Main Fork of Deer Creek**.

Left Starting down the only rappel in the **Northwest Fork** of Deer Creek. This one is right at the end of the **South Branch**. **Right** Coming down the same 2-part rappel. This rap is 20m from webbing around a chokestone. You avoid this rappel by getting into the North Branch.

Both shots above showing 2 of half a dozen simple downclimbs while doing the lower end of the **Northwest Fork of Deer Creek**.

Left Downclimbing in the lower end of the **Northwest Fork of Deer Creek**. In one place, you can either help each other down; or set an Ibis hook in a hole in the wall and rappel. **Right** The **Northwest Fork** of Deer Creek is a nice slot.

One of the better rock art or petroglyph panels around is this one in the **West Fork of Left Hand Fork** of Deer Creek. The **Big Horn Panel** shows mostly big horn sheep plus some human images. On this day, a rainstorm had washed sand off the top covering the panel.

An aerial view of the northern part of **Kodachrome Basin State Park**. Notice the 2 sand pipes which are best viewed from the **Nature Trail** which covers the left and middle part of the picture. Also notice the red-roofed building in the lower left--that's the shower house. Foto taken 12/9/2003.

One of the best, and one of the few, pictographic panels around, is this one in **lower Deer Creek**.

Hogeye & Starlight Canyons, Carlow Ridge--from Old Pahreah

Location & Access This area is about halfway between Kanab & Page and north of Highway 89. **Hogeye Canyon** is located due north of Old Pahreah. It drains into the Paria River from the northeast just north of where Kitchen Canyon enters from the west. **Starlight Canyon** is found just east of Mollies Nipple, northwest of Old Pahreah, and not far north of Highway 89. The route to Starlight Canyon discussed here is from the southeast and the Paria River.

To get to the trailhead, turn north from **Highway 89** between **mile posts 30 & 31** and at the sign stating *Historic Marker*. From this parking place & tall monument, drive northeast on a good dirt road. Even though this road is graded, it can be slick in wet weather because of the presence of the Chinle & Moenkopi clay beds. It's 7.6 kms (4.7 miles) to the former Paria Movie Set; 8.4 kms (5.2 miles) to the Pahreah Cemetery; and **9.5 kms (5.9 miles)** from the highway to a **shaded trailhead**. You'll park on the west side of the Paria, while what's left of the townsite of Old Pahreah is on the east side of the river.
Trail/Route From where you park, simply walk north in the flood plain of the Paria River. You'll cross the creek many times. Along the way are ruins of old ranches and petroglyphs & cowboy signatures as shown. Read more about the history of these sites under **Map 18, Upper Paria River Gorge**.
Starlight Canyon At the mouth of Kitchen Canyon, head west about 2 kms along a small stream. About 100m below Kitchen Falls, turn left or south and walk up Starlight. About 1200m into Starlight, the canyon constricts and you'll find a short narrow section; climb up a chute to a widening canyon above. Continue upcanyon about 2 more kms to the 2nd side-canyon coming in from the right. Walk up this short drainage about 200m to find **Starlight Cave** on the right facing south. In this deep alcove, you'll see where pot hunters or archeologists have been digging in the floor, as well as some pictographs inscribed with charcoal on the walls. The ceiling is black with soot indicating aborigines built fires in this cave for a long time in the distant past.

On the ridge opposite the mouth of the cave is a **man-made cattle trail** running uphill to the west. You could use this trail to get out on top of the mesa, then head for Mollies Nipple. This means you could reach Starlight Cave combined with a hike to **Mollies Nipple**, coming in from the west. Another thing to keep in mind, the old wagon road which ran from Pahreah up Kitchen Canyon to the Kitchen Cabins has now been wiped out where it used to bypass Kitchen Falls. Over the years, floods have undercut the slope causing it to slide. As of 2009, you could not hike up Kitchen Canyon to the Nipple Ranch.
Hogeye Canyon From the mouth of Kitchen Canyon, continue north, perhaps stopping to see 2 panels of cowboy signatures & petroglyphs as shown on the map. Just over 1 km above Kitchen will be a rincon (abandon meander), an old ranch site, and the mouth of Hogeye Canyon. Just into this major canyon will be running water and lots of trees. About 1 1/2 kms upcanyon will be a mossy cataract with running water. About 300m above that will be a big wall collapse & boulders you'll have to climb around. For the next 800m or so you'll find a fairly narrow canyon with high walls, and tall slender cottonwood trees trying to reach the sun. These trees have branches on top--but few on their lower trunks.

About halfway up Hogeye is a dryfall you can easily climb. Beneath it is where water begins to flow. Above that, the canyon is totally different--it's dry with no cottonwood trees. This goes on for about 1 km, then for about another 500m will be more running water and cottonwoods. Beyond that it's dry again.

You could turn back there, or return to Old Pahreah via cow trails in **Lower Death Valley** and along the **Carlow Ridge** down to **The Box** and the Paria River. Near the upper end of Hogeye, you'll come to the confluence of 4 canyons. Turn right or SSE and walk up that drainage following this map carefully. Just north of the butte that looks like a beehive, head east, then south and climb up just east of this beehive rock. Continue south but veer right or southwest and get up on a big hogsback ridge.

This ridge, the southern part of which is called **Carlow Ridge**, runs all the way south to where the Paria River cuts through The Cockscomb in what is called **The Box** or **Paria Box**. You could head southeast and visit Sam Pollock Arch, but that would make a very long day--so stay on the ridge line following various cows trails south. Further along you'll pass just east of what this writer is calling the **Rock Garden** on Carlow Ridge. Soon after that is a trail junction: the **Yellow Rock Trail** heads east into lower **Cottonwood Wash**, while The Box Trail continues south. There are lots of stone cairns in this part marking the way. Once in The Box, turn right or northwest and walk up along the Paria River again. Just south of where Old Pahreah once was, and on the far right or east side near the canyon wall, are the remains of 3 stone structures built by **Charles H. Spencer in 1912**. Spencer was trying to extract gold from the Chinle clay beds. Read more about this is the chapter, **Mining History: The Paria River Drainage**, in the back of this book.
Elevations Old Pahreah townsite & trailhead, 1440m; lower Starlight & Hogeye Canyons,1525m; upper Hogeye, 1755m; high point along Carlow Ridge, 1856m.
Time Needed It's about 11 kms from Old Pahreah to the cave in Starlight Canyon; this might take 6-9 hours, depending on side-trips to the historic sites along the way. From Old Pahreah to the head of Hogeye is roughly 13 kms. This could take 8-11 hours round-trip, maybe a little longer if returning via Carlow Ridge & The Box (?). These are pretty long hikes, but walking is generally fast & easy.
Water There's running water year-round in the lower part of Starlight, but there may also be cattle around, so beware. There's no chance for cattle to get above the cataract in Hogeye, so above that, water should be reasonably good to drink (?), especially from or near the spring source.
Maps USGS or BLM maps Kanab & Smoky Mountain (1:100,000) for driving & orientation; Deer Range Point, Fivemile Valley & Calico Peak (1:24,000--7 1/2' quads) for hiking.
Main Attractions A short but interesting narrow section & pictographs in Starlight Canyon; cowboy signatures & petroglyphs and old ranch sites along the Paria; and in Hogeye, narrows, running water, total wilderness and great views from Carlow Ridge. Also, about 100m north of the old Carlow Ranch house chimney, is a large boulder with dinosaur tracks embedded in the south side.
Best Time to Hike Spring or fall. Winter has ice water wading; summers are hot as a pistol.
Boots/Shoes Waders along the Paria River; dry-weather shoes elsewhere.
Author's Experience Here are his major hikes in these parts. Years ago he walked from Old Pahreah, up to the Kitchen Cabins in Kitchen Canyon, up Starlight to where the water first begins to flow, then about halfway up Hogeye Canyon and back to his car, all in about 9 1/2 hours. A 1997 hike went up Starlight to the cave, then up into lower Hogeye Canyon and back to Old Pahreah in 8 hours. His hike in 2003 was from Old Pahreah, up Hogeye and back via the Carlow Ridge to The Box, plus a quick peek at Spencer's stone cabins, all in 8 2/3 hours. In 2009, he did the exact same hike in 8 3/4 hours.

Map 12, Hogeye & Starlight Canyons, and Carlow Ridge-
-from Old Pahreah

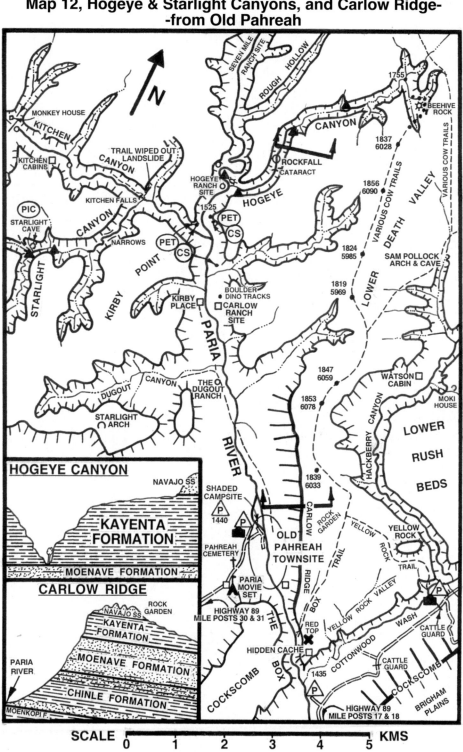

SEVEN MILE RANCH SITE

ROUGH HOLLOW

1755

BEEHIVE ROCK

CANYON

MONKEY HOUSE

KITCHEN

1837 6028

VARIOUS COW TRAILS

KITCHEN CABINS

TRAIL WIPED OUT: LANDSLIDE

CANYON

ROCKFALL CATARACT

HOGEYE RANCH SITE

HOGEYE

1856 6090

DEATH VALLEY

KITCHEN FALLS

1525

PIC

STARLIGHT CAVE

PET CS

STARLIGHT CANYON

NARROWS

PET CS

1824 5985

SAM POLLOCK ARCH & CAVE

LOWER

STARLIGHT

KIRBY POINT

1819 5969

BOULDER DINO TRACKS

KIRBY PLACE

CARLOW RANCH SITE

PARIA

1847 6059

WATSON CABIN

MOKI HOUSE

CANYON

THE DUGOUT RANCH

1853 6078

HACKBERRY CANYON

LOWER

DUGOUT

STARLIGHT ARCH

RUSH

BEDS

RIVER

1839 6033

HOGEYE CANYON

NAVAJO SS

SHADED CAMPSITE

P 1440

P

CARLOW

ROCK GARDEN

YELLOW ROCK

YELLOW ROCK

KAYENTA FORMATION

MOENAVE FORMATION

PAHREAH CEMETERY

OLD PAHREAH TOWNSITE

TRAIL

TRAIL

CARLOW RIDGE

ROCK GARDEN

NAVAJO SS

KAYENTA FORMATION

PARIA MOVIE SET

BOX RIDGE

THE BOX

RED TOP

YELLOW ROCK VALLEY

P

HIGHWAY 89 MILE POSTS 30 & 31

PARIA RIVER

MOENAVE FORMATION

CHINLE FORMATION

HIDDEN CACHE

COTTONWOOD

CATTLE GUARD

CATTLE GUARD

WASH

COCKSCOMB

MOENKOPI F.

COCKSCOMB

1435

P

BRIGHAM PLAINS

HIGHWAY 89 MILE POSTS 17 & 18

SCALE 0 1 2 3 4 5 KMS

Both of these pictures are from **Hoyeye Canyon**. To the left is the **cascade** with all the running water, and the upper shaded area with lots of tall **cottonwood trees** and good campsites.

Right at the head of the narrows in **Starlight Canyon** is this short slot and minor dropoff.

Starlight Cave showing black soot on parts of the ceiling indicating that aborigines had lots of camp-fires here for many years. Also notice the pictographs made with charcoal.

Both pictures are from **Starlight Cave**. The pictographs were made with charcoal, but some of them have disappeared, or nearly so. Since it's inside a cave, corncobs have survived nearly 1000 years.

Cannonville Slot Canyons

Location & Access   The author was introduced to these 2 short slot canyons by Bob Ott of Cannonville, the man (mostly his wife) who runs the camper's concession at Kodachrome Basin State Park. These **Slots** are located very conveniently about 1 km southwest of Cannonville. All or most of these canyons are on public domain, but the only way to get there is across **Bob Ott's private land**. If it's done right, he doesn't mind having hikers cross his property to see the slots, but he does want people to call him first at Tele. 435-679-8787 just so he knows who is there. Or call Bob or his wife at Kodachrome Basin Cabin rentals, Tele. 435-679-8536. For the latest access information, you're asked to stop at the visitor center in Cannonville and talk to someone there (Tele. 435-679-8981). They can update you on the private land situation.

To get there, drive south from the **visitor center** on the **Kodachrome Basin Road** about **1.1 km (.7 mile)** and as the highway begins to curve southeast, look for a open area for parking on the right or west. There you'll see a gate which is the entry to the southeast corner of Bob's alfalfa field. Park either on the inside or the outside of that gate.

Trail/Route   From just inside the gate at the southeast corner of the alfalfa field, walk south until you come to the dry wash draining the land to the west, then simply head westward and into the 2 main slots. Or walk west along the south side of the alfalfa patch until you're close to the slots, then walk & route-find cross-country until you're there. Walk up each drainage as far as you can; you'll eventually be stopped by a dryfall. In the upper end of each, will be a short narrow section of canyon and a slot.

These canyons are made from the same geologic formation as seen in Kodachrome Basin State Park to the east. The slots are in the lower levels of the **Entrada Sandstone Formation** called the **Gunsight Butte Member**. The color is red, and it's more of a hardened mud, than sandstone--best to leave the "stone" off this one! When it rains, part of the outer surface melts away and ends up in the Paria, then the Colorado River. Inquire at the visitor center as to the best way to get up on top of the mesa just to the west for some interesting fotos looking down onto these red rocks.

Elevations   Visitor center, Cannonville, 1792m; mouth of each slot canyon, same as in town, 1792m.

Time Needed   To do the hike into each slot and return is to walk about 3 kms. This should take 1-2 hours, maybe a little more if you want to set up a camera & tripod for pictures.

Water   Take you own. There are water taps at the visitor center, Cannonville town park, or the Grand Staircase gas station, store & motel just a block north of the visitor center on Highway 12.

Maps   USGS or BLM map Panguitch (1:100,000) for driving; and Cannonville (1:24,000--7 1/2' quad) for hiking.

Main   Attractions
Bright   red-colored slot canyons that are easy to reach.   No need for a 4WD here!

Best Time to Hike
Spring or fall are best, but these can be hiked 12 months a year.

Boots/Shoes   Any comfortable boots or shoes.   You'll never need   wading-type shoes here.

Author's   Experience   In 2003, he parked   at   Bob's house   and   walked into each canyon. He set up his camera at the head of each of the main forks, and took the time needed to come back with some   pretty   good shots.   Round-trip took   about   1 2/3 hours. If you're in a hurry you can do it much faster than that. In 2009, he parked at the alfalfa field and did the hike in 1 1/2 hours.

The upper end of one of 2 main canyons in the **Cannonville Slots**. They're short, but easy to get to and don't take a lot of time.

Map 13, Cannonville Slot Canyons

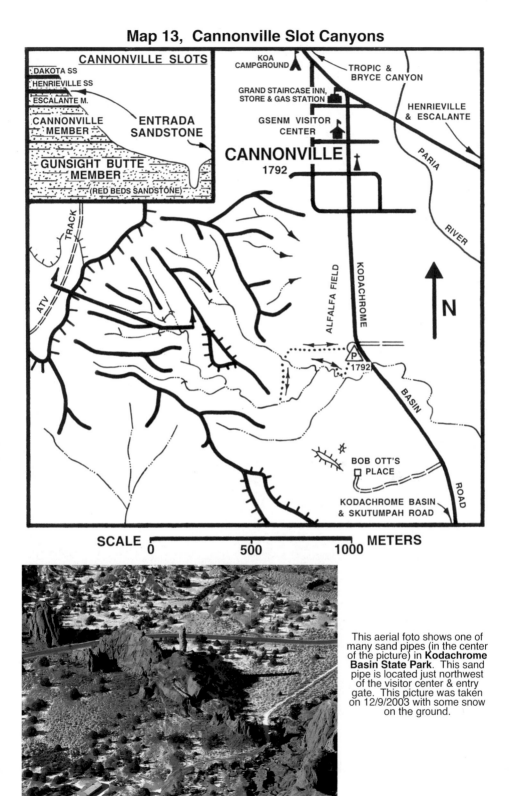

CANNONVILLE SLOTS

DAKOTA SS
HENRIEVILLE SS
ESCALANTE M.
CANNONVILLE MEMBER
ENTRADA SANDSTONE
GUNSIGHT BUTTE MEMBER
(RED BEDS SANDSTONE)

KOA CAMPGROUND
TROPIC & BRYCE CANYON
GRAND STAIRCASE INN, STORE & GAS STATION
HENRIEVILLE & ESCALANTE
GSENM VISITOR CENTER
CANNONVILLE
1792
PARIA
RIVER
TRACK
ATV
ALFALFA FIELD
KODACHROME
N
P
1792
BASIN
BOB OTT'S PLACE
KODACHROME BASIN & SKUTUMPAH ROAD
ROAD

SCALE
0   500   1000   METERS

This aerial foto shows one of many sand pipes (in the center of the picture) in **Kodachrome Basin State Park**. This sand pipe is located just northwest of the visitor center & entry gate. This picture was taken on 12/9/2003 with some snow on the ground.

85

Trails, Hikes & Sand Pipes in Kodachrome Basin State Park

Location & Access This map includes most of **Kodachrome Basin (KB) State Park**. It's located only about 3-4 kms directly south of Henrieville, but you can't approach it from there--except by trail. This park was first discovered by the outside world (National Geographic Magazine) in 1948 and was published in the September, 1949 issue. For about 60 years prior to that so-called expedition, Kodachrome Flat was known as **Thorley's Pasture**. Jack Breed, the author of that article, forgot to ask the locals what the name of the place was. The best things to see here are the **sand pipes**--read more below.

To get there, drive south out of **Cannonville** and the **visitor center**, and follow the signs along the paved KB Road. Drive a total of **11.7 kms (7.3 miles)** to the **Kodachrome Basin Turnoff (KBT)**. At that point, if you continue east, you'll be on the graded Cottonwood Wash Road--but instead turn left or north staying on the paved road going into KB. At the visitor center you must pay a fee to enter (the author paid $3 for half a day in 8/2009). Inside the park is a camper's store and fully-equipped cabins (with camping supplies and horseback rides), a campground with showers ($2) & dump station, a picnic site and several constructed trails, some level enough for mtn. bikes (Panarama Trail only). This state park is open year-round (there is an additional fee for camping and/or a shower). A national park service pass does not get you into KB. If you have good weather & sunshine, and you're there at the right time of day, fotographing the sand pipes will be very much worth while. As you enter the park, pick up their latest free map at the visitor center showing all the trails and facilities. This map is updated to 2009.

Trail/Route Most of the hiking trails are located north & northwest of the new visitor center. Right next to the campground, is the beginning of the **Eagles View Trail**. It takes you up a steep path to Eagles View Pass, at 1935m (in 2009 it was closed). Immediately south of the campground is the paved **Nature Trail** which takes you past a couple of sand pipes. East of the showers is the **Angels Palace Trail**, and a couple of more sand pipes (you look down on one). East of the cabins is the **Grand Parade Trail**; and to the west is the **Panorama Trail**, which features **The Ballerina**, one of the most-fotogenic sand pipes around. At this trail's western end is **Panorama Point**, an overlook situated on a rock outcropping. In the last several years, this trail has been extended westward and is called the **Big Bear Geyser Trail**. This walk or mtn. bike ride, is along a mostly-flat trail and is well-signposted. On the eastern side of the park is a short trail through some low cliffs to the **Shakespeare Arch**. Another site to see, but which you can drive to, is **Chimney Rock**, the biggest sand pipe in the park. Get there by driving northeast from the visitor center on a graded & graveled road. About 600m northwest of the visitor center is another fotogenic sand pipe right next to the paved park road.

Elevations Visitor center, 1756m; the Eagles View Trailhead, 1804m.

Time Needed The walk to **Eagles View Pass** should take only 10-15 minutes, one-way. The **Nature Trail**, about 10 minutes or so. The **Angels Palace Trail**, 15-20 minutes. The **Grand Parade Trail** about 15-20 minutes. The **Panorama Trail** is a longer loop and you could do this in about 1 or 1 1/2 hours, but you may want more time if you continue west on the **Big Bear Geyser Trail**. The walk to **Shake-**

From along the **Eagle's View Trail** looking back at the trailhead. About 20m from the parking place is one of many **sand pipes** for which Kodachrome Basin is famous.

Map 14, Trails, Hikes & Sand Pipes in Kodachrome Basin S.P.

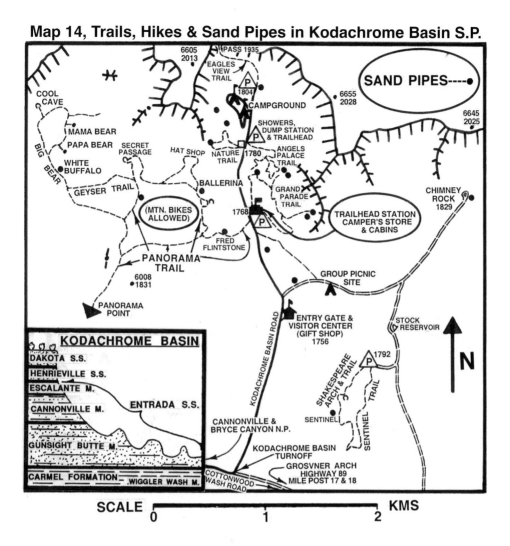

SAND PIPES----•

COOL CAVE

MAMA BEAR

PAPA BEAR

SECRET PASSAGE

HAT SHOP

WHITE BUFFALO

GEYSER TRAIL

6605 2013

PASS 1935

EAGLES VIEW TRAIL

P 1804

CAMPGROUND

6655 2028

SHOWERS, DUMP STATION & TRAILHEAD

6645 2025

NATURE TRAIL

1780

ANGELS PALACE TRAIL

BALLERINA

(MTN. BIKES ALLOWED)

1768

GRAND PARADE TRAIL

CHIMNEY ROCK 1829

TRAILHEAD STATION CAMPER'S STORE & CABINS

FRED FLINTSTONE

PANORAMA TRAIL

6008 •1831

PANORAMA POINT

GROUP PICNIC SITE

ENTRY GATE & VISITOR CENTER (GIFT SHOP) 1756

STOCK RESERVOIR

N

KODACHROME BASIN

DAKOTA S.S.

HENRIEVILLE S.S.

ESCALANTE M.

CANNONVILLE M.   ENTRADA S.S.

GUNSIGHT BUTTE M.

CARMEL FORMATION   WIGGLER WASH M.

SHAKESPEARE ARCH & TRAIL

P 1792

SENTINEL

SENTINEL TRAIL

CANNONVILLE & BRYCE CANYON N.P.

KODACHROME BASIN TURNOFF

GROSVNER ARCH HIGHWAY 89 MILE POST 17 & 18

KODACHROME BASIN ROAD

COTTONWOOD WASH ROAD

SCALE 0   1   2 **KMS**

speare Arch should take less than 10 minutes for the one-way trip. There are no official trails around the sand pipes just northwest of the visitor center, but you can see and fotograph them from the road. If you hurry, it's possible see most of the fotogenic sites in this park in half a day.

Water At the visitor center, camper's store and at the campground.

Maps USGS or BLM maps Panguitch & Escalante (1:100,000) for driving; Cannonville & Henrieville (1:24,000--7 1/2' quads) for hiking; a Utah State Highway map and sketch map from the visitor center.

Main Attractions Red rock spires and cliffs, plus cabins and a well-developed campground with showers. Also, a rare geologic feature known as sand pipes. Read more below.

Best Time to Hike Spring or fall, but the park is open and can be visited year-round.

Boots/Shoes Any light-weight boots or shoes.

Author's Experience In 2009, the author walked almost all trails on this map in about half a day.

Sand Pipes of Kodachrome Basin

Within this state park are a number of unusual geologic features called **sand pipes,** which occur almost nowhere else. In the park, they're found mostly in the red-colored **Gunsight Butte Member** of the **Entrada Formation**. They seem to be concentrated in the area north & west of the visitor center. These red rock spires are lighter colored and more weather resistant than the surrounding rock. They average about 20m in height and 4-6m in diameter. The sand making up the pipes is normally more coarse than the surrounding rock. It's been thought they were created by the injection of liquefied sand maybe from a tidal flat, perhaps triggered by an earthquake and possibly initiated by cold water springs. Later erosion left these sand pipes standing high & dry.

Road Map: Rock Springs Bench Trailheads

Location & Access **Rock Springs Bench (RSB)** is located southeast of Cannonville, immediately south of Kodachrome Basin State Park & the Cottonwood Wash Road, east of the upper Paria River drainage, and west of the upper part of Hackberry Canyon. From the north and the Cottonwood Wash Road, the RSB slopes up to the south and ends at **Rock Springs Point**, which is part of the White Cliffs, a prominent feature running east-west across this part of southern Utah.

Use this map and driving information to gain access to: **(1) Johnson Hole Canyon & Trail**, including the Upper Paria River Gorge, Red Slot, Asay Bench & Canyon, and the middle part of Deer Creek; **(2) Johnson Hole, Snake Creek & the CCC Trail** into the Upper Paria River; **(3)** the technical slot in **Stone Donkey Canyon**; **(4)** and part of **Upper Hackberry Canyon** and/or the Upper Trail into Hackberry. If conditions are right, a 2WD pickup can make it to all these trailheads, but it's best to have a HCV & 4WD.

To get to these RSB trailheads, drive south & east out of Cannonville (check road conditions at the GSENM visitor center before leaving town) on the paved **Kodachrome Basin Road**. After 11.7 kms (7.3 miles) you'll come to the **Kodachrome Basin Turnoff (KBT)** with a pullout & information board on the right or south side. Instead of turning left or north on the paved road going to KB, first set your tripometer at 0, then head **east** on the unpaved but graded **Cottonwood Wash Road**. After 1.3 kms (.8 mile) turn right or south onto Watson Ridge. After a ways, you'll pass the **BLM** or **CCC corral** (Km 2.1/Mile 1.3) on your left, then will arrive at Rock Springs Creek (RSC) crossing (if there's been a flood in the previous day or two, this could be a problem even for 4WD's. About 200m past this normally dry creek bed, you'll arrive at **Wallace Ott's Corral** at Km 3.8/Mile 2.35.

To reach **(1) Johnson Hole Saddle & Trailhead,** make a hard right turn immediately south of the cattle guard & fence next to the corral and continue west along the fence. Soon you'll cross RSC for the 2nd time, then will be heading west. Shortly you'll cross RSC (Km 4.5/Mile 2.8) for the 3rd time, this time with a little water. Just beyond that is where the old **Rock Springs Shearing Corral** used to be situated. Nearby are 2 boulders with **signatures** of **early-day sheepmen**.

From the old corral site, head straight south up the sandy track upon RSB. At Km 6.5/Mile 4.1 will be a road coming in on the left or east (If you have a 2WD, and are heading for the other 2 trailheads, turn left or east at this point as this is likely the easiest route). Finally, 10 kms (6.2 miles) from the KBT, you'll reach a low divide called here, **Johnson Hole Saddle**, and another road coming in on the left. In about 2008, this road was graded and in 2009 was in pretty good condition for 2WD cars (but this changes with each storm). At that road junction are big P/J trees you can park & camp under; or you can continue south past a **very sandy** area for another 300m or so to the beginning of the actual horse trail running down into Johnson Hole Canyon.

To reach the trailhead for **(2) Johnson Hole, Snake Creek, the CCC Trail or (3) Stone Donkey Canyon,** start at Ott's Corral 3.8 kms (2.35 miles) from the KBT. Drive on the main road southeast into what Wallace Ott calls **Rough Canyon**. At Km 5.4/Mile 3.3 is a junction. If you continue straight ahead, you'll come to what used to be a very rough & steep section which challenged the best 4WD's; but now it's been graded and as of 2009 was good for 2WD's. Or you can turn right and go west up a steep sandy ridge. In the past, the author has taken his old VW Rabbit & newer Golf TDI up this section, but lately it's gotten worse, so the last time up with his Chevy Tracker, he had to shift into 4WD. In the right conditions a 2WD can make this, but gear down, rev up, and go as fast as possible.

Just out of Rough Canyon going west, you'll pass a **gate** & a chained area, then at Km 7.9/Mile 4.9 you'll come to a 4-way junction--turn left. After another 600m (.35 mile), is another junction--turn left again (if you turn right at this point, you'll end up at the Johnson Hole Saddle & Trailhead, #1 above). After another 400m (.25 mile), and at Km 8.9/Mile 5.5, is a 3-way intersection--turn right and drive south another 5.4 kms (3.35 miles) to the end of the road, which is 14.3 kms (8.9 miles) from the KBT. This last section of road runs straight south and straight up RSB and is rutted because flood water runs right down the track. In the past the author took his VW Rabbit & Golf up this, but both were high-centering a lot in sand. But as of 2009, there were 3 flood-gutted places on this track--the 3rd of which was a meter deep!--but by the time you get there, it surely will have been graded (maybe?) or vehicles will find/make bypasses around the washed out places. The author had to stop at the 3rd bad spot at Km 11.6 (Mile 7.2) and walked from there 30 minutes to the end of the road. In the opinion of this writer, the best thing to happen here is to have it graded every few years and fix it so flood waters are diverted. It seems better to have one track instead of many. Or close the RSB to all motor vehicles.

To reach the **(4) Death Valley Draw Trailhead,** let's start at the junction just below where the rough & steep section used to be. Head southeast up and out of Rough Canyon, hoping the road stays good. About 7 kms (4.3 miles) from KBT, is another junction--continue straight ahead to the southeast. After another 600m (.35 mile), and just beyond **Sam Pollock's little shack** & small trailer house on the left, the road veers left or east. Finally at the head of Death Valley Draw will be a junction and a fence & gate at Km 8.5/Mile 5.2--turn right or south and continue to where the road is blocked off at Km 9.1/Mile 5.6. Park there or nearby.

Regarding that old shack & small trailer house, here's what Wallace Ott of Tropic had to say: *That cabin was put there by Sam Pollock in about the late 1930's [Sam's son Afton Pollock says it was built in 1941]. He was a sheepman and he's the guy I bought the grazing rights from. I camped in that cabin quite a bit. I took that trailer in there in the 1960's.*

For those with a 2WD only, your best chance to reach all these trailheads might be to head west from Ott's Corral in the direction described above going toward the Johnson Hole Saddle Trailhead, then use the connecting roads shown on the map to reach the other 2 parking places. There's a fair amount of sand in this county, so keep moving as fast as conditions allow when you see deep sand ahead. Also, **carry a shovel** at all times. In winter, or when the sand has some moisture, it's a lot easier to drive through; when it's extra dry, more difficult--even for 4WD's!

Map 15, Road Map: Rock Springs Bench Trailheads

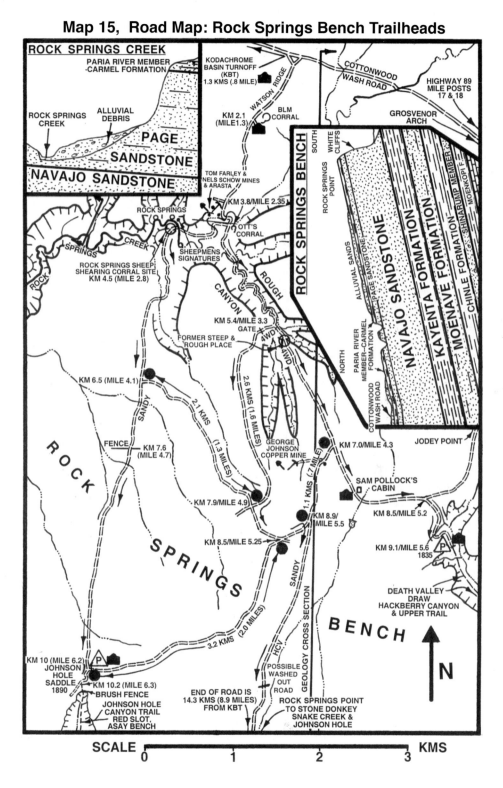

ROCK SPRINGS CREEK

PARIA RIVER MEMBER
-CARMEL FORMATION

ROCK SPRINGS
CREEK

ALLUVIAL
DEBRIS

PAGE
SANDSTONE

NAVAJO SANDSTONE

KODACHROME
BASIN TURNOFF
(KBT)
1.3 KMS (.8 MILE)

WATSON RIDGE

COTTONWOOD
WASH ROAD

HIGHWAY 89
MILE POSTS
17 & 18

KM 2.1
(MILE1.3)

BLM
CORRAL

GROSVENOR
ARCH

TOM FARLEY &
NELS SCHOW MINES
& ARASTA

KM 3.8/MILE 2.35

ROCK SPRINGS

OTT'S
CORRAL

SHEEPMENS
SIGNATURES

ROCK SPRINGS SHEEP
SHEARING CORRAL SITE
KM 4.5 (MILE 2.8)

SPRINGS   CREEK

ROCK

CANYON

ROUGH

KM 5.4/MILE 3.3
GATE

FORMER STEEP &
ROUGH PLACE

4WD

4WD

ROCK SPRINGS BENCH

SOUTH

ROCK SPRINGS
POINT

WHITE
CLIFFS

NAVAJO SANDSTONE

ALLUVIAL SANDS

PAGE SANDSTONE

KAYENTA FORMATION

MOENAVE FORMATION

CHINLE FORMATION

SHINARUMP MEMBER

MOENKOPI F.

NORTH

PARIA RIVER
MEMBER-CARMEL
FORMATION

COTTONWOOD
WASH ROAD

KM 6.5 (MILE 4.1)

SANDY

2.1 KMS
(1.3 MILES)

2.6 KMS
(1.6 MILES)

FENCE   KM 7.6
(MILE 4.7)

GEORGE
JOHNSON
COPPER MINE

1.1 KMS (.7 MILE)

KM 7.0/MILE 4.3

JODEY POINT

SAM POLLOCK'S
CABIN

KM 7.9/MILE 4.9

KM 8.5/MILE 5.25

KM 8.9/
MILE 5.5

KM 8.5/MILE 5.2

KM 9.1/MILE 5.6
1835

P

R O C K

S P R I N G S

SANDY

DEATH VALLEY
DRAW
HACKBERRY CANYON
& UPPER TRAIL

N

GEOLOGY CROSS SECTION

B E N C H

3.2 KMS (2.0 MILES)

HCV

KM 10 (MILE 6.2)
JOHNSON
HOLE
SADDLE
1890

P

KM 10.2 (MILE 6.3)

BRUSH FENCE

JOHNSON HOLE
CANYON TRAIL
RED SLOT,
ASAY BENCH

POSSIBLE
WASHED
OUT
ROAD

END OF ROAD IS
14.3 KMS (8.9 MILES)
FROM KBT

ROCK SPRINGS POINT
TO STONE DONKEY
SNAKE CREEK &
JOHNSON HOLE

SCALE

0   1   2   3   **KMS**

Johnson Hole Canyon & Trail, Asay Bench Trail & Canyon, the Red Slot, and Middle Deer Creek Canyon

Location & Access This area is due south of both Cannonville & Kodachrome Basin State Park, south & west of Rock Springs Bench, and also along both sides of the upper Paria River drainage. Read the driving instructions to this trailhead under **Map 15, Road Map: Rock Springs Bench Trailheads.**

Trail/Route From where ever you park at Johnson Hole Saddle, walk south down the shallow drainage on an emerging ATV & hiker's trail to the first little dropoff. There you'll find the remains of a brush & log fence which is the beginning of the **Johnson Hole Canyon Trail.** This canyon & trail are named after an old-timer named **Sixtus Johnson.** Wallace Ott of Tropic had this to say: *That old trail through Johnson Hole Canyon was there for years & years, and it was named after Sixtus Johnson. But later I was the one who did most of the work on that trail. I took powder down in there. and in one place it was so slick, that the horses would slip. One old gray horse slipped and by the time he got down to the bottom he was dead. Then I blasted some up at the top and fixed it.*

Go through the gate and follow the well-used trail along the left side of the upper drainage. Further along, you'll drop down into the dry creek bed. Continue down the wash bottom until you come to a dropoff. Actually, if you're paying attention near that point, you may have seen one trail head south toward **Johnson Hole** about 200m above the dropoff. If you follow that one, it will take you past a small butte with the elevation marked **6188** (1886m) on the *Bull Valley Gorge 7 1/2' quad.* That trail is easy to follow until you reach a point halfway between **Sugarloaf**, and what this writer calls **Little Sugarloaf**, then the path fades away to almost nothing.

However, don't take that route; instead, look for another trail bypassing the dropoff on the left or east side. Once back in the wash bottom, continue for another 200m or so, and be looking for the trail running up to the left. Hopefully you'll find a small stone cairn there. Once out of the drainage, the trail is easy to follow due south down a prominent **hogsback ridge** just west of the above-mentioned butte. Further down, you'll begin to veer to the right or southwest about 500m north of the elevation marked **5652** (1722m) on the *7 1/2' quad.* This is where you'll have to watch closely for the trail as it runs southwest, then west down a minor ridge (someone needs to put up some cairns in this part). If you want to see **Balanced Rock**, about halfway down this smaller ridge, and near a couple of cairns going due west, look SES about 300m. It's also about 200m WNW of elevation **5652** (1722m).

Soon the trail levels some, then makes an abrupt turn to the left 135° and heads southeast and off a minor point into the **Paria River** 15m below **Lone Rock**. Right at the bottom are willows & Russian olive trees, and the initials HS 1913. This stands for Harmon Shakespeare. According to Wallace Ott: *There's also an AD nearby, put there by Amond Davis. Harmon Shakespeare was my neighbor in Tropic, and he was down there in 1914 herding buck sheep. There used to be about 20 herds of sheep down here, and they'd take the bucks out alone, away from the ewes. And they took a herd of bucks down into Johnson Hole and Harmon and his brother was a herdin'um.*

Now before getting down into the Paria River at Lone Rock (which has some historic cowboy signatures), let's head for a narrow section in the lower end of **Johnson Hole Canyon**, a place this writer is calling the **Red Slot.** From Lone Rock, retreat back up the trail about 200m and walk cross-country just about due north until you drop down into the lower end of Johnson Hole Canyon, then walk up the sandy wash bottom. Roughly 1 1/4 kms from Lone Rock you'll come to a slit in the wall in the bottom of the Navajo Sandstone, which in this area is bright red in color. Walk into the slot and after 30m you'll see Wallace Ott's signature on the right. After another 50m, the slot widens into what appears to be a tiny rincon immediately below where flood waters drop about 45m into the Red Slot. This is an interesting place, and well worth the visit.

Once at Lone Rock, you can head down the Paria River to **Crack Spring** (about 1 km and on the west side); or walk upcanyon and into what this writer is calling **Asay Canyon**, which is the 1st drainage northwest of **Asay Bench.** Also, about 500m northwest of Lone Rock and on the left or west side will be the **Asay Bench Trail.** It's behind some cottonwood trees and you may see an old **fence** around a section at the bottom of the trail. It's the only place around where the cliffs give way to a slope where a cattle trail can exist. This will be the way you get on or come off Asay Bench.

According to Wallace Ott: *It was a rancher named Ed Asay who built that trail upon Asay Bench. He was my uncle and he lived in Woodenshoe. He was born in 1873, same as my Dad, and left the country in the 1910's, so it would have been built in the early 1900's.*

About 1 km upriver or north of the Asay Bench Trail, will be the mouth of **Asay Canyon.** Walk straight upcanyon and into a nice shallow narrows with a little running water. After about 200m, it slots-up into a crack and you'll have to chimney straight up about 2-3m to continue. With 2 or more people, this is easy--or you'll need long pants & long-sleeved shirt, or **knee & elbow pads**, to save skin! Just above this one little dropoff is a short slot, then the canyon opens some. Or, if you can't or don't want to chimney up, return to the mouth of the canyon, climb up on the bench to the north, and head upcanyon along a ridge for 300m or so, then drop back down into the canyon bottom just above the **lower slot.**

About 1 km above the mouth of Asay Canyon is a major fork; turn right into the longest of the 2 tributaries. After about another km, will be the short & sweet **upper slot** barely shoulder width. This one is only about 50m long, but it's fotogenic. About 500m above this upper slot the canyon forks; take the fork to the left which comes down from the southeast. Getting out of this fork will take just a little climbing, but anyone can handle it; it's more a matter of route-find than hard climbing. If you stay in the bottom of this fork, the canyon narrows and you'll find a small stand of **quaking aspen**, the only ones the author's ever seen in such a low altitude semiarid environment. Just above these trees is a dryfall, so retreat to the last aspen and climb the slope on the northeast side. This has steep slickrock in a place or two. Once out on top, you could retreat back downcanyon; or walk across **Asay Bench** and down the cow trail to the Paria. But before going anywhere, be aware there is a minor **petroglyph panel** on the west face of a black colored wall about 6-7m above the bottom. See map.

Or once on top of the bench, walk south 600m and down a broad drainage into the middle part of **Upper Deer Creek Canyon.** You'll enter this drainage just above **2 gooseneck bends**. Once down in, you can walk down to about 3m rappel into the lower end of the canyon. Hikers regularly walk up to the bottom of that big dryfall from the Paria. In Lower Deer Creek Canyon is running water, lots of cottonwood trees & campsites, and 2 panels of pictographs. Or you can head upcanyon and into the lower end of the **Northwest Fork.** There you'll find a nice 100m-long slot before coming to a 7m sloping dryfall. Or if you turn left instead, and into the **Main Fork of Deer Creek**, you'll soon come to a 100m-long deep dark slot and perhaps a couple of pools. That will be the end of upcanyon travel. To do the en-

Map 16, Johnson Hole Canyon & Trail, Asay Bench Trail & Canyon, the Red Slot, and Middle Deer Creek Canyon

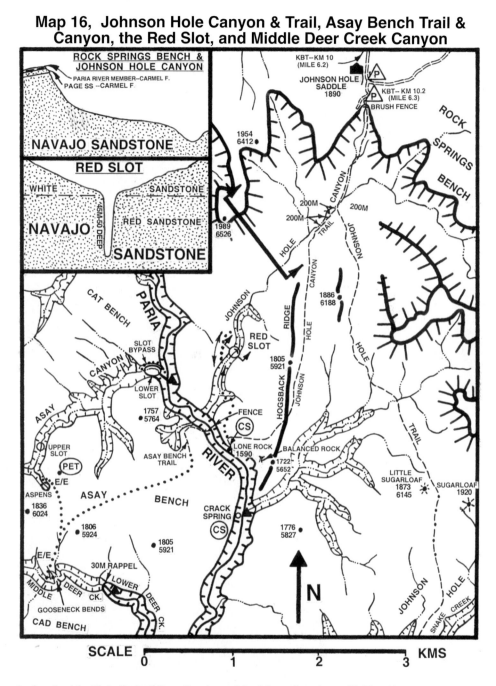

ROCK SPRINGS BENCH &
JOHNSON HOLE CANYON

- PARIA RIVER MEMBER--CARMEL F.
PAGE SS --CARMEL F.

NAVAJO SANDSTONE

RED SLOT

WHITE   SANDSTONE

NAVAJO   RED SANDSTONE

45M-50 DEEP

SANDSTONE

KBT--KM 10
(MILE 6.2)

JOHNSON HOLE
SADDLE
1890

KBT--KM 10.2
(MILE 6.3)

BRUSH FENCE

ROCK SPRINGS BENCH

1954
6412

200M   200M

200M

1989
6526

1886
6188

CAT BENCH

PARIA

JOHNSON

SLOT
BYPASS

RED
SLOT

RIDGE

1805
5921

HOGSBACK

JOHNSON

HOLE

JOHNSON

CANYON

HOLE CANYON

TRAIL

JOHNSON HOLE

HOLE

LOWER
SLOT

1757
5764

FENCE

CS

CANYON

ASAY

UPPER
SLOT

PET

E/E

ASPENS

1836
6024

ASAY

BENCH

LONE ROCK
1590

BALANCED ROCK

1722
5652

LITTLE
SUGARLOAF
1873
6145

SUGARLOAF
1920

ASAY BENCH
TRAIL

RIVER

CRACK
SPRING

CS

1806
5924

1805
5921

1776
5827

E/E

30M RAPPEL

LOWER

MIDDLE

DEER CK.

DEER CK.

GOOSENECK BENDS

CAD BENCH

N

JOHNSON HOLE

SNAKE CREEK

SCALE   0   1   2   3   KMS

tire length of the **Main Fork of Deer Creek**, read the information along with **Map 11**.
 After your trip to the middle part of Deer Creek, head northeast a little over 2 kms to the top of the Asay Bench Trail which drops off the northeast side of Asay Bench as shown on the map. You won't see this trail on top of the bench; only when it starts down from the top.
Elevations Trailhead, 1890m; Lone Rock & the Paria River, 1590m; top of Asay Bench, about 1770m.
Time Needed To do the entire hike suggested above will take from 10-13 hours, maybe more for some people (?). A long all-day hike! Or you might backpack in and camp at Crack Spring or near the lower end of Asay Canyon and do it in 2 days.
Water Paria River water must be treated; water from lower Asay Canyon may be drinkable as is (?); and water from Crack Spring has been drank straight from a little pipe for more than a century.

Maps USGS or BLM maps Kanab, Panguitch & Smoky Mountain (1:100,000) for driving & orientation; and Bull Valley Gorge & Slickrock Bench (1:24,000--7 1/2' quads) for hiking.
Main Attractions Several short & sweet slots, historic cattle trails & cowboy signatures.
Best Time to Hike Spring or fall, but can be done in summer. This is sandy country, so the only place where wet roads can be a problem might be along the bottom of Rock Springs Creek with clay soil.
Boots/Shoes Along the Paria River, you'll need wading boots/shoes; elsewhere, dry-weather shoes.
Author's Experience He camped at the trailhead and did the described loop-hike in 10 1/4 hours in 2003. On 7/24/2009, he did the same thing but didn't include the walk to Crack Spring; instead, he explored a new route into the upper part of the Northwest Fork of Deer Creek. That trip took 10 1/2 hours.

Above Left This is the **sand pipe** called the **Ballerina** located along the Panarama Trail in Kodachrome Basin State Park. It's one of the most fotogenic spires or sand pipes in the park.

Above Right Balanced Rock is located about halfway between the Johnson Hole Canyon Trail and the Paria River. It's also due west and up a bit from Lone Rock.

Right Lone Rock, located at the bottom of the Johnson Hole Canyon Trail and next to the Paria River. Look around the sides and you'll see some old cowboy signatures.

Above Left Looking back down at the beginning of the **Asay Bench Trail**. This constructed cow trail is easy to find & follow in the lower parts near the Paria, but once on top of the Asay Bench, it disappears in the sand.

Above Right The lower end of **Asay Canyon** has some nice narrows and running water. If you take water from the spring source, and there isn't any cow-manure in it, it may be drinkable as is (?).

Left Aerial view of the **Upper Paria River Gorge**. This picture was taken on 12/9/2003 with some snow in shaded places. In the center bottom of the foto, and just to the right of the snow & shadows, is **Lone Rock**.

Above Left Looking downstream at the head of **Asay Canyon**. These are aspen or quaking aspen trees, the lowest altitude site of these trees the author has seen.

Above Right The **Upper Slot** in **Asay Canyon**. If the light is just right, you'll find some interesting curves and erosional features.

Right Very near the end of **Asay Canyon** is this tight slot. You can chimney up or down 2-3m, but you'd want long pants and a long sleeved shirt or you'd loose skin; knee & elbow pads work better. Halfway through this short slot, the canyon opens to the left into the **Lower Narrows**.

Above Left Inside the **Red Slot**, which is in the lower end of **Johnson Hole Canyon**. Notice the log jammed into the slot.

Above Right This is where the **Red Slot** comes out of the Navajo Sandstone wall. The slot is only about 150m long.

Left Just inside the **Red Slot** is the signature of Wallace Ott. He was(born in 1911 and was still alive in 2010.

Johnson Hole, Snake Creek & the CCC Trail to the Paria River

Location & Access This area is due south of Kodachrome Basin State Park & Rock Springs Bench, and east of the Upper Paria River Gorge. Read the driving instructions for this hike under **Map 15, Road Map: Rock Springs Bench Trailheads.**

Trail/Route There are 2 possible ways into Johnson Hole & Snake Creek from the north. **Approach 1:** From the end of the road on **Rock Springs Point**, route-find due south with compass & map in hand, first along a faint winding ATV track, then along an emerging hiker's trail for about 1 km. About 200m before the actual end of the point, look for a cairn (single pointed standing rock) on the left marking a trail-of-sorts angling down over the rim heading southeast. This is **Wallace Ott's Horse Trail** (he only had a horse on it about 3 times!), but it's only visible in the upper part; further along, head straight down a sandslide. Consider caching a bottle of water at the bottom for the return hike--especially in hot weather. You'll hate climbing back up the sand!

Once in the drainage at the bottom of the sandslide, simply walk downcanyon--which happens to be the head of **Snake Creek.** After a ways, the drainage veers southwest, then in the area southeast of **Sugarloaf,** and near where 3 upper tributaries of Snake Creek meet, you'll come to a **40m dropoff & bypass**. From there, turn back to the left about 50m or so, and walk down in on the east side. Below the dryfall, the canyon gradually becomes more shallow again. Finally, you'll come to a **big dropoff of 40-45m.** From there, backtrack 100m to find a **cow trail** angling up a few meters to the south on the east side of the drainage. Get on it, walk south, and after 300m or so, you'll start down several short sections of constructed trail. This takes you down to where the main fork of **Upper Snake Creek** meets the **East Fork** (there are several other routes into the East Fork 1-2 kms east of this cattle trail as shown on the map). Wallace Ott of Tropic says this **Snake Creek Trail** was first built by Eli LeFevre and Layton Jolley during the 1930's, but after Ott bought their grazing rights in 1945, he upgraded it. His son Sherrell Ott now runs cows down Snake Creek during the cooler half of the year. Today you'll see fresh cut steps in the trail made with a cordless saw.

Approach 2: From **Johnson Hole Saddle**, at the head of Johnson Hole Canyon, start down the obvious trail heading south (read more information under **Map 16**). After less than 2 kms and while walking in the upper drainage bottom, continue on a trail straight ahead to the south instead of following the dry creek bed southwest to a dryfall about 200m away. Follow the trail that runs south along the east side of a small butte labeled **6188** (1886m) on the *Bull Valley Gorge 7 1/2' quad* and Map 16. Follow this well-used trail south, then southeast to between **Sugarloaf** and what this writer calls **Little Sugarloaf.** Watch carefully as the trail fades between these 2 peaks. From there, veer right or south and from the top of a low ridge, continue down a good trail into Upper Snake Creek as shown on this map. This is the trail the Otts use to take cows into Johnson Hole & Snake Creek for water. This route, Approach 2, is the easiest, but a little longer.

Once into **Lower Snake Creek**, you have several route choices. One would be to go up the **East Fork** and explore **2 alcove-type caves.** The 1st is about 400m up from the bottom of the trail and on the left or north side; the 2nd is about another 500m upcanyon and on the right. The back ends of both caves have black soot-covered ceilings, indicating they were used a lot in the distant past by fire-building aborigines. There seems to be no pictographs or petroglyphs around, but archeologists or pot hunters have been busy as beavers digging holes in the floor of each cave looking for something!

If you walk up each of the 3 main tributaries of East Fork, you'll come to dryfalls, or brush-choked narrows. Not so interesting, but you could route-find out of the canyon to the north and back to the Rock Springs Bench Trailhead as shown on this map.

About 150m downcanyon from where the 2 upper forks of Snake Creek meet, you'll come to the 1st of **3 dropoffs.** Get around the 1st via a constructed cattle trail on the right or west side. Wallace Ott once did some cement work in this section so cows could get down to a spring and running water for a drink. Below this **1st dropoff** is where cattle stop; and about 50m below there is a minor 7m-high waterfall. Route-find (no trail) around this **2nd dropoff** on the right or west side.

About 500m below the 2nd dropoff is a big **wall collapse** which surely fell sometime around the year 2000 (?). The upcanyon-side of this dam is filled with sand and right after each flood will likely be a small temporary lake. About 250m below this **wall collapse** is a 3rd dropoff which is a mossy cascade. Getting around this can be a problem so take a short rope or cord. Start on the left or east side. Walk 2m on a ledge, then help each other down, perhaps using a rope. For 2-3 people this shouldn't be a major obstacle. The author looped his pack rope around a small root and jumped down about a meter; the small rope kept him from sliding in the slippery moss below. From there to the Paria you'll find an emerging hiker's trail coming upcanyon, running water & cottonwood trees and some campsites.

At the **Paria River**, look for a panel of cowboy signatures behind willows on the left or east side right where the 2 canyons meet. From there you could go all the way downcanyon to Old Pahreah and Highway 89, or head upstream. About 2 kms above Snake Creek on the left or west side is **Oak Canyon.** It has good running water in its lower end. About 500m above Oak, and again on the left or west side, is the bottom end of the **Deer Trails Trail.** This constructed cow path begins near the end of the Nipple Ranch Road on Oil Well Hill. This trail and Oak Canyon are discussed in detail under **Map 11, Deer Creek.... and Oak Canyon.**

About 100m north or above the bottom of Deer Trails Trail, and on the right or east side of the Paria, is the lower end of the **CCC Trail.** At its beginning, this trail is well-constructed and was used to run cows from the Upper Death Valley & Johnson Hole areas down to water in the Paria River Canyon. According to Wallace Ott, this trail was built by the CCC's sometime in the mid-1930's. At that time, they had their main camp northeast of Henrieville near the old Smith Ranch, but while doing various projects along the Upper Paria River Gorge, they may have had a temporary spike camp near the mouth of Deer Creek, which is another 300m upcanyon. If you have time, you could visit Deer Creek with its pictograph & petroglyph panels. But this may take an additional hour or two (?).

Or, for this hike, climb the CCC Trail which zig zags up and to the south along several benches. Soon it rounds a point just above the mouth of a short side-drainage Wallace Ott calls **Red Creek,** then just inside this minor drainage, it angles up to the left. It's easy to follow until it reaches the mesa rim, then it disappears in the sand. At that point, route-find north about 600m until you're above or north of the steep part of Red Creek, then turn east and walk about 1 km back to Snake Creek. At that point, you should be just above the **big dropoff** where the Snake Creek Trail begins. While in this area, you'll be passing through colorful **teepee-shaped rocks** which can be fotogenic. Once in Snake Creek, follow your tracks back to your vehicle, perhaps taking a look at the east side of Sugarloaf & some ponderosa pines situated back there. This is another colorful scene. Or climb Sugarloaf for some nice views from

Map 17, Johnson Hole, Snake Creek & CCC Trail to Paria River

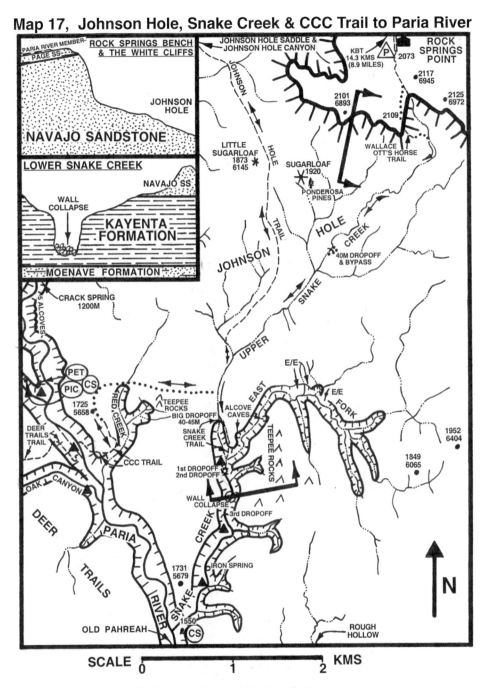

on top. That's where sheepherders spent time watching their flocks.

Or if you started hiking at the Johnson Hole Saddle, you could continue upcanyon along the Paria. About 3 kms above the bottom of the CCC Trail will be **Crack Spring** (good drinking water) on the left or west side. It comes from a crack in the wall behind some small cottonwood trees; look for clear water flowing from the bank, plus grass. Also, look at all the **historic signatures** of cowboys and freighters who ran teams & wagons between Cannonville and Pahreah.

About 1 km north of Crack Spring is **Lone Rock** on the right or east. About 15m below it will be the beginning of the **Johnson Hole Canyon Trail**. Follow it as shown on **Map 16** back to your car at the Johnson Hole Saddle Trailhead. This is the same trail you use if going to Asay Canyon & Bench, and Red Slot.

97

Elevations Trailheads, 2073m & 1890m; top of Wallace Ott's Horse Trail, 2109m; end of Snake Creek, about 1550m; Lone Rock & lower end of Johnson Hole Canyon Trail, 1590m.

Time Needed To do either of the loop-hikes suggested will take from 9-12 hours (longer if going via Lone Rock), but you can shorten the hike by going down Snake Creek only to the 3rd dropoff and re-turning; or make it longer by visiting Deer Creek Canyon. Or you can backpack in for 2-3 days, perhaps seeing Asay Canyon and coming out via Johnson Hole Canyon Trail. Lots of hiking options here.

Water Take plenty in your car & pack. Otherwise there's running water in Snake Creek and the Paria River (treat it). Also in Oak Creek, Deer Creek, Crack Spring (best) & Asay Canyon, if you go that far.

Maps USGS or BLM maps Panguitch, Kanab & Smoky Mountain (1:100,000) for driving & orientation; Bull Valley Gorge, Slickrock Bench, Deer Range Point & Calico Peak (1:24,000--7 1/2' quads) for hiking.

Main Attractions Seldom-seen canyons, interesting caves, an old CCC-built trail & cowboy signatures.

Best Time to Hike As usual in spring or fall, but with the higher altitudes, hiking in summer isn't so hot. Winter hiking is also possible but with some frosty nights and possible wading!

Boot/Shoes Wading-type shoes in Snake Creek, Deer Creek and Paria River; dry-weather shoes else-where.

Author's Experience He's been in these parts many times, but on 2 trips in 2003, he car-camped at the end of the road on Rock Springs Point, then (1) hiked down Ott's horse trail to Sugarloaf, down into middle Snake Creek, explored all tributaries of the East Fork, visited the 2 caves, and returned basically the same way. Round-trip 7 1/3 hours. On the other trip (2), he went straight down Snake Creek to the Paria, upriver to the CCC Trail, then returned via Sugarloaf (and the lower end of the trail discussed under Approach 2--Johnson Hole Trail), all in 9 hours. In 2009, he left his Jeep Patriot where the road was washed out on Rock Springs Point, then walked 30 min. to the end of the road, and up to Ott's horse trail and down Snake Creek to the 2 caves & the 2nd dropoff and back in 7 3/4 hours.

This is the upper-most cave in the **East Fork of Snake Creek.** Back in-side, the ceiling is covered with soot indicating Indians used it for camping, and had lots of campfires, for a long time.

This is the inside of the 2nd or upper-most cave in the **East Fork of Snake Creek**. Notice all the remnants of soot on the walls and ceiling which indicates Indians camped here for a long time.

At the base of Rock Springs Point is this butte called **Sugarloaf**. The yellow rock, plus ponderosa pines and blue sky make for an interesting picture.

This is the 1st cave you come to if going up the **East Fork of Snake Creek**.

The pool below the 2nd dropoff going down **Snake Creek** from the mouth of East Fork. To get down to this pool from above, carefully walk along the bench in the upper left-hand side.

This picture was taken somewhere in **Little Dry Valley (near Kodachrome Basin)** sometime during the winter of 1936-37. That winter had some of the deepest snow in the history of southern Utah. On the caterpillar is Hasle Caudill; in the snow is foreman Rex Thompson, both from the Henrieville CCC Camp. On that day, this Cat cleared a road to Watson Ridge so the CCC boys could deliver 14 tons of cottonseed cake to a big tent at the CCC/BLM Corral. The cottonseed cake was for Sam Pollock's sheep herd, which was in Upper Death Valley at the time. (Hasle Caudill foto)

This cow trail leads down between the 1st and 2nd dropoffs in **Snake Creek** where water begins to flow. This is as far as cows can go, but you can route-find around the 2nd dropoff on the right side. See the picture on the opposite page which shows the pool below the 2nd dropoff, and the ledge you walk on to get down.

Upper Paria River Gorge

Location & Access The **Upper Paria River Gorge** is that part of the drainage between Cannonville and the Old Pahreah townsite. Some might extend this upper gorge on down to Highway 89. The Lower Paria River Gorge is from Highway 89 down to Lee's Ferry and the Colorado River. Unlike the Lower Gorge, this upper part has mostly easy access, but with some wild & wooly places in between.

You can start at either end of this section and walk all the way through, but you'd need a car shuttle. Or you can park at either end and head for the middle part of the gorge and return the same way. To reach the upper part, drive south then east out of Cannonville on the paved road in the direction of Kodachrome Basin. After crossing the Paria River bridge, park at one of several little side-canyons which can be used to reach the main drainage. Near **Shepherd Point** would be one entry; or walk down **Road Hollow**--which used to be the main wagon route until the road was built around Shepherd Point; down **Little Dry Valley**; or from **Ott's Corral** (see Map 15) and walk down Rock Springs Creek as shown. Other possible places to begin would be from along the Skutumpah Road at the **dam crossing** on Sheep Creek; on Willis Creek; or the more difficult and exciting Bull Valley Gorge.

To enter at the lower end of the gorge, drive along Highway 89 about halfway between Page & Kanab. Between mile posts 30 & 31, and at the sign stating *Historic Marker*, turn northeast and drive 9.5 kms (5.9 miles) to near the Old Pahreah townsite on a rather good dirt & clay road (it's slick when wet!).

Another possible way into the middle of the upper gorge or canyon would be to drive along Highway 89, then very near mile post 37, turn north onto the **Nipple Ranch Road.** Drive northward to Oil Well Hill, but when the road turns east, stop and park there where a very sandy ATV track heads northwest. This would be near he beginning of the Deer Trails Trail. It takes you down to a point just below where Deer Creek enters the Paria. Read all about this under **Map 11**.

Elevations About 1750m along the Upper Paria trailheads; about 1850m at Willis Creek and Bull Valley Gorge; and 1440m at Old Pahreah.

Time Needed Old timers who talk about using the gorge as a road between Cannonville and Pahreah say it was 30 miles (48 kms) between the 2 settlements. But you can shorten that a lot by beginning from one of the side-canyon drainages. This entire distance, say from Sheep Creek or near Shepherd Point, can be walked in one very long day, but you'd need a car at both ends. However, it's recommended you take several days because there are many side-canyons to see such as Asay Canyon, the Red Slot, Deer Creek, Snake Creek, and some old cattle trails to explore. In 3-4 days one could have an enjoyable hike.

All the Upper Paria River Gorge or Canyon is within the newly created GSENM, but since the main canyon corridor has been an old wagon road since the 1870's, some people think they, and their vehicles, still must be allowed entry. The GSENM has tried to close the canyon to motor vehicles, but with little success. Finally in 2009, the 10th Circuit Court of Appeals rejected a county lawsuit and upheld the BLM's right to close the canyon to motor vehicles. Shortly afterwards, on Memorial Day weekend, 2009, a large group of 300 ATV riders showed up at Old Pahreah and took off up the canyon in defiance. Apparently nothing happened to them, but this Upper Paria River Gorge is closed to all motor vehicles, even those of stockmen who have cattle in the drainage during the winter months (approximately November 1 to May 1). There are periodic patrols to check on compliance.

Water There is a year-round flow in the Paria, but during the irrigation season, which is from sometime in late April until about the first of October, there's little or no water flowing downcanyon past Cannonville. Each year is different. Most or all of the water in the gorge at that time seeps out from the bottom of the Navajo Sandstone or the top layers of the Kayenta Formation. This is in the area below the White Cliffs, which begins near the bend of the river known as the **Devils Elbow.**

There are many small seeps in the upper part of this map and in the gorge near Devils Elbow, which should be drinkable as-is (?). Also, most major side-canyons have a small stream. If you walk up any of these canyons to where the spring or seep begins, then that water is normally drinkable as-is (?). In winter months there are cattle in the canyons, so some precautions should be taken, such as taking water directly from a spring, using Iodine tablets, or filtration. However, in the summer months, from about mid-May until the end of October or the first part of November, there are no cattle in the canyon. They are taken out during this time and put on higher summer pastures in the mountains. With the steeper gradient & monsoon floods, the stream flows fast and will wash out the microbes which can give hikers stomach troubles.

It's during this time of year, and when there has been a long dry spell, that the water in this upper gorge is as clear as any mountain stream and which the author has drank many times. About the only sediment entering the creek at this time is the small amount of sand being washed down by Kitchen Canyon Creek. However, when you get into mid or late summer, and with the presence of thunder shower activity, the water is often times very muddy.

For those who want to be on the safe side and drink only spring water, there are 2 fine springs on the west side of the canyon about straight across from the mouth of **Hogeye Canyon**. Another good source, perhaps the best in the gorge, is the historic **Crack Spring**. This spring is about 2-3 kms upstream from the mouth of Deer Creek Canyon and about half a km downcanyon from Lone Rock. Walk close to the west wall and look and listen carefully for the water coming out of a pipe in a cluster of small cottonwood trees.

Maps USGS or BLM maps Kanab & Smoky Mountain (and a small corner of Panguitch)(1:100,000); Calico Peak, Deer Range Point, Bull Valley Gorge, Slickrock Bench & Cannonville (1:24,000--7 1/2' quads). Be sure and carry either of these sets of maps, as this hand-drawn sketch is not that accurate. The 2 metric maps at 1:100,000 scale are recommended.

Main Attractions Sites of the old Dugout, Carlow, Kirby, Hogeye and Seven Mile Flat Ranches. Petroglyphs & Cowboy signatures or etchings are at the mouths of Kitchen Canyon, Snake Creek, Deer Creek and Rocks Springs Creek. Inside Deer Creek are the only pictograph panels in the area. Cowboy signatures are at Crack Spring, Lone Rock and other sites. You'll also have a number of old historic cattle trails, and many good campsites and solitude.

Best Time to Hike Spring or fall, with the very best times being from late March or early April to mid or late May, and from mid or late September to late October. Summers are hot, and late spring and early summer (late May through June and into July) usually brings small gnats and large horse flies. If you go too early in the spring, or late in the fall, your feet will be blocks of ice with some wading.

Boots/Shoes Wading-type boots or shoes. If you're planning to do the entire gorge hike, which is rather long, take a sturdy pair of shoes. Many people take an old pair of shoes to *wear out* on a trip like this, but if they're too old or battered, they fail to give support to the feet and may not last to the end of

Map 18, Upper Paria River Gorge

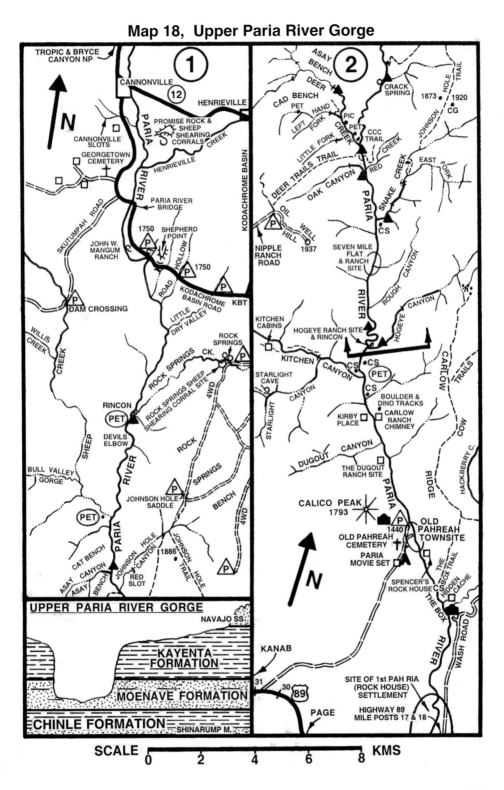

the hike. So take a pretty good pair of shoes, even though the wading will shorten their life.

Author's Experience The author has been upcanyon from Old Pahreah 7-8 times visiting the old ranches and trails, and Hogeye, Deer Creek and Kitchen Canyons. These were all day-hikes, which took from 8 to 9 1/2 hours. Another day he walked from Road Hollow down to Crack Spring, had lunch, and returned, in 7 1/2 hours. Another time he walked down Willis Creek to Deer Creek Canyon on a 2-day trip, which should have taken at least 3 days. On one of his last visits, he walked from Old Pahreah to as far as Deer Creek and the cow trails in that area, in less than 8 hours, round-trip. One trip was a hike off Rock Springs Point. He walked down past Sugarloaf and into the middle part of Snake Creek, then over the hump west and down the CCC Trail, and up Deer Trails to the west side bench. Then he returned to his car on Rock Springs Bench, all in about 7 1/2 hours. In 2003, he was in this area with his 4WD Chevy Tracker and from Rock Springs Bench and Oil Well Hill to the south on no less than half a dozen hikes. In 2009, he did 5 more trips starting on Oil Well Hill, Old Pahreah, Johnson Hole Saddle and on Rock Springs Bench, walking into the middle part of this canyon and side-canyons.

Trail/Route As you enter this canyon, you'll likely see some motor vehicle tracks (mostly ATV's) in the north & the south. In the lower end just above Old Pahreah, you'll likely be using some of the original old wagon roads which went from Pahreah to some of the ranches upcanyon. The *Smoky Mountain 1:100,000 scale metric map* shows the old road accurately to where it ends below the Kirby Place. Today there's an occasional ATV using this track (but which is **now illegal**) which is scarring parts of the canyon bottom and entering side-canyons.

There are also grazing permit holders who go into the middle part of the canyon occasionally in 4WD's to take in or bring out cattle--but this is now officially illegal. This is usually about May 1, and in the first part of November. These permit holders have a reason to be there, and aren't just out joy riding, as most recreation vehicle owners are.

At about the Kirby Place and going north, these tracks fade away as the canyon narrows; then you'll be walking in the flood-gutted canyon bottom. Grazing permit holders now get into or out of the upper part of this gorge via Sheep Creek, but the early day wagon road was right down the Paria past Devils Elbow. Walking is easy all along this creek bed.

Beginning now in the upper end of the gorge. You'll first be walking in a shallow canyon or drainage, but soon it narrows and deepens as the river begins to cut down into the Navajo Sandstone. Remember, while the river is downcutting, the walls are rising; that is, the top of the Navajo is higher in the south than to the north. In other words the rock formations slope down to the north.

At the mouth of **Rock Springs Creek**, you'll see an isolated, lone standing butte, which must be a part of an old abandoned meander or river channel. On the west side of this butte, and 6-8m off the ground, you'll see some pretty good petroglyphs. They were apparently put there when the river bed was much higher.

Downriver from Rock Springs Creek, is a big bend in the canyon, which old timers call the **Devils Elbow.** At that point the canyon is getting deep and moderately narrow. The white sandstone walls are the Navajo Sandstone, which form the White Cliffs all across the region.

In the area of the Devils Elbow, you'll begin to see many small seeps along the sides of the stream channel, and the creek begins to grow in volume. In early summer, the upper part can be totally dry, or nearly so, and the water you see in the Paria downstream actually begins here.

As you near where **Sheep Creek** enters from the west, you begin to see red sandstone in the canyon

Aerial view of the butte at the junction of the **Paria & Rock Springs Creek**. The Paria River flows from right to left, and Rock Springs Creek enters from the lower right-hand corner of this picture.

bottom. This is the lower part of the Navajo Sandstone. Then just a bit further downstream and in the area of Lone Rock, you'll see the top part of the Kayenta Formation emerging. The Kayenta forms little benches or terraces. As you walk south, the river continues to downcut, and the beds rise at the same time. From the Lone Rock area on down, most of the major side-canyons have some kind of water supply, either a flowing stream or good springs. If you walk up Sheep Creek a ways, maybe 300-400m, look for a nice panel of petroglyphs on the south side. Walk up a sandy slope to reach them.

About 2 kms below Sheep Creek will be **Asay Canyon** coming in on your right or west side. It will have some running water and there's a nice slot about 200m upcanyon. About 1 km below Asay Canyon is the **Asay Bench Trail**. It's an old cattle trail built in the early 1900's, and it's on the right or west side behind some cottonwood trees. It's the only place around where you can easily get up on Asay Bench. Read more about this canyon & trail along with **Map 16.**

About 400m downstream from the Asay Trail, and on your left is a big rock standing out in the river channel. This is what old timers called **Lone Rock.** Look closely on its sides and you'll see numerous old cowboy signatures or etchings. Some of these date back to the late 1800's, but some of the older ones are now becoming indistinct. About 15m downstream from Lone Rock and up against the willows & Russian olives to the north, is the bottom of the **Johnson Hole Canyon Trail.** This begins at Johnson Hole Saddle and is discussed along with **Map 16.**

To see what the author is calling the **Red Slot,** walk north up this trail about 200m and where it starts to turn east, you continue in a NWN direction. After another 600m or so, you'll drop down into the lower end of Johnson Hole Canyon. Walk up this dry wash another 700m to find a nice slot in the lower red-colored Navajo Sandstone. This is also covered in more detail with **Map 16**.

About 850m below, or south, of Lone Rock, and on the west side of the canyon, is **Crack Spring.** You'll have to walk close to the west wall and watch carefully to be able to see or hear clear water coming out of a crack in the wall. It's on a narrow little bench with many small cottonwood trees, and is hard to see unless you're close by. In the old days, when wagoneers & freighters were running between Cannonville & Pahreah, they always made this place their lunch stop, thus making the whole trip in one long day.

Years ago someone placed a 5-cm pipe into the crack, making it easier to get a drink. The pipe is still there, and it always has a good flow. Since the space right at the spring is both wet & small, it's best to camp on the opposite side of the river and upcanyon about 100m under some big cottonwood trees. Camping there would also leave the spring clean and pristine.

The late Kay Clark of Henrieville, remembered a trip he took with his father in April, 1920. They started in Cannonville and headed for Pahreah. They were carrying several sacks of grain, evidently to be sold to sheep herders in the lower valleys. When they made their lunch stop at Crack Spring, there were several other wagons already there. Since they were riding in comfort in a white-topped buggy with fringes, some of the other drivers made comments as to how they were really traveling in style. In those days, a white-topped buggy was like a Mercedes; and ordinary wagons used by most local people, were like Model T Fords.

On either side of Crack Spring, are many very old **cowboy etchings** or **signatures of travelers**. Those which are black in color, were made by placing axle grease on a finger, then writing a name. This grease prevented the sandstone from flaking away, so what you'll see there today are many raised letters or signatures which literally stand out on the wall like Braille writing. Other people carved their names into the sandstone with a sharp metal instrument.

About 2 kms below Crack Spring are **5 big coves** on the east side of the canyon high above. One

Left In the middle of the **Red Slot**. This is easily reachable from Lone Rock. **Right** The **2nd dropoff** in the middle part of **Snake Creek**. Get down from this ledge on the left side of this picture.

105

Left Crack Spring is the best water source along the Upper Paria River Canyon. It comes out of a pipe now. **Right Lower Deer Creek Canyon**; under a ledge just left of the tree are pictographs

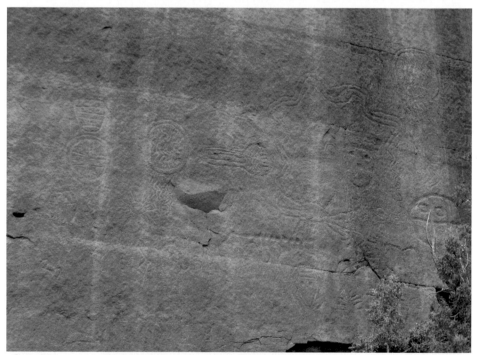

One of the more unusual rock art panels around. These petroglyphs are located at the point where **Deer Creek** and the **Paria River** meet, and on the east side. There are no big horn sheep here, which is a little different. These are up on the wall about 4m, or higher.

seems to have developed into an arch. Just below these is the mouth of Deer Creek Canyon, one of the best side-trips you can take while hiking the Upper Paria River Gorge, so plan to camp and spend time in this one.

Deer Creek Canyon

Deer Creek Canyon is moderately narrow, with high vertical walls made of the red-colored lower Navajo Sandstone & Kayenta Formation. This canyon is similar to places in the Lower Paria River Gorge or even the lower end of the Buckskin Gulch, where the campsites are located.

Inside the canyon is a crystal clear, year-round stream, which begins flowing at the base of a 30m dryfall about 2 1/2 kms up from the Paria. Along the stream are many fine campsites under large cottonwood trees. The walls of the canyon are red, but the benches you'll be camping on are white Navajo sands, which have blown off from the White Cliffs above.

As far as Deer Creek water is concerned, cattle may be in this canyon from early November to May 1. By May the cows are taken to their summer ranges. After the cattle leave the water should be much better, but you'd better purify it anyway, unless you take it directly from the spring at the bottom of the big 30m dryfall.

If you're interested in petroglyphs & pictographs, this is one of the best canyons around to see them. Right at the mouth of the canyon is one long panel of **petroglyphs**, including one glyph which is like a tic-tat-toe box. You'll have to climb a cedar tree to have a close look at this one.

Just inside Deer Creek about 200m, and on the right or east side, are several **pictographs** and petroglyphs. At one time, it looks as though someone tried to chop one of them out of the wall with an axe--but was unsuccessful. About 200m above this panel is what the author calls **Little Fork** coming in on the left or west. You can walk up this drainage for about 650m, skirt one dryfall, and climb another. Above that are ways to climb completely out of the canyon.

About 400m above Little Fork and on the right or east wall are signatures of Kay Clark & Byron Davis from 1935. Just above these signatures and on the opposite or west side, is a place you can **climb out** of the canyon. There are 2 routes out, but you'll have to bushwhack a little just getting to the base of the cliff. Once above the brush, it's a simple climb. See **Map 11**.

About 1200m upcanyon from the Paria (and 200m below Left Hand Fork), is the **best pictograph** panel around. There are actually 2 panels: one you can crawl up to and see close-up, the other is reachable, but you'll have to climb up a wall that appears to be on the verge of collapse.

About 200m upcanyon from these pictographs, the **Left Hand Fork** of Deer Creek enters on the left or west. Walk about 250m into this well-watered canyon, turn right or north, scramble up a steep trail in oak brush to the next ledge, and turn back east. This is the **Left Hand Fork Trail**. Right at the corner of the 2 canyons, and following stone cairns, turn northwest and walk up to Cad Bench. Read more about it, the Main Upper Fork of Deer Creek, Little Fork and Oak Canyon under **Map 11**.

About 2 1/2 kms up Deer Creek Canyon you'll come to a blocking dryfall. This is as far as you go from inside the canyon. At the bottom of this 30m dryfall is where the water begins to flow. It's in this upper part, that you'll find many white sand benches and large cottonwood trees, which combine to make some of the best campsites anywhere. Immediately below the dryfall is a large alcove-type cave on the north side which would make a good camp.

Continuing down the Paria Canyon now. About 850m below the mouth of Deer Creek, and on the east side, is the beginning of the **CCC Trail**. In the beginning, this trail is well-constructed, and was used to run cows from the Upper Death Valley, Johnson Hole and Snake Creek areas, down to water in the Paria Canyon. This one is easy to find and follow.

According to Wallace Ott of Tropic, this trail was built by the CCC's sometime in the mid-1930's. At that time, they had their main camp northeast of Henrieville at the old Smith Ranch. While doing various projects along the Upper Paria River, they may have had a spike camp near the mouth of Deer Creek Canyon. However, in talking to several of the enrollees of the Henrieville camp, none could remember a spike camp actually being in this canyon. They may have been driver there on day-trips out of their main camp (?).

About 100m below the beginning of the CCC Trail, and on the west side of the canyon, is the beginning of the **Deer Trails Trail**. Over the years, various cattlemen & sheepmen constructed this trail, at least that part up to the rim, then it's a well-worn cow path in the sand. Wallace Ott says Jim Henderson, who at one time owned the Nipple Ranch, was probably responsible for most of the rock-work you see there today. This trail was used as a link between the Bryce Valley towns and the Nipple Ranch. Henderson, who lived in Cannonville at the time, would take a wagon load of supplies down the Paria to Deer Trails, then transfer it to pack horses for the rest of the trip. This trail begins or ends on Oil Well Hill to the southwest. By using this trail, you can quickly get into this middle part of the Upper Paria River Gorge, but you'll need a 4WD vehicle to reach the trailhead. Read more on this trail along with **Map 11**.

Roughly 350m downcanyon from the Deer Trails Trail, **Red Creek** comes in on the left or east. This is a short drainage, and according to Wallace Ott, in the spring of some years, there used to be a little stream come out of it. In times of flood, the water came out red, thus the name. Just below the mouth of Red Creek, **Oak Canyon** comes in on the right or west. You can walk up Oak about 1 km to a big dryfall of about 25m (?). Below that is a good spring and that water runs all the way to the Paria. This is a deep narrow gorge with cottonwood trees and willows, but not a lot of room for camping. As of 2003, there were old signs of beaver in this gorge, but nothing new, so this water should be reasonably safe to drink (?), although to be sure, walk up to the dryfall and take it from the spring source (or purify it downcanyon).

Snake Creek Canyon

About 2 kms below Oak Canyon, and on the left or east, is the mouth of **Snake Creek**. Right there on the south side corner is a nice panel of cowboy signatures hidden behind some willows. Snake Creek has a good, year-round flowing stream for more than 2 kms along its lower course. This part has trees and campsites. You can walk up Snake Creek for about 2 kms along hiker & cow trails, then you'll come to a waterfall or cascade. This one may be a little difficult to get around, but 2 or 3 people with a short rope should be able to help each other up. Above this first waterfall is a wall collapse and subsequent dam (it's easy to climb over). Beyond that is a section with more trees, then you'll come to 2 more dropoffs. Climb around the first on the left.

Between these 2 dropoffs, the water begins to flow, and there's an old constructed cattle trail down between the two. Wallace Ott once did some cement work between these 2 dropoffs to enlarge one pothole and make a better trail.

About 125m above these dropoffs is where 2 upper tributaries of Snake Creek come together. Coming down the point between the 2 forks is another constructed cattle trail. Wallace Ott says this **Snake Creek Trail** was first built by Eli LeFevre and Layton Jolley during the 1930's, but after Ott bought their grazing rights in 1945, he upgraded it. If you walk up the East Fork of Snake Creek, you'll come to 2 big caves which were occupied by aborigines hundreds or thousands of years ago. See **Map 17** for more details.

There are 2 other ways you can enter this middle part of Snake Creek. One way is to walk up the CCC Trail from the Paria. Once that trail reaches the rim, it disappears going north. From there, and with a compass & map in hand, continue north for about 600m, then turn right or east and cross the upper part of Red Creek Canyon. When you come to the second drainage, which is the upper part of Snake Creek Canyon, turn right and head south downcanyon. When you reach a big dropoff, back up about 100m to find the Snake Creek Trail on the east side. Walk south on it and into the main canyon as described above.

The 3rd way into the middle and upper parts of Snake Creek, Johnson Hole and Stone Donkey Canyon is to drive to the end of the track on Rock Springs Point. If you're interested in that trip, see **Map 15, Road Map: Rock Springs Bench Trailheads** for more information.

Seven Mile Flat Ranch

About 2 kms below the mouth of Snake Creek is a place where the canyon opens up and becomes wider. This is **Seven Mile Flat**. It got its name because it was about 7 miles, or 11 kms, above the town of Pahreah. The late Kay Clark, an old-timer and cattleman from Henrieville, was too young to remember much, but was told this is where a man by the name of John Wesley Mangum had a small ranch which people referred to as the **Seven Mile Flat Ranch**. As the story goes, it was a summer-time place, with a cabin and corrals. At the ranch, they raised among other things, sugar cane, from which they made molasses. In winter the family lived in Pahreah for several years of its early history.

Kay Clark did remember that at the northern end of the flat area and on the west side of the river, he once saw the remains of a small molasses mill. There was some kind of a foundation and the old rollers, which were used to squeeze juice out of the sugar cane. It's possible you might find something there today, although the author saw nothing. If anything was there, it's surely been washed away by now.

No one can say for certain what the exact dates were when this ranch was occupied, but Kay thinks it must have been at about the same time Pahreah was prospering, which was in the late 1870's and up until about 1883 & '84. That's when the first big floods roared down the Paria which started the migration out of the valley. It must have been one of these first floods (later floods occurred in 1896) which may have taken out facilities at Seven Mile Ranch, and started washing farmland away from Pahreah. Today at Seven Mile Flat, there's nothing more than a broad washed-out river flood plain.

Rough Hollow, and the Hogeye Ranch & Canyon

From the Seven Mile Flat area down to the mouth of Hogeye Canyon, there isn't much to see, except one side-canyon entering on the east. The author still hasn't been into this, but Wallace Ott says there's no water in it, so for a cow man, it wasn't very interesting. From the top end, it was too rough to get a horse into, although Wallace went in a couple of times on foot. For that reason he nicknamed it **Rough Hollow.**

Left The **Kirby Ranch chimney** located not far below the mouth of Kitchen Canyon. **Right** The **Carlow Ranch chimney**, which is about 300m due east of the Kirby chimney.

At the very mouth of **Hogeye Canyon,** is a rincon (abandoned meander or river channel). Right out in the middle of the rather flat area is a rounded butte, which apparently resembled a hog's eye, thus the name, Hogeye Canyon. Hogeye is another of the major side-canyons of the Paria River, which is discussed in more detail on another hike, see **Map 12**. In its lower end, it does have a good year-round running water supply and many good campsites.

Right at the mouth of Hogeye Canyon and on the flats surrounding the Hogeye Butte, is the location of another old homestead known as the **Hogeye Ranch.** The late Marian Clark, who was in his 90's when interviewed in 1987, thought it was John Wesley Mangum who may have had some farmland and corrals there. The late Herm Pollock of Tropic thought Ernest Mangum, son of John Wesley Mangum, was there, which may be true, but Ernest wasn't born until January, 1894.

Both sources believed this summer ranch was occupied in the years after people started leaving Pahreah, but no one knows for certain when it was first used. Herm remembered a small wooden shack on the north side of Hogeye Butte, and Marian Clark remembered a small 2m-square stone storage building of some kind. Goats were raised, and some farming was done in summer. The big floods of 1883-84 and/or 1896 must have lowered the creek bed to the point they could no longer get water up to their farmland. Nothing remains today, except a lot of Cheat or June grass, indicating the place was over used or heavily used by someone at some point in time.

Just northwest of the Hogeye Butte is a good spring coming out of the west side of the canyon; and just southwest of the butte is another spring, which made the site a good one as far as water is concerned. About 800m south of Hogeye Butte, and on a point of land jutting out from the eastern canyon wall, are 2 panels of mostly **cowboy signatures,** including Roy Twitchell and Arthur Chynoweth, a couple of early-day cowmen in this country.

About 1 1/2 kms below Hogeye is **Kitchen Canyon** coming in on the right or west. This is discussed in another hike, but right at the mouth of this canyon is a good panel of petroglyphs & cowboy signatures. Be careful of Kitchen Ck. water; it drains the Nipple Ranch which has grazing cattle year-round.

On the east side of the Paria Canyon, opposite the mouth of Kitchen Canyon, is where the Marian Mangum family may have had a dugout, and what must have been a garden and summer ranch area. The author was made aware of this place after his early hikes were finished, but as late as 2003, he saw nothing that would indicate a ranch was ever located there. Maybe it's been washed away (?).

However, about 1 km below the mouth of Kitchen Canyon, and on the north side of the mouth of a side-canyon coming into the Paria from the east, is a large boulder with more cowboy etchings; *Arthur Chynoweth, Nov. 24, 1925, and X Land + Cattle Co., Jos. + Geo. Graf.* The Grafs were former Cannonville sheep & cattlemen; and Author Chynoweth came into this country in the fall of 1892 with his parents and 3 brothers; Will, Sam and Harvey. The Chynoweths are still one of the more prominent families of Bryce Valley today.

Kirby Ranch

About 1200m below the mouth of Kitchen Canyon, and on a bench just west of the creek and under a cottonwood tree, are the ruins of the **Kirby Place or Ranch.** The only thing left to see is a rock chimney. The old cabin was either burned down or the logs were hauled away to build another house or barn someplace else.

As with the other ranches in the area north of Old Pahreah, not much is known for sure about this

These petrified tracks on a boulder about 100m north of the Carlow Ranch chimney would likely be classed as **dinosaur tracks**, but they're not much larger than a human hand.

ranch site. But everyone agrees that it is the Kirby Place, and that it was first occupied from the years of about the mid-1870's on through about the time of the first flood to hit the valley. The late Kay Clark said it was the typical summer ranch site. Apparently the Kirby family lived in Pahreah during the winters, then had cows and a small garden at the ranch in summer. Herm Pollock believes the Kirby family left for Arizona after the 1883 & '84 floods, which left their irrigated land high & dry.

Carlow Ranch
About 300m due east of the Kirby Ranch house chimney on the opposite side of the canyon, and sitting out in the middle of a sagebrush flat, is the foundation and chimney of the **Carlow Ranch house**. Herm Pollock remembered this family when he was just a boy of 12.

The year was 1922 and it was Christmas time. For most of that fall Herm and his father Sam Pollock, had stayed in what was left of the town of Pahreah. The Pollocks lived in Tropic, but they were in the Pahreah area with a sheep camp, and were also in the business of supplying food & supplies to other sheep camps in the region.

On Christmas morning with nearly half a meter of snow on the ground, Sam loaded up 2 boxes of food and other supplies and put them on 2 mules. He instructed 12-year-old Herm to go up the canyon about 5 kms to the Carlow home, and present the family with the gifts of food. Herm vividly remembers the time, because it was the first time he ever played Santa Claus.

He also remembered the time well because of how poor the Carlow family was. Their home was a one-roomed cabin made of logs & rocks. At that time it had no door, only a piece of canvas covering the opening. The only heat they had was from an open fireplace. When Herm first went in, he placed one hand on the inside of the door frame, which was covered with thick soot. When he pulled his hand back, it was black.

The several small children were dressed in rags, and were absolutely filthy. Their normally red hair was black, covered with soot from the open fire, and because they had gone so long without bathing. Mrs. Carlow was dressed in clothes made from flour sacks. Herm also remembered a story of one of the young boys. He had found an old blasting cap somewhere and was playing with it when it exploded. He lost 3 fingers on one hand.

Herm Pollock went back home a week after this experience, but his father helped the Carlow family get through the winter. When spring finally came, Sam took a wagon to the ranch and helped them get out. Later in the spring of 1923, the family left the country, and no one remembers where they went or if their old cabin was ever occupied again.

If looking for the old Carlow Ranch site, first find the Kirby Place, which is easier to locate. Then walk 300m due east across the creek, which is a low flood plain, then upon a sagebrush-covered bench. It must be about 50m or so west from where the steeper canyon wall on the east comes down to the tall sagebrush. About 100m north of the Carlow Chimney, is a large boulder, and on the south side of it are dozens of animal tracks, most of which are the 3 toed variety. Most would call these **dinosaur tracks**.

Going downcanyon from the Kirby Place, and on the west side of the river, you can get onto one of the old original roads and walk most of the way to Old Pahreah. At the mouth of Dugout Canyon, the 2 tracks meet. If you continue on this single track about half a km south or below the mouth of Dugout, you'll see on the right, just as you go down a little decline, several old logs, posts and a depression in the ground. This is believed to be what is called The Dugout and the Dugout Ranch.

The Dugout (Dugout Ranch)
The Dugout is just one of several old ranches or homesteads along the Paria River just above the old townsite of Pahreah. The site was situated up against a low embankment which was along the edge of an old river channel. First, earth was removed, then logs were built up on the sides and on the top. Dirt may or may not have been put on the roof, but inside it must have been cool in summer and warm in winter, because it was at least partly underground.

No one knows who first settled the Dugout Ranch, but in the life story of Sam Pollock (complied by Afton Pollock of Tropic) mention is made that William Swapp & his wife were living there in August of 1901. They helped a couple of young cowpokes with a bed and a little food as they were heading north back home to Bryce Valley.

Years after that, several old-timers from Tropic and Henrieville remember the time John (Long John) William Mangum (another son of John Wesley Mangum) and family lived there. This was in the late 1920's and early 1930's, and may have extended to about 1934, according to Wallace Ott and the late Kay Clark. The wife of Long John Mangum was named Oma, and her maiden name was Carlow. Mr. Carlow of the Carlow Ranch was her brother.

As one story goes, in about 1934 the Mangums, either Long John (or brother Marian?), had a cabin at the mouth of Kitchen Canyon. At that place, they once had a fine corn field out on the flat. Herm Pollock remembered this time period well, because the Mangums lived there for 2 years, then were washed out by a big flood which rolled down Kitchen Canyon and the Paria on July 10, 1936. During this same flood, Pollock was stranded for 2 1/2 days on the Carlow Bench (surrounding the old cabin) with a herd of sheep. He had nothing to drink but muddy flood water. An interesting side-note to Mangum brothers, Long John and Marian; they married Carlow sisters, Oma and Edna.

Some time in the early or mid-1930's, Long John Mangum began working on a ranch in Fivemile Valley south of Pahreah, which he homesteaded. Long John's son Herman Mangum got title to it in June, 1937, according to courthouse records. This was at Cottonwood Spring and was called Fivemile Ranch by most people, but some called it Cottonwood Ranch. One or both of these Mangums lived there until 1942, then high-tailed-it for Idaho and greener pastures. See the **Hattie Green Mine story** along with **Map 27,** for the location of Fivemile Valley & Ranch, and how they got lumber for their ranch house.

Continuing south from The Dugout. Perhaps the last thing to see in the Lower Paria River Gorge, besides the Old Pahreah townsite, is the line of cottonwood trees marking what appears to be the original ditch or canal which provided water for Pahreah homes & gardens. This canal began about 1 1/2 kms below The Dugout, and about 2 kms above Pahreah on the east side of the river. It's where the stream is pushed to the west by a rocky buttress from the east. You can still see the very faint remains of the canal by following the broken line of cottonwood trees down to the townsite.

Read more about the history of Old Pahreah under the **History of Ghost Town along the Paria River**, and the **Mining History,** in the back of this book.

Layton Smith and his sister **Iris Smith Bushnell**, standing in front of the **last cabin** to be lived in at **Old Pahreah**. This picture was taken sometime in the 1970's. This cabin was taken apart and re-assembled back from the river aways in the early 1990's, then it burned down in the winter of 1994-95. (Iris Smith Bushnell foto)

The **last cabin** standing at **Old Pahreah**, but it along with all other dwellings have washed away or burned down. This picture was taken sometime in the 1970's. (Iris Smith Bushnell foto)

Death Valley Draw, Upper Hackberry Canyon & Upper DV Trail

Location & Access   **Death Valley Draw (DVD)** is one of the main tributaries to **Upper Hackberry Canyon**. If you're planning to hike all the way through Hackberry, you could use this upper side-canyon as the starting point; or the Slickrock Bench Trailhead (the best starting point) discussed with the Round Valley Draw hike. DVD is located west of Hackberry & Round Valley Draw, on the east side of Rock Springs Bench, and southeast of Kodachrome Basin State Park. Read the driving instructions for this hike under **Map 15, Road Map: Rock Springs Bench Trailheads.**

Trail/Route   From the end of the road, or wherever you park in upper DVD, walk south along an old road for roughly 1 km, then this vehicle track enters & disappears in the dry creek bed. For the next 1 1/2 kms, walk in the dry wash, or along a cow trail, then be watching carefully for the trail as it crosses the creek bed and climbs up the other side. Hopefully a **cairn** will still be there in the sand.

But let's stop there for a moment. If you want to enter Hackberry via the lower end of DVD, then continue downcanyon another km. There you'll find a chokestone and a 3m+ dropoff; chimney down and help others if necessary. This is the beginning of a short **50m slot**. Beyond that it opens up wide and after another 100m or so is where flood waters drop into a **very tight crack** with a number of tree trunks wedged in its upper part. The top of that crack is more or less horizontal for about 30m with logs stuck on top and down inside. You can't get in at the very beginning of the crack, but if you have two tools ropes, you might tie webbing to one of the logs near the end of the crack and rappel to the bottom. Don't try to get in at or near the beginning of the crack--you won't make it through--it's too tight.

Or if you're not prepared to rappel, backtrack to the beginning of, or just above, the 50m slot. About 15m above the 50m slot, is a walking route around it just to the west. Once in the area, work you way south and route-find down into another little **side-canyon** that runs north/south parallel to the tight crack. Getting through this little canyon requires downclimbing in 2 places, but anyone who calls him/herself a hiker should be able to handle it. Or help each other, and/or have a short rope to lower packs, then downclimb into and through this drainage. At the bottom, turn the corner to the left and view the lower end of the tight crack, then walk 350m to Hackberry Canyon which is a walk-through from top to bottom.

Now back to the trail leaving DVD. Once out of the bottom of DVD, the trail heads nearly due south below big Navajo Sandstone cliffs to the west. Soon you'll cross a sizable side-canyon coming in from the right or west; not much to see up there. Beyond that, the trail passes west of a couple of monoliths on your left--see the **Round Rocks** on the map, then continues south into Upper Death Valley. It's in this region you'll see a prominent peak known locally by at least 3 different names; **Cottonwood** (USGS map name), **Big Horn or Death Valley Peak.** This will be straight ahead as you walk south. Also, **Twin Knolls** will be ahead but to the left a little; and a peak that has no name on any map, but which Wallace Ott of Tropic calls **Little Mollies Nipple.** This is straight ahead but to the right a little (not on this map).

Eventually you'll come to a fence running east-west. This separates grazing pastures. Walk through the open gate and continue south and a little east toward Twin Knolls. In this area you'll have to watch closely for the trail. Eventually the trail runs south along the west side of both knolls, crosses one shallow drainage with several big potholes, then south to another minor drainage where the **Upper Trail** or **Upper Death Valley Trail** runs down into Hackberry Canyon. When you arrive, you'll see some cairns, plus a path worn smooth by the hooves of cattle & horses going down slickrock. In several places, steps are cut, then the trail turns left or northeast and runs upcanyon along a ramp to the bottom. There you'll find an old fence & gate and lots of cottonwood trees, water & shade.

Nearby are some cowboy signatures: **E.M. Bolton 10/22/13, HS & JH 1913.** These stand for Harmon Shakespeare & Jim Henderson, and one of the Boltons from Tropic. Wallace Ott (born in 1911 and still alive in 2010!) remembered the Bolton family: *There was a Bolton family living here in Tropic about 2 blocks from where I'm living. The old man died before I knew 'um, but I knew the family. And he had one son named Eplapapas, and another one named Lindonaflis, and the one that was my age was Wayne Bolton. It may have been the old man who put his signature there--or it could have been his son Eplapapas, because he run cattle and sheep down there too. Lindonaflis worked at the first sawmill which had power up here on the East Fork of the Sevier River. He was the first man that I know of that got killed at a sawmill. He got jerked into the saw and it sawed him right in two. He was just a teenager.*

Here's a little history on the Upper Death Valley Trail as told by Wallace Ott: *That Upper Trail was built by **Samson Chynoweth** [who arrived at Pahreah with his family in the fall of 1892], he was about the first one who ever used powder in this country. He had quite a herd of cattle--as many as 200 head of cows. He lived down at the Old Pahreah town, that's where he raised his family. He had his cattle in there and they had a terrible drought. There wasn't any way for the livestock to get down to Hackberry Creek, except for the Upper Trail. Then one cow dropped down and died right there on the trail, and the others was up on top and couldn't get by, and they figured between 80 & 100 head of cattle choked to death. That's why they now call it* **Death Valley.**

The late Herm Pollock of Tropic thought that originally some stockmen from Panguitch were the first to build & use this trail, but that anyone who ever ran cows in that country since then has made some improvements to it. Today it's a good trail and wide enough for 2 cows to pass..

Elevations   Death Valley Draw Trailhead, 1835m; bottom of Upper (Death Valley) Trail, 1622m.

Time Needed   Without any side-trips or much exploring, you could walk down DVD & Trail to the Upper Trail, then up Hackberry and back to your car via DVD and the little side-canyon in 8 -12 hours.

Water   Carry your own, but water begins flowing just above where the Upper Trail enters Hackberry.

Maps   USGS or BLM map Smoky Mountain (1:100,000) for driving & orientation; and Bull Valley Gorge & Calico Peak (1:24,000--7 1/2' quads) for hiking.

Main Attractions   An historic cattle trail, and 2 of several ways into upper Hackberry Canyon.

Best Time to Hike   Spring or fall. Pretty warm in summer, cold in winter.

Boots/Shoes   Dry-weather shoes--except if you hike down Hackberry beyond the Upper Trail, you'll need wading-type shoes as there's water (normally very shallow) throughout most of Hackberry.

Author's Experience   He hiked down Death Valley Draw, checked out the route around the tight slot at the end of that canyon, continued south along the Upper Death Valley Trail to the Twin Knolls, then returned and explored the big side-canyon to Hackberry about 1/3 the way down to the Upper Trail. Round-trip took 9 3/4 hours. Next day he went down Wallace Ott's Horse Trail, and finished the hike to the Upper Trail, walked up to the beginning of running water, then returned--but did lots of exploring around all sides of Cottonwood Peak, and finally back to his Tracker in 9 2/3 hours. On 7/26/2009, he camped at the DVD TH, walked down the Upper Death Valley Trail to the Upper Trail, then all the way up Hackberry to the end of DVD & the little side-canyon, and back to his Jeep Patriot in 7 1/2 hours.

Map 19, Death Valley Draw, Upper Hackberry Canyon, and the Upper Death Valley Trail

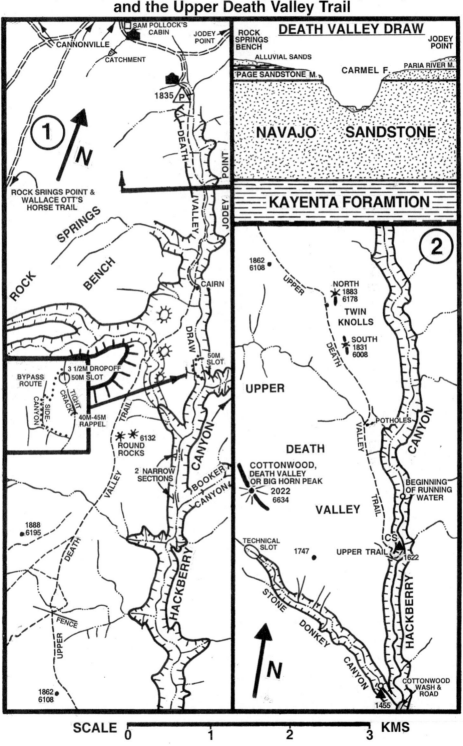

DEATH VALLEY DRAW

CANNONVILLE
SAM POLLOCK'S CABIN
JODEY POINT
CATCHMENT
1835
ROCK SPRINGS BENCH
ALLUVIAL SANDS
PAGE SANDSTONE M.
CARMEL F.
JODEY POINT
PARIA RIVER M.

NAVAJO SANDSTONE

KAYENTA FORAMTION

ROCK SRINGS POINT & WALLACE OTT'S HORSE TRAIL
ROCK SPRINGS BENCH

DEATH VALLEY
JODEY POINT
CAIRN
50M SLOT

BYPASS ROUTE
3 1/2M DROPOFF
50M SLOT
TIGHT CRACK
SIDE CANYON
40M-45M RAPPEL
6132 ROUND ROCKS
2 NARROW SECTIONS

DRAW
TRAIL
VALLEY
CANYON
BOOKER CANYON
HACKBERRY

1888
6195
DEATH
FENCE
UPPER
1862
6108

UPPER
DEATH
VALLEY
TRAIL

1862
6108
NORTH 1883 6178
TWIN KNOLLS
SOUTH 1831 6008

UPPER
DEATH
VALLEY

POTHOLES
CANYON

COTTONWOOD, DEATH VALLEY OR BIG HORN PEAK
2022 6634

VALLEY
BEGINNING OF RUNNING WATER

TECHNICAL SLOT
1747
UPPER TRAIL
CS
1622

STONE DONKEY CANYON
HACKBERRY

COTTONWOOD WASH & ROAD
1455

SCALE   0   1   2   3   KMS

113

From the north and from along the Upper Death Valley Trail, looking south at **Cottonwood, Death Valley or Big Horn Peak**. Just on the other side of it is Stone Donkey Canyon with its nice slot.

Left The beginning of the **Upper Death Valley Trail** as it first runs down a little side-drainage, then into Hackberry Canyon. Notice the steps cut in the Navajo Sandstone. **Right** The **Upper Death Valley Trail** as it runs along the rim of Hackberry Canyon. To the left and looking south is Hackberry with its many trees and running water.

Left Inside **Hackberry Canyon** just above where the Upper Death Valley Trail enters from the west. **Right** The big dropoff near the end of **Death Valley Draw**. Done right, it may be downclimbable; or it's a rappel of about 40-45m.

The **Sam Pollock cabin** built in 1941. It's located on Rock Springs Bench near the head of Death Valley Draw and the George Johnson Copper Mine. Sam's son Afton Pollock is on the left, while Afton's son Steve is to the right.

Round Valley Draw and Upper Entry to Hackberry Canyon

Location & Access Round Valley Draw is one of the main upper tributaries to the much larger Hackberry Canyon and is located about halfway between **Kodachrome Basin (KB)** and **Grosvenor (Butler Valley) Arch**. To get there from the Bryce Canyon area, drive south out of Cannonville (this town now has a GSENM visitor center) on the paved KB Road. When you arrive at the KB Turnoff (11.7 kms/7.3 miles), continue straight east on the graded **Cottonwood Wash Road**. From the KB Turnoff, drive another 11 kms (6.9 kms); this should put you at the bottom of **Round Valley Draw.**

Or if you're coming from the south and Highway 89, turn north onto the Cottonwood Wash Road between mile posts 17 & 18. Drive north for 51.4 kms (31.9 miles). Once there, turn south onto the Rush Bed Road, which is immediately east of the dry wash. After **2.7 kms (1.7 miles)** you'll cross Round Valley Draw, then drive south up the hill 100m to a parking place & trail register. You can camp there or drive south up the road 300m to the Round Valley Seep and camp there with water in a metal trough.

Trail/Route From the Round Valley Draw Car-park, walk down the dry creek bed 1200m to the ponderosa pine on the left bench. There you'll see the top layer of Navajo Sandstone (more likely the Page Sandstone?) exposed; and the beginning of the slot 100m beyond. Get down in the tight crack and chimney/downclimb right where the slot begins. Some less-experienced hikers may need a helping hand, so take a short rope just in case.

About 500m into the slot, and right where the **North Fork** comes in on the right or north, you'll come to several large boulders. Every flash flood through this canyon rearranges the route through this section, so look for the footprints of others. You'll surely have to do some downclimbing in which some may need a helping hand. For some, this will be just difficult enough to be fun. Once through this little obstacle course, and after another 75m or so, you come to the deepest & darkest section. In the middle of this narrow part, you may have to wade between more boulders, as this part changes with every flood too! Continue downcanyon; there are still more narrows, but no more difficult obstacles. After passing through the narrows, you could return the same way back upcanyon; or climb out to the north toward the **Slickrock Bench Car-park** (the way to this car-park is discussed in detail along with **Map 23, Hackberry Canyon**), then rim-walk back to your car on a hiker-made trail as shown.

Elevations Car-park/trailhead, about 1850m; end of slot and exit route, 1775m.

Time Needed Hiking this slot, then exiting at the Slickrock Bench Route (a walk-up), and rim-walking back to your car, will take about half a day, depending on how long you want to enjoy the slot.

Water Round Valley Seep is just up the road 300m from the trailhead, but it's not reliable. Best to take your own water and have a good supply in your car at all times. Sometime in the mid or late 1930's, a small **CCC spike camp** was located there while the boys worked on several projects in the area. If you look at the sandstone wall west of the metal water trough, you'll see a hole that's been blasted out. This is where the camp stored perishable foods.

Maps USGS or BLM map Smoky Mountain (1:100,000) for driving & orientation; and Slickrock Bench (1:24,000--7 1/2' quad) for hiking.

Main Attractions One of the best non-technical slot canyons around.

Best Time to Hike Spring or fall, but it's cool in the slot in summer, and usually dry in winter (?).

Boots/Shoes If you're there right after rains, expect to wade several shallow pools (or mud holes).

Author's Experience On one trip he went down in late March and found half a meter of snow on the narrow's floor. There was no water in any of the potholes then. He went down again in June, a week after heavy rains, and found some mud in the low places, but no pools of water. Another trip was in 8/2003, a few days after a flood, with mud everywhere and a few shallow pools. Round-trip took 3 1/2

This old mid-1930's foto shows the **Round Valley Neck (or Draw) CCC spike camp**. These watering troughs at **Round Valley Seep** (some locals call this Rush Bed Seep) are in the same place as some newer troughs todays. This site is about 600m south of the Round Valley Draw Trailhead.
(Willy Bryant Foto)

Map 20, Round Valley Draw/Upper Entry to Hackberry Canyon

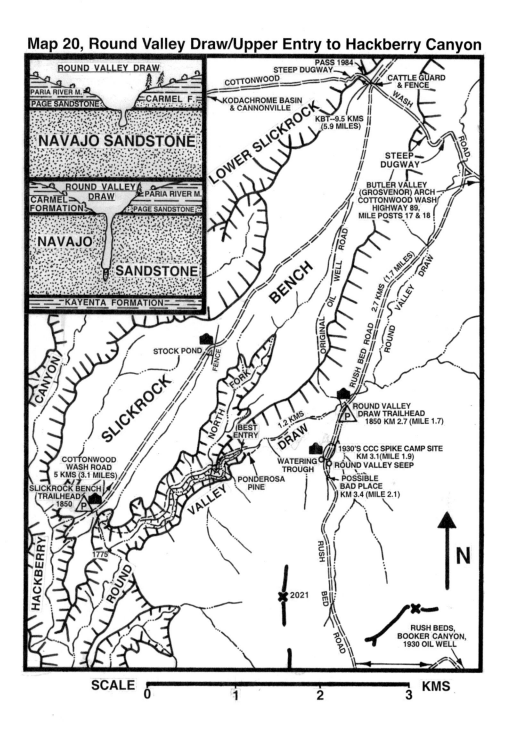

hours. In 8/2009, he found some mud & pools, but kept feet dry. He returned via the rim route in a total of 2 2/3 hours. Not many people were using the rim trail, so they must be returning back up the canyon bottom (?). According to the trail register for 8/2009, most hikers were in the canyon for 3 hours.

Above Left The beginning of the slot in **Round Valley Draw**. Best to crawl or chimney down in right at the beginning slot.

Above Right Downclimbing right at the beginning of the slot in **Round Valley Draw**. Often times there's a little mud and sometimes water at the bottom, but it's never deep.

Right This is what it looks like about 200-300m down the slot in **Round Valley Draw**.

Above Left Just below where the big boulders are and where the North Fork enters, is the deepest & darkest part of the **Round Valley Draw**.

Above Right From the rim of **Round Valley Draw**, looking at where the canyon begins to open a little for the first time.

Left From the rim looking directly down at the big boulders you'll have to crawl through. To the lower right is where the **North Fork** enters; to the left is where the main canyon is coming down; and straight ahead is downcanyon and the deepest & darkest part of **Round Valley Draw**.

Booker Canyon

Location & Access   The locals never had a name for this canyon but people at the BLM office in Kanab, once referred to it as **Booker Canyon**, after one of their staff, Bill Booker. It's the first canyon south of the narrows of Round Valley Draw, and is southwest of **Grosvenor (Butler Valley) Arch**. To get there from the Bryce Canyon area, drive east then south through Tropic to Cannonville (Cannonville now has a GSENM visitor center), then continue south on the paved Kodachrome Basin Road for 11.7 kms (7.3 miles). At that point is an information board on the right and the paved road turns left or north. This is the Kodachrome Basin Turnoff (**KBT**). From there, continue straight east on the graded **Cottonwood Wash Road**. Drive 11 kms (6.9 kms) from the KBT until you arrive at **Round Valley Draw**. Once there, turn south onto the **Rush Bed Road,** which is immediately east of the dry wash. After 2.7 kms (1.7 miles) you'll cross Round Valley Draw, but continue south uphill past the parking place & trail register for Round Valley Draw. Next is Round Valley Seep with a water trough on the right or west. Not far from the Seep is a little wash cutting across the road (at Km 3.4/Mile 2.1)--be sure to have a shovel handy because you may need to fill that wash in to get by--even with a 4WD!

About **5.7 kms (3.5 miles)** from the **Cottonwood Wash Road**, stop and park on the south side of the road. You may need a HCV/4WD for this last part. While there are a number of ways to enter Booker Canyon, beginning at this place is the quickest and involves the least amount of driving.

If you're coming from the south and Highway 89, turn north onto the **Cottonwood Wash Road** between mile posts 17 & 18. Drive north for about **51.4 kms (31.9 miles)**. At Round Valley Draw, head south along the Rush Bed Road past Round Valley Seep and to the parking place just described.

Trail/Route   From where you park, walk due south across a shallow valley. This will put you on a point between 2 upper drainages of Booker Canyon. Once there, walk southwest down the nose of the point. With a little zig zagging & route-finding, you can walk all the way down to the canyon floor. About 500m below where you reach the bottom will be an **6m dropoff & bypass** and a short narrows section. Skirt left and walk around the dryfall on the south side before re-entering the dry creek bed. Continue down-canyon. About 2 kms below the 1st dropoff will be a **7m dropoff & bypass.** To avoid this, walk along the right or north side and re-enter the wash about 150m below. It's in this area you'll find some interesting fotogenic places with green ponderosa pines growing out of cracks in the white Navajo Sandstone slickrock, and hopefully with blue skies above.

From there to the beginning of the **Booker Canyon Slot** will be another km. This slot is less than 1m wide, so to get down in, simply span it--with one foot on one side, your other foot on the other. Do this for 10-15m, then downclimb to the bottom just below several chokestones. Some beginners may feel a little uncomfortable here, so having an experienced hiker along may be helpful (for the experienced canyoneer it's nothing!). This shallow, but fairly tight slot, lasts for about 200m, then opens.

About 300m below the slot will be a **7m rappel**. This means you'll either have to stop there and return the same way; or rappel. There are 2 ways to rappel--**this will be for someone who has a little experience!** (1) Walk back upcanyon 75m and look for several fist-sized cobblestones to be jammed into a groove just above the dropoff. Once a cobblestone is wedged in, wrap a short piece of webbing around it, add a Rapide/Quick Link, and use a rope at least 20m long to rappel/or handline down. But doing it this way will be leaving trash in the canyon. (2) Or, take with you what climbers and canyoneers call an **Ibis Hook**, which you can buy in climbers supply stores. It's shaped like a large fish hook. Tie a short rope to it, and place the hook somewhere in that groove. If it doesn't feel secure, use the hook's sharp point to create a small hole so the hook can't pop out, then rappel/handline from the hook. Once everyone is at the bottom, give the rope some slack, then flip it, and the hook should come right out, and you'll be on your way.

At the bottom of this simple rappel, you'll encounter a couple of minor dropoffs you can downclimb or slide down. About 1 1/2 kms below the rappel will be **Hackberry Canyon**. You can either continue down Hackberry to the Cottonwood Wash Road (this will involve spending one night in the canyon); or head upcanyon and enter Round Valley Draw. If doing this, look at the previous map of Round Valley Draw to see how you can get back to the Rush Bed Road. You can do that by getting up on Slickrock Bench and rim-walking; or walk straight up the narrows of Round Valley Draw and eventually back to your car (a 2nd car would save 45 minutes walking).

The remains of a food storage cave at the site of the former CCC camp next to the **Round Valley Seep**. This dates from the mid or late 1930's. Nearby is an old water trough made from a hollow log, plus a metal water tank.

Map 21, Booker Canyon

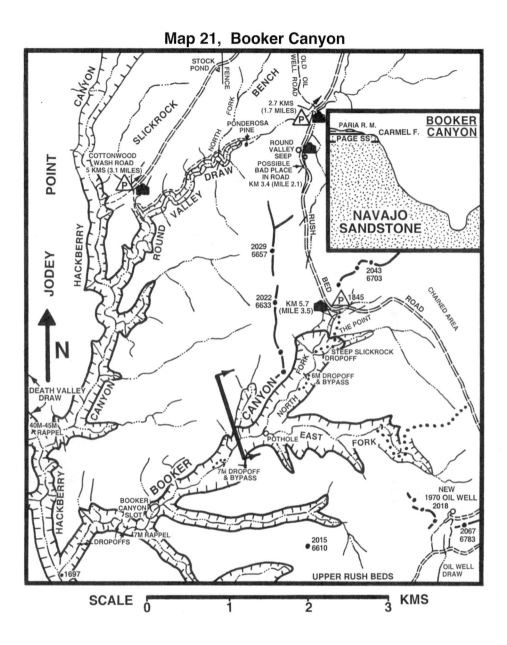

SCALE 0 1 2 3 **KMS**

Elevations Normal entry car-park, 1845m; junction of Hackberry & Booker Canyons, 1697m.
Time Needed If you walk down to the 3rd dropoff/rappel point & return the same way, about 4-6 hours round-trip. The 2nd option would be to make the simple rappel/handline into lower Booker, walk down to Hackberry, then up through Round Valley Draw and back to your car. This will likely take somewhere between 7-11 hours (?), a full day's hike.
Water This is a dry canyon, so take plenty of water in your car and pack.
Maps USGS or BLM map Smoky Mountain (1:100,000) for driving & orientation; and Slickrock Bench (1:24,000--7 1/2' quad) for hiking.
Main Attractions One short slot, possible rappel and solitude in a canyon that's never been grazed.
Best Time to Hike Spring or fall, but anytime the clay-based entry roads are dry.
Boots/Shoes Dry weather-type boots or shoes.
Author's Experience Once he came up from Hackberry Canyon and stopped at the 7m dryfall. His next trip was down from the top to the 7m dryfall/rappel, then back and out the East Fork as shown. That trip took less than 5 hours. In 2009, he hiked down to the rappel point and back in 3 1/3 hours.

Halfway through **Booker Canyon**, and on the north side, you'll see ponderosa pines growing out of cracks in the Navajo Sandstone canyon wall.

Left Another scene in the middle part of **Booker Canyon**, with ponderosa pines growing out of cracks in the canyon wall. **Right** In the **Booker Canyon Slot** just above the 7m rappel.

These 4 cooks are standing in front of the mess hall at the **Henrieville CCC Camp**. One or more of these enrollees likely worked at the spike camp located at Round Valley Seep, which is on the way to the Upper Rush Beds and Booker Canyon. From the mid or late 1930's. (Hasle Caudill foto)

This is **Ilan Pollock**, one of the sons of Sam Pollock, and brother to the late Herm, and Afton (still alive in 2010). This sheep camp dated 1938, was somewhere in **Upper Death Valley** just west of the upper end of Hackberry Canyon. (Afton Pollock foto)

Stone Donkey Canyon

Location & Access Stone Donkey, which is unnamed on USGS maps, is an upper west-side tributary to Hackberry Canyon, which in turn is a tributary to the Upper Paria River. It got the name because of a rock which resembles a donkey. **Stone Donkey Canyon** is a technical slot requiring ropes & rappelling gear. It's located south & southeast of a prominent landmark called Cottonwood Peak.

There are 2 ways to reach this canyon. First, read the driving instructions along with **Map 15, Road Map: Rock Springs Bench Trailheads.** That map & description shows you the way to reach Stone Donkey from Rock Springs Bench. The author once got to the end of this track in his old VW Rabbit & newer Golf TDI, but since then, heavy rains have made the road even worse and now you'll likely need some kind of HCV, or better still, a 4WD. In 2009, the author failed to reach the roads end in his Jeep Patriot, and had to walk for 30 minutes (about 2 1/2 kms/1 1/2 miles) to get to the normal trailhead. Because of this problem, the **2nd way** to Stone Donkey is recommended. For this, drive north from Highway 89 on the **Cottonwood Wash Road** for **23.3 kms (14.5 miles)** and park opposite the mouth of Hackberry Canyon (HC) which is the HC Trailhead. Parking there in **Cottonwood Wash** will allow you to reach Stone Donkey from the lower end. See **Map 23**. This may or may not mean a longer hike, but driving, and the route in from there, is much easier and a lot less complicated.

Rating After a pretty long hike you come to a tight slot with one or several rappels totaling about 40m, then some steep & tight downclimbing in a 250m-long slot. This rates a **3B III**.

Equipment Rappelling gear, a 60m & a 15m rope (if you intend to pull your ropes and drag them with you through the slot, then take also two 60's), one 6-8m rope/cord for lowering each pack, one headlamp per/person, and of course a compass & map, ascenders, etc.--as always! Also knee & elbow pads especially in warm weather; in spring or fall, take a wet/drysuit--there's almost always water in the slot.

Route Rock Springs Bench Route From or near the end of the road, and with the two 7 1/2' maps listed below in hand, follow a recently-made illegal ATV track south about 700m to the rim & first overlook. From there continue south to near the southern tip of **Rock Springs Point** as shown. About 200m before the actual end of the point, look for a cairn or single standing rock on the left marking the beginning of the trail angling down over the rim heading southeast. This is **Wallace Ott's old horse trail** but is only visible in the upper part (he only took a horse up or down this route about 3 times!); further along, head straight down the sandy slope. Consider caching a bottle of water at the bottom of this steep slope for the return hike--especially if it's warm weather.

Once at the bottom of the big cliff & sandy slope, walk down the dry wash for about 5 minutes, then route-find SSE. After about 2 kms, you'll pass west of **Little Mollies Nipple** labeled **6825** (2080m), and immediately under the elevation marked **6444** (1964m) on the *Slickrock Bench 7 1/2' quad.* Continue south along a **hogsback ridge**, but eventually veer southeast and drop down into the upper part of Stone Donkey. If you can't read a topo map, or use a compass, you're in the wrong place!

Once into upper Stone Donkey, walk about 4 kms with scattered ponderosa pines until you're almost exactly due south of **Cottonwood Peak** (other local names for this are **Buckhorn or Death Valley Peak**) marked 2022m (6634). When you reach the beginning of the slot, you'll have 3 choices of how to get started. (1) Tie a 15m rope to a small bush, then a 60m rope to the end of that. From there you can handline or rappel down over 2 dropoffs, then rappel over a chokestone and down another 20-25m to a walk-out pool. Leave ropes and pick them up later. (2) Or, you can help each other down into the slot, set up webbing & D-rings on chokestones, then rappel down to the pool just mentioned. This way you'd be pulling your rope and dragging it down the remainder of a tight slot.

(3) Look southeast from the head of the slot to a cedar (juniper) tree which is about 30m from the edge of the slot. From it you can rappel in immediately below the pool mentioned above. To do that, first tie a short rope of about 15m to the tree, then attach the 60. Rap in from there, but tether your pack to the front of your harness and let it dangle down between your legs; this is because you'll have about 30m of free rappel. This will be a fast rap on a single rope, so better have a **variable speed control ATC**, or run the rope through an extra carabiner on a leg loop on your harness--anything to slow the descent! Leather gloves will help. Leave the ropes to be picked up later on the way back to your vehicle.

At the bottom and just beyond the pool, remove your rappelling harness and tie it to the rope to be hauled up later--otherwise you'll scrape the hell out of it going downcanyon. After a short walk, comes several interesting downclimbs in a tight slot. This is where you'll want the **smallest pack possible.** This is also where either a wet/drysuit, or long pants & long sleeved shirt; or **knee & elbow pads** will save skin. Later, you'll come to a dark slot where **a headlamp is required.** This goes on for about 35m. There will always be deep water here, so chimney over the deep places to avoid swimming. A short distance below that, the canyon opens quickly. This entire slot is only about 250m long--but it's a good one.

About 1 km below the slot, turn left and exit the canyon at one of 2-3 places heading north. Once out, route-find northwest between the slot and Cottonwood Peak back to your ropes and return the same way back to your car.

Hackberry Canyon Route If coming up Hackberry, one plan would be to backpack during an afternoon about 13 kms to the mouth of Stone Donkey, then walk 400m upcanyon to a spring. That's your waterhole. Camp in that area somewhere. This should take about half a day. Next morning, from the spring, continue upcanyon just over 1 km, exit as suggested above, route-find to the upper end of the slot and head downcanyon taking your ropes with you. Walk back to your car in the afternoon.

A 2nd plan for would be for strong hikers only. Camp at or near the trailhead on lower Cottonwood, then with an early start, head up Hackberry and do this in one long day. You can shorten the day some, if you forget the ropes & rappel, and upclimb the slot to the bottom of the rappel, then return.

Elevations Crossing of Rock Springs Creek, 1725m; Rock Springs Bench Trailhead, 2073m; high point of hike on Rock Springs Point, 2109m; exit in Stone Donkey, 1627m; junction of Hackberry & Stone Donkey, 1455m; end of Hackberry Canyon at Cottonwood Wash, 1440m.

Time Needed To ensure success, camp at the Rock Springs Bench Trailhead, then take from 9-13 hours for the round-trip day-hike. If coming up Hackberry, you'll likely need about 1 1/2 days for the hike; but if you camp at the mouth of Hackberry, get an early start, strong hikers can do it in 11-14 hours (?). But less if you upclimb the slot and forget the rappel; this one would be for experienced hikers only.

Water Take plenty in your car and pack. There's always some water in potholes and in the slot, and it's always at the spring in lower Stone Donkey. Take purification tablets for pothole water as there's always cow poop in the valley above the slot.

Maps USGS or BLM map Smoky Mountain (1:100,000) for driving & orientation; and Calico Peak & Slickrock Bench (1:24,000--7 1/2' quad) for hiking.

Flash Flood Danger High risk in the short 250m slot, but no danger elsewhere.

Map 22, Stone Donkey Canyon

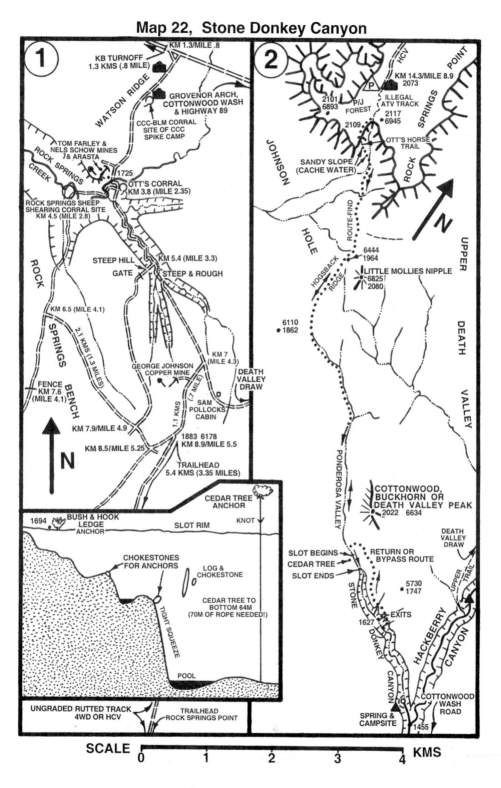

1

KB TURNOFF
1.3 KMS (.8 MILE)

KM 1.3/MILE .8

WATSON RIDGE

GROVENOR ARCH,
COTTONWOOD WASH
& HIGHWAY 89

CCC-BLM CORRAL
SITE OF CCC
SPIKE CAMP

TOM FARLEY &
NELS SCHOW MINES
& ARASTA

ROCK SPRINGS CREEK

1725

OTT'S CORRAL
KM 3.8 (MILE 2.35)

ROCK SPRINGS SHEEP
SHEARING CORRAL SITE
KM 4.5 (MILE 2.8)

ROCK SPRINGS BENCH

STEEP HILL

GATE

KM 5.4 (MILE 3.3)

STEEP & ROUGH

KM 6.5 (MILE 4.1)

2.1 KMS (1.3 MILES)

FENCE
KM 7.6
(MILE 4.1)

GEORGE JOHNSON
COPPER MINE

KM 7
(MILE 4.3)

DEATH
VALLEY
DRAW

.7 MILE

1.1 KMS

SAM
POLLOCKS
CABIN

KM 7.9/MILE 4.9

1883 6178
KM 8.9/MILE 5.5

KM 8.5/MILE 5.25

TRAILHEAD
5.4 KMS (3.35 MILES)

N

2

HCV

KM 14.3/MILE 8.9
2073

2101
6893

P/J
FOREST

P

ILLEGAL
ATV TRACK

2117
6945

ROCK SPRINGS POINT

2109

OTT'S HORSE
TRAIL

JOHNSON HOLE

SANDY SLOPE
(CACHE WATER)

ROUTE-FIND

6444
1964

HOGSBACK RIDGE

LITTLE MOLLIES NIPPLE
6825
2080

UPPER DEATH VALLEY

6110
1862

N

PONDEROSA VALLEY

COTTONWOOD,
BUCKHORN OR
DEATH VALLEY PEAK
2022 6634

DEATH
VALLEY
DRAW

SLOT BEGINS
CEDAR TREE

RETURN OR
BYPASS ROUTE

SLOT ENDS

5730
1747

UPPER TRAIL

STONE

EXITS

1627

DONKEY

CANYON

HACKBERRY CANYON

COTTONWOOD
WASH
ROAD

SPRING &
CAMPSITE

1455

CEDAR TREE
ANCHOR

BUSH & HOOK
LEDGE
ANCHOR

1694

SLOT RIM

KNOT

CHOKESTONES
FOR ANCHORS

LOG &
CHOKESTONE

CEDAR TREE TO
BOTTOM 64M
(70M OF ROPE NEEDED!)

TIGHT SQUEEZE

POOL

UNGRADED RUTTED TRACK
4WD OR HCV

TRAILHEAD
ROCK SPRINGS POINT

SCALE

0   1   2   3   4   KMS

Best Time To Hike You can hike this canyon any-time between late March or early April through October. If going in the spring or fall, a wet/drysuit is required; this is because any little shower puts water into the slot from the surrounding slickrock. Late spring/early summer is best because of longer days.

Boots/Shoes Wading boots or shoes for the slot, but any kind of shoe outside it.

Author's Experience On this first trip, he car-camped at Wallace Ott's Corral, then after an hour of wandering on top of Rock Springs Bench, he finally found the right road and got to the trailhead. His hike to the technical slot (but not down it) and into the canyon below to as far as the spring and back, took 8 hours.

On his second trip (9/23/2002), he carried a ton of ropes plus wetsuit, then attempted to go down from the head of the slot. He attached a 60m rope to the bush, backed up by an Ibis hook in a crack, then handlined down to the last big drop above the pool. He wasn't sure if the rope reached the bottom, so being alone he jumarred back up and went in from the south side as Scott Patterson & friends had done. After the slot, he retrieved his ropes (60 & 17m) and returned to his Chevy Tracker in 9 1/2 hours. He drank 4 liters of water on the hike which was an average day temperature-wise for September.

On 8/31/2003, he hiked up Hackberry and up-climbed the slot to the pool & bottom of the rappel. On the way back, he left Hackberry Canyon at the Ken Goulding Trail and after trial & error and some backtracking, made his way to the west side of Castle Rock, then east along the drainage south of this peak. He finally got back to Cottonwood Wash Road and his car after 11 hours. Staying on the Goulding Trail would have been easier & faster. Quicker & easier than that would be to stay in Hackberry going both ways.

Above Right Just below the big rap into **Stone Donkey** it's narrow & dark; head lamp required.
Below Right The pool at the bottom & the beginning of the slot. This is the end of the rappel if you come right down the slot instead of from the side. **Below Left** If you come up the slot from the bottom, you may have a pool here which is near the end of the slot in **Stone Donkey**.

Above This is in the lower end of **Stone Donkey Canyon** not far above Hackberry. Below the spring in lower Stone Donkey, there is running water year-round, plus some good campsites.

Left Rappelling from the cedar tree above and into the upper part of **Stone Donkey Slot**. If using this route in, you'll land immediately below what is sometimes a pool. Tom Martin took this picture while standing in what is often a pool--but on that day, it was a hole in the sand and bone dry.

Hackberry Canyon, Watson Cabin & Sam Pollock Arch

Location & Access Hackberry is one of 3 long canyon hikes in this book, and it's one of the best when considering availability of water, good scenery, pleasant campsites and interesting things to see along the way. **Hackberry Canyon** lies just east of the Upper Paria River Gorge and runs south roughly parallel to it. The road you'll be using, whether you go in at the head of the canyon or enter from the bottom, is the **Cottonwood Wash Road**. For a better look at the lower end of the canyon, see **Map 26**.

To get there from the north & the Bryce Valley area, drive south through Tropic to Cannonville. One block south of the Grand Staircase Inn & gas station is one of the **visitor centers** for the Grand Staircase-Escalante National Monument **(GSENM)**. Stop there and check on the latest road conditions and other information. They are open from 8-4:30 every day during the 9 warmest months of the year (Tele. 435-679-8981). From Cannonville, head south & east on the paved **Kodachrome Basin Road** to the Kodachrome Basin Turnoff **(KBT)**, a distance of 11.7 kms (7.3 miles). From the KBT, continue east on the graded **Cottonwood Wash Road** for 9.5 kms (5.9 miles). At that point you'll be on top of **Slickrock Bench** at a cattle guard & fence. See **Map 20, Round Valley Draw** for a better look at the driving route to this trailhead.

If you're coming from the south & Highway 89, drive to a point roughly halfway between Page & Kanab. Between **mile posts 17 & 18** turn north onto the same Cottonwood Wash Road (if coming from Page, stop at the GSENM visitor center (Tele. 435-675-5868) in Big Water, Utah, between **mile posts 7 & 8** for an update on the Cottonwood Wash Road. Most of this road has a clay base and when it's wet, it's impassible even for 4WD's! When dry it's fine for cars). Drive north up through Cottonwood Wash, past the mouth of Hackberry (this is 23.5 kms/14.6 miles from Highway 89; or 39.6 kms/24.6 miles from the KBT), past the turnoff to Grosvenor (Butler Valley) Arch, across Round Valley Draw and to the same cattle guard & fence mentioned above. This is 53 kms (32.9 miles) from Highway 89.

On the east side of the cattle guard & fence, turn south on a reasonably good 2WD track. Drive south & southwest past a fence & stock pond (Km 3.2/Mile 2) to the end of the road at Km 5/Mile 3.1.

Trail/Route From the **Slickrock Bench Trailhead** marked 1850m, and with compass in hand, **walk due south** on a minor trail for about 150m or less; there you'll begin to drop down into a minor side-canyon of lower **Round Valley Draw** (don't head southwest on another faint trail which ends at the rim of Hackberry and some impassible cliffs!). This side-canyon entry gets a little steep in places, but should be easy even with a large backpack. Once at the bottom of Round Valley Draw, simply walk downcanyon.

About 2 kms below the trailhead, **Hackberry Canyon** comes in on the right or west side (at one time, you could drive down upper Hackberry about 4 kms to begin hiking, but that route seems to be washed out or blocked off and isn't used anymore). About 3 kms below the confluence of Round Valley & Hackberry, the lower end of **Death Valley Draw** comes in on the right or west. You can walk up this drainage about 300m; there you'll come to a crack where flood waters fall about 40-45m to the canyon floor. There is a way up around this in a canyon to the left--read about it with **Map 19, Death Valley Draw.**

About 2 kms below Death Valley Draw, **Booker Canyon** comes in on the left or east. If you walk up Booker roughly 1 1/2 kms, you'll come to a couple of dryfalls, which you can bypass, then some pretty good narrows, and finally another dryfall you cannot climb. That's the end for people coming up Booker Canyon. About 4-5 kms below Booker is another fairly long **side-canyon** coming in on the left or east side. Ken Goulding Jr. of Henrieville, the rancher who runs cows up on the Rush Beds, says there's a route somewhere near this canyon where you can ride a horse off the rim and down into Hackberry. So far, the author hasn't been in that canyon or on that route up to the east-side rim, but there are a number of places a hiker could climb out of Hackberry either on the east or west sides.

About 3 kms below that side-canyon, you should see water starting to seep into the creek bed. From that point on, all the way down to Cottonwood Wash, you'll have running water most of the way. About 800m below where water starts to seep out, will be lots of cottonwood trees, willows and a bench on the right or west. On it you should see a fence, and behind it a constructed cow trail in or out of the canyon. This is called the **Upper Trail** or **Upper Death Valley Trail**. See **Map 19, Death Valley Draw** for more details.

The late Herm Pollock of Tropic, believed this Upper Trail was first made by a group of Panguitch cattlemen in the late 1800's (Wallace Ott thinks it was built by Samson Chynoweth? The truth may be that many cattlemen did some work on it over the years). It was on this very narrow path, as it runs along the rim of the canyon, that a cow once laid down on the trail and died. Because it was so narrow, the other cows wouldn't step over her body to get to water. The end result was the choking death of many cows in the area which is now called **Upper Death Valley**. Since that disaster, the trail has been improved by different cattlemen who ran stock in the Upper Death Valley area. Today it's a good trail.

A little over 2 kms below the Upper Trail, **Stone Donkey Canyon** comes in on the right or west side. This canyon divides the Upper from Lower Death Valley. Walk up this drainage about 400m to find a low dryfall with a potty-type arch above a spring. You can bypass this little dryfall on the left. If you continue up Stone Donkey, you'll come to a very good slot as described with **Map 22**. If coming from above, you'll have to rappel in, but if coming up from Hackberry, you can wade in from the bottom. If you have a headlamp, knee & elbow pads (and a wet/drysuit in spring or fall), and have the strength to chimney up a narrow crack, you can reach the pool at the bottom of the rappelling section. If you can make it to that point, you'll have seen about 95% or more of the slot. You can also get out of lower Stone Donkey on the north side, walk around to the upper end of the slot and rappel in, as described in the separate chapter mentioned above.

Less than 2 kms below Stone Donkey, is another cow trail out of the canyon to the right or west. This is called the **Lower Trail** or **Lower Death Valley Trail**. As you near this area, you'll notice the wall on the right gets lower & lower with sand on top. Right at the bottom of the trail and high on the wall in front of you, are several cowboy signatures. The best & most famous one reads, **W.M. Chynoweth, 1892.** It's about 4m above the creek and 30m from the bottom of the Lower Trail.

The Lower Trail is mostly along a natural break in the cliffs, but minor work has been done in the very lowest part. Just above the cliffs is a long sand slide which cows walk on going to or from the creek for water. This is still used by cattle today in the Lower Death Valley area during the winter months.

About 400m below the Lower Trail and on the left or east side is another low bench. Get upon this at the north end to find the beginning of the **Goulding** (pronounced Golding) or **Ken Goulding Trail.** There should be a stone cairn at the beginning (?). This trail was likely first built by the **Chynoweths** beginning sometime after their arrival at Pahreah in the fall of 1892, but much more work was done on it by the **Ken Gouldings**, both father & son, both of which are now dead.

The Goulding Trail zig zags back & forth up the east side of the canyon wall, then once on top, it runs

Map 23, Hackberry Canyon, Watson Cabin & Sam Pollock Arch

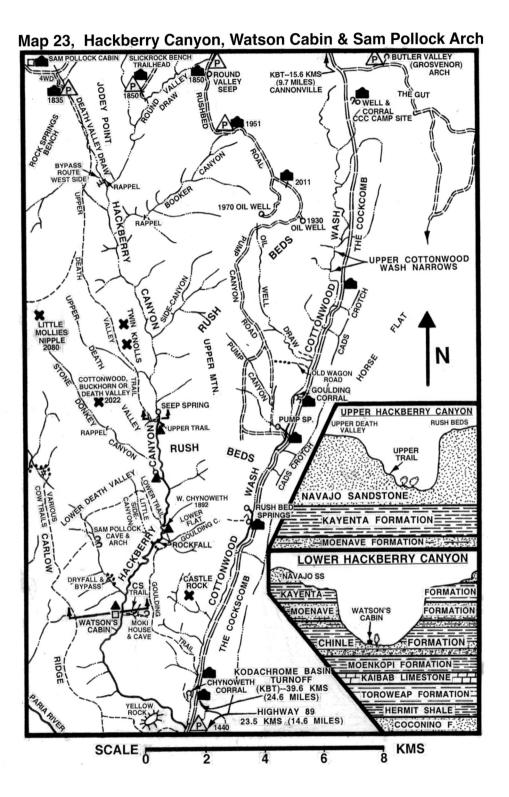

SAM POLLOCK CABIN
SLICKROCK BENCH TRAILHEAD
4WD
1835
JODEY POINT
ROCK SPRINGS BENCH
DEATH VALLEY DRAW
BYPASS ROUTE WEST SIDE
RAPPEL
UPPER
HACKBERRY
RAPPEL
DEATH
LITTLE MOLLIES NIPPLE 2080
TWIN KNOLLS
UPPER
DEATH
VALLEY
SIDE CANYON
CANYON
STONE DONKEY
COTTONWOOD, BUCKHORN OR DEATH VALLEY 2022
RAPPEL
DEATH VALLEY
TRAIL
SEEP SPRING
UPPER TRAIL
RUSH
CARLOW
VARIOUS COW TRAILS
LOWER DEATH VALLEY
LOWER TRAIL
LITTLE SIDE CANYON
W. CHYNOWETH 1892
LOWER FLAT
GOULDING C.
SAM POLLOCK CAVE & ARCH
ROCKFALL
HACKBERRY
DRYFALL & BYPASS
CS TRAIL
GOULDING
CASTLE ROCK
WATSON'S CABIN
MOKI HOUSE & CAVE
TRAIL
RIDGE
PARIA RIVER
YELLOW ROCK

ROUND VALLEY DRAW
1850
1850
RUSHBED
ROUND VALLEY SEEP
1951
BOOKER CANYON
CANYON ROAD
1970 OIL WELL
RUSH
UPPER MTN.
PUMP CANYON ROAD
PUMP CANYON
PUMP SP.
RUSH
BEDS
COTTONWOOD WASH
RUSH BED SPRINGS
CADS CROTCH
COTTONWOOD
THE COCKSCOMB
KODACHROME BASIN TURNOFF
CHYNOWETH CORRAL
1440

KBT--15.6 KMS (9.7 MILES) CANNONVILLE
2011
1930 OIL WELL
OIL WELL DRAW
BEDS
THE COCKSCOMB
WASH
UPPER COTTONWOOD WASH NARROWS
CADS CROTCH
OLD WAGON ROAD
GOULDING CORRAL
HORSE FLAT

BUTLER VALLEY (GROSVENOR) ARCH
WELL & CORRAL CCC CAMP SITE
THE GUT

N

UPPER HACKBERRY CANYON
UPPER DEATH VALLEY   RUSH BEDS
UPPER TRAIL
NAVAJO SANDSTONE
KAYENTA FORMATION
MOENAVE FORMATION

LOWER HACKBERRY CANYON
NAVAJO SS
KAYENTA   FORMATION
MOENAVE   WATSON'S CABIN   FORMATION
CHINLE   FORMATION
MOENKOPI FORMATION
KAIBAB LIMESTONE
TOROWEAP FORMATION
HERMIT SHALE
COCONINO F.

KODACHROME BASIN TURNOFF (KBT)--39.6 KMS (24.6 MILES)
HIGHWAY 89 23.5 KMS (14.6 MILES)

SCALE
0   2   4   6   8   KMS

southeast down into a little drainage we'll call **Goulding Canyon**. From there it runs southwest up the other side to the top of the mesa. You can follow it on the map. Once out of Hackberry, it runs south past the head of a little side-canyon with some Anasazi Indian ruins called the **Moki House** (read more below), then curves to the east south of Castle Rock. It's in this section you'll likely see a few stone cairns marking the trail. Finally, it zig zags down a little side-canyon into Cottonwood Wash about halfway between Castle Rock and the mouth of Hackberry. That last steep section was man-made, as was the part where it leaves Hackberry. In between, the trail runs through sand but it's visible most of the time. This trail and the ruins are described in more detail with **Map 26, Lower Rush Beds, etc.**

About 400m below the Goulding Trail is a relatively new feature in the canyon. Where there was once a minor 1m-high ledge & waterfall right at the contact point of the Kayenta & Navajo Formations, there's now a large **rockfall** in the canyon. On October 25 1987, part of the Navajo Sandstone wall on the west side broke away creating a dam across Hackberry Creek. This was heard by Ralph Chynoweth who was deer hunting & camped on the little bench at the very beginning of the Goulding Trail at the time. The dam is about 8m high and at first created a sizable lake above the dam for perhaps 100m or more. However, the waters finally seeped through the debris and over the years has created a new stream course on the west side of the dam. Slowly over the years, flood waters have carried away most of the sediment that had backed up behind the dam. There's now a hiker's trail around the dam on the east side.

About 75m below the rockfall is a route to the canyon rim up a steep gully on the east side. You can climb up this to meet the Goulding Trail, but it's choked full of unstable rocks & boulders, and is **not recommended**. In places you have to climb on all-4's and one of the large rocks could dislodge at any time! Immediately opposite this steep gully, there's another **little side-canyon** coming in from the west which has a small stream. A km below that are 2 gooseneck bends where the canyon is about as deep as it gets. Just below that, you may see a nice spring on the right or west side.

Further along is **Sam Pollock Canyon**. About 3 kms up this drainage is an **arch** with Sam's name on it. At one point, you'll have to route-find up to the right or north side, to get around a dryfall which otherwise blocks the way. It's an easy climb. Once you reach the arch, which is on the east side of the canyon, look to the north or upcanyon side less than 100m to see a big alcove-type cave, maybe called **Pollock Cave (?)**. In the back are cowboy signatures such as Art [Arthur] Chynoweth, 1918, and black soot from aboriginal fires.

About 1 km downstream from the mouth of Sam Pollock Canyon, and on a bench on the west side of the creek, is the old **Watson Cabin**. Read the full story about it and Frank Watson below. In the summer of 2009, the BLM, with a helicopter, ferried in supplies to fence-off the cabin to do rehab work.

Due east of the Watson Cabin is a minor drainage. If you go up this, you can bypass a dryfall on the left or north side and find lots of **cowboy signatures**. Further up you'll pass another cliff band on the right or south side, then if you veer north again--and with some route-finding--you might see the **Moki House** in an alcove **cave**. See **Map 26** for more details.

About 3-4 kms below the cabin and where the gorge turns east, Hackberry cuts dramatically through the Navajo Sandstone part of **The Cockscomb** before reaching Cottonwood Wash. This is the deepest and narrowest part of Hackberry Canyon. Just to the south of the mouth of Hackberry is a very colorful dome of Navajo Sandstone called **Yellow Rock**, which is discussed in detail on **Map 26**.

Elevations Slickrock Trailhead, about 1850m; bottom end of Hackberry Canyon, 1440m.

Time Needed This hike is around 28-30 kms long. It can be done in one long day with a car on each end, but most people normally take 2-3 days, depending on how many side-canyons they visit along the way. If you're going all the way through the canyon, consider leaving a mtn. bike at one end to substitute as a car shuttle. But riding a bike back to your car might take 3-4 hours--or more (?)! Hitch hiking is another option. In October, 2003 there were 200-300 cars a day using Cottonwood Wash Road, but in 2009, there were fewer cars because of terrible road conditions. As this book goes to press, Kane County and the GSENM are in the middle of a turf war and the road wasn't being maintained.

Water It begins to flow in the creek bed about 800m above where the Upper Trail comes in. It then flows nearly all the way to Cottonwood Wash. There's a good spring up Stone Donkey Canyon, and there are several seeps or springs just below the rockfall, including the little side-canyon to the west.

From the first of November through April, there can be cattle in the canyon--depending on the drought, so take water directly from a spring, or purify it first. In summer when the cattle are gone, it should be better--a lot better after a flood has washed out all the cow pies and cleaned the canyon.

Maps USGS or BLM map Smoky Mountain (1:100,000) for driving & orientation; and Slickrock Bench & Calico Peak (1:24,000--7 1/2' quads) for hiking.

Main Attractions Good (?) water, shady campsites, narrow side-canyons, old historic cattle trails, an old homesteader's cabin, and solitude.

Best Time to Hike Spring or fall. In late spring and early summer, you'll be plagued by large gray horse flies (from late May into July). To survive these pests, wear long pants.

Boots/Shoes Wading boots or shoes, but the stream really is small.

Author's Experience He's made 15-20 trips into the canyon, but only once did he walk all the way through. On that occasion, he left in the evening from the road to Round Valley Trailhead, then rim-walked above Round Valley Draw to the route down in, and finally camped near the confluence with Hackberry. Next day he hurried all the way through and hitched a ride back to his car.

The Story of Frank Watson and the Watson Cabin

There's a rather well-built and well-preserved cabin in the lower end of Hackberry Canyon and an interesting story behind it. It's called the Watson Cabin, after a man known locally as Frank Watson.

The man's real name was **Richard Welburn Thomas** who came from Wisconsin. As the story goes, Thomas apparently had a quarrel with his wife one night, then early the next morning, he got up, left the house and walked to the railway station where he boarded a train for the wild west. This is the story that's told, but he could also have been a fugitive from the law. Why else would he change his name?

After some wandering, it seems he ended up at **Lee's Ferry** under the employment of **Charles H. Spencer**. Spencer was the big-time mining promoter who got lots of money from investors and tried to find a way to separate gold from the Chinle clay beds at Lee's Ferry. Spencer worked at Lee's Ferry between 1910 & 1912. It was at this time Thomas changed his name to Frank Watson. Evidently, Watson was a good all-around handy man and mechanic. It's been said by several men in Bryce Valley, that Watson was involved in the running of the paddle wheel steamer *Charles H. Spencer* up the Colorado River to Warm Creek, where they were to load coal and ship it by barge down to the gold diggings at Lee's Ferry. This whole operation failed in the end, and the miners left in 1912.

From Lee's Ferry, Spencer and his men went up the Paria River to the old town of Pahreah, and were involved in mining gold from the Chinle clay beds from 1912 to about the end of World War I. Watson was also there at that time, and it appears that at some point he went over **Carlow Ridge** to the east and into lower Hackberry Canyon and built this cabin. It's been said that he had a rough trail or route from the cabin, over the ridge, and down to Pahreah, but no one seems to know of its whereabouts today.

The late Herm Pollock, a rock hound from Tropic, remembered the Watson Cabin as being well-built. Watson made the wooden hinges on the door with only a pocket knife. About 150-200m south or downstream from the cabin, Watson had a flume and a sluice box, both of which were painted bright yellow when Herm saw the place in 1922. Apparently, Watson had tried to do the same thing in lower Hackberry, as Spencer tried to do over the ridge at Pahreah, because the Chinle clays are exposed in both places. Frank's operation failed too.

George Thompson of Cannonville remembered a little about the cabin and the time when his father, Jodey Thompson (Jodey Point between Death Valley Draw & upper Hackberry carries his name), tried to homestead the bench land where the cabin is located:

We used to go down there when I was just a little feller when he had water out there on the ground, then a big flood came down and lowered the wash 'till he couldn't get it out into the ditches anymore. So Dad gave it up. I was 4 or 5 when we were down there, about 1926 or '27, and it was soon after that that he decided it was a useless effort. After that, they went down several times and put the water back in the ditches--they hauled trees into the wash and made dikes, and got the water back up there, but the wash was so deep that every little flood would take it down and wash everything out on 'um, so they finally decided it wasn't worth the effort.

For a year or two, Dad planted corn. [They also attempted to grow peach trees.] I remember he brought up corn for the cows in winter. There was a road down there--not much of a road, but it was travelable. I do remember that we went in a wagon--he'd load the kids and away they'd go. I don't know how they got past that little jumpup, but there was a way around it in those days.

There's an interesting story about one dark night in the cabin, as told by several old-timers in Bryce Valley. Jodey and one of his brothers either got to the cabin late at night, or were sleeping there, when they heard rattlesnakes in the darkened room. With only a candle for light and a pitch fork with 5 prongs, they somehow managed to spear one rattler with each prong. In the morning they stood the pitchfork up against the cabin wall with the 5 snakes dangling from it. The longest nearly reached the ground.

According to the late Ken Goulding, Sr. of Henrieville, Watson was employed by the Goulding family off and on for several years herding sheep, apparently during the mid to late 1910's (?). At one time Watson lived in a tent, which was pitched behind the Goulding house in Henrieville. Ken recalled one winter, Watson tore down an old Model A Ford, and put it back together again the next spring.

At about the end of World War I, and after the time Watson built his Hackberry Cabin and had worked for the Gouldings, he built a small store on what is now known locally as **Watson Ridge**. Watson Ridge is south of Henrieville, and due south of Chimney Rock, which is in Kodachrome Basin State Park. The store was small, and catered to the sheepmen who were numerous in the area at that time. He sold all kinds of supplies, but Ken Goulding remembered him selling candy, Bull Durham tobacco, and a bootleg whisky everyone called *Jamaica Ginger*.

The **Watson Cabin** in the lower end of **Hackberry Canyon**. It's believed this cabin was built by Frank Watson sometime in the 1910's.

This was in the early days of prohibition, and selling this rot-gut whisky was forbidden. The lady who owned & operated the only store in Henrieville, bought it from someone, then it was transported out to Watson's store, where they used to have some wild parties. It was sold and drank openly at Watson's place, because it was so far away from the law.

To get to Watson's old store site, drive east from the Kodachrome Basin Turnoff on the Cottonwood Wash Road for 1.3 kms (.8 mile). At the first road running south, turn right, and drive another 150m, then veer right again. Beyond that aways, turn right or west again. It was near the crest of the hill, but on the west side. Today there's only a few scattered tin cans, etc., marking the spot. Just beyond his old store site is a corral built by the CCC's in 1937 or '38. It's now called the BLM Corral. A CCC spike camp was located nearby.

The last time Goulding saw Watson was in about 1921. Herm Pollock and some of the Otts pick up the story from there. After leaving the store on Watson Ridge, he likely went to the bottom end of **Heward Canyon**, a tributary of **Sheep Creek**, which is just east of Bryce Canyon NP, and southwest of Cannonville. About 2 kms west of the old Johnson Ranch on Sheep Creek, is a very well-built stone house along the road running up Heward Creek. This may have been built by Watson, since it was so well-constructed and is still in very good condition except for the wooden roof, which has collapsed under its own weight. Watson lived there, or perhaps just downcanyon at the Johnson Ranch. While there, he apparently tried to develop a coal mine just west of the cabin for one or 2 winters (see **Map 47, Bryce Valley & Skutumpah Road Ranches**, in the back of this book for the location).

To get to the Heward Canyon rock house, drive south out of Cannonville on the Kodachrome Basin Road for 4.2 kms (2.6 miles), and turn west. Drive past the **Georgetown Cemetery** toward the old townsite of **Georgetown**. From the Yellow Creek Road just west of Georgetown, turn south and head for Sheep Creek and the sites of the old Henderson and Johnson Ranches, and Heward Creek. About 2 kms west of the old Johnson Ranch, is the rock house on the right side of the road. It's **12 kms (7.45 miles)** from the Kodachrome Basin Road and on the right about 75m from the road. It's hard to see because of several cedar trees, so look closely.

Later, Watson landed at the old W. J. Henderson Ranch, which is about 1 1/2 or 2 kms southwest of the Georgetown site, and just up the hill from where the James R. Ott Ranch was located. At this ranch, Watson lived with an old man named Hyrum "Hite" Elmer. Wallace Ott remembers when old Hite died, because Watson came down to their ranch to get a wagon to haul him off.

From the Henderson Ranch, Watson went back to Wisconsin to see his aging mother sometime in the mid-1920's. She was apparently very happy and surprised to see him, according to Ken Goulding Sr. Since he had been gone for so long, and had lost touch with the family, his mother thought he surely must have been killed by Indians.

Right Joseph (Jodey) Wallace Thompson and his wife Rachel in about 1900. He was 5 years old when his parents settled in Bryce Valley in 1876. In about 1926, Jodey attempted to farm the area around the Frank Watson Cabin, but that scheme only lasted for a couple of summers before flood waters lowered the creek bed. Jodey Point, located just west of the upper end of Hackberry Canyon, is named after this man. He is the father of George Wallace Thompson, presently of Cannonville. (George & Joe Thompson foto)

Below This is the signature of *Will Chynoweth, 1892*, located at the bottom of the **Lower Trail**. It's 3m above the creek bed and about 20m southeast of the bottom the trail.

Left **Sam Pollock Arch**. **Right** The **Watson Cabin** below, and looking due east at the little drainage which leads up to the **Moki house** ruins & cave. To get to the Moki house from the cabin, walk up the drainage to near the ledge, veer left or north for nearly 100m and get up on the little bench that's visible below the wall in shadows. Walk that bench into the drainage again, and be looking for cowboy signatures on your left. From there, go upcanyon but veer right to get upon the next series of ledges, then head left or north again and hunt for the alcove cave which holds the Moki house ruins. It's not easy to find, but it's there. The cave faces southwest. See pictures, and read more about the Moki house ruins, along with **Map 26**.

This is the alcove **cave** just north of **Sam Pollock Arch**. Notice the black soot on the ceiling; this comes from thousands of campfires built & used by aborigines. On the back wall is the signature of *Art Chynoweth, Feb. 20, 1918*. There are also pieces of bone, flint chips, and pottery fragments in this cave.

Upper Cottonwood Wash Narrows & Grosvenor Arch

Location & Access Featured here is a short narrow section in the upper end of Cottonwood Wash. These narrows aren't very long, but they are nearly as deep and narrow as parts of the Buckskin Gulch, against which many slot canyons are judged. This hike is located about 7 kms south of the **Butler Valley Arch** (this was the name of the arch before the National Geographic Society arrived in 1948 and changed the name to **Grosvenor Arch** after the NGS President). To get there, drive south from Bryce Canyon on Highway 12 through the towns of Tropic and Cannonville. From Cannonville head south & east on a paved road following the signs to Kodachrome Basin. At the **Kodachrome Basin Turnoff (KBT)**, continue east (instead of going north to KB) on the graded **Cottonwood Wash Road**. From the KBT, drive **21.4 kms (13.3 miles)**. This will put you at the bottom of a steep dugway going south. Just in front of you will be some very colorful red & white rocks, and just beyond a 2nd pass. Park where a sign indicates the **Upper Trailhead**. If coming up Cottonwood Wash from the south, turn north from **Highway 89** between **mile posts 17 & 18**. From the highway to the Upper TH is **41.7 kms (25.9 miles)**. South of the Upper TH **1.3 kms (.8 mile)** is the **Lower Trailhead** at the end of your hike. When this Cottonwood Wash Road is wet, stay away--it's impassable, even for 4WD's! However, it tends to dry quickly in summer after rains. Check the nearest visitor center for a road report. Or call the one in Cannonville (Tele. 435-679-8981) or the Big Water Visitor Center (Tele. 435-675-5868).

Trail/Route From the Upper TH near the culvert over Cads Crotch Wash, scramble down into the drainage. After just a few meters, you'll have a choice of going up Butler Valley Draw a ways, or down the Cottonwood Wash. Go up first, as that part is perhaps the best. It's not as deep as the canyon to the south, but it's more narrow. Then head downcanyon. There are 2 very short side-canyons and some high dryfalls to see along the way. After about 2 kms, you'll come out the bottom end heading east back toward the road and the Lower TH. From there, it's a 20 minute road-walk back to your car. These narrows are formed by a strange twist of the dry stream channel which is further west than the road; which is where you'd think the normal water drainage should be. This is called an *antecedent stream*, which means the channel was there before The Cockscomb was fully uplifted.

Elevations Upper Trailhead, 1735m; Lower TH, 1685m; picnic site at Grosvenor Arch, 1900m.

Time Needed There's about 600-800m of interesting narrows up Butler Valley Draw, then about 2 kms of Cottonwood Wash narrows. You can do the whole hike in 1-2 hours.

Water Carry water in your car and pack. There's no water at the little developed picnic site (with toilet & paved trail to the arch) 300m from the base of Grosvenor Arch.

Maps USGS or BLM map Smoky Mountain (1:100,000) for driving & orientation; and Butler Valley (1:24,000--7 1/2' quad) for hiking.

Main Attractions A short, but interesting & easily accessible narrow canyon, plus Grosvenor Arch.

Best Time to Hike About anytime, but summers are a little warm, and cold winter weather prevents the road from drying quickly after storms (best to get there via Cannonville). Spring or fall are ideal times.

Boots/Shoes Dry-weather boots or shoes.

Author's Experience Once in early April, and again in mid-October, the author did this entire hike in about 1 hour round-trip. On 8/29/2003, he entered the drainage about 2 kms north of the normal entry point and walked down Butler Valley Draw first, then the lower narrows. This scouting hike and road-walk took 3 hours. He did the Narrows hike in 7/2009 in 1 1/2 hours.

To the right, the **Cottonwood Wash Road**, and next to it the **Upper Cottonwood Wash Trailhead**. Just out of the picture to the right is the beginning of Upper Cottonwood Wash Narrows. But maybe the best thing to see here are these very colorful rocks and clay beds.

Map 24, Upper Cottonwood Wash Narrows & Grosvenor Arch

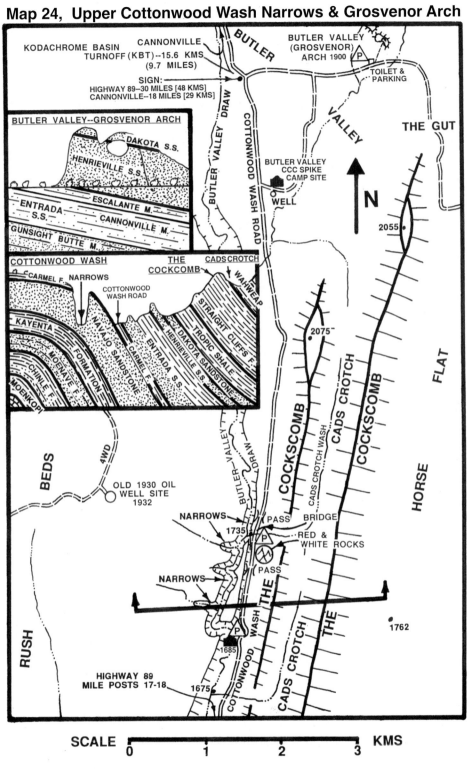

KODACHROME BASIN
TURNOFF (KBT)--15.6 KMS.
(9.7 MILES)

CANNONVILLE

BUTLER VALLEY
(GROSVENOR)
ARCH 1900

P

TOILET &
PARKING

SIGN:
HIGHWAY 89--30 MILES [48 KMS]
CANNONVILLE--18 MILES [29 KMS]

BUTLER

BUTLER VALLEY DRAW

COTTONWOOD WASH ROAD

VALLEY

THE GUT

BUTLER VALLEY--GROSVENOR ARCH

DAKOTA S.S.

HENRIEVILLE S.S.

ESCALANTE M.

ENTRADA
S.S.

CANNONVILLE M.

GUNSIGHT BUTTE M.

BUTLER VALLEY
CCC SPIKE
CAMP SITE

WELL

N

2055

COTTONWOOD WASH

THE
COCKSCOMB

CADS CROTCH

CARMEL F. NARROWS

COTTONWOOD
WASH ROAD

KAYENTA

MOENAVE F.

NAVAJO SANDSTONE

CHINLE F.

MOENKOPI

FORMATION

CARMEL F.

ENTRADA S.S.

HENRIEVILLE S.S.

DAKOTA SANDSTONE

TROPIC SHALE

STRAIGHT CLIFFS F.

WAHWEAP

2075

CADS CROTCH WASH

CADS CROTCH

COCKSCOMB

COCKSCOMB

HORSE

FLAT

BEDS

4WD

OLD 1930 OIL
WELL SITE
1932

BUTLER VALLEY DRAW

NARROWS

1735

P

PASS

BRIDGE

RED &
WHITE ROCKS

PASS

NARROWS

THE

COTTONWOOD WASH

P

1685

CADS CROTCH

THE

1762

HIGHWAY 89
MILE POSTS 17-18

1675

COTTONWOOD WASH

CADS CROTCH

RUSH

SCALE

0   1   2   3   KMS

Upper Rush Beds Cattle Trails and the Old 1930 Oil Well

Location & Access The high country south of Round Valley Draw, and in between Hackberry Canyon & Cottonwood Wash, is generally known as the **Rush Beds**. This information & map covers the northern or Upper Rush Beds from about the head of Booker Canyon south to Lower Flat & Rush Bed Spring, which is in Cottonwood Wash. Shown here is the road to the New Oil Well drill site, the Old 1930 Oil Well, the 4WD roads extending south from the oil wells, Upper Mountain, the Old Wagon Road, Pump Canyon & Trail, Rush Bed Spring & Trail and the Narrows of Upper Cottonwood Wash.

To get there, follow the signs south from Cannonville on the road running to Kodachrome Basin. At the junction or turnoff where the paved road heads north to Kodachrome Basin (Kodachrome Basin Turnoff--KBT) continue straight ahead to the graded **Cottonwood Wash Road** (From the KBT (Km & Mile 0) to Highway 89 is 63.3 kms (39.2 miles). Or if coming from the south and Highway 89, turn north onto the Cottonwood Wash Road from between mile posts 17 &18).

To reach the Old 1930 Oil Well, drive east from the KBT to **Round Valley Draw** (RVD) at Km 10.9/Mile 6.8 (54 kms/33.5 miles from Highway 89), and turn south onto the **Rush Bed Road** as if going to RVD & Booker Canyon. You'll pass RVD Trailhead at Km 2.7/Mile 1.7, then go south past Round Valley Seep. Just after that may be a bad place in the road, so having a shovel is a good idea. After that the road is generally good, but has a rough place or two and is best to have a HCV. Continue south, then veer east & south around the head of Booker Canyon, which is along a chained & reseeded area. At **Km 8.5/Mile 5.3** is a junction; to the left or east is the track running down to the Old 1930 Oil Well site; straight ahead is the road to the **New Oil Well**. If you turn left, after about 1 km will be a fence & gate & bad place in the road. Signs indicate this road may be blocked off there at some time in the future. About 1 1/2 kms from that gate will be the **Old 1930 Oil Well** site down a short road to the left or east. From this well is an old 4WD track running down to Pump Canyon. Read more on the history below. In the future, if you want to go down to Pump Canyon from the Old Well, you may have to park at the well site, or back up the road at or near the gate, or even at the junction mentioned above (?). This will depend on future GSENM policy and lawsuit #2477 which will determine if they block off these roads or not. Stay tuned!

If you continue south toward the New Oil Well, at Km 9.5/Mile 5.9 will be a fence & gate (leave it as you find it--open or closed), then the road goes down to the southwest and ends in a sandy sagebrush flat at Km 10.5/Mile 6.5. Inscribed on the well's metal pole/plug is *"Butler Valley Gov. #1, Marathon Oil Co., Sept. 14, 1970, Sec. 22, T39S, R1W"*. From this site are 2 very sandy tracks heading south to join the track from the Old Well, but the BLM has them blocked off (ATV's are still driving past the signs illegally!). This will be one trailhead.

To reach the **cattle & oil well trails off the Rush Beds into the middle Cottonwood Wash,** drive east from the KBT to Grosvenor Arch Turnoff (Km 15.6/Mile 9.7) and veer south into Cottonwood Wash. Continue south past the Cottonwood Wash Narrows Hike to Km 26.2/Mile 16.3 (36.9 kms/22.9 miles from Highway 89) and park right on the road. Just west of that point should be the bottom end of the **Old Wagon Road** (300m north of that will be the mouth of what this writer calls **Oil Well Draw**).

Or continue south to Km 28.7/Mile 17.8 (34.5 kms/21.4 miles from Highway 89) and turn west onto a little side road & camping place at the mouth of **Pump Canyon, Spring & Trail.** Park and/or camp in the little loop-road. Or continue downcanyon to **Rush Bed Spring & Trail** at Km 31.1/Mile 19.3 (32 kms/19.9 miles from Highway 89), and park at one of 2 pullouts on the west side of the road. Not far to the south of Rush Bed Spring is Castle Peak and other trails & hikes which are on the next map.

Trail/Route Depending on monument policy, you'll likely have to walk a short distance to the **Old 1930 Oil Well,** as described above, and below.

The **Old Wagon Road** is where wagons loaded with lumber from the Old 1930 Oil Well were taken off the Rush Beds into Cottonwood Wash. The late Ken Goulding, Jr. of Henrieville said: *I guess they put trees on 'um--put drags on 'um to hold 'um back, and went right off there. They must of had 'um fixed up pretty good, because it's steep.* From the bottom, John (Long John) W. Mangum & Jim Ed Smith, without a road, hauled the boards in wagons down to Old Pahreah & Fivemile Ranch (read more below).

From where you park on the Cottonwood Wash Road, look west at the steep slope where you'll see a long vertical mound of red dirt or clay sitting on top of the white Navajo Sandstone slickrock. Walk west about 200m to the southeast base of the red dirt mound and first look for a couple of small piles of old boards. Once you find those, walk northwest 75m to find the bottom of the Old Wagon Road which is on the south side of the long red dirt mound. This wagon trail isn't used too much, but it's clearly visible. Walk up this to where it starts to level off, then it fades and disappears. If you continue cross-country to the west, you'll cross an old drift fence, which is now on the ground. About 200m west of that is the road the oil drillers used to get down to Pump Canyon and their water pumping operation.

According to Ken Goulding, Jr., there's another old cattle trail running east off the Rush Beds about 400m north of the Old Wagon Road. This one is on the north side of Oil Well Draw, but is barely visible in just a few place as it comes off the steeper slope.

From where you park near the mouth of **Pump Canyon,** cross Cottonwood Creek (usually with a little water) to the west to find the end of Pump's drainage. Climb out of it to the west and onto the lower end of an old unused & washed-out road. Follow it west to the bottom of the steep slope. From there, you can turn right or north, reenter Pump Canyon and walk up to the spring; but there's no sign of where the oil well's water pump & pond may have been. Or, you can continue west up the very steep **Lincoln Lyman or New Pump Canyon Road** along the south side of the canyon. At the top of the steep part is a fence & gate. This road runs west, then north to meet the original track running south to Pump Canyon as shown on the map. You can follow this north, then make a loop coming south on the north side of Pump Canyon where the road peters out next to the drift fence, which at that point is still standing. From there follow cow trails south down into Pump Canyon and up the other side back to the gate (or route-find down the steep slickrock to the spring).

Ken Goulding, Jr. remembered when the Pump Canyon Road was built: *I think the BLM built it. They had Lincoln Lyman go down there and blade it off with his Cat. About that time, I had an old 2-ton 4WD dump truck, and I took it off of there. And it was steep! You'd have to stand there with your feet on the brake & floor boards! It was built not long after we got the Rush Beds grazing rights, and that was in 1958. It must have been in about 1960 that Pump Canyon Road was built. That was Lincoln Lyman from Escalante, he was workin' for the BLM.*

There's another old cattle trail just southwest of **Rush Bed Spring.** From where you park, walk west across the small creek, then route-find a little north to an old road running below the power lines west of the creek. Once on that track, head south past power pole #88. About 75m south of that and in an

Map 25, Upper Rush Beds Cattle Trails & the Old 1930 Oil Well

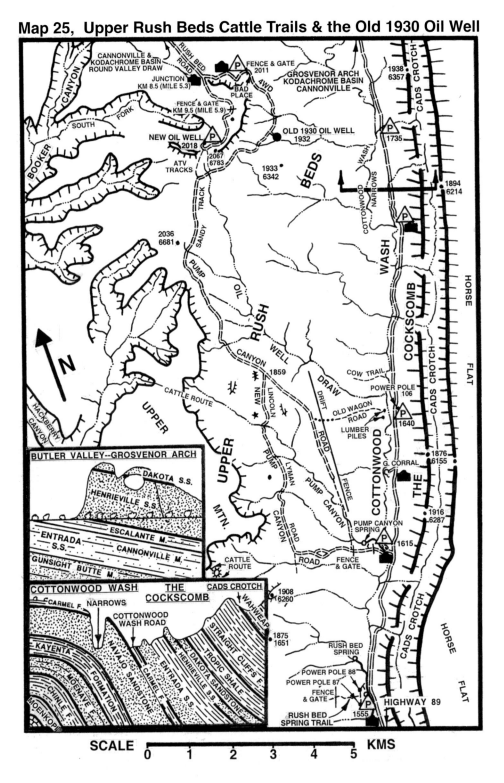

SCALE   0   1   2   3   4   5   KMS

area that's seen some flooding, head west straight up the rocky & shaley slope. After another 200m or so, you should begin to see some stone cairns marking the lower end of the **Rush Bed Spring Trail**. Follow it up--the further you go, the easier it is to find & follow. Near the top of the steeper slope you'll be in a minor drainage, then you'll come to a drift fence & gate. Beyond that, the trail disappears in the sands of the Lower Rush Beds.

Elevations New Oil Well, 2018m; Old 1930 Oil Well, 1932m; bottom of the Old Wagon Road, 1640m; bottom of Pump Canyon Road, 1615m; Rush Bed Spring, 1555m.

Time Needed You can hike along these historic trails for just an hour or two, or spend all day. You may be able to take a 4WD to the Old Oil Well, or maybe you'll have to walk in from the fence & gate (?). You'll want an hour or two at the **Old Well**--it's the most interesting place to see on this map.

Water None on the Rush Beds, so take your own. Water can be found at Pump & Rush Bed Springs (2 parts--one in a little canyon, the other in the marshy grass across from the Cottonwood Wash Road). But you'll have to purify this water.

Maps USGS or BLM map Smoky Mountain (1:100,000) for driving & orientation; Slickrock Bench, Butler Valley, Horse Flat, Calico Peak & Fivemile Valley (1:24,000--7 1/2' quads) for hiking.

Main Attractions Historic cattle trails and an old oil well in a little known country.

Best Time to Hike Spring or fall, but can be hiked anytime the roads are dry. The Cottonwood Wash Road is often wet & closed in winter--sometimes in summer. Check at the nearest visitor center.

Boot/Shoes Any comfortable light weight boots or shoes.

Author's Experience Once he hiked west up the New Pump Canyon Road, north to the road junction at 1859m, then down the Pump Canyon Trail and back to Cottonwood Wash in about 2 1/2 hours. Another time, he parked his Tracker at the New Oil Well and hiked south then east on the track to the Old 1930 Oil Well while looking for a "Jeep Trail" shown on the Butler Valley quad--that road does not exit! Then it was road-walking back to his vehicle, all in 2 1/2 hours. Later, he found the old lumber at the base of the Old Wagon Road, along with the trail north of Oil Well Draw. Later he found the Rush Bed Spring Trail. That hike lasted about 1 1/2 hours.

History of the Old 1930 Oil Well, and old Roads & Trails

One of the more interesting historic places to see in the Paria River Country is the Old 1930 Oil Well in the northern part of the Rush Beds. The Rush Beds is the higher country between Cottonwood Wash & Hackberry Canyon. At the well site you'll find 4 large cement footings, one for each corner of the derrick, plus a metal pipe in the middle. Nearby is a pile of half-melted bricks which once lined the steam boiler, and several piles of hugh timbers which were part of the derrick. Also nearby is the rotting remains of a large wooden wheel, again part of the derrick complex, and some scattered junk. About 60m uphill to the west from the drill hole is a large pile of wood cut into lengths just right for the boiler. About 200m north of the drill hole, are 3 smaller piles of wood (2 are almost covered by sand, in addition to what may have been a cellar (?).

In the **official records** about this well, a mistake has evidently been made. According to the American Petroleum Institute (API), there were 2 drill holes very near each other in this area and both were done by the Midwest Oil Company. The first was called the **Midwest Butler Valley Well** and was in the SW1/4, SE1/4 of Section 14 (just to the north of the ruins you see today). According to their records, drilling began January 1, 1930 and ended on July 21, 1930. They reached 4436 ft. or 1352 meters. It's API number is 4302505000.

The second well was called the **Midwest Government #1**. It was located in the SW1/4, NE1/4 of Section 23. Both sections were in T39S, R1W. For this so-called second well, drilling began on October 27, 1930 and ended December 15, 1930. It was reported to have reached 4436 ft or 1352 meters, same as the other one, but something isn't right! It's API number is 4302510726. This second well is the site with all the relics you actually see today.

After reading these records, the author returned to the site and walked through the area with map & compass in hand. However, there is no second oil well, the one supposedly in Section 14! Somehow, someway, someone made a mistake in recording the event. The well in Section 23 is the one you see on the ground today.

In 2003, there were several old-timers in the Bryce Valley area who knew something about this old oil well. One man was the late Desmond L. Twitchell of Cannonville. He was 8 years old when his father, **Loren E. Twitchell** was hired to haul some or most of the supplies & equipment to the well. Here's a few things Desmond remembered:

I rode out there on an old 1926 Cat, a trawler cat. I rode on the seat with the driver. That was Midwest Oil Company's Cat. They pushed the road out there and my Dad followed the Cat. They had to hook the Cat onto the truck to pull 'um for about 1/2 a mile before they got out to near the oil well.

Dad had a 1927 White truck, and a 1929 White. He bought that 1929 White because he couldn't pull those hills with that 1927 model. That was the fall of 1929. It took us 2 days to go from Cannonville to Marysvale, which was the end of the railway line, then out to the well, and back to Cannonville.

Once, they buried one truck out there in the creek, in the mud. We went down and tried to pull out #4--we called it #4, it was an old Jeffrey truck. It got in the flood and we tried to pull it out, but we couldn't with the other truck we had. Anyway, they finally got it out and stripped it down and used it for a trailer to haul supplies. The old chassis is still out there in Lower Slickrock north of the main road. The 1929 White truck had duel wheels, and 2 transmissions, so it could pull up the hills. When we'd get to the bottom of some hill, we'd hook a cable from the duel-wheeled truck onto the other one and pull both of 'um over. They worked on the road in 1929, drilled in 1930, and hauled stuff out in 1931.

The bunkhouse was uphill from where that pile of wood is. They had a couple of guys, all they done was cut wood. The bunkhouse had 2 rooms; it housed their main crew which was there, the driller and a couple of helpers. They had a separate building for their tools and oil that they used on the rig. That big round wheel was on the top to the rig. It was used to hoist the material up. It was pretty well worn out so Dad didn't haul it out.

Another man who knew something about the operation was Charley Francisco of Tropic (his wife used to have a little bed & breakfast place on the southeast side of town). Charley's father worked on the well from start to finish. Here are some things Charley remembered about the place:

*My Dad's name was **Charles Edward Francisco**. He came to this country from Kansas as a oil driller. He came down along the Colorado River to Wagon Box Mesa [by Capitol Reef N.P.]. They drilled a well over there on Wagon Box Mesa. My Dad fired a boiler for years. He was a fireman, then a driller. They drilled that one before my time. I was born in 1925. Then my Dad came here for I don't know how many years, but I can remember when they were drillin' out there on the Rush Beds. Dad lived here a* *while, then met my mother and married her. He lived here for a few years before all this happened.*

To begin, they built that road out there all the way by hand. A fellow out here in Cannonville by the name of Loren Twitchell had a big old White truck. He had a grocery store and he freighted for everybody in this part of the country at that time. And he went and bought another truck to haul all the equipment for that well in. I remember they said he got out here in Round Valley Neck [just north of Round Valley Seep] and buried one of those trucks in mud. And they had a hell of a time! I guess they had every man in this country trying to help lift that stuff off that truck so they could get it out of the mud. They brought that drillin' equipment down from the railroad in Marysvale, then through Panguitch--about the same route as we have today.

Now they made that road from The Shepherd [Shepherd Point--the gap you drive through on the way to Kodachrome Basin] all the way out there. They worked everybody they could get when they was building that road. Every man that was available had a team or had anything they could work with--they hired. They had fresnos & scrappers, and 2 or 3 guys was a usin' dynamite.

And everybody wanted to work. There was no such thing as a little cash down in this country! And them [oil company] guys paid good money according to what people was a makin' in this country, or could even think about makin'! I know them guys made more money out there in 5 months than they made in a year & a half herding sheep or cows or what ever they was doin'.

[After the road was built and all the equipment was hauled in], they had men a choppin' wood and a haulin' wood and cutting it in lengths. That was for the boiler because all the power they had for drillin' was steam. Everything was steam powered [they had a small gasoline engine which ran a generator for electric lights]. They used bricks in the fireplaces [boilers]. When those bricks would burn through, then you'd burn your metal out, so you had to replace the bricks to line the boiler.

The derrick was made of wood, and they had some steel for bracing, but it was made of great big heavy timbers. Them homes was back from the well a ways. Two or 3 of the crew lived there, where the other pile of wood is. Dad pumped water for a year up to the oil well site; he run that pump station at Pump Spring down in Cottonwood Wash.

Wallace Ott of Tropic had a little more information about the well and the pump in Pump Canyon, or at least in Cottonwood Wash: *I went down there to get a job on that road when I was 18 years old. That was in 1929. They had quite a big camp, I ate with them; they had a cook and a kitchen outfit; it was quite a crew of guys. I'd say they had as many as 10 men altogether. I took a touring car out there a number of times--they had a pretty good road then. They had a gas engine pump in the canyon and you could hear it for miles around.*

Now back to Charley Francisco's story: *I was 7 or 8 years old when we went back out there after the drillin' had shut down. My Dad and a guy named Jack Seaton went out there to tear down all those buildings and stack up that lumber. We cleaned out all the nails--I pulled nails for days! Then they sold a lot of the lumber to Long John Mangum and Jim Ed Smith. I think they about got it for nothing. They hauled that stuff over and down over them ledges along the Old Wagon Road down into Cottonwood Wash and back up to Piaria [Old Pahreah], and took some down to Five Mile. Jim Ed Smith had some beautiful sheds and stables and corrals at Piaria. He built stables enough for 20 head of horses. [Long John Mangum took his share of lumber down to Five Mile and built a house. It's still standing today at the Five Mile Ranch which is just north of the Hattie Green Mine]*

[After all the workers left], Carl Syrett hauled some of that wood up here to Ruby's Inn for several years. He had a great big truck and he hauled wood out of there--from those stacks at the old oil well. Oooh, there was ricks of wood! That was Ruby Syrett's boy Carl. Fred Syrett [Carl's son] told me they'd go out there and have a picnic and load a big load of wood on his truck and haul it home. It was still good wood, and it was all cut! They had a big fireplace at Ruby's Inn, and it was cut to the right length. At that time it was still a decent road, so it was easier doin' that than goin' out and choppin' it.

Wallace Ott again: *When the oil well quit, the town of Tropic bought that pipe [which ran from Pump Canyon up to the well] and used it up here to pipe their water. I think it was a 4" metal pipe. A crew went down and brought it up. When I was mayor here in Tropic, they was using the same pipe.*

This truck (nearest) is one of the original **White trucks Loren Twitchell** used to haul drilling equipment from the end of the railway at Marysvale, to Bryce Valley and on to the **oil well** site in the **Upper Rush Beds**. Later Ruby Syret, the man who built Ruby's Inn, bought it to haul lumber. To see both trucks, drive east from Ruby's Inn about 200m to the Bryce View Lodge. The 2nd truck is a 1920's International.

139

All old fotos on these 2 pages are from **Charley Francisco** of Tropic.

Top This foto is of the **Old 1930 Oil Well**, but the background seems different (?). Perhaps the negative is backwards (?).

Right Charles Edward Francisco (Charley's father) is one of the 2 drillers in the middle. This is also supposed to be the **Old 1930 Oil Well**, but the background doesn't seem correct--but it's a good picture of an early oil well & drillers.

Below This appears to be the 1927 or the **1929 White truck** used by Loren Twitchell to haul this boiler, among other things, to the oil well in the Rush Beds. It also appears to be the same White truck you can see just across the road to the east from Ruby's Inn. See the picture on the previous page.

Left This is supposed to be a picture of the Rush Beds Wells, but the background seems different--perhaps because they must have cut down all the cedars around the place for fuel for their boiler (?).

Middle This is one of 2 piles of wood, called *ricks of wood* by miners & rough necks (oil drillers), at the **Old 1930 Oil Well** on the Rush Beds. The wood is slowly rotting away.

Below These are the 4 cement bases of the derrick at the **Old 1930 Oil Well** on the Rush Beds. Nearby are parts of the oil derrick itself.

Lower Rush Beds Trails & Hikes: Castle Rock, Goulding Trail, Moki House, Yellow Rock, Hidden Cache & The Cockscomb

Location & Access One of the most striking land forms of southern Utah is the feature known as **The Cockscomb.** The Cockscomb is a fold in the earth's crust, more properly called a monocline, which has created a rather sharp erosional ridge that runs north-south. It begins just south of Canaan Peak in the north, and continues south far beyond Highway 89. The part shown on this map stands the highest, has the sharpest ridges, and is the most fotogenic.

This same feature continues south past Coyote Buttes and along the east side of House Rock Valley Road. In the area of Highway 89A, in the House Rock Valley, you see it continuing south to Saddle Mountain and into the Grand Canyon. There it goes by the name of the East Kaibab Monocline.

Access to this area is via the **Cottonwood Wash Road.** It runs right down the middle of The Cockscomb Valley which is Cottonwood Wash; this begins just south of Grosvenor Arch and ends at the Paria River. While the highest and most rugged part of The Cockscomb is east of this road, there is also a less-dramatic ridgeline on the west side formed mostly by the Navajo Sandstone. The most prominent feature on the west side of The Cockscomb is **Castle Rock,** at 1850m elevation. It stands up like a sore thumb above all its neighbors. Another prominent feature is **Yellow Rock.** It's located just south of the mouth of Hackberry Canyon. Between Yellow Rock and **The Box** of the Paria, is a small valley right on top of the western ridge. Most of the rocks there are yellow, but some peaks are capped with red sandstone. The author is calling this place **Yellow Rock Valley,** for lack of a better name.

All these places between Cottonwood Wash and Hackberry Canyon are on top of a plateau or mesa called the **Rush Beds.** In this case the Lower Rush Beds. The north or Upper Rush Beds is discussed on the previous map.

Besides all this scenic stuff, there are other interesting places to visit. On top of the lower or southern end of the Rush Beds is the **Ken Goulding Trail,** which was likely originally built by Sampson Chynoweth or his boys; Will, Sam, Arthur or Harvey (the family arrived in Pahreah in the fall of 1892). This fairly good cattle trail connects the lower end of Cottonwood Wash with the middle parts of Hackberry Canyon. It also runs close to an alcove with Anasazi ruins--locally known as the **Moki House.** Just south of this trail is a short section of another trail or route sometimes called the **Chynoweth Trail,** which begins near what used to be the **Chynoweth Cabin** (before it burned down) **& Corral.**

There's one last interesting place to visit. The author is calling it the **Hidden Cache.** It's on top of the western side of The Cockscomb not far from where Cottonwood Wash and The Box of the Paria River meet. The story of this place is told below. Nearby, and from inside The Box, is the beginning of **The Box Trail.**

To get to the Hidden Cache & The Box Trail, leave Highway 89 between mile post 17 & 18, and drive northwest on the Cottonwood Wash Road for 19.2 kms (11.9 miles). At that point (about 44 kms/27.4 miles from the Kodachrome Basin Turnoff--KBT), the road begins to run north along an eastern branch of the Cottonwood Wash. This will be just below where The Box and Cottonwood Wash meet which is just to the west. At that place, which is now sign-posted, leave the main road and drive west along a side-road about 150m to where the river floods on occasions, and stop at a new trailhead. By parking, and perhaps camping there, you'll have access to the Hidden Cache and The Box Trail.

If you continue north in Cottonwood Wash, you'll eventually pass 2 cattle guards. Just north of the 2nd, and at Km 23.2/Mile 14.4, you'll come to the **Brigham Plains Road** on the right or east side (39.9 kms/24.8 miles from the KBT). This road zig zags eastward up the main Cockscomb Ridge to Brigham Plains on the other side. Walk or drive this steep road to access the top of The Cockscomb for great views & fotos. Or, you can park at or near this road junction and have access to the **Yellow Rock Trail.**

If getting into the lower end of **Hackberry** is your goal, then park at the trailhead just east of the mouth about 200m north of the Brigham Plains Road (23.5 kms/14.6 miles from Highway 89; or 39.6 kms/24.6 miles from the KBT). Some people park here when going to Yellow Rock as well. To see the **Chynoweth Cabin site, corral,** and the beginning of the **Chynoweth Trail,** turn west from the Cottonwood Wash Road 24.3 kms (15.1 miles) from Highway 89; or 38.8 kms (24.1 miles) from the KBT. To get to the **Ken Goulding Trail,** turn west off the main road about 25.3 kms (15.7 miles) from Highway 89; or 37.8 kms (23.5 miles) from the KBT. You can park and camp at all of these trailhead parking places. Or if going to **Castle Rock,** continue north on this road to a point about 27.2 kms (16.9 miles) from Highway 89; or 35.9 kms (22.3 miles) from the KBT. Park right on the road.

Trail/Route From where you park just east of **Castle Rock,** head west across Cottonwood Wash, and walk into the prominent little canyon coming down from the south side of Castle. Just inside the bottom of the drainage, veer left and scramble up a steep slope to the southwest. Higher up, contour north across the upper face of the slope, go around a little corner or pass of sorts, then scramble down to the dry creek bed below. There is no trail--just rugged route-finding. Continue west up this drainage until you can walk out on the right side onto the southeast buttress or ridge. Once on this smooth, rounded buttress, head northwest up toward the summit area. This will involve a little route-finding, but this part is easy. To get fotos of the back side of Castle Rock, use the drainage on the south and west sides. There you'll find some pretty good cattle trails in some places.

From where you park near the beginning of the **Ken Goulding Trail,** walk west 50m along a fence to the bottom of Cottonwood Wash and immediately turn northwest into a dry wash coming out of a minor canyon. Head that way for 200m; you may see a trail on the left. There at the very bottom of the steep part will be the trail straight ahead and against the vertical wall on the right. This part has been constructed, but once on top and heading north & northwest, you'll just follow a trail marked with cairns. Soon you'll turn west a ways, then north again, then slowly it veers northwest and west again; in this area it's sandy, but the trail is generally easy to follow. Just before you reach the high point marked **5770** (1759m) on the *Calico Peak 7 1/2' quad,* the trail will be running north again along the ridge top. From that mark, it's 200m to a narrow little gap or pass.

From there, continue north on a fading trail for 400m, then if you want to see the **Moki House** or Anasazi ruins, turn down to the left or west & southwest and follow a shallow drainage. After about another 400m, you'll be in big Navajo Sandstone bluffs or domes, and a dropoff of a couple of meters. The author tied a short rope to a bush and got down, then back up OK, but with 2 or more people, you should be able to help each other down & back up without a rope, if you choose.

From that little dropoff, walk northwest along a small canyon for 75-100m and look to the right. There should be an alcove with some ruins and the Moki House underneath. There are also a number of fairly recent signatures of cowboys *(Ken Goulding, June 1, 1929)* and a small pictograph. This site is about

Map 26, Lower Rush Beds Trails & Hikes: Castle Rock, Ken Goulding Trail, Moki House, Yellow Rock, Hidden Cache & The Cockscomb

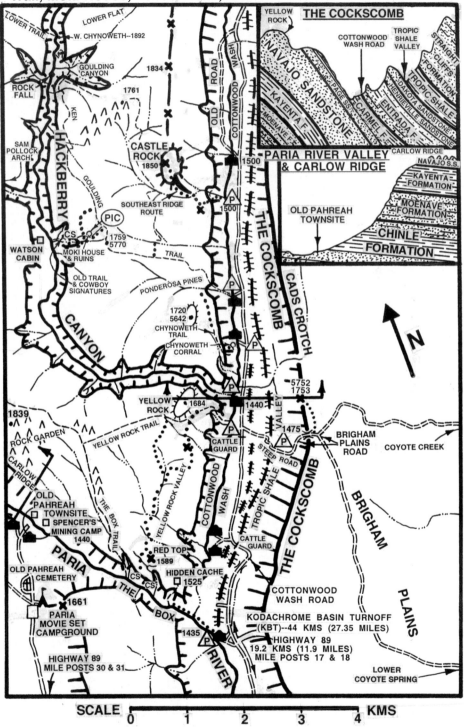

LOWER FLAT
LOWER TRAIL
W. CHYNOWETH--1892
1834
1761
GOULDING CANYON
ROCK FALL
KEN
SAM POLLOCK ARCH
HACKBERRY
CASTLE ROCK
1850
GOULDING
SOUTHEAST RIDGE ROUTE
PIC
CS
1759
5770
WATSON CABIN
MOKI HOUSE & RUINS
OLD TRAIL & COWBOY SIGNATURES
PONDEROSA PINES
TRAIL
CANYON
1720
5642
CHYNOWETH TRAIL
CHYNOWETH CORRAL
YELLOW ROCK
1684
YELLOW ROCK TRAIL
1839
ROCK GARDEN
CARLOW RIDGE
OLD PAHREAH TOWNSITE
SPENCER'S MINING CAMP
1440
OLD PAHREAH CEMETERY
PARIA
THE BOX TRAIL
YELLOW ROCK VALLEY
RED TOP
1589
CS
CS
HIDDEN CACHE
1525
THE BOX
1661
PARIA MOVIE SET CAMPGROUND
HIGHWAY 89 MILE POSTS 30 & 31
1435
RIVER

OLD ROAD
COTTONWOOD WASH
1500
P
1500
P
P
P
1440
CATTLE GUARD
1475
COTTONWOOD WASH
CATTLE GUARD
1589

THE COCKSCOMB
CADS CROTCH
5752
1753
TROPIC SHALE VALLEY
STEEP ROAD
THE COCKSCOMB
BRIGHAM PLAINS ROAD
COYOTE CREEK
BRIGHAM
PLAINS
COTTONWOOD WASH ROAD
KODACHROME BASIN TURNOFF (KBT)--44 KMS (27.35 MILES)
HIGHWAY 89 19.2 KMS (11.9 MILES) MILE POSTS 17 & 18
LOWER COYOTE SPRING

N

THE COCKSCOMB
YELLOW ROCK
COTTONWOOD WASH ROAD
TROPIC SHALE VALLEY
STRAIGHT CLIFFS FORMATION
NAVAJO SANDSTONE
PAGE SS.
CARMEL F.
TROPIC SHALE
DAKOTA SANDSTONE
HENRIEVILLE SANDSTONE
ENTRADA F.
KAYENTA F.
MOENAVE F.
CARLOW RIDGE
NAVAJO S.S.

PARIA RIVER VALLEY & CARLOW RIDGE
KAYENTA FORMATION
MOENAVE FORMATION
OLD PAHREAH TOWNSITE
CHINLE FORMATION

SCALE
0   1   2   3   4   KMS

143

Castle Rock from the west and the ridge where the Ken Goulding Trail runs. In this area, you can leave the trail to reach what locals call the Moki House. Notice the toadstool rocks in the foreground.

From the top of **The Cockscomb** near the Brigham Plains Road, you'll have one of the best views of the **Cottonwood Wash** and **Castle Rock**. In the far background to the right side is Table Cliff Plateau. Can you also see the Cottonwood Wash Road in the middle of the picture?

From the top of **The Cockscomb** looking west at **Yellow Rock**, mouth of Hackberry Canyon to the right & Mollies Nipple in the far background. The Yellow Rock Trail goes up the drainage to the left.

850m due east of Frank Watson's Cabin down in Hackberry Canyon. There is an old cowboy trail or route from the cabin up to these ruins, but they are not easy to find regardless of your approach. To read about the route (with cowboy signatures) from the Watson Cabin, see **Map 23**. Also, from this site, you can get back to the Ken Goulding Trail by walking north along the western face of some ledges for 500m, then veer east or northeast. This is the route taken by anyone riding horseback.

Now the Ken Goulding Trail again. For the first little ways north of the Moki House area, it'll be a little hard to follow this trail in the sand, but it heads due north with a few turns in & out of gullies. As you near the **Rockfall** (in the canyon bottom), the trail begins to veer a little to the northeast, then east as it drops down into what might be called **Goulding Canyon**. It's easy to follow in this region. At the bottom of the drainage, the trail immediately cuts back to the northwest on the north side. You'll see parts of a constructed trail there, then it runs north along a bench, and finally zig zags down the eastern wall of Hackberry Canyon on various benches. Several places have been rocked-up for cows. At the bottom, the trail veers north on the last or lowest bench and hits the creek almost exactly halfway between the **Rockfall & the Lower Trail** as shown (400m either way).

Going back up into Goulding Canyon for a moment. Right where the trail crosses the dry wash, if you walk upcanyon a little, you should see another constructed cow trail heading north and a little eastward. Ken Goulding Sr. and his son Ken Jr., cobbled-up a trail there somewhere (the author wasn't aware of it on his last hike) which runs up through some ledges and out on top of what they call the **Lower Flat.** This continues to be a pasture for Steve Goulding's (Ken Jr.'s son) cows in winter.

There's a good campsite right across the wash east of the **Chynoweth corral & old cabin site.** Just west of the corral is the foundation of a cabin. Here's what Ralph Chynoweth of Henrieville remembered about the first Cottonwood Wash Road, and their family cabin & corral: *We used to camp there before we built that little house. And one time we had some wild cattle out there and we had this great big old steer and my dad told me I could have it if I'd go get 'im. We went down there and camped in a trailer that night--this would have been late November, 1957. That cabin wasn't there then, and that road goin' down Cottonwood wasn't very good either. In most of the places where it is now is not where it was then. For most of the way above that old cabin, the road used to be on the west side of the wash, but over the years, they just kept improving it a little at a time. It was just a Jeep trail the first time they built it. We only had that trailer there about a year when we built that cabin. We had a ton and a half truck with a load of lumber on it--and I don't know how we ever got down there! It was my brothers Jack, Gene, Wade and myself who built the cabin. As near as I can remember, we built it in about 1958. We built the corral at the same time.*

I'd say that cabin burned down in the early 1980's. We don't know who burned it down, but it may have been the BLM, because they burned some others at the same time. Ours was burned down quite a while before those line cabins in the Escalante country were burned.

Regarding the building of the Cottonwood Wash Road, the best source is from the unpublished family history of Sam Pollock. His story went something like this. The road was built in 1957 by a cooperative effort organized by then 72-year-old Sam Pollock of Tropic, who wasn't paid a dime for his efforts. It included people from Bryce Valley, Escalante and Antimony. That group of people wanted a shortcut to the Lake Powell area to increase tourism in their own little area.

For the job, Pollock leased a bulldozer from the Soil Conservation Service and it was operated by Harvey Liston; a road grader was borrowed from Garfield Country, and it was driven by Loral Barton;

This is what locals in Bryce Valley call the **Moki House**, with only one structure still standing. It's hard to find whether coming to it from the Ken Goulding Trail, or up from the Watson Cabin.

Aerial view looking north up though the **Cockscomb Valley** holding Cottonwood Wash; to the left is Yellow Rock; up from there is Castle Rock; and in the far distance is Table Cliff Plateau.

Byron Davis donated a compressor and helped run it (it was used for only 9 days, and they blasted in only 2 places). Doyle Clark also helped on the operation. It took 100 days for planning, engineering and construction, but only 70 days to complete once they got rolling. The project was started on June 28, and completed in early October of 1957. At that time, they had a dedication ceremony at Rush Bed Springs.

The state of Utah had surveyed 2 routes for a road to Page and the Glen Canyon Dam. They chose the route east from Kanab because it was cheaper. The other more direct route through Cannonville and Cottonwood Wash would have cost $9.5 million. The road Sam Pollock built cost $5500. They got the money to build it from Garfield County, and from donations & sales of various kinds. Today it's a maintained county road. But it wasn't maintained at all in 2009, because of a squabble between the Monument BLM and the Kane County officials. Sooner or later things should improve again.

About 150m south of the cabin's foundation is the beginning of a very faint trail running west up to the top of the first little ridge. From the ridgetop, it heads north up on the Lower Rush Beds where it disappears. After about a km of no trail at all, one route heads west again. From there Ralph says: *That trail goes up a little canyon with lots of slickrock and some big ponderosa pines, then it heads north and connects with the Goulding Trail.* This trail/route isn't that good, so it's recommended you use the Ken Goulding Trail to get up on the Rush Beds.

The Cockscomb If you've parked at the base of the steep part of the road going up toward Brigham Plains, then you have only to walk about 2 kms to the pass overlooking The Cockscomb Valley. Or you can drive up, but it's 1st gear all the way on a clay surface, so don't try it when it's wet! From the pass, walk north along the eastern base of the ridge for about 500m, then climb straight up to the west. You'll soon reach the highest part of the ridge in this immediate area marked **5752** (1753m). This is the easiest part of The Cockscomb to get to and fotograph from. This is due east of Yellow Rock.

To reach the area between Hackberry and The Box, which is **Yellow Rock Valley,** leave your car parked near the junction with the Brigham Plains Road, and walk west on an emerging trail across Cottonwood Wash. Enter the first little drainage 450m south of the mouth of Hackberry. Once inside this tiny canyon, veer northwest and climb straight up an **old horse trail**. This is the beginning of the **Yellow Rock Trail.** Once on top, the trail is marked with stone cairns; so just head west toward the big dome which is **Yellow Rock**. It's made of the Navajo Sandstone, and is bright yellow with swirls of red, maroon, pink & white on the south side which resembles a *marble cake.* This is a marvelous place for color fotos. From the top of Yellow Rock, you'll have nice views looking north. There's another yellowish dome-like rock just to the north of lower Hackberry at 1720m altitude, and of course Castle Rock is in the distance. Looking south, you'll see lots of mostly-yellow dome rocks, plus **Red Top** in the distance.

There are no trails down through **Yellow Rock Valley**, so pick the route that suits you best. Two possible routes are shown on the map. At the southern end just above The Box, is a another colorful sight. It's what this writer calls **Red Top.** The top is as red as the brightest autumn leaves, the lower parts are all varicolored Navajo Sandstone. Red Top soars above everything else in the immediate area. You can also get into the Yellow Rock Valley from the Paria River and The Box Trail, as shown on the map.

Now for the trail to the **Hidden Cache.** From the car-park near the confluence of the Paria & Cottonwood Wash, walk northwest along the Paria to the beginning of The Box. This is about 800m from the car-park. About 300m into The Box, and on your right or north, is the 2nd minor drainage you come to. Head up and into this mini canyon. You should see 1 big cairn at the bottom, then a trail heading up the left side first, then it crosses over to the right side. Once on top and after the terrain levels, it's another 100m to where you'll see the first gray **metal shelter**. Just behind it 15m away, are the remains of a second metal box and the **rocked-up opening** of a **cave.** The story is told below.

Less than 1 km from the beginning of the Hidden Cache Trail, you'll come to the beginning of **The Box Trail** (halfway between the 2 is a panel of cowboy signatures & an old fence on the right or north side). It begins just above the middle of The Box and heads up a steep inclined ramp in a NNW direction. Once on top of the southernmost Rush Beds, this good trail heads north to a point due west of Yellow Rock. From there, one branch heads northwest, then north and follows Carlow Ridge all the way north to upper Hogeye Canyon. Read more about this trail under **Map 12**. But you can also turn east and walk along the **Yellow Rock Trail** back to Cottonwood Wash and the main road.

Elevations For The Cockscomb Hike, from 1475m altitude up to 1753m, or higher further north. Climbing Castle Rock, from just over 1500m where you park, up to 1850m on top. For Yellow Rock, you'll walk from 1440m up to 1684m, and for the Hidden Cache, it's from about 1435m to 1525m.

Time Needed From the Cottonwood Wash Road to the pass in The Cockscomb, is less than 2 kms. From the pass to the high point is another 700m. The round-trip hike can be done easily in a 2-3 hours--much less if you drive up to the pass. For Castle Rock, it should take up to about 2 hours to climb, 3-4 hours round-trip--maybe more. To explore the country between Yellow Rock and Red Top, you'll need no less than half a day and you'll want to be there in the middle part of the day. It's only about 1 1/2 km from the car-park to the Hidden Cache, and can be done in 20-25 minutes, one-way, or a couple of hours round-trip.

Water Take your own, and always have extra water in your car. There's usually water in both Cottonwood Wash and the Paria which can be used for washing.

Maps USGS or BLM map Smoky Mountain (1:100,000) for driving & orientation; Calico Peak & Fivemile Valley (1:24,000--7 1/2' quads) for hiking.

Main Attractions An interesting look at an unusual geologic feature fully exposed. Geology students shouldn't miss this one, as these are some of the most interesting hikes in this book. The view from the top of The Cockscomb, Yellow Rock or Castle Rock is spectacular. It's also one of the most fotogenic places covered by this book. Also, a short hike to what has become a local legend at the Hidden Cache.

Best Time to Hike Spring or fall, but this area can be visited anytime the Cottonwood Wash Road is dry.

Boots/Shoes Any boots or shoes, but a rugged pair for climbing The Cockscomb Ridge and Castle Rock. For Yellow Rock Valley, use running-type shoes because of the slickrock. You'll have to wade the Paria several times on the way to the Hidden Cache, so go prepared for wading.

Author's Experience The author parked at the bottom of the ridge, then walked up the road to The Cockscomb. Round-trip was about 1 1/2 hours. He climbed Castle Rock 3 times, with a lot of exploring along the way. He did some exploring around the west side on the second hike, and that took about 3 hours round-trip. One of his 3 hikes to Yellow Rock was south through the Yellow Rock Valley to Red Top, and back the same way to his car; that took about 3 1/3 hours. On 3 trips to the Hidden Cache via The Box route, it took about 1 hour each, round-trip. Another time he hiked to the Hidden Cache, up The Box Trail to an overlook of Old Pahreah, down the Yellow Rock Trail and back to his car in about 5 1/2 hours.

Above Aerial view of **Castle Rock** looking NEN with the Cottonwood Wash and Cockscomb Valley in the far upper right of this foto. We're looking at the southern side of the Castle Rock with the big slickrock ramp running from the lower right up to the summit area. To climb it, that's the route to take.

Right This is the south slope of **Yellow Rock**, one of the more colorful scenes anywhere. Be there about high noon on a clear day-- no clouds!

The Story of the Hidden Cache

The last hike to be added to the 1st Edition of this book happened quite by accident. While interviewing one of the old timers in Tropic, the story about a possible German spy and a cache of food and equipment was told. Later the author tracked down the people who originally found the cache, and got the full story.

It began on **February 8, 1953**. Harvey Chynoweth of Cannonville, his 4 sons, Jack, Gene, Wade & Ralph, and Harvey's brother Will Chynoweth, were running cows in the lower Cottonwood Wash and out to the east of The Cockscomb on the flats called Brigham Plains. They had worked all day, and arrived back at camp late. Camp was in the lower Cottonwood Wash, not far above where it flows into the Paria River, at the bottom end of The Box.

Since the bottom of the valley had been grazed-out by cows and there wasn't much feed for the horses, it was common practice for cattlemen working in the area to run their riding stock up on top of the Carlow Ridge or Rush Beds to the west where they could pasture at night. Up there they couldn't go far because of rough terrain and there was plenty of grass. Since Ralph was the youngest of the boys, he was chosen to take the horses up above the cliffs.

It was after dark, but there was a full moon and the sky was clear. Ralph recalls having trouble with one little sorrel pony which was trying to run away or something. At any rate, when the horses were left in the upper pasture, they were always hobbled so they could be found and caught easy the next morning. When Ralph finally got a hold of the little sorrel, he began putting the hobbles on it. But then something caught his eye. The moonlight was so bright, it reflected off something made of metal. He went over to investigate and found a couple of small metal sheds or boxes. He could see inside one of them and saw that somebody had lived there. He returned to camp a little spooked and told the story. No one believed him. They thought he was dreaming or just telling stories.

The next morning they all went back up to get the horses and saw in full light what was there. It was some kind of camp but hadn't been lived in for a long time. There were 2 galvanized metal boxes or shelters, measuring only about 1 1/4m x 2m x 2 1/2m each, and a cave which had the entrance cemented up with a little rock wall.

Inside one of the boxes was a bed with blankets on it, all tucked in neatly; a small metal wood burning stove which was new and apparently hadn't been used; and an old .22 rifle which hung above the door. The .22 was a hex-barreled single shot, which broke in the middle to load, like some single-shot shotguns. There were also several new denim shirts, underwear, socks, pajamas, 2 pair of boots, toothbrush, toothpaste, and neatly folded napkins. The clothing items were neatly put together and folded, like what you'd find in the military and ready for inspection. Besides these clothes, was some kind of a

The **Hidden Cache**. This foto shows the little **cave** that was walled-up at the front to create a warm and comfortable shelter. Nearby is what remains of one of the little metal shelters that was used to store food and other supplies. Time and gravity are slowly having an effect on it.

Inside the **cave** at the **Hidden Cache**. The outside face is shown in the foto above. The author is holding one end of the electric wire that ran from a windmill outside, to an electric hot plate inside. In 2009, a little wood burning stove was still inside as well. The cement used to mortar-up the wall must have been the best quality, because it looks like it could have been built a month ago.

149

military uniform. One man swears it was from W.W.I.

In the other metal shelter, and very neatly packed away, was a food cache of sizable proportions. The food cache included jars or buckets of peanut butter, canned milk, chocolate, sugar, rice, flour, raisins, canned fish, sardines, corned beef, and other canned goods. Most of the cans had rusted badly, from the inside out, and had leaked, spoiling the contents. Indications were that it had been there for some time. One witness said they found one can of corned beef dated 1942.

Just behind the 2 metal shelters, was a small cave. The front of this cave, measuring about 1m x 2m, had been sealed up with a rock & mortar wall. The job was so well done, that in 2009 when the author last saw it, it appeared as if it could have been made only a month or so before. The entrance passage was a small metal-framed window, like the kind you see in some homes or buildings of W.W.II vintage. The inside of the cave had been dug out some, and it measured about 1 1/2m x 2m at the front end, and it tapered back to the rear about 4m. Not much headroom, but cozy.

Inside the cave, the Chynoweths found an electric hot plate and several 5-gallon (19 liter) water storage jars full of water. The fact that they hadn't frozen and broken, indicates how well insulated the cave was in winter. There were also a bunch of batteries of various kinds.

Right in the corner next to the entrance, are 3 wires which were built into the rock & mortar wall. These wires led outside to a windmill contraption and a generator mounted on a rock behind the cave. The single blade propeller was 4-5m long, and mounted horizontally (instead of vertically as is usually the case with most windmills). The cave had built-in wiring so electricity generated by the windmill generator outside could be used for lights or cooking inside.

According to the newspaper report in the March 19, 1953, *Garfield County News* in Panguitch (a week later in the Kanab paper), all identifiable marks on the generator and other equipment found, had been scratched off. Even the numbers on a thermometer had been removed! Jack Chynoweth also stated that all labels from canned goods and from all clothes were also removed.

About 16 years after this story was told to the author, and in 2003, he went back to Ralph Chynoweth in Henrieville and asked more questions about the place, and he had this to say about what happened after they found the cache: *We went down there on horseback, down through Cottonwood, but my Dad, Harvey Chynoweth couldn't ride a horse, his hips was gone. So he came on down there in the Jeep so he could be with us. There wasn't no road in there then, not down Cottonwood Wash. He came right down through the Piree Crik, past Old Pahreah and through the Paria Box and up to our camp. If there would have been a road, we would have fed the horses hay; that's the reason we took the horses up on top to feed.*

We got all that stuff out of there and down to camp--we hauled it off with a pack horse. We carried everything that we thought was of any value at all, and carried it out of there, Dad carried some of it out in the Jeep, and we hauled some of it on pack horses. And we went down there several times to haul that stuff off. We had an agreement between the bunch of us that we'd never say nothin' to nobody. We were going to keep it a secret, because we wanted to go back and look around more. Maybe find something else (?).

Now, Dad and my Uncle Will and brothers, felt like them people had robbed a bank, or got into something like that, and they were going to come back there and have a place to stay. Well, we brought this stuff home and had it stored here for quite a long period of time before we told anybody about it. We kept that stuff in my Dad's shed down here. I didn't get to go after that first trip because I was just 16 and still going to school; but my brothers [and Darrel Blackwell & George Thompson] and my uncle and Dad, they all went down and they spent several days down there and searched that whole area. But it was some length of time after that before anybody else knew anything about it.

It was about a month and a half after they found the cache--Ralph thought it was longer--that they finally called the Sheriff of Kane County, Mason Meeks, and told him the story. Shortly thereafter, the Sheriff and Highway Patrolman Merrill Johnson, Merle (Peaches) Beard, and others, went to the Chynoweths place in Henrieville and took all the booty away.

At the time, Ralph told the Sheriff, that he had found the cache, including the .22 rifle, and that he wanted it back. That was the only thing he cared about. OK, no problem! But in the end nothing was ever returned to the Chynoweths--and this has been a burr under Ralph's saddle ever since.

Sheriff Meeks sent a report to the FBI. Later those investigating the case contacted Meeks and it was their speculation that whoever set up the place had likely been a spy during WWII (?).

But there were several different theories advanced as to who built the cache: (1) Who ever built it was a deserter from the army and on the run; (2) That he was a draft dodger; (3) He was just an old hermit, who happened to have been in WWI; (4) He had worked for Charles H. Spencer in the gold diggings at Old Pahreah, and had returned to hide out; (5) And because some of the clothing items had foreign labels (French), some thought he may have been a spy of some kind. The radio and generator equipment prompted this idea.

There was also endless speculation as to how this person may have gotten all the equipment and food there without being detected At the time the man was there, which must have been in the early to mid-1940's, and during WWII, there were no roads into the area except the one to Old Pahreah. When this story finally came to light, there was all kinds of talk about it, and then people started remembering events that had happened in the previous years which may have had a connection with the cache.

The one which seems to hold the most credibility is the story told by Calvin C. Johnson of Kanab, the man who presently (with sons) owns the Nipple Ranch. He remembered the time as being in 1944 or '45. On several occasions he and other cattlemen in the area of Old Pahreah, had seen a Willeys Jeep parked inside The Box, and at the bottom of the cliffs where the cache was later found. Calvin also remembers: *My brother and I were the first ones who knew of him when he was out there. My brother knew him better than I did. He would occasionally come to town in his old Jeep. Out there we would wave at 'im and he'd stop and say hello, but he had a heavy accent and we kinda figured he was a German spy or something. He was just a real odd, quiet type of fellow. All he'd do is stop and we'd say hi--we didn't ask him many questions, and he just wouldn't answer--he wouldn't talk. We just talked about the time of day, or the weather, how he was doin'. He really had a real heavy German accent. I think he was maybe 30-35 years old at that time. He had army camouflage-type clothing with a hood. He had a heavy beard with a medium complexion. He was about 6 foot tall and weighed about 180 lbs.* Calvin also recalls the boys he rode with on the range used to call this fellow, *"our little German spy"*. Apparently this had more meaning in 1953 after the cache was discovered, than it did earlier.

Another event happened in 1963, which may have had a connection with this place. At that time, the Sheriff of Kane County was Leonard Johnson. His family lived in the polygamist community of Short Creek, now called Colorado City, Arizona, and/or Hildale, Utah. He had a pilot's license and once, while flying in the area between Hurricane Mesa and Short Creek, spotted something from the air. Later, they went to it on the ground, and found another small metal cabin full of food similar to the cache near Old Pahreah. Nothing else was found in that cache, but everyone familiar with the 2 sites seemed to think there was a connection.

This picture shows the same metal box or shelter at the **Hidden Cache** as the one below which was taken in 2009. This old foto was taken in February, 1953. Shown here are L to R--Will Chynoweth, Harvey Chynoweth (behind), George Thompson and Jack & Gene Chynoweth.

This is the 2nd metal box located at the **Hidden Cache**. This one is still in good condition and it was the one with the bed, most of the clothing, blankets, and the .22 rifle that Ralph Chynoweth never got back from Kanab Sheriff Mason Meeks.

From in front of the cave at **Hidden Cache**; **Left** Bottled water, batteries, etc. **Right** L to R--Jack Chynoweth, his father Harvey inside the cave, and brother Gene.

Above This is the metal box at the **Hidden Cache** that had the bed and .22 rifle. It also had a shelf above the bed, and a small window at the back as shown.

Above Right Inside the cave at the **Hidden Cache** were large bottles of water and batteries and what looks like bottled fruit or preserves.

Right Having lunch down in Cottonwood Wash. These are the guys who carried all the supplies out of the Hidden Cache in late February, 1953. L to R are Harvey Chynoweth, Gene Chynoweth, Darrel (Browny) Blackwell, Jack Chynoweth and Will Chynoweth. George Thompson took this picture. (All old pictures on this page are from Darrel Blackwell, former CCC enrollee, now of Layton, Utah)

These are members of the **Thompkins Expedition** of 1939, who rode horses all the way from Bryce Valley into what locals call the *Lower Country*, which is Wahweap and the Lake Powell area. From L to R are: Earl Smith, Thompkins, the leader & organizer of the expedition, Tom W. Smith (Earl's brother, and son of the 2nd and last Mormon Bishop of Pahreah), Kay Clark and Byron Davies. This picture is in the possession of LaKay Clark Quilter of Henrieville. She is Kay's daughter and was born after the group went on this trip, but she can't remember the purpose of the expediltion. A good guess is, Thompkins was after fotographs of the canyon country, as the camera that took this picture was a good one.

Left Inside the alcove cave that holds the **Moki House** in the lower Rush Beds. Notice the single pictograph on the wall. **Right** This is the beginning of the **Box Trail**. In the background is The Box of the Paria River, which is only about 2 kms south or downstream from the former townsite of Old Pahreah. The part you see here is a constructed cattle trail.

153

The Hattie Green Mine and Fivemile Ranch

Location & Access Perhaps the easiest hike, and the one with the easiest access in this book, is the trail to the **Hattie Green Mine**. The Hattie Green is an old copper mine sitting right on top of The Cockscomb, sometimes known further south as the East Kaibab Monocline. This mine consists of 2 main tunnels and 3 other pits, prospects or adits. The first claim on the site was filed in 1893. Get more information on this mine under **Mining History** in the back of this book.

The location of this hike is just off Highway 89 about halfway between Kanab & Page. It's also about 11 kms (7 miles) northwest of the Paria Ranger Station & Visitor Center. Stop at the parking place next to the highway & gate about 100m south of **new mile post 28**. That gate marks the beginning of the road to the mine. If you have a low clearance car, it might be best to park there and walk.

Or with a HCV (in 2009 it was a pretty good road, even for cars), and if the gate near the highway is not locked, drive through and shut the gate behind you. Proceed across the dry sandy wash heading south. After about 500m (.3 mile) turn east onto the most-used road. Follow this fairly well-used track into the small north-south running canyon leading to the mine. About 1.4 kms (0.9 mile) from the highway, park under a big piñon pine (this makes a good campsite as well). To reach this place you'll be **crossing a small piece of private land,** so if you see any **Private Land** or **No Trespassing signs,** park in the parking place next to the highway and walk--hopefully that won't bother anyone (?).

Trail/Route If you have a LC car, it might be best to park it at the gate and walk along the road beginning near mile post 28. Follow the track as described above, around the southern end of a low minor sub-ridge of The Cockscomb.

From where the road ends at the piñon pine & campsite, walk north about 750m, then be looking to the left or west for a small man-made stone structure (a pile of rocks). About 25m north of that stone pile, look uphill to the east for some cairns marking the lower part of the trail. Further up, you'll see a real trail, which may have been an old wagon road. This 1st trail takes you to the top of **The Cockscomb** where some of the mining activity took place, including the **Eastern Tunnel**, located 50m down the east side, and a pile of copper ore located right on the crest of the ridge.

A 2nd trail runs up to the **western tunnel**. It begins about 50m north of where the 1st trail takes off. The bottom of this trail is marked by cairns, but a little further up, it turns into a real trail as well. At the entrance to the western tunnel is a pile of what looks like old stove pipes, but which must have been used to circulate air inside the tunnel (?).

Until 2008 or so, you could explore the tunnels, but then the Utah Division of Natural Resources, closed both entrances for safety reasons; the **east-side tunnel** was bricked-up, the **west-side tunnel** has a metal cage installed. But here's what the author found in 2003; about 25m inside the **eastern tunnel** is a wooden doorway with 1920 inscribed on it; just beyond that is a 4m-deep vertical shaft. Above it is a wooden hand-cranked hoist which brought ore from a 2nd lower tunnel up to the main passage. Both tunnels go back only about 10m beyond the hoist. Inside the **western tunnel** are wooden rails (you can still see these) for small ore cars, then after maybe 40m, one tunnel goes left or north a short distance only, another heads straight ahead another 25m or so, and the one going right or south, goes on for a long ways, but to reach the end you'll have to crawl as it's caved in further along. This one has some old miner's signatures on the walls going back to the 1940's, maybe older (?). In 2009, the author found a **3rd tunnel** on the west side, but it only goes back about 15m and has nothing to see.

Elevations Highway parking, 1500m; end of HCV road, 1550m; the ridge-top ore heap, about 1675m.

Time Needed From the highway to the mine is only about 2 kms, and should take 2-3 hours, round-trip. If hiking from the piñon pine & campsite, only 1-2 hours will be needed, round-trip.

Water There's none around so take water in your car & pack.

Maps USGS or BLM map Smoky Mountain (1:100,000) for driving & orientation; and Fivemile Valley (1:24,000--7 1/2' quad) for hiking.

Main Attractions A couple of old heaps of copper ore.

Best Time to Hike Spring or fall, but can be done year-round.

Boots/Shoes Any comfortable boots or shoes. Simple running shoes are best.

Author's Experience The author has been there 6 times.

The Fivemile Ranch

Added to the Hattie Green Mine hike is a little history on one of the nearby ranches. The **Fivemile Ranch** is one of the least-known outposts mentioned in this book. It's also one of the very last places to have been homesteaded in the entire region. The ranch is located in what is called Hattie Green Valley, about 8 kms (5 miles) due south of Old Pahreah--thus the name Fivemile. At least one old-timer from Tropic says the original name of the place was the Cottonwood Ranch, as it's located immediately below **Cottonwood Spring.** The ranch is located west of The Cockscomb and east of Highway 89.

To get there, turn east off Highway 89 between **mile posts 28 & 29**, and possibly park at or near the gate where the road enters the **electric substation** site. If that gate isn't locked, you can drive through but always close it behind you. From the highway, drive 250m north past the substation and to a fence & gate; from there turn east for 40m and park. If you have a 4WD, you can get closer to either spring shown on this map, but the main roads are all washed-out and ATV's have created a maze of tracks going nowhere. So, best to park along the old fence and walk from there.

The earliest written record the Kane County courthouse has on the Fivemile Ranch is dated May 11, 1913. That's when William J. Henderson filed a claim on the water rights to one or both of the springs involved with the Fivemile Ranch spread. To the north is the Fivemile Spring; to the south about 1 km is Cottonwood Spring--this is where the old ranch house is located.

The next recorded information about Fivemile Ranch was on June 17, 1937. This was when **Herman Mangum** got a patent deed on it from the government under the Homestead Act. To have gotten it under the Homestead Act, he would have had to live there, or made improvements to the place for 5 years, before getting title to the land, which apparently came in 1937. Herman was the son of Long John W. Mangum.

The John Mangum family lived in or around Old Pahreah after it was mostly abandoned in the early 1900's. Later on, Herm Pollock, Wallace Ott, and Kay Clark remembered the family when they lived in The Dugout, 2-3 kms north of Old Pahreah. That was in the late 1920's and early 1930's (?).

Here's a short history of the little house located just west or below Cottonwood Spring. In 1930, a crew of roughnecks from the Midwest Oil Company was drilling a test hole in the northern end of the Rush Beds, in the area south of Round Valley Draw, and south and a little west of Grosvenor (Butler Valley) Arch. That outfit pumped water to their camp & drill site from what has been called ever since,

Map 27, The Hattie Green Mine and Fivemile Ranch

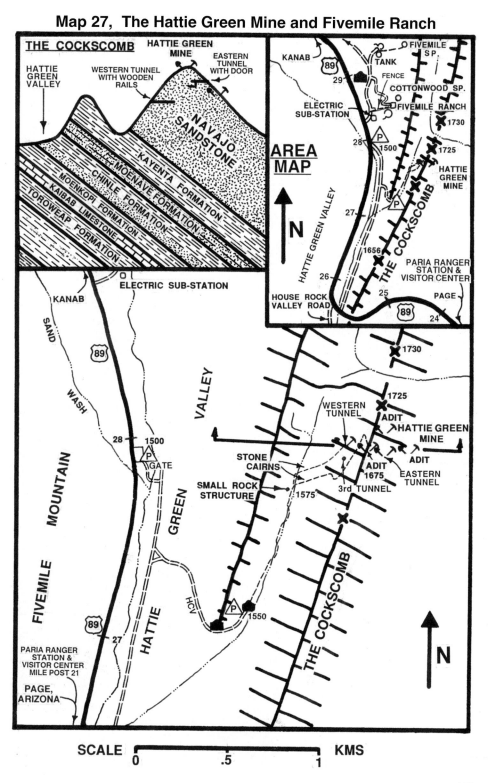

SCALE
0   .5   1   KMS

155

Pump House Spring & Canyon. That place is located in upper Cottonwood Wash where the water begins to flow. When their hole came up dry, they abandoned the site and sold parts, equipment and lumber to various local people. One of those people was Long John W. Mangum, who bought one or more wagon loads of used lumber.

Long John and his son Herman, along with Jim Ed Smith and his son Layton, hauled the lumber off the Rush Beds along the **Old Wagon Road** and down Cottonwood Wash to Cottonwood Spring in the Hattie Creek Valley, before a road was built. That was sometime between 1932 & '35. Just southwest of the Cottonwood Spring, they built a small frame, 2-room house out of the used lumber. It wasn't too fancy, and had no insulation. The back room wall used to be papered; not with wallpaper, but with pages from 1930's magazines. This homemade wallpaper job is gone today, but before, you could read up on events from the 1930's. The author once saw an advertisement for new Dodge cars selling for $640.

Throughout the years, the area around the Fivemile Homestead has been owned by 2 individuals. Apparently the Fivemile Spring was held by Jim Henderson through 1945, but before that, Delmar G. Robinson of Kanab, bought out the Fivemile Ranch and Cottonwood Spring from the Mangums in May, 1942. The Mangums then headed for Idaho and greener pastures.

Later on, in September 1959, it was deeded over to Delmar's son, Don R. Robinson. Finally in 1963, the Litchfield Company obtained a Quit Claim Deed on at least part of the property around the spring and ranch house. In the late 1980's, Jeff Johnson of Kanab leased the place and ran cows there.

If you want to visit the old ranch, best to park at or just north of the substation, and walk; just don't go in hunting for some kind of souvenirs because both are on private land. From the parking place suggested, walk east right along the fence line; that will take you straight to the ranch. There's not much to see, just the shack and some wire corrals & fences. If you see any **No Trespassing** signs, **Stop.**

Above Left This is all you'll see about 5m into the **eastern tunnel** at the **Hattie Green Mine**. Some time in about 2008, mining people bricked-up the entrance so no one could enter--they claim it was done for safety reasons.

Above Right And this is what you'll be greeted by only about 3m into the **western tunnel**. They claim it was for the safety of the general public.

Right The **western tunnel** opening with pipe that appears to have been used for moving fresh air into the mine. The entrance to this tunnel is now closed.

Above The little house at **Fivemile Ranch**. This was made with lumber from the **Old 1930 Rush Beds Oil Well**. It was brought down the Old Wagon Road in Cottonwood Wash before a real road existed. Read more in the text on the opposite page; or along with **Map 25**, page 136.

Left This is the soft red clay beds over which the **Old Wagon Road** ran in the upper end of Cottonwood Wash. You can just barely see the trail at the top between 2 small bushes, then running down the middle of the foto. In the lower half of the picture, it veers to the left and near the edge of the red clays. This is where Long John Mangum and his son Herman, along with Jim Ed Smith and his son Layton, hauled the lumber off the Rush Beds along the Old Wagon Road and down Cottonwood Wash to Cottonwood Spring in the Hattie Green Valley. This was all before a real road was built.

The Rimrocks and Wahweap Creek Toadstools, Side Step Canyon, the Yellow Toadstool & Chimney Rock

Location & Access Featured here are some short hikes to several groups of **toadstool (TD)**, hoodoo or mushroom-like rocks. Several groups of these are located immediately north of Highway 89, north & east of the Paria Ranger Station & Visitor Center, and in the area known as **The Rimrocks**. To get to this area using **Map 28A**, drive along Highway 89 about halfway between Page & Kanab. Between mile posts 19 & 21 are 4 minor valleys running north from the highway into The Rimrocks. Use this map to locate the various parking places. The most popular hike, and most-used starting point, is at the bottom of **Valley 4**. This parking place is halfway between mile posts **19 & 20**; going there will take you to the **Red Toadstool**. Another starting point begins just north & across the highway from the Visitor Center called here **Valley 1**. For closeup views of the **best** group of TD in this area, drive along Highway 89 to between **mile posts 17 & 18**, then turn north onto the **Cottonwood Wash Road**. After 4.6 kms (2.9 miles), stop & park next to the road on the left or west where a little side-road is found.

Another area with perhaps the most interesting group of TD is located just outside the boundaries of the Paria River along **Wahweap Creek**. To get there using **Map 28B**, drive along Highway 89. Between mile posts 17 & 18 turn north onto the Cottonwood Wash Road (Km & Mile 0). Drive 2.25 kms (1.4 miles) and turn right or east onto another good graded road. If weather is threatening, or the roads are already wet, stay out of this area--**this is clay country which means slick roads when wet!**

Almost immediately you'll pass under some big power lines heading northeast. At Km 6.1 (Mile 3.8) is a road turning off to the right; this 4WD track runs south along Coyote Creek to some TD or chimney-like towers below. But continue eastward; you'll soon cross Coyote Creek which is the only real rough place on this road, then at Km 7.3 (Mile 4.55) is a large catchment called **Blue Cove Pond**. At Km 13 (Mile 8.1) the **White Sands Road** turns south toward Big Water--but it's sandy in places! Read more below. At Km 15 (Mile 9.3) is a fence & gate just beyond another stock pond; just beyond that is a steep dugway made of gray Tropic Shale. Finally, at Km 17.1 (Mile 10.6) you'll come to Wahweap Creek and a gate in the fence on the right. If things are dry and you have a HCV, you can continue south along Wahweap from there, but that gate in Section 8 is the end of the road. Be aware, if you drive a vehicle south down the creek bed, you'll be in a wilderness study area (WSA), which is **illegal**.

To reach what one German website is calling **Side Step Canyon**, turn south onto the White Sands Road and drive for 1.9 kms (1.2 miles) to a fence & gate. Park there 600m west of Side Step.

If the weather is bad and the road to Wahweap Creek is too muddy, there is another way. To do that, drive along Highway 89 to **Big Water** (formerly known as Glen Canyon City). Just west of **mile post 7**, head north along the main road in town. Follow this as it veers northwest, then descends to the valley below and the Wahweap State Fish Hatchery (4.1 kms/2.6 miles from the highway). Continue northwest on the generally good road to Km 6.2 (Mile 3.8) and park at the **Wahweap Trailhead**.

To reach the **Yellow Toadstool** near **Chimney Rock**, drive to **mile post 13** on Highway 89 and turn north. Continue north under some big power lines, past a corral and stock ponds, then at **Km 5.8 (Mile 3.6)** is a fence & gate with a sign "wilderness area beyond". However, everyone seems to be ignoring the sign and continuing north (?). If it's actually blocked off, you'll have to walk from there; or drive on as everyone else was doing in 6/2009! If driving, continue north to **Km 7 (Mile 4.4)** and veer right into a little side-drainage of Chimney Rock Canyon. After another 300-400m, turn right or east and drive to the end of the road at **Km 7.9 (Mile 4.9)** and park. This is 650m northwest of Chimney Rock.

Trail/Route Map 28A--From the bottom of **Valley 1,** hop the fence carefully and walk north or northeast for a little over 1 km. The area northeast of the trailhead has many TD rocks high on the shoulder of a buttress. In Valley 2, you can just barely see some TD high above, while Valley 3 has nothing of interest. From the trailhead in **Valley 4,** walk through a hiker's gate heading north on a well-used trail; this is the most popular TD hike in the area. You'll soon pass a trail register. At the head of this valley is one very prominent TD, then several more just beyond that. Other TD can be seen to the west.

If starting from the north & the Cottonwood Wash Road, walk southwest for 1 km along an emerging hiker's trail in the direction of the highest point on the horizon--better have a compass to do this! Once on the rim, one group of TD should be just below and to the left (east). Follow the map--there's now a trail down to the next level or bench. From that group, you can bench-walk southwest and around the corner of a jutting point to see a 2nd group which is the same bunch you see if walking northeast up Valley 1. There are other scattered TD in the area.

Map 28B--From the gate on **Wahweap Creek**, walk south along the right or west side of the dry wash. After 2 kms, you'll come to the first group of TD on the right or west in a little hollow formed by the white cliffs of the Gunsight Butte Member of the Entrada Formation. This is the **best group**. Around the corner 400m in the next indentation of the canyon wall is another really good group. These are both in the NE 1/4 of Section 17, T42S, R2E. Others are just south of that. If you walk in from the Wahweap Trailhead, it will take a couple of hours of walking up Wahweap Creek to reach this same area.

From the **gate** on the White Sands Road, walk ENE along the fence line toward the head of **Side Step Canyon**. Route-find around the south rim of this indentation to the **West Fork** of Wahweap Creek. There are ways to the bottom, and ways to get up to the rim on the east side. Shoot fotos from inside, or from either rim. Nice place.

From the trailhead in Chimney Rock Canyon, walk east a ways then veer north on an emerging trail to the base of **Yellow Toadstool**. From the same trailhead, hike to **Chimney Rock** as well, but instead of turning north, turn south and make your way along more than one trail. There are some cowboy signatures on Chimney Rock, including *Sam Pollock, Nov. 29, 1919* and *Art Chynoweth, May 1, 1917*.

Elevations Highway trailheads,1335m; Cottonwood Wash Road parking, 1470m; Wahweap Creek, 1310m; Side Step Canyon Trailhead, 1399m; Yellow Toadstool Trailhead, 1335m.

Time Needed In The Rimrocks, about 45 minutes to an hour round-trip for each hike--maybe longer for serious fotographers. Along Wahweap Creek, maybe 2 hours, perhaps longer for foto hounds. Two or 3 hours for the area around Side Step Canyon, and 1-2 hours for Yellow Toadstool, and nearby areas.

Water There's a well & tap about 40m west of the Visitor Center. Take plenty if going to Wahweap Creek.

Maps USGS or BLM maps Kanab & Smoky Mountain (1:100,000) for driving & orientation; West Clark Bench, Bridger Point, Lower Coyote Spring & Nipple Butte (1:24,000--7 1/2" quads) for hiking.

Main Attractions These fotogenic Toadstool/Mushroom/Hoodoo-like features were created by 2 types of rocks with contrasting erosional characteristics. The pedestal part of the TD is white sandstone and believed to be the Gunsight Butte Member of the Entrada Sandstone Formation. This is the white fine-grained massive sandstone with a red layer at the bottom forming most of the higher cliffs in The Rim-

Map 28A, The Rimrocks Toadstools

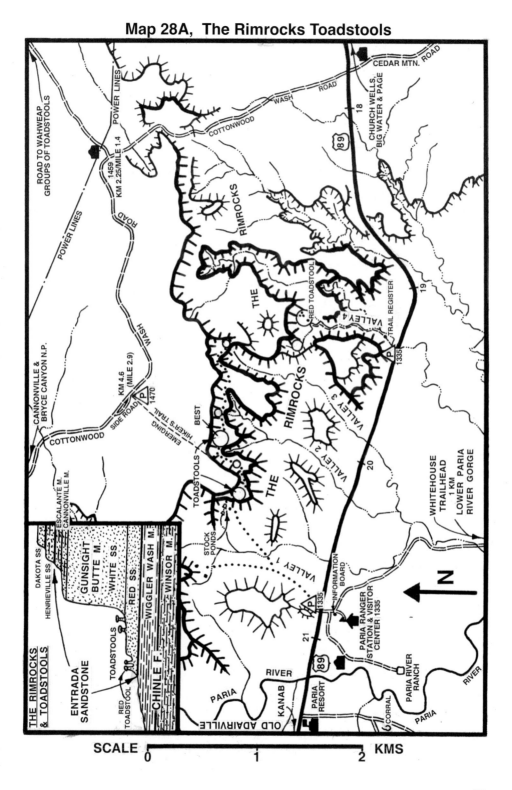

SCALE

0   1   2   KMS

Map 28B, The Wahweap Creek Toadstools, Side Step Canyon, the Yellow Toadstool & Chimney Rock

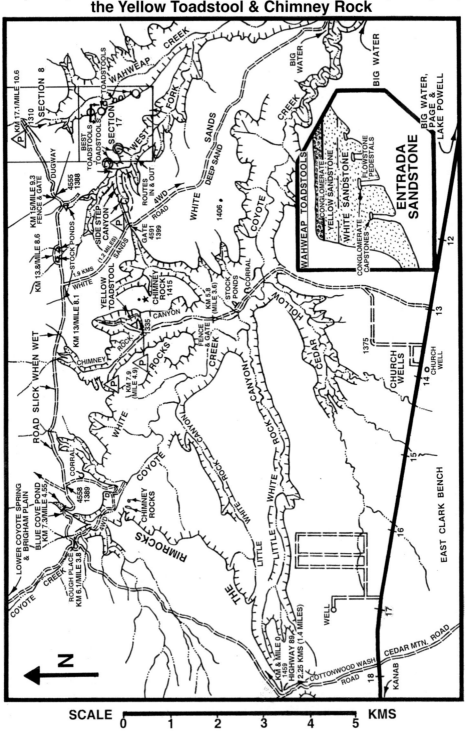

SCALE

0   1   2   3   4   5   KMS

rocks. The capstone in The Rimrocks is a gray more weather-resistent sandstone with some limestone--at least the erosional features look like limy sandstone (?). This could be from an upper layer of the Entrada or Henrieville Formations, or perhaps part of the Dakota Sandstone. For sure, it's from one of the layers above the Gunsight Butte, and below the Tropic Shale. See the Geology Cross-Section of the Paria in the back of this book.

The Wahweap Creek TD have reddish conglomerate capstones or topknots. On the canyon wall this is the layer immediately above the white Gunsight Butte Member. This white fine-grained friable (which means the grains of sand can be rubbed off easily) sandstone is the pedestal. The unique thing about this rock is, when it rains and the outer surface of the pedestal gets wet, gravity pulls the outer one centimeter down and it looks just like flowstone in most limestone caves. It's as if these pedestals are made of sugar and with each rainstorm are slowly melting away. This is truly a unique place.

BYU geologist Tom Morris says this sandstone appears to fall into the category of **Quartz arenite** (more than 90% of the grains are derived from quartzite). The cement or matrix holding the grains together is calcium carbonate, a kind of limestone.

Over thousands of years, parts of the limy sandstone or conglomerate caprock broke off and rolled downhill to rest on top of a bench or a more eroded part of the Gunsight Butte Member. Then the caprock, being more weather-resistent, shielded the softer white fine-grained sandstone below from eroding away. After many years, all that's left is a pedestal and a chunk of capstone balanced on top.
Best Time to Hike Spring or fall, or anytime the roads are dry.
Boots/Shoes Any comfortable shoe will do as these are very short & easy hikes.
Author's Experience He spent about 1 hour in Valley 1, about 45 minutes going up Valley 4, and 1 1/4 hours exploring the best group from the Cottonwood Wash Road. About 1 1/2 hours at the Wahweap site; Side Step Canyon area, 4 3/4 hours; Yellow Toadstool & Chimney Rock, 45 minutes.

Left This is one of the toadstools just behind or north of the more-famous **Red Toadstool**, located in Valley 4, just north of Highway 89. There are several in this area. **Right** This toadstool is in the 2nd group you come to when walking south from the **Wahweap Trailhead** in Section 17. See Map 28B.

Left This little cluster of toadstools is in the **best** group within the **Rimrock Toadstools**. Get to these from the Cottonwood Wash Road. **Right** This cluster of toadstools are high on a buttress, and near the head of **Valley 1** in the **Rimrocks** just north of the Paria Ranger Station.

Left The **Yellow Toadstool**, located due north of **Chimney Rock** and 5-6 kms due west of the Wahweap Toadstools. **Right** One of many toadstools labeled **Best Toadstools** on Map 28B. These are part of the first group you come to while walking down Wahweap Creek from the trailhead. The soft white fine-grained friable sandstone appears to flow or melt like sugar after rains.

Above Left A nice tower or toadstool located just east of the mouth of **Side Step Canyon**.

Above Right This is the well-known **Red Toadstool**, located in the Rimrocks section just northeast of the Paria River Ranger Station.

Left This is perhaps the most famous toadstool of all. It's located in the **first group** as you walk south down along **Wahweap Creek** from the trailhead. The 2 clusters along Wahweap are among the most-fotogenic of all. Be in this area in the morning to mid-day hours for the best sun & light.

The Buckskin Gulch & Paria River Loop-Hike--Part 1

Location & Access This section, **Map 29 and Part 1,** includes the upper part of what is traditionally known as the Paria River hike, and its best-known tributary, the **Buckskin Gulch**. This map covers the upper part of the **Lower Paria River Gorge** down to The Confluence which is where the Buckskin Gulch enters from the west. It also shows the entire Buckskin Gulch and its 3 trailhead entry points.

Map 30 and Part 2 begins at **The Confluence** and includes that part of the Paria River Gorge down to **Wrather Canyon & Arch**. This is the best part of the Paria because it has many springs, good narrows, excellent campsites, an old historic trail to the rim, and at least one good panel of petroglyphs.

Map 31 and Part 3 shows the Paria River from **Wrather Canyon** down to **Bush Head Canyon**. This is where the gorge begins to open up and becomes wider. This is also where it begins to look more like the Grand Canyon. This section has one of the best arches in the world, 4 routes to the rim for fine views of the canyon below, more good springs & water, campsites, and more petroglyphs.

The last part of the Paria River Gorge is shown on **Map 32 and Part 4**. It begins at **Bush Head Canyon** and ends at **Lee's Ferry** on the Colorado River. The canyon in this section opens up wide and has old ranches, some abandoned uranium prospects, adits or mines, and some of the best petroglyphs or rock art on boulders the author has seen. Each of these segments could be a one-day hike, but to see all the side-canyons, and do side-trips, it may take 5-6 days. Most people do the entire hike in 3-4 days.

In 1984, all of this Lower Paria River Canyon and the Vermilion Cliffs, was put aside as a wilderness area. Now this one large crescent-shaped region is officially called the **Paria Canyon--Vermilion Cliffs Wilderness Area**. It includes all of the Paria Canyon from about the power lines below the White House Trailhead and the Buckskin Gulch, down to Lee's Ferry, then west following the Vermilion Cliffs to the upper House Rock Valley to the west. Then in 2000, the **Vermilion Cliffs National Monument** was created. It includes all of the Sand Hills (Paria Plateau), the wilderness area mentioned above, plus almost all land between the House Rock & Coyote Valleys on the west, Highway 89A on the south, the Lower Paria River Gorge on the east & northeast, and the Utah-Arizona state line on the north.

There are 4 ways to get into this gorge, all of which are from Highway 89 which runs between Page & Kanab. The normal entry point for the Paria is the **White House Trailhead.** It's the easiest to access and can be used regardless of the weather conditions, as it's at the end of a graveled road. The other 3 entries are into the Buckskin Gulch. They are; the **Middle Trail/Route** on top of West Clark Bench, **The Buckskin,** and the **Wire Pass**. All these are discussed later.

The real starting point for all hikes in the Paria River & Buckskin Gulch is at the **Paria Ranger Station & Visitor Center.** It's located about halfway between Kanab & Page and between **mile posts 20 & 21** on Highway 89 (and 200m to the south). Be sure to stop there before entering the canyons and talk to a BLM employee or volunteer. They sell a limited number of books, maps and post cards, etc. It's open from 8:30 am to 5 pm daily from about March 15 to November 15. At some time in the future, and because of the new Grand Staircase-Escalante National Monument (GSENM), it may remain open year-round (but not as of 2010, or in the near future). Usually someone lives behind the office in a trailer house, and they keep the latest information on weather & hiking conditions posted outside on an **information board.** That information comes from the Kanab BLM office, Tele. 435-644-4600. The visitor center has a radio telefon but it's used for emergencies only--and not available to the public.

If a ranger is not at the visitor center or it's closed, you can pickup & fill out the **Recreation Fee Permit Envelope** at the self-service pay station or information board. After filling it out, drop it in the metal box provided. As of 2010, **day-hikes** down the Paria and/or Buckskin cost $6 per day (no reservations needed); as well as $5 a night for camping in the canyons. Reservations are required to camp in either canyon. See more details and the **latest regulations in the introduction to this book**. But for the very latest information, go to the website **www.az.blm.gov/paria**. Every year the BLM makes some kind of change in policy and going to the internet for updates is the best way to be current.

Also, after leaving the visitor center, you're requested (voluntary) to sign in at any of the 4 trailheads, whether you're going on an overnight trip, or day-hiking. Because of the heavy visitor use around The Confluence of the Paria & Buckskin everyone is urged to day-hike only, rather than camp in that area. If you need to **fill water bottles**, do that at the **tap 40m west of the visitor center building**, as all the trailheads are dry.

Now, to reach the normal trailhead for entry to the Paria River; turn east then south just before the Paria Ranger Station, and drive 3.4 kms (2.1 miles) on a good gravel road to the **White House Trailhead**. This place has picnic tables, fire pits, toilets, and a campsite--but for a fee! However, for a quiet & uninterrupted night's sleep, it's recommended you camp anywhere but there! Best to pull off the highway on any side-road in the region. This area is almost all public land. About 1 km north of the trailhead, and on the west side of the access road, are a couple of cottonwood trees and a good campsite.

If you arrive at the trailhead without water, go back to the ranger station. If you have time, you can visit some petroglyphs across the river to the west and north 2 minor draws. That rather **hidden** rock art **panel** is on the left or south side just after you enter a minor drainage; it's also located between the canyon wall and a detached slab or boulder. The white sandstone seen at or near the trailhead is the Thousand Pockets Tongue of the Page Sandstone (although almost all maps still show it as the upper part of the Navajo Sandstone).

The White House or Clark Cabin Ruins

The story behind the name of this trailhead, and the White House Cabin & Spring, was told to the author by the late **Kay Clark**, formerly of Henrieville. The story begins in the Luna Valley of New Mexico. In February, 1887, Wilford Clark (Kay's father) was born to Herriet & Owen Washington Clark. Soon after this child was born and Herriet strong enough to travel, the small family moved from Luna Valley to southern Utah and set up a homestead on the Paria River just downstream from where the White House Trailhead is today.

They arrived in June, 1887, and immediately built a small cabin. The family lived there only about a year, then in 1888, moved upriver a ways to the Adairville site (Adairville existed only from about 1873 until 1878, then was abandoned because of lack of summertime water). Largely because of water problems, that place didn't work out either, so in 1889 the family moved further upstream to Pahreah, which at that time was in the process of losing population. The first big floods to come down the Paria River, which caused many people to have second thoughts about living at Pahreah, roared down the canyon in 1883 & '84. Another big flood came in 1896.

In 1892, Owen W. Clark moved the whole family once again, this time to a safer and more promis-

Map 29, The Lower Paria River Gorge--Part 1
The Buckskin Gulch & Paria River Loop-Hike

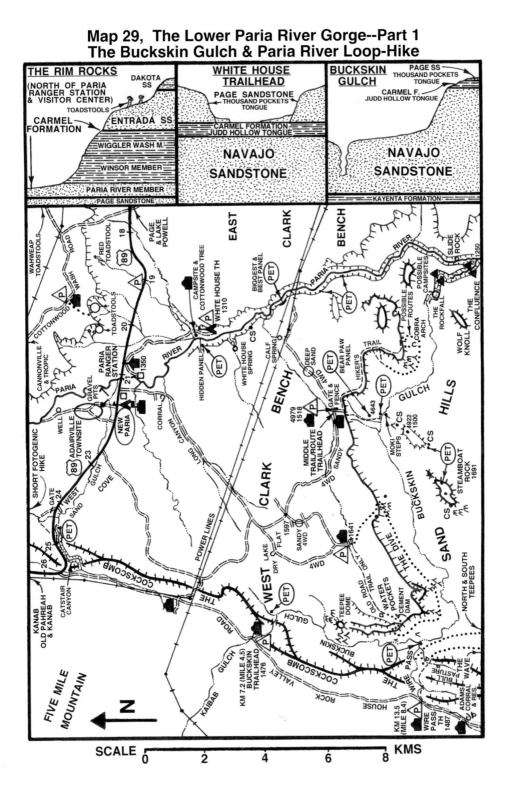

Left Owen W. Clark (picture taken in the early 1900's) and his family arrived in Southern Utah in June of 1887 and built the cabin downstream from the White House Trailhead. **Right Owen W. Clark** and **wife Herriet** in the early 1940's. (LaKay Clark Quilter fotos)

ing land around the town of Cannonville. The family has been in Bryce Valley ever since.

Now back to the name of White House. After the Clarks left their original cabin, sheep herders used the place as a camp and a supply depot when they had their flocks out on top of East Clark Bench just to the southeast (both the East Clark and West Clark Benches appear to be named after Owen W. Clark?). Sometime in the 1890's, the cabin burned down, apparently due to carelessness on the part of a sheepman.

It was the sheepmen who gave the place the name, **White House Cabin** and **White House Spring.** When they were out on the range for a long time, and had to drink any water they could get, they always enjoyed going back to the Clark Cabin because of the good-tasting water they could get from the little spring located just upstream and into a little draw to the west. As the story goes, someone commented that this water was so good, it could have come directly from the White House (in Washington DC). Thus the name stuck, on both the cabin & spring, and later the trailhead.

To find the White House Ruins today, walk south from the parking lot along the east side of the Paria. Best to stay on the bench, not in the flood plain. After almost exactly 1000m or 1 km, and 400m south-east of the canyon holding the White House Spring, look for an inconspicuous pile of rocks--this is re-ally not worth the effort. This is said to be the remains of the cabin's fireplace. There were at one time some corrals just north of the ruins, but they were washed away long ago by floods. About 40m east of the pile of stones and at the base of the cliffs, is a cowboy etching which looks like someone's brand.

Buckskin Gulch Trailheads

The other 3 trailheads are for entry into the best slot canyon on the Colorado Plateau and the world--the Buckskin Gulch. To reach the **Buckskin Trailhead**, drive west from the Paria Ranger Station & Vis-itor Center on Highway 89 and through The Cockscomb. Just west of where the highway cuts through the monocline and between **mile posts 25 & 26**, turn south on the **House Rock Valley Road (HRVR)**. This road is well-traveled, sometimes-maintained and generally good for any car even in light rains. If you drive this road south, you'll end up at **House Rock** on Highway 89A between **mile posts 565 & 566** in the House Rock Valley. Highway to highway the distance is about 47.7 kms (29.6 miles). From High-way 89 south to the first car-park, the Buckskin Trailhead, is 7.2 kms (4.5 miles); or 40.5 kms (25.1 miles) from the south & Highway 89A. At that point, turn east and drive 250m and park and/or camp at the trailhead which is just behind a low hill. This is where Kaibab Gulch (which turns into the Buckskin Gulch at or near the trailhead) cuts through The Cockscomb.

From the Buckskin Trailhead, continue south for a total of 13.5 kms (8.4 miles) from Highway 89, to the **Wire Pass Trailhead** (34.2 kms/21.4 miles from the south & Highway 89A). This is the more pop-ular starting point of the 2 entries at the head of the Buckskin Gulch, because it shortens the walk by a couple of hours. The Wire Pass Trailhead is located in the lower end of Coyote Wash or Valley, but for some reason that part of the drainage below the trailhead is not called Coyote Wash. Instead, it's just called the Wire Pass. You can camp at either trailhead, but both are dry, so take plenty of water with you. The BLM has installed a pit toilet at each of these trailheads.

The 4th and last entry possibility into the Buckskin, is from the **West Clark Bench** and the **Middle Trail/Route (MT/R).** Until recently it was really more of a route than a trail. Get there by driving along Highway 89 between mile posts 21 & 22. Immediately east of the **Paria River Guest Ranch** and **Paria Outpost & Outfitters,** turn south onto a good graded road. This is public access, but you pass through some private land and 2 gates & corral in the first 1 1/2 kms. Leave the gates as you find them; either open or closed, then drive southwest up **Long Canyon** (which has some moderately good narrows) on a maintained road which can be slick & muddy in wet weather. At the head of the canyon, stay on the most-used road, the one which veers left at the first 2 junctions, then continues south, then east. The last part will be down a very shallow & broad drainage towards the Middle Trail/Route Trailhead near a fence & gate, as shown. In the last km or so before the trailhead, **beware of deep sand!** If the sand has a little moisture, 2WD's can make it OK. If the **sand is dry**, it's for **4WD's only!** The author made it several times in his VW Rabbit, but 4WD's are highly recommended. If you're driving a car, stop a little ways before the trailhead. In June, the driest month, sandy roads tend to be their worst, so a shovel in the trunk should be standard equipment! This trailhead is 12.6 kms (7.8 miles) from Highway 89.

This trailhead and the Middle Trail/Route is the least-used of the entries to the Buckskin, but it affords a different view of the country you'll be walking through, and the access road is generally good for most vehicles. It also allows you access to **Cobra Arch**, one of the most unique around.

Trail/Route--FROM WHITE HOUSE TRAILHEAD Most people going down the Paria just to the lower Buckskin and back, or all the way to Lee's Ferry, usually begin at the **White House Trailhead**. Many people walk down to The Confluence, up the Buckskin Gulch a ways, then return the same way. This part of the hike down the Paria is very easy, and normally there are no obstacles.

In the first 2 kms or so, the bed of the Paria is wide with the creek meandering all over, then the Navajo Sandstone walls slowly rise and come closer together. You'll have to cross the creek several times in this first part, so get used to the idea of wet shoes! After about another 2 kms (see the cowboy signatures on the right) will be a short side-canyon coming in from the right or west. About 1 km below that, and again on the right or west, will be a big rounded curve with a high smooth wall that's covered with desert varnish. All around that wall will be scattered etchings of **rock art,** but the **biggest & best panel** will be on the south side.

A little over 2 kms below these petroglyphs, and as the river is running southeast in a straight line, will be more rock art on the right or west side. Look for a crack in the wall opening to the north about 200m from the river. Walk inside this crack to find more **etchings** 3-4m above on the east facing wall. Another km below these, and again on the right or west side, and up 4-5m, will be more hard-to-see petroglyphs. About 50m below these is a paleface-made **+** & **1/4** high on the wall. Just above that is an image of a big horn sheep.

About 5-6 kms below these last petroglyphs will be **Slide Rock.** This is where a section of the Navajo Sandstone wall was undercut, then broken off and slid straight down into the river. Presently, the river flows behind it, making a short tunnel or bridge. Below Slide Rock, the canyon constricts and in 2 places the creek fills the slot from wall to wall. These 2 places are about 50m & 300m from The Confluence with the Buckskin Gulch.

Please be aware that in the past, and after some floods--but not all--these 2 short sections can be extra deep. Having at least one air mattress with your group would help ferry packs across deep water. For this reason, be sure to stop and look at the **information board** located in front of the Paria River Ranger Station & Visitor Center. Rangers will alert you to any problem areas in the canyon on that information board; however, 99% of the time there's little or nothing to worry about. Now let's stop at The Confluence and go to the trailheads for the Buckskin Gulch.

FROM BUCKSKIN TRAILHEAD From the **Buckskin Trailhead,** you have an unobstructed walk into the Gulch. About 1 km from the trailhead, and just after you walk through a gate-like narrow constriction, veer left and look almost due east. About 125m away is a good panel of big horn sheep **petroglyphs** on a wall on the bench above the creek bed. After the petroglyphs, the canyon is open for a ways

then begins to narrow as you near the confluence of the Buckskin & Wire Pass drainages. There's not a lot to see before you arrive at the Wire Pass drainage.

FROM WIRE PASS TRAILHEAD In the first km, you'll pass through open country, then the trail going up to the right to the Coyote Buttes and The Wave. Read about this with **Map 37.** From there, the wash narrows quickly. Soon you'll come to a narrow place where there can be a minor obstacle, a chokestone or two, which can create one or more dropoffs of 1-3m. This situation changes with every flood. If there's a problem here, the rangers will let you know by posting a message on the information board in front of the Ranger Station. Right where the Wire Pass & Buckskin Gulch meet, are a number of **etchings** of big horn sheep on your right-hand or south side.

From the Wire Pass/Buckskin Confluence, the real Buckskin Gulch begins, and doesn't end until The Confluence with the Paria. This part of the canyon is nearly 20 kms long, and averages 4-5m in

This is in one of 2 tighter parts of **Wire Pass** just before you reach the **Buckskin Gulch.** There are times when floods rearrange boulders or logs in this section, but so far, nothing has happened to make any serious impediments for hikers.

width for its entire length. At times the gorge may open to 8-10m in width, then narrows down to no more than a meter wide. The author recalls something like 40-50 places in the Buckskin where logs were seen wedged into the slot high above--mute evidence of nature on the rampage, and a grim reminder of the danger of walking this gorge. One last word of caution: **HAVE A GOOD WEATHER FORECAST BEFORE ENTERING THIS CANYON!** Normally this slot is somewhere between 20-30m deep, but downcanyon near the Paria, the walls seem closer to 100m in height! This is the longest slot canyon in the world, and certainly one of the best.

For the most part, walking down the Buckskin is uneventful, but normally there are several small pools of water or mud you must wade through. These pools occur where the slot constricts and flood waters gush through and scour out holes. Most of these are concentrated in the 3-4 kms upcanyon from where the Middle Trail/Route enters. There's no running water in the Buckskin Gulch, except in times of flood. Since the bottom is so hidden from the sun, and the temperatures so cool, there is little evaporation, even in the heat of the summer, therefore muddy pools are usually there all the time. One such place is called the **Cesspool**. It's about 1 km upcanyon from the MT/R. Right after any big flood, you may have to float your pack across this pool (this would be something very rare), so taking an air mattress is a good idea. Once again, check for messages on the information board at the Paria Ranger Station for the latest word concerning the depth of this pool and others. Then at the last minute make the decision to take an air mattress or possibly an inner tube.

FROM THE MIDDLE TRAIL/ROUTE (MT/R) From the parking place, follow the fence due south to some minor cliffs. Hop the fence to the west side, then follow footprints to the right and down over the first ledges. A trail is slowly developing along a drainage veering a little southwest from the trailhead. This takes you right to the rim of the Buckskin. About 300m before the Buckskin, walk left or east and look for a big, black, south-facing wall that's about 100m from the dry wash you followed coming down (on the *West Clark Bench 7 1/2' quad*, it's about 100m south of elevation **4643**/1415m). On that face about 3 & 5m up, are 2 small panels of rock art. One has 2 bear prints, so we'll call this the **Bear Paw Panel**. Lots of erosion has taken place since this one was made--or they made a ladder to stand on (?).

From where you reach the Buckskin, turn east and walk about 200m for the final route into the bottom of the slot. You may have to look for an easy way down the first stage. **WARNING:** From the lip of the narrows, and the second stage of this route, you'll have to downclimb about 30m over **fairly steep downsloping slickrock** that's always covered with loose windblown sand. This means you'll have to remove packs and lower them by hand to a companion, or use a short rope. ***Short people, inexperienced hikers and anyone carrying a large pack may find it difficult getting up or down (especially down!) this last 30m.*** On one of the author's trips, it had been raining, the sand was wet and sticking to the soles of his shoes. This was the worst he has ever seen it! He slipped near the bottom and slid a couple of meters, and although no harm was done, it was a wakeup call that this route can be risky! If using this MT/R as an entry point, be sure to take a short rope and help each other down.

For anyone hiking the Buckskin in 2 days, this is a good place to camp, as it allows you to take another look at the weather situation halfway through the gorge. This is obviously a hike you don't want to do in a monsoon weather pattern. The MT/R also allows you to exit and take a 3 km side-trip to **Cobra Arch** (best to do that on a separate hike; read more below). From this entry/exit point, you can also scramble up a steep slope to the south rim for a hike to the fotogenic **Steamboat Rock** and other

From an intermediate ledge looking down on the bottom of the **Middle Trail/Route**. Just to the left and out of sight, is where you crawl down to the bottom; and just to the right of the hiker in the red shirt is where the moki steps are, and the route up the south side of this old Indian trail. The level place in the middle is a campsite 3-4m above any possible flood waters.

landmarks on top of the Sand Hills (Paria Plateau).

COBRA ARCH Might as well describe the routes to Cobra at this point. In the past, most people going there, started down the MT/R, then walked cross-country southeast between the cliffs to the north, and the Buckskin to the south, until they reached this unusual arch. But in the summer of 2009, the author noticed an emerging **hiker's trail** heading east from the end of the fence and above the first ledge going down to the Buckskin. He followed this wondering where it might lead. And sure enough, people were rim-walking east & southeast aways, then working their way down over several little ledges to the sandy flats below, then south and east around a corner to Cobra Arch. Sometimes this trail disappears in the sand, but follow it as best you can as shown on the map. The author stayed on the rim, and later had a good look directly down on the arch from the north. In that area was a cairn, likely indicating a route down steep slickrock straight to Cobra Arch. The author didn't try this, but the route looked doable.

STEAMBOAT ROCK If you're just going to Steamboat Rock, then starting at the **MT/R** would be your shortest walk. Head down into the Buckskin (notice 2 big horn etchings on your left near the bottom), then immediately on the other side of the canyon wall will be a sloping ledge you'll have to get on to start up the other side. But notice the little cups or rounded holes on top of that ledge--these are genuine **moki steps** and they're close to 1000 years old, or older (?). This, and the petroglyphs, proves this is

Left Part of the **Bear Paw Panel** located just north of where you drop down the Middle Trail/Route into the Buckskin Gulch. This part is up 4-5m, so either they made ladders to get up to it, or the ground was higher when they put their art/grafiti here.

Below The south side of **Cobra Arch**, one of the prettiest, unusual and fotogenic arches around.

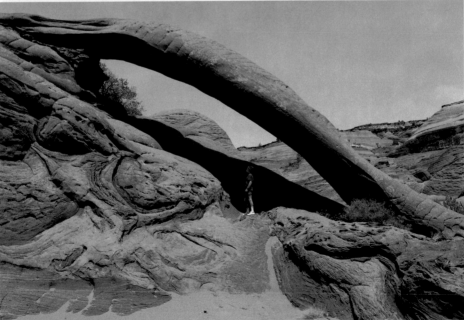

These are the Big Brain & Cauliflower Rocks (**BB&CR**) around the southwest corner of **Steamboat Rock**. In the foto below, they are found in the lower right-hand corner.

Steamboat Rock from the air and looking northeast. If you're good at reading maps & topography, you can see where the MT/R comes off the ledge in the left background, and where Cobra Arch is. In the lower right corner are the BB&CR shown in the foto above. If you can climb up on top, there are more teepee-like rocks and other fotogenic sites. Get on top via the southern slopes. In the lower left-hand corner of this picture and along the cliffs, is the signature of *Lee Averett, Oct. 31, 1925.*

an old **Indian trail or route** across the Buckskin.

To get on top of that ledge, you may need a push from a partner; or pile up some rocks to stand on if you're alone. Route-find up over several ledges, some with more moki steps. Once on top and out of the canyon, walk southwest about 1 km to find some fotogenic rocks in the area surrounding elevation **4922** (1500m). In this area, you'll find 2 places with **cowboy signatures (CS)**, plus a small rock art panel. From these rocky outcrops, head southwest again for 1-2 kms to **Steamboat Rock**. There you'll find one rock art panel just inside a mini canyon on the east end, cowboy etchings to the west, and best of all, some **Big Brain/Cauliflower Rocks (BB&CR)** at the extreme southwest end of Steamboat. You can also get there from the west and the area east of The Wave (North & South Teepees), but it's a little shorter walk from the MT/R. No permit needed here.

Now back to the Buckskin Gulch. A couple of hours downcanyon from the MT/R entry/exit point, is what is normally the only obstacle in the Buckskin. This is **The Rockfall**, created by some large boulders falling off the canyon wall about 3 kms up from The Confluence. The worst part is a 3-4m-high climb or descent, over one of these boulders. During the 1980's, someone chopped several steps into one of the boulders which you might use, but you'll normally find a rope nearby as well that you can hand-line down. BLM rangers normally cut out ropes that appear to be unsafe, so be prepared to install a new one (with knots or loops) to help you get down and/or to lower packs. To ensure you have no problems, take **a rope 10m long**. Without packs, hikers can sometimes slide, jump or wiggle down through this dryfall but it's a little risky without a rope (in 2009, the steps appeared to have been newly enlarged making this a safer descent).

In 1991, there was an unusual short-lived obstacle in the lower Buckskin between **The Rockfall** and the campsites in the lower end. This was a rare swimming pool. Apparently a bigger-than-normal flood roared down the Buckskin in the winter of 1990-91 and scoured out deep holes where the walls constrict. At the deepest pool, the author had to hold onto a log with one hand, while holding his day-pack up with the other to keep it dry. People taking big packs down had to float them across, while others just swam. Later floods filled in these holes and by 1997, 2003 & 2009, everything was back to normal, with ankle-deep water. Expect big changes with every flood and go prepared!

About 300m above **The Confluence** with the Paria River, are several campsites in the lower Buckskin on a couple of sandy benches high above the creek bed. This is a heavily-used area, and at times in the past has been closed to camping. The reason for the closures was to allow the vegetation to re-cover, and the toilet poop to disintegrate. If you're camping there, please tread lightly and use existing paths and tent sites. Also, be careful where you use the toilet and dispose of waste. **The toilet problem in the lower Buckskin is perhaps the primary reason the BLM instigated the policy of allowing only 20 hikers per/day to backpack & camp in the Buckskin/Paria drainage.** If camping or day-hiking, try to do your toilet duties anywhere but at this site in the lower Buckskin. Here's another option. There are 2 possible campsites about 750m below The Rockfall. You'll have to carry water back up from downcanyon, but it will lessen the impact on The Confluence campsites.

Elevations White House Trailhead, 1310m; Buckskin Trailhead, 1476m; Wire Pass Trailhead, 1487m; Middle Trail/Route Trailhead, 1518m; The Confluence of the Buckskin & Paria, about 1250m.

Time Needed The distance from the Buckskin Trailhead to the confluence of Wire Pass is about 7 kms, or a couple of hours. From the Wire Pass Trailhead to this same confluence is about 3 kms; about 1 hour. From that point to The Confluence with the Paria is another 19 kms. From The Confluence back up to the White House Trailhead is another 11 kms or so. This makes the total distance from the Buckskin to the White House Trailhead about 38 kms (23.6 miles). From Wire Pass to White House is about 33 kms (20.5 miles). This can be done in one long day, but it's not recommended for everyone. You'll need 2 cars, or a car & mtn. bike to be used as a shuttle. If doing this, start at Wire Pass Trailhead.

The author once left a mtn. bike at White House, then drove to Wire Pass. He walked down the Buckskin and up the Paria to White House in 8 hours 13 min. This wasn't too bad, but the bike ride back to Wire Pass was--being at the end of an otherwise long day and peddling against the wind. It turned out to be a very tiring 10-hour day. Despite its length, it's recommended you do this in one day to cut down on the number of campers near The Confluence.

Or you can do this same hike in 2 days; but the problem with camping (likely at the **MT/R**) would be that you'd have to carry at least a gallon (3.78 liters) jug full of water; more in hot weather, less in cooler conditions. Most people however, make it all the way through the Buckskin in 1 day and end up camping near The Confluence where there's a permanent water supply.

Water The Buckskin is normally bone-dry, but with an occasional pool of water or mud to wade through. Since most people don't have the courage to drink this, count on it being a dry hike. Carry all the water you'll need. Normally, about 2 kms up the Buckskin from The Confluence, you'll begin to see pools of water; and about 1 km from the Paria, and just above the campsites, water begins to flow. This is a year-round water supply. But since this campsite area and the lower part of the Buckskin is so heavily used, and with people walking in the water all the time, especially in the spring and fall months, plan to filter or purify it first.

Another option for those camping near The Confluence is to take empty jugs (always have plenty of empty water bottles, as they weigh almost nothing) down the Paria a ways, and fill them up at **Wall Spring** or at the spring just above it (see the next map of the Paria, Part 2). This is about 3 1/2 kms below The Confluence. Still another alternative is to purify or filter the Paria River water. Since most of this water seeps out of the bottom layers of the Navajo Sandstone in the Upper Paria River Gorge and below the town of Cannonville, it's really not that bad; it's just a little muddy at times, especially if there's any storm activity upcanyon. The author has never used filters, but it seems they would clog-up badly if used in muddy water. So let muddy water settle overnight first, then filter it. A bottle of Iodine tablets might be the best idea.

The Paria below The Confluence flows year-round, but between the old Adairville town site and the Buckskin it's often dry in the early summer. Part-time rancher Charley Hepworth of Page, who owns the ranch just north of Highway 89 and the site of old Adairville, has leased part of his property to Western Rock Products which has several gravel pits near the Paria River. At times they divert the river water with temporary dams and store it in several ponds. However, in dry conditions and/or in the heat of the summer, water in the Paria doesn't even reach old Adairville. In July, or after the first flood of the season, the Paria River then flows again, usually until the next spring or summer. To check on the Paria water, just glance at the creek bed as you drive across the bridge on Highway 89 near mile post 21. Also, it's important to check on the water situation at the ranger station, or ask other hikers of its whereabouts.

Maps USGS or BLM maps **Kanab** and especially **Smoky Mountain** (for the Buckskin Gulch only), and to these add **Glen Canyon Dam**, which shows the Paria River from the state line, or The Confluence, down to Lee's Ferry (all at 1:100,000 scale). The Glen Canyon Dam map also shows the Vermilion Cliffs and Sand Hills. Or you might try the 1:62,500 scale maps Paria, Paria Plateau, and Lee's Ferry. These are now out of print, but there may be a few still around in some sales outlets.

The BLM has recently published a new map/guide called **Hiker's Guide to Paria Canyon.** It's in book form with 30 small maps covering the Paria and Buckskin down to Lee's Ferry. But it's not just one map showing the entire canyon. Their old map with the same title at 1:62,500 scale is a good one if you can find it. Hopefully at some time in the future that one will be reprinted.

Another excellent map is one of the series of 4 field study maps which were prepared by the BLM, USGS, and others, covering the Sand Hills (Paria Plateau). These maps are in the series titled **MF-1475, A, B, C & D.** Each map is at 1:62,500 scale, and very much the same, except each has a different emphasis such as (A) geology, (B) geochemical data, (C) mines & prospects, and (D) mineral resource potential. Get these maps from any USGS outlet. Each of these covers the entire Lower Paria River Hike from White House to Lee's Ferry, plus the Vermilion Cliffs & Sand Hills, and all of the House Rock Valley Road (which is the access to the Buckskin Gulch and Sand Hills).

Main Attraction The best slot canyon in the world. Also, with an exit at the Middle Trail/Route, you can have a look at Cobra Arch (and Steamboat Rock) one of the most unique around. Be sure you read the part on **Fotography in Slot Canyons** in the Introduction to this book, which will help you take home better fotos of this dark chasm.

Best Time to Hike Because of possible cold water in the pools of the Buckskin, May & June have become the most popular time to visit this canyon. It's getting hot by June, but once inside the narrows, it's very cool. You'll seldom see the sun; and it's that way for 19 kms! So the heat of the outside world doesn't really matter, except for the walk back up the Paria to the White House Trailhead. June is the driest month of the year, not only for this region, but for the entire state of Utah. Kanab receives about 31 cms (12 in.) of rainfall annually, most of it in winter. With the low temps and lack of sun in the gorge, the pools of water, especially the Cesspool, simply don't evaporate. Pools seem to stay in the Buckskin most of each winter, and often times until about June, then sometimes dry-up for a time. Each year is different. If you were to go down the Buckskin right after a summer storm, you may have to float your pack across one or more pools on an air mattress or inner tube. See the information board at the Paria Ranger Station for the latest word on the Cesspool situation and hiking conditions in the Buckskin.

You can hike the Buckskin throughout the summer, but you'd want a good weather forecast. If you're there in a dry spell, then fine. But if you arrive in a wet period, with daily showers around, stay out of this canyon! Southern Utah has 2, 3 or 4 wet monsoon periods each summer, each lasting a few days. These periods usually occur sometime between mid-July to mid-September. This is the period you should be most cautious with the threat of flash floods.

Actually, as narrow as the place is, there are still many high places you could crawl up to and away from raging flood waters. But when the floods do come, they usually come in a surge, and you may not have time to look for a hideout. Always listen to the local radio stations for the latest weather forecasts as you drive into the area. The **Buckskin Gulch** is the **worst place in the world** to be in a flash flood!

Boots/Shoes Best to take wading-type boots or shoes for the entire hike.

Author's Experience The author has been all the way through the Buckskin twice, and at least part way through on about 20-25 other occasions, and from each trailhead. On 1 trip he made it from The Confluence campsite to the Wire Pass Trailhead, with a large pack, in less than 6 1/2 hours. On 4-5 trips, he walked from the White House Trailhead, down the Paria, up the Buckskin to The Rockfall, then back the same way, all in about 7 hours. Another time he left the MT/R parking, walked down to the bottom of the entry/exit point, then to Cobra Arch, and back to his car, all in 3 1/2 hours. Twice he has hiked down the MT/R and up the other side to Steamboat Rock. Round-trip was about 4 hours. Most people will want more time than that taken by the author. Some may want to double the author's hike times.

All fotos on these 2 page are from the lower **Buckskin Gulch**.

Opposite Page
Left Helping each other down through the **Rockfall** using a rope.

Right Climbing up through the **Rockfall** in the lower Buckskin Gulch using steps cut in a boulder. In 2009, these steps were in good condition.

This Page
Above Left Two hikers just walking out of the **Cesspool** not far above where the **MT/R** reaches the bottom.

The other 2 shots are in the **lower end** of the **Buckskin** where water begins to flow. The walls are really getting high in this section.

Lower Paria River Gorge--The Confluence to Lee's Ferry

Location & Access The Lower Paria River Gorge is so long and has so many interesting sites to see, it's been broken down into 4 parts with 4 different maps. Part 1, covers mainly the Buckskin Gulch and the trailheads leading into it; and the upper part of the Lower Paria River Gorge or Canyon. The 2nd, 3rd & 4th maps cover the canyon from The Confluence of the Buckskin Gulch and the Paria River all the way down to Lee's Ferry. This is where the Paria empties into the Colorado River.

If you plan to do this entire canyon hike from top to bottom, call the BLM Field Office in Kanab, 435-644-4600, and ask if they have a list of people who perform shuttle service between Whitehouse Trailhead (or any of the Buckskin Gulch trailheads) and Lee's Ferry. Or better still, go to the website **www.az.blm.gov/paria/**, and click on **Shuttles.** Here's what you may find: Barry Warren, PO Box 7041, Page, AZ, 928-640-0191; Betty Price, 928-355-2252; Canyon Country Outback Tours, Wally Thomson, 888-783-3807 or 435-644-3807; Marble Canyon Lodge, Catalina Martinez, 928-355-2295 or 928-355-2225; Paria Outpost (immediately west of the Paria River & Paria Ranger Station) Susan & Stephen Dodson, PO Box 410075, Big Water, Utah, 84741, 928-691-1047.

Once you get someone lined up, the normal procedure is for you to drive to **Lee's Ferry** and park in the **Long Term Parking Lot** which is 300m west of the boat launching site at the end of the road. There's a sign telling everyone of the right place to park. Then your shuttle drives you back to Whitehouse or Wirepass, and you hike back to your car at your own pace.

Most people who do the entire canyon hike, start at the White House Trailhead. To get there, leave Highway 89 between mile posts 20 & 21, and drive south for 3.4 kms (2.1 miles) on an all-weather gravel road. Read more about this and the 3 other entry points under **Part 1, The Buckskin Gulch**.
Elevations The White House Trailhead, 1310m; The Confluence, 1250m; Paria River at the bottom of Wrather Canyon, 1165m; the mouth of Bush Head Canyon, about 1100m; and Lee's Ferry, 950m.
Time Needed Here are the latest BLM calculations for distances in the Paria River Canyon. From the White House Trailhead to Lee's Ferry, is about 39 miles (62 kms). From the Buckskin Trailhead to Lee's Ferry, about 48 miles (77 kms). From Wire Pass Trailhead to Lee's Ferry, around 45 miles (72 kms). A long hike anyway you look at it, but a fun one, and one which has several side-canyons or routes to the canyon rim to explore.

An extra fast walker could get through the canyon in 2 long days, others have trouble doing it in 4. Most do it in about 3, but this book introduces some new hikes out of the canyon and up to the rim, so some may want 5-6 days. It you're the type who likes to take it easy, do a lot of exploring, and likes to set up nice camps and relax, then a week isn't too long. However, the longer you plan to stay, the heavier your pack will be.
Water From The Confluence to Lee's Ferry, you'll have year-round water all the way, but you can only drink river water if you purify it with Iodine tablets or filter it. During the irrigation season in the Bryce Valley (Tropic, Henrieville & Cannonville), which extends from about mid-April through the beginning of October, there's very little water flowing down the Paria below Cannonville. Most of the water you see entering the Lower Paria Gorge during this time period seeps out of the bottom layers of the Navajo Sandstone as the river cuts through the White Cliffs below Cannonville. So it's pretty good water, but there are cows in the canyon, usually in the cooler 6 months of the year, so therein lies the danger.

Left Part of the **Hidden Panel** located just northwest and across the Paria River from the White House Trailhead. **Right** Looking up the Buckskin Gulch from the **first campsite** in the lower end.

Map 30, Lower Paria River Gorge--Part 2
The Confluence to Wrather Canyon & Arch

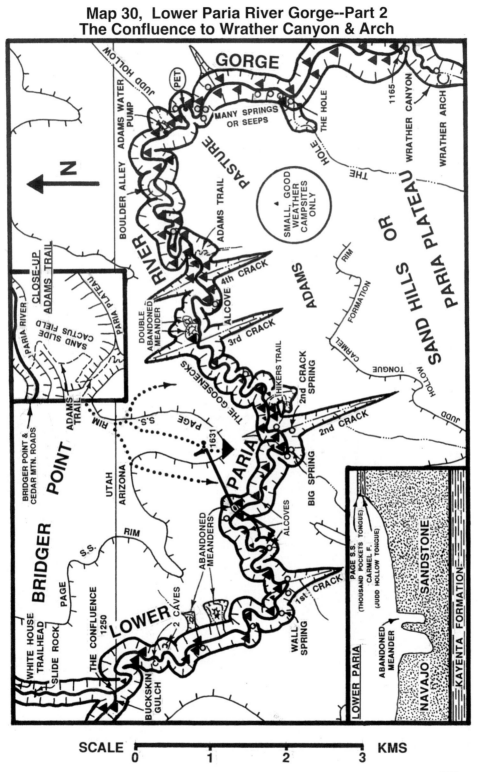

SCALE

0   1   2   3   KMS

In the heat of most summers, or at least in June and July, the water in the upper gorge (between The Box, where the Paria cuts through The Cockscomb, and Highway 89) disappears in the sands. Then it begins flowing again in the lower canyon at the bottom end of the Buckskin Gulch near The Confluence. It then flows year-round to Lee's Ferry. The amount of flow changes from year to year, and from season to season.

For those who prefer to drink good spring water without filtration or chemicals, take it from **Wall, Big, and Shower Springs,** and from springs inside Wrather and Bush Head Canyons. However, between The Confluence and Bush Head, are a number of minor seeps, which likely will have flowing water most of the time. The author always carries a small $4 bottle of iodine tablets in his pack for emergency situations.

The alternative to chemicals is filtration. The latest REI catalog lists filters designed for hikers ranging in price from about $35 to $130, but there are cheaper ones than that. Some manufactures are making a fistful of dollars on the scare tactics of some people, but the BLM and the NPS are required to tell hikers to boil or treat all water--even spring water--to stay away from possible lawsuits. The author prefers spring water, and iodine tablets as an emergency backup.

Another thing to remember, carry several empty water bottles or plastic jugs. They don't weigh much, and can be thrown away at the end of the trip. By having a couple of gallon (3.785 liters) jugs, you can carry good water from springs to you camps site.

Maps Read about maps under the previous chapter, **The Buckskin Gulch & Paria River Loop-Hike.**
Main Attractions A deep and narrow canyon gorge, several places to climb out to the rim, interesting side-canyons, one of the best arches in the world, a chance to see desert big horn sheep, and many good campsites and petroglyphs. It's a great trip for those who have time off work in the spring or fall. More later under **Trail/Route.**
Best Time to Hike If you're doing this hike from the White House Trailhead straight down the Paria to Lee's Ferry with just a quick look into the bottom of the Buckskin, then spring or fall is best. More specifically, the best time is from about the first of April through May; and again from about mid-September through mid or late October. If you go too early or late in the season, the icy water you'll be wading in all the time will make your feet feel like blocks of ice! The author prefers the spring months because the days are longer. Remember, March 21, has the same amount of daylight as does September 21.

By June 1st, the temperatures are getting up there to around 30°C (86°F) on average, and that's pretty warm while walking in the sun all day with a big pack. You can count on temps of about 40°C (104°F) all through July and into August at Lee's Ferry. In the narrowest parts, and when wading in the creek, the heat doesn't affect you so much; but in the lower end of the canyon near Lee's Ferry, the altitude is only about 950m, and you'll be walking in the sun constantly.

Another reason to stay out of the area in about June, is because there are big gray **horse flies** which bite the back of bare legs. The solution; wear long pants. Horse flies seem to congregate in the more open areas in the bottom end of the canyon with water & tamaracks around. You'll also be hindered by very small gnats which get in your hair and bite. In the spring and fall, these 2 pests don't exist. Neither do they seem to exist in the narrow parts of the canyon; instead, just in the more open places.

Boots/Shoes You'll be walking in or crossing the Paria River hundreds of times on your way to Lee's Ferry. In the narrower places you'll be hiking right in the stream continually. Your footwear will be wet all the time, so some kind of wading boots or shoes is recommended.

In the last few years, a number of new hiking boots or shoes have been on the market, designed es-

Slide Rock as seen from upstream, but on this day there was no water in the Paria River.

pecially for this type of hike. The very best kind is something that isn't affected by water. In other words, a shoe that's **not made of leather**. For use in places like the Zion Narrows in Zion NP, shoes by the name of 5-10's are really the best, but they're expensive. The Converse All Star basketball shoes, made of rubber and canvas, are good, but they have a thin sole and low heel. Then there are the plain ordinary running shoes. They are very good, but some may have leather parts which shrink after they've been wet. This means you may want to apply boot oil to the leather parts after the hike. Best to buy a good pair of running shoes without any leather parts. Most running shoes are that way these days.

Another tip, since this is such a long hike, start with a pair of shoes in good condition. Or if you have an old pair, and are trying to put them out of their misery, it might pay to take along a newer and light weight pair as a back-up. This is an especially good suggestion if you intend to climb out of the canyon. It takes a lot out of shoes to be used under strenuous conditions when wet all the time.

Author's Experience The author has been into the canyon from the White House Trailhead and up from Lee's Ferry many times. On each trip, he went to somewhere in the middle of the canyon, and returned the same way to his car, thus avoiding a car shuttle or hitch hiking. In addition, in 2003 and 2009, he entered half a dozen times from the north rim via the old Indian trail. On several occasions he went up-canyon to about as far as the 2nd Crack; other times went down to Bush Head Canyon, climbed out, rim-walked to Wrather Canyon and returned from there. On his last trip, he found the Indian trail up to the south rim and Sand Hills via the moki steps. Read more about this later.

Trail/Route--The Confluence to Lee's Ferry The first half of the way between The Confluence and Lee's Ferry is narrow, but it's not the slot-type canyon you find in the Buckskin Gulch. There are many springs, campsites, running water year-round, and no obstacles. If you were caught by a flash flood in this section, you would have very little trouble finding a high place out of the way of the torrent. There are many good campsites, and always one site near each of the good springs. Taking fotos is in some ways easier here than in the darker Buckskin, because here you'll see the sun part of the time. There are several abandoned meanders (abandoned stream channels) to explore, and there are some petroglyphs, an historic pumping site, and several trails or routes to the canyon rim.

If you arrive at The Confluence, near mile P7 on the BLM log-type map, and find the campsites just inside the lower Buckskin too crowded or noisy, then you could walk downstream about 1 km to find several other places, high and dry and safe--near mile P8. Some might prefer this campsite to the Buckskin sites anyway, as it's closer to the springs located another 2-3 kms downcanyon. Just a couple of bends downriver from this campsite are a couple of alcove-type caves.

About 3 1/2 or 4 kms below The Confluence, is a nice campsite and a usually good spring the author calls **Wall Spring**--near mile P9. It's had a good flow of water each time the author was there, but Skip, the former Paria Ranger, recalled times where its flow was so low, it was hard to get a safe drink. But normally you can rely on this spring.

About 500m below Wall Spring is a good campsite and another spring, which may in the long run be more reliable than its neighbor upstream. This spring, near mile P10, is at or near a side-canyon this author calls the **1st Crack**. It's the result of a minor fault, as are all 4 of the Crack Canyons shown on **Map 30.**

From Wall Spring, the canyon runs a little northeast, then southeast. Between the 1st & 2nd Crack Canyons, you'll pass 3 large alcoves or overhangs. These undercuts are similar to those found in West Canyon, Coyote Gulch and elsewhere. A km or so beyond the first overhang or alcove is another over-

Wall Spring, the first good spring you come to when hiking downstream from The Confluence. There's a good campsite just across the river to the north.

hang where the river undercuts the Navajo Sandstone wall. About 800m beyond that is a feature known as an **abandoned meander**, or an abandoned stream channel--near mile P11. A few thousand years ago, the Paria River ran through this channel, but it slowly undercut one of its walls in the process of making a gooseneck turn. It finally abandoned the old loop for a new one. The former stream channel is 5-6m above the present level of the river. It may be worthwhile to take a break from wading and check this out. The access is easy and there are camping possibilities on the north side of the meander. About 350m below this is the last of the 3 undercuts and the possibility of a minor seep.

Just before you arrive at the **2nd Crack**, you'll come to the best spring in the canyon. This one is called **Big Spring**. Across the river is another good, very popular campsite--near mile P12. If that site is full when you arrive, just go downstream a ways to find still more camping places and springs--near mile P13.

Right at the very end of what the author calls the 2nd Crack, is another possible spring. It flows out of this little side-canyon with a good discharge--at least when the author saw it several times. If you're a rock climber, it might be fun to look for a route out of the canyon to the south and up this 2nd Crack. Someone who is experienced with chimneying might be able to get out of or beyond the first set of ledges, and find a way up this crack canyon to the south rim. It looked promising, for a real tough climber.

Beyond the 2nd Crack, the Paria heads northeast again, and you enter a section of the canyon where there are few if any springs. Between 2nd Crack and the Adams Pump, there are no springs of any consequence, just river water. The author has placed several springs on the map, but they are mostly just minor seeps, and may or may not be of any use. This part of the canyon has some very tight turns, very high walls and it's as narrow as any part of the Paria River below the area just above The Confluence. The author has labeled this section **The Goosenecks**--even though the entire gorge is one gooseneck bend after another! You'll be walking in the stream as often there as anywhere along the hike.

About 600m below the 2nd Crack is a bench on the right or south, and a big horn sheep & **hiker's trail** going up into what is likely yet another abandoned meander high above the present stream channel. Here's a corner of the canyon the author didn't fully explore when he first found it, but in 2009, he did have a good look at it from the rim. A tough climber might get out, but with some hard climbing.

Near the end of The Goosenecks is the **3rd Crack**--about mile P14. It, like the other 2 upstream, is a little inconspicuous. It's hard at times to follow the river channel on the map; that's part of the reason these crack canyons are not easily seen. It's also a little difficult to keep your orientation (north-south) as you walk down this narrow gorge. A compass is helpful and should be standard equipment for all.

Just beyond the 3rd Crack and on your left is another abandoned stream channel. It's maybe 10-15m above the river level, and easy to get into. The author followed it for a ways, then returned the same way. But it appears on the *Wrather Arch 7 1/2' quad*, to be a kind of **double abandoned meander**--that's just below mile P14. It might be worthwhile to take the time to check this one out. It could also make an interesting campsite if you can get up inside it.

Less than 2 kms below the 3rd Crack you'll come to the **4th Crack**--near mile P15. This one is more obvious than the previous 3, partly because the canyon is beginning to open up and become wider. From the rim above, it appeared that a good climber could possibly make it out of the canyon to the north, using this very narrow slit in the wall, but the author didn't take the time to try it. In the 4th Crack running south, there are some ledges to skirt and a little climbing, but from the top of the Adams Trail, where the author looked down on it twice, it appeared to be climbable (?), at least for an experienced and well-equipped group.

About 500m beyond the 4th Crack, and on the south side of the creek bed, is the beginning of the old **Adams Trail**. More interesting than the trail itself, is the hard-luck story behind it.

Big Spring, one of the best water sources in the Lower Paria River Gorge. There are a number of good campsites both up & downcanyon from this spring.

Above Left The narrows in the Paria River just above **The Confluence**. This can have deep water, depending on the previous flood, but on this day, all these Koreans had was deep mud to wade through.

Above Right Desert varnish staining the walls of the **Paria River Gorge**. This part is between Wall & Big Spring.

Left This is the first of the 3 big **alcoves** between **Wall & Big Springs**. This section is one of the more-foto-genic parts of the Lower Paria River Gorge.

The Adams Trail and Water Pump

The area south & west of the Lower Paria River Gorge is called the Sand Hills by all the local cattlemen; the Paria Plateau by others. The name Sand Hills is very fitting, as the top-most layer of rock is made up mostly of the Navajo Sandstone. When it weathers away, it forms very sandy conditions. Because of the sand, the only way to get around the plateau is to walk, ride a horse or use a 4WD.

Despite the poor travel conditions, the area has been used for cattle and sheep & goat grazing since about the mid-1880's. It's fairly high, rising to 2043m on the southern edge at Powell's Monument and elsewhere above the Vermilion Cliffs. This means it has good pasturage, and it's surrounded on 3 sides by impassable cliffs or canyons. To the north is the Buckskin Gulch, on the north & east is the Lower Paria River Gorge, and on the south are the Vermilion Cliffs, which rise up 500-600m above the valley floor. The only easy way onto the plateau is from the west and the Coyote or House Rock Valleys.

Throughout the years, cattlemen slowly but surely began to develop water facilities in the Sand Hills, as there is no running water, and not one good reliable spring on the Plateau. They built small dams below exposed slickrock slopes to catch whatever rain fell, and of course there were already natural potholes or tanks in the slickrock. The number of cattle was always small and limited by the available water. Most livestock grazing was done in winter with snow on the ground, and animals removed in the warmer months. Despite all the hardships, things went well for 50 years or so. Then a long drought began in the early 1930's which coincided with the Great Depression.

During this drought period, there were several different cattlemen who had livestock on the Sand Hills range. The northeast quarter of the plateau was used by a man named Johnny Adams. As he began to see his cattle die of thirst, he started looking down into the Paria River Canyon for water. He must have pondered long and hard as to how he might get his cattle down to the year-round flowing river--or how he might get some of that water up to his cows.

Finally he thought he had the problem solved. He investigated pumping equipment and had come to the conclusion that with available technology and pumps, he could move water from the river to the rim, a vertical distance at one point of about 215m. So in the winter of 1938-39, he made the decision to build a rough access trail to install pumping equipment. After searching the rim, he found a place, which with a little dynamite and work, could be used.

The **Adams Trail** was hacked out of the canyon wall in the **spring of 1939**, and the pump, gasoline engine, and 300m of 5-cm (2") pipe were trucked in over the Sand Hills access road. For the last part of the journey, pack animals were used to haul the equipment in.

According to P.T. Reilly, the man who researched the history of this pumping station (which is written in the **Utah Historical Quarterly, #2, 1977**), it was Dean Cutler who straw-bossed the job for Adams who was rather elderly at the time. The remaining crew members were Lorin Broadbent, Eugene McAllister, and Lynn Ford (Trevor Leach also had a hand in transporting the pipe to the head of the trail). The country was very rough, and getting the equipment to the rim was a major undertaking. Water and food were packed in, and the most luxurious comfort was one's bedroll spread out on the ground, even though rattlesnakes were numerous after the weather began to warm up.

Their first job was to construct a rough trail to get the motor and pump down to the river. It was never intended to be a good trail, only good enough for men to scramble up & down. Horses were apparently never taken up or down the trail. The men lowered the pump and motor down the cliffs with ropes, one step at a time. Finally the pump and engine were in place, then pipe was carried down one section at a time and attached.

Left The bottom of the **Adams Trail**. There are moki steps to the left (this is an old Indian trail), but the easiest way is right up the crack in the middle. **Right** The upper part of the **Adams Trail**. This crude path runs from lower right to upper left. A horse can't make it, but a big horn sheep can.

It was well into summer when they installed the last section of pipe. They had intended to fill several potholes which were just above the rim. When the pipe was finally in place, they climbed down to the river to give it a try. But the river was very muddy, the result of storms upstream. They decided to abandon any pumping until the creek cleared. But that night it rained. It filled all the stock tanks and potholes. The drought was over, and the pump was never even tested. There it sat for 2 years.

In 1941, Adams sold the pump to another cattlemen, **A.T. Spence**. But Spence never used it. He ended up selling it to **Merle Findlay** in 1944 (more likely 1945). The pump continued to sit and gather dust & rust. Findlay owned the unused pump for 4 years, then sold it to **Gerald Swapp** in 1948.

Gerald Swapp's cattle range was the area north of the Paria, called the Flat Top and East Clark Bench. It was, and still is, a good grazing country, but lack of a good water supply has always restricted the potential of the range. After mulling over the idea of pumping water from the Paria up to the benchland for 10 years, Swapp finally bought the unused and untested pumping rig to give it a try. His intention was to pump water into the lower end of **Judd Hollow**, which is about 3 kms downstream from where the pump was originally set up at the bottom of the Adams Trail.

To do the job, Swapp hired Eugene McAllister, who was one of the original members of the crew who put the pipe & pump in place, and **Tony Woolley** (this may have been the guy who helped build the cement dam in Shed Valley). In December, 1948, the 3 men walked down into the canyon along the trail, got the engine running and got a good flow of water out the upper end of the trail.

Later, in January of 1949, under some rather cold conditions, Woolley rode a horse down the Paria Canyon, in similar fashion to the feat performed by John D. Lee in 1871. The pipe was all disconnected and placed in bundles, then tied together at one end. A rope was tied to the cross-tree of the saddle, and the pipe was dragged down the partially frozen stream to Judd Hollow. The 4 cylinder, Fairbanks--Morris flathead engine and the pump, were carried on horseback downstream, one at a time.

To avoid damaging the pump by using it with muddy water, the crew dug a sump at the edge of the north bank of the stream. It was a hole, lined with rocks, which would allow water from the river to filter in slowly, thus avoiding the muddy water when the stream was running high. Their intention was to run the pipe directly up to the bottom of Judd Hollow, a rise of 300m. Then they hoped to run it northeast for another 3 kms to a tank in the area where cattle were located. This would require much more pipe. So Woolley rode the horse downcanyon to Lee's Ferry, while Swapp and McAllister hiked back up the Adams Trail to the truck and drove back to Kanab to get more pipe and a booster for the pump.

But things just didn't work out for Swapp. He had been ill throughout the ordeal of replacing the pump & pipe, so he decided to remain in Kanab until he felt better. However, he got worse instead. Finally he was taken to the hospital in Cedar City, where he died on March 28, 1949.

After this second effort to pump Paria River water up on the benchland surrounding the canyon, no one ever tried the feat again. And there it sits today; the engine, pump and one length of pipe running into the ground where the sump was dug. You can still see it on the north side of the stream, on a low bench, at the mouth of Judd Hollow between miles P17 & P18 on the BLM log map. More on this later.

Now back to hiking. To find the **Adams Trail**, walk downstream about 300m from where the south arm of **4th Crack** drains into the canyon. On the south side of the creek, on a minor bench, and in an area which is rather broad, look for yet another rounded bench rising about 10m above the embankment. You may first notice some moki steps notched into the sandstone wall. It's possible these could be old

This shows about all of the **Adams Trail**. On the right it goes up the side of the wind-blown sandune, then to the left behind the sand, then cuts back to the right, and finally angles up to the left before reaching a ramp which runs up a minor drainage to the top of the Sand Hills

Indian-made steps, because they're very smooth and worn today. The author never climbed the steep part using these steps. But just to the east or left (as you look at the sloping rock wall), is a near-vertical 1-2m-wide crack in the sandstone bench. You have to use all-4's to make it up, but it's easy climbing. For a closer look at this trail, see the little insert on **Map 30, Lower Paria River Gorge--Part 2.**

Once you arrive on this first bench, walk east along a good trail, gradually turning to the right or south. Almost immediately you begin to walk up a steep sandslide covered with cactus. To avoid damaging this pristine cactus field, follow the established hiker's trail as it veers to the right and southwest, then turn south into a minor drainage. Further up you'll come to the base of a talus & sandy slope on the right or west. Head straight up this slope which comes down from where a minor drainage comes off the wall in front of you. As you arrive near the top of this sandy slope, you begin to see part of the original constructed trail. Near the top, and almost next to the canyon wall, turn right or northwest, and walk along the base of the cliff. After about 100m, you come to more cliffs and at first it appears to be a dead-end. At that point, look to the left, or south along the cliff face, and you'll just be able to make out a faint line indicating the trail angling up along the cliff face. Walk up this ramp, which is a little steep in a place or two, but which is easy walking. An unloaded burro may or may not make it up, but a big horn sheep or deer would have no trouble.

Further along, you come to a level section, then less than 100m away, you'll again come to what is obviously a constructed trail. It zig zags up one last steep place to the southwest before running due south up the minor drainage you saw from below. At the top of this draw, the trail vanishes in the sand.

This is an easy walk, and it seems a pity no one took the time to finish the trail. Just a little more work, and it would be good enough for a horse to use. Once you get on the trail, anyone can make it to the top in about half an hour. From the top, you can walk along the rim in either direction for some fine views of the canyon below. Just south of the top of the trail are some fotogenic sandstone fins.

Now going downriver again. Between the Adams Trail and the mouth of Judd Hollow, the river makes several tight bends and is again enclosed in high walls. After about 1 1/2 kms, you'll come to a 250m section where several large boulders have fallen off the canyon wall and landed in the stream channel. In this part, the river meanders back and forth between rocks. In times of flood and high water, deep holes are scoured out next to some of these boulders. If you're there not long after a flood, you may encounter the deepest water of the entire hike. A walking stick would be helpful, but on the author's last trip in 2009, there was a trail around all these boulders mostly on the north bank, so deep wading may be a thing of the past.

An Episode of Military Explorations and Surveys--October, 1872

This place, which the author calls **Boulder Alley,** may have been the place which inspired a story to be written about the Paria Canyon by a member of the October, 1872, military expedition to the region. The author found this story, **An Episode of Military Explorations and Surveys,** in the **October, 1881** issue of **The United Service**. It was written nearly a decade after the event, and for obvious reasons. The author is identified only as T. V. B., and it goes like this (edited slightly for this book).

I know that the hero of the following narrative would rather lose his tongue than speak of a noble deed performed by himself. Nevertheless, every noble action deserves to be known. I beg the Lieutenant's Pardon.

In the month of October, 1872, the different field-parties composing "explorations and surveys west

The **Adams Water Pump**. The flathead engine on the right, pump with pipes on the left.

of the one hundredth meridian," rendezvoused near St. George, in Southern Utah, and after a week spent in preparations for the final work of the season, again broke camp, the writer being assigned to the "party of the southeast," of which Lieutenant W. L. M., of the corps of engineers, had charge. The duty assigned to this "party" was the exploration of the "rim of the Great Basin" of Southern Utah, thence to go to the Colorado River, ascend and explore the Canyon of the Paria, and return.

After a couple of days' march, the greater number of packers and escort were left in camp, as it was thought that a smaller party could do more effective work, and the number of explorers was reduced to ten,--Lieutenant M., Mr. W., topographer, a cook, two packers, two soldiers, a Mormon, a Pah-Ute, and myself. The Indian was to be our guide, but as he only knew enough English to ask for whisky, the Mormon was taken along as interpreter.

In those high regions the nights were already disagreeably cold, so that after making camp we would pile up half a dozen dead pine-trees and start a fire that lit up the pine woods for miles, and sometimes even compelled us to shift camp, much to the disgust of our Pah-Ute, who was fearful of a visit from his dreaded foes, the Navajos, and did his best to convince us that one could warm himself better over a small fire than a large one, generally finishing the pantomime by telling us that "whitey man big fool!"

In due time we struck the "Great Navajo Trail," used by the Navajo Indians in their annual trading expeditions to the settlements of Southern Utah, and here our Indian became quite frantic with anxiety to go back to his own hunting-grounds, pleading that "his father never went farther;" but he had to stay with us, and every morning, without fail, he mysteriously showed us the footprints of savage enemies who had been lurking about the camp through the night--though we failed to see an Indian during the entire trip, or had even a mule stolen.

The party derived considerable amusement from the repugnance of the mule ridden by Lieutenant M. for the Pah-Ute: neither did time do much towards reconciling the two. Whenever the Indian made his appearance unexpectedly before the lieutenant's charger, off came the lieutenant and away went the mule, a maneuver to which our chief at last became so accustomed that rather than be violently ejected from the saddle, he would gracefully slide off when he saw "coming events cast their shadows before," and he owned, good-naturedly, that when that mule wanted him off he might as well come. So the Indian was quite as much a trial to the lieutenant as the mule.

We encamped on the Paria River two miles from its junction with the Colorado. I speak of the Paria as a river because it is honored with that rank on the maps, but feel as though I owe the reader an apology for deceiving him, for in a less arid country it would scarcely be dignified with the name of creek. But in this respect the pilgrim of the great trans-Rocky Southwest cannot afford to be fastidious. In these water-scarce regions everything having the appearance of running water is at least a creek, and the imagination delights in exalting a creek into a river. So on all the maps of New Mexico and Arizona, the Rio Colorado Chiquito [Little Colorado River] figures prominently, and would readily impose itself upon the unwary as a second Mississippi, yet memory vividly and lugubriously recalls the times when, not in one particular locality but in many, I boldly straddled it with my legs, and in that position washed my soiled undergarments; and worse, for too often it contained no water to wash with at all.

Two miles from our camp, at the junction of the Colorado and Paria, amid that weird scenery, isolated from all the world, was the ranch of John D. Lee, late bishop and major in the Mormon Church. The martial bishop was not often at home, and Mrs. Lee No. 17, with her nine children, garrisoned the ranch and battled with the elements for a livelihood.

In the mean time we had lost our Indian and his adjutant, the Mormon, much to the relief of Lieutenant M.'s charger. The two worthies had, from the beginning, overloaded their stomachs with ham and bacon, articles of diet to which the Indian and Mormon stomach is not accustomed, and had brought upon themselves severe bilious attacks.

The canyon of the Paria, which we were now to explore, was estimated to be about thirty two miles in length, and it was said that no human being had ever succeeded in getting through it. A flock of geese, the Mormons told us, had swam through the canyon, from the Mormon settlement of Paria to the Colorado River, and though we did not succeed in getting through it ourselves, our very failure, methinks proves that we were not geese.

Early on the morning of November 20 [1872] we started on the performance of what we all knew would be a difficult and dangerous task. At first the gorge was several hundred yards wide, the walls of the canyon sloping and not more than seven hundred feet in height; but with every mile the canyon narrowed and its walls became higher and more vertical, until at the end of five miles it did not average more than thirty yards in width, while the walls had attained a vertical height of fifteen hundred feet. The creek occupied the middle of the chasm, and often the entire space, from wall to wall, so that we were obliged continually to cross and recross it, as well as ride against the stream, a task which was rendered more difficult by oft-recurring patches of quicksand in which our animals became mired, obliging us to make frequent halts to dig them out. In this way we accomplished ten miles the first day, camping in a cottonwood grove where the canyon had widened, and where enough grass grew to feed our animals.

The next day the difficulties increased. Occasionally the walls met overhead forming caverns dark as night, through which we waded and half swam, often compelled to bend over the saddle, so low was the rocky ceiling. Nor was the labor of urging the bewildered mules through these dark passages an easy one. That night we encamped, wet and chilled, on a peninsula of rocks large enough to accommodate ourselves and our animals.

The third day was bitter cold. Soon after starting the mule, ridden by the cook, Kittelman, a middle-aged German, whose duty on the march it was to lead the burdenless bell-horse, sank, belly-deep, in quicksand, and stuck fast, keeling over on his side and lying on Kittelman. We were occupied half an hour digging out the mule, during which time it required the strength of two men to keep the mule's head above water, and of one to perform a similar office for the poor cook. The mule, in his struggles, frequently struck Kittelman in the face, so that the latter, when extricated, was badly bruised and stupid from cold and excitement. No time was to be lost, however, and in his half-frozen condition the man had to mount the bell-horse and follow the party.

We now found ice formed in localities where the water was deeper and less rapid. This increased in thickness from one-eighth to one-half inch, when our mules refused to take to it farther, and we found ourselves compelled to dismount, wade up the icy stream, often to our armpits in water, and here and there break the crust of ice by means of our carbines, rocks, etc. This task was performed by Lieutenant M. and myself, for which purpose we kept a few hundred yards ahead of the party, leading our mules.

About 3 P.M. we came to a sharp bend in the canyon, where the water had cut into and undermined a portion of the wall, forming a large and deep pool about fifty feet wide and forty feet long, which was also covered with a crust of ice, half an inch thick. This pool we must needs cross. After breaking up the ice with large rocks, I attempted to wade through it, but when about ten feet from the edge sunk knee-deep in quicksand and was fain to scramble back. I then mounted my mule and attempted to ride him in, but no amount of either urging or coaxing would induce the otherwise tractable animal to take to the water. Lieutenant M. then made the attempt with his mule, with the same result; the animals instinctively shrank back. By this time the remainder of the party had come up. The bell-horse had been ridden by the cook since the accident of the morning, and was saddled. I was about to mount him to ride him through the pool, knowing that he would obey under all circumstances, when Kittelman, though shivering with cold and scarcely more than half conscious, anticipated the movement, saying that he was not afraid to ride his horse where any other man was willing to go. The animal entered the pool without hesitation, and had gotten nearly halfway across when, as if sucked down, man and horse disappeared. In about twenty seconds the man's head again came to the surface, as well as that of the horse, Kittelman no longer on the horse but evidently still clutching the bridle,--his gaze vacant. After a few seconds, to our horror, man and horse again disappeared, and now it was that we began to realize that a human being, our companion and servitor during months of exploring, was about to perish before our eyes--almost within reach of our hands--and we utterly powerless to help, for who would plunge into that ice-covered pool, occupied as it was by a horse struggling for life?

Among the party was a packer by the name of Evans, a large, powerful man. He had passed most of his life in Oregon, and his swimming-feats on the Columbia River, as related by himself, surpassed those performed by Leander and Byron. To him all eyes were now turned and there he stood, the picture of sickening fear and cowardice. Lieutenant M. now called out in agonized tones, "My God! will nobody save that man?" and hearing no response, without waiting to disencumber himself of overcoat or boots, he plunged, head foremost, into the awful hole. After fifteen seconds of terrible suspense, during which the horse had regained the surface and crawled to the rocks on which we were assembled, Lieutenant M. reappeared, holding the body of Kittelman in his arms. The latter was still alive, but only drew breath four or five times after leaving the water. We at once placed him on a pile of blankets, and four of the party chafed him vigorously for an hour and used other means of resuscitation, but in vain--he was dead.

In the mean time one of our packers had scaled a crevice in the rocks, to a point where a lot of stunted cedars could be seen, of which he threw down a sufficient quantity to keep up a fire during the night. Though not unused to hardships and stirring scenes, I shall never forget that night's camp. We were upon a peninsula of rocks, just large enough to accommodate the party; beside us flowed the dark stream; over us rose to a vertical height of over three thousand feet the rocky walls of the chasm, but a few stars being visible. The body of Kittelman lay a few feet from the fire, covered by a blanket. The glare of the fire served only to intensify the weirdness of the scene. Added to this was the knowledge that should tomorrow be an unusually warm day the snow would melt in the mountains, the stream would rise, and we should be drowned like rats in a cage before the end of the canyon could again be reached.

So we waited anxiously for morning. The body of Kittelman was sewed up, sailor-fashion, in a piece of canvas and packed on a mule, the frozen bones cracking horribly during the process. We carried the body with us for about two hours, when we came upon a crevice in the rocks, some twelve feet above low water, and into that we laid the remains and covered them with rocks, assured that no human hands would ever disturb them.

And though we returned to the mouth of the canyon unsuccessful, and with a life less, we had gained a hero more.

T. V. B.

Portions of this military episode in the Paria Gorge are obviously exaggerated and were written to entertain. Very seldom is there quicksand in the canyon, but horses could easily get quagmired. Their feet cover less area than do humans, but they might have 10 times more body weight. John D. Lee however did take a herd of cows down this same canyon, almost exactly one year before this military expedition, and it took him 8 days to get from Pah Ria (Rock House) to the Colorado River.

Going downstream again. About 700m below Boulder Alley, where the big rocks are in the stream channel, you'll come to the **Adams Water Pump** on the left, about 5m above the creek. Just behind the pump is another of many abandoned meanders in the canyon. Less than 1 km below the pump and on a sharp bend in the river, are several good campsites, possibly a good spring and a panel of petroglyphs--between miles P18 & P19.

Just below the petroglyphs, you'll normally begin to see seeps along the stream's edge. Along the river between the petroglyphs and The Hole are many places where you can camp and get water--just above mile P19. Each time the author visited this part of the canyon they were flowing.

The next feature of interest is **The Hole**, which is near mile P19 on the new BLM map. The Hole is the very bottom end of a canyon draining off the Sand Hills which flows into the Paria. All you'll see from the river is this lower end. At the very bottom of this drainage, and right next to the river, the seeping waters have eroded away the sandstone, making an alcove or cave-like feature shaped like an inverted key hole; thus the name.

You can walk into this dark recess about 40m, where you'll find a seep at the very back end, right where the water falls when it comes off the slickrock country above. Near the entrance to The Hole, you can set up camp on a little bench, which is completely under a big overhang. This would be a good place to camp for those hardy souls who prefer to travel without a tent. The seep will likely have water when you arrive, although it's not on anybody's *"best springs list"*. Upstream about 50m or so, is another seep, which had a good flow upon each of the author's visits.

It's in the area below the Adams Pump that the canyon begins to widen, and from The Hole down, it continues to open up even more. Between The Hole and Wrather Canyon there isn't anything special to see, except there are many places with scattered cottonwood trees which could make good campsites. Only problem is, the author doesn't recall seeing many good seeps.

Wrather Canyon and Beginning of Map 31

Wrather Canyon is one of the real gems of the Lower Paria River Gorge. It's a short side-canyon, only about 1 km long, but it has one of the most interesting & impressive arches in the world called **Wrather Arch**. There's also a spring not far below the arch, which provides water for a small year-round flowing stream in the lower part of the canyon. This is between mile P20 & P21 on the BLM map.

As you approach this canyon from upstream, you'll be looking right into it. But as the stream inside

Wrather comes near the Paria, it turns abruptly east and parallels the Paria for maybe 250m. You'll have to reach the very mouth of Wrather Creek before you can enter this drainage. Inside the canyon, a hiker-made trail runs up to and underneath the arch. Along the way is a good example of riparian vegetation. There are several huge cottonwood and box elder trees, water cress, mosses, cattails, and other plants this author can't describe. It's a little green paradise in the middle of the desert.

Because the bottom of Wrather is so narrow and fragile, the BLM asks that hikers not camp in the canyon. There's not much space anyway. Instead, camp at the mouth of the canyon across the river to the north, and/or in one of several groves of cottonwood trees nearby. When you go up to the arch, take your empty water jugs to be filled. By not camping inside the canyon, you can also help preserve the good quality of water for those who follow in your footsteps.

Wrather Canyon Overlook Hike & South Rim Indian Trail

For those with a little time who like climbing and want a break from trudging along in this seemingly endless gorge, here's a diversion. Take a hike to the canyon rim right above Wrather Arch.

From the campsites at the mouth of Wrather, head downcanyon about 750m. At about that point you'll be passing through an area of tall grasses, sort of like bullrushes. On the right or south side, will be a low bench which you can breach easily. Above this low bench is a triangle-shaped sandslide coming down from the southeast; walk straight up this toward its apex. Since about 2003, there has been an emerging hiker's trail; follow it up. At the top is a steep gully coming down to the top of the sandslide. But don't climb up that gully; instead just above the sandslide, look for a little bench to your right or south side. Get on it and walk west. In 2009, the author placed several cairns there; hopefully they'll stay as this new found route is much easier & safer than climbing unstable rock at the head of the gully.

After walking 50-75m along this bench, turn left or south, and using real honest-to-goodness **moki steps**, climb over a couple of fins and up a tight crack, and out. The Indians apparently used moki steps to go straight up one fin, but it's exposed and the steps are slowly eroding away, so look for a crack to climb which is safer. Once over this hump, contour south until you're in a shallow drainage, then route-find straight up to a saddle, then turn right or south and scramble up to the canyon rim.

Upon arriving at the top, rim-walk west towards the edge of Wrather Canyon. You should reach the rim directly above the arch. It looks a lot smaller from above than when you're in the canyon, indicating the great height of the wall you're standing on. On one trip to the rim, the author spotted 3 desert big horn rams on the rim directly above the arch. This hike may be one of the best side-trips in the whole canyon. Take fotos of the arch from about midmorning through midday.

North Rim Overlook Hike & Indian Trail

If you're a natural bridge watcher, here's a hike that will place you high on the north rim of the Paria

directly across from the mouth of Wrather Canyon. From this overlook, you can see right up Wrather for one of the best views of the arch.

Begin at the campsites at the mouth of Wrather and walk downcanyon about 300m. As you pass the last corner, look straight north and to the left a little, and you'll see a kind of crack canyon, similar to the fault-made cracks further upstream. It's shape and geologic origin become very clear when viewed from the south rim.

Head straight for the crack, passing where you can through the low cliff or bench made by one of the lower layers of Navajo Sandstone. Just as you're about to enter the bottom of the crack canyon, look to your right and at the corner, and you'll see a good panel of **petroglyphs.** In about the same area on your left or west, is a single rock art figure which is hard to see. To the author and others, this rock art, (along with the **moki**

This niche in the canyon wall is known as **The Hole,** or sometimes Keyhole. It's located a couple of kms upstream from Wrather Canyon. There's always good drinking water seeping out from the bottom of this big dryfall.

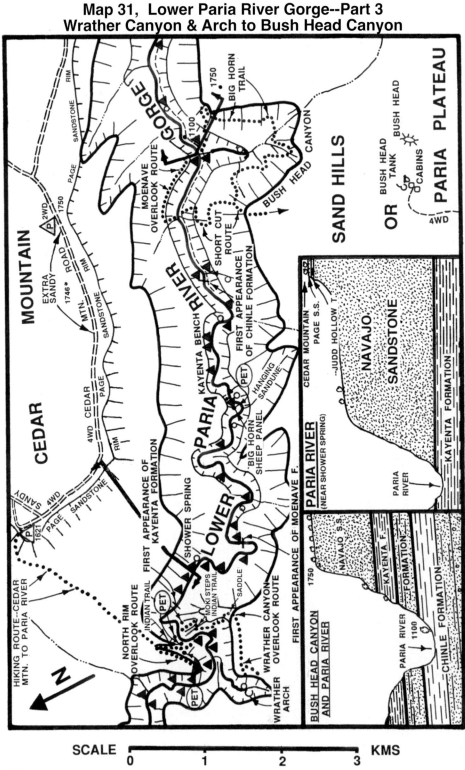

SCALE

0   1   2   3

KMS

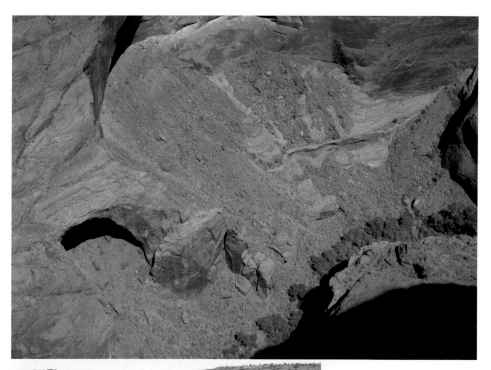

Above From the rim of the northern Sand Hills, you have a good look down at the head of **Wrather Canyon** and **Wrather Arch**. Running water begins flowing in the green bottom toward the right-hand side of this picture. Also there are trails up to and under one of the more unusual arches in the world. To get a good foto from this site, be there about mid-day.

Left Wrather Canyon with **Wrather Arch** dead center in the middle of the foto. This picture was taken from the **North Rim Overlook** as shown on Map 31; this is immediately next to an old Indian trail or route going down and across the canyon to the Sand Hills on the other side. For best foto results, be there around mid-day, and in late May or June with high sun. This means fewer north face shadows.

187

Left From the south rim of the Paria looking north at the **Indian trail & North Rim Overlook**. The Indian trail runs from lower left to upper right. **Right** From the north rim looking south at the **Indian trail** to the south rim. Go up the sandslide to the middle of foto, turn right, cross a couple of fins (where the **M** is in Moki) using **moki steps**. Continue right aways, then up to the saddle & rim.

Looking southeast at the south-side **Indian trail** up to the **Sand Hills**. Go up the sandslide to the left, then come back toward the camera on a little bench (below the words Moki **Steps**), cross a couple of fins using **moki steps** (see foto page 189). Continue route-finding right, then up to the saddle & rim.

steps mentioned above located on the opposite side of the canyon), indicates an old **Indian trail**, as they normally made etchings along well-traveled routes. This is the only place in the canyon where you can go from rim to rim, with a quick river crossing in between. There's another panel of petroglyphs on the other side of the river (the author didn't find this on his last trip), at about the place you begin the hike up to the Wrather Canyon Overlook, lending more credibility to the idea that this is an old Indian trail or route across the canyon.

As you enter the narrow chasm, you'll be climbing due south. The way is easy at first, then it steepens and narrows. The upper part is almost vertical, but since it's right on the fault line, there was a buildup of minerals in the crack, which is now exposed. This new rock, different from the Navajo Sandstone, is harder and has numerous hand & footholds. So although it's nearly vertical, and somewhere between 12-14m high, it's quite easy to climb. Just at the very bottom of the pitch is a chokestone you must pass on the right. With a little help from a friend, most people should be able to chimney or wedge their way up this 2m-high obstacle. Take a short rope for less-experienced hikers, especially on the way down. The author had no problems in his 7-8 trips up & down this, and he was always alone.

After the steep pitch, it's just a scramble to the rim where you'll then make a hard left turn, and walk southwest to a point overlooking the river and the mouth of Wrather Canyon. Late morning to midday, and in late spring or early summer, would be the best time for taking fotos of the arch. Take a telefoto lens.

Another way to reach Wrather Arch and this part of the canyon is to come down this old Indian route from above. Read all about that under **Map 34, North Rim Hikes: Lower Paria River Gorge,....**

Going downcanyon again. The next important stop is **Shower Spring**, 2 kms downcanyon from the mouth of Wrather and on the left or north side. It's at mile P22 on the BLM map. Throughout the years this one has proved to be a good reliable waterhole. Water drips off a mossy ledge into a knee-deep pool, which you'll have to look for it (and listen) behind some willows--just follow the trails in the area on the left/north side of the stream. This important spring comes out of the rock right at the contact point between the Navajo Sandstone above, and the Kayenta Formation below. This indicates the permeability of the Navajo, and the impermeability of the Kayenta. Across the river is a fine campsite.

Below Shower Spring, the canyon widens still further, and the Kayenta Bench becomes more prominently exposed. Between Wrather & Bush Head Canyons, there are several minor seeps or springs, including one which comes out of the wall on the south side of the river below a big **hanging sandune** in a basin above. As you near the cliffs below the hanging sandune leave the creek bed and get on the bench to the left or northeast side. At the same time, be looking up to your left at the smooth wall covered with black desert varnish. There you'll see perhaps the best petroglyph panel in the canyon. That wall is covered with etchings of big horn sheep, thus the name, **Big Horn Panel.** About 1 1/2 kms below the hanging sandune & rock art panel, is the last seemingly-reliable spring in the main canyon before reaching Lee's Ferry. There's also a place to camp near mile P25.

Bush Head Canyon, Transplanting Big Horn Sheep & the Big Horn Trail

The next major stop is **Bush Head Canyon,** between miles P26 & P27 on the BLM log map. Like Wrather, this one is very short, less than 1 1/2 kms from the river to its headwall. At the mouth of this canyon are several campsites, and best of all, normally good clear water. It may or may not be flowing

Left Part of the **Big Horn Panel** located about halfway between Wrather & Bush Head Canyons. **Right** Real old & well-worn **moki steps** along the **Indian trail** up to the south rim of the Paria River Gorge just downcanyon from Wrather Canyon. Some steps were really big at one time.

down to the Paria when you arrive, but even if it does, it might be best to walk 700-800m upcanyon to where a very good spring comes right out of the bottom of the Moenave Formation. The water in this little canyon is surely good to drink as-is, because cattle don't quite make it up that far. However, the water has a kind of swampy taste to it in the lower end near the river. This is caused by decaying cottonwood and box elder leaves lying in the creek bed. At the spring itself, it's *puro agua dulce!*

Immediately above the spring, is a dryfall and you can't go up any further in the bottom of the canyon. But, for the adventurous hiker who enjoys a little climbing, here's a fun side-trip. The author calls it the **Big Horn Trail.** Actually there are no real trails involved, just a couple of routes to the canyon rim that are occasionally used by desert big horn sheep.

But the story behind the desert big horns must first be told. As indicated by the hundreds of petroglyph panels in the region, almost all of which show etchings of big horn sheep, one can conclude this magnificent animal has long been a part of the scene in this canyon & mesa country. But in the period of a little more than a century since the white man first began exploring the region, their numbers have gradually shrunk. Local ranchers believe the big horns caught diseases from domestic sheep and were hunted to near extinction. It appears these virtually disappeared in the Paria Canyon, so it was decided to reintroduce desert big horn sheep to this gorge.

In July of 1984, the Arizona Game & Fish Department, in cooperation with the BLM, started to carry out the plan. Because of the overgrazed desert big horn sheep range on the south shore of Lake Mead, which is part of the Lake Mead National Recreation Area, it was decided to capture some of those sheep and place them in other areas suitable for their existence. The places chosen were the Lower Kanab Creek (between Kanab and the Colorado River), the Paria River Canyon and the Vermilion Cliffs.

Altogether, 53 sheep were captured in July of 1984, of which 16 were taken to the Kanab Creek area. The remaining 37 were taken to Lee's Ferry. Nineteen were taken to and released at Fisher Springs, not far west of Lee's Ferry, and up against the Vermilion Cliffs. The remaining 18 sheep were transported by helicopter to the Bush Head Canyon area and released.

In the Bush Head Canyon release, there were 11 females or ewes, and 7 males or rams. Of the 18, five females were equipped with radio-telemetry collars. These special radios have the ability to send out a signal, not only when the sheep is alive and well, but can also detect when the animal dies with a mortality sensor. The radio signals are then monitored periodically by aircraft.

In the weeks and months following the transplant, numerous flights were made over both release sites to monitor their movements. Very little movement or migration was detected at first, but in the time since, the herd of sheep at Fisher Springs has moved out along the base of the Vermilion Cliffs, with several going into the Marble Canyon region. Those at Bush Head seemed to stay nearer the release site. About 8 months after the release, 2 sensors noted fatalities in the Bush Head area. In late February, 1985, with the help of a helicopter, the 2 big horns were found dead, apparently having fallen from icy cliffs.

After about a year's time, it was observed that the Bush Head sheep had started migrating, perhaps on a seasonal basis, to other locations along the Paria River and to the mesa top, or the Sand Hills/Paria Plateau. But each time the Game & Fish people fly over the region, it's been found that the sheep stay pretty close to the initial release site, indicating that location is a good one. In November, 1984, a volunteer group from Arizona State University helped to build a slickrock water catchment basin somewhere on the plateau above Bush Head Canyon. In 11/2003, while hiking up the Dominguez Trail just

Left From the south rim north of Bush Head Tank is this **hanging sandune**, which resembles a hanging glacier in other locals. **Right** The same **hanging sandune** as seen from the north rim of the Lower Paria River Gorge. From where this foto was taken, you can almost get to the bottom.

above Lee's Ferry, the author saw, at fairly close range, 2 groups of big horns totaling 11 head. In 7/2009, he also saw a single full-curl ram running up the west side of The Big Knoll in the Sand Hills.

Over the years, the author made several trips up from the bottom and the Paria, just to check out the ways these sheep were getting up & down the canyon wall from the river to the rim. On an earlier trip, he saw at close range, 3 big horns on the lip of Wrather Canyon, which sparked this curiosity. In the end, he found 2 routes from the river to the rim and to the Sand Hills rock feature called Bush Head. Here's one way to the canyon rim. **See Map 31, Lower Paria River Gorge--Part 3.** From the very mouth of Bush Head Canyon, look southeast up the steep hillside You'll see a talus slope, then a green place with tall grasses and bullrushes, indicating a wet spot or minor seep just below the first bench. Head that way, straight up to the southeast. From the first little ledge, make your way up through several more benches and minor cliffs. Remember, you're heading for the big bench, just below the massive Navajo Sandstone wall. There's an easy way through each little bench, but you'll have to zig zag a bit, and route-find on your own to find the easier places to pass through. As you near the big terrace, bench-walk or contour to the left or east a little and into a minor drainage. On the other side of this gully is one last step or cliff to get through, which is again easy. Once on top of this, bench-walk or contour first around to the west, then south, heading toward the big south wall of upper Bush Head Basin.

As you near the headwall, you'll have to walk down through a break in the top layer of the Kayenta to the mini valley below, then route-find back up to and into the most western of the 2 alcoves at the head of the canyon. Go straight for some trees, which appear to be near a spring (but there's no spring or water).

From the head of this second draw, turn right and walk due north, still contouring or bench-walking along the top of the Kayenta. In one little mini canyon, you'll come to a cliff where it appears that'll be the end of your hike; but from there simply walk uphill to the west, then down a little ramp to the bottom, thence again contour to the north.

As you near the area southwest of the mouth of Bush Head Canyon, you'll see in front of you another small canyon coming down from the left, or west, and a sandslide just beyond. Head up this canyon, but just into it, veer to the right or northwest, and route-find up through some minor cliffs. This part is nearly a walkup all the way to the rim.

From the rim, you might choose to walk due south about 2 kms to Bush Head, or the **Bush Head Stock Tank**. At that old stockman's camp are 2 old cabins, a stockade-type corral, and a small concrete dam, located at the base of a little slickrock valley. If there's been rain in the region recently, this stock tank will have some water. But don't drink this, it's full of cow poop! Cattle graze this area during the winter months, making the water unfit to drink. Read more about it in the Sand Hills History.

Back at the Big Horn Trail. The longer and more scenic route has been described. If you've come up this one, but want a shorter way down, take the **Short-cut Route** back to the river. Begin at the very last part of the first route described. Walk straight down the cliffy slope, but when it becomes less steep, veer to the left or northwest, and make your way around some of the intertongued beds at the contact point of the Navajo & Kayenta. There is no way of describing the route, except to say you may have to zig zag a little to reach the river. At one place, the author chimneyed down a 10m-high crack in one of the ledges. If he had walked still further west, he may have found an easier way and walked down through this bench.

Looking northeast from the **Bush Head Tank** or reservoir, toward **Cedar Mountain** on the north rim of the Paria Canyon. A dirt tank may have been built in the 1930's by Glen Hamblin; the cement dam was put in later. Read more about its history in the **History of the Sand Hills** section of this book.

As you work your way down this slope, you'll see a minor drainage below. Head for it. But just as you think you've got it made, you'll come to one last cliff. The author jumped down this one, but you can walk through it if you'll veer to the right and bench-walk to the east until you come to a mini-dugway, where you walk down to the north and to the river and trail.

Whichever route you go up or down, it'll involve some route-finding. There are no serious obstacles, but you may have to do some zig zagging on either of these routes to find the easy way up or down through the Kayenta and Moenave Formations. Take all the water you'll need for the day, as there's none above Bush Head Spring, and you can't get to the spring from either of the routes just described. Also, take a lunch, as you can spend a day on this one. The author lost time exploring around for the Big Horn Trail, then went all the way to Bush Head Tank, finally returning via the Short-cut Route, arriving back at camp in just under 9 hours. Without the side-trip to Bush Head Tank, it would have been an easy day-hike. Most people would be happy to just get to the rim and return directly to camp, taking most of a day. If you have a 4WD, you can drive to Bush Head Tank anyway.

In 2003, the author came down the old Indian trail from the North Rim to the river, walked down-canyon to this Short-cut Route, then climbed to the top, rim-walked northwest to view Wrather Arch, went down the south-side Indian trail with moki steps to the river and finally up the other Indian trail back to his Chevy Tracker on Cedar Mountain. That took 9 1/4 hours. In 2009, he did the same hike, but visited Bush Head Tank along the way, returning in 10 1/3 hours.

While interviewing some of the old-timers in the region about the early-day history of the canyon, the late Mel Schoppman of Greene Haven (northwest of Page), told the author about a scheme by his fa-ther John, and Rubin Broadbent. It seems they were looking for ways to either get water up to their cat-tle on top of the Sand Hills, or take cattle down to the river below. They searched, and finally found a way off the plateau and down to the river at Bush Head Canyon. The route they made on horseback was along what has just been described as the Short-cut Route. They considered constructing a cat-tle trail, but it turned out to be too big a job. Years later Mel Schoppman also made it up through the cliffs on horseback. With a little scouting around, this is an easy walkup route.

According to everyone the author talked to, there are no routes up through the Vermilion Cliffs to the Paria Plateau between Bush Head Canyon and the Eastern Sand Hills Crack, discussed under **Map 42**. Rock climbers could surely find a route, but it likely couldn't be climbed by ordinary hikers.

Now back to hiking down the Paria. As you leave Bush Head Canyon on your way to Lee's Ferry, you'll be walking along the south side of the river on an old cattle trail, which over the years has gradu-ally gotten better and more distinct with the increase of hikers. Actually, from 3-4 kms above Bush Head, you can get on the south side of the river and stay there until you're in the area of the first of many prominent boulders with petroglyphs, as shown on **Map 32**. In this section of about 10-12 kms, you won't have to cross the stream once--unless you want to.

The reason for the trail winding its way up and above the river is that in this part of the canyon the softer beds of the Chinle Formation are beginning to be exposed. When this occurs, the canyon auto-matically widens, and the cliffs made of the Navajo, Kayenta and Moenave Formations, begin to pull apart. As this happens, large boulders break off the canyon walls and roll down into the stream chan-nel. In this section, the stream channel itself is choked with these house-sized rocks, therefore it's been easier to walk on the bench above, than right along the river.

About 2 1/2 kms below Bush Head Canyon, you may see where **F.T. Johnson** left his inscription on **May 30, 1912**. It's on a boulder just south of the trail (to your right) with the etching facing northwest. No doubt, Frank was chasing cows! Farther downcanyon and just before you get back down to the river, look to the right or west to see a large boulder with rock art on the south side and top. That boul-

Frank T. Johnson was the son of Warren Johnson. The Johnsons ran Lee's Ferry for many years. They also farmed and ran cattle to about as far as Bush Head Canyon.

Map 32, Lower Paria River Gorge--Part 4
Bush Head Canyon to Lee's Ferry

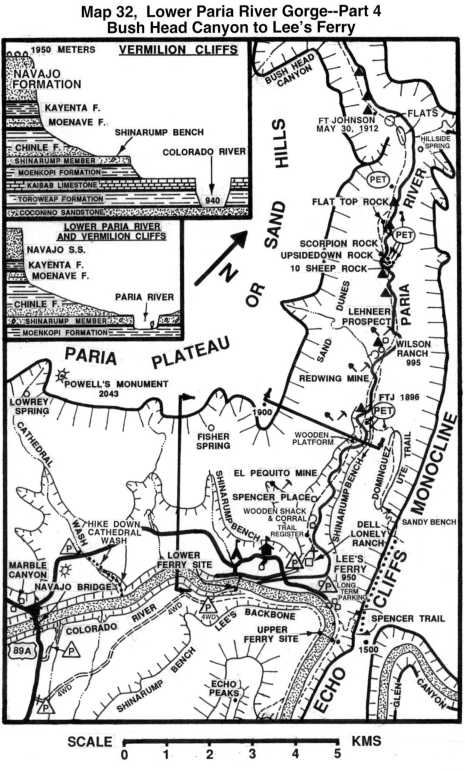

This is either **Flat Top Rock**, or the one up the trail a ways. Rock art is on all boulders in the area.

This boulder is called **Scorpion Rock**; can you see the scorpion on the left?

der is 6-8m west of the trail.

Further along and about 750m below where you first reach the river, you'll be walking along a bench made of whitish sandstone. To your left 25m or so, you may see a red-colored boulder on top of the lighter slickrock bench. On top of that square-shaped rock are more petroglyphs. This is near mile P31. This the author calls **Flat Top Rock** on **Map 32.** From about that point, look up and to the east side of the river, and you can see a couple of boulders standing alone on the sandy hillside. One of these also has petroglyphs.

This is called **Upsidedown Rock**, and for obvious reasons. It seems to have rolled down the slope halfway through an etching party.

The author calls this one **10 Sheep Rock**. All or most of these boulders are within a kilometer or two of each other. Almost every large rock or boulder in that area has some kind of rock art on it.

The **Wilson Ranch** site. The house was located to the right of the trees in the background. The corral must have been for horses because the highest logs are about 2m above the ground.

About 1 km below Flat Top Rock, and as you first cross over the river to the east side, are at least a dozen large rocks or boulders with panels of petroglyphs. These are between miles P31 & P32. One is called **Scorpion Rock**, because of a large scorpion-like figure on it. Another is **Upside Down Rock,** because half the glyphs are upside down. The rock must have rolled down the slope halfway through an etching party. These last 2 boulders are immediately left of the well-defined trail. Just around the corner and up the slope about 30m to your left is another good one. This might be called **10 Sheep Rock**. It has, among other glyphs, 10 big horn sheep in a line. If you spend a little time there, you may find even more rock art. These *boulderglyphs* are some of the best the author has seen, and up till now, there's no paleface graffiti on them. There's a good campsite under 2 cottonwood trees just across the river and down a bit from these boulderglyphs, but you'd have to purify and drink river water.

The Wilson Ranch and old Uranium Mines

About 2 kms downstream from the petroglyphs, you may see at a point where the river turns east, some old fence posts, some minor seeps, and an old mine test hole called the **Lehneer Prospect**. Another 200m further and on your right as the trail turns south, is an old road running up on a bench. This looks like a rock wall. This may be part of the old **Wilson Ranch** (?). About 500m below that, you'll come to some large cottonwood trees on the west bank, where the old Wilson Ranch house once stood. It's between miles P33 & P34 on the BLM log map. The house foundations can still be seen, as well as a cement trough of some kind. At that point, and just behind you to the north are the remains of a small wooden shack built next to a large boulder.

The Wilson Ranch was first built by Owen Johnson and Sid Wilson in about 1918. They gathered lumber from a sawmill on the Kaibab near Jacob Lake, and logs from Lee's Ferry, and hauled them in wagons about 8 kms upriver to this site. With this material they built a rather large 2-room cabin, in the shape of an "L". According to the late George W. Fisher, each room measured about 6 x 8m.

It was Sid Wilson who lived there and claimed the rights to the place. Throughout the years, no one ever actually owned the ranch, but each person who lived there was able to claim and sell his squatter's and water rights. While at the ranch, Wilson ran some cattle, but worked at other jobs too. At one time he was the one who measured the water levels of the Paria and Colorado Rivers at Lee's Ferry.

In 1927, Wilson left and sold his rights to Pete Nelson, but Nelson didn't actually live at the place until after about 1930. In 1933, George W. Fisher bought out Nelson, and lived there until he was drafted into the military in 1944. The BLM, which in the days before 1947 was called the Grazing Service, allowed Fisher to run about 200 head of cattle during his stay at the ranch.

It was the Fishers who installed a rough wooden floor to the house and covered it with Navajo rugs. They also built a windmill and hooked it up to a small generator. The electricity first went to several batteries for storage, then was used for lights and a radio. They had a pump, which pumped water from the nearby spring to their house in a 10-cm (4") pipe. Water from the spring was also used to irrigate a small garden.

When the Fishers left in 1944, they sold it to a Navajo man by the name of Curly Tso, who lived mostly on the reservation. Curly had it for a number of years until his death, then his son sold it to the Grafs of Hurricane, Utah. Sometime while Curly owned the place, the house burned down. Then in

The **Spence Place**, or one of the structures there; it's not a lot to look at, but it may have been lived in. To see this, be sure to take the trail to the west of the Paria a ways, otherwise you'll miss it.

1974, the National Park Service bought out all the private holdings at Lee's Ferry, including the Lonely Dell Ranch. Since no one had any ownership papers on the Wilson Ranch, and it was part of the public domain, it just became part of the Paria Canyon--Vermilion Cliffs Wilderness Area. In 2000, this entire canyon became part of the Vermilion Cliffs National Monument.

Almost next to where the old ranch house stood is Wilson Spring. This spring usually has a good flow, but it seeps out of the hillside for about 30m and hasn't been cared for in many years, so you can't expect to get a safe drink there. You'd do better to go to the river for water. At one time part of the spring was developed and put into a pipe, and fenced off so cattle couldn't pollute it, but now the spring is full of cow pies and the water undrinkable. Immediately south of the willows, grass & trees is a corral made of posts at least 2m high; it must have been used for wild horses.

Next to this corral is a rocked-up pit looking something like what mechanics use to get into when working underneath cars. Next to it is a pile of what appears to be uranium ore. This was likely part of the local mining operation. From there look south, and on a hill just to the west of the creek, can be seen a couple of mine tunnels. This was known as the **Red Wing Mine**, which dates from the uranium boom days of the early 1950's.

About 2 kms below the Red Wing, you'll see on your left a faint track running up the hill to the east. This hill is actually the Shinarump Bench, and the track is the beginning of the **Dominguez or Ute Trail**. Actually, the track you see is another 1950's uranium prospecting track (Trevor Leach claims he built that short road), but it's apparently in about the same place as the old trail. Right where the trail begins to climb, you may see on a 1 1/2m-high boulder, more petroglyphs, including a **F.T.J. 1896.** This glyph was etched by Frank T. Johnson, who grew up at the Loney Dell Ranch and who helped run the ferry in the years after 1910. Read more on this Dominguez Trail along with **Map 33.**

About 600m below the beginning of the Dominguez Trail, and on the west side of the river, is another old mining road running up on the Shinarump Bench. There are no doubt other test prospects up there to the west. At the bottom of that road is a raised & sagging **wooden platform** with uranium ore samples stacked on top.

The Spencer Place

About 2 kms before you arrive at Lee's Ferry and the Lonely Dell Ranch, is another old building with the remains of a very old car (from the 1920's) lying there rusting away. This is what the late George W. Fisher called the **Spencer Place.**

In the period between the 2 world wars, there were as many as 10 families living at Lee's Ferry, mostly in the vicinity of the old Lonely Dell Ranch. Most of them were polygamists; some of whom had been, or soon would be, excommunicated from the Mormon Church. One of these families belonged to Carling Spencer (no relation to Charles H. Spencer). It was from Carling Spencer that Fisher bought this old house or cabin in about 1940. Fisher put it on skids and dragged it up to the place where it's seen today. In those days it was simply called the Spencer Place. Fisher fixed the place up to live in part time when he wasn't up at the Wilson Ranch. Part of Fisher's time in those days was spent working on constructing roads in the area because he couldn't make a living on ranching alone.

In 2009, the author found the **stone cabin** seen above, but didn't see a wooden cabin in that area. It's possible floods have taken it away, or the trail bypassed that site; with every big flood, the trails

This is the **wooden shack** near the corral in the lower end of the Lower Paria River Gorge not far above Lee's Ferry.

along the Paria change locations. But that stone cabin may be part of the Spencer Place.

Less than a km below the Spencer Place is another **wooden shack & corral**, which are part of some of the later development of the Lonely Dell Ranch. This corral is used periodically today by cattlemen who still retain grazing rights in the area.

Just beyond this corral, and in the middle of a big flat, is a **trail register** where hikers are encouraged to sign in or out of the canyon (to get a count on visitor use). From that point continue straight ahead on the right or west side of the river. Soon you'll walk along a trail built along the face of a cliff. Immediately after that are the remains of several old water pumping schemes. Whenever dams were built to divert water to the fields at the Lonely Dell Ranch, they were soon washed out by floods. So later on, and to this day, water is pumped from the Paria up to a ditch, then to orchards further along.

Just beyond the pump site is the cemetery, some old farm machinery and finally the Lonely Dell Ranch where you can see some old ranch houses. Beyond that is the day-parking lot with toilet, then nearly a km past it is the **long term parking lot**. That's where you leave your car if hiking this entire canyon. See Map 32 & 33.

Lonely Dell Ranch

The Lonely Dell Ranch really started on December 23, 1871, when John D. Lee and wives Emma & Rachel arrived at the place late in the afternoon. Early the next morning, Emma looked around and made a comment about how lonely the place was, thus the name. It was John D. Lee who was sent to the Paria to make and run a ferry for the Mormon Church. Read more about this man in **The Story of John D. Lee and Mountain Meadows Massacre,** in the back of this book starting on **page 340**.

After Lee was captured in November of 1874 in Panguitch, the Church had to send help, because Emma Lee--wife No. 17, couldn't handle the job by herself. So they sent **Warren M. Johnson** to take charge and run the ferry service. That was in March, 1875. At first Johnson took his first wife, then about a year later, brought his younger second wife to the ferry. After he arrived, he built a large 2-level house, which stood until 1926.

At the time Johnson arrived, Emma owned the ferry and had squatters rights to the Lonely Dell Ranch. So she and the Johnsons both profited from the ferry service. But in 1879, the Mormon Church bought the ferry rights from Emma for a reported $3000. She then moved south into Arizona and eventually settled at Winslow, where she died in 1897.

Warren Johnson's family lived at the ranch and ran the ferry from 1875 until 1896. At that time the church decided he had completed his mission and released him. It had been a long struggle living at this almost-forgotten desert outpost for so many years. Just one of the hardships he had to suffer through, was the loss of 4 of his younger children.

In May 1891, a family passing through the area traveling from Richfield, Utah, to Arizona, told Warren about a child of theirs which had gotten ill and died in Panguitch. No one thought about it then, but 4 days later, one of the Johnson children became ill and died. A few days later other children were struck with the same sickness. All together, 4 Johnson children died between May 19 & July 5, 1891. The disease was diphtheria, which 3 other children got, but recovered from. One large grave stone, with all their names on it, can be seen in the cemetery today just north of the ranch houses.

The Church replaced Warren M. Johnson with a man named **James Emmett**. Emmett arrived in

1896, along with his 2 wives. While he ran the ferry he talked the Church into building a cable across the river, to which the boat could be fastened. This made things much safer and easier. Before that time there had been a number of accidents and drownings associated with the crossing.

While running the ferry, Emmett also did a little farming and ran cattle, part of which were in the House Rock Valley to the west. Even though that area was mostly public domain and open to all, he had troubles with the **Grand Canyon Cattle Company** (GCCC), which was run by B. F. Saunders and Charles Dimmick. At one time in about 1907, Dimmick accused Emmett of stealing cattle, and it went to court. Emmett was found innocent.

But later, the GCCC got back at Emmett, by buying the ferry service from the Mormon Church in August 1909. Shortly thereafter, Emmett sold his land and property to this same company. At first the ferry was run by any GCCC cowboy who was staying at the Lonely Dell Ranch at the time. But things changed after less than a year, because the service was unreliable. In early 1910, the Grand Canyon Cattle Company hired the best men for the job--the sons of Warren M. Johnson.

Jerry Johnson arrived at the ferry in February, 1910, and was joined by his brother **Frank** in July, and both ran the ferry. It was these men and their families who lived at the Lonely Dell Ranch and assumed responsibility for the ferry until the **Navajo Bridge** opened across Marble Canyon in **January, 1929**. Actually the last ferry crossing was on **June 7, 1928**. That's when the boat tipped over with 2 cars on board. All 3 men running the ferry were drowned, and the boat floated down into Marble Canyon. Because the bridge was so near completion, the ferry was never replaced.

Because of the way the ferry was handled in 1909-1910, Coconino County became concerned about keeping this important link open. So the county bought the ferry service from the Grand Canyon Cattle Company in June 1910. **Coconino County** became the owner, but they hired the Johnsons to run it until the bridge opened.

In December of 1926, clothes drying near a stove caught on fire and burned down the 2-story Johnson home at Lonely Dell. It had been built by Warren M Johnson in about 1877 and had stayed in the Johnson family until it burned.

After the bridge opened, there wasn't much traffic in or around Lee's Ferry, but several polygamist families lived there during the 1930's. The Church owned the ranch for a time, then the polygamist families of **Lebaron, Spencer and Johnson** bought it. Still later on, the Church got it back, but then **Leo & Hazel Weaver** bought the Lonely Dell Ranch in the late 1930's and attempted, unsuccessfully, to run a dude ranch and raise Anglo-Arabian horses. While there, they constructed the long white stone building which sits just northeast of Samantha Johnson Cabin.

The Weavers stayed at Lonely Dell until the early 1940's, then moved out. **Essy Bowers** owned the ranch for a couple of years, then in 1943 sold it to a man name **C. A. Griffin**, a stockman from Flagstaff, who had a big herd of cattle on the Navajo Nation lands to the east. It was Griffin who first attempted to pump water out of the Paria onto farm land, rather than to build dams, which always washed out. In later years the **LDS Church** once again held title to the ranch.

In about 1963, Lee's Ferry was included in the **Glen Canyon National Recreational Area**, but the 65 hectares (160 acres) of private land remained private. In 1974, the private property of the Lonely Dell Ranch was bought by the U. S. Government and National Park Service. Lonely Dell Ranch was put on the National Register of Historic Places in 1978.

For a lot more detailed information about Lee's Ferry, read **Desert River Crossing,** by Rusho & Crampton; **Lee's Ferry**, by Measeles; and 3 books by Juanita Brooks: **John D. Lee, Zealot--Pioneer Builder--Scapegoat; A Mormon Chronicle: The Diaries of John D. Lee;** and **Mountain Meadows Massacre**. Also read **Lee's Ferry**, by P. T. Reilly.

If you're hiking up the Paria for more than one day, or doing the entire Paria River trip from the Whitehouse Trailhead, be sure to park at the large paved **long term parking lot** southeast of Lonely Dell instead of at the small visitor parking place at the ranch entrance.

This picture of the Warren Johnson family was fotographed from a larger one located at an information board at the Lonely Dell Ranch parking lot (Glen Canyon NRA foto). It was taken by Frank Nims of the Stanton Survey in December, 1889. L to R: Mary, Jonathan, Polly, wife Permelia holding LeRoy, Jerry, Millie (Permelia?), Frank Warren, Laura Alice, Nancy, and Melinda. About 1 1/2 years after this foto was taken, 4 of these children (names underlined) died of diphteria. They are buried in the Lonely Dell Ranch Cemetery with one tombstone.

Aerial view of **Lee's Ferry**. Lonely Dell Ranch is just left of center; Lee's Ferry Upper Terminal, right; long term parking, just right of center; Lee's Backbone far right; Spencer Trail, above and left a little.

The gravestone for **John Green Kitchen.** He was the man who created the Kitchen Ranch in the area north of Mollies Nipple. The gravestone reads: *Born in Canada, March 25, 1830. Died July 18, 1898.*
According to P.T. Reilly's book, he probably died of euthanasia (suicide?).

The grave of Warren Johnson's 4 children who died of diphtheria in the spring and summer of 1891.

Farm equipment dating from the 1930's or thereabouts. These are located just south of the Lonely Dell Ranch Cemetery, and a short distance north of the ranch buildings and the present fruit trees.

Part of the **Lonely Dell Ranch** built by Leo Weaver in about 1940. This stone building was used as part of his dude ranch operation. The National Park Service now uses it. Just to the right and out of site is an new orchard.

This is the blacksmith shop apparently built by Jerry Johnson in the late 1920's. It's now called the **Jerry Johnson Cabin**. For a time it was used as a school.

The National Park Service is now calling this the **Samantha Johnson Cabin**. This came after Lees time. Some of the tools seen here date from the late 1800's. A cellar is seen on the far right.

Looking south at the Colorado River from the lower **Spencer Trail**. In the lower left is the **Upper Ferry Terminal** site; across the river with the old road is the south-side Upper Ferry site.

The **Warren Johnson home** at the **Lonely Dell Ranch**. It burned down in 1926.
(New Mexico State Archives)

Unloading at the **Upper Ferry Terminal** at **Lee's Ferry** in the early 1900's. Beyond is the south side
of the Colorado River. You can still see some of the ruins at the ferry terminal today.
(Arizona State Library)

Ox teams pulling a wagon up the dugway toward the **Upper Ferry Terminal** near Lee's Ferry.
(Arizona State Library)

This picture was taken at the **Upper Ferry Terminal** by Charles Kelly (author of *Outlaw Trail*) in 1932. According to W. L. Rusho, who wrote the book, *Lee's Ferry, Desert River Crossing*, the cabin was deliberately burned down in 1959 by the USGS to prevent vandalism. The fireplace in that cabin is surely one of the 2 chimneys left standing today.

The Dominguez & Spencer Trails, Glen Canyon Overlooks, and the Lee's Ferry Historic Sites

Location & Access Both trails featured on this map begin at Lee's Ferry. In 1776, Spanish padres Dominguez & Escalante used the **Dominguez Trail** when looking for the Ute Ford (later called the Crossing of the Fathers) to cross the Colorado River on their historic journey back home to Santa Fe. This same trail (sometimes called the **Ute Trail**) was used by Navajos & Utes in the early days, when they would cross the Colorado River to trade with the Mormon settlers in southern Utah. The **Spencer Trail** was built by big-time promoter Charles H. Spencer, partly as a short-cut from Lee's Ferry to coal fields along Warm Creek to the northeast, and partly to impress investors who were given the grand tour and big sales promotion of his mining operations at the Ferry.

To get there, turn off Highway 89A at Marble Canyon/Navajo Bridge and drive northeast to Lee's Ferry. After 8.4 kms (5.2 miles) turn left or north and continue for another 350m and park at the Lonely Dell Ranch parking place. This is where you park if hiking to the **Dominguez Trail**. Or if climbing the **Spencer Trail**, park where they launch boats at the end of the road which is 9.3 kms (5.8 miles) from Highway 89A.

In addition to these 2 hikes at Lee's Ferry, another interesting side-trip would be to the south side of the Colorado River to the **Lower & Upper Ferry Terminal sites**. But don't do this without the *Lee's Ferry 7 1/2' quad*, which you can buy at the Navajo Bridge Visitor Center. To get there, drive east across Marble Canyon on the Navajo Bridge. From the bridge, continue southeast roughly 2 1/2 kms (1 1/2 miles). About halfway between mile posts 536 & 537, turn north and go through a gate (close it behind you please). From the gate you must have a HCV & 4WD. This route is used by Navajos going to the Lower Ferry site to fish, and they have churned up the steeper hillsides pretty bad, evidently using 2WD's and spinning like hell! Also, in several places, the road splits into a number of tracks; these were made by people looking for an easier way over some ledges, so stay on the most-used road. Finally, after 5.4 kms (3.35 miles), you'll come to the edge of a flat bench where you can look down on the Colorado to the left, and the 4WD road going down straight ahead. That's a good place to park, because beyond that the road does a lot of zig zagging and you can walk about as fast as driving. Park or camp there.

Read more about the mining history at Lee's Ferry in the chapter about **Mining History: The Paria River Drainage**, in the back of this book.

Trail/Route To hike the **Dominguez Trail**, walk from the Lonely Dell Ranch parking lot upstream along the Paria River Trail for about 5 kms. On the right, you will see an old mining track running up a minor slope to the east and through a break in the Shinarump Conglomerate Formation. It begins next to a boulder with some petroglyphs. Once on the bench, head southeast past another boulder with rock art, then go over a hill and down past a north-south running mining track. Cross it and head straight up slope to the east. There's nothing in the way of a visible trail here. Higher up, and on a 2nd terrace, you'll come to a big **sandy bench** stretching out to the southeast. Walk southeast toward a low place on the canyon rim; either route-finding or following big horn sheep trails. At the south end of the sandy bench, head east straight upslope. When you reach the cliffs, you should pick up the constructed part of a trail as it zig zags up the slope, then turns south at or near the ridge crest. There are 2 constructed cattle trails through the cliffs to the rim; no doubt the work of the Johnsons when they were at the Lonely Dell Ranch.

The **Spencer Trail** begins just east of **Lee's Fort**. The bottom of the trail veers left from the more-traveled route to the Upper Ferry Terminal. Once on this path, you can follow it easily as it zig zags up the steep cliffs. If you'd like to do both trails together on the same hike, then walk up the Spencer, route-find north along the ridge crest, then head down the Dominguez. It's easier to locate the Dominguez Trail from the top than from the bottom. Another thing you can do while at the top of the Spencer Trail, is route-find about due east and to one of several good viewpoints of the lower end of **Glen Canyon** and the Colorado River. With about one extra hour, you'll return with some nice fotos.

Before heading up the Spencer Trail, spend some time exploring around **Lee's Fort**. There are several stone buildings in that area and you can pickup a map & guide at the parking lot. Among other things, you can see part of Spencer's old 1911 mining operation, including **2 boilers**, several stone buildings, plus the sunken remains of the streamboat *Charles H. Spencer*. Just upriver from that, is what's left of the **Upper Ferry Terminal**. There's more to see there than on the south side of the river.

From the suggested parking place on the south side of the Colorado River, walk down along the twisting road. After roughly 600m, be looking over the rim to the left for an old road running down to the river and the **Lower Ferry site.** This lower site is nearly 1 km below where the Paria meets the Colorado. This is a favorite fishing place for Navajos.

Or, stay on the track going up along a dugway below Lee's Backbone. This old wagon road runs up along the chocolate-colored clay beds of the Moenkopi, then gradually descends to the river across the way from the rafters launching place at the end of the paved road. Beyond the gauging station & cable, the faint track crosses a flat area on its way to the **Upper Ferry site** and beyond.

Elevations Lee's Ferry, 950m; top of the Spencer Trail, 1450m; Dominguez Pass, 1500m.

Time Needed The Spencer Trail is about 2 1/2 kms, one way, and will take about 2-4 hours round-trip. From the trailhead to Dominguez Pass is about 8 kms, one way. Most could do this in 5-6 hours or more round-trip, returning the same way. If a loop-hike is made using both trails, it's close to 16 kms. With the ruggedness of the ridge-top, it'll likely take the average person all of one day to make the trip. If you're in a big hurry, you can walk the 4-5 kms to the Upper Ferry site (on the south side of the river) and back in 2 hours, but most people will want 4-5 hours for this hike.

Water Always take it with you, but there is water available at several places around the Lee's Ferry area.

Maps USGS or BLM map Glen Canyon Dam (1:100,000) for driving & orientation; and Ferry Swale & Lee's Ferry (1:24,000--7 1/2' quad) for hiking.

Main Attractions Historic trails in an historic region, with fine views from the rim of the canyon.

Best Time to Hike Spring or fall. Summers are hot as hell, winter time can be pleasant.

Boots/Shoes Dry-weather boots, except waders for the walk up the Paria to reach the Dominguez Trail.

Author's Experience He first climbed both trails on separate trips, then in October, 1997, he parked at the end of the paved road at the boat launching site, and made the loop-hike suggested above in just over 5 hours. In 2003, and racing the setting sun, he made the top of the Spencer in 38 minutes. Later, on the Dominguez Trail, he spotted some new petroglyphs as shown, and 2 herds of big horn sheep totaling 11 head on the sandy bench below the pass. On his 2nd trip to the south side of the Colorado River and the 2 ferry sites, he parked at the suggested place and did the trip in just over 2 hours, but he was in a hurry. He also explored the Lower Ferry site the evening before.

Map 33, Dominguez & Spencer Trails, Glen Canyon Overlooks, and the Lee's Ferry Historic Sites

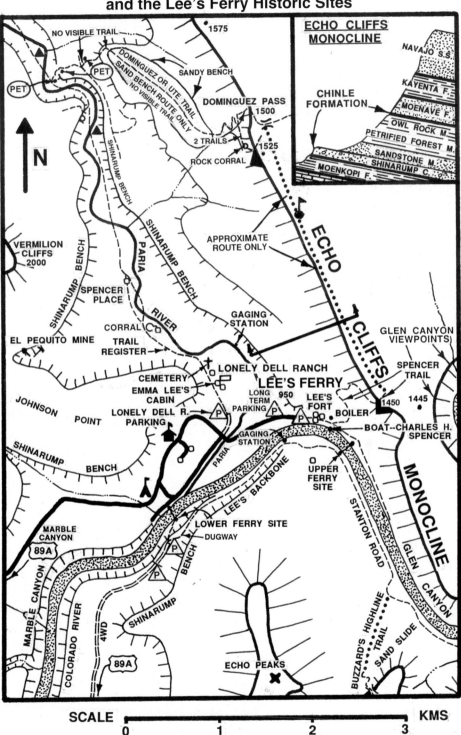

ECHO CLIFFS MONOCLINE

NAVAJO S.S.
KAYENTA F.
MOENAVE F.
CHINLE FORMATION
OWL ROCK M.
PETRIFIED FOREST M.
SANDSTONE M.
SHINARUMP C.
MOENKOPI F.

NO VISIBLE TRAIL
1575
PET
DOMINGUEZ OR UTE TRAIL
SANDY BENCH
SAND BENCH ROUTE ONLY
PET
NO VISIBLE TRAIL ONLY
DOMINGUEZ PASS 1500
N
2 TRAILS
1525
ROCK CORRAL

SHINARUMP BENCH
PARIA
SHINARUMP BENCH
VERMILION CLIFFS 2000
SHINARUMP BENCH
APPROXIMATE ROUTE ONLY
ECHO

SPENCER PLACE
RIVER
GAGING STATION
CORRAL
TRAIL REGISTER
EL PEQUITO MINE
GLEN CANYON VIEWPOINTS
CEMETERY
LONELY DELL RANCH
SPENCER TRAIL
EMMA LEE'S CABIN
LEE'S FERRY
CLIFFS
1450 1445
LONG TERM PARKING
950
LEE'S FORT
JOHNSON
LONELY DELL R. PARKING
P
P
BOILER
POINT
P
BOAT--CHARLES H. SPENCER
SHINARUMP
GAGING STATION
PARIA
BENCH
UPPER FERRY SITE
MONOCLINE
LEE'S BACKBONE
BENCH
STANTON ROAD
MARBLE CANYON
89A
LOWER FERRY SITE
DUGWAY
P
GLEN
P
SHINARUMP
CANYON
MARBLE CANYON
4WD
BENCH
BUZZARD'S HIGHLINE TRAIL
SAND SLIDE
COLORADO RIVER
89A
ECHO PEAKS

SCALE 0 1 2 3 KMS

From near the top of the **Spencer Trail** looking straight down on **Lee's Ferry**; Lonely Dell Ranch upper right, long term parking in about the middle, boat launching & Colorado River in the lower left.

About 8-10 minutes walking east from the top of the **Spencer Trail** is this scene overlooking lower **Glen Canyon**. This section has clear & cold water and is a great trout stream.

Above An aerial view looking down on most of the **Dominguez or Ute Trail**. The Paria River runs from left to right across the bottom of this picture, with the Dominguez Trail beginning in the canyon to the lower left, then on top of the big **sandy bench** and angling up to the right where it tops out on the rim of the plateau.

Left Halfway down **Cathedral Wash**, which is along the paved road to Lee's Ferry. See **Map 32** for a look at the parking place along the highway running between Marble Canyon & the Navajo Bridge, and Lee's Ferry. The trailhead is signposted and you can't miss it. It's an easy & fun walk with a little scrambling which will take you down to the Colorado River. The hike to the river & back, should take from 1-2 hours. In summer or in hot weather, take a little water.

North Rim Hikes, Old Indian Trail & Thousand Pockets:
Lower Paria River Gorge

Location & Access Featured here are some hikes from the high country north of the Lower Paria River Gorge. Three parts of an area known generally as the **East Clark Bench** are; Flat Top, Cedar Mountain & Thousand Pockets. There are several 4WD-type roads running up to **Cedar Mountain** from the Big Water area, but the normal way is to drive along Highway 89 east of the Paria Ranger Station. Between mile posts 17 & 18, and directly across the highway from the start of the Cottonwood Wash Road, turn south onto the **Cedar Mtn. Road**. It's generally good for cars up to Cedar Mtn., but there is one little rocky place with a short sandy section below. However, the author's VW Rabbit & Tracker (using 2WD in the months of October & November with a little moisture in the sand) and later his Jeep Patriot, did fine. Staying on the most-used road, drive a total of 17.4 kms (10.8 miles) to a **4-way junction**. There are 2 ways to reach the trailhead from there; **shortest & fastest** is to head southwest; the 2nd power line you drive under will be at Km 20.9/Mile 13 (from Highway 89); at Km 25.3/Mile 15.7, turn right at a junction and continue west to Km 28/Mile 17.4, and park at the trailhead (1621m) for a hike along an old **Indian trail or route** down to the river and up the other side into the Sand Hills.

Or, you could drive along a loop-road around Cedar Mtn. from the **4-way junction**. That loop road is sometimes graded up to the communications facility at Km 21.7Mile 13.5, then it gets very sandy soon after that and is less-used. It's also a longer way to reach the trailhead, a total of 32.7 km (20.3 miles) from Highway 89.

In the **Flat Top** area are 2 side-roads; one is out to the north side of **Judd Hollow** to some metal tanks & a trough; another is down toward **Bridger Point**. See distances from the highway on the map. Both of these side-roads are sandy in places, but with a little moisture, even cars can be driven there. **But be sure to take a shovel**, especially if things are dry.

Another interesting place near the rim of the Lower Paria River Gorge is a small area known as **Thousand Pockets**; get there from the northeast and from near Lake Powell. First, drive along Highway 89 northwest of Page, Arizona. Near the entry roads to Greene Heaven, leave Highway 89 between mile posts 555 & 556, and first drive along the old highway, then turn southwest & south on a pretty good well-used road in the direction of Ferry Swale. At Km 3.9 (Mile 2.4) veer left; at Km 4.3 (Mile 2.7) veer left again; at Km 5.6 (Mile 3.5) continue straight ahead--don't turn left; at **Km 7.4 (Mile 4.6)** park on a bench just before going downhill. With a good 4WD, you could continue downhill aways, but it's sandy.
Trail/Route The best hike here, and one for an experienced outdoor person, would be down an old **Indian trail or route** to the Paria. From the parking place at 1621m, walk west over the rim, hopefully following 6-8 cairns marking the route to the bottom of the steep Page Sandstone bench & rim. Once at the bottom, continue southwest about 2 kms to the canyon rim and a steep crack-like chute going down to the river. Use Wrather Canyon as a landmark to find this steep gully from the rim. Also, see **Map 31,** and read the nearby description of how to climb up from the river under the heading, **North Rim Overlook Hike & Indian Trail.**

If you plan to take a big pack & camp in the canyon, include a short rope to lower packs in several places, and to help beginners down & back up. Or, you can just day-hike down this route to see some of the best parts of the Lower Paria River Gorge. Also, take the more detailed USGS maps for this hike. Once at the Paria, you can head downstream to Bush Head Canyon, cross the creek to see Wrather Canyon & Arch, climb the steep **Indian trail** with **moki steps** up to the south rim not far below Wrather, or walk upstream to the Adams Water Pump and/or Trail.

Here are some other hikes. From the southeast side of Cedar Mtn., you can route-find down into a side-canyon to a place called **Water Pockets.** However, you can't go too far as there are some big dropoffs halfway down. You'll also have some good views from the rim. From the north side of **Judd Hollow** and the **metal tanks & trough**, route-find down over the rim via some old ladders and a pipeline. Once into Judd Hollow, it's an easy walk down to the edge of the canyon for a look straight down at the old Adams Water Pump site located next to the river.

There are also some interesting rim-hiking possibilities from the end of the pretty good road down onto the south peninsula of **Bridger Point.** It's easy to get off the Page Sandstone Rim and to the very edge of the gorge. See **Map 30.** There might even be a route down into one of the 4 Crack Canyons from along the north rim. If you find one, please email the author.

Thousand Pockets If you stop on the hill, walk down the road to the 4WD parking, and head west up the valley. Higher up, the best parts of the Thousands Pockets area will be to your left or south. Just wander around. There are 2 parts that seemed best to the author; one was on a high point marked **4753T** (1449m) on the *7 1/2' Ferry Swale quad.* This one has the **Big Brain & Cauliflower Rocks (BB&CR).** Another nice area is near elevation **4785** (1458m). There may be more. Also, you might head up to the west and have some nice views down into the Lower Paria River Gorge.
Elevations Cedar Mountain 1800m; bottom of gorge at Bush Head Canyon, 1100m.
Time Needed It's about 2 1/2 kms from the parking place at 1621m to the Paria, but finding the old Indian trail to the bottom may take a little time. Plan on staying all day, depending on how far you go once you reach the river. The other hikes to the rim would likely take about half a day, or less.
Water Take plenty in your car, but there may be some at the Bunting Well (?), Trough & Corral on top of Flat Top. Be prepared to purify it first, unless you can get water before it reaches the cow trough.
Maps USGS or BLM maps Smoky Mountain & Glen Canyon Dam (1:100,000) for driving & orientation; perhaps the USGS maps MF-1475, A, B, C or D (1:62,500); and Bridger Point, Glen Canyon City, Wrather Arch & Water Pockets (1:24,000--7 1/2' quads) for hiking.
Main Attractions An unregulated way to reach the middle part of the Lower Paria River Gorge from the rim and different views of the canyon from either the north or south rims.
Best Time to Hike Spring or fall, and hopefully soon after some rains, as some roads are sandy.
Boots/Shoes Any dry weather boots if rim-walking, wading shoes if going to the canyon bottom.
Author's Experience In 2003, he once drove his Chevy Tracker to the parking place at 1621m, climbed down to the Paria, headed downcanyon to Bush Head, climbed to the rim, rim-walked to an overlook of Wrather Arch, down the Indian trail with moki steps and back to his car, all in 9 1/4 hours. Next day, it was down to the river again, up Wrather Canyon to the arch, upcanyon past the Adams Pump, up the Adams Trail a ways, and almost to the 2nd Crack Canyon, and finally back to his car, all in 10 hours. In 2/2008, he spent 5 hours in Thousand Pockets. In 2009, he duplicated his feats of 2003, but this time he found moki steps on the route to the south rim just below Wrather Canyon.

Map 34, North Rim Hikes, Old Indian Trail & Thousand Pockets: Lower Paria River Gorge

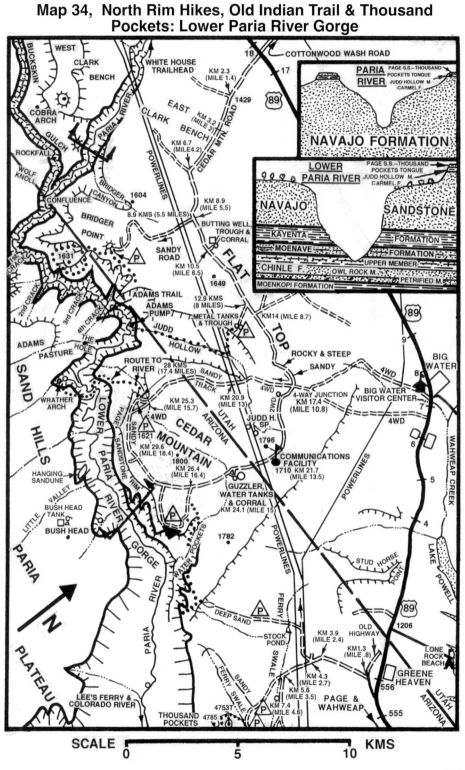

From the air looking up the **Lower Paria River Gorge**, with the lower end of **Bush Head Canyon** in the lower left. The route out of the gorge is up the sandslide at the center bottom part of this foto. **Cedar Mtn.** is just visible on the right with the Page Sandstone rim clearly showing.

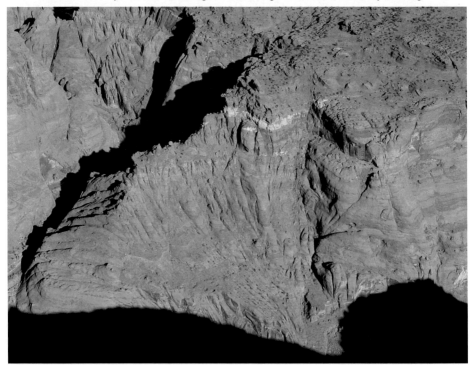

From the air looking down on the north rim and the **Indian trail** down to the Paria in the center right.

One of the 2 better parts of what is known as **Thousand Pockets**. It's located due west of the Glen Canyon Dam and Page, Arizona.

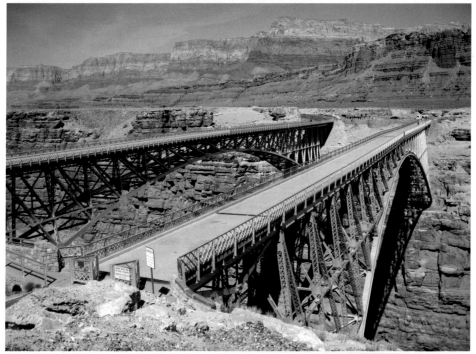

The **Navajo Bridges** over **Marble Canyon**. The old one is on the right, and it was finished in January, 1929. It's now a foot bridge only. The new Navajo Bridge is on the left. Between the bridges on the far side is a new visitor information center. In the far background is the Sand Hills/Paria Plateau.

The Water Pockets, West Clark Bench

Location & Access The location of this hike is in the southwest corner of the **West Clark Bench (WCB)**. This elevated mesa or plateau is north of the Buckskin Gulch, west of the White House Trail-head and the Paria River, and south of Highway 89. This area has colorful slickrock with many shallow depressions or potholes. The local cattlemen & BLM call these features, along with the area, **Water Pockets** or just **Pockets**. After heavy rains, the pockets fill up with water which can be used by both wildlife and cows. The area also has many interesting and colorful rock formations including **Big Brain & Cauliflower Rocks (BB&CR)**, and features that resemble **rock logs** lying next to each other.

To get there, drive along **Highway 89** just west of the Paria River between **mile posts 21 & 22**, and turn south next to the **Paria Outpost & Outfitters,** and the nearby **Paria River Guest Ranch & Campground**. Head south on a graded road past a corral on the right, then into and through **Long Canyon** (see **Map 29** for the first part of this drive). Once on top of the WCB, and 6.7 kms (4.2 miles) from the highway, veer left at a junction; at Km 7.2 (Mile 4.5) veer left again; at Km 8.2 (Mile 5.1) turn right or south at the junction shown on this map labeled **1597m**; at Km 8.4 (Mile 5.2) go straight ahead--don't turn right or west; at Km 8.9 (Mile 5.6) go straight--don't turn right or left; at Km 10.7 (Mile 6.6) veer left; and at **Km 11 (Mile 6.8)** is a blocked-off road on the right--that's the **Water Pockets Trailhead**. Best to have an AWD/4WD for the last part of this drive, but most cars, driven by an expert, can get there with 2WD only (there's one short, but real sandy place--so **rev up and go as fast as conditions will allow!**).

Trail/Routes From the barricade & trailhead, walk southwest along an old sandy road. After a little more than 2 kms, you'll come to slickrock and an old **wooden feed trough** on the right. Water Pockets is the area beyond that and all over the southwest corner of the WCB. Observe the map carefully. Southwest of that feed trough and in about the middle of that slickrock flat is a large water pocket which has been enlarged by a **cement dam**. To capture more water, the MacDonalds & BLM of Kanab built a low cement wing running south about 100m in order to divert more rainwater into the dam & water hole.

From the dam, walk south & southeast along or near the rim of the WCB. Along the way you'll see a number of water pockets--if you're there after a storm, you'll find plenty of water and maybe some pools big enough to swim in. Two of these have cattails and other grasses and are important for wildlife.

Now back to the cement dam. From there, walk west about 100m to find a **little hogsback ridge** veering down and to the right or northwest. Climb down that steep slickrock to an **intermediate bench** on the west side of the WCB; on this map it's labeled **rock log bench**. Once there, continue north to find a number of places with fotogenic BB&CR, rock logs & teepee-like peaks or features. Some of these are pretty close to the upper part of Buckskin Gulch; infact, you can see or visit some of these if you hike downstream from the Buckskin Trailhead going toward Wire Pass.

To make a loop hike of the area from the **little hogsback ridge**, make your way to the bottom of the big cliffs as shown and walk south, then east along the base of the big cliffs and/or **The Dive**. If you continue far enough, you can climb back up beginning **just west** of the number **31** on the *West Clark Bench 7 1/2' quad*; this is Section 31, as shown. This is where elevation 1463m and the BB&CR are shown on this map (It was while walking the base of The Dive in this area that the author found 4 broken arrowheads in about 2 1/2 hours!) There are a couple of steep places on slickrock above the BB&CR, but anyone can climb back up to the rim there. It involves a little route-finding.

If you make this loop-hike, once back on top, either walk directly back to your car; or walk west along the rim back to the water pockets, then to your car. Or if you stay on the **rock log bench** on the west side, head north, then climb back up east just before the big **teepee dome** with lots of teepee-like rocks on top. That area has BB&CR & rock fins, but don't walk on the fins. Use the old road to return.

Elevations Water Pockets Trailhead, 1641m; base of The Dive, about 1460m.

Time Needed Depending on how far and where you go, from 3-7 hours.

Water Take your own, there's none on top; except after rains then you'll find plenty in pools.

Maps USGS or BLM map Smoky Mountain (1:100,000) for driving & orientation; and West Clark Bench (1:24,000--7 1/2' quad) for hiking & driving.

Main Attractions Fotogenic rocks and good views to the south at The Wave and Coyote Buttes.

Best Time to Hike Cooler weather in spring or fall; winter is best for driving on sandy roads.

Boots/Shoes Any comfortable light weight boots or shoes.

Author's Experience The author has been to this area several times over the years. On his last trip, he walked southeast from the trail-head, found the route down over The Dive, then rim-walked west to the cement dam and other water pockets, then used the little hogs-back ridge to get off the top and to the flats below. He then walked around the corner and east along the base of The Dive to the exit route, climbed back up on top of WCB and directly back to his car in 6 1/2 hours.

This is one of 2 **big water pockets** shown on the map at the extreme southern end of the southwest corner of the West Clark Bench known as Pockets or **Water Pockets**. It has water most of the time, otherwise it's a small sea of green grasses, including cattails.

Map 35, The Water Pockets, West Clark Bench

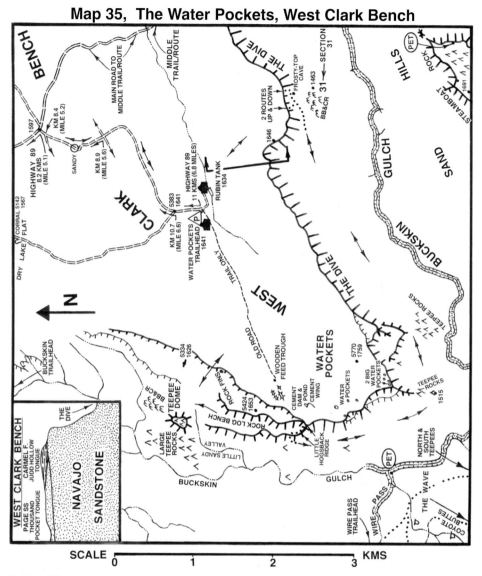

Cowboy History of the Water Pockets On top of that little cement dam are some signatures: *Noel 77, Lanny Talbot, Berch 77, & M. Pierce.* And on top of the 100m-long cement wing is scratched *Dec 1976, BVO/UGS/RC.* This indicates all that cement work was put there in late 1976 & early 1977.

The author talked to several people about who built that little dam & wing. One was **Lanny Tabot** of Kanab, a former BLM range conservation officer. He stated: *There was a Robinson, and a Chenoweth and a BLM maintenance crew. It was for Toby or Merrill MacDonald. The BLM paid for the building of that little dam. We used to go out and do quite a few little water reservoirs, water catchments & pipelines and stuff like that. It was the BLM who done it, or paid for the work back in the old days. Then in the mid-1980's, they turned it over to the permittees. During my little trips around, I'd check their pipelines and get'um goin' for 'um, stuff like that; wasn't supposed to, but did it anyway.*

Brent Robinson also of Kanab, who is a partner to Tyson Johnson, both of whom have permits to graze cows in the Sand Hills just south of the Buckskin Gulch, had a little more to say about the Water Pockets: *I bought that permit from Dennis MacDonald, his dad was Merrill, and that was a joint project with the MacDonalds and the BLM. I got permission from the BLM to repair that, but that's all wilderness, so it's kinda difficult to go out there and do much. That's definitely a water source that we need.*

Then just to the south [of the cement dam] is another little water pocket down near the ledge. It's a natural pothole, a pretty good sized one, and MacDonalds dropped a line off the edge and siphoned water down to the bottom about 500 feet [150m] underneath to the little plateau between the Pockets and Wire Pass. And there's an old 1000 gallon ring tank down underneath The Dive at the foot of the ledge. They had a 2 inch [5 cm] poly or plastic line drapped off there, with a float bulb-value at the bottom. Dennis MacDonald said they let that ring tank off the ledge with an old Willys Jeep.

215

Looking west at the **cement dam** & former natural water pocket. In the distance is Buckskin Mountain; to the far left is the Wire Pass Trailhead; to the near left and beyond is the **cement wing** to the dam you see here. This dam was built in December, 1976 and January, 1977.

This picture was taken looking north from along what this writter calls the **Rock Log Bench**. In the distance is the **Teepee Dome**, and the many BB&CR seen in the foreground.

Scenes like this are all over the **Water Pockets** landscape. This area has lots of BB&CR, rock logs and teepee-like rocks, and is easily in the top 4-5 most-fotogenic places in the Sand Hills region.

Looking north at **Teepee Dome** (just to the right of the upper center) from this **little sandy valley** just to the south. This area is probably the most-fotogenic in the **Water Pockets** of West Clark Bench. If you can get on top of Teepee Dome, there might be something even better.

Introduction: Driving, Touring & Fotography in the Sand Hills

Location & Driving Problems The **Sand Hills** (local rancher's name) or **Paria Plateau** (geologist's name) is located immediately south of the Utah-Arizona line and between the Buckskin Gulch & Lower Paria River Gorge, the big Vermilion Cliffs parallelling Highway 89A, and the House Rock Valley Road (HRVR) to the west. You can get there from either Highway 89 in Utah, or Highway 89A in Arizona.

CAUTION: THIS IS SANDY COUNTRY AND FIT FOR 4WD's ONLY. Actually, popular **AWD's** like the CRV, Forester & Rav 4 would do well, but most have **less than 20 cms (8")** of clearance. It's best to have about 22.5 cms (9") or more. Solve this problem by installing **oversized tires**. That's what the author did with his **AWD Jeep Patriot** with 5-speed manual transmission, and it worked fine. With oversized tires, his Patriot now has about 22.5 cms of clearance. The clearance is needed to avoid the sandy hump in the middle of some roads; however in the last few years and with more ATV's roaming this place, that high spot between the ruts has been flattened some.

Once there, one **important thing** to do is **let about half the air out of your tires**. Go from **35-40 lbs for highway driving**, down to **about 20 lbs** in the **Sand Hills**. This makes tires more flexible which grips the sand better and puts more rubber to the road. Here's perhaps the most important **driving tip**: when you see deep sand ahead, **GEAR DOWN & REV UP--before you get into a sand trap--then go AS FAST AS CONDITIONS ALLOW**--until you reach firmer ground on the other side. If you have to change gears in middle of one of the long & deeper traps--you're screwed, and you may not make it out!

Late winter is the best time to visit the Sand Hills, because normally there's more **moisture in the sand** at that time. With moisture in the sand, your chances of getting stuck are minimal, even with a 2WD. If the sand is **frozen**, that's even better. **Late February and March** (with the longer days & warmer temperatures) might be the ideal time for traveling the Sand Hills. Or anytime **right after heavy rains**. A little snow in shaded places would probably help. Normally, there's some snow at higher altitudes--that's the country in the southern part of the plateau--for about 3 months or more of the year.

Here are some other things to keep in mind when traveling this region. Remember, the southern parts of this plateau near the Vermilion Cliffs, are higher than the northern sections near the Buckskin Gulch & Paria River. So, when you drive from **Pine Tree Pockets** (locals just call it **Pine**) to **White Pockets** (**WP**), you'll be going downhill slightly which is easier than going back uphill in the **SANDY TRACKS**. In this **SANDY COUNTRY**, that can be a problem if you don't have the right vehicle, have never driven in deep sand before, and the sand is really dry.

Regardless of the season, when going into the Sand Hills, always do so with a new or nearly new vehicle--or at least one that's well-maintained and **reliable**. Also, have **new or nearly new tires**, and a **good battery**. If you have to, spend $100 or more and get the best battery available--that's a small price to pay for a trouble-free/worry-free trip. For the most part roads are not rough & rocky, just **SANDY**. A **shovel** is your best piece of equipment to take, but also have a **battery jumper cable & tow rope/chain**. And/or travel in **convoy**--with **more than one vehicle**. If you have a **cellfone**, the only way to get reception is to get on top of a butte--but this is **unreliable** at best. Sometimes you can stand next to a big metal water tank, or wind mill tower and get reception. And last, always take more **water, food and FUEL** than you think you'll need; running in **4WD/AWD** and **pushing sand around all day long** and almost **all the time, really sucks gas!**

Access The **House Rock Valley Road (HRVR)** is your access route, but in **winter** it can be muddy because of clay beds in some locations, especially if you're coming from the north and the Utah side, and Highway 89. If it's wet & muddy when you arrive, wait until early morning and do as the ranchers do-- **drive the frost**--when the mud is frozen. Call the **BLM in Kanab (435-644-4600)**, and they'll update you on the condition of the HRVR; or they may inform you of local cowboys who know the road conditions even better. If it's really muddy, come in from the south, the House Rock Valley & **Highway 89A**. On that side, the road is more gravelly and better maintained than in Utah (Arizona seems more willing to upgrade their half of the HRVR than Kane County, Utah). But the minute you arrive on the Plateau, it's sandy, and it's best to have some moisture in it.

There's only one way to reach this isolated plateau by road and that's from the west and the **HRVR**. From the **north** and **Highway 89**, turn south from between **mile posts 25 & 26**. Drive about **32.7 kms (20.3 miles)** to a major junction and the road running east to **Pine**. At that T-Junction is **Bowman's Corral** on the west side of the HRVR--the best landmark to look for.

If coming from the **south** and **Highway 89A**, turn north at the old stone ranch house & corrals called **House Rock** which is between **mile posts 565 & 566**, and drive **15 kms (9.3 miles)** to the above-mentioned T-Junction and Bowman's Corral. From there turn east onto the partly-graveled **Entry Road**. After **10.1 kms (6.3 miles)** you'll come to the ranch house at **Pine**. In most cases, Pine will be your jumping off point to the rest of the Sand Hills.

In the heart of the Sand Hills is a circular **Loop Road**. From this main Loop Road, you can visit all corners of the plateau. Here's a road log from **Pine to Joe's Ranch** along the southern half of the Loop Road. Start by driving west on the south side of the ranch house on **Road #1105**. Southeast of Pine **500m (.3 miles)** is a junction; veer left staying on Road #1105 (the other road heads for Jim's Tanks). At **Km 3.3/Mile 2** is another junction; stay right. Not far after you pass through a gate with a corral on the left or north, is another junction at **Km 8.3/Mile 5.1**; for kilomage/mileage purposes we'll take the road to the right--but going left at that point will give you a chance to see **Pinnacle Valley well & corral** at the northern end. At **Km 10.8/Mile 6.7** is a junction with a big metal water tank called **Tank in the Flat** just ahead; veer left or east at that point which is in the southern end of Pinnacle Valley. If you veer to the right or south, you'll end up at the **Jarvis Ranch** and at the beginning of the **White Knolls Loop**. From there, you could drive the roads at the south & west end of the Sand Hills including **Jim's Tanks** and the **Bonal Road**. More on that area later.

Continuing along Loop Road. At **Km 12.9/Mile 8**, is another junction. If you had taken the turn into upper Pinnacle, this is where that road meets the Loop Road. From the south end of Pinnacle Valley you'll be heading northeast. At **Km 19.3/Mile 12**, is a junction about 200m south of **Tombstone Tank** and a **fence & gate**. This is the other end of the White Knolls Loop Road. At **Km 21/Mile 13** is another junction; the road to the right or south runs eastward to **The Beehives** and **Soap Creek Tanks**. Instead veer left next to a small stock pond (normally dry). Finally, at **Km 22/Mile 13.7 is Joe's Ranch** (everybody just calls it **Joe's**) on the right. **Attention:** For a total of about 250m, and on either side of this historic ranch, is **DEEP SAND**, so be ready to gear down, rev up & increase speed. This is definitely one of the **BIGGEST & WORST SAND TRAPS** in the Sand Hills.

Now let's start at **Pine** again, but take the northern part of the **Loop Road** to **Joe's**. Drive east from the north side of the **Pine ranch house**. Soon it turns north. **After 6.3 kms (4.1 miles)** is the **Big Sink**

Map 36, Sand Hills Area Map

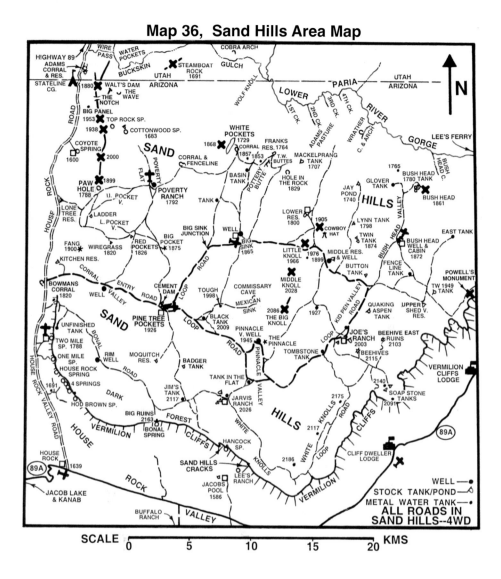

Junction; straight ahead or left is the road to **White Pockets** (more on that later), but turn right or east instead and at **Km 9.6/Mile 6.1** you'll be at the bottom of **Big Sink**. In that area are some Big Brain/Cauliflower Rocks (**BB&CR**), something the Sand Hills are famous for. Continuing northeast out of Big Sink, gear down & rev up, because that section has more **deep sand**. On top, you can turn left or northeast and drive past a cinder block house with nearby corrals & well. This is where cowboys often stay. If you head north from there, you can get to White Pockets.

But for now, head east from Big Sink on the Loop Road. Immediately past a gate at **Km 10.3/Mile 6.4** is a junction; if you turn left or north, you'll be on another loop running down to Hole in the Rock, Twin White Buttes, the real Frank's Reservoir, Pottery Butte (1863m) and White Pockets. But continue east on the Loop Road. At about **Km 13.5/Mile 8.4** is another junction; if you turn left or north, you'll be on a road that's not on any USGS map. It runs down to the Lower Reservoir. At **Km 15.6/Mile 9.7**, you should be on the south side of **Little Knoll**. Continue eastward down the east side of Little Knoll to find another **deep, sandy section**. At **Km 16.3/Mile 10.1** is another junction--in the middle of the sandy area just mentioned; going left or north will get you to Lower Reservoir. At **Km 18.2/Mile 11.3** is a fence & gate with corrals to the left or east. Just before that is a road running east 400m to **Middle Reservoir** with a **windmill & well** and big metal water tank. We'll cover this area later. Continue southeast passing through the 3rd most-fotogenic region in the Sand Hills after White Pockets & Coyote Buttes. **At Km 23.6/Mile 14.5**, is a junction; if you veer left or north, you'll drive toward Bush Head Valley with Bush Head Cabin & Well, and at the end of the road, Bush Head Tank. Just past that turnoff is another junction at **Km 23.8/Mile 14.6**. If you head left or east, you'll pass the Fenceline Tank, and again end up in Bush Head Valley. But for now continue south. Finally, at **Km 27.6/Mile 17.2**, will be **Joe's**. Be ready for the **250m-long sand trap** on either side of that place.

There are several other shorter loop roads that should be covered here. There are 3 ways to reach **White Pockets**, which is the most-popular destination in the Sand Hills. One is to drive south from **Highway 89 for 26.3 kms (16.4 miles)**, turn left or east and continue past **Lone Tree Reservoir** and the **Commissary Trees & Camp** (see Map 37) to a junction at **Km 2.2/Mile 1.4** (at this point you'll be in **deep sand**, so gear down & rev up), turn left and continue northeast past **Paw Hole (for 200m south of Paw Hole is the WORST Sand Trap in the Sand Hills)**, then east to **Poverty Flat & Ranch (Poverty)**. Let's stop here for a moment and look at a 2nd way to Poverty and White Pockets.

Drive along the HRVR and turn east at Bowman's Corral as if going to Pine. From the HRVR, drive east **5 kms (3.1 miles)** to **Corral Valley**; just beyond the windmill & **well** (the mill itself is gone now) on the right, turn left or north and drive past **Red Pocket (Km 10.5/Mile 6.5)** and to **Poverty at Km 14.6/Mile 9.1**. From the old ranch buildings & windmill site, head northeast to a corral & fenceline at **Km 18/Mile 11.2**. From there head due east up & over a low divide to intercept the road which runs north from **Pine**. That junction will be at about **22.7 kms (14.1 miles)** from the HRVR. Be aware that along the last part of this route from Poverty, and as you're going over the low ridge, you'll likely find **one bad spot** that requires lots of clearance--or lots of RPM's to skirt through sand around one steep rough place. This 2nd route is the one used by most guides out of Page.

Here is the best way, and the **normal way**, to **White Pockets**. Start at Pine (Km & Mile 0), then drive east from the north side of the ranch house. Soon that road turns north. **After 6.3 kms (4.1 miles)** is Big Sink Junction; continue north. At **Km 10.7/Mile 6.6**, is a small metal water **tank** on your left at a minor road junction. At **Km 13.1/Mile 8.1** is a junction; coming in from the left or west is the other route to **White Pockets** from **Poverty**. Continue north. At **Km 14.4/Mile 9** is another junction; the road running east goes on to Pottery Butte and Hole in the Rock, but continue north. About 300m before the parking at White Pockets is a small **corral**; open, drive through, then close the wire gate and stop at the parking place which is **15.3 kms (9.5 miles) from Pine**.

The **White Knolls** located in the southeast part of the Sand Hills has lots of **hill-top Anasazi Ruins**. Get there from the south end of **Pinnacle Valley**. From along the Loop Road where you see the big metal **Tank in the Flat** in front to you to the left, veer right and drive along Road #1104 for **2.4 kms (1.5 miles)** to the **Jarvis Ranch**. From just inside the fence and just before the white house, turn left or south. Set your odometer at 0. Head southeast for 600m to a road veering off to the right. This goes south to near the top of the **Northern Sand Hills Crack**. But continue southeast. Eventually you'll come to a fence & gate at **Km 11.2/Mile 6.9** from Jarvis. Just beyond that, almost every hill on the left has hill-top ruins, or crude granaries in small caves around the sides. At **Km 12.2/Mile 7.6** is a junction, drive straight ahead north; don't veer to the right or east. From there on, follow the most-used track which does not conform to the roads shown on the *7 1/2' quads*. The maps in this book are very close to correct. The road shown on USGS maps was used by cattlemen, but the one used now by everyone was created by people just driving around looking for ruins; this is now the most-used track.

At the north end of the White Knolls Loop Road, and at a junction **21.3 kms (13.2 miles)** from Jarvis, continue straight ahead toward the northwest. Finally at **Km 25.1/Mile 15.6** you'll come to the main **Loop Road** about 200m south of the **Tombstone Tank** and a fence & gate.

Another loop road runs from the **Jarvis Ranch** west to **Jim's Tanks**, then either northwest back to **Pine** along **Road #1104**; or continue west toward the trail which drops down to **Bonal Spring**. From that area, you can head northwest along what the ranchers call the **Bonal Road** (Road #1100) and back to the **HRVR 2 kms (1.25 miles)** south of Bowman's Corral and the main Entry Road to Pine and the Sand Hills. These are the main tracks most people will be interested in, but there are lots of other less-used roads around the Sand Hills; most of these will be covered in the next part.

Trails, Routes, Important Landmarks & Fotogenic Places Let's start in the north with the most-popular attractions on **Map 38, North Central Sand Hills**--(for now let's bypass **Map 37**, Coyote Buttes and The Wave for the moment and concentrate on the introduction to fotogenic places the Sand Hills.

White Pockets From the parking place next to a fence, walk west into the middle of White Pockets. After 300m you'll be there; head south to find the all-white **BB&CR**, or north to get into the same white BB&CR with lots of reds & yellows in the layer below. Just wander around. To the northeast and under the big cliffs is a cave with small fragments of pottery & corn cobs (**Corn Cob Cave**) and cowboy & goat herder's signatures. Also in the north end is a small **cement dam** built by ranchers to enlarge a natural water pocket to hold more rain water for cows. It has water most of the time, because there are grass & reeds growing in the pond. Just to the west is **White Pocket Butte** (all or most of the neat fotos are found east of this butte). Photographers can spend a full day here getting the right light & shadows. This is surely the most-fotogenic place in the Sand Hills--easily as good as The Wave area.

Butte 6093T About 1 km east of the main White Pockets Road is a **fence & gate** just south of the end of a low mesa with no name; but it's marked with the altitude of **6093T (1857m)** on the *Poverty Flat 7 1/2' quad*. If you walk north along that fenceline, then scramble upslope a ways, you'll come to a smooth, vertical sandstone wall and a nice **rock art panel**, and *Harvey Judd's* signature 30m to the east. Somewhere around the base is supposed to be a small ruin in a cave and broken pottery, but the author looked twice and never found it.

Frank's Reservoir USGS maps show this as being just east of **Butte 6093T (1857m)**, but it's actually 1 km northeast of Pottery Butte. Where the *7 1/2' quad* shows Frank's is only a **water trough**, but just to the south is an old **historic rip gut or stake & rider fence** running east/west across the valley. This fence was made by piling cedar (juniper) posts is such a way as to make it stand on it's own without barbed wire. At the east end and on a wall is a cowboy signature, *Lynn Ford Nov. 13, [19]27*. Now the real Frank's Reservoir (see map). This old water storage pond or tank is named after Frank Mackelprang, one of the early ranchers who helped develop the Sand Hills range for cows.

Pottery Butte (author's name) This is the unnamed butte marked **6079T (1853m)** on the *Wrather Arch 7 1/2' quad*. It's located about 1 km southwest of where the real Frank's Reservoir is. The only thing to see here are lots of **pottery fragments** along the east & south sides. But no ruins or rock art (?). It's possible some ruins may be buried in sand; or this may have been a popular stopping/camping place for Anasazi Indians on a trail running between the Middle Trail/Route crossing the Buckskin Gulch, and the more populated areas in Joe's Valley and White Knolls.

Twin White Buttes (author's name) These are about halfway between Pottery Butte and Hole in the Rock, and directly south of Frank's Reservoir. On the east side of the south tower is a detached boulder next to the main wall. In 2 places on that boulder is some rock art and cowboy signatures; one is *Hugh Farnsworth Feb. 12, 1932*, and a *K--- Judd*.

Hole in the Rock This is just another butte, but in the middle is a nice **arch** worth seeing.

A typical scene in a cluster of Big Brain & Cauliflower Rocks **(BB&CR)** that is called **White Pockets**. At the bottom of the high point in the background is the Corn Cob Cave. See **Map 38**, page 261.

Another typical scene in the **White Pockets**. White dominates the BB&CR on top, then other colors, mostly reds & yellows lie below.

Above A typical scene in the middle and southern parts of **White Pockets**. Looking northwest from the southern parts at the big dominant rock we'll call **White Pockets Butte**. By climbing this butte around mid-day, you might get some interesting shots.

Right This picture was taken in the middle part of **White Pockets** just west of the parking place.

From the air looking eastward at about the middle of the **White Pockets**. In the far left, and just visible, is a small pool created by the building of a **cement dam** to catch rainwater for cows.

Part of the **rock art panel** located at the southern end of butte or mesa labeled **6093T (1857m)** which is just east of White Pockets. See Map 38. Park at the gate and walk a short distance from there. The larger image is nearly life size. To the right of this is the inscription, *Harvey Judd, Jan. 6, 1926*.

The **rip gut or stake & rider fence** running east-west across the valley that's north of Pottery Butte. On the left side of the little mesa in the background is the rock art panel at 6093T (1857M).

Just a sample of pottery fragments/potsherds found at the southern and eastern side of **Pottery Butte.** They come in all shapes and colors, and archaeologists can probably tell us where they came from. Pottery Butte is the author's name, and it's located not too far east of White Pockets.

Looking north at the **Twin White Buttes** or Knolls. The corral in the foreground is the one you drive right through. See Map 38. To the right and out of sight is Hole in the Rock Butte & Arch.

Mackelprang Tank This is just northeast of Hole in the Rock and the road is blocked off at the wilderness boundary part way there. There are 2 tanks or water storage ponds or reservoirs there, but one dam is washed out. There's nothing to see in the area, but just to the northeast of Mackelprangs, are the remains of an old cattle trail zig zagging up through the ledges to the top of the southern part of **Adams Pasture**. If you go up there, you'll see where someone has piled up rocks along the rim of the mesa to keep cattle on top--or away from the top.

From this area, and from a corral between Twin White Buttes & Hole in the Rock, a road heads south to the main **Loop Road** located just east of **Big Sink**. You can make this loop while on a visit to White Pockets. This loop road was fine upon the author's visit, but the area south of **Basin Tank** and up to the **Cutoff Road**, has 2 long sections of **deep sand**.

Big Sink In the bottom of this valley with no outlet are some white rocks similar to the BB&CR at White Pockets, but they're not as extensive. Also, on 2 hills to the south & southwest are ruins and cowboy signatures on top of both. There are also surveyors cairns--made with rocks borrowed from the Anasazi ruins. On the north side of Big Sink is a cinder block house that's sometimes used by cowboys or other travelers. Please don't mess up a good thing! There's also a corral, windmill and well nearby. Water from that well flows by gravity down to Basin Tank, then on to the trough to the south.

Mexican Sink & Commissary Cave The best way to Mexican Sink is to head west from Pine, then turn or veer left after **3.3 kms (2 miles)**. That track isn't used much--depending on the time of year, but one branch heads to & past **Black Tank**, then north, and east to the water trough at 1998m (**6.2 kms/3.8 miles** from Pine). At that point you could drive north and end up at Big Sink along a good road--by Sand Hills standards--no sand traps. Or head east to Mexican Sink (**8.4 kms/5.2 miles**)--that's also a good road with little sand. Northeast of the middle of Mexican Sink is a 250m-long cliff with a couple of ruins, an alcove where Indians built a lot of fires--or where livestock men camped a lot, plus the **Commissary Cave**. To get there, drive northeast out of Mexican Sink about 600m to a gate in the fence (**9.1 kms/5.7 miles** from Pine); the old track going northeast from there hasn't been used in years, so why not park at the gate and just walk due north about 900m? Or, if you can see the old track, walk along that to the center of a little basin with the altitude of **6369T** (1941m). From there walk 200m magnetic west to find the cliff with Commissary Cave on the far right or north end. Read more about it in the History of the Sand Hills section. In the middle of Mexican Sink are a couple of fotogenic pinnacles.

Little Knoll The first thing to see east of Big Sink is Little Knoll. Park on the south side and walk north up to the big smooth sandstone wall to find a 2-part **rock art petroglyph panel**. There's no desert varnish, so the art is hard to see and fotograph, but one part goes up to 4-5m. There are also some cowboy signatures; *Kay Wilson Oct. 11, 1927; Chas. J. Ford 2-19-[19]13; and Lynn Ford Jan. 7 1947; also F. L. Farnsworth*, but no date. On the west side of Little Knoll is small panel of rock art and on the east side under a ledge is very crude shelter--not worth visiting.

Just south of Little Knoll is an unnamed butte with **Five Tops**. It's marked **6483T (1976m)** on the *7 1/2' Wrather Arch quad*. Just south of that are some orange & white BB&CR and teepee-like rocks.

Lower Reservoir, cabin & corrals There are 2 roads running north from either side of Little Knoll to this place. This pond is one of the biggest in the Sand Hills, at least it had a lot of water on the author's visits, maybe 2-3m deep. It's also the biggest dam the author has seen on the plateau. The catchment area for this reservoir is a **big slickrock area** made of nothing but pure **white BB&CR**. An interesting place for fotos. Just to the north of the reservoir is a cabin (some call it Dunk's but while Dunk Findlay may have stayed there some, it was built by A.T. Spence), a small horse barn & corral. Both have good roofs, but the cabin now lacks windows. To the north of that is a big stockade-type corral; in the wash bottom below the dam are at least 5 ponderosa pines.

Cowboy Hat Buttes (author's name) Just northeast of Little Knoll is a butte and a cluster of teepee

Looking at the east side of what USGS maps label **Hole in the Rock**. Add to that, Arch, and it pretty well tells the story. This is halfway between Mackelprang Tank and Twin White Buttes.

In the bottom of **Big Sink** are these interesting rocks. There used to be a little dam here which caught rain water, but it's no longer used. Looking SSW at 2 high places on what maps refer to as **Pinnacle Ridge**. There are Anasazi ruins on top of both. There's also an old airstrip in the bottom of Big Sink.

Above From the air looking down on **Lower Reservoir** and its all-white catchment made of BB&CR. The summer and fall of 2009, were dry, so there isn't much water in the pond which is on the lower left-hand side of this foto. When there's lots of water in the reservoir, you can come up with some interesting pictures here. Also interesting are the cabin, corrals and barns located just off this picture to the lower left. See more pictures of this place in the **History of the Sand Hills** part of this book.

Left This is part of the big rock art panel located on the south side of **Little Knoll**. From where you park, it's a short walk north up to the bottom of the big cliff. It's hard to see the petroglyphs because there's no desert varnish on this face. It also has some cowboy signatures like **Chas. J. Ford, 2/19/[19]13**, one of the oldest the author has seen in the Sand Hills.

227

Above The little pond that is **Middle Reservoir.** Just to the right of the picture to the west, is Middle (Reservoir) Well & Windmill. To get all of these in a nice foto, be there in the morning to mid-day. There's water here most of the time because of 2 little dams just to the left and out of sight. They were built by Joe Hamblin likely sometime in the 1890's.

Right This is what the author calls **Cowboy Hat**. See Map 38. It's just northeast of Little Knoll, and south of an un-named butte with the altitude of 6251T **(1905m)**. Just to the right and out of sight, is a cluster of BB&CR which might be interesting.

rocks; and in between is an interesting rock that looks like an upside down **cowboy hat** on a pedestal, thus the author's name for the buttes. Both have some interesting rocks; the northern butte marked **6251T** (1905m) has white layers with yellow & orange streaking or swirling. The other is a cluster of white BB&CR.

Middle Reservoir Area See **Map 39, Northeast Sand Hills**, for this little part. Within 3 kms of Middle Reservoir on all sides are lots of fotogenic rocks, mostly **BB&CR**. One thing that makes this area different from all the others, are the **orange rocks**, or white rocks with **orange swirls** or streaking. This area must rank as the 3rd best place in the Sand Hills for fotographers. A good place to start is at the well, windmill & big metal water tank just east of the gate & corral on the main Loop Road. Immediately east and below the well (it sits on top of the end of a low mesa) is the Middle Reservoir itself. Some time just before 1900, Joe Hamblin built a couple of **tiny rock dams** at the bottom of a small drainage basin so when it rains, all runoff is caught in a pond. The catchment is made of white BB&CR with orange swirls. There should be water in the pond most of the time, and that makes a nice fotographic scene in the morning or mid-day hours.

South of the windmill are more of the same BB&CR but these are in long rows like **log rocks** stacked next to each other. From the well & windmill, you can see lots of other clusters of BB&CR to the south and east. To the south a ways are some teepee-like rocks, and the Loop Road runs right through the middle of a couple of clusters. Further southeast are several other clusters about halfway between Middle Reservoir & **Button Tank**. The catchment for Button Tank has lots of white & orange rocks, and about 3 kms due north of Button are **Twin Tanks**. You can walk there on an old seldom-used road. It's catchment is a wall of white & orange sandstone with yellow & orange swirls. This one is worth seeing in the afternoons. Also, a little more than 1 km northwest of Twin Tanks is **Lynn Tank**. Just east of it are some colorful rocks, and 500m to the north is another nice cluster of BB&CR.

Cathedral & Pinnacle Valleys If you drive south from the gate & corral at Middle Reservoir, you'll find more of the same type of rocks in the northern part of **Cathedral Valley**, especially on the east side of the road. On *The Big Knoll 7 1/2' quad*, and just north & south of the word *Valley* (as in Cathedral Valley), are 2 pretty good areas. In the southern part are some ponderosa pines, and right on top of that low rock cluster and at a place where water ponds-up after rains, you'll find a bunch of pottery fragments. This was a natural waterhole and more than one crockpot was dropped & smashed.

If you continue south on the same **Cathedral/Pinnacle Valley Road** you'll end up in the north end of Pinnacle Valley. But before you get there, you could stop and walk west into the area south of the south end of **The Big Knoll**. Or if you're riding along the Loop Road in the northern end of Pinnacle Valley, stop at the **Pinnacle Valley Well**. Between that and the south end of The Big Knoll are more BB&CR. Also, throughout Pinnacle Valley are scattered small rock outcroppings; thus the name.

The best thing to see in **Pinnacle Valley** (see Map 40) is **The Pinnacle** itself. It's located 500m due east of the well and is the most-prominent feature around. Walk over there and on the west side is a **small cave** with a black ceiling (indicating it was used a lot by Indians with fires) and next to it are a bunch of cowboy & goat herder signatures including Willy & Trevor Leach, Findlays, Spence and Frank L. Farnsworth going back to 1911. On the southeast side are pottery fragments and more cowboy signatures.

Although The Pinnacle looks like a sharp peak from the west, it's actually a tall cluster of BB&CR. If

These are what the author calls **rock logs**, and they are on the south side of the little point where the **Middle Reservoir Windmill** sits. These types of rocks are found all around this area,

This is part of the slickrock catchment just above **Twin Tanks**, which is about 2 1/2 kms northeast of Middle Reservoir. This area is a mixture of white & orange slickrock with lots of swirls like you see here. There are also some beehive or teepee-like rocks.

you go to the east or north sides, you can climb up on top. There you'll find **3 water pockets.** One has water almost all the time, the other 2 were just wet on the author's visits. The bottoms of both of these were lined with **pottery fragments**. This tells us Anasazi Indians were using this as a water source about 900 years ago; and the pottery is still visible. An interesting place.

Bush Head Valley See Map 39 again. Continue east from Middle Reservoir on the Loop Road. If going into Bush Head Valley, take the most-westerly of the 2 roads running north to **Bush Head Cabin & Well**; it's a little shorter (5.2 kms/3.2 miles), but the quality of road is the same for both routes. There's an old **truck & drilling rig** at the cinder block cabin (this is lived in periodically) that's interesting, plus a granary, corrals and the well. On both sides of this little valley are lots of orange rocks.

If you continue north down toward the little butte called **Bush Head**, you'll eventually come to **Bush Head Tank** (it's **5.5 kms/3.4 miles** from Bush Head Cabin to Bush Head Tank). This is an interesting place. Glen Hamblin built a dam with a **cement core** at the bottom of a large slickrock catchment so now you'll find water there most of the time. Nearby is an old stockade-type corral, plus **2 old cabins**. One has a cement wall up about a meter, then a frame house on top of that. On the cement part someone scratched the date 12/7/1942. The other is a simple wood frame cabin, but someone installed metal sheeting on the walls and roof which is badly rusted now. Neither cabin has a door and wouldn't provide a lot of protection as an emergency shelter in a snow storm.

Roughly 2 kms northwest of Bush Head Tank are some pretty good, white & yellow, beehive-like rocks near elevation **5791T (1765m)**. A km west of that is another cluster of tilted beehive rocks. You can get to this area from the Paria River next to Bush Head Canyon as shown on Map 30 of the hike going down the river.

Shed Valley, Powell's Monument & Paria Needle There's not a lot to see in the east end of the Sand Hills, but there are a couple of places. Best to start at **Fenceline Tank** and head southeast; or take the sandier shortcut route that passes by the **Upper Shed Valley Reservoir**. This reservoir is washed out and the sand left in the roadway (gear down and rev up if you take that road). Otherwise where these 2 routes meet, head southeast along a fenceline. After 200m or so, and next to a low butte, stop and walk eastward. There you'll find the **TW 1949 Tank** which is a cement dam at the bottom of a slickrock catchment. On it are the initials **TW 1949**, apparently that's when the cement was laid by one of the Woolleys--perhaps Tony Woolley (?).

Continue southeast along the fenceline. Right at the edge of the plateau, the fence ends with a gate. Drive through it and head northeast to find the butte called **Powell's Monument** and next to it the **Paria Needle**. On the southwest side of Paria Needle are 2 small panels of petroglyphs. Also in that area is a nice granary, but the author failed to find it. Along the road to this area is a wildlife guzzler and some spectacular views down on the Colorado River & Marble Canyon.

Joe's Ranch & Tanks This is the oldest, and the only ranch in the Sand Hills. It may have had it's beginnings in 1884; read its history in the history section. This is **160 acres,** or a quarter section, of **private land**; but no one minds if you trespass, as it's now owned by the **Grand Canyon Trust**. There's a corral, 2 metal water tanks, a cabin, saddle shop & blacksmith shop which are in bad shape. Behind the cabins are 4 small stock ponds or reservoirs. One of these is pretty big and usually has water in it. These ponds are at the bottom of a large, circular basin or catchment; and it's all made of **white BB&CR**. There are also lots of Ponderosa pines, and the 2 combined, plus blue skies, make some nice pictures--best to be there in the afternoons. This has to be the 4th best place in the Sand Hills for pictures.

Joe's Horse Pasture, Brush & Rip Gut Fences, and Ruins If you walk south about 250m from Joe's cabins, you'll find a horse/cow trail zig zagging up the slope to the east. It's hard to see, but it's in the only place that's easy to get on top of the mesa behind the ranch. From on top, you'll have the best view of Joe's Ranch, stock ponds and catchment basin. If you head straight for The Beehives to

Looking east at the **Pinnacle Valley Well**, with **The Pinnacle** in the background. There's an Indian cave on the west side, plus lots of cowboy signatures. On top are 3 water pockets with potsherds.

Looking down at **Joe's Ranch**, the biggest of 4 reservoirs, and the lower part of the water catchment. This is perhaps the 4th best place in the Sand Hills for shooting great fotos. Water is in the biggest pond almost all the time, but cattle wade right in to drink. Behind the camera is **Joe's horse pasture**.

the east, you'll eventually come to an old brush fence that generally runs north-south. This is the work of Joe Hamblin, and it enclosed his horse pasture. If you follow it north, it turns into a rip gut or stake & rider fence. Just north of where it turns west are some unimpressive ruins in the flats. There's also another brush fence around the rim of the slickrock catchment for Joe's stock ponds. Also, out in what this writter calls Joe's Valley and in front of Joe's Ranch, there are 4-5 ruins, as shown on Map 39.

The Beehives & Soap Creek Tanks About 1 km (.6 mile) southwest of Joe's Ranch on the main Loop Road is a junction next to a small stock pond (normally dry). From there, head south then east toward **Soap Creek Pasture** and an overlook of the **Cliff Dwellers & Vermilion Cliffs Lodges**. The first point of interest along the **Soap Creek Road** will be after **3.3 kms (2 miles)**. At that point is a side-road turning left or north. Drive this for 500m and park next to a fence. Just west of that are **The Bee-hives**. There you'll find 5 mini buttes, with 2 small **ruins/granaries** on the 2 buttes to the west. There's also some crude rock-top ruins on the biggest butte, plus there are **pottery fragments** or potsherds everywhere, especially in the middle of the group.

Going east again. Soon after you cross over a pass or divide and head down the other side, you'll come to the 2nd road to the right at **Km 4.5/Mile 2.8**. Drive this through an open valley and up a pretty good track for about 2.7 kms (1.7 miles) to near an overlook of the valley below near elevation **7022T (2140m)**. From there you can work your way down over minor ledges to the east to find the **Soap Creek Tank #2** and another reservoir, Soap Creek Tank #1, plus lots of **BB&CR** which are white with red, purple or pink swirls. This is a pretty nice place for fotos, partly because you can usually combine blue sky & ponderosa pines with all the varicolored rocks.

Go east again on the Soap Creek Road. About **4.8 kms (3 miles)** from the main Loop Road is the 2nd road to the left. Drive this for **2.1 kms (1.3 miles)** and park/camp in big cedar trees next to a small butte maybe 20-25m wide, and about 15m high. On top is a small **pueblo (Beehive East)** which formerly housed a small band of Anasazi. There are pottery fragments all over the place. **A reminder; taking potsherds home is illegal!** So please leave them there for others to discover and enjoy.

If you continue to the end of the Soap Creek Road, which is at about **Km 6.7/Mile 4.1**, you'll be in the bottom of a basin (this could be hard to get back out of if the sand is dry, so you may want to walk from the one steep place to the road's end). This puts you near Soap Creek Tank #1, which is normally dry, but also in the heart of the Upper Soap Creek Fotogenic area.

White Knolls The discription above pretty well tells the story here. See **Map 40, Southern Sand Hills**. There are ruins on top of almost every knoll or hilltop in this region. The author marked 11 sites or sets of ruins on his map, but there are lots more. You can read about part of this area (Section 35) in an archaeological report (White Knolls Survey) by the Vermilion Cliffs National Monument headquartered in St. George, Utah. Try this website from a German guy named Steffen Synnatschke; **http://www.synnatschke. de/files/Paria-Plateau-Report-Draft-2007.pdf**. It's a big file, but if this doesn't work you should have access to it from the monument's office in St. George.

Jarvis Ranch See **Map 40**. Read about the history of the Jarvis Ranch in the history chapter. Near the well-built white frame house is a barn & 2 metal water tanks, plus corrals. If you drive west (set your odometer at 0) from Jarvis on **Road #1104**, you'll pass a road on the left at **Km2.4/Mile 1.5**; further along is another road to the left at **Km 3.6/Mile 2.2**. These less-used tracks make a loop up to near the rim of the Vermilion Cliffs and to the wilderness boundary. In that area are some teepee-type rocks. See

Part of the Anasazi ruins on top of a butte the author calls **Beehive East** (it's about 2 kms east of The Beehives). There are lot's of pottery fragments here, so please leave them for others to enjoy.

These are just some of the rocks & colors you'll see in the area of **Soap Creek Pasture** and tanks. Soap Creek Tank #2 has water most of the time, and there are lots of BB&CR in this area.

The **Jarvis Ranch house** from the back side. It was built in about 1935. This picture was taken on 2/18/2008; normally there's more snow than this at that time of year. You can normally get into most of the Sand Hills by about March 1. Read more in the section on **History of the Sand Hills**.

more of those tracks with **Map 42** on Jacobs Pool and the Bonal Spring Loop-Hike.

Jim's Tanks These are located at **Km 4/Mile 2.5**. There you'll find a couple of metal tanks partly underground. Just to the west is an area covered with corrugated roofing which collects rainwater, which in turn flows downhill and into the tanks. That's what it used to do; but today it's unmaintained and doesn't collect water. This is called a guzzler (or trip tank), the kind usually built to supply water to wildlife--but this one's for cows. From Jim's, you can drive northwest on **Road #1104** back to Pine.

Or, drive west on **Road #1102**. At **Km7.3/Mile 4.5** (from Jarvis) is a junction; turn sharply to the left and head back uphill to the south on the **Bonal Road**. After another **1.1 kms (.7 mile)**, you'll come to where the road is blocked off at the wilderness boundary. From there, walk up a trail 300m to the place you'll reach if climbing up from **Bonal Spring**. There you'll find 3 cement watering troughs and nearby a large complex of hilltop **Anasazi ruins**. This is like a small village, and may be the biggest site in the Sand Hills. You could climb down the crack to the south to Bonal Spring, or drive northwest again past the last junction previously mentioned. From there on, you'll be on **Road #1100**, what old timers called the Bonal Road. If you use this, it will take you back to the **HRVR**, a distance of about 13.8 kms (8.5 miles) from the big ruins. Along the way are a number of roads going in all directions, but there's nothing to see or fotograph in those parts.

Elevations T-Junction & Bowman's Corral--HRVR & Entry Road to Sand Hills, 1820m; Pine Tree Pockets Ranch House, 1926m; White Pockets Trailhead, 1729m; Poverty Ranch, 1792m; Big Sink, 1865m; Middle Reservoir, 1899m; Lower Reservoir, 1800m; Bush Head Well & Cabin, 1872m; Bush Head Tank, 1780m; Pinnacle Valley Well, 1945m; Joe's Ranch, 2003m; The Beehives, 2115m; hill by Soap Creek Tanks, 2140m; Hilltops in White Knolls Area, about 2175m; Jarvis Ranch, 2026m; cliff-top ruins above Bonal Spring, about 2163m.

Time Needed Few hikes are very long, just wander around the slickrock with your camera to find the best shapes, colors or shadows. One, 2 or maybe 3 hours for each location.

Water Take lots of water with you, there are **No Springs or Running Water in the Sand Hills**. However, and only in an emergency, you may find some water in troughs if cows are in that area; ranchers pump it from several wells (or in some cases the Home Ranch Reservoir at Joe's Ranch), and into metal tanks & troughs where their cows are grazing (it's estimated there are between 100-150 kms of water pipeline buried in the Sand Hills). Or in small man-made reservoirs after heavy rains. **Treat or filter any water you might see/use.**

Maps USGS or BLM maps **Glen Canyon Dam** (mostly this one) & Fredonia (1:100,000) for driving & orientation; and Poverty Flat, Wrather Arch, Water Pockets, House Rock Spring, One Toe Ridge, The Big Knoll, Emmett Hill & Emmett Wash, plus parts of West Clark Bench, Coyote Buttes & Navajo Bridge (1:24,000--7 1/2' quads) for hiking, driving and finding all the sites & elevations found in this and the next chapter on History of the Sand Hills.

Main Attractions The Sand Hills is a **Fotographer's Dream** with unusual rock formations & colors. Not counting Coyote Buttes, White Pockets is the best place (these 2 places are tied for 1st/best places in this writer's mind), then the Middle Reservoir area is 3rd best. After those places, it's behind Joe's Ranch, Lower Reservoir & Soap Creek Tanks (Also, the Water Pockets on West Clark Bench is really good). The White Knolls & The Beehives area have most of the ruins. Also the rock art panels on Little Knoll & Butte 6093T are good. The biggest rock art panels seen anywhere will be discussed with the House Rock Valley & Hod Brown Spring hike, and the Sand Hills Cracks & Bonal Spring hikes.

Author's Experience He was taken to Jarvis & Joe's Ranches in the late 1980's by someone at the request of former owner Dunk Findlay, then got back in 2/2008 with a Chevy Tracker and saw White Pockets, Big Sink, Jarvis, Joe's & Soap Creek Tanks. In 2009, and using a Jeep Patriot, he explored all parts of the Sand Hills on about 8 trips from April to October.

This is just one part of the big Anasazi ruins located at the top of the route up through the Vermilion Cliffs above **Bonal Spring**. Not far away are 3 cement water troughs used when water was pumped up to the plateau from Bonal Spring below.

234

Above Just one of many **hill-top Anasazi ruins** you'll see in the southern part of the Sand Hills. These are in the **White Knolls**.

Left One of several mini buttes or pinnacles in the valley known as **Mexican Sink**. This one is located on the eastern side and right in the bottom.

Looking north at **Wave 2**, located southwest of, and a little higher, than the top of **The Wave**. It's also in Sand Cove and just above and east of **Butte 5215T** (1590m). (see Map 37)

Teepee-like rocks just east of elevation marker **5697T** (1736m) at the north end of **Top Rock** (see Map 37). In this area are several Ponderosa pines and the same kind of rock you see at **The Wave**.

Left **Grosvenor Arch**, located in the upper part of Cottonwood Wash. The yellow is a tongue of Henrieville Sandstone. (See Map 24, Upper Cottonwood Wash Narrows). **Right** One nice scene in the **Tiny Northwest Cove** area of the southern **Coyote Buttes**. (See Map 37)

Left These colorful rocks are found on the high ground between **Cottonwood Cove** & Cottonwood Cove Trailhead. (See Map 37) **Right** Colorful clay beds in the upper part of **West Cove**, located north of **mile post 24** along Highway 89 not too far west of Paria Ranger Station. (See Map 29)

Northwest Sand Hills: Coyote Buttes & The Waves

Location & Access Before going anywhere, read the part below about the **required permit system** for the central part of the **Coyote Buttes**. Also, see **Map 36, Sand Hills Area Map**; and read the previous part; **Introduction to Driving, Touring & Fotography in the Sand Hills** before doing any driving in the Sand Hills, or attempting to use the southern or southeastern approaches to Coyote Buttes.

Map 37A features a place called Coyote Buttes, which is a part of The Cockscomb Ridge immediately south of Wire Pass Trailhead (one entry point to the upper Buckskin Gulch). In the early 1990's, someone went there, made a motion picture, and showed it in Germany. Ever since, there's been a stampede of Europeans, mostly Germans, heading that way, along with American fotographers. The color & striations of some rocks, notably **The Wave & Wave 2**, is spectacular, making Coyote Buttes high on the gotta-go-to list for foto bugs.

To get there, you could come in from the south and Arizona. About halfway between Jacob Lake & Marble Canyon and the Colorado River, is a place called House Rock between **mile posts 565 & 566** on **Highway 89A**; from there turn north and drive along the **House Rock Valley Road (HRVR)** to the **Wire Pass Trailhead**, a distance of **34.2 kms (21.2 miles)**. When conditions are dry, this is a good road for any car; when wet it can be slick in places where the road runs across clay beds. However, as of 2009, Arizona had improved the road on their side of the state line, so it isn't as bad as it once was. See **Map 36, Sand Hills Area Map**, for a look at the entire region including the HRVR.

But the more popular and most-used way to get there is to drive along **Highway 89** about halfway between Kanab & Page. Immediately west of The Cockscomb, and between **mile posts 25 & 26**, turn south onto the same **HRVR**. Drive **13.5 kms (8.4 miles)** until you reach the Wire Pass Trailhead. This is also the most popular entry point to the Buckskin Gulch. Wire Pass Trailhead now has a large parking lot, public toilet, and you can camp there too, or anywhere else in the area. Hiking from Wire Pass Trailhead is the fastest, easiest and shortest way to reach the heart of Coyote Buttes and **The Wave**--the number 1 destination. Another nearby foto shoot is **Wave 2**.

Here are several other ways into Coyote Buttes via the HRVR. Not far south of Wire Pass Trailhead is the beginning of a route/trail into the heart of the Buttes through **The Notch**. To get there, drive south from Highway 89 a total of **17.5 kms (10.9 miles)**; or north **30.2 kms (18.7 miles)** from Highway 89A. As you near this area, watch for a big prominent notch, gap or pass in The Cockscomb to the east. Park where there are some roads & campsites on the west side of the HRVR; or perhaps near the old rusty **metal water tank** 200m northwest of the HRVR (it's hard to see).

Or, here's a **better way** to The Notch. Drive south from the parking place just described about **320m** (.2 mile) and park under some cedar trees on the east side of the HRVR. You should see a sign stating you need a permit, and another small one indicating archaeology sites nearby. Parking & hiking from there will allow you to pass some old tumbled-down Anasazi ruins and the biggest & best rock art panel in the Coyote Buttes area. Both will be on your way to The Notch.

To reach the southern end of the **Coyote Buttes & Paw Hole**, drive south from Highway 89 on the HRVR for **26.4 kms (16.4 miles)**; or **21.3 kms (13.2 miles)** north from Highway 89A. At that point, a road heads east for 320m to **Lone Tree Reservoir**. If you have a 2WD, continue east to a point about 1.6 kms (1 mile) from the HRVR and park & camp. Beyond there the road is **very sandy** and for **4WD's**. Or if you have a good 4WD and want to try to drive there, then continue ESE uphill for about **2.2 kms (1.4 miles from the HRVR)** and turn left or northward at a **"T" junction**. After about another 1 1/2 kms (1 mile) you'll be just south of Paw-Hole. In that area is a **200m-long section of very deep sand--maybe the worst sand trap in the Sand Hills**, so gear down, rev up and start going like hell just before you hit the sand trap. Don't slow down or stop until you're on *tierra firma*. From the Paw Hole area, the track heads east to the **Poverty Ranch (Poverty)** then north to the **Cottonwood Cove** area.

Here's a better way into the Cottonwood Spring & Cove area. Using **Area Map 36**, turn east from the HRVR onto the **Entry Road to Pine Tree Pockets (Pine)**. That junction is **32.7 kms (20.3 miles)** from the north & Highway 89; and **15 kms (9.3 miles)** from the south & Highway 89A (on the west side of that junction is the **Bowman's Corral**). Head east on a partly-graveled road in the direction of the ranch house at **Pine**--but after 5 kms (3.1 miles) turn northeast from the **Corral Valley Well** heading in the direction of **Poverty**. Once you leave the Entry Road, you must have a **4WD**.

Now follow this map carefully. After passing **Red Pockets & Corral**, and at a junction 8.8 kms (5.4 miles) from the Entry Road, you could veer right and end up at the old Poverty Ranch; but now there's only a barn & well and not much to see (plus lots of deep sand on the east side of where the ranch houses once stood), so it's best to veer left bypassing the ranch. Continue north running along side Rawd Sander's old airstrip. After that you'll go through a gate (close it behind you--that gate & fence separate 2 grazing pastures) and up past a corral near the **pass, camping area and trailhead marked 1737m**. The sand gets real deep on the north side of that pass, so park in some cedars which is now the trailhead **13.4 kms/8.3 miles** from the Entry Road and Corral Valley.

Because of deep sand on all roads surrounding Poverty, the best time to go into that region, or anywhere else in the Sand Hills, is right after a good rainstorm, or in the winter season (November through March) when there's normally more moisture in the sand. When deep sand gets really dry, even the best 4WD's have a hard time.

Trail/Route The normal starting point for the route to **The Wave** is the **Wire Pass Trailhead**. On the east side of the parking area is an information board & sign-in place. Read instructions, do what you have to do, then walk east across the road on an obvious trail; or along a marked & well-used trail. About 1 km from the trailhead, and as you're heading in a northerly direction in the dry creek bed, you should see an **old road/trail** and many footprints going up the steep hill to the right or east--this is an old Cat track. Go up this hill (if you continue along the Wire Pass dry creek bed you'll soon be in the **Buckskin Gulch**). About 300-400m from the creek bed will be the trail register for Coyote Buttes. Continue southeast on the old wagon road to the bottom of the first drainage (there used to be 2 stock ponds in that area called **Bull Pasture Reservoirs**) then veer left and follow tracks east over a low divide in a slickrock ridge. About 50m after you cross the little pass, veer right or southerly and route-find along the eastern side of the same north-south running ridge. Follow this map and other people's tracks as best you can over mostly slickrock.

Roughly 9/10 of the way to The Wave, you'll look down on a sandy valley with 3 medium-sized **cottonwood trees**, and not far beyond, a dry wash running from the southwest out of **Sand Cove**. From there, you should see a **vertical crack** in the distance which is above and just south of The Wave. This is something you can see as you get close to The Wave. It's also the best landmark to shoot for. From the wash, you'll see 2 sandslides coming down from the south, also 2 trails; walk up one of these fol-

Map 37A, Northwest Sand Hills: Coyote Buttes & The Waves

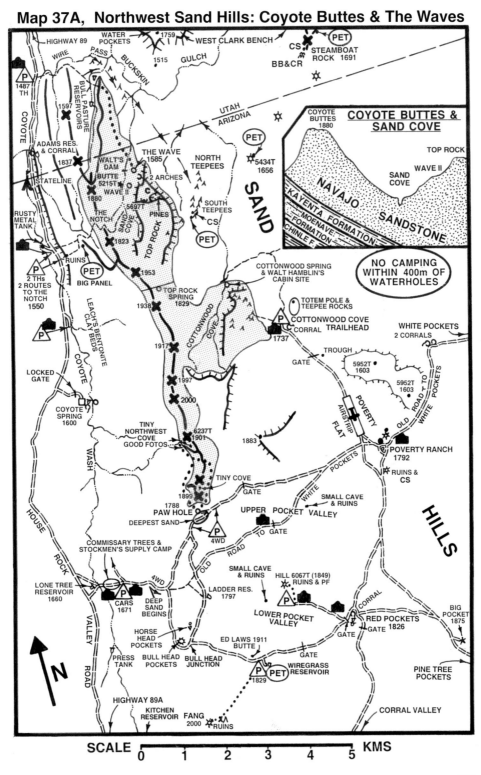

HIGHWAY 89

WATER POCKETS

1759

WEST CLARK BENCH

CS

PET

WIRE PASS

BUCKSKIN

1515

GULCH

STEAMBOAT ROCK 1691

BB&CR

P 1487 TH

BULL PASTURE RESERVOIRS

UTAH ARIZONA

COYOTE

1597

ADAMS RES. & CORRAL

1837

STATELINE

THE WAVE 1585

WALT'S DAM

BUTTE 5215T

WAVE II 1880

THE NOTCH

5697T

SAND COVE

1823

NORTH TEEPEES

2 ARCHES

PINES

TOP ROCK

SOUTH TEEPEES

CS

PET

PET

5434T 1656

COYOTE BUTTES 1880

COYOTE BUTTES & SAND COVE

TOP ROCK

WAVE II

SAND COVE

NAVAJO SANDSTONE

KAYENTA FORMATION

MOENAVE FORMATION

CHINLE F.

RUSTY METAL TANK

RUINS

PET

BIG PANEL

1953

P 2 THs 2 ROUTES TO THE NOTCH 1550

LEACH'S BENTONITE CLAY BEDS

COYOTE

1938

TOP ROCK SPRING 1829

COTTONWOOD COVE

COTTONWOOD SPRING & WALT HAMBLIN'S CABIN SITE

TOTEM POLE & TEEPEE ROCKS

P COTTONWOOD COVE CORRAL TRAILHEAD 1737

NO CAMPING WITHIN 400m OF WATERHOLES

WHITE POCKETS 2 CORRALS

P

1917

GATE

TROUGH

5952T 1603

5952T 1603

OLD ROAD TO WHITE POCKETS

LOCKED GATE

COYOTE

1997

2000

COYOTE SPRING 1600

WASH

TINY NORTHWEST COVE GOOD FOTOS

6237T 1901

1883

WHITE POCKETS

POVERTY FLAT

AIRSTRIP

POVERTY RANCH 1792

RUINS & CS

TINY COVE

GATE

SMALL CAVE & RUINS

UPPER POCKET VALLEY

HILLS

1899

1788 PAW HOLE

DEEPEST SAND

P 4WD

ROAD TO GATE

HOUSE ROCK

COMMISSARY TREES & STOCKMEN'S SUPPLY CAMP

4WD

OLD

SMALL CAVE & RUINS

HILL 6067T (1849) RUINS & PF

CORRAL

LONE TREE RESERVOIR 1660

P CARS 1671

DEEP SAND BEGINS

LADDER RES. 1797

P

LOWER POCKET VALLEY

RED POCKETS 1826

GATE

BIG POCKET 1875

VALLEY ROAD

HORSE HEAD POCKETS

PRESS TANK

BULL HEAD POCKETS

BULL HEAD JUNCTION

ED LAWS 1911 BUTTE

GATE

GATE

WIREGRASS RESERVOIR

PINE TREE POCKETS

P PET 1829

N

HIGHWAY 89A

KITCHEN RESERVOIR

FANG 2000 RUINS

CORRAL VALLEY

SCALE

0 1 2 3 4 5 KMS

lowing footprints directly into The Wave. It's located about 200m from the dry wash, and about 50 vertical meters up the north end of a ridge called **Top Rock**.

Other nearby fotogenic sites are in **Sand Cove** and what some are now calling **Wave 2**. To get there, follow the dry wash into Sand Cove about 1 km, instead of climbing up to The Wave. Aim for the tiny cluster of buttes labeled **5215T** (1590m) on the *Coyote Buttes 7 1/2' quad*. Wave 2 is 250m ENE of this butte, but 70m above it on a bench. Climb up steep slickrock. You can also get there by bench-walking southwest from just above The Wave, and onto a bench to Sand Cove. At Wave 2, you want shadows, so be there just after the sun comes over the ridge to the east, maybe 9-10 am; and just before the sun drops below the western ridge. Be at **Butte 5215T** around mid-day--you don't want shadows there. Butte 5215T has some nice striations on it's south side. See picture. This site even rivals The Wave & Wave 2. Other good places are North & South Teepees, and east of Cottonwood Cove.

If you don't have a permit for Coyote Buttes, you can still go to **The Teepees** which are outside of the **Special Management Area: North & South Coyote Buttes**. Instead of taking the trail to The Wave, continue down the Wire Pass drainage toward Buckskin Gulch for about another 800m or so, then look for one of several ways out of the canyon and up to a bench to the south. This will be just before you enter the 1st Wire Pass Slot; or in between the 2 short slots in lower Wire Pass. Once out of the drainage, and on top of any high point, look SSE and you should see the **North & South Teepees** on the horizon. Walk cross-country east, then south along the approximate route shown on the map.

Perhaps an even better way to the Teepees is to use the old road going toward The Wave, but skirt left or north at the north end of the slickrock mentioned above, which is away from the Special Management Area boundary--check the boundary carefully, it's easy to avoid the *forbidden zone* where you're supposed to have a permit. You can also get there by walking east from The Wave.

Another emerging trail into **The Wave & Sand Cove** is through **The Notch**. From the HRVR and 320m (.2 mile) south of the turnoff to the rusty **metal water tank**, head east on a developing hiker's trail. At the top of the first ridge, you should see a couple of piles of rocks; these are old **hill-top Anasazi ruins**. From there set your compass on 60° and head ENE across a sagebrush-covered flat for 600m. Be looking for a trail--there's a pretty good one there somewhere. As you near the main part of The Cockscomb, be looking up about 30m for a big west-facing pertruding rock. On it is one of the best **rock art panels (petroglyphs)** around. It consists of one large and 3 smaller panels.

After viewing the rock art, walk north along the base of The Cockscomb for about 200m, and head eastward into an obvious canyon along an **old cow trail**. Once into that minor canyon, continue east & southeast on a good trail, then veer north cutting across the bottom of The Notch. Soon you'll turn south and eventually reach The Notch (there are several minor trails in the area). From there, veer right on a sandy hiker's trail contouring south, then east and downhill into the slickrock valley called **Sand Cove**. Head northeast down the drainage to see **Wave 2**, but don't forget to see the foto op just south of **Butte 5215T** (1590m) on the quad. Or, near the bottom of the drainage is an old historic rancher-made sand-filled reservoir and **Walt's cement dam** and maybe some water (?). About 150m below the dam, turn right or south with all the other tracks, and climb up to The Wave. South of The Wave at the north end of **Top Rock**, and in the NE 1/4 of Section 6 (where elevation **5698T**/1737m is located), is a little cove with ponderosa pines and nice fotos.

For **Paw Hole**, and if you have a 2WD, walk the road discussed above all the way. Paw Hole is a sometimes-water-filled semi-natural pocket or depression surrounded by teepee-shaped rocks (read about how this depression came about in the **History of the Sand Hills**). You can visit the area around Paw Hole and for about 250m to the north **without a permit**. But to go further north and to the 1st big butte, you're supposed to have a permit for the **South Coyote Buttes**--which is still easy to get on a walk-in basis at the Paria River Ranger Station (in winter at the Kanab BLM Field Office).

Here's a nice hike just north of Paw Hole. From or near Paw Hole, walk north and around the east side of the first really big butte. Between that 1st butte and the next one just to the north is a **Tiny Cove** draining to the east with some really nice yellow & white sandstone with streaks of maroon, plus erosions features like those at The Wave & Wave II. Here's another fotogenic place; if you continue north on the east side of the main ridge crest, then cut down to the left or northwest to the west side, you'll soon come to the same **yellow, white & maroon rocks** as in Tiny Cove; let's call this the **Tiny Northwest Cove**. This area is about 300m south of elevation **6237T** (1901m). Plan to spend at least half a day in the Paw Hole area for the right light & shadows; but it's best in the mid-day hours.

From the road, pass & trailhead north of the **Poverty Ranch**, walk northwest on a newly-created **hiker's trail** into the area east of **Cottonwood Cove** and south of **Cottonwood Spring**. There you'll find the **Cottonwood Teepees**, but be careful wandering around--in some places there are small fins of rock sticking up that go crunch when you step on them. Right where that sandy trail disappears in the first bunch of rocks & buttes are some really nice colors--in this case lavender, purplish or pinkish rocks and lots of swirling, plus all other colors. You can spend several hours in that area. Or if you don't have a permit, you could legally walk due north from the trailhead to the **Totum Pole** (see map), and **North & South Teepees, or Steamboat Rock** avoiding the Special Management Area.

Elevations Wire Pass Trailhead, 1487m; The Notch Trailheads, 1550m; pass near Cottonwood Cove, 1737m; high point in the Buttes, 2000m; The Wave, 1585m.

Time Needed It's less than 4 kms from Wire Pass Trailhead to **The Wave**, and if no stops are made, should take up to 1 1/2 hours; most people spend 4-6 hours (or more) for the entire hike. From Lone Tree Reservoir to **Paw Hole** is about 3 1/2 kms uphill in sand; this can be done in a couple of hours, or all day for fotographers. From Wire Pass Trailhead to **The Teepees** via the Lower Route should take 1 1/2-2 hours one-way. From the HRVR to The Wave via **The Notch Trail** should take 1 1/2 hours or so one-way. Time and distance to the **Cottonwood Teepees** area will depend on how far you can drive.

Water Always take plenty in your car and in your pack, especially if 4WD'ing north of Poverty.

Maps USGS or BLM maps Kanab, Smoky Mountain, Glen Canyon Dam & Fredonia (1:100,000) for driving & orientation; Pine Hollow Canyon, West Clark Bench, Poverty Flat & Coyote Buttes (1:24,000--7 1/2' quads) for hiking. Sorry, The Wave and Coyote Buttes are right where 4 maps meet!

Main Attractions The Navajo Sandstone in the Coyote Buttes is colored red, yellow, white and maroon, plus it has interesting shapes and erosional features plus striations. The Wave seems to get all the attention, but Wave 2 & just south of Butte 5215T, the Tiny & Tiny Northwest Coves north of Paw Hole, the various Teepees and other similar sites are great too. Steamboat Rock has some interesting rocks.

Tips for Fotographers Take plenty of memory space & batteries. **The Wave** has a NNW to SSE component, and you don't want shadows! So from early November to early February, be there between 10:10am & 10:50am for best results. A month or two on either side of these dates will give you a slightly larger window. In the 2 months before or after June 21, which is daylight savings time, be there from about 10am to 2pm. Also, be there on a day with 100% pure, clear, unfiltered & unadulterated sunshine--something that's difficult under the present booking & reservation system! **Write and complain! Read more below.** For the **Tiny Coves** north of **Paw Hole**, plan to be there for several hours in the middle of the day, or maybe spend an entire day in that area if you're a photographer.

Best Time to Hike April, May and early June, and September & October. Summers are pretty hot, plus there's desert haze. Winters can bring crystal clear skies and it's easier to get reservations or a walk-in pass, but it can be pretty cold, plus there's a very small window for foto ops during the short days of winter. Plus, muddy conditions along parts of the HRVR could be a problem.

Boots/Shoes Running or athletic-type shoes that won't leave black scuff marks on rocks. Also, you'll be walking in sand in most places so don't take running-type shoes that have the light-weight mesh around the toes--that mesh allows sand into your shoes.

Author's Experience Once, he left his VW Rabbit at the Corral Valley Well and walked to Cottonwood Spring and back in 8 hours. Later he drove his Chevy Tracker to the pass & corral at 1737m and spent 4 hours in that area. He walked from the Wire Pass Trailhead to The Teepees via the Lower Route and returned, all in 4 hours. He walked from near Coyote Spring to Paw Hole (not a recommended route!) and back in 3 1/2 hours. Using The Notch Trail, he made it to The Wave and back in 3 hours, but was in a big hurry. Once he hurried into The Wave via the normal route but missed the best time frame with the sun. Round-trip was 2 hours, but you'll want lots more time than that. Another trip to The Wave via Wire Pass took 5 1/2 hours round-trip, but that also included a quick trip down the Buckskin for pictures. Walking to Paw Hole from near Lone Tree Reservoir took 1 1/2 hours round-trip; a 2nd trip with his Jeep Patriot and parking at Paw Hole, then into the Tiny Coves took 2 1/3 hours round-trip.

Permit Requirements for Coyote Buttes
Special Management Area for 2010

Before going into the heart of Coyote Buttes, which is the shaded area on the map, you're supposed to have a permit. Below are the latest rules & regulations as outlined in a BLM handout for 2010. However, be warned! BLM policy can change at the drop of a hat, so see the website **www.az.blm.gov/paria** for the latest changes or updates! Or **https://www.blm.gov/az/asfo/paria/coyote_buttes/permits.htm.** Below are rules & regulations in the simplist of terms. Or call the BLM in Kanab at 435-644-4600.

Permits Required--Coyote Buttes North (this includes **The Wave, Wave 2 & Sand Cove**)--20 people/day--10 with advanced reservations done online via the internet, 10 for walk-ins. US$7 per person & per dog. **Coyote Buttes South** (north of **Paw Hole, & Cottonwood Cove**)--20 people/day--10 with advanced reservations, 10 for walk-ins. US$5 per person & per dog.

Group size limit 6 people. Coyote Buttes are for day-use only. No overnight camping permitted. Dogs are allowed in the Coyote Buttes--but for a fee--read above. Campfires or burning of trash/toilet paper prohibited. Please carry out all trash. Guides, outfitters and certain organized groups require a separate Special Recreation Permit.

To Make Reservations Most of the time, there is only 1 way you can get one of the 10 reserved permits issued daily, up to 3 months in advance, for the North & South Coyote Buttes:

Online To quickly view available hiking dates, secure a reservation, and pay fees (credit card only), visit the Paria Canyon Project Website at: **www.az.blm.gov/paria.** If you do not have access to the internet or cannot obtain access at your local library, call the Arizona Strip Interpretive Association (ASIA) at 435-688-3246; or the Kanab BLM Field Office, 435-644-4600 and a staff member may access the web for you--or will more likely tell you you're out of luck! As of 2010, you can only apply for a permit ONLINE; no mail-in or faxed applications allowed.

Permits for available hiking dates may also be purchased in person at one of several BLM office locations including Kanab, St. George and the Paria Ranger Station & Visitor Center near mile post 21 on Highway 89 about halfway between Kanab & Page (this would be in the summer season only).

Once your hiking date is reserved, a permit & map will be mailed to you, or you may choose to pick it up at one of the locations listed above. It's easier to get a permit in June, July & August, and from mid-November to mid-March--than it is in April, May, September & October--the busiest months.

To Get Walk-in Permits 10 Walk-in Permits for the **North Coyote Buttes** and **The Wave** are available every day for the **FOLLOWING DAY**. Between **mid-March & mid-November**, drive to the Paria Ranger Station & Visitor Center located near mile post 21 on Highway 89. The Paria Ranger Station opens at 8:30am. If more than 10 hikers are present, they will draw permits from a hat at 9am. Walk-ins are not on a first come, first serve basis--all applications received before 9am will be given the same priority. Fewer people go to the **South Coyote Buttes**, so they will give you a permit on the spot for the same day, or the next day if less than 10 people show up.

In the winter months, from **mid-November to mid-March** (subject to change), obtain a walk-in permit at the Kanab BLM Field Office, 318 N. 100 E. Call 435-644-4600 for further information (or call the Arizona Strip District Office in St. George, Utah office at 435-688-3246), or about any changes in policy which is about a 100% possibility!

Comments on How to Change Public Policy on
Coyote Buttes Permit Reservation System

The above stated requirements for 2010 are constantly being re-evaluated as this is being written and will surely be modified as soon as this book goes to press! In the opinion of this writer, that part of the BLM which sets the policy for Coyote Buttes is now being dominated by the **lunatic fringe** of the **Southern Utah Wilderness Alliance (SUWA)**, an organization this writer has been a member of for many years.

The BLM policy of permits and especially reservations, has turned this into the biggest **bureaucratic nightmare of all time**, all because a few radicals in the environmental movement want everyone to have a **true wilderness experience in the Coyote Buttes.** But, is going to a so-called wilderness area with up to 19 other people a real wilderness experience?

Surely those making the policy for Coyote Buttes work for the BLM and they have the right to go there anytime they want without getting a reservation or permit. They don't have to jump through all the hoops the rest of us are required to. It seems some BLM employees want to keep this place a big secret, and part of their own little private sanctuary. But remember, it's our land, not the BLM's!

One of the legitimate issues BLM policy makers worry about in allowing more people to visit **The**

Wave, is that everybody walks right on the places they want to fotograph. In time, some black-soled shoes may leave scuff marks--but none have ever been observed by this writer. Even if scuff marks do occur, the next rainstorm wipes them away--this is soft sandstone remember, and it's continually erod-ing away. Instead of asking hikers to just wear soft-soled shoes into the area, this writer suggests every-one remove shoes entirely while at The Wave; that way 500 people a day could visit the place and would do no more harm than with the present policy. Beyond The Wave, there are few other places in Coyote Buttes where walking all over colorful rocks would have a detrimental effect, but some policy makers use this argument to justify their actions. What this present policy seems to be doing is creat-ing a type of *forbidden fruit*, which everyone wants to taste, just to see if it's really poison. In the end, and with this type of bureaucracy in place, people will just go out there anyway, with or without a per-mit, and not pay the user-fee.

Here are some suggestions this writer offers the BLM.

1. Have everyone pick up a one-day user-fee permit when they arrive at the Kanab BLM Field Office, the Paria Ranger Station & Visitor Center; or with the increased fee collections, install a small trailer house at **Wire Pass Trailhead** and have a seasonal ranger sell permits there--on the spot. That per-son could also inform hikers on proper ethics in the more sensitive areas, and recommend other places to get great pictures. That person could also make periodic hikes to The Wave to make sure everyone has a permit. This would eliminate the old Soviet-style bureaucratic nightmare of getting reservations.
2. Charge $5 a day for a user-fee per person, and have no limitations on visitor numbers. If the sky turns cloudy, they can buy another permit and go out again the next day with better light & sun. If things get too crowded on weekends or holidays, charge a higher fee for those days.
3. Install a sign at the entrance to The Wave asking that all shoes be removed. A solar-powered toilet could also be placed near The Wave, but out of sight, to eliminate that potential problem.
4. The BLM should erect a line of cairns or markers of some kind to show the way to The Wave--instead of kicking them over like some rangers are presently doing. That way everyone would stay on one narrow path instead of wandering all over the place. The route to The Wave seems to be the only place on the planet, or at least in any wilderness area in America, where the custodians don't want to make an easy-to-follow trail!
5. For every rule or regulation the BLM makes, someone has to be hired to go out and enforce it. By eliminating the reservation system, more money could be used for onsite personnel to educate the pub-lic on the potential problems.
6. Since the Utah Olympics (2002), there have been 20 permits issued each day for The Wave (North Coyote Buttes), 10 of which have been walk-ins. But in talking to no less than a dozen hikers who have been there, none saw anywhere near that many people out there. Rumors say that some wilderness radicals are grabbing up reservations with no intention of going to the Buttes (?). They just want to keep people out. Or, fotographers are reserving 3-4 days in a row to ensure they have a sunny day (?). This is another good argument for eliminating the reservation system.
7. For those who want a *true wilderness experience*, why not go to a million other places! By eliminating the reservation system, everybody who gets a permit will likely go and enjoy it. And Europeans who come from halfway around the world will at least have a fighting chance to see The Wave.

Why not try a new policy with no quotas and see what happens. If there ever were crusty fins at The Wave, they are now long gone--so little if any more damage can occur. The only problem that could occur is that fotographers may have to direct traffic to get shots without people. And the only thing that will be lost is the *true wilderness experience* as defined by SUWA and other radicals. Please keep in mind, this world is getting smaller by the day, and the population getting larger. So we're all going to have to get used to the idea that some special places, like The Wave & Coyote Buttes, are going to be pop-ular destinations, even though they're in a wilderness area. Also, there are at least a million other places, just on the Colorado Plateau, where people can enjoy solitude. The way it is now, with 20 people al-lowed to visit The Wave daily, can this be called a *true wilderness experience?* Not quite!

This writer has never heard of anyone trying to deny tourists the right to go to Delicate Arch in Arches NP., just so there wouldn't be so many people in their picture. There's never been anyone try to limit the number of tourists walking all around Bryce Canyon's hoodoos, just so some can have a wilderness trip. Same with Zion Narrows; on a hot summer day, there may be several thousand people walk up the Virgin River Canyon, but everybody accepts that and no one has ever tried to limit the numbers! In most of our national parks, better facilities have been created to handle bigger crowds and more traffic.

This writer would much rather be at one of these places with a crowd, than to be required to make reservations months in advance. People still have to walk 4 kms to The Wave, and the access road will remain dusty or muddy, so the herd heading that way will never be that large.

If you feel the same way about this nightmarish reservation and/or quota system as this writer, please write a letter with your opinions to the BLM, 345 East Riverside Drive, St. George, Utah, USA, 84770, Tele. 435-688-3246; or to the Kanab BLM Field Office, 318 North, 100 East, Kanab, Utah, USA, 84741, Tele. 435-644-4600; or the Utah State Headquarters of the BLM, 324 South State Street, #301, Salt Lake City, Utah, USA, Tele. 801-539-4010.

The BLM sets policy on your public land, so please write letters or make telefon calls. If they don't hear from you, they think everyone approves of what they're doing. In the past, the BLM has been more responsive than some other government agencies when it comes to incorporating public comment into policy; hopefully that same trend will continue.

Here's what this writter has added to this edition. This should disperse some of the traffic wanting to go to The Wave. He finally got a pretty good 4WD vehicle and has seen all of the Sand Hills and is introducing some new areas especially for fotographers. A place that is likely better than **Coyote Buttes** is **White Pockets**, not far east of The Wave. The 3rd best place in the Sand Hills has to be within a 3 km circle around **Middle Reservoir**. Perhaps the 4th best area is the **Water Pockets** on the West Clark Bench northeast of The Wave. After that the little drainage basins or catchments surrounding **Joe's Ranch or Soap Creek Tanks** would have to be 5th & 6th. The catchment for **Lower Reservoir** is an-other neat place. For those who like **Anasazi Ruins**, head for the **White Knolls**.

For those who want giant **Rock Art Panels**, hike to **Hod Brown Spring** and the **Eastern Sand Hills Crack**; no need for a 4WD to reach these last 2 places. Read more in the other sections covering the Sand Hills and House Rock Valley.

Above From the air looking down on the **North Teepees**. You don't need a permit to visit the North or South Teepees, that's one good reason to visit these places. **Right** This scene is just around the corner and to the **southwest of The Wave**. Shadows are all important here, but not in The Wave (In the far background is West Clark Bench, and the Water Pockets). To get here, get on top of The Wave, then walk southwest toward **Sand Cove**. If you stay on this level, you'll eventually come to Wave 2.

This is what is labeled the **Big Panel** on Map 37A or B. It's one of the best petroglyph sites anywhere. It's on the way to **The Notch**, which is one of several ways to reach The Wave. It's about 200m south of the little canyon & trail you first use in getting up to The Notch.

This is **The Wave**, one of the better-known fotographic scenes in the world. The hikers are right in the bottom. Wander around, there are other great places, in both North & South Coyote Buttes.

The south side of **Butte 5215T** in **Sand Cove**. Wave 2 is to the right a ways and up on a bench.

Inside the **Tiny Northwest Cove**. No color enhancement here--just a northeast facing wall and sun from the opposite side reflecting into these shadows. Around the corner to the south is nice too.

Left This is what the author calls, the **Totum Pole**, located just northeast of the Cottonwood Cove Trailhead. No permit needed to see this place. **Right** One of several fotogenic scenes in what this writer calls the **Tiny Cove**, in the South Coyote Buttes just north of **Paw Hole**.

History of the Sand Hills: The Anasazi Indians, Angora Goats, and History of Grazing Goats & Cattle in the Sand Hills and House Rock Valley

Anasazi Indians

It's only been in recent years that the world beyond Kanab and southern Utah became aware of what was to be found in the Sand Hills or Paria Plateau. This place is so sandy, isolated and hard to reach that it wasn't until 4WD's came along that very many people went there. Before that, ranchers took sheep, goats and cattle to graze, but that was mostly in the winter when there was snow on the ground; and they did it riding horseback, or in wagons. Tourists didn't discover the place until about the time the Vermilion Cliffs National Monument came into existence. One of the things they found was evidence of prior occupation by native Americans.

The first archaeological investigations of the Sand Hills were conducted in the 1960's, then after a gap, more studies were done in about the decade of the 2000's. What they found were a number of **hill-top ruins**, which, quite frankly, are not very fotogenic, and for the most part, not very interesting to look at. But maybe that's a good thing.

Other than the information personally gathered by this writer in 2008 & 2009, and on about 9 trips to the Sand Hills, most comes from a study titled, **Archaeological Investigation on the Paria Plateau, Vermilion Cliffs National Monument, 2007**. It was published in April, 2008. Archaeologists studied Section 35, T39N, R5E in the White Knolls, and the West Bench Pueblo located 3 kms north of Two Mile Spring in the upper House Rock Valley.

Most of the ruins on the plateau are found in the southeast corner and the **White Knolls**. This is the highest part of the Sand Hills, so it would have had the most rainfall. Another populated area was **Joe's Valley** (author's name)--lots of Indian signs around Joe's Ranch. Then there is a line of hill-top ruins running east-west across the middle of the plateau. Later in this chapter, most of the ruins the author found will be discussed in more detail.

Here are some of the conclusions archaeologists found. Most habitation sites are on top of low hills or small buttes, quite often with a nice view in at least one direction. Most of the larger ruins or **pueblos**, of which there are only about 12-15 on the entire plateau, are squarish in shape, with a central courtyard similar to an Asian caravansary. The walls were little more than a meter high, and must have had logs & limbs for the roofs, which are now long gone. Researchers believe the largest pueblos only had 3-4 family units at any one time; but the different pueblos may or may not have been occupied at the same time. So the population was never very large, due mostly to the lack of good water sources.

Other smaller ruins are found under ledges, but none are anything like the cliff dwellings found in the Grand Gulch/Cedar Mesa country to the east. There are a few small caves, most with soot-blackened ceilings, indicating campfires were used. Other small sites were what researchers called **field houses**. These are found below the hill-tops and closer to agriculture areas which were in **closed basins** (no outlets). These little basins or sinks are found everywhere in the Sand Hills. In Joe's Valley near Joe's Ranch are found a number of these small ruins at the foot of little buttes, indicating the Anasazi farmed that valley which was next to one of the best water catchments in the Sand Hills.

From the type of pottery found and other artifacts, archaeologists place the bigger ruins in the **Late Pueblo II period A.D.1050 -1150**. They also are calling those who lived in the hill-top pueblos **Kayenta & Virgin Anasazi Indians**. But there is some evidence that people were there earlier than the Anasazi, which are classified as **Archaic**; they predate the Anasazi by perhaps a 1000 years (?). The Archaic people were hunters & gatherers and used larger projectile points; whereas the Anasazi engaged in some agriculture with less hunting, so they used smaller arrowheads. One thing is for sure, the Sand Hills has lots of arrowheads.

Regarding agriculture, the main crop they grew was corn. This was done in the bottoms of the closed basins, but in the case of the White Knolls, the average elevation of the basins is 2100-2150m (7000'), which means they had a short growing season. At the same time, and at that altitude, there was more rainfall, but less evaporation, which means they could have done it with less rain. Researchers believe

the average rainfall in the White Knolls is 30-40 cms (12"-16"). Since there are no springs or running water any-where near, they had to rely totally on rainfall--which is never reliable. Their existence must have been a hit & miss proposition.

Most of their drinking water was

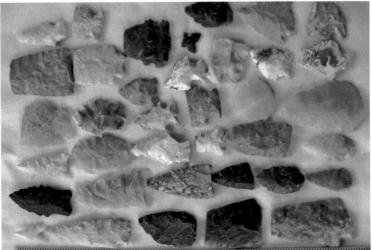

Part of one summer's collection of arrowheads in the **Sand Hills**. Most are pretty small and broken--but they're still man-made & nearly 1000 years old.

obtained from rain which funneled into natural water pockets in the slickrock. Two of the better known water pockets which have water most of the time are at **Big Pocket** and **The Pinnacle**. More will be said of these later. Another thing they surely did was dig what we would call wells. These were more than likely in the same places that early-day cowboys built their reservoirs. Three of the reservoirs Joe Hamblin built were below large slickrock catchments at **Lower & Middle Reservoirs**, and at his place, Joe's Ranch--which is normally referred to as **Joe's**.

Also, most habitation sites in the Sand Hills were fairly close to natural routes down off the plateau to springs at the base of the big Vermilion Cliffs; or to the Paria River. In long periods without rain, these were their life-lines to survival. It's only a couple of hours walk from the White Knolls down the **Eastern Sand Hills Crack** to what was later called Lee's Ranch & Jacobs Pool. Others closer to the middle of the plateau could escape to drinking water by going down the **Northern Sand Hills Crack** south of the Jarvis Ranch; that would put them at Hancock Spring. Those who lived at the big ruins further to the west could crawl down the crack above **Bonal Spring** to water there. Still further west, the Anasazi could escape down to what is known today as **Hod Brown Spring**, which isn't too far from **House Rock Spring**. Still further to the west were a number of small springs in the upper House Rock Valley. They could also get down to the Paria River through the Buckskin Gulch and the **Middle Trail/Route**, the **Adams Trail**, the **Indian Trail** near Wrather Canyon, and at **Bush Head Canyon**.

One of the more interesting things about the Sand Hills is, there are pottery fragments or potsherds everywhere, and not just around the bigger ruins. They are also found on the slopes below the springs mentioned above. This indicates there haven't been that many visitors taking them, and that those people relied heavily on pots for carrying and storing water. Also, the Sand Hills have many teepee-type rocks or small buttes, and if you walk around these to the south or west sides and in the **wind moat**, you'll almost always see pieces of pottery. **But remember, it's against the law to take some home!**

Angora Goats

No one alive in 2009 knew for sure when Angora goats were first introduced into southern Utah or the Sand Hills of northern Arizona, but it appears to have been in the mid or late 1890's. This under-appreciated and almost-forgotten animal was looked down on with distain by most cattlemen and was only around for about 50 years, but it was an important source of income to a small group of livestock men of Kanab. But first let's look at the history of these goats and the mohair industry.

There are several different types of goats in the world. Some are large and raised primarily for their **meat**. Another type is the **dairy goat**, which is milked, then the milk is drank or made into cheese. Some people can't tollerate cow's milk, but goat milk is often digested with ease.

Other goats are raised for their **hair or fleece**. One of these is called **Cashmere goats** and they appear to have come from the Central Asian Himalayan region. Their hair is soft, warm and luxurious. The other kind raised for their fleece are called **Angora goats**. What they produce is called **mohair**, and it too is soft and some of it is made into fine apparel; courser hair was used in car upholstery until foam rubber and other synthetics came along.

Here's a short history of Angora goats and how they got to the US. The following comes from several internet sources. Archaeological records indicate that the Angora goat was one of the first animals domesticated. The fleece of the Angora was revered in biblical times as it is today for its strength, luster and versatility, and it came to be known as mohair. Although Angora goats are believed to have originated in the mountains of Central Asia and Tibet, the mohair industry really got started on the Anatolian Plains of Turkey near the capital city of Ankara (Turkey's capital city and province was called Angora up until 1930).

White fleece for clothing obtained from goats and their kids is first recorded in the cuneiform tablet writing of the Sumer people living in Turkestan between the 14th-12th century B.C. Further mention is made regarding the use of mohair at the time of Moses (ca. 1571-1451 B.C.) in the Old Testament book of Exodus.

The birth of the **mohair industry** eventually got started in Angora after the goats had traveled thousands of kilometers from Turkestan (east of the Caspian Sea). During the 13th century, Genghis Khan drove Suleyman Shah and his goats out of Turkestan to the Euphrates River, where he drowned as he attempted to cross the river. His son Ertrugul, escaped to neighboring Konya (part of today's Turkey) to become a loyal follower of Sultan Aladdin. Ertrugul was rewarded for his loyalty with a large dominion which included todays Ankara. It is there that the Angora goats finally settled, with climatic conditions perfect for their breeding and the production of a fleece that became a staple in the region.

Rumors about this white goat whose fleece was both exquisite and versatile led to the rediscovery of the Angora goat by a Dutchman in 1550, and the subsequent demand generated the first mohair industry in Europe.

Unfortunately, soaring demand led to the practice of cross-breeding, and both the Angora goat and its mohair fleece faced extinction. Finally in 1838, 30 Angora goats were successfully exported to South Africa, and by 1856, South Africa became an important supplier of high quality mohair due to refined selective breeding. Today, South Africa is one of the 3 leading mohair producing countries in the world, exceeded only by Turkey and the United States.

The majority of goats and the mohair fleece in the United States, comes from Texas. The introduction of the Angora goat into America happened by accident in the mid-1800's, when the Sultan of the Ottoman Empire (now Turkey) asked President Polk for advice on the production of cotton. Dr. J. B. Davis was asked to perform and document a series of experiments on cotton growing in Turkey. In 1849, Dr. Davis returned to the United States with 9 thoroughbred Angora goats. It appears that the Angora goats that eventually made it to Utah came from Texas, some perhaps via South Africa (?).

The history of the first Angoras to Utah is a little unclear, but quoting from the *Daughters of the Utah Pioneers* book, **History of Kane County**: *The Johnsons were the first to have Angora goats in the southern part of the state.* Problem is, it doesn't state which Johnson.

It seems there are several Johnsons who could be the likely candidates, but the one most likely to be the first or most involved with Angoras was **Jesse N. Johnson**. According to the book, **Utah Since Statehood, Historical and biographical**, Volume IV, printed in 1920, Jesse was born in Virgin, Utah in 12/1968, the son of Nephi Sr. & Coradine Mariger Johnson and the grandson of Joel Hills Johnson. Jesse's father was the one who first contracted the mail route from Johnson (Canyon) & Kanab to the Santa Clara/St. George area and it seems Jesse was one of the young riders. Jesse stayed at home with the family in Johnson (his father made tracks for Mexico in 1889 because the Feds were rounding up Mormons for having too many wives and were attempting to disenfranchise the LDS Church) until

Left **Jesse N. Johnson**, the man who may have been the first to have Angora goats in Utah. (*Utah Since Statehood*) **Right** Angora goats. These would likely be wethers. (Trevor Leach foto)

he was 25, then in 1893: *He started out in business independently, specializing in handling sheep and Angora goats, being the first to introduce the South African Angora goats into Utah. In later years he sold his goats and concentrated his attention upon sheep and cattle raising....* It appears these goats first came to Utah sometime in the mid or late 1890's (?).

Another man who was instrumental in raising some of the first Angoras in Utah was a half brother (half brothers or sisters in southern Utah usually means they came from polygamist families) to Jesse. He was **Justin Merrill Johnson**--but he was always know as **Jet Johnson**. He was born in Virgin in 11/1862 to Nephi Sr. & Mandana Merrill Johnson and the family later moved to Johnson Canyon. As a teenager, he too was instrumental in carrying the mail to Kanab & Johnson. More will be said later about Jet as he was one of the first to have Angoras in the Sand Hills.

Not too many years after the Angoras came to Utah, and especially Southern Utah, Kanab seems to have been the center for the goat & mohair industry. Quoting again from the book, *History of Kane County: On January 29, 1906,* The **Utah Angora Goat Association** *was organized at Kanab to promote the mohair industry in this country. Its officers were Benjamin Hamblin, president; David Robinson, vise-president; F. A. Lundquist, secretary; and directors Joseph R. [Roscoe or Rock] Hamblin [son of Joe Hamblin], Edwin D. Woolley, Jesse N. Johnson, Frank Little and John M. Ford. It was active for a time, but finally ceased to function.* Benjamin Hamblin was one of 3 sons of Jacob Hamblin (**Ben &**
Joe from one of Jacob's wives, and **Walt** from another wife) who settled in Kanab and were involved in goat & cattle raising in the Sand Hills.

About this time someone in the Frank Little family (?) took a picture of men shearing Angora goats in 1904 north of Kanab. That foto shows Frank and his son Knowlton in a corral with the shearers. Knowlton (the boy sitting on the fence in the upper right of the foto) was 7 in 1904, but looks older (?), so that picture may have been taken a couple of years later.

Besides those mentioned above, other men who owned Angora goat herds from Kanab were: Ben Hamblin, Neaf Hamblin (son of Joe), Fay Hamblin (son of Walt), Art, Frank & William (Billy) Mackelprang, Albert (Bert) Leach (Trevor Leach's father), Lewis Jepson, Alex Merle Findlay, Ren Flanigan, Nephi M. Johnson, Tom Robinson, Murray Averett, Frank L. Farnsworth and son Hugh (?), and Joseph W. Chatterly. There were many others who had

Shearing **Angora goats** north of Kanab in 1904. On the far right middle, and shearing a goat, is Frank Little. The boy in the upper right and on the fence is Knowlton Little. This foto comes from the Kanab Heritage Museum & Sandra Little Chatterly.

smaller herds but these were the main herd owners in the Kanab area and those involved in the mohair industry.

Before moving on, **Bessie Averett Mackelprang** (Art's wife & Murray's daughter) did an interview in 1999 as part of the **Southern Utah Oral History Project**. In it she explains (with some editing) a few things about goats and commonly used terms: *All male kids (young goats) were **castrated** because they were not purebred--castrated goats are called **wethers**. The purebred male breeding goats (**billy goats**, but were sometimes called bucks, which are male sheep) would be bought and shipped in to mate and they cost at least $50 (1930's price) each; but would last for years. A lot of breeding billy goats came from Texas or were imported from the Mediterranean. The purebred billy goat would be separated from the **nannies** (female goats) until breeding time. The wethers were sometimes called **dries**, because they couldn't make kids. These wethers had very long hair or fleece and were used for shearing to obtain **mohair** (Angora goat hair). Sometimes one of these wethers would be killed for meat. At the goatherd someone might say, "I'm going to kill a mutton", but they really meant to kill a goat; whose meat is called **chivon**. Meat from sheep is called **mutton**.*

A couple of articles in the **Kane County Standard (KCS)** out of Kanab mentions goats. In the 7/19/1929 issue it talks about Lewis Jepson and his son Dell going to Texas and bringing back 22 purebred Angora bucks or billies. These were direct descendents of a billy goat imported from South Africa.

Another article from 2/20/1931 was titled, **Growers of Mohair have Organized:** *The mohair growers of southern Utah and northern Arizona met at Kanab recently and perfected an organization to be know as the Southern Utah-Northern Arizona Mohair Growers.* Neaf Hamblin was chosen president, with Wm. J. (Billy) Mackelprang (both of Kanab) as one director. Several other men from other parts of southern Utah were members of the organization. It's not known how long this 2nd organization lasted.

There were several other articles in the **KCS** during the year 1931 regarding Angoras and their byproducts. These seemed more like advertisements for mohair than anything else. One explained the different uses for goats. The meat was for human consumption, the hide was used mostly for fine leather gloves, the hoofs were turned into glue, their horns were used to make knife handles, and the fleece or mohair was used in upholstery padding in cars & train seats. The mohair coming from younger animals was softer and used for fabrics and clothes. By 1931, there were about 3,500,000 goats in the US.

Shearing Corrals From roughly the late 1890's to the early 1940's, there was easily as many goats in southern Utah as sheep. But even though these were 2 different animals, they fit nicely in the same niche as far as shearing, transportation of fleece and overall care and equipment were concerned. Goat herders used the same sheep camps or wagons when tending goats, the clippers used for shearing were the same for goats as for sheep, and the same sacks were used for transporting wool or mohair.

As for shearing, goats were generally sheared a little earlier in the spring than were sheep. When the weather started warming up, they had to shear the goats quickly because the mohair would begin to fall out or shed just like all other animals do in springtime. Goats were sheared beginning in late March and into early April; sheep were shorn right after that, sometime in mid or late April. The shearing pens or corrals were generally the same for both. One of the biggest shearing pens in southern Utah was **Goulds**, located south of La Verkin in Gould's Wash and at Gould's Spring. Articles from the **KCS** for March & April, 1931, told about some of the buildings burning down, but they were rebuilt in time for spring shearing. That season they sheared 40,000 sheep.

Another corral was located in the Glendale area near Highway 89 north of Mt. Carmel. The Littles used that one, as well as one found in upper Kanab Creek at the Robinson Ranch north of Kanab. It was located somewhere in the area which today is the Best Friends Animal sanctuary. While going through old newspapers, other sheep & goat shearing corrals were mentioned. In 4/1912, 13,000 goats were sheared at **Dry Lakes** (somewhere east of Alton and near the north end of Johnson Canyon), with no loss due to storms or cold. That was in the **Kane County Independent**. In the 1/23/1914 issue of the **Kane County News** it stated: *NOTICE TO SHEEPMEN I will run a 24 machine shearing plant this spring either at Dry Lake or Pine Spring. Will be prepared to shear all the goats and sheep that come. Am ready to book your herds. Write for information* **J. N. Johnson**.

In the 4/15/1932 issue of the **KCS** was an article which read: *....shearing began last Wednesday April 13. Thomas Jensen and R. A. Jackson are in charge of the shearing at the **Bull Rush Corrals**. Mart Chatterley at **Harry (Hod) Brown's Ranch** [Muggins Flat east of Kanab] and Don Millett is in charge of goat shearing at the **Lewis Jepson ranch**.*

The goats which were grazed in the Sand Hills, which was quite a ways east & southeast of Kanab, were sheared in a number of places, one of which was the old Jepson Ranch or place. It's located just south of Highway 89 near mile post markers 39 & 40 and in the south part of Telegraph Flat. Not a lot to see there, but it is private property belonging to Calvin C. Johnson of Kanab. Here's what Calvin had to say about that place: *All I know about the [Lewis] Jepson Place is [first acquired 6/12/1912], Art Mackelprang bought it [9/30/1938] and built a water tank so they could water their goats while shearing them right there. Today, there's a cement block where the shearing machine was bolted to. After the Mackelprangs sold their goats, they sold the place to Tom Robinson [6/17/1943], then I bought it from Tom [4/5/1945]. I built those reservoirs below the old shearing corrals. We still call it the Jepson Place.*

Bert (Albert) Leach and his son **Trevor** were there at the Jepson Place and here's what Trevor remembered about shearing there one year: *We had our own herd of goats, we used to bring Dad's goats in there and shear 'um. Back in those days there used to be a pretty good little spring, but it's dried up now. When Art Mackelprang got it, they built a big cement water tank so they'd have water for shearin' time. Art & Frank Mackelprang bought it in about 1938, and my Dad and I and my brother Willy helped 'um built a shearin' corral there. We had a hell of a time building it--it's all rock, no soil. Lynn Ford probably helped build it too; he was herdin' goats for the Mackelprangs. We sheared our goats there at least 1 year, but we sheared in a lot of different places.*

Another important shearing area for Angora goats which used the Sand Hills as their winter range, was in **Johnson** or Johnson Canyon about 15 kms east of Kanab. This is the canyon you drive through when going from Kanab to Cannonville via the Skutumpah Road. Johnson was a farming community created by the descendents of Nephi Johnson, Sr. and was located in the southern end of Johnson Canyon or Valley. **Neaf Hamblin**, one of Joe's boy (read more below), was a big time goat herd owner and he had equipment and shearers at his place in Johnson for many years. But there were others too. Here's a short article from the **KCS** for 3/16/1934: *Work began Friday at the Millet shearing plant in Johnson Canyon, employing about 20 men for 20 days. During this time more than 12,000 goats will be shorn. The goats belong to residents of Kanab.*

Another corral specifically built for shearing both sheep & goats was erected by the **Telegraph Flat CCC Spike Camp** which was located in lower Park Wash across from Pottery Knoll. During their stay,

Left Part of the **CCC Sheep & Goat Shearing Corral** located near the road to Mollies Nipple and the Nipple Ranch. **Right** Part of the **Kitchen Reservoir** & rip gut fence. This was the first water storage reservoir built (by John G. Kitchen Jr.) in the Sand Hills and likley the Arizona Strip.

they built the corral as shown on **Map 9,** page 53. We think it was built in 1937, but wasn't used much, because the last goat herd in the area was sold in about 1943 or '44, and sheep didn't last much longer (many sheep and all goats in Utah disappeared in the early 1940's, because the army drafted all the herders).

The Leaches apparently used this corral at least once, and Trevor says: *That corral is divided into pens. Each herd had 4 shearers, and each one would have a place they'd put the goats, then they'd shear'um, then they'd put'um back in the pen so they could be counted. And they'd get so much a head for shearin' 'um. In our time it was just local guys who done it. I used to shear--just our own goats--it's a back breakin' job! They would be less than a 100 pounds, and sometimes you'd get one that would fight, and that was kinda bad. Some of 'um would bite some too; bite ya on the rear end while you was holdin' 'um!*

Many of the goats which wintered in the Sand Hills had their summer range in the high country south of Bryce Canyon National Park and north of the Skutumpah Road. Here's what Trevor had to say about how he and his father handled the shearing operations on their goat herd in the late 1930's & early '40's: *At the end of winter we sheared out on **Buckskin Mtn.** We called it the **Shearin' Corral**. It's on the old road, the Honeymoon or Navajo Trail, that used to come from Piree [Paria River & Lee's Ferry] to House Rock and Kanab. It's by **Shearin' Corral Reservoir**, and the old shed's still up there, but it finally just fell down. It's north of **Middle Reservoir** about 2-3 miles. So we'd shear there in the spring, in March before they started shedding hair; then we'd usually stay in that area, on Buckskin Mtn. or in the Sand Hills [waiting for the kidding season].*

We pulled off the mountain one spring and sheared, and went back on the mountain and lost 200 head in one night! They just froze, they didn't have nothin' on 'um--that was in about 1940-'42. If you sheared 'um only once a year, the hair would be dragging on the ground. But we used to shear twice a year. If you didn't, in winter time, they'd walk through the snow and it would build-up on the hair and you'd have to take a hammer and brake up the balls of snow. Our dogs would be the same, the hair would ball-up because snow would stick to 'um.

***Kitchen Reservoir** used to be kind of our headquarters at that time--that was before we had Coyote Spring. That's where dad had a **kiddin' corral**; so we'd kid the goats there. After kidding, we'd take 'um down to Coyote and hold 'um until about the first of June, then we'd trail 'um north up to the ranch [near Bald Knoll & Alton].*

At the end of summer, in September, we'd shear up there at the ranch. I used to shear a lot of 'um myself. We made a shearin' plant up there and it had a shaft and everything. I've still got it up there in a shed at the ranch today. We'd shear just before going south to the Sand Hills. We used to go about halfway down Johnson Canyon--down to where the houses first started--then cut east across to Seamons Point & Wash and down that way [10 kms east of Johnson Canyon]. They've got a road down there now, but in those days there was just a kind of trail through there. There used to be a lot of water out through Seamons. From the ranch, it would take 4-5 days to get to the Sand Hills.

History of Grazing Goats & Cattle in the Sand Hills

At this point, let's move more towards the history of the Sand Hills, otherwise known as the Paria Plateau, as well as continuing the discussion about Angora goats.

Within the Sand Hills there is only one small piece of private land, a 65 hectare/160 acre (quarter section) plot that may have been the first non-Indian habitation site in the entire Arizona Strip. This became known as **Joe's Ranch (Joe's).** What made this place so unique was; it was in a very isolated place, there was no live or running water or permanent springs anywhere near, and because of the deep sand, getting there was always difficult. The only real springs anywhere near Joe's are at **Two Mile** and **Coyote,** located at the western edge of the Sand Hills, and a full day's ride on horseback from Joe's Ranch.

This ranch was created by, and got its name from, **Joe Hamblin.** Joe was one of 3 sons of **Jacob**

Joe Hamblin as a young man. Also Joe's Ranch in about 1920 and looking northeast. It appears he had a cabin and 2 tents--perhaps belonging to visitors. The big pond of today is in about the middle of this foto.

Left Joe Hamblin in 1920, probably at his ranch. Above Joe as a younger man. All the pictures on this page are from Rock Burgoyne of Kanab. Rock is a greatgrandson of Joe Hamblin,

Hamblin who made significant contributions to the history of the Sand Hills and Angora goats. The 3 were Joe & Ben who came through Jacob's 1st wife Lucinda; and Walt (a half brother) who came through Louisa Bonelli, Jacob's 4th wife. Polygamy was popular with Mormons in Utah in those days!

Joe Hamblin was born October 6, 1853, and along with at least one of his father's families, moved to Kanab in 1870. Not long after that he began working for John W. Powell on his surveying expeditions (but not the early river trips). This lasted on & off for about 15 years. He married Elsie Albertina Johnson, the daughter of Nephi Sr. & Condradina Johnson on February 14, 1879. They had 2 sons; Nephi Junius (Neaf) and Joseph Roscoe (Rock), but Elsie died giving birth to a third son. Joe had no way to care for the 2 little boys, so they were raised by various members of his wife's family. As grownups, these 2 men were a couple of the more prominent citizens in Kanab & Johnson (located in lower Johnson Canyon 16 kms east of Kanab). Each son was also into raising sheep, goats & cattle.

It was about the time his wife died that Joe went to the Sand Hills looking for a homestead. He had been in the area before with one of the Powell expeditions (?) and knew the place. According to the late Dunk Findlay, he went there looking for a ranch site for the first time in about 1884. Because of its isolation and lack of water, it must have taken years before it could be called a real ranch. And since it was the only ranch of any kind in the Sand Hills, it was always called The Ranch or Joe's Ranch by local cowboys, sheepmen & goat herders. Today it's simply refered to as Joe's. Joe Hamblin had cattle, as well as sheep & goats at various times.

In those first few years of building his ranch, and before he built his cabin, Joe apparently lived in a cave or overhang with a tarp stretched out over the front. This according to Trevor Leach and Jay Findlay. This was an Indian cave located about 250m south of the present-day buildings. Joe lived there until he built a cabin. The cave faces west, is about 3m deep and 3-4m wide across the front and has signs that Indians once lived there. The author failed to located it but wasn't looking in the right place at the time, and couldn't return in the late very snowy winter of 2009 & '10 to find it.

In the last year of Joe's life, it must have been apparent that his health was failing, so, according to Coconino County courthouse records in Flagstaff, Arizona, he signed his ranch over to his sons; **Neaf & Rock** (Rose Hamblin, the wife of, and representing **Rock Hamblin**, signed for Rock). That **Bill of Sale** was dated **May 7, 1924**. Joe signed his name with an "X"; apparently he never learned to read or write (?). It was witnessed by his brother Ben and Walt's son Fay Hamblin. The hand-over or sale included the 160 acres of private land which was his ranch, 270 head of cattle, and the water rights to **Hamblin Ranch, Middle & Lower Reservoirs**. This tells us it was Joe Hamblin who built the first little dams to form reservoirs below 3 of the best slickrock water catchments in the Sand Hills. Later owners enlarged all 3 of these reservoirs with bulldozers. Joe died December 3, 1924.

According to the memory of **Rock Burgoyne** of Kanab (**Rock** Hamblin's grandson), while brother Neaf got the Sand Hills and 8 hectares (20 acres) in lower Johnson Canyon; Rock got land that now holds the old movie set in lower Johnson Canyon, plus land in the Deer Springs area (?) somewhere along the Skutumpah Road.

On the very next line below where Neaf got Joe's Ranch, it states that Neaf & Rose (Rock) sold the Ranch & water rights to **William B. Adams**, who was the brother of **Johnny Adams**. It's dated August 14, 1941. Apparently, the Adams brothers bought out Neaf Hamblin's Sand Hills estate in about 1928, but perhaps full payment wasn't made until the Adams brothers were in the process of selling out to the next owner of that part of the Sand Hills which was **A.T. Spence**. That **deed & bill of sale** was dated **September 9, 1941**. Going back another step, courthouse records show that John A. (Johnny) Adams officially filed on the water rights to the 3 reservoirs mentioned above on July 27 & September 27, 1928, but it wasn't confirmed (?) until October 31, 1929. It was finally recorded on November 9, 1929.

In 1987, the author interviewed Dunk Findlay several times. Here's some information he gave at that time. It was during the time Johnny Adams was at The Ranch in **1934**, that the **Taylor Grazing Act** was passed. In the years after that legislation, the Sand Hills was slowly broken up into a number of grazing areas, pastures, or allotments, much to the consternation of the old-timers. Other cattlemen got in on the western part of the Sand Hills range, and over the years fences were erected. This changed the whole setup.

Quoting now from a letter by Dunk Findlay: *The only water Adams had was at Joe's Ranch, and the Middle and the Lower Reservoir. There was no other water on the Plateau. Other people had to graze when there was snow on the ground. That's when the sheep and goats were in there. Most times it served only as a winter range other than around the Ranch. That's why it was not over-grazed.*

The Ranch was a permanent ranch used year-round by Hamblin, Adams, Spence, and the Findlays. There were several times the cattle had to be moved away on account of lack of water, that's why we drilled a well. After the Taylor Grazing Act [and with all the fencing], there was no place to move; before that, cattle were moved any place there was water on the public domain. No one owned anything then.

While going through the history of grazing & water rights in the Sand Hills, keep a few things in mind. First, almost all livestock men using the Arizona Strip were from Utah, and going all the way to Flagstaff to do any business was extremely difficult until after the road was built to and from the bridge over Marble Canyon which was completed in January, 1929. Almost nothing was recorded in the courthouse until after that date. Also, the Sand Hills is a big area, and there were dozens of people coming and going with their sheep, goats & cattle. For example, on September 3, 1937, there were 35 signatures (some were wives) on a document claiming a percent of water rights to **Two Mile Spring**. Tracking all the owners or those who had grazing or water rights in the Sand Hills is impossible.

For now, let's put the history of Joe's Ranch aside and take up some stories and history about other parts of the Sand Hills in general. The most important source of information for this part comes from **Trevor Leach** of Kanab, the son of **Albert (Bert) Leach**. Trevor was born in July, 1920 and was nearly 90 years old as this edition went to press. In 2009, he was the oldest and most-knowledgeable person alive in regards to Angora goats and the history of the Sand Hills. He as well as many others will be quoted throughout this chapter.

Map 37B, Northwest Sand Hills: Coyote Buttes, Poverty R. & Red Pockets

If going to The Wave at the north end of Coyote Buttes, you'll be walking along an old road for about 1 km. Trevor Leach talks about how he gave the name **Bull Pasture** to part of that area: *I put that Cat trail up that hill and I built them reservoirs. I built 3 reservoirs, but they're all filled in now. There used to be trees all up through there, but I pushed 'em all over and burned 'em. That was before the BLM was like they are now. That was what I called Bull Pasture. I wanted to homestead the place, but the homestead act went out before I was old enough. That was sometime in the 1940's. There's no real springs up there, but there's water; you can go in there and dig for water anytime. I used to run my bulls in there, that's how it got the name.*

In the early days, one of only 2 permanent waterholes in or near the Sand Hills was **Coyote Spring**, which everyone refers to as just Coyote. It's located in Coyote Valley just west of the southern end of the Coyote Buttes Special Management Area. Here's some of what Trevor remembered about Coyote: *My dad bought it from Justin Merrill (Jet) Johnson [half brother to Jesse N. Johnson, the one who is credited with bringing goats into Utah]. Nobody had that spring before Jet, he developed it. How it got it's name was the coyotes had dug a hole back in there and a little water was comin' out. Then he went in there with a team & scrappers and dug it all out and put perforated pipe in there and got that water to flow out. The original pond was on the other [east] side of the wash--that's where Jet had it. I piped that water over to the west side of the wash and built that reservoir. I run water in it for 2 years and couldn't get it to hold, so I went down the valley a ways and got that bentonite clay with my Cat and hauled it in to line that reservoir and it filled right up. It holds water good now. Before we got it, Jet's daughter married Lloyd Chamberlain and he tried to homestead Coyote; he went out there and built that original cabin but he never proved up on it.*

Jet is the one who filed on the water first [September 27, 1905], then he sold that to my Dad [Albert Leach, January 28, 1930]. And Dad sold it to me [Trevor Leach, September 1, 1961]. That was done in Flagstaff--I know I had to go to Flagstaff for everything when I was there. We only had a cabin there, because I moved the cattle in summer up to the Ranch [near Bald Knoll], and we'd take 'um out there to Coyote in winter. We lived in a sheep wagon most of the time there, but finally I lined that little cabin and built cupboards and things in it.

I built the 2 little sheds that are next to the pond. That lumber I built those barns out of came from the movie set, the Greatest Story Ever Told. They filmed it out at Wahweap. I and Dale Mont McCal-

Map 37B, Northwest Sand Hills: Coyote B., Poverty, Red Pock.

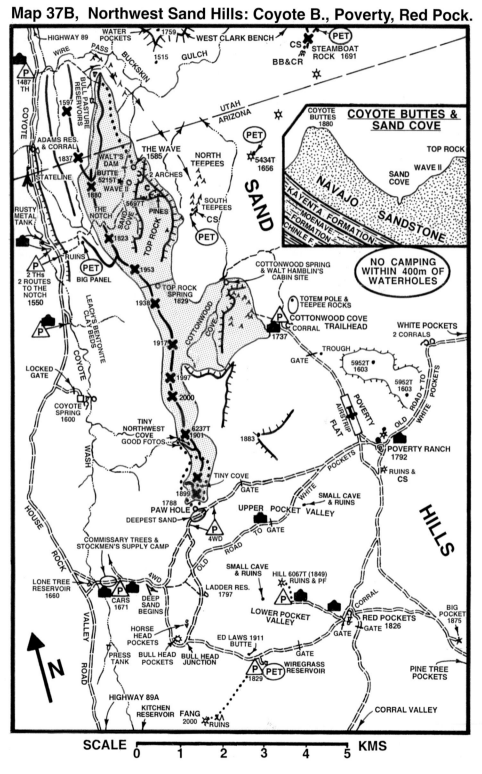

HIGHWAY 89
WATER POCKETS
1759
WEST CLARK BENCH
CS
PET
STEAMBOAT ROCK 1691
WIRE PASS
1515
GULCH
BB&CR
P
1487 TH
COYOTE
BUCKSKIN
1597
BULL PASTURE RESERVOIRS
UTAH
ARIZONA
COYOTE BUTTES 1880
COYOTE BUTTES & SAND COVE
1837
ADAMS RES. & CORRAL
THE WAVE 1585
NORTH TEEPEES
PET
5434T 1656
TOP ROCK
STATELINE
WALT'S DAM
BUTTE 5215T
2 ARCHES
SAND
WAVE II
SAND COVE
WAVE II 1880
5697T
SOUTH TEEPEES
NAVAJO SANDSTONE
RUSTY METAL TANK
THE NOTCH
SAND COVE
PINES
CS
KAYENTA FORMATION
MOENAVE FORMATION
CHINLE F.
1823
TOP ROCK
PET
RUINS
P
2 THs 2 ROUTES TO THE NOTCH 1550
PET
BIG PANEL
1953
NO CAMPING WITHIN 400m OF WATERHOLES
1938
TOP ROCK SPRING 1829
COTTONWOOD SPRING & WALT HAMBLIN'S CABIN SITE
LEACH'S BENTONITE CLAY BEDS
P
COYOTE
COTTONWOOD COVE
TOTEM POLE & TEEPEE ROCKS
WHITE POCKETS 2 CORRALS
1917
P
COTTONWOOD COVE CORRAL
TRAILHEAD
1737
TROUGH
GATE
5952T 1603
LOCKED GATE
WASH
1997
5952T 1603
COYOTE SPRING 1600
2000
TINY NORTHWEST COVE GOOD FOTOS
6237T 1901
1883
AIRSTRIP
POVERTY FLAT
OLD ROAD TO WHITE POCKETS
POVERTY RANCH 1792
TINY COVE
WHITE POCKETS
RUINS & CS
GATE
SMALL CAVE & RUINS
1899
1788 PAW HOLE
UPPER POCKET VALLEY
HILLS
DEEPEST SAND
P
4WD
WHITE POCKETS
COMMISSARY TREES & STOCKMEN'S SUPPLY CAMP
OLD ROAD TO GATE
HOUSE ROCK
SMALL CAVE & RUINS
HILL 6067T (1849) RUINS & PF
LONE TREE RESERVOIR 1660
4WD
LADDER RES. 1797
P
CORRAL
BIG POCKET 1875
P
CARS 1671
DEEP SAND BEGINS
LOWER POCKET VALLEY
RED POCKETS 1826
GATE
HORSE HEAD POCKETS
ED LAWS 1911 BUTTE
GATE
PINE TREE POCKETS
VALLEY ROAD
PRESS TANK
BULL HEAD POCKETS
BULL HEAD JUNCTION
P
PET
WIREGRASS RESERVOIR
1829
N
HIGHWAY 89A
KITCHEN RESERVOIR
FANG 2000
RUINS
CORRAL VALLEY

SCALE
0 1 2 3 4 5 KMS

253

From a hill on the west, looking eastward down on **Coyote Spring**. The spring is in the far background on the east side of Coyote Wash somewhere and the water is piped to the water trough & pond you see here. Just about everyone who owned water rights added to the facilities you see.

An old foto of **Paw Hole** from Trevor Leach. This must have been taken sometime after it had been bull-dozed into an artificial pond or tank. In the 1990's and early 2000's, the author saw water here, but in 2003 & 2009, and while the ground was wet, had no surface water. Surely the Indians dug for water here and made a well similar to what Jet & Walt did centuries later. Read the history below.

lister and my boy tore that movie set down. Then **Bud & Dixie Northcott** got it from me [December 22, 1981] and remodeled the whole thing. Later, the Northcotts sold it to **William Nelson** on February 1, 2006 (both Northcotts are dead as this book goes to press), then on March 30, 2009, **Ron & Sherrie Finicum Henderson** bought it.

About 3 kms down Coyote Wash to the north, and just to the east, are the bentonite clay beds Trevor mentions above. If you walk east into a cove, you'll find lots of very **colorful clay beds** and a loading chute he used when loading clay. Be there in the late afternoon, with full sunshine, for nice fotos.

Another landmark hikers & fotographers are familiar with is **Paw Hole**, located at the southern end of Coyote Buttes. Here's what Trevor had to say about its history: *Wild horses would come in there and paw out a little hole with their hoofs, dig down in the sand a little, so water would seep up, that's how it got the name--**Paw Hole**. Some time in the early 1900's, Jet Johnson and Walt Hamblin took 2" x 12"s in there and tacked 'um together and made a well--and they dug it out down to bedrock. Then they could come in there and take a bucket and dip water out for their horses.*

Years later, and while the Leaches had the Coyote Spring Allotment, Trevor bought a bulldozer (in

Looking in a northwest direction at **Paw Hole** on the morning of 5/17/2009. The ground was wet, but no water. You can visit this place without a permit, as the boundary of the South Coyote Buttes is about 250m north of here.

those days they only used Caterpillars or Cats) and did a lot of work for miners in the area during the uranium boom in the late 1940's and early 1950's (**Jack Mognett** of Kanab was the other local Cat skinner; members of Jack's family state it was their dad who taught Trevor how to run Cats). Here's more of what Trevor remembered: *It was probably in the early 1950's, when I went in there with a Cat and cleaned the whole thing out down to bedrock. Now the water seeps in from all around those rocks.* What you see there today isn't quite a natural waterhole, but there are lots of pottery fragments around indicating the Indians may have dug a well there themselves.

There were survey crews in the Sand Hills in May, and the fall of 1936, in addition to April, May & June, 1937, and some of the roads they used are different than the ones used today. Trevor remembers something about them and the original road, the **Joe Hamblin Road**, that ran out to Joe's Ranch: *It started right there where Lone Tree Reservoir is today, then it went up the Ladder where Ladder Reservoir is, across Lower Pocket Valley, across Red Pockets, east and passing right next to Big Pocket, then past Edwins [Pockets], south of the Big Sink, through Mexican Sink, south of the Big Red Knoll [on most maps it's shown as The Big Knoll] then across Round Valley and finally to Joe's Ranch. That was the first road in the Sand Hills.* Most of that old track is no longer used today, and in many areas, there's no trace of it. But there is an old track shown on the *Miscellaneous Field Studies Map MP-1475-A (1:62,500 scale)*, which follows the description given by Trevor. This is a good map covering the entire Sand Hills, but most of today's roads aren't shown accurately on it.

West, and just a little south of Paw Hole about 3 kms, is **Lone Tree Reservoir**. This is another stock pond that Trevor Leach built sometime in the late 1940's or early 50's--that's when he had his Cat, but he can't remember dates. About 200 & 400m east of Lone Tree and on the road you take to Paw Hole, is an area with a little history. Trevor again: *What the old timers would do was load their wagons up pretty heavy here in Kanab, then they'd go out there to the goat herds or to the cattle, but when they'd get there, they couldn't pull up that hill because it was too sandy. So they'd dig a hole in the sand and wrap stuff in a tarp and bury it. Then the herders would come and get their supplies. That was the* **Stockman's Supply Camp**, *and they all used it. And sometimes, they'd hang stuff in the trees too-- there was some big trees, cedar trees, along in there. They put canned stuff and stuff like that up in the trees too. It would freeze in winter, but that didn't hurt it. We also called that place* **Commissary Trees**.

We used to have this **supply box** *right at the edge of the sand. Dad or somebody would haul supplies out there in a wagon from Kanab, then we'd come from the herd and get'um in a wagon when we needed 'um. It was all wagons in them days. Later you could get out to the supply camp in a truck.*

There are a number of interesting things to see along the road running between Lone Tree Reservoir and Red Pockets. Once above the Commissary Trees, turn right or south at the sandy junction (if you turn left or north you'll wind up at Paw Hole) which is **2.2 kms (1.3 miles)** from the HRVR and continue south, then a little east to **Bull Head Junction** at Km 4 (Mile 2.5) from the HRVR. Just before you reach that junction will be a cluster of teepee-like rocks to the north. On top of these are what old timers called **Bull Head Pockets**; some bull got up there once looking for water and died. If you climb up, you'll find 4 pockets or depressions which hold rain water. Each of these pockets have pottery fragments in the bottom. If you turn north at Bull Head Junction and drive about 500m, you'll find **Horse Head Pockets** on your left to the west which consists of several natural rain-filled water pockets. If you poke around those rocks, you'll find more pottery fragments and another little reservoir built by Trevor Leach with a Cat. North of there about 800m is **Ladder Reservoir**; Trevor Leach built that one too.

Upper left is **Ed Laws 1911** signature out by Wiregrass Reservoir. Ed Laws and his wife Orpha. Ed on a horse, probably in Kanab. And one of the men in the buggy is Ed Laws while he was working for the CCC's during the 1930's. (all fotos from Hollis Jones)

From Bull Head Junction drive east to about Km 5.7 (Mile 3.5) and look to your left or north about 50m to see 2 short pinnacles or tiny buttes about 8-10m high. On the west side of one is the signature *Ed Laws 1911*. There's an interesting story behind this man. Much of this story comes from Ed's youngest daughter **Grace Laws Jensen** of St. George, and **Hollis Jones**, Ed's nephew.

Ed Laws was born in Johnson in 1889 and would have been 22 years old when he left his name on that rock. It's believed he was working for A.M. Findlay herding sheep, goats or cattle at the time. In 1912 & '13, he was on a mission for the LDS Church in Wisconsin. Sometime later he worked for the Forest Service on the north rim of the Grand Canyon somewhere. In the 1930's he was a supervisor for the CCC's and was stationed at the Phantom Ranch in the bottom of the Grand Canyon for a while. After that he was a ranger for the National Park Service stationed at Tuweap, near Toroweap Lookout in the western Grand Canyon.

The entire Laws family had gathered in Kanab for the Christmas Holidays of 1946 when disaster struck. A front page story in the *Kane County Standard* for January 3, 1947, tells some of what happened: *Edward Laws, 59, and his son Berkley Laws, 20, were the second and third victims of the mysterious poisoning which at first was believed to be caused from drinking bad whiskey. After the death of Russell Brooksby on December 26, the two men were rushed to the Salt Lake General Hospital, where they died on December 29.*

Grace Laws recalls some events. She states that it wasn't the wine (nor whiskey) they drank, but they did die of botulism. At supper a day or two before Christmas, the 3 men had eaten some pickled beets that Ed's wife Orpha had home-bottled; no one else had eaten them. Grace says the beets looked funny and were softer than normal, so she threw them out. By the time Brooksby died, all the evidence had been thrown out and the bottle washed--that's the reason they thought it was the wine or whiskey.

Grace had been married to Brooksby for 3 months & 17 days when he died. After that, and when her father & bother got really sick, Grace said: *There were no ambulances in those days so it was [the late] Merrill Johnson [of Kanab] with the Highway Patrol who took them as far as Panguitch. Then the Highway Patrol in Panguitch picked them up and took them as far as Richfield, I think. Then the Richfield people took them as far as Nephi, then other police took them into Salt Lake City.*

They were taken to the Salt Lake General Hospital because their throats were swollen and that was the only facility which had iron lungs at the time. They died within 10 minutes of each other.

From **Ed Laws Butte**, continue east about 300m and look for a faint track turning right or south. Follow this track about 250m and stop under a large cedar tree. At that place are 3 teepee-like rocks or buttes forming a triangle. Two have north facing petroglyphs along a kind of crack or faultline. On the west side of those is a mound of dirt with pottery fragments and signs of some ruins. In the middle of

Wiregrass Reservoir The foto on the **right** is from the air. The reservoir is near the center and in the deep shadows surrounded by 3 pinnacles. The largest pinnacle is to the upper left a little and that's where the picture on the left was taken from. **Left** Notice the little cement dike in the lower left, and the watershed above the top of the foto. There are petroglyphs on the walls in shadows.

the 3 buttes is **Wiregrass Reservoir**. This is what Trevor Leach told the author: *I also made Wiregrass Reservoir; it's more of a water pocket than reservoir. I took a front end loader down there--damn near tipped 'er over, and cleaned out the sand and dumped it off to the east somewhere. There was a big crack there, and...., there was a big watershed, a good one, drains into it. But with that crack, it wouldn't hold water, so I went down there north of Coyote Spring and got some bentonite clay, and loaded it, and put it in there and it's held water ever since.*

Since Trevor was there, someone has put a small cement dike across the lower end of the water-pocket. The reason it got the name Wiregrass, when it overflows it does so out in a little flat east of the pocket itself; as a result that little flat is covered with short wirey grass.

While visiting Wiregrass, and if you have the time, you might take a hike to a high point labeled Fang or **Fang Peak** (2000m/6234') on the *Coyote Buttes 7 1/2' quad*. From Wiregrass, walk southwest with a compass in hand because it's hard to see your destination for much of the way. On the south side of that butte are some crude **ruins**, plus pottery fragments. There are also some teepee-like rock just to the northeast which have pottery fragments as well. The whole hike can be done in about an hour.

Just southwest of Fang Peak is the **Kitchen Reservoir**. It's not shown on this map, but is on **Map 36**. There's little or nothing for the average visitor to see there, but it has a little history that should be told, this time by Trevor Leach again: *Kitchen's Reservoir is the oldest reservoir on the Arizona Strip. It was built by old Johnny G. Kitchen Jr. [he was the son of John G. Kitchen Sr, the man who began the Kitchen Ranch north of Mollies Nipple]. It was built before I was here, probably in the early 1900's. It still has an old stake & rider fence around it, but it has been cleaned out at least once since it was first built. Now my dad owned Kitchen Reservoir, he bought that first and then he bought Coyote. So we watered there, and from other pockets, there's a lot of water pockets in the Sand Hills.*

From Wiregrass, continue east. A little further on, you'll pass through a gate, always close it behind you--it separates pastures or allotments. Right next to the **Red Pockets** watershed is another gate, but before going through it, turn left or west and drive about 1 1/2 kms (1 mile) to the middle of **Lower Pocket Valley** and stop at a fence. Park there and walk north along the fenceline to the hilltop with the elevation **6067T** (1849m). On top of that prominent hill between Upper & Lower Pocket Valleys, are some **ruins** (not much to look at), and thousands of **pottery fragments** everywhere.

One more short walk. From where you park at the fence, walk west along the northern side of Lower Pocket Valley. At several locations, you'll find small buttes or teepee rocks with pottery fragments, and **1 small cave** with soot on the ceiling indicating it was inhabited, or people camped there, at one time. Or, if you drive along the original road to **White Pockets** (see Map 37A or B) part of which runs through **Upper Pocket Valley**, you'll find at least 1 small cave with **crude ruins** and more pottery fragments. Trevor Leach also mentioned that somewhere in the western end of that valley, next to the road and a pinnacle, is a small pile of rocks which his brother Willy (Bill) thought was an Indian well. This writer failed to find it, partly because the first description wasn't very good, and he never got back a 3rd time.

Richard Cothern, the son of the late **Beeb Cothern** mentioned something about a well being drilled at **Red Pockets**: *Floyd Maddox had Poverty, but he drilled at Red Pockets too, but he didn't get any water, I think his little old rig didn't go deep enough or something, so he give up. It was a dry hole.* There were 8 wells successfully drilled in the Sand Hills; this was the 9th, but it never produced.

257

Pottery fragments from the top of **Hill 6067T (1849m)** just northwest of Red Pockets. There are also ruins on top, but they aren't worth looking at. But there are thousands of potsherds.

Above The **Big Pocket** that's on top of a small butte or cluster of BB&CR. On this day the water was only half a meter deep.

Right From the air looking westward down on the small butte which is famous for it's big water pocket. Notice how it's hollowed out on top. The **Big Pocket** is on the left, and you climb up the opposite or west side.

One of the more intriguing things about the Sand Hills are the many **water pockets**. These are small natural depressions in slickrock. After a big storm, some hold water for months. Most of the bigger water pockets are associated with what looks like Big Brain & Cauliflower Rocks (**BB&CR**), something that's widely seen in the Sand Hills, but almost nowhere else. In many, if not most cases, what you'll have is a raised cluster of these BB&CR, which from a distance, look like a teepee rock, or ordinary butte. Sometimes these appear flattish on top, other times they appear to be like a mountain peak. But first looks can be deceiving, as is the case with both The Pinnacle (discussed later) and Big Pocket.

Big Pocket is the most famous of the natural water pockets in the Sand Hills. Here's how to get there. From the west side of the Red Pockets slickrock catchment & corrals, turn east onto the road shown on Map 37. Drive 1.9 kms (1.2 miles) to a junction and veer right heading southeast toward Pine. At Km 3.1 (Mile 1.9) from Red Pockets, turn left or east. This little **side-road** is hard to see so be looking eastward for a small butte or pinnacle about 250m from the main road.

If going there from Pine, set your odometer at 0 at the ranch house, then head west on the Entry Road for 150m, and turn north and drive about 5.1 kms (3.2 miles) to find the same side-road. Drive east 250m and park at the western base of **Big Pocket Pinnacle**. Scramble up the west side to find about **10 moki steps** before coming to a 15x20m depression right on top; it's just like the top of a volcano, but this one's made from Navajo Sandstone. At the south end of that depression is a 2x3m pocket that has water most of the time. You'd never know it was there unless you climbed up to see it. There are also pottery fragments around the south & west base, so the Indians were aware of this place.

The cowboys also knew about it and it was right on Joe Hamblin's original road to his Sand Hills ranch. Here's what Trevor Leach remembered about it: *It's a big lone rock and it's got a little water-*

Left This is **Red Pockets**, with the slickrock water catchment on the right or south. Most of the water running off the catchment runs into these ponds. To the left are the corrals.

Below Aerial view of **Poverty Ranch**. To the left are the barns, corral and water troughs; lower right is what remains of the houses; on the right is what's left of the windmill tower (the windmill is gone).

shed which drains into a big pocket--it's always got water. That's where we used to water our horses and camp. Joe Hamblin just about drowned there once. It was winter and it had a little ice on it, and he went to get water for his horses and he fell in and he damn near drowned trying to get out it chilled him so much. That's along where the old road used to go out to Joe's Ranch.

From Red Pockets, drive north to the **Poverty Flat & Ranch**, which is just called **Poverty** by local cowboys. About 600m, south of what buildings there are left at Poverty, is a little butte next to the road on the east. Walk to the top to see some crude Anasazi **ruins** and the signature of *Chas. Ford, Feb. 28, 1916* at the southern base of the butte.

No one alive in 2009 seemed certain when the buildings were put in at Poverty, but on January 19, 1945, **Walt Hamblin** sold his holdings in the Coyote Buttes, just to the north, to his son **Fay, and Floyd Maddox** (read below). It was in early 1957, when Hamblin & Maddox drilled the well, and several buildings were erected. The Poverty Well was the 2nd to be drilled on the plateau. All together, between 1953 and about 1963, there were 8 wells drilled in the Sand Hills.

About the time the well was drilled, **David DeHaven** bought Poverty from Hamblin & Maddox on 3/30/1957, but then on 2/13/1958, sold out to **Ben** (JR Jones' step father) **& Mannie Foster**. Then the Foster Brothers sold out to A.P. **(Rawd) Sanders** 1/16/1959. Rawd Sanders had it almost 20 years, selling out on 7/18/1978 to **Jim Byrant** (JR's father in law). On 6/28/1982, Bryant sold out to **Vern Carner**, who soon after that, consolidated all grazing in the Sand Hills under one owner. Read about the own-

This appears to be **Walt Hamblin's Cement Dam** in the little drainage coming out of **Sand Cove**. It's full of sand now, but there's always water seeping out the bottom. Whenever there's a big storm and water comes down the drainage, the sand absorbes some of it, then releases it slowly at the bottom of the dam as if it were a spring. There are parts of another little cement dam below this, but it's about washed away.

ership of Joe's Ranch and water rights to other allotments in the Sand Hills later in this chapter.

One bit of work which had little to do with ranching was the building of an **airstrip** at Poverty Flat, located just east of the southern end of the Coyote Buttes, and just north of the Poverty Ranch. The man who built that and the only one to ever use it was **Rawd Sanders**, who used to be a crop duster pilot. More on this man, and more on the other airstrips in the Sand Hills & House Rock Valley later.

There's one last former ranching area located on Map 37. This was the development of several springs inside, and just east, of the Special Management Zone in the Coyote Buttes. You can get to this area via Wire Pass, The Notch or from the south and Poverty. If you're getting there from Poverty, it's best to use the road running north/south west of the ranch; it bypasses some **deep sand** especially on the east side of the former ranch buildings. It also parallels the old airstrip just to the north. There are remains of the old road running north from the present-day **Cottonwood Cove Trailhead**, but it's extremely sandy so walking is the best option.

It appears the very first person to file for water rights in this area was **Walt Hamblin**. He was one of the sons of Jacob Hamblin, and half brother to Joe & Ben. The first time we know that Walt was there is a document stating that on September 2, 1908, he filed for water rights to the **Cottonwood Spring**. This is the same spring that's in Cottonwood Cove. Another document states he filed for water rights to **Sand Spring** on April 2, 1909. On a surveyors map dated May, 1937, it shows Sand Spring in the same location as the little dam & seep seen today just west of The Wave, and up the little drainage coming out of Sand Cove--not the Sand Spring located northeast of The Wave. Years later, Walt sold these to his son **Fay Hamblin & Floyd Maddox** on a courthouse document dated January 9, 1945. That document lists Sand Spring & **Sand Reservoir** (that's the little dam, Walt's Dam, mentioned above) as well as **Top Rock Spring**.

Trevor Leach knew something about all of these sites starting with Cottonwood Spring: *About 100 yards south of the dam I built sometime in the 1950's, and on the west side, is where Walt Hamblin used to have an old cabin. He just had a few boards put up--not much of a cabin. In Sand Cove, it was Walt who built that little cement dam. There's sand backed up behind it, and there's water coming out from underneath it. It would have been put in in the 1920's, or maybe the '30's [maybe the 1910's?].*

I and Lynn Ford put a pipeline off that ledge from Top Rock Spring. We drug the pipe from Wire Pass on a mule. We put 2 pipes on each side. Old Walt Hamblin hauled it down to Wire Pass and we got it there, and took it around and up to Top Rock. But it was no good; the thing of it is, we put a box in there, made of 2"x12"s, tacked 'um together and piped that water off. But by the time a cow would get over to it, it would be gone in the sand. It used to run quite a bit of water.

Map 38, North Central Sand Hills: Pine, White Pockets & Pinnacle Valley

Here's some history associated with Map 38. As you drive west on the Entry Road from the HRVR, the first place you come to is the ranch complex at **Pine Tree Pockets**, but everybody just calls it **Pine**. In the late winter of 2008 & '09, Coconino County road crews hauled gravel and dumped it on this Entry Road, making this the only place in the Sand Hills where you won't need a 4WD.

At Pine you'll find a barn & corrals, a well, a big metal water tank and a house; the eastern half of which was built by **Elmer Rider** in about 1964 or '65 (?) according to Elmer's son Richard. The original cabin was built by Roy Woolley or Harold I. Bowman in the 1950's (?) while one of them had grazing rights to that immediate area. Bowman bought about half of the grazing & water rights to the Pine area on 5/26/1953. By 6/2/1958, BLM records in St. George indicate that H.I. Bowman owned all the grazing & water rights to South Two Mile, Pine Pockets, Moquitch Tank and Frank's Reservoir (Mackelprang Tank)(These last 2 names are actually 2 reservoirs, but the BLM seems confused).

The well was drilled in the mid or late 1950's (?) by **Roy Woolley**, according to Dunk Findlay, but here's a little more of what **Beeb Cothern's** boy **Richard** remembered: *Pine Pockets Well was already there, then Dad deepened it. I understand it was 600-700 feet [about 200m] then he went down a couple of hundred feet to get more water out of it. Then I pulled it and repaired this last spring [2009] and it's about 900 feet [275m] deep.*

While discussing the story of Pine, a little should be said about the Bowmans first; and that starts with **Harold I. Bowman, Sr**. His story starts with **Jacob Lake**, which is not exactly in the Paria River drainage, but pretty close; and there was a connection between Jacob Lake, the Bowmans, House Rock Valley and the Sand Hills. **Harold I. Bowman III**, a grandson of Harold Sr., tells a little of what he remembered, and was told, about how his grandparents got started: *When Harold Sr. came out of the*

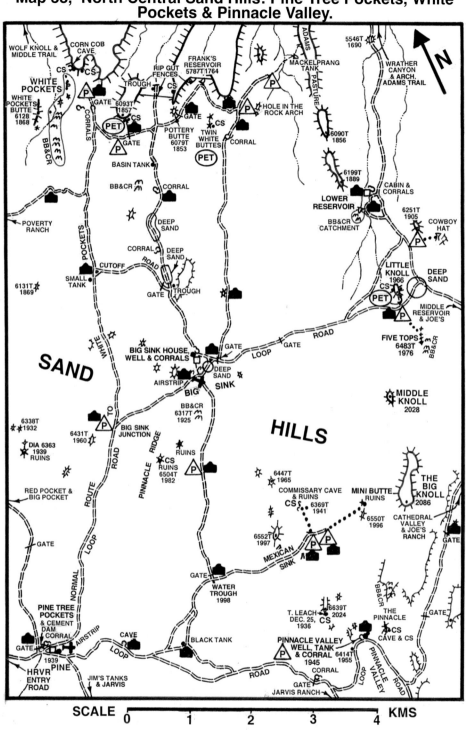

SCALE 0 1 2 3 4 KMS

colonies of Mexico and went to Kanab, he set up a mercantile store there. And Nina, his wife, my grand-mother, took a 55 gallon barrel of gas [up to that junction] and started pumping gas for the truckers--at least that's how the family tells the story. Grandmother started with just a leanto and a barrel of gas. [For many years they were building and improving a road from Kanab up to the north rim of Grand Canyon & VT Park, and down toward Lee's Ferry and the site of the then-future Navajo Bridge across the Colorado River.] That must have been in 1923, but by the '50's, our family had a lodge up there. So Grandmother was out there in the early 1930's getting things started and by the time I came along in 1952, there was a lodge & cabins, and we improved it constantly and built bigger and built more.

Now Harold Sr. & wife had 2 kids; **Harold Jr. and Effie Dean**. Effie Dean married John Rich Sr. He's dead, but she still lives in 2010. It's Effie Dean and their children who still runs Jacob Lake, and owns land, grazing & water rights in the upper House Rock Valley (in 2010). Harold Jr. had 4 kids, including Harold III; who has provided most of this information.

Harold Jr. got interested in flying, and in the mid-1950's the business bought their first plane. For many years the families were living in Salt Lake during the winter months so the kids could go to school, then were at Jacob Lake in the summers. The reason the business got the plane was so they could com-mute back & forth quicker. The first plane was a Cesna 172. It was used to commute from Kanab to Salt Lake. Later they traded the Cesna for a **Piper Comanche**, then that one was used to fly to/from Salt Lake. Then sometime in the late 1950's, they bought a **Super Cub**, which was just a 2-seater; with the pilot in the front, and one passenger in the back. It was about that time Harold Jr. began thinking of ways to take care of the cattle in the Sand Hills, and get back to Jacob Lake in a hurry. So they began building short runways or **airstrips** in the Sand Hills.

Immediately east of Pine, and running east-west, is a long narrow flat area just south of the road you take when you start driving toward White Pockets. During the late 1950's, the Bowmans had a landing strip built there. Here's what Jack Mognett, remembered about that proj-ect: *I was probably in junior high when we did that; sometime in the late 1950's when we worked on that airstrip at Pine. It began at their house & well and ran east. We knocked out all the trees and sagebrush and roughed it out with a little D-4 Cat, then we got Bowman's blade [old road grader] to kinda smooth it up a little more.*

During the same time frame, 1958 or '59, they build another landing strip at **Bush Head Well**. It began at the little barn & corrals just northeast of the present-day cinder block house & well. It ran southwest to northeast. Harold III, can't remember much about the 3rd airstrip which was located in the bottom of **Big Sink**, but Ron Glover could.

Ron Glover, who's father **Jim Glover** worked for the Harold I. Bowman& Sons for many years, had a few memories of when he flew in or out of the Sand Hills with Harold Jr. Here's what he remembered: *The Bowmans had 3 airstrips; at Pine, Bush Head and at Big Sink. It was Harold Jr. who used to fly in[to Kanab] and pick me up over UEA weekend, and other weekends, so I could go out and gather cows with 'um. I was out there the day he crashed the Super Cub. This was in the late 1950's. I would have been 12-15 years old, and I was still in school. I wasn't old enough to drive because he had flown in and got me. We had finished gathering early and these guys wanted to go see if there were any deer over around Bush Head. So Harold Jr. and Dean Bogadol took off in the plane and landed at Bush Head-- they just looked to see if there were any deer because it was in the fall when the hunt was on, but they didn't find any. I remember Dad being worried because it got after dark, and they weren't back. Then we could hear 'um come and they circled, so we ran out and got 3 of the trucks parked along the airstrip to try to get 'um enough light to see how to land. They got down right close to the ground, maybe 8-10 feet [2-3m] above, when he just kinda dropped it. And it just spread the landing wheels on it, just popped them out, didn't hurt anybody. They put it on a trailer and brought it in to the Kanab airport. It sat here in this airport for a long, long time, but it eventually got fixed.*

At Pine they had a wind sock mounted on a tree, but there at Big Sink is a metal post and it had a wind sock on it for years and years. I think the metal post is still out there in that flat at the bottom.

Harold III again: *After the business bought a 2nd airplane, an old crop duster Super Cub, it was housed there at House Rock. We used to own a little gas station & grocery store there. And right across Highway 89A is where the airstrip was, on the south side of the highway. So Dad would drive downhill 13 miles [21 kms] from Jacob Lake and park there at House Rock, then fly out to the ranch to check the cattle and water and whatever, and work with the cattle--rather than taking the time to drive all the way. So that's why those airstrips were built and used, because of that Super Cub.*

Flying was a good way for a busy husband & father of 4 young kids to take care of a ranching oper-ation, but it eventually killed him. According to Harold III; *My Dad was up really late the night before. And the next morning he got up early, from Jacob Lake, and went to Salt Lake.* That was Monday, **June 5, 1961**.

In the **6/8/1961** issue of the **KCS**, it mentions that Harold hit a mountain peak just northeast of Pan-guitch at about 6:45am while flying his Piper Cub to Salt Lake. Harold III again: *Yes, Jim Glover who ran the ranch for us, was with Uncle John when the plane was spotted [sometime Monday afternoon]. The Utah Highway Patrol who helped Kim and I when we made the hike to the plane a few years ago, Ortho "Buck" Buckley told us that due to the payroll Dad was carrying, only sworn peace officers were allowed at the plane until it was recovered.* The paper went on to say, the auto pilot had been on, and if he had been 100 ft. (30m) higher, or to the right or left the same distance, he wouldn't have hit the mountain. Harold was raised in Salt Lake, and was an athlete playing football at East High, and the Uni-versity of Utah during WWII.

Later, the Bowmans & Riches, sold or divided their grazing & water rights, and improvements in the Sand Hills in the early 1980's. We believe it was sold to **Dan Ramsey** and the Ramsey Cattle Company (?). For the moment, go to the transfer of ownership of Joe's Ranch, which in this period of time may be the same as for Pine. Ramsey sold out to **Vern Carner** and the Two Mile Corporation at 4/13/1984. Carner quickly bought out others and put all of the Sand Hills under the ownership of one man.

From the north side of the Pine ranch house, drive east, then north in the direction of White Pock-ets. This is now the least complicated way and **standard route** to **White Pockets**. In the area where one road turns east toward Big Sink--let's call this the **Big Sink Junction**--you can stop & park, and hike east and see crude **ruins** on top of 2 summits at the north end of what is shown on USGS maps as **Pin-nacle Ridge**. During at least one of the surveys of the Sand Hills, the survey crews borrowed rocks from these ruins to erect their own cairns. There are also the usual pottery fragments and cowboy signatures on the western-most summit. You can also wander to the west of the Big Sink Junction and visit more **ruins** and a small west-side cave on what is labeled **Dia Peak**, at **6363** (1939m). That area is all just northeast of Big Pocket.

This picture was taken at **Jacob Lake** in 1931 or '32. It shows Harold Bowman Sr., wife Nina (who died in 2/1959), and Harold Jr. and his sister Effie Dean. The family had just finished constructing the new inn, or part of the inn. (all pictures on this page are from Harold I. Bowman III)

This is the **Super Cub**, just a 2-seater, and the only plane the Bowmans had that landed in the Sand Hills. This pictures shows the landing strip at **Bush Head Well**. The plane is ready for takeoff going in a north-east direction.

Branding with the **Harold I. Bowman Jr.** family. From Left to Right: Kent on the horse, Harold III, father Harold Jr. branding cow, mother Afton, daughter Genene and Kim on the horse to the right. This was at the corral at Bush Head Well in about 1959.

Harold I. Bowman Sr. and son **Harold I. Bowman Jr.** This picture was taken in about 1959 or '60.

Looking eastward over **Pine**: upper right is the road to **Jarvis & Pinnacle Well**; upper left is the road to **White Pockets**--and just to the right of that is the **airstrip** the Bowmans had built. The slickrock in the lower half of the picture are the **Pine Tree Pockets** with a **cement dam** in the middle.

This **cement dam** & small reservoir as seen in the foto above, is located about 100m west of the corrals at **Pine**. At one time, there was a pine tree here somewhere, but it's long gone. However, there are several water pockets in this slickrock area, thus the name **Pine Tree Pockets**. Behind & below the camera are 2 water troughs (one cement) and a ledge where Anasazi Indians used to camp.

Looking due east while flying over the north end of **Pinnacle Valley**. Below is the well, corral and water tank. To the right is Pinnacle Valley, and due east up the barely-visible fenceline is **The Pinnacle**, the butte with 3 water pockets right on top. In the far, far distance left is Navajo Mountain.

From the air looking north at the **Middle Reservoir** area: the well, **windmill** and metal water tank are in the upper left, while the slickrock water catchment covers most of this picture. On this day, the reservoir was dry; it's barely visible in the upper right just left of the orange cluster of BB&CR.

Continue north toward White Pockets. There's not a lot to see north of Big Sink Junction until you pass through the middle of a small corral with a gate; always close the gate behind you. About 350m beyond that corral & gate is the parking area for **White Pockets**. From there you just wander around taking pictures. Foto bugs will want all day with lots of sun to see this area because of the **BB&CR** which are white with streaks of orange, reds, yellows & maroon.

Besides all the fotogenic rocks, there are some historic places too. About 700m north of the parking lot and at the bottom of the big cliff is a **cave** once occupied by Anasazi or Fremonts with scattered pottery fragments, flint chips, corncobs and **cowboy signatures** from *Fay Hamblin, and Willy & Trevor Leach, 1937*. About 300m southeast of the cave are more cowboy signatures; *Lyle, Hugh Woodard, & Vernon Huff, 8/13/41*.

In the north end of the White Pockets is one natural water pocket that's been enlarged by a dam. Here's what **Calvin C. Johnson** remembered about his experience working there in the early summer of 1937 at the age of 14: *We were camped there at White Pockets for several days and they were building that reservoir with a team & scrapper. It was a one horse scrapper with 2 handles but it was narrower than a Fresno. And I broke one of the handles--they was drivin' the team and I was dumpin' the scrapper. It was just a dirt dam when I was there. The cement part was put in after I was there in 1937. I was working for* **Walt Hamblin** *and the 2 other men there was* **Frank** *and* **Art Mackelprang**.

Danny Mognett is the one who put a cement dam in that little reservoir and here's what he remembered about the place: *When we got there it was just an old dirt dike, then I put the cement core in it. Rawd Sanders had the Halversons working there, but I did most of the work by myself. We used the sand that was there, and we hauled in some cement, and I think we hauled some gravel in with a loader; couldn't get a truck down in there. It was about a 6 foot [2m] wall across there, then we run a pipe out the back and the Halversons [Adaline & Ray] was supposed to put in a trough and a float valve below it sometime later. That was in 1972; I remember that because I bought a loader in 1972. It was a front end rubber tire loader, and I was using it to clean ponds out for the cowmen around the country.*

Here's Calvin C. Johnson again telling more of his experiences in the Sand Hills that summer of 1937: *I was born in 1923, and I had just got out of school. School was out about the 25th of May, and I left about the 1st of June, and stayed with* **Walt Hamblin***; I didn't come back until the 24th of July. But for 2 years before that, in about 1934 or '35, or '36, I would take Walt Hamblin's horses from Kanab, and would ride them out there and he would meet me in his place up at Coyote Spring or Two Mile Spring. I would take 2 horses and a mule most of the time; sometimes 3 horses and a mule. I would go over Buckskin Mountain and usually meet him at* **Two Mile Spring***; there was an old rock house there. Two Mile had some of the best water, and that's where they would camp to start their trips into the Sand Hills.*

In those days, some cattle was out there year-round. At that time, the cattle would come in to Two Mile and Coyote Spring, and since it was open range, some of 'em would even go down to House Rock Spring. And sometimes there would be water in Buckskin Gulch. They would come to those springs for water when it was dry, but when it rained, they would scatter back out all over the place.

What we was doing was goin' out there to catch the cattle and brand the calves, that was the main thing. We was brandin' Walt's calves, and he did a lot of range roping in those days; it was usually a long ways to any corral, which were usually just a holding-type corral.

Walt would leave Kanab in about a **1933 half ton Chev pickup** *with 2WD and he would meet me at Two Mile, then we took horses from there and we went all over the range with pack horses--no one took vehicles out into the Sand Hills at that time. Now I'm sure that Jarvis must have hauled some lumber out there to build that house & shed, but I didn't see them with a vehicle. I don't think he'd been there more than a couple of years when I was there in 1937. He went in there around 1935, I think. He leased a state section and had a permit for only a few cows, and there wasn't much water there at that time. Now there were roads and wagon tracks all over--most everyone went out there in a* **sheep wagon***. Now Walt didn't have a sheep wagon; we just camped right out on the sand. We all had a bedroll, and we had a tarp--they used a tarp over their pack horses, and we'd stretch that tarp out to eat on and sleep on, and stuff like that. One thing we did, we'd push the sand down under the tarp and make a little depression, then we'd wash in that depression to wash our faces.*

We ate an awful lot of sardines & raisins out of cans. Boy, old Walt and them old boys wasn't very heavy eaters. And I'll tell you, I had quite a time with my eating; being a young boy and active I required more food. So I'd get in the pack and help myself to a can of sardines and raisins. And we had some rice, and of course you had sugar and flour and lard so you could make gravy and bread. It was just biscuits--just flour and water and bakin' powder and grease. At that time we didn't make sourdough bread. Now when we camped with other cowboys, they'd do the cooking and we'd have a pretty good meal. We did kill a beef while we was out there so we ate quite a lot of meat--about 2 times a day. What we'd usually do is eat a good breakfast, then we wouldn't eat again until the late afternoon, and that was it. Then I'd sometimes get a can of sardines or something. And we had quite a few potatoes.

What we did when we killed that beef--Fay Hamblin, Walt's boy, took most of it to town to keep it. But what we kept, which was most of the hind quarters, we'd hang it out at night and let the air cool it, then we'd wrap it up real good in blankets and the tarp and keep the temperature cool through the day and you'd be surprised how long that meat would keep. We never did throw any of it away that summer. And as soon as the sun went down, all the flys would disappear.

Then your water was quite scarce too. There was a little seep behind Coyote [Buttes]. Walt and I put that little dike [near The Wave] in there; we camped there and it was only a little sand seep, and we dug into that pretty good so the horses could get a drink, and that's all the water we had. We hobbled our horses up in that little cove [Sand Cove]. It was Walt Hamblin and I who put the first cement dam in there. We carried a sack of cement from Coyote Spring on the west side of the Cockscomb, over and around and up what they called the Ladders on the back of a mule. One sack is all that we could carry and we started that little dam with it. After we were there, others went in and did a lot of development.

Now in those days, they all ran cattle in common, or together. At that time **Johnny Adams** *was about the biggest cow man in there. He ran about 700 head at that time. Walt ran about 400 head.*

We didn't carry any grain or oats for the horses, we just hobbled 'em out at night. Usually they'd stay close to camp. Once I had to follow 'em about 3 miles while we was camped at White Pockets--they was headed for Two Mile. We always tried to camp near some water; in fact, one time Walt wouldn't let me throw the dish water out. I never will forget that. I went to throw the water out, and he wouldn't let me and he says, "boy, dirty water washes clean".

Down at Two Mile Spring, they had an old **rock house** *[read more about this in the chapter on House Rock Valley] and it had to have been built in the late 1920's or earlier '30's (?). It never had any doors in it, just a big rock building with big open doorways on each side, and windows. Walt Hamblin and I*

These 3 pictures were taken 9/17/2009 at **White Pockets**. The main part of White Pockets everyone wants to see is east of the big butte shown in the upper foto. If you can get on top of White Pockets Butte, you might find something interesting there. The dam is to the right in the upper foto.

267

stayed in there, and some of the other boys slept outside. Otherwise we just slept outdoors under the stars.

During June of 1937, while we was down at Two Mile; there was no water out there in the Sand Hills, and those cattle were trailing in to Two Mile and Coyote Springs. And those springs are about 10 miles apart. And those cattle were real small and not doing very well; you could almost reach around 'em. And they'd come in there and load up with water; at both of those springs they had little reservoirs, and they were big enough to take care of all those cattle. At Two Mile, the water would drip off those ledges and into that pond.

And while we was there--and I'll never forget it--we had a heavy electric storm come in there and it rained all that one day and that night. It was in the first part of July, 1937. And the cattle just disappeared! You see, it rained all over those Sand Hills and there was water in all those pockets like White Pockets and Joe's, and those cattle knew where they was--and they was gone! And when we saw those cattle again after only about 10 days or so, why they were filled out and looked like different animals. Those Sand Hills is just like a flower garden after it storms; and it has a whole variety of plants, and they start growing. The day after it rained, the plants would start comin' up through that sand.

Calvin C. Johnson finished his summer of 1937 at the Jarvis Ranch, but that part is told under **Map 40, Southern Sand Hills**.

Building Stock Ponds This is a good place to mention other important people associated with the development of livestock grazing and water storage projects in the Sand Hills. One person was **Jack Mognett**; his son **Danny** tells a little about his father: *Dad was building roads for them uranium people when they had that big uranium boom out there in the late 1940's and early '50's. Dad run D4's all over and then he finally bought a D6C Cat.... We were out there in the Sand Hills mostly in summer. What I was doing was cleanin' out some ponds with a front end loader, while Dad and my brother Melvin was making new reservoirs.*

While some stock tanks or reservoirs were built, or cleaned out, by Jack Mognett, or his sons **Melvin** and **Danny**, **Trevor Leach** was there too. After Trevor and his father Albert sold their goats in the early 1940's and started running cattle in the Coyote Spring Allotment, Trevor bought a D4 Caterpillar and joined Jack in building roads for the uranium miners throughout southern Utah and the Arizona Strip. At that time, they were the only *cat skinners* around. Trevor was the one who built 8-10 reservoirs in the Coyote Buttes area and the Coyote Spring Allotment.

In addition to these men, **Jay Findlay** as a teenager, built a number of reservoirs in the eastern Sand Hills for his father Lynn, and uncle Dunk. More will be said about these later. **Frank & Art Mackelprang** are credited with building Franks & Mackelprang tanks/reservoirs (read more below), while **Jim Glover** supervised the building of Jim's and Glover Tanks for Harold I. Bowman. And going way back in time, **Joe Hamblin** built at least 2 ponds at his ranch, plus Middle and Lower Reservoirs.

From White Pockets, let's head back up the road to the south a short distance, then east. Right at the south end of mesa with the altitude of **6093T** (1857m), is a **rock art panel** at the bottom of the cliff; this is one of the better panels around. Best way to get there is to park at the gate about 300m south of that cliff face and walk north along the fenceline. From the end of the fence, scramble directly up-slope to the big smooth sandstone face. There you'll find some nice **petroglyphs** with one image being almost life size. From there, walk 30m to the east to see the signature of *Harvey Judd, Jan. 6, 1926*.

From that gate & rock art panel, continue east 600m or so, then north. If using the *Poverty Flat & Wrather Arch 7 1/2' quads*, you'll see they have Frank's Reservoir shown there along with an old **rip gut or stake & rider fence** running east-west. However, there's no reservoir of any kind there; **Frank's Reservoir** is actually on the other side of another little mesa to the east--as shown on this map. But while you're there, have a look at that old fence; not many of those around today. If you walk east from the road along that fence (there's a new barb wire fence as well), you'll come to a smooth cliff wall with another signature of *Lynn Ford, Nov. 13, [19]27*.

Lynn Ford's signature is seen all over the Sand Hills, probably more than anyone else's. Lynn was a goat herder and a cowboy--mostly working for other herd owners, but he apparently owned a few goats & cattle himself. He once owned a few shares of the water rights to Two Mile Spring, but he sold them to Delwin F. Hamblin 2 1/2 years before he died on November 14, 1955 at age 49; so he must have had some livestock. As a younger man, Lynn married Bessie Averett, who's family had come up from New Mexico. Her father owned a lot of goats at one time. After Lynn & Bessie had a baby girl, they divorced and Bessie married the guy Lynn was working for at the time, Art Mackelprang. There are some intriguing stories floating around Kanab just under the surface regarding that triangle, but those stories can't be told here. Trevor Leach remembered him: *Lynn Ford spent about half his life out there, he used to punch cows and herd sheep & goats. He worked for Walt Hamblin and Art Mackelprang at different times. Lynn and I worked together for years, camped together, and when he died at 49, I thought he was an old man. He had a bad heart.*

From that old rip gut fence, head east again in the direction of the real Frank's Reservoir--the one on this map. At the gate shown, park and walk about 100m northwest to what this writer has named, **Pottery Butte**, at **6079T** (1853m) altitude. Around the south & southeast side of that little butte are thousands of **pottery fragments**. There may or may not be some ruins too (?) at the base of the butte on the east side. If they ever did exit, they're covered by sand now. Another explanation for so much pottery would be that it's about halfway between the Middle Trail/Route crossing Buckskin Gulch and the more populated Joe's Valley, and White Knolls region of the southeast Sand Hills. Maybe this was an Anasazi camping place and they broke more water-carrying pots there as a result (?).

From Pottery Butte, head northeast to find the real **Frank's Reservoir**. Look around there and you'll see another rip gut or stake & rider fence running from wall to wall across the valley, and maybe some cowboy signatures (?). This place is named after Frank Mackelprang and it was likely built in the early 1930's. Trevor Leach was there too and talks about it: *Frank and Art Mackelprang had cattle after they sold their goats, and they had their headquarters there at Frank's Reservoir. They had a kind of tarp over a frame--kind of a tent up in there and they kinda lived in that when they was out there. Frank had cattle before they had goats. Lynn Ford, Frank Mackelprang and I spent a lot of time together out there.* Read more below.

From Frank's, drive southeast and be looking for **Twin White Buttes** (author's name). On the southeast side of the southern-most butte is a boulder separated from the main wall. Around that are cowboy signatures of *F. Hugh Farnsworth, Feb. 12, 1932*, and others, plus several Anasazi images. On one occasion, Hugh, the son of **Frank L. Farnsworth**: *was herding either goats or cattle in the Sand Hills, and [according to his nephew Dennis Farnsworth Judd of Kanab] somehow broke a leg, and had to ride horseback all the way back to Kanab.* Hugh also left his signature on the big rock at the begin-

This is the little **cement dam** in the northern part of **White Pockets**. It was put in by Danny Mognett in about 1972. An earlier dirt dam was built in 1937 as mentioned by Calvin C. Johnson. Just below the peak in the upper right is what this writer calls the Corn Cob Cave, with cowboy signatures.

Left This is the **Home Ranch Reservoir** at **Joe's Ranch**. This is an enlargement (the Bowmans) that Joe Hamblin originally built. This picture was taken on 2/17/2008, with snow on part of the catchment behind. **Right** Looking west at one of 2 little dams Joe Hamblin built at **Middle Reservoir**. Just behind the dams is the little pond, with the well, windmill and water tank on the hill.

An aerial view of **Hole in the Rock** looking west. The arch is a little hard to see, but it's just above dead center in this foto. The roads you'll be using are in the upper left-hand corner.

Another aerial view looking down on **Frank's Reservoir**, but its real location is east about 1 km from the place it's shown on the USGS maps. Notice the rip gut or stake & rider fence running across the valley; and the road in the upper left making the dog's leg turn. Twin White Buttes is beyond the upper left-hand corner of this picture. The road, and all motorized traffic ends in the lower right-hand corner at the wilderness boundary.

ning of the trail to Hod Brown Spring in House Rock Valley. Hugh's father Frank once had 5000 Angora goats, but later traded them in for cattle which was his main business after World War II.

From the Twin White Buttes, head east to **Hole in the Rock**, which is a pretty neat **arch** in the middle of a small butte. East of that, the road soon ends--actually blocked off at the wilderness boundary. From the road's end, you can walk along the old original track to **Mackelprang Tank** which sits up against the west side of **Adams Pasture Mesa**. This reservoir was built by **Art Mackelprang**, Franks older brother. Art was a single man until he was 44, then he married Bessie Averett, who at one time was married to Lynn Ford. Art & Bessie had 2 boys; Roy, born in 1939, and Van 2 years later in 1941. Even though **Roy** was born late in the time his father was in the Sand Hills, he remembered lots of stories & history of how his father got into the goats & mohair business: *Everybody told him, oh hell you're a damn fool with these goats, and laughed at 'im and all this, but he just said I thought this would be a good deal, and as it turned out, I did damn good. And then a lot of people wanted into goats. Dad bought Angora goats for the first time in about 1925, I think (?), and he was one of the earlier ones in this country who got into the goats & mohair business [in the 45-50 years Angoras were in Utah, Art bought goats in about the middle of that time period].*

I know he had goats for some time before 1929, because he told me, I had sheared, and I had my mohair in the warehouse at the [railroad] dock in Cedar City to be shipped. And he said the buyer came around--I think they had been paying 5 cents [a pound], and then they was goin' up to 7 cents or maybe even a dime a pound. They thought they was gettin' a lot of money, just like property was here 2 years ago. And the buyer said, I'll give you 2 bits [25 cents]. Dad says I'll take it. And everybody said to Dad, wait and it'll go to 4 bits [50 cents], but he said I'll take 2 bits. And the buyer said, I'll be back by in 2 weeks and give you a check or a draft on it and I'll get a release for the hair. Dad says fine. And bingo! In that 2 weeks Wall Street crashed, and then we was in The Depression and Dad had to pay storage on the mohair and everything else. Dad said if I had got my money on that 2 bit deal, I'd a went through The Depression flying high.

In the Sand Hills, the **herd owners** had what they called a **commissary**; it was mostly just a wagon, but they would go out and take supplies in it to the herders. When they moved the goat herd to different places, the owner would hook it onto the sheep wagon and would move it to where ever they had agreed and would set it up. So when the herder came in, they would off-load supplies, and see what the herder needed for the next week or so. My dad would go out to the herders every week or 10 days. Dad could sleep in the commissary, or on the ground. With the sheep wagon we had, you could pull the table out--it was rather wide--and it slid right in under the bed. You could sleep several people in there if it was rainin'.

When they were using mules or horses from Kanab to go out to the Sand Hills it would probably take 2 days--a couple of days each way. Then he'd be a couple of days out there, so most of his time was just restocking his goat herders out in the Sand Hills. As my father came out of the Sand Hills--there was a lot of good wood out there, mostly juniper--he always loaded his wagon or truck with fire wood. He'd haul it in for his family and his mother. So he spent part of a day loading wood when he was comin' back; he spent quite a lot of time behind a team. Then later on, he started using pickups--boy he was rough on them--he traded and got a new one about every year! They didn't have 4WD either, so that limited them. Then he got a little Ford tractor when they came out; that was in the 1930's. He thought they'd pull a wagon out there but I think he only made one trip with the commissary--it was too dang cold in the winter to drive that tractor.

One time I asked dad, and he said, the wethers produced the best hair [mohair] of any of 'um. They didn't go nuts about breeding and didn't have any kids, so all their energy went into production of hair. Also, Dad told me that they tried shearing at **Gould's Shearing Corral** down by Hurricane. It was a big shearing station--they'd shear a herd a day. To shear there, you'd pick a number for an assigned date to be there, but some guys would try to beat it. And the next thing you'd have was a whole day's traveling that was grazed off completely--no feed. Then you got into the shearing and you was another day getting sheared, then you were a day getting back out to feed & water.

So my Dad built his own shearing station. That's a place Calvin C. Johnson owns now, but it's called **Jepsons**. My father bought that from Lewis Jepson in 1938. Jepson apparently tried to homestead the place, but they left to go mining in Idaho, and we have letters from Jepson to my Dad asking to be paid quickly, but nobody had money in those days. It was only about $500 for the property I think. Dad said I ain't got no money either!

Dad sold the Angora goat herd out a little after 1941, maybe 1942. You see, when the war started, they drafted all the herders. And mother said she'd herd the goats, because her family [the Averetts] had had goats, but Dad said he didn't want his wife herding goats! So he sold the goats to somebody in Texas and went into cattle. And that left the Leaches, Bert and his son Trevor, as the only goat herd in the country. So Bert said, only one goat herd in the country can't make it--there was kind of an infrastructure thing there you see. So they sold their goats sometime after that. We kept our goats up in the upper country in summer [Skutumpah Country] and moved 'um, down to the Sand Hills in winter.

Now, let's go back to the building of **Mackelprang Tank**, Roy was there not too long after his dad built it: He built the Mackelprang Tank with that little Ford-Ferguson tractor. It had a little scrapper behind it,

Both of the pictures of water were taken at **Mackelprang Tank**, with **Art Mackelprang**. The boys by the tent are **Van** on the left, and **Roy** on the right with father Art in the middle. **Wes Averett** is standing next to some sacks of mohair. All fotos here were taken in about 1944. (Roy Mackelprang fotos)

271

Shearing Angora goats with a motor driven rotating shaft above, and rigged to clippers for doing the clipping. **Art & Bessie** Averett Ford Mackelprang, baby Van and toddler Roy. The 1930-something **truck & sheep wagon** that belonged to Art Mackelprang. And Art Mackelprang **camping and cooking** a meal with frying pan & coffee pot, in the Sand Hills. The youngster is Roy, Art's oldest boy. All fotos here are from Roy Mackelprang and believed to be taken in 1941 or '42.

a full-width scrapper, and he used that to drag the sand around.

That may have been first built in the late 1930's (?) but he enlarged it in 1944 not long before both Mackelprang brothers sold 3/4's of their **water rights** to Frank's Reservoir & Mackelprang Tank to **Royal (Roy) B. Woolley**. The date was *October 23, 1944,* according to documents in the St. George BLM office. They also sold some of their water rights to Two & One Mile Springs over in upper House Rock Valley on the same date. Then on *February 2, 1945,* Art sold most of his rights to Horse Pasture Reservoir (somewhere in Section 10 due north of Frank's Reservoir) and Two & One Mile Springs to **Harold I. Bowman Sr**. It appears the Mackelprang brothers were out of business in the Sand Hills at that time.

Here's something to keep in mind when researching history of the Sand Hills; it's been very difficult to keep track of who owned what in the way of **water rights** throughout the years. In Arizona, it's water rights that are bought & sold, and not so much with **land ownership**, as it is in Utah. Another problem has to do with having some records in the St. George, Utah, BLM office which handles all grazing business on the Arizona Strip; while other records are in the Coconino Country Courthouse in Flagstaff. Nearly all livestock graziers on the 'Strip are Utah residence which brings up the question; why didn't Utah take the 'Strip when Arizona apparently offered it to them several times? Had Utah taken the 'Strip, the state boundary would have been the Colorado River. Also, the 2 Mackelprang reservoirs mentioned above had several different names & spellings on BLM documents. In at least one case, the location in a particular Section wasn't correctly stated. Apparently the bean counters & paper shufflers in St. George often times were confused with poor communications between livestock men and the Grazing Service (after 1947, the BLM), as to what was actually going on at ground level in the Sand Hills.

Let's move up the valley southwest of Pottery Butte. On one little divide is **Basin Tank**; when cows are in that particular pasture, it and a water trough next to it, will be filled with water which flows north by gravity down from Big Sink Well. South of Basin Tank is a corral in a basin (no outlet), and just west of that are a few fotogenic rocks, then a couple of places with **DEEP SAND**--so gear down, rev up if using that route. Actually, when the sand has some moisture, it's not so bad, so kick your boot in the sand occasionally to check for moisture.

Next stop is **Big Sink**. This is a perhaps largest & deepest of all the many **closed basins** (with no outlets) in the Sand Hills. Right in the bottom is a small area with BB&CR and teepee-like rocks, but they aren't very colorful. There's even a small man-made dam in one cluster of BB&CR, but it hasn't been maintained in years, and certainly not since the well was drilled. Also, just to the south and just west of the road running south toward Black Tank and Mexican Sink is another cluster of BB&CR that look fotogenic from a distance.

If you're on that road running northeast out of the bottom of Big Sink, rev up good as you'll come to a short patch of **deep sand**. On the north side of Big Sink are **corrals**, a **well** & **water storage tanks**, and a **cinder block house**. We're not exactly sure when the well was drilled, but several sources have stated that all 8 wells in the Sand Hills were drilled in about a 10 year period beginning with the Pinnacle Valley Well in 1953. Let's say it was drilled in the early 1960's. Like most of the wells in the Sand Hills, this one was drilled by **Beeb Cothern** who worked for a guy named **Bud Mersenfelter** after they come up from Tucumcari, New Mexico. Beeb ended up living in Kanab. Richard Cothern, Beeb's son told this writer: *Dad drilled it all the way down, from start to finish, and it's 1200-1400 feet [400m] deep.*

According to **Richard Rider** of Fredonia, who is one of the sons of the late **Elmer Rider**: *the well was already there at Big Sink when dad built the cinder block house.* Richard was born in 1948 and was in junior high or high school when Elmer built that house in about 1963-'64 while being employed by **Harold I. Bowman Sr.** There was never any private land at Big Sink, but all the range improvements, facilities, grazing & water rights now belong to the Grand Canyon Trust.

Speaking of the Bowmans, here's another piece of history they are responsible for. Jay Findlay, son of Lynn Findlay, and grandson of Merle, remembers the **airstrip** at Big Sink: *Bowmans had that, because they had a little plane..... **Harold Jr.** flew in there all the time, and I flew with him sometimes, flying around looking at different places. The strip ran from NW to SE right in the bottom. They brought a Caterpillar in there that I think **Jack Mognett** had; he was doing work for us and he did some work for the Bowmans, and I think he's the one who cleaned off that airstrip. Mognett cleaned off both airstrips, the one at Pine and Big Sink. I would say they were fixed up in the mid-1950's.*

The road running north-south from just east of Big Sink and downhill to Hole in the Rock is good; in other words it isn't used as much as the Loop Road, so it hasn't been churned up by vehicles into any big deep sand traps. Also, from Big Sink there's a good road, by Sand Hills standards, running south to the **gate & water trough** at **1998m**. From there another good, and less-used track runs east to **Mexican Sink**. This basin is easily as large as Big Sink, and there are some colorful & fotogenic spires and small buttes in the area.

While at Mexican Sink, you can visit a couple of interesting places. From the center of this closed basin, drive east on the only road. When you come to the fence & gate on your immediate left, stop and park (there used to be an old track running northeast from there, but it's no longer used by stockmen and has small trees going up in it, so why not let it go back to nature and walk from the gate?). From that gate, walk due north about 900m until you see a line of low cliffs maybe 250m long (this is about 300m west of the middle of a little basin marked **6369T** (1941m) on the *One Toe Ridge 7 1/2' quad.* In the middle of those cliffs is a small alcove with black soot on the ceiling, blackish sand below with lots of pottery fragments, and some interesting colored walls. From there, walk northeast along the base of the cliffs about 100m to find some **Anasazi ruins** at ground level, again with lots of pottery. Immediately beyond that is a small **cave** opening in the wall, and several rocks piled up at the opening. Inside, it's about the size of the inside of a small car or pup tent. On the inside wall is the signature *Dud. A 1939,*

The **well** on the hill south of **Big Sink**; it used to have a windmill, but not now. **Elmer Rider** stands beside the **cinder block house** he built in the early 1960's while working for the Bowmans (Richard Rider foto). Inside the block house at **Big Sink**.

Above Commissary Cave is just a hole in the wall, but it has an interesting past. Inside is what looks like a brand engraved on a wall, a kind of Rocking-L.

Right Sam Judd is the grandfather of Ron Glover, who tells the history of Commissary Cave.

and an -L with a bow or crescent underneath; seems like a brand, and similar to a rocking L (see foto directly above). Near the entrance is some soot on the ceiling, indicating Indians once had fires inside.

This place we'll call **Commissary Cave**. Here's the story behind it as told by **Ron Glover** of Kanab: *I remember my grandfather, **Sam Judd,** telling me about that cave. One time, we left Big Sink heading east and were gathering cows up through there west of Dunk's fence, when he showed it to me. We walked over to it and he said, stockmen from all the little parts of the Sand Hills would put all their letters and notes in the cave; it was like a mail box. And whoevers turn it was to go to town, would pick up all the stuff and go into Kanab and when they came back, they would leave stuff for different people in this same little cave. Then everybody from all over the Sand Hills would drop by and pick up their stuff. For example, if someone needed tobacco, they'd leave some money in a tin can along with a note for whoever was going into town next, then they'd pickup the tobacco some time later. It was a small cave and nobody lived in it, but they had it rocked-up in front to keep the weather out. Grandpa was born in 1895, so they were doing this in the early 1900's until maybe about 1920--somewhere along in there, and before trucks and cars were being used.*

From that first gate and trailhead for Commissary Cave, drive east along the fenceline to another fence running north-south. There's another gate there, and although the *7 1/2 quads* show an old road continuing east, there's no sign of if today (what those maps show is the original road running to Joe's Ranch but it's disappeared in most places). So why not park your ATV's there and walk about 1100m (.65 mile) to more **ruins** on top of, and at the base of, a **mini butte** (10-12m high & wide) which is just north of another long narrow butte marked **6550T** (1996m) on *The Big Knoll 7 1/2' quad*. There are lots of pottery fragments around too.

For now, let's head northward. The author chased a full-curl big horn ram up onto **The Big Knoll**, but never saw any ruins, rock art or cowboy signatures there. On some maps, this is called **Red Butte**, which is the name of the bench mark on top. He also walked completely around **Middle Knoll** and

Top This is the **cabin** that **A.T. Spence** built just below the dam at **Lower Reservoir**. It's in good shape except for the doors & windows. **Below** Part of the watershed for **Lower Reservoir**. Looking southeast at the little butte labeled 6251T (1905m). The dam is just to the left of this foto.

found nothing of interest. Halfway between Middle and Little Knolls is a line of 5 little buttes the author is labeling **Five Tops**. Nothing there either, but just to the south and east are a couple of small clusters of BB&CR; the ones to the south are fairly fotogenic. Just 2 kms due east of Five Tops is Middle Reservoir & Well, which is covered in the next section, and on **Map 39**.

Just north of Five Tops is **Little Knoll**. Park on the south side and on the high point of that road, and walk due north straight up to the south face and the smooth sandstone wall. There you'll find another good **rock art panel**, plus several cowboy signatures: **F.L. Farnsworth, Lyle J[udd?], Kay Wilson, Oct. 11, 1927; Chas. J. Ford 2-19-[19]13; and Lynn Ford, Jan. 7, 1947**. Some petroglyphs are up 4-5m on facing walls. On the west side is another small petroglyph panel not worth looking at, and on the east side is a small ruin under a ledge. Be aware of possible **deep sand** on the east side of Little Knoll and around the junction of the Loop Road and the road running north to Lower Reservoir.

Northeast of Little Knoll about 2 kms is an unnamed butte with the elevation of **6251T** (1905m). The south side of that butte has some nice colors, but there's better stuff 500m southeast of that. There's a cluster of teepee or BB&CR and one nice pinnacle that looks like an upside down *cowboy hat*.

Continue north downhill on a good road to **Lower Reservoir**. This is another very interesting place. Joe Hamblin started the little dam at the foot of a big slickrock water catchment made of pure **white BB&CR**. Very fotogenic when shot with low sun and some shadows. After Joe died, his son Neaf sold

These are the **2 old rusty coyote traps** the author found in the summer of 2009 in the Sand Hills. According to Trevor Leach, they almost certainly belonged to **Cecil Cram** who trapped in that country in the 1930's & '40's. Both traps have chains so they can be tied down, but the one on the right also has home-made hook which, if dragged very far, would snag on something. The little tags on both chains read GF1720.

it to Johnny Adams, then it went to A.T. Spence, Merle, and Lynn Findlay, then to the same owners as we saw at Joe's Ranch. North of the dam, which has been enlarged and cleaned out several times, is a well-built cabin believed to have been built by A.T. Spence sometime between 1941 & '45. Next to it is a horse barn, half a dozen Ponderosa pines just below, then a couple of stockade-type corrals just to the north. Today, some of the local cowboys call the 2-room house **Dunk's Cabin** (but it's doubtful he stayed there very often because he never had that area as his grazing allotment, or had water rights to the reservoir), which was built with a rain catchment and pipes on the roof which channels water into a cistern standing nearby.

During the summer of 2009, this writter found **2 old rusty coyote traps** in the Sand Hills; one near Wiregrass Reservoir, the other not far from Big Pocket, and near Edwin's Pockets. He showed them to Trevor Leach and here's what he said: *Cecil Cram used to trap out there, these are likely his traps. These is government traps, they're not regular traps. The others which we all used to use was Victor traps; they've got 2 handels, one on each side. But these are hard to set I'll tell ya. The government used to pay the trappers a salary, then they could sell the pelts too, but I don't know how that worked. Cecil was out there in the 1930's & '40's, because he camped with us once in a while. He stayed in that sheep camp at Lower Reservoir quite a lot before that cabin was built.*

If you continue down the gradual slope to the north, the road ends less than 3 kms from the upper part of **Wrather Canyon** and its big arch. From the end of that road, it's an easy walk to **The Hole**, the area above **The Keyhole**, as seen from down in the gorge. In the vicinity of Wrather Canyon are several areas with nice teepee-like rocks with the same colors as on Steamboat Rock. It's also an easy way to reach the top of the **Adams Trail** going down to the Paria; in fact, this is surely the route of the old wagon road that Johnny Adams used when he built that trail. Trevor Leach had a little story to tell about working for Johnny Adams and that trail: *I worked for **Johnny Adams** when he had that place. When he was there, he kept his headquarters there at Joe's. I was there when Johnny pumped water out of the crik, I helped haul the pipe down there. We hauled it from Kanab out there to the Sand Hills with old trucks, then we loaded it into wagons and took it down there to the beginning of the trail where they took it down to the river. We put that pipe off down to the river, and old Gene McCallister got on that 2" [5 cms] pipe and slide down it--from top to bottom! They had a pump in the bottom and the water came up. But just after we got it started, it rained, so they quit. But they did get water up there, I was there.*

Beeb Cothern pulling pipe at the **Pinnacle Valley Well**, and repairing the pump at the bottom. In the background is where Trevor Leach put his signature Christmas Day, 1936. (Richard Cothern foto)

Left From near the top of **The Pinnacle**, for which Pinnacle Valley is named, looking down at the main pocket that has water almost all the time. In the background to the west is the Pinnacle Valley Well. **Right** The other **2 pockets** on The Pinnacle usually don't have water, but do have **pottery fragments** that have been there for nearly 1000 years!

Now back to the south and **Pinnacle Valley** which has to be the widest & longest unbroken such place in the Sand Hills. Throughout this wide open valley are many small outcroppings of Navajo Sandstone but nothing really big except for one in the north end called **The Pinnacle**. The valley is covered with grasses and sagebrush-like shrubs and was always a top grazing area for goat herders, then cattlemen and because of that, **Merle Findlay** had a **well** drilled in the northern end in **1953**. **Jay Findlay**, the son of Lynn, and grandson of Merle, fills in a lot of gaps in information about this place and the wells all over the Sand Hills: *All those **wells** were drilled in a 10 year period, because the same driller was out there. It was **Beeb Cothern**--he worked for a guy who came up here from Tucumcari, New Mexico, named **Bud Mersenfelter.** Beeb was the main driller. The well at Pinnacle Valley is over 1200 ft. (365m) deep. Beeb Cothern **welded** all those **steel tanks** too, at least the vast majority of them. The big tank in Pinnacle Valley he put together in 1965. Beeb was the one who serviced all the wells for most of the years he was alive. He was the only one who could pull the pipe and fix 'um. Beeb died about 2 years ago.* His son **Richard** took over the business of drilling wells, and continues today (2010).

At the well are corrals, a small shed, a fotogenic windmill no longer in use, the new well & propane powered pump and a big metal water tank. Just to the east is **The Pinnacle**, which if lined up with the corrals & windmill, makes a nice picture. Park at the well and walk to The Pinnacle; there you'll find a **cave** on the west side with soot on the ceiling, meaning the Anasazi built fires in it. Also, there are a number of old cowboy & goat herder signatures. One is the oldest this writer has seen in the Sand Hills--**F.L.F. 1-11-1911**, this can only belong to **Frank L. Farnsworth**. Also there are initials of Willy & Trevor Leach in 1937, an Averett, S. Spence, 1941, Lynn Findlay, etc. On the southeast corner of The Pinnacle is another alcove with more goat herder & cowboy signatures, plus lots of pottery fragments.

Here's something that's hard to believe until you see it with your own eyes. The Pinnacle looks like a peak with a sharp point on top, as seen from ground level, but it's actually an elongated cluster of BB&CR. If you circle around to the north or east side and climb it, you'll find what Trevor Leach calls **Pinnacle Pocket**. Actually there are 3 pockets; one holds water almost year-round--it's on the west side, while the other 2 are on the northern end, and don't hold water for very long after good rains. The bottoms of these 2 are lined with **pottery fragments**. The amazing thing about this is, the fragments still haven't been covered with sand since a bunch of poor thirsty Anasazi Indians broke their water jugs there about 800-900 years ago! Interesting place. Please leave the potsherds there! It's the law.

Best place to see Pinnacle Valley is from on top of The Pinnacle itself. Also, north of Pinnacle Well are a number of places with BB&CR--they're just about everywhere in these parts. If you drive west from the well about 300m, you'll come to where the road turns south. Park there near the altitude marked **6414T** (1955m) on the *One Toe Ridge 7 1/2' quad*. It was somewhere in this area that 16-year old **Trevor Leach** was camped on Christmas day, 1936. Before telling his story, take a short 1 km walk north, northwest from that parking place and up to the end of a mesa or buttress with the altitude marked **6639T** (2024m). On the south side of that buttress is a bunch of goat herder & cowboy signatures, and lots of pottery fragments. The most important signature reads **Trevor Leach, Dec. 25, 1936**. Also clearly visible is that of **Lynn Ford, Dec. 6, 1930, and W. Leach, 1937**. See fotos on next page.

This is a good place to let Trevor tell about being snowbound for so long, and a lot more about **Angora goats** and general **history of the Sand Hills**: *I was about 10 years old when I first went out there to the Sand Hills; must have been about 1930 [he was born in July, 1920]. You see, I spent the entire* *summer of 1936 out here with Junior Brown. My Dad had bought Neaf Hamblin's goats, and I and Junior was out on the Sand with a dry herd. We spent that summer out on the mountain [Buckskin Mtn.], and out there to Coyote and finally in the Sand Hills for winter. That's how come* **I got snowed in in 1936-37** *and didn't see no one for* **32 days**. *My dad, Bert Leach, had Angora goats and I had 3200 head of 'um in that one herd. It was there by Dunk Findlay's place [Findlays came in 10 years later] where I got snowed in. It was there in the Pinnacle Valley, and I was camped just west upon that hill above where the Findlay Well is now. I went out there to relieve the herders that was with the herd because it was during Christmas holidays, 1936. When school let out for Christmas, I rode a horse out there and I was 16 years old. The regular herders there was Lynn Ford and Junior Brown. And they got on their horses and headed for town, and it started to snow in the next couple of days. Junior Brown finally got back to me the 2nd of February; he damn near froze to death trying to get back out there on his horse. Lynn Ford never did come back that winter.*

And it started to snow the day after Christmas and I never seen anybody until the 2nd of February. The wells wasn't there then, nothing was there then. It was all open country. It was in 1936, and that's when they surveyed it. There was a **survey camp** *a little ways from where I was camped. And when it started to snow the surveyors took off for town. And they give me a sack of sweet potatos and a few other things like that, and I had goat meat and a sourdough jug and flour.*

The snow was close to 4 feet deep on the level everywhere. I lost about 1200 goats; just about lost 'um all. They crowded into them trees because there wasn't any feed, the snow was so deep. I laid out there 7 nights with a little fire under a limb, and with 2 dogs. I had a sheep wagon, but I'd take them goats in bunches to try to get'em to split up. I tried to split 'em up into 500 head to a bunch, and I'd cut limbs, and we'd go through the snow, me and my dogs. I made me some skis--something like snowshoes is what they was. I had a 6 foot board, the only board in camp, and I sawed it down the middle with a meat saw and made me 2 snowshoes, more or less. And I took mutton tallow and cooked that to the boards so the snow wouldn't stick to 'em. I took an old pair of overshoes and bolted 'em to the boards, and that's what I'd put on my feet to try to get around. I turned my horses loose cuz I didn't have no feed; put the horse blankets on 'em, and turned 'em loose.

The goats, they eat anything out there, the cedar trees, browse, sage brush, old man brush, bitter brush--but nothin' eats rabbit brush--only rabbits, I guess (?). Goats eat about the same as a deer. Some cedar trees they eat up--others they wouldn't touch--I don't know why (?).

I'd go along with my dogs and I'd cut a limb off and they'd try to get to it. But I couldn't make it back to camp a lot of times--it was 7 nights I didn't make it back to the camp wagon. Sometimes I'd find a big tree and set it on fire; or build me a small fire underneath some limbs and get up in the tree and the heat would come up under me--that's the way I slept. The goats would get under them trees and towards morning, they crowd in there and some would lay down and others would pile on top of 'um

When I first went out there, before the storm, it was dry and I was pourin' water--there's a big water pocket just up from that Findlay Well, up on that big white rock [The Pinnacle] that's east of there. And that's where I was pourin' water off to water my horses. Then it started snowin' and it never quit! Pinnacle Pockets, is what's that's called.

Later, my dad came out there in March [of 1937]; he was snowed in up at Bald Knolls. He got with Bill Adams and they come out there with pack horses. We had dead goats everywhere. I had 3200 head in the herd to start with, and I wound up with about 2000. So we lost about 1200 head. I went out there later with a wagon and gathered 'um up after spring broke and put'um on the north sides of trees, then Dad had some guys come out--they had hair about that long on 'um--and these guys sheared 'um, so we could get something out of 'um. We sheared the dead ones, then I piled 'um up under them trees. But you know, I've been out there since, and I can't even find a horn. They must deteriorate fast.

If you think Trevor was stretching the depth of the snow, here are the rain/snowfall amounts for Kanab that winter. For **December, 1936**, the total precipitation was **3.52"(nearly 9 cms)**, nearly triple the nor-

The 3 gray colored signatures above are located at the end of the **mesa or buttress** marked **6639T (2024m)--Trevor Leach, Dec. 25, 1936, Lynn Ford, Dec. 6, 1930,** and **W. Leach, 1937**. The **Chas. Ford** signature (just above) is on one of the hills south of **Big Sink**. The **Frank L. Farnsworth** etching is near the cave on the west side of **The Pinnacle**.

mal. The 2 biggest surges came on the 28th & 31st. For **January, 1937**, Kanab got **2.4" (6.1 cms)**, that's about double the norm. For **February, 1937**, they got **3.77" (9.6 cms)**, mostly rain and about triple the norm.

Snow reports began with the **January 8, 1937** issue of the **KCS**. As it turned out, the storm was considered the worst in southwestern Utah history. There must have been 8-10 CCC camps in southern Utah at the time, and many were stranded. CCC bulldozers worked for a couple of months getting roads cleared and rescuing people and livestock. Some students were stranded at home or in schools for days. A train ran into snowdrifts west of Cedar City and was derailed. There were 32 men working at Bright Angel Point--North Rim of the Grand Canyon--and were stranded for 6 weeks, another family was stranded for the same time period at a sawmill south of Jacob Lake. Losses with livestock weren't as bad as originally thought, but thousands of sheep & goats died. Southern Utah basically stood still for upwards of 2 months. January, 1937, was the coldest month in recorded Utah history up to 2010! The average temperature for the state was 10.3°F (-12.1°C); that was 14.7°F (-9.6°C) below average.

Here's more of Trevor's story: *My dad first got goats in about 1922 or '23, then when I was 5 years old [1925] was the first time I went out on the mountain [Buckskin Mtn.]. He bought his goats from Mackelprangs, and he ran 'um in with Billy Mackelprangs [brother to Art & Frank] in the beginning.*

Sheep Wagons *I spent 40 years out there in a sheep wagon, I and my brother **Willie Leach** [later on in life he preferred to be called **Billy**--more on Willy later]. Dad actually bought our sheep wagon from the Swapps, up there just this side of Alton. Swapps had sheep, and he bought their sheep wagon when he went into the goat business. My boy's got it now out to Page, he took it out there and he's got it displayed at Ken's Old West (see picture below).*

Inside, it had a wood stove in the corner, and you had your cupboards, then you had your table--it would fold up, and bins in the side, and in the back you had it so you could put stuff under the bed--from outside. They're not very big, but they were handy. Then we made it so you could make an extra bed in there, we'd take the door out of the sheep wagon and if we had company, we could have another bed.

*Horses pulled it out there, wagons was all there was then in the Sand Hills. I worked teams for years, **mules** first; my dad had mules. After that time I got snowed in 1936-'37, then that's when we got **horses**. The mules all died; they got distemper, so I had to get a team of horses. Distemper for them is like the flu is for us. If they get it nowadays, you can give them a shot, and it'll dock it; but back then we didn't and they'd just keep gettin' sicker & sicker, and finally die. One died at Red Pockets, one of 'um died just as you go into Pinnacle Valley, another one died in Mexican Sink, and the other one which was raised in Tropic, went back there and died suddenly. He went right up the Piree Crik.*

For food, we'd eat goats; hell ya, had mutton all the time. You can't tell the difference between that and sheep mutton. And I always had a sack of flower for sourdough biscuits. I've made enough sourdough biscuits to pave the road from here to Page! I used to make 'um 3 times a day.

*For **water**, now my dad owned [the water rights to] **Kitchen Reservoir**, he bought that reservoir first and then we bought Coyote after that. So we watered there, and from pockets; there's a lot of water pockets in the Sand Hills. But once it snowed, then we'd depend on snow for the rest of the winter. We'd melt it for camp water and the goats they'd eat the snow--sheep & cattle eat snow too. I've seen cows come off the mountain, and in the spring they'd be pretty thirsty when they'd get down to Coyote--and they'd try to eat the water instead of drinkin' it! They'd keep bitin at it, because they'd been eatin' snow all winter. Then after a while they'd start to drink it.*

The **original sheep wagon** that Bert Leach bought from Swapps sometime in the 1920's (?). It's also the one that Trevor lived in for so many years. It's now on this pedestal beside the dinner club of Ken Leach (Trevor's son), Ken's Old West, in Page, Arizona. **Right Angora goats** somewhere near the Leach's Ranch north of Johnson Canyon near Bald Knoll. (Trevor Leach foto)

Albert **(Bert) Leach**, Trevor's father, in a field of wheat (?) in later years, and as a young man in the chair. Bert was born in England in 12/1887 and came to Utah in 1911 and worked on the boat *Charles H. Spencer* at **Lee's Ferry**. He worked in a sawmill near Jacob Lake, then homesteaded a place near Bald Knoll, north of Johnson Canyon. There, he opened a coal mine, but later went into Angora goats, then cattle. He owned the water rights to Coyote Spring for about 30 years.

Up until about Christmas you'd have to water the goats, we'd usually come into Coyote. During those times we's stay on the east side of the mountain [Buckskin Mountain] or up in the Sand Hills not too far so we could come back to water. We'd water 'um, then after about 5 days, we'd take 'um back to water. That was the goats; they'd drink every day if they could get it, but they'd go 5 days pretty good without water. But we'd stay close in, try to water 'um every 2 or 3 days.

One question this writer had for Trevor was; why did you have to tend or herd sheep & goats, and not cattle? His answer was: *Because the coyotes would get 'um all; that was the main reason. They'd go and come, but a bunch of goats would go off and make 'um a bed ground, and they'd stay there for a week or so without nobody around--then they'd come back to the same place and bed. But if the herders weren't around, the coyotes would get into 'um and raise hell; and kill a whole bunch of 'um. If you had a goat in a sheep herd, the coyote would kill the goat! The dogs was there mainly to just take care of 'um--they might run out and bark at the coyotes--but they didn't bother the coyotes that much.*

Our **dogs** *was just like humans. We trained 'um and you could send 'um for miles around them goats. We had Australian shepherds and crossed mostly with collies. My daughter has one now, it's the same kind of dogs we used to have. And we had a couple or 3 all the time. We raised our own dogs, but we had one litter of pups that was crossed with a coyote--they was half breeds. And I took a herd of goats from up there at Bald Knoll over to Cedar City and I was 14 years old, and I had a half breed coyote dog with me when I done that. They was sneaky' buggers, but they was good dogs. You could just wave your hat or your arms, or whistle, or somethin', and they'd go circle the herd. They'd come back and you'd say, "well, did you get'um all? Go check your tracks", and they'd go out and circle with their nose on the ground. Oh, they were good dogs, but we had to keep an old one around to kinda learn the young ones what to do. We'd work the older one with the young ones. I don't know where they come from originally, but we just raised all ours.*

Pure bred **breeding billy goats** *were brought from Oregon & Texas; Dad used to give $500 & $600 for a good billy goat. We used to have 1 billy for about 30 nannies. Goats have a breeding season like deer, so sometime in September you had to take the billies out of the herd and put 'um somewhere else, then we'd put 'um back with the herd about Christmas time--end of December. Dad used to take the billies over to Johnson [Valley at that time]. It was at that time of year that the Jepson's used to put their billies upon No Mans Mesa.*

The reason we'd take the billies out of the herd from September through early December was that the nannies would be in heat and we didn't want the kids born in late winter or early spring. It takes 'um 6 months for the kids to come and we wanted them born in warmer weather, in May or June. For the rest of the season, except for September through early December, we just left the billies with the herd.

The **wethers, the castrated goats**, *would produce 10-12 pounds of hair [mohair] a year--we kept them in the dry herd. We'd run nannies and kids and wethers, and the ones that didn't have kids.*

We used to haul our mohair over to Cedar City to the railroad. Before I ever got a driver's licence, I was about 14, I took a truck load of hair over there. It was a 1 ton International and we put 3-4 sacks on it, then I'd take a 1935 Ford pickup with a couple of sacks in it. The sacks with mohair was about 3 feet across and 9 foot long [1x3m]. They weighed about 500 pound [225kg] a piece. The hair would be tromped tight in the sacks, and we'd put some boards down and roll'um into the trucks. We had to go through Zions and around that way to get to Cedar. We went through the tunnel and there used to be big windows in it. I don't know where they shipped it to after Cedar City.

Mohair *used to be a pretty good thing here; it was worth as high as a $1 a pound when wool was sellin' for 30 cents. That was just before the stock market crashed [in October, 1929]. They used to use mohair for car seat cushions, for clothes, lots of things. Your couches was made out of mohair years ago.*

In March, 1999, **Bessie Averett Ford Mackelprang** was interviewed for the Southern Utah Oral History Project. She concentrated on goats and goat herding. One of her stories had to do with the Angora goats getting **lice** and had to be dipped: *Ren Flanigan and my dad Murray Averett was out with the goats getting ready to dip them..... They had a tub with some water and they put arsenic in it and boiled it.... Then they'd put it in this big vat [dug in the ground] that they had built--put so much water in it and so much poison, and bring the goats into the corral and take one goat at a time and put it down in that dipping vat and shove 'em down with a big stick. Then they could climb up the other side, they had steps so they could get out.... It took us 2 or 3 days to get them all dipped. I was on one side to help push them in the dip, but then Dad wouldn't let us get around there where we could get poison on us. We got those dipped and then instead of leaving, I stayed and lived with Mrs. Flanagan for, oh a year or two. Then Dad decided he had to have someone help herd those goats 'cause the Flanagans had just about 3000 head. That was quite a big herd. So they told me, that if I helped him herd goats they would pay me for it. So I did and I rode a mule with a packsaddle and a pillow on the packsaddle..... I'd go around those goats and get it [the mule] on the run and they'd see something black [off to one* side], and they'd stop to look at that and I'd a keep a goin' over it's head and down I'd go. I got throwed quite a few times but I didn't get hurt. I thought that was a heck of a note--having to ride a mule with a packsaddle! I spent most of the next summer there helping Dad with those goats..... Well I helped until school, when of course I had to quit and come into town.

Trevor Leach remembered dipping goats too: We went over there to Lamb Springs [west of Kanab] to dip our goats once. Just below Sink Valley [up by Alton] they had a dippin' vat, and we dipped there one year. And Art Mackelprang had one over there at Quinceys too--that's Roy Mackelprang's place now. That's up above Skutum[pah]. Then Dad built our own dippin' vat on our place at the ranch [near Bald Knoll]. We dipped the goats in the late summer or fall before going to the Sand Hills.

One of the sadder times in livestock history of southern Utah, and for other parts of the west as well, culminated in the fall of 1934. This was the slaughter of about 10% of the total livestock from many of the western ranges. The reasons were, in the years prior to that time, there was a big increase in the number of sheep, goats & cattle using the public domain in the western US. The result was overgraz-ing and overall degradation and erosion of Forest Service and Grazing Service (BLM after 1947) lands. Adding to this problem, there were several very dry years leading up to 1934. On top of that, there was an over supply of all livestock resulting in deflation in prices. The Great Depression was also rearing its ugly head, plus segments of the goat herd in southern Utah were infected with a form of **Brucellosis** known locally at the time as **goat fever** (or Malta disease or undulant fever).

Because of these problems, the Roosevelt Administration passed the **Taylor Grazing Act** in 1934, which began the process of setting up for the first time, controls on grazing, and how many animals would be allowed to use public land. One of the first things they did was to reduce the livestock num-bers. Here are several quotes from the **KCS**. In the 11/9/1934 issue it states: GOAT PURCHASES OR-DERED INCLUDED IN DROUGHT RELIEF ....the Washington administration Saturday agreed to the purchase of 6000 goats, chiefly in southern Utah.... The Utah FERA undertakes to dispose of the goat skins by preparing them for shipment to whatever point the federal surplus relief corporation may des-ignate, and in the meantime it is preparing estimates as to the cost of canning the meat of a number of the animals to be purchased....

In the 11/23/1934 issue it states: SLAUGHTER OF SURPLUS GOATS STARTS AT KANAB Three hundred twenty-five head of goats were slaughtered in Johnson canyon Saturday, under the government program. These goats were the oldest ewes [nannies] in the flock owned by Neaf Hamblin. The next herd to be culled and slaughtered belongs to the Richfield bank and is now at the Kitchen corral [located on the road to Mollies Nipple]. If necessary arrangements can be made with government officials, this whole herd of more than 3000 head will be slaughtered. Read more about this herd below.

Two articles from the 12/14/1934 issue pretty well tell the tale: UTAH TO PURCHASE TEN [THOU-SAND] GOATS Utah has received an additional allotment for the purchase of goats that has been al-located to the counties as follows: Washington, 5000; Kane, 2500; Carbon, 700; Iron, 500; Garfield, 300; San Juan, 300; Grand, 150; and Duchesne, 150. There are still 400 head to be allotted to lesser goat counties.... The purchases which have already begun are confined to females one year old and over. The price to be paid is $1.40 per head. The goats must be pelted and the pelts cured and deliv-ered to the county FSRC agent. Those goats fit for food will be processed in local plants, with no out-of-state shipments. It is hoped that this purchase will eliminate the old female goats and that this number will relieve the goat situation in the state.

U. S. WILL BUY 50,000 EXTRA HEAD OF UTAH CATTLE The federal government will spend $684,500 for the purchase of cattle in the state,... bringing the grand total to approximately two million dollars applied to this particular type of drought relief. In addition, the goat buying program will be aug-mented to the extent that it is believed it will be possible to purchase all female goats in the state for slaughter.... In all, 50,000 cattle will be purchased under the new order bringing the grand total up to 155,000 head. An average of about $13.50 a head will be paid for the cattle....

Largely as a result of Governor Blood's representation to federal officials of the danger from Malta or undulant fever contracted from goats, the program has been extended in order that Utah may be rid of this dangerous contamination. Humans, cows, pigs or other animals have been known to contract Malta fever through contact with goats afflicted with the disease and in the southern part of Utah a mild epidemic of this contagion has been reported....

Left Trevor Leach standing beside one of his dad's (Albert or Bert) 1930-something trucks in 1941. (Roy Mackelprang foto) **Right Trevor Leach** on one of his favorite steeds. In the background left is the old stone house at **Two Mile Spring**. (Trevor Leach foto)

Regarding the **3000 goats** belonging to the Richfield Bank, this may have been the same herd that Lewis Jepson put on top of No Mans Mesa to hide them from the bank. Trevor Leach was there and explains: *It was the females they wanted to kill, they wouldn't take the males. The bank had all the female goats of Jepsons; but they didn't kill them up at the Kitchen Corral, they killed them at the Jepson Place, and all them washes was full of dead goats. Then the Buntings took their pigs out there and turned 'um loose to eat the dead goats.*

They had to skin'um first, and they wasn't supposed to take any of the meat, but a lot of 'um did. It was pitiful, them poor buggers toward the last was pert near starved to death. They never fed 'um a damn thing from the time they started it, then there was blood all over the corral! I was just a kid, but I remember goin' down there and it would just make you sick. It was the damnest thing you ever seen!

Goat fever was a relatively mild disease, but it left some people with some long-term health issues. Many people who owned goats or worked with goats during the kidding season got it in the early 1900's, but usually only those who were involved with goats during the kidding season took precautions. Trevor explains: *We never had no trouble with our goats all the time Dad had 'um, but my mother got goat fever up at Bald Knoll and she lost her hearing. In the kidding season, every time we'd go into camp we'd wash our hands in lysol water. And we always put an apron on before we cooked anything. The only time we did this was when we was kiddin' the goats.*

About the time the Grazing Service was scaling down the number of livestock on the public ranges, there was a push by local ranchers to get rid of the wild horses as well. Trevor remembers a time in the mid-1930's when they went out to Joe's Ranch to get rid of some of them: *At that time there used to be a lot of wild horses out there in the Sand Hills. When I went out there to Joe's one time, we was gathering wild horses. We gathered 'um and we put a bell on an old mare, and put 'um in that old horse pasture above Joe's--Shellings was doing it, I just went to help. When we left there to go to Two Mile, they had about 30 head of horses that they had water trapped by the reservoir. Before we left, we roped the rest and put a gunny sack over their heads, so they could follow the bell. And we headed out for Two Mile; we lost a few of 'um, but we got there with most of 'um. I had about 7 of my own in there, that's the reason I was with 'um, I was trying to get my horses too. I had caught 'um when they was colts and branded 'um out there. That was about 1935 or around in there (?). After we got 'um to Two Mile, we shipped 'um to Cedar City, then somebody used 'um for dog food.*

*Wild horses was the ones who made them trails into White Pockets--horses & cows that made them. You can see where they wore foot steps in the rocks. We didn't bother the horses too much--but we shot a lot of 'um--I didn't but ol' Lynn Ford and a bunch of 'um did. I shot a few on [Buckskin] Mountain. But later on, when the BLM was going to protect 'um [after the **Wild Horse & Burro Act of 1971** was passed], then we all went out there and got rid of 'um so they couldn't keep 'um on our range.*

Trevor tells about his half brother, **Willy Leach**, but keep a couple of things in mind; Trevor, when being interviewed, used 2 names, Willy and Bill when talking about him, but his brother always signed his name **Willy** on the rocks in the Sand Hills (that's why this writer always uses the name Willy). After he finished his military obligation in the army during World War II, he somehow decided he liked the name Bill better. Still later, he may have even changed his last name back to Clem (?). Here's the story: *Willy's mother was an Australian and she got a divorce from her husband while living there. She was married to a man named **Clem**. She got in with some Mormon missionaries in Australia, and she and her mother and her sister came over here and brought Bill (Willy) when he was young. Willy was born in October, 1914, in Brisbane. So Willy's name was Clem at that time. And they bought a house up here at the other end of Kanab, then they sold it and moved to Salt Lake.*

Later they lived in Alton, that's where my dad, Bert Leach met Willy's mother; they were married in 1919, and Willy took up the name of Leach. When he was about 14, he dropped out of school, and that's when he first went out there in the Sand Hills. Bill was out there from when he was about 14 (1928). He spent about 7 years out there at one time without coming to town; until the army got 'im. But then he made Sargent in the army. He was an airplane mechanic; but he didn't know nothing about mechanics when he went in. He had spent his whole life herdin' goats.

He was drafted in about April of 1942, and was one of the first guys they took when the draft started. He got to be a First Sargent in the Army--that's a pretty good rating. When he got back from the service, he herded some of the cattle. We had goats until 1944 or '45, then we got cattle and we run them in the Sand Hills, and around Coyote.

Later, he went out to Page to work in the water department and the hospital in Page [until he retired

Willy or Bill Leach in the US Army in 1942; and Willy & Trevor Leach sometime in the 1980's.

in 1985--some of these dates are from his obituary]. He bought a home there. He worked there in Page, and worked with the cows too, then he got alzheimers. It was terrible. He had it for 8 years, he should have died 8 years sooner--he just kept walkin', he wouldn't stop. You'd be talkin' to 'im and he'd walk off and leave ya.

Willy had about 7 kids; one of 'um was Donny Leach and he lives in Page. He bought Bills house when he died. Donny changed is name back to Clem, at least that's what I've heard.

Willy wrote a diary every night [in the Sand Hills], what we done and what happened out there for 10 years. But I don't know what happened to those diaries. And you can't beat how he could draw maps.

Roy Mackelprang wasn't born until 1939, but he remembered stories told to him by his mother Bessie who was about Willy's age and knew the family well: They took Willy out there when he was maybe in the 8th Grade and he stayed on a goat herd until somebody pulled into camp, then he'd run and hide-- even people he played with as kids, like my mother. And they left 'im there.

But Willy was drafted with my mom's oldest brother, **Wesley Averett**, and another fellow here in town. And Willy was scared to death [to be so far from home]. And they told us that he'd stick so tight to them--he knew 'um, somewhat, and he'd be almost steppin' on their feet tryin' to stay close to peo- ple he knew--all the time. And one of 'um would find the other, and say, "good hell, will you take him for a while".

But [going in the service] did him a world of good. Later the army split 'em up, and Willy went in the aircorp. When he came back he was a different man. When he came out of the army, he was around here a little while and then when they started the Glen Canyon Dam he signed up for the Bureau of Reclamation, and went to Page and worked there until he retired.

The last goat herds in the Sand Hills and the Kanab area may have belonged to the Flanagans, Art & Frank Mackelprang, then Bert Leach--Trevor's dad was apparently the last goat man to sell out. Bessie Mackelprang (Art's wife) gives perhaps the best account of the last days of goats and goat herd- ing in the area in her *Southern Utah Oral History Project* interview of March, 1999. Here's part of her story: Old man **Ren Flanagan** had a big herd of goats and he couldn't find a herder. It was when the war started [and all the herders got drafted], so he had his goats up where they called the **Red Knoll** [northwest of Kanab]. He said he'd auction them off. I don't know who all was there, but there was a bunch, and he said he'd sell them to the highest bidder. And **Ivan Ford**, my cousin, said six bits [75 cents]. And Ren said, "sold". So Ren left. Before that he had all those goats, about 3000. But all they [Fords] did was just take what they wanted for mutton, and there was goats scattered all around this country for quite a while until the bank finally sent somebody out to get what was left.

[So just after the start of World War II] **Art Mackelprang** and **Bert Leach** was the only ones left with a herd of goats. Art had been trying to sell his for a couple of years. When Roy [Mackelprang] was about 2 years old [born in January, 1939], he finally found a guy in Texas that wanted them, so he delivered them over the north end of the [Buckskin] mountain and down into House Rock Valley. They loaded them on trucks and shipped them to Texas. That left Bert Leach with his herd and Willy [his adopted son] that had herded for him for so many years; but they drafted him, so Willy had to go [in the army]. So there Bert was with just Trevor left and he had to have a herder. He had to have somebody move the camp. So I don't know who Bert sold his to.....

But [my husband] Art took his money and bought some cows. Art just got $3 a head for his goats and a cow cost a lot more than $3, but he started his herd of cattle that way. He had a place in the Sand Hills that he'd take down in the wintertime, and then we'd bring them back in the spring, and take them up to the ranch [in Skutumpah country] in the summer. He'd drive the cattle and I'd drive the truck. He had his brother **Frank,** who was his partner and both had cattle, help drive them.

Trevor remembers the last herd his dad sold: Dad sold some goats and they were shipped to Cali- fornia, then a big old flood came and killed 'em all, and he never got paid for 'um. He just lost it. I think it was about 1800 goats, or something like that. We trailed 'um to Alton and loaded 'um into trucks, and that was the last I seen of 'um.

Map 39, Northeast Sand Hills: Middle Reservoir, Bush Head & Joe's Ranch

This section and Map 39 covers the eastern 1/5th of the Sand Hills. Let's start with **Middle Reser- voir & Well**. Within about 3 kms in most directions from this place is probably the **3rd most fotogenic** area in the Sand Hills. Located there is a well situated at the east end of a low bench; it still has the old windmill & big metal water tank, plus a new pump powered by propane.

Let's stop here a moment to hear what Richard Cothern said about this well and **windmills** in gen- eral: Some of them windmills are 20 footers [6m], they rate 'um by the diameter of the wheel, but they don't make 20 footers anymore. Dad told me they put a mill on the Bush Head Well that just wasn't pumpin'; couldn't get enough water out. Then I think they put that one on the Middle Reservoir Well. And they used it, but they got water lines running to different places out there and they needed more water, so they put the propane powered pumpjack on it so they could get more water. But that mill turned it alright, and pumped water. You can get 16 foot [5m] mills now and they're probably good down to 1200-1400 feet [about 400m]. If you start gettin' past that you won't get nearly as much water out of it. The reason they went to the pumpjacks was they needed a little more volume quicker. Dad [Beeb Cothern] drilled that one from scratch, and I'm thinking it might be 1400 feet [425m] deep.

Immediately down the short slope east of the well & windmill is a slickrock water catchment made of white BB&CR with orange swirls. At the bottom of that catchment is Middle Reservoir which has 2 little dams made of rock & old logs. The original dams were built by **Joe Hamblin**, which likely goes back to the 1890's, maybe earlier. This and Lower Reservoir and the ponds at Joe's Ranch were the reser- voirs built by Joe and handed over to his sons **Neaf & Rock Hamblin** on May 7, 1924.

Only at the end of long dry spells does this reservoir go dry, so most of the time you can get some really neat fotos with the water & reflections of the windmill in the background. Also, just to the south of the well & windmill, and just off the south side of that low bench, are more BB&CR, and some that are more like a cluster of **rock logs** instead of BB&CR. Also, within a km or so to the south and east are several more clusters of BB&CR or rock logs.

If you drive east about 1 km from the gate & corral at Middle Reservoir, you may see another faint track heading north toward Twin Tanks, Lynn Tank and finally toward Jay Pond. You could also park at Middle Reservoir and walk, and save a lot of sand driving & gas. As for fotos, **Twin Tanks** has some really nice colors & swirls on the slickrock catchment wall, and **Lynn Tank** has some nice stuff just to the east, and to the north a little. **Jay Pond** has nothing of interest for fotographers. **Button Tank** is just to the east and it has some nice colors; walk north to it from the Loop Road.

Map 39, Northeast Sand Hills: Middle Res., Bush H. & Joe's R.

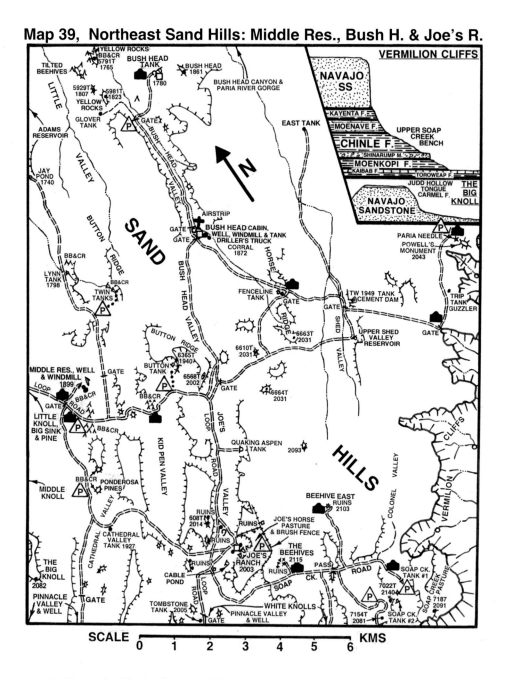

SCALE   0   1   2   3   4   5   6   KMS

As for history, **Jay Findlay** (born in 1943), youngest son of Lynn, and grandson of Merle, tells how he made many of these stock tanks: *We had a D4 Cat and I took it out there and spent time cleaning some old tanks; then I built **Lynn Tank** and **Jay Pond**. North of Jay Pond, I increased the size of **Adams Reservoir**. I also made **Button Tank**, and the **Upper Shed Valley Reservoir**. I also did **Quaking Aspen Reservoir**. Near there was the only quaking aspen tree out there. Then south of Joe's about half a mile [800m] is **Cable Pond**, we Findlays made that one. I was out there 2 different times, in the fall of 1959 & '60; and I was out there 2 years ago, and noticed all of 'um have filled up or washed out.*

From the northern end of **Joe's Valley** (this writter's name), drive north to **Bush Head Cabin & Well**; there are 2 different roads heading that way as shown on the map. You'll also find a corral, storage barn, metal water tank and an old truck that was used in drilling wells, or cleaning them out and pulling pipe. Richard Cothern told the author that his father, **Beeb Cothern** drilled that well a year or so after 1962, and before the house was built.

Middle Reservoir Well & Windmill was drilled and installed by Beeb Cothern in the early 1960's. The windmill is disconnected and now water is pumped with a propane powered engine. From the edge of the little point with the well, looking south at **teepee & BB&CR**. The road to Joe's and Bush Head Country runs through the middle of the far off rocks.

This little upsidedown **D-4 Caterpillar** belonged to the **Findlays**--it's the same one the **Jay** used to build so many ponds in the Central Sand Hills. It tipped over coming off a trailer in 12/1970. And **Lynn Tank**, 4 kms north of Middle Reservoir. There are colorful rocks in the background to the east.

Here's a good place to tell the story of the guy who drilled most of the wells in the Sand Hills. Son Richard tells us: *Dad's name was **William Lloyd Cothern**, otherwise known as Beeb. He had that name for 80 years, because he got it when he was young, but I can't remember how or why. He was born in Amarillo, Texas, but wound up in Tucumcari, New Mexico. Dad worked for a guy named **Bud Mersenfelter**; he owned the rig and the company. Then Dad came into Utah with Bud and was drilling for uranium over by Moab. That was back in the 1950's. Then we moved to Kanab and I was in the 1st grade here in Kanab [age 6--1958-'59], then we moved away for a while, then came back to Kanab in 1962, and I would have been 10. He may have done some drilling in the Sand Hills before we left-- around 1958-'59 (?). So we've been here all the time since 1962, and most of the wells he drilled from scratch were drilled in the first 2, 3 or 4 years after that. Dad drilled **Big Sink, Corral Valley, Rim, Bush Head and Middle Reservoir Wells**, that's 5, then he **deepened Pinnacle Valley and Pine Pockets Wells**. That Bush Head Well wound up being 1800 feet [550m] deep, that's the deepest one out there.*

Basically what he done was, they'd drill a well and then put in a metal water tank right after. I can't remember about the Bush Head tank, it's a bolt-together one. That one at Pinnacle Valley, Dad built it. There's a tank right there at Jarvis itself, I built that one. There's also a bolt-together one there at Jarvis, but then it got to leakin' so I built the other one right close to it. I put up about 6 tanks since dad was out there in the '60's.

*The metal tank at Pine Pockets, I built it. I built the one up on the hill north of Poverty, then there was a loop down to the north and there's about 4 tanks around it that I put up. This is all north of the Poverty Well. All the tanks we put up are **welded**, that's why I was thinking Dad didn't put that one in at Bush Head because it was bolted together.*

Cothern's Drilling Dynasty
Far left is **Beeb Cothern** as a young man sometime in the 1940's; he drilled most of the water wells in the Sand Hills. Next is Beeb's son **Richard Cothern** in high school, 1970. He is now continuing the drilling business began by his father and Bud Mersenfelter. **Cothern & Son Drilling** sign on the door of the truck on the left. This is one of the drilling rigs cobbled together by Beeb-- it's home-made all the way. Both Beeb & Richard could drill & weld, and build anything from scratch.
(Richard Cothern fotos)

We wound up going out in the Sand Hills any time of year--different times for different wells-- depending on where they moved their cattle. We went out fairly regularly in the winter too. We could get around year-round, that truck we had was 2WD. Most of the time we just lowered the pressure in the rear tires--the drive wheels--and it helps a lot. And we drove that country enough so we knew where those sandy spots were and we'd gun it right on through.

There's about 60 miles [100 kms] of **water lines** *running around out there. What they did was they'd rip a trench with a lipper on the back of a Cat, then they had a tube that they mounted on the lipper, then they just fed that plastic pipe down in that ripped trench as they went along, and it covered it up at the end. That's how they done most of it--it was done in one step. It was a lot cheaper that way. That's how they bury these telefon cables and things like that these days, same way. I think they tried to get'um down about 3 feet [1m]. Even then they still have problems of freezing during a real cold winter. Most of the time they run 'um down the middle of the roads, from what I know of it.*

Everyone in Kanab who is familiar with the Sand Hills has stated it was **Jack Mognett** who laid all the water lines on the Plateau. He did it with a D6 Cat with a ripper and pulling a trailer behind carrying the plastic pipe.

Richard Cothern again: *We've lived here ever since 1962. Dad died April 20, 2007 and he's buried in Kanab. He was 86, and the first time he got sick was the fall before he died. We were headed for Bush Head to work on that well. And we got out there and broke a radiator hose on the truck, so we stayed at Pine Pockets that night and we come back, and he was telling me he didn't feel very good. He had lung cancer and had to drain fluid out of his lungs 3 times and they finally gave him about 6 months to live and that's about all he did. But he worked clearn up 'till then. He never smoked.*

Richard Cothern mentions more about Bud Mersenfelter: *I think he helped on some jobs, but I got the impression Dad done a lot of the work. Bud wound up in California, and he was consulting for some-one out there. I think they kinda went out of the drillin' business after they went out there. He moved on anyway, but Dad stayed in Kanab. Then he came by the shop a few years ago when he was 86 years old. That was 10 years ago, and he was about 10 years older than Dad.*

Regarding that old truck at Bush Head Well, here's what Richard said: *The winch on that truck is a little small and I think it wasn't powerful enough for what they needed. I think Dad told me Harold Bowman, who had that area for grazing at that time, had a guy doing mechanic work and I think he overhauled the engine in it, but hadn't done anything to pull that well, so they just parked it there and it's been there ever since. It's actually a 6WD, an old Dodge army truck. We never owned it. As the place got sold & bought, that truck went with it. Later, Dad made up a truck out of a 1953 Chevy with a winch on it and that's what we've been usin' over the last few years to pull the wells.*

But **Ron Glover**, son of Jim Glover who worked as foreman for the Bowmans for many years, had a little different version of the story about the **6WD Dodge Power Wagon**: *That was an old truck that we used when we pulled wells. Beeb Cothern had it fixed it up so we could pull the pipe and casing out of the wells. It used to have an A frame on it and the cable would go up and over the top. The drillin' rig itself Beeb kept on his own truck when he'd come in. It was that old Dodge Power Wagon that we had rigged up for 2-3 different purposes. At one time we had it rigged up with an A frame on the front, and that would have been in the late 1950's and early 1960's, and whenever they brought heifers down from Montana we put 'um all over there at Bush Head. When they were calving, the calves were com-*

ing out too big, and we were loosing a lot of 'em. So we used that Power Wagon with that A frame and we'd drive around and pick'um up--the cows were breaking down in the back when they were calvin'--so we'd pick'em up on a sling we had rigged and we'd haul'em into the corral and get 'em up to water and feed. We lost a lot, but we saved a lot too. So we used that Dodge Power Wagon throughout the '60's & '70's and then Beeb was pullin' wells out there one time and it broke down and so they just left it there at the Bush Head Cabin & Well. See the picture.

The cinder block house at the Bush Head Well was built by **Elmer Rider** in about 1963 or '64, according to his son Richard of Fredonia. Richard Rider was out there the summer his dad built it. Elmer was working for Harold I. Bowman at the time.

There's not a lot to see around the Bush Head Well except for some orange rocks on either side of the valley, so head north again down Bush Head Valley. After about 4 kms (2 1/2 miles), you'll come to a fence & gate; pass through it and immediately turn right or east. Soon you'll be at the **Bush Head Tank**, a reservoir with a cement dam at the bottom of a slickrock water catchment. Also there is an old stockade-type corral and 2 small, one-room cabins.

A document, a deed, from the Coconino County courthouse in Flagstaff tells us that water rights from Bush Head Wash were filed on by **Charles G. Cram** on October 10, 1928. The same document talks about Bush Head Reservoir as well, so it appears that Charley Cram is the one who first built the dam & reservoir at Bush Head. Also, most of the old-timers seem to think it was **Glen Hamblin** and his brother **William F. (Billy) Hamblin**, who built the **2 cabins**. The Hamblins apparently came to this area sometime around 1930 (?). There was an article in the 11/18/1932 issue of the **KCS** that states: *Mr. and Mrs. Glen Hamblin left for the Sandhills last Saturday where they intend to stay three weeks.*

Calvin C. Johnson was there in the summer of 1937 and this is what he remembered: *When I was there in 1937, Glen & [wife] Pruda Hamblin had made a little ol' rock house; it was one room and small, right there on the rock at Bush Head. And he ran about 100 head of cattle right around Bush Head. It was kind of the heart of the range and those other cowboys didn't bother him any--they worked with him and he just kept his cattle right around there all the time. But he'd have to come to Two Mile in the dry times, but we had enough rain then. I don't remember any cement in the dam when I was there. They stayed in a rock house the way I remember it, built of native rock, and the rock was up about 4 feet (?).*

What you have there today are 2 little cabins; one has cement up from ground-level about 1 meter. The cement pony wall likely covers the rock foundation Calvin remembered. In 2009, the author saw the inscription 12/7/1942 written in that cement wall; apparently that part was put in exactly one year after Pearl Harbor. Above that short cement foundation was a simple framed wall. This could have been built about the same time they built a cement dam for the reservoir (?).

There's a second cabin as well. It's a frame shack and covered with rusty tin siding of some kind. About half the siding was gone in 2009. **Ira Schoppman,** who was born in 1935, was there in 1945 or '46 and this is what he remembered: *We used to stay in the cabin at Bush Head, my dad [**John V. Schoppman**] and I, when we worked and gathered cattle for **Roy [Royal] Woolley**; he ran cattle in the Sand Hills. He was from Ogden. We stayed in the cabin that's covered with tin. That would have been in about 1946; that's when my brother Mel was in the service. Glen & Billy Hamblin were brothers and they worked for someone out in the Sand Hills.*

We always lived in Cedar and my dad had to go all the way over to House Rock to take care of things, and he'd be gone for a month at a time. During the summers, he started to take me with him when I was about 10 years old, and I was there for a lot of years. I wasn't in the Sand Hills much, I was always in House Rock [Valley] except when we helped Roy Woolley move his cattle out of the Sand Hills. When we went to Bush Head, we left House Rock at daylight riding horseback and [Glen] was waiting there at Bush Head with the grub ready and the beds made. It was 50 miles from House Rock Valley out there to Bush Head Tank, and by gad I'll tell ya they used a 2WD 1937 International pickup to get out there--he'd let the air partly out of the tires.... I can't believe he could do it.

Trevor Leach was down that way a time or two, and knew Glen & Pruda: *Glen hauled all that stuff in there in a little dodge pickup--and it wasn't a 4WD! Glen used to bring his cattle in to Two Mile Spring to ship the calves, and I helped him & Pruda get their cattle out to Joe's.* **Pruda Woolley Hamblin** was

Both fotos are from **Bush Head Well**. **Top** From the corrals looking southeast at the well (left) and former windmill, with the cinder block house on the right. **Below** The same Bush Head Cabin built by Elmer Rider in the early 1960's; and the old 1940's **Dodge Power Wagon**.

Glen's wife. They never did have any kids, but they did have a great big old dog.

Glen Hamblin was a descendent of Frances Marian Hamblin, a brother to Jacob. Pruda Woolley Hamblin was the daughter of Edwin D. Woolley, Jr., and according to her obituary (7/2/1997--KCS), a half sister to Royal (Roy) B. Woolley (apparently the same fellow mentioned above), who ran a lot of cows in the Sand Hills in the 1940's & '50's.

According to some documents dug up at the BLM office in St. George, *Billy Hamblin **quit claimed** to Royal B. Woolley 2/3 interest in Bush Head Reservoir in April, 1940*. That's the reason Roy Woolley was grazing cattle in the Bush Head Allotment along with Glen. Later, and about the time Ira Schoppman went out there that summer of 1946, *Glen & Pruda Hamblin quit claimed to Royal B. Woolley 1/3 interest in water rights for Bush Head Reservoir on August 17, 1946*. This was apparently the time Glen & Pruda got out of the cow business in the Sand Hills.

Still later, and on the same document, *Roy Woolley quit claimed Bush Head Reservoir Allotment to Harold I. Bowman, a relative Melvin G. Bowman & son-in-law John P. Rich, April 17, 1959*. The next owner of the Bush Head Allotment may have been **Dan Ramsey** (?) & the **Ramsey Cattle Company**.

Bush Head Well & Cabin from the air looking west. The cabin & old truck left; well & water tank, bottom center; the corrals & small barn or shed in the upper right.

Bush Head Tank, with the corrals in the background to the left. The cement part was put in sometime after 1937, according to Calvin C. Johnson. It was surely **Glen Hamblin** who put it in.

Glen & Pruda Hamblin, likely about the time they were married which was on June 26, 1927 (or July 27, 1928-- depending on whose obituary you're reading!). They never had children, so it was hard rounding up these fotos from the *Kanab Heritiage Museum*. They lived at Bush Head Tank & the little cement & frame cabin shown on the next page, for the better part of the 1930's, and perhaps into the '40's (?). Glen died in April, 1971; his bother Billy Hamblin died 4 months later. Pruda Woolley Hamblin, who attended the U. of Utah and Utah State U. before she was married, died in June, 1997 at the age of 94.

The one **cabin** at **Bush Head Tank** that was rocked-up, then cemented-up, apparently in 1942. In the left background is the other cabin that's covered with some kind of rusty sheet metal.

Paria Needle left, **Powell's Monument** right. Access road is in the lower left. In the far background left, and below the cliffs, is Lee's Ferry and Marble Canyon.

After Ramsey, the entire Sand Hills was put together for the first time with **Two Mile Corp & Vern Carner**. More on Sand Hills ownership is discussed later under Joe's Ranch history.

In that general area, there's supposed to be a metal water tank named **Glover Tank**, which this writter wasn't aware of at the time of his visit. This could only be named after Jim Glover (Ron's father) who worked as foreman for the Bowmans for many years. North of that are some colorful rocks at the end of some ridges not far from the Lower Paria River Gorge. You can get down into the canyon via 2 routes in this area; next to Bush Head Canyon, and the Moki Trail near Wrather Canyon.

From Bush Head, let's go back to the south to **Shed Valley**. There are a couple of reservoirs there, the **Upper Shed Valley Reservoir** (built by Jay Findlay as a high schooler in about 1960) is washed out. The sand is really deep just below that as the water which took out the dam, dumped the sand right in

Ranchers probably call this the **Lower Shed Valley Reservoir**, but it has the initials **TW 1949**, on top of the dam, thus this name. Behind the camera is what appears to be a wall of **Stromatolites**--perhaps a buildup of blue green algae in an interdunal lake, swamp or wet place, which trapped carbonate crystals which gradually enlarged layer upon layer, and was finally replaced by iron (petrification).

the road. The lower Shed Valley tank is a cement dam with the initials, **TW 1949**; thus the author's name of this tank (TW may be Tony Woolley, who worked on the Adams water pump along the Paria River). Some may call it Lower Shed Valley Tank (?). It's now filled with sand and useless for water storage. Surely it must have been one of the Woolleys (?) who put that one in. Next to that dam is an outcropping that has the appearance of a **reef** (read above)--but in the middle of Navajo Sandstone (?).

From there, drive southeast along a fenceline to a gate right where the bottom drops out of the Sand Hills. From there it's only about 3 kms to the **Paria Needle & Powell's Monument**, a couple of big Navajo Sandstone buttes. There's supposed to be one Anasazi granary on the other side of the obvious canyon, but the author missed that one. There are also a couple of small rock art panels on the southwest side of the Paria Needle, but there's not a lot to see in that part of the Sand Hills either in the way of Anasazi ruins or picture taking. But you will have some nice views of the valley below.

Way back to the west is **Cathedral Valley** which has a big metal water tank & trough. There are some pretty good BB&CR in the north, then just to the south of those, a few more, with one water pocket on top that's filled with pottery fragments. That's the little high ground which has a dozen or so ponderosa pines. In the southwest corner of the map is **The Big Knoll**, sometimes called **Red Knoll**, or **Big Red Knoll**. It has several pinnacles on the south side, but it's not worth the hike.

Kid Pen Valley doesn't have much to fotograph, but here's what Trevor Leach stated: *Pert near everybody out there had goats at one time, and I think Joe Hamblin had a **kiddin' corral** there. They was really worth something back then--I mean the mohair was.*

In **Joe's Valley** (author's name) south of **Quaking Aspen Tank**, and on either side, are a number of crude **Anasazi ruins**. Those on the west side are found at the base of the low buttes. None of these are big, and they aren't very interesting, but there are pottery fragments at all sites. The reason for this concentration of habitation sites is the proximity to the big slickrock watershed above **Joe's Ranch**. At Joe's you'll find 4 ponds or reservoirs, but one has water almost all the time. Lots of pottery there too. This catchment is perhaps the 4th best fotogenic place in the Sand Hills. Most of these are like log rocks and almost pure white.

The buildings you see there now we think were built by **A.T. Spence** (he bought the place on September 9, 1941) then he sold out to **Merle Findlay** on **March 3, 1945**. Joe's original cabin is long gone, but some of his stockade-type fences may still be there. Walk up through the catchment and you'll see either a **brush**, or **rip gut fence** running right along the rim of the watershed. It looks real old. Also, walk in any direction from the catchment rim, and you'll eventually come to another brush or rip gut fence. That was apparently built by Joe Hamblin, and Trevor says that was his **horse pasture**.

Jay Findlay was a little too young to remember personally, but other members of his family have told him about what was there at Joe's when his grandfather, Merle Findlay, bought the place: *That old cabin of Joe's and all that stuff had been taken down and that new house & barn and a saddle shed was made with lumber that was hauled off the Kaibab Forest. But the **blacksmiths shop** was made out of the lumber from the old **Joe Hamblin cabin**. This was all done by A.T. Spence just before the Findlay's bought him out in March of 1945.*

Now the old **crib**, something like a **well**, that Hamblin had there was still in existence when we came in; that's where he got his drinking water. There was a wooden crib down in there about 25 feet [8m] deep, all wooded up, about 6'x6' [2x2m]. From the upper pond where the water came off the slickrock, they had a little cement dike and the water settled in the sand and seeped underground. Just south the cabin there's a pond dug there, then just east of it was another little pond, and right in the center of it

291

Aerial view looking eastward, down at **Joe's Ranch**, stock ponds or reservoirs, and most of the water catchment. Lower left are the ranch houses built between 1941 & '45. The big pond, known in the courthouse and BLM records as **Home Ranch Reservoir**, is in the middle.

February 17, 2008, with ice on the **Home Ranch Reservoir** at **Joe's Ranch**. This is the main pond at Joe's, but there are 3 other smaller ones in the immediate area.

Just east of the buildings & main stock pond at **Joe's Ranch**, is part of the **water catchment**, one of the best in the Sand Hills. There are no springs here, but there's always water in the sand below.

The ranch buildings at Joe's were built in the early 1940's by **A.T. Spence**, just before the Findlay's bought the private ranch property and the water rights.

Just south of **Joe's Ranch** buildings & stock ponds is the southern part of the water catchment.

Part of the enclosure fence to **Joe's Horse Pasture**. Some is rip gut or stake & rider like this, other portions are made of trees & limbs just laid on the ground to form a fence to keep horses in.

Left Merle Findlay beside his 1950-something Dodge Power Wagon, the first 4WD vehicle after the Jeep at that time. **Right Lynn Findlay** & his wife in 1935-'36.

Left Dunk Findlay just south of the **Pinnacle Valley Well** repairing a leaky pipeline. The well was the first to be drilled in the Sand Hills in 1953. **Right Jay Findlay**, one of the sons of Lynn Findlay. Jay, as a high schooler, built most of the little reservoirs in the central Sand Hills with a D4 Cat.

Soap Creek catchment near the edge of the Sand Hills. Looking west at the little butte labeled **7022** (2140m) on the map. On this day, 2/18/2009, snow was covering some of the better formations.

was where the crib was. The Bowmans dug that great big pond that wasn't there when we were there; water run out of the upper pond then into the crib pond, then into the lowest one. And we used to pump water out of that crib for cows when it was dry.

Now if you go up the fenceline south about 200 yards [180m], there's a **cave** in there. And it had a lot of Indian sign in it and my grandfather said that some of the old timers used to sleep in there. As you drive up from Jarvis right into Joe's on the right-hand-side there's a new fence that goes up to the pasture that they made. And about 200 yards up that fenceline on the left is a big cave. I found some little corn cobs and different things in there. It was south of where the houses are.

Now let's finish the history of ownership of Joe's Ranch. Merle Findlay and his sons Lynn & Dunk (Duncan) had it from 1945, then Merle died on **April 1, 1959**. After that, the 2 sons managed the place as one unit and for a while, but according to everyone familiar with the Findlay family, those 2 brothers fought like mules. So finally they split up, and according to courthouse records, that date was **September 19, 1962**. **Dunk** got Pinnacle Valley & Well, and the Jarvis Ranch & pasture; while **Lynn** got Joe's, Middle & Lower Reservoirs and the Shed Valley area.

Then on **May 31, 1963**, Lynn sold Joe's Ranch and all the other reservoirs & water rights to the **Vermilion Cliffs Cattle Company**; that was **Harold I. Bowman** and his son-in-law John Rich, Sr. At that time the Bowmans, as everyone calls that outfit, had the Bush Head country and the eastern Sand Hills, plus what they got from Lynn Findlay, and White Pockets, Pine Pockets, Big Sink, Frank's Pasture and Moquitch Pasture Allotments.

In the **A. D. (Dunk) Findlay Case File** from the BLM office in St. George, there's a memorandum dated August 28, 1981. Part of what it stated goes like this: Closure of A. D. Findlay Case File. On March 5, 1981, an application of transfer from A. D. Findlay to Ramsey Cattle Company was approved.... This transfer included all of Mr. Findlay's grazing privileges on the Arizona Strip.... deeds can be found in the **Ramsey Cattle Company** Case File.... Any future business on the Home Ranch Allotment should be refereed to **Dan Ramsey**, Winslow, Arizona.

But, on a document from Coconino County courthouse dated **December 16, 1983**, the actual sale of Joe's Ranch which is in Section 31, T40N R6E was filed. It went to Ramsey Cattle Co. Inc. Keep in mind, this plot of land was the only private property in the Sand Hills, which is filed differently than water rights--but the 2 go hand-in-hand. Next transfer was on **April 13, 1984**. Dan Ramsey sold out to the **Two Mile Corp**, and **Vern Carner**. At that time or shortly there after, Vern obtained other allotments & water rights, and for the first time, put the entire Sand Hills under the ownership of one outfit.

The next transfer took place on **June 18, 1988**. That's when **Mark Stephensen** and **Jay Wright** bought the Sand Hills from Two Mile Corp & Vern Carner. Then on **June 2, 1992**, Stephensen & others sold out to **Kay Sturdevant** from Springville, Utah (he now lives in nearby Benjamin). Sturdevant had it only 6 years and during those years he stated they ran between 1200 & 1500 head of cattle on the Paria Plateau & the Two Mile Allotment. Finally on **October 26, 1998**, Kay sold out to **David Gelbaum** and the **Kane Ranch Land Stewardship & Cattle Co**. After that, and on **September 28, 2005**, the entire Sand Hills was bought by the **North Rim Ranch, LLC**. This was some kind of conservancy organization. But then on **January 29, 2009**, there was a name change, now it's the **Grand Canyon Trust**. This outfit would like to take all cattle off the Sand Hills, but prior bylaws require they keep cat-

Above According to one source this is a foto of 4 Johnson brothers and (?)--L to R; Sixtus, Seth, Joel, Nephi (**Neaf**) **Hamblin (?)** & Justin (**Jet**) **Johnson** (he developed **Coyote Spring**). The younger boy in the upper right, who looks a lot different than the others, is supposed to be Neaf Hamblin who was raised by Nephi Sr. & Mandana Johnson after his mother, Joe Hamblin's wife, died when he was a baby. But there is contradictory information about who is in this picture! (Kanab Heritiage Museum foto) **Above Right Fay Hamblin** in white, son of Walt (Joe's half-brother--same father, different wife--lots of that in polygamy Utah), hob-nobbing with Utah Gov. Calvin H. Rampton in the 1960's (?). Fay was a ramrod for bringing movie makers to southern Utah to make cowboy shoot'um-up picture shows (Jeff Frost foto). **Right Joseph Rosco (Rock) Hamblin** was the brother of Neaf Hamblin, both of whom were the sons of Joe Hamblin (Rock Burgoyne foto). **Below Right Walt Hamblin** in his younger days. Walt was born in 1868, so if he were 22 here, it would be 1890 when this studio picture was taken (Jeff Frost foto--Fay Hamblin's grandson). **Below** This is part of what the author calls the **Best Ruins** in the White Knolls. Almost all ruins in the Sand Hills are the hill-top variety.

Just northwest of the **Jarvis Ranch**, and just off the road to the north, is this **cement dam** immediately below a slickrock catchment. It likely has water all the time, plus it's full of cattails.

tle there, so they lease it out.

In 2005, 18 or 19 allotments were awarded to **Tyson Johnson** (grandson of Calvin C. Johnson) and **Brent Robinson**, both of Kanab. They run cattle there year-round, but move the cows from one pasture to another every 2-3 months **JR Jones** has 2 winter pastures or allotments; but he has to move his cows out in the summer. Read the early history of Joe's near the beginning of this chapter.

If you're in this part of Joe's Valley, remember there's a **big deep sand trap** just before arriving at Joe's and going in both directions for a total of up to 250-300m. If things are dry and it's been churned up by lots of traffic, that can be one of the **worst places** in the Sand Hills, so **gear down and rev up good!**

Southwest of Joe's and in the area west of Tombstone Tank are a bunch of fotogenic little buttes or mesas that are often bypassed. Also, on the bottom part of Map 39, are some interesting places. Southwest of Joe's about 1 km is a junction. From there head south from the Loop Road at a little usually-dry pond or tank that looks like just a depression. The **Soap Creek Road** runs southeast to near the edge of the Vermilion Cliffs and the Soap Creek Pasture. Along the way are **The Beehives** and **Beehive East**, both with ruins. Those on **Beehive East** are some of the best in the Sand Hills. Further along, you'll eventually reach **Soap Creek Tank #1**. In that area are lots of BB&CR with various colors, including perhaps 4th or 5th best place in the Sand Hills for taking pictures of colorful rocks.

History wise, Trevor Leach tells part of his experience there: *Soap Creek Pasture & Tanks, that's where they used to wean their calves. There's kind of a rip gut fence out there too. Johnny Adams may have built those dams (?) [or perhaps A.T. Spence?]. I helped 'um take their weaners out there one time. Those earth tanks was built with a team & fresno scrapper. I went out there and helped Johnny Adams for a week or two once.*

Map 40, Southern Sand Hills: Jarvis Ranch & the White Knolls

In the southern Sand Hills, one of the more interesting places to visit is the **White Knolls** (a knoll is a hill, butte or small mesa). What makes this place interesting are no less than a dozen **Anasazi ruins**, most of which are on hill-tops. There are no real cliff dwellings in alcoves like you see in so many other places on the Colorado Plateau. As you drive along the White Knolls Loop Road, be looking for places where others, looking for ruins, have parked. In 2009, there were few such places, but this area will become more popular soon. Also in 2009, there was a new road running along the base of the knolls instead of out in the valley along the old now-unused road shown on the USGS maps. Only in recent years has this place seen any visitors. As you drive along, have a map handy and match the ruins (marked with an R) with altitudes shown. All walks are short and easy. The site titled, **Best Ruins** on Map 40--next page--just north of the elevation **7173T** (2186m), are less than a km from the Loop Road. They have walls over a meter high.

For anyone looking for an interesting hike, try this. About halfway between Jarvis Ranch and the southern White Knolls is a minor depression marked **6757T** (2060m). Park there, then using a map & compass, head southwest for the rim of the Vermilion Cliffs and the **Eastern Sand Hills Crack**. It's less than a km. Walk down a ways to find half a dozen good **rock art panels** on the north side of a minor

298

Map 40, Southern Sand Hills: Jarvis Ranch & the White Knolls

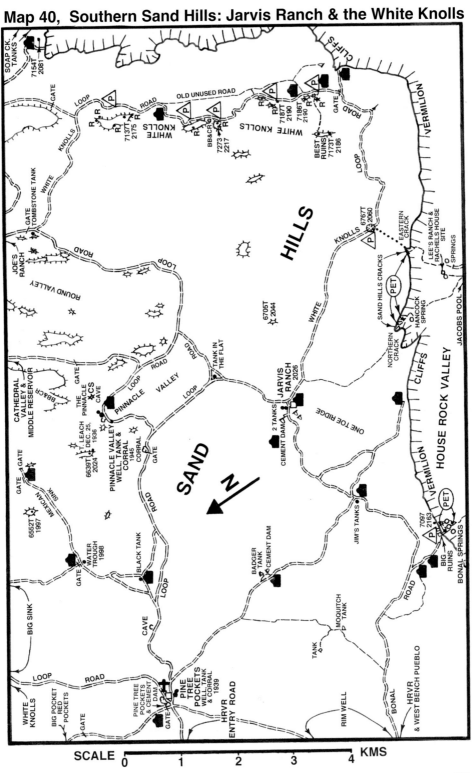

SCALE 0 1 2 3 4 KMS

drainage facing south. You can also get to this crack from Jacobs Pool & Lee's Ranch located below.

The **Jarvis Ranch** is an interesting place. Located there is a rather nice home--it used to be a lot better than it is now--a storage barn, and a couple of metal water tanks. Just west of the white house is what used to be a nice cellar. Still further west are a couple of dams & reservoirs but they're both partly washed out. If you drive west on the road heading for Jim's Tanks about 300-400m, look to the right or north to see a little road running less than 100m to a **cement dam** in the drainage below a slickrock catchment. That has water in it year-round, along with cattails. It's also a nice place to camp.

The Jarvis Ranch came about and had something to do with the grazing rights changes back in the mid-1930's as a result of the **Taylor Grazing Act** of **1934**. The late Dunk Findlay said: *Arthur Jarvis never got a permit to run cattle--he was not there in the priority period [If you hadn't been grazing cows in a given area during the period of 1928-'34, then you weren't allowed to have grazing privileges unless you bought someone else out]. Jarvis was working for Walt Hamblin (Fay's dad) when the BLM finally gave him a small allotment of 3 or 4 State Sections.* (Another version of this story states that Jarvis leased land from a state section.) According to Dunk, Jarvis never had many cows, maybe 15 or so, but they built a fine ranch house anyway, which is just north of the Northern Sand Hills Crack. That was in 1935.

The Jarvis house isn't just a line cabin or a bunk house, but a nice home; or it was. It's painted white, has five good-sized rooms and a propane gas lighting & cooking system. There was even a refrigerator, which was run on propane. Water was collected by the use of roof rain gutters & down-pipes, which funneled rainwater into a cistern below the house.

On the Water Resources map drawn by the **S.M. Miera Survey** of **April, May & June of 1937**, it shows the cement dam and a 2000 gallon galvanized water tank and the place was called the **Tres Piños Ranch**. Just after this survey was made, Calvin C. Johnson was there in the early summer of 1937 as a 14-year old kid. Here's what he remembered: *At Arthur Jarvis's Ranch, we stayed inside this old shed, then Mrs. Jarvis had me come in the house--she was like my 2nd mother for a while. In 1937, it was a nice home. Jarvis had deer horn furniture, which he made himself, but he had an old fellow who helped 'im. That old man must have been in his 60's, but I don't know if they were related or not. I think that house had been there a couple of years when I was there, it must have been built in about 1935. I don't remember the propane lighting, that was put in later. They had coal oil lamps when I was there.*

Jarvis may have had a vehicle, because he had a lot of lumber in there. And I don't remember him having a team [of horses]. So someone hauled it in for him, or he owned a truck. There was no vehicles out there when I was there.

When **A.T. Spence** got a hold of the ranch on **March 31, 1941**, he (according to Dunk Findlay) used the *house for his main headquarters. He had built the house at the Lower Reservoir, and it and the house at Joe's were used as line cabins. Spence added 2 more rooms to the original Jarvis house. He said not to spoil a good thing he put hard wood floors in them too.*

After Dunk and his brother Lynn divided the range in 1962 (after their father Merle died in 1959), Dunk made this house his headquarters. It was Dunk Findlay who put the propane lights and refrigerator in the house in about 1962. He installed a bolt-together metal tank next to the barn, and pumped water to it from the Pinnacle Valley Well after 1953. This was done by a small portable gasoline engine.

Richard Cothern, son of Beeb Cothern, states that he did some work at Jarvis: *There's a tank right there at Jarvis, I built that one. But there's an older bolt-together tank there too, but then it got to leaking, so I built another one close by.*

Just northeast of Jarvis is the **Tank in the Flat**. This is a welded job and was built by Beeb Cothern. Son Richard has told this writter that all the welded metal water tanks in the Sand Hills were constructed by Beeb earlier on, or himself after the 1960's.

In the area southeast of Jarvis, along the road to the White Knolls, you may notice a small area that's been chained. That area is called the **Jarvis Pasture**. While going through old files in the St. George BLM office, the author found a document in the A.D. (Dunk) Findlay Case History File. It was a form titled, *Assignment of Cooperative Agreements or Range Improvement Permits*, and it lists several range projects that had been approved by the BLM. One project was titled, *Sand Hills Juniper Eradication*, and it was in Sections 19, 20, 29, 30, in T39N, R5E. It was signed by Lynn F. Findlay, but it was in his brother Dunk's allotment. The date was 9/19/1962. The chaining likely took place that fall or winter (?).

Ron Glover mentioned 2 other places in the Sand Hills that had been chained. One was near the Rim Well located along the Bonal Road (see **Map 41**): *They had it chained when I was there in the late 1950's or early '60's; we (the Bowmans and their foreman, Jim Glover) had 2 cats come in and chained that and the Pine Pasture for us. They did chaining on all of those areas in about the same time period- -Jarvis, Rim Well and the Pine Pockets Pastures.*

Regarding range improvement projects like chaining, building fences, corrals or water storage reservoirs, wells, etc. on the public domain, **Whit Bunting**, formerly of Kanab, but who was the head Range Conservation Officer in the St. George BLM office for the Arizona Strip in 2009, had this to say: *A Section 4 Permit, which they don't have anymore, but back in the time you're researching now, were projects that were 100% funded by the operator or permittee. So the permittee had ownership; they didn't own the ground, but they owned the project. And that's one of the things that's bought & sold when they're transferred to another permittee or livestock man.*

But most of our projects now are Coop Agreements; this means the government owns the project but there's still whatever proportion that the permittee contributed to the project they will have ownership in it. In other words, whatever the labor was to construct a fence for instance, the permittee would have that portion of the project, and then the government would own the other portion. In other words, the cost of doing a project is shared by the BLM and the rancher grazing cows out there somewhere.

Moving west on a well-traveled road we find **Jim's Tanks**. This is different than most of the metal tanks in the Sand Hills. What you'll find there are 2 metal water storage tanks partially underground. These are situated about 75m below a water catchment made of galvanized roofing panels which is about 30-40m in size. Rain or snow falls on this raised catchment, then it flows down to the 2 tanks and is stored. Below that somewhere will be watering troughs which operate with a float valve. When cows drink so much water, more water comes in, just like the float valve in a toilet's tank. Sometimes these are called trip tanks or guzzlers.

Ron Glover says: *They were installed by my dad, Jim Glover, who worked for Harold I. Bowman. It would have been in the early 1970's when they put it in.*

If you drive west from Jim's Tanks 3.3 kms (2 miles), you'll come to a junction with a hard left turn to the south. Drive another km or so, and you'll come to a trailhead at the wilderness boundary. Walk from there about 250m and you'll come to the rim and the top of the route down to Bonal Spring. Located

These old **1920-something trucks** are hauling either sheeps wool or Angora goat mohair to the railway line in Lund, Utah (in Utah's West Desert west of Cedar City). (Kanab Heritage Museum foto)

there are 3 cement water troughs and perhaps the biggest **Anasazi ruins** in the Sand Hills.

Before going further, the name **Bonal** needs to be explained. In previous editions, the author called & spelled it **Bonelli**--that's what Dunk Findlay called the guy and the spring. However, in researching this 5th edition, a collection of 10 maps were found in the BLM office in St. George. They were hand drawn by a survey crew signed **S.M. Miera, March 25, 1937**. They spelled the name of this place **Bonal Spring**. Surely this is correct (?), and will be used from now on. Other documents have this name.

A better history of Bonal Spring will be told along with the hikes to the Sand Hills Cracks, but for now let's hear what Trevor Leach had to say about his experience in about 1935: *We went out there and Johnny Adams had me punching cows, and Lee Averett pumping water from Bonal Spring to up on top. He had to go down that crack and start that pump to get water up. Lee was working for Johnny Adams because Bonal was out of it at the time. We called it the **Bonal Spring & Bonal Road** in the mid-1930's when I was 15 years old.*

The road Trevor mentioned is the one that Bonal built/used in the short time he was there. If you follow it northwest, you'll end up at the West Bench Ruins and the House Rock Valley Road (HRVR). But for now let's head north from Jim's Tanks about 3.6 kms (2.3 miles) and be looking closely to the right or east. Somewhere there is a track running to a couple of reservoirs or tanks. One is washed out, a second is a cement dam in a little mini canyon in the slickrock. In the early days these were called **Badger Tanks**. From this place continue northwest toward Pines. After about an other 1 1/2 kms (1 mile) is the turnoff going west toward Moquitch Tank. There's nothing to see there and it's washed out. But Ron Glover was there: *At **Moquitch Tank**, you could usually dig down and find water, so we dug down and put in some of that leech line pipe and covered it with rock, gravel rock, and for a while we had water--until a flood came down and took everything out.*

Sand Hills as of 2010

Tyson Johnson, grandson of Calvin C. Johnson informed this writer of the status of Sand Hills cattle grazing as this book goes to press: *There are **18 or 19 fenced pastures** in the Sand Hills, and 4 or 5 smaller trap-type pastures. And me and Brent Robinson, my partner, have all of them but 2. JR Jones has 2 winter pastures--Poverty, White Pockets and Cottonwood are the 2 pastures he uses in the winter time. He takes his cows out somewhere else for the summer.*

We change the cows to a new pasture about every 3 months, but a lot of that is dictated by the BLM; they come up with the management plan. They go out and check the feed, and make changes according to what's available. The spring of 2009 was excellent, lots of real good feed.

In the past, some of the fences were put in by the BLM--or a private contractor put them in for the BLM--and some were, and still are, put in by the ranchers. It's not like all the fences went in at the same time; they fence off pastures, then they might decide to cut one in half.

We've got about 600 head [of cows] out there right now, but that all depends on the BLM [and the amount of rain]. The AMP, the Area Management Plan, has it rated for up to 1400 and some change--just under 1500 head. But we've been in a pretty bad drought in the last few years, so there haven't been that many cows out there. We have our 600 cows in 3 herds, and so they're in 3 pastures right now.

*For any capital improvement that needs to be done the **Grand Canyon Trust** does that. They put the liner in the tank at Joe's, but it's not holding up. We've been out there since 2005, about 4 years. The Trust bought it I think in 2005, and there weren't any cattle on the place then. They bought it from a guy named Gelbaum and he had taken all the cattle off [because of the lack of feed caused by the drought] so there hadn't been any cattle there for about 4 years before I got out there.*

Next stop will be House Rock Valley and a new map.

Hike to Hod Brown Spring & Rock Art Panel, History of House Rock Valley, and the Condor Release Program

Location & Access The **House Rock Valley** is located immediately south & southwest of the Sand Hills, south of **Coyote Buttes** & the Wire Pass Trailhead, and due north of what used to be a gas station & store, now just a rented ranch house, called **House Rock** on Highway 89A.

The best way to get to this area is to drive along **Highway 89A** about halfway between Jacob Lake and the Navajo Bridge over the Colorado at Marble Canyon. When you come to House Rock (now a white stone ranch house) between **mile posts 565 & 566**, turn north onto the **House Rock Valley Road (HRVR)**. This is a good graded county road and maintained well enough for cars. Drive 4.5 kms (2.8 miles) to the Condor Viewing site on your right; at Km 5.9 (Mile 3.7) is the turnoff to the Curtis & Delwin Hamblin Ranch, and Hod Brown Spring; at Km 8.9 (Mile 5.5) is the turnoff to One & Two Mile Springs; at Km 12.8 (Mile 8) is the turnoff to the Bonal Road and the big ruins of West Bench Pueblo (that road is graveled up to the ruins, but it's sandy beyond that). If you continue north along the HRVR, at Km 15 (Mile 9.3) will be Bowman's Corral & the turnoff to the main Entry Road for the Sand Hills.

Trail/Route The only real hike here is up to **Hod Brown Spring** and one of the biggest rock art/petroglyph panels found anywhere. From where you turn off the HRVR, head east about 150m past a couple of sheds or barns, a water trough & corral (next to the old chimney--more on this later), cross a dry wash, and after about 500m (.3 mile), turn south as shown on the map. Finally after 2.1 kms (1.3 miles) park where the road is blocked off at the wilderness boundary. From there, walk roughly 1 km to the old **Hod Brown Ranch** site, the history of which is discussed on the following pages. At Hod's Place, you'll find a cement water trough, small pen next to a large boulder with cowboy signatures (one is F.H. Farnsworth 1936--this was F.L. Farnsworth's son), and a kind of a rip rap water storage reservoir (?).

From Hod's Place scramble up the steep slope in a northeast direction following an **old pipeline**; one line is made of steel, the other is plastic. When you reach the first **cliff band**, either turn left a ways to find a route up through it; or, **best** to turn right or east. Immediately, you'll see the pipe running up through a wooden sleeve leaning against the cliff face. From there continue east 40m to find a good **rock art panel**. Just beyond that is a steep climbing route up the cliff. If that's too much for you, continue east along the base of the cliff until you come to a sandy area which covers the ledge, then scramble straight up to the **Hod Brown Spring**. Along that sandslide are what seems like millions of **pottery fragments**. The only thing to see at the spring is a bunch of reeds & grasses along a 100m section that's always wet. In the past, 3 little springs were developed at the base of that cliff, which is just to the right or east of the **condor roosting site** with all the white manure running down the rocks.

The best thing to see in this area is a big **rock art panel**, all petroglyphs, that's close to 150m long. The first part begins about 100m east of the where the pipe comes out of the hole & spring. If you walk east past the rock art and along the base of those big cliffs, you'll find 2 routes up to the top of the plateau. The first is a little steep and it goes up through a tight crack. Best to continue southeast along the base of the cliff. If you watch carefully, you'll see occasional **pottery fragments**, which tells this writer, this is a trail or route used by Anasazi going to or from the top of the Sand Hills. Roughly 600m from the spring, watch closely for one last rock art panel--it's small but a nice one. At that point, scramble & route-find zig zag fashion up the slope to the top. Return the same way.

NOTE: You'll be crossing private land (John Rich of Jacob Lake & St. George) where the barns & old chimney are, so please don't mess with anything there--or this access route may be closed.

Elevation Trailhead, 1695m; Hod Brown Spring, 1890m; Rim of Sand Hills/Paria Plateau, 2012m.

Time Needed To the big petroglyph panel is only about 1 1/2 kms, with a rise of about 200m, so it can be done in an hour, but you'll want 2-3 hours or more to see all the rock art and return.

Water The pipeline from Hod Brown Spring is completely broken and hasn't been used in years, and you'd have to work to get a drink from the spring, so take your own water.

Maps USGS or BLM maps Fredonia, but also have Glen Canyon Dam (1:100,000) for better regional coverage for driving & orientation; and House Rock Valley (1:24,000--7 1/2' quad) for hiking.

Main Attractions Historic ranch sites and one of the biggest & best rock art panels anywhere.

Best Time to Hike Spring or fall, but you can hike here year-round.

Boots/Shoes Any comfortable hiking boots or shoes.

Author's Experience He discussed this place with Bob Ford & Dixon Spendlove of Fredonia, and Trevor Leach & Mark Hamblin of Kanab in conjunction with the history of several of the places in the House Rock Valley. It took 2 hikes to the spring & mesa top to see everything; the trips lasted 1 3/4 hours & 3 3/4 hours, but both trips were for scouting & exploring so a lot of time was spent backtracking, etc.

Other Interesting Sites and History

Bowman's Corral Just off the upper or northern part of this map is the Bowman's Corral on the left at the junction of the House Rock Valley Road and the **Entry Road** running east into the Sand Hills. Trevor Leach tells a little about the corral which is a good land mark in that area: *That's Bowman's Corral, and they used to ship their cattle from there. In fact, I've shipped from there myself. They used to have scales there and trucks would come up from House Rock to get the cows. The Bowmans built it, or had it built anyway. It was probably in the late 1940's or around in there when they did it. There was an old boy who built it--what he done was bored holes through them posts and put rebar in the holes and bent the rebar down--instead of using nails or spikes.*

West Bench Pueblo If you're not so much into hiking, or you don't have a 4WD and are not quite ready for the Sand Hills, you can still see one of the more impressive Anasazi ruins around. This one's called the West Bench Pueblo. If coming from the south, the turnoff from the HRVR is 12.8 kms (8 kms) from Highway 89A; if coming from the north, it's 2.1 kms (1.3 miles) south of Bowman's Corral and the turnoff for the Entry Road to the Sand Hills. From the **HRVR**, drive any car northeast 1 km (.6 mile) along a **graded & graveled road** to the ruins which will be on your left or north, just before the **Bonal Road** turns east. These ruins are very typical of others found in the Sand Hills. This one is on the rim of an escarpment with a nice view to the west; the Anasazi always liked an unobstructed view in at least one direction. This site is within walking distance of water at Two Mile Spring, and it's laid out in a rectangular pattern with a courtyard in the middle. It was studied in 1967 & 2007, and it appears to have been influenced by both the Virgin & Kayenta Anasazi cultures to the south and from across the Colorado River. When built, many rooms appear to have had walls about a meter or a little more in height, then logs and brush must have been laid on top. The roofs have long since decayed because most ruins in the Sand Hills are hill-top sites. Nearby along the rim are at least 2 more insignificant ruins as shown.

Map 41, Hike to Hod Brown Spring & Rock Art Panel, History of House Rock Valley, and the Condor Release Program

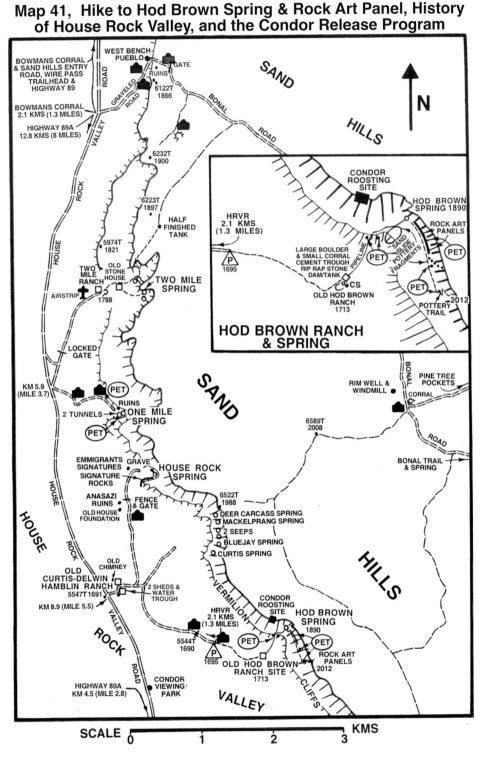

BOWMANS CORRAL & SAND HILLS ENTRY ROAD, WIRE PASS TRAILHEAD & HIGHWAY 89

WEST BENCH PUEBLO

GATE

RUINS

6122T 1866

SAND

HILLS

N

BOWMANS CORRAL 2.1 KMS (1.3 MILES)

HIGHWAY 89A 12.8 KMS (8 MILES)

GRAVELED ROAD

VALLEY ROAD

BONAL ROAD

6232T 1900

6223T 1897

HALF FINISHED TANK

ROCK

5974T 1821

HOUSE

TWO MILE RANCH

OLD STONE HOUSE

AIRSTRIP

1788

TWO MILE SPRING

CONDOR ROOSTING SITE

HOD BROWN SPRING 1890

ROCK ART PANELS

HRVR 2.1 KMS (1.3 MILES)

P 1695

LARGE BOULDER & SMALL CORRAL CEMENT TROUGH RIP RAP STONE DAM/TANK

PIPELINE

SAND SLIDE

PET

POTTERY FRAGMENTS

PET

CS

OLD HOD BROWN RANCH 1713

PET

2012

POTTERY TRAIL

HOD BROWN RANCH & SPRING

LOCKED GATE

KM 5.9 (MILE 3.7)

PET

RUINS

2 TUNNELS

ONE MILE SPRING

PET

SAND

HILLS

RIM WELL & WINDMILL

PINE TREE POCKETS

CORRAL

BONAL

6589T 2008

ROAD

BONAL TRAIL & SPRING

EMMIGRANTS SIGNATURES

GRAVE

SIGNATURE ROCKS

HOUSE ROCK SPRING

ANASAZI RUINS

OLD HOUSE FOUNDATION

FENCE & GATE

HOUSE

ROCK

6522T 1988

DEER CARCASS SPRING

MACKELPRANG SPRING

2 SEEPS

BLUEJAY SPRING

CURTIS SPRING

OLD CHIMNEY

OLD CURTIS-DELWIN HAMBLIN RANCH

5547T 1691

2 SHEDS & WATER TROUGH

KM 8.9 (MILE 5.5)

VALLEY

VERMILION

CONDOR ROOSTING SITE

HOD BROWN SPRING 1890

HRVR 2.1 KMS (1.3 MILES)

5544T 1690

P 1695

PET

OLD HOD BROWN RANCH SITE 1713

PET

ROCK ART PANELS 2012

CLIFFS

HIGHWAY 89A KM 4.5 (MILE 2.8)

CONDOR VIEWING PARK

VALLEY

SCALE

0   1   2   3   KMS

Above From just above and looking down on the old **Hod Brown Ranch** site. Left is the boulder with some cowboy signatures & a small pen next to it. Also the square cement water trough. In about the middle of the foto is a rectangular feature that can only be a stock pond (?), but how would the water stay in? Maybe the bottom is lined with clay (?). This picture was taken from along the **pipeline** which runs from Hod Brown Spring down to the water trough shown.

Right The **pipeline** running from Hod Brown Spring down to the ranch site below, runs through this **wooden sleeve** that protects it as it drops off the **1st cliff band** mentioned in the text above. Get up through this cliff band by heading left a ways, or turn right to see a nice rock art panel about 40m away. Just beyond that you might climb up the cliff, or continue to the right or east until you're on the sandslide, then scramble straight up to the Hod Brown Spring.

Above This is the best **rock art panel** along the **1st cliff band** just to the right or east of the pipeline & wooden sleeve shown on the opposite page.

Left From the 1st cliff band, looking up at the big Navajo Sandstone wall. Immediately below the big cliffs is **Hod Brown Spring** where all the green is. Just off the picture to the right is the beginning of a 150m-long petroglyph or rock art panel. It's one of the biggest & best around. As you scramble up the slope below the spring, be looking on the ground for lots of pottery fragments or potsherds.

Above An old picture of **House Rock** and the **gas station & store** located on Highway 89A. This was how it looked sometime in the early 1960's (?). It certainly looks different now. Today, the white stone house is still there, but there are no gas pumps or store. It's still owned by the Rich family which owns & operates the Jacob Lake facilities to the west. In 2010, a renter was living here. (Harold I. Bowman III foto)

Right This picture is from the big **rock art panel** beginning about 100m east of the **Hod Brown Spring**. This and the one on the opposite page, show a variety of art.

Above This is the stone house on Highway 89A known as **Rock House** on maps. This is where you turn north onto the **House Rock Valley Road**. The Vermilion Cliffs are the background to the NNE. Look at the cliffs directly above the solar panel on the left; that's where you'll find Hod Brown Spring and the big rock art panel. Behind the camera and on the south side of the highway is an airstrip that the Bowman family established in the mid or late 1950's. From there they flew into the Sand Hills to take care of their cattle.

Left These **Hod Brown panels** have all kinds of images, from snakes, birds & humans to the ever present big horn sheep. This one has 3 cross-like etchings, which makes one wonder if the Spaniards didn't pass this way before the Mormons or trappers arrived. The highest etching is 5-6m up with nothing to stand on. Either they built and used ladders, or sand & rocks at the base of the cliff have since washed away.

307

Part of the **West Bench Pueblo** located about 3 kms north of Two Mile Spring. It was in the process of being studied when time and/or money ran out (?). Please don't disturb what researchers started.

From a small hill near **Two Mile Spring**, looking down to the west at the Grand Canyon Trust's facilities at Two Mile. On the right is the old stone house built by Frank Rider. Beyond are the 2 newer houses, corrals, water troughs & tanks, and somewhere out there is Rawd Sander's airstrip.

Two Mile Spring The next major site in the upper House Rock Valley going south is Two Mile Spring. Just below the spring itself there is a 16 hectare (40 acre) plot of private land. It's now owned by the **Grand Canyon Trust**, the same conservation outfit that has the entire Sand Hills. This being in Arizona, land & grazing on the public domain is water based. Early land ownership & water rights to all the little springs and parcels of private land in the House Rock Valley were taken up by the **Grand Canyon Cattle Company**. That seems to have been long before 1916. Documentation wasn't filed until the fall of 1930, then they officially filed on it, but then it was sold in November of 1930--perhaps a result of the stock market crash the previous year (?).

From that point on, it's impossible to track all the people who owned a percentage of water rights to Two Mile Spring. Basically, everybody who had sheep, goats or cattle in the Sand Hills between about 1934, when the **Taylor Grazing Act** was enacted, to about the mid-1950's, owned some shares to that water. The reason was, it was about the only reliable waterhole around, and when things got real dry, that was the only option for their livestock. Coyote Spring was a good waterhole too, but it was always owned by just one person. Read about that in the chapter *History of the Sand Hills*.

Beginning in the 1950's, most fencing began to go up, and wells were being drilled, so that changed the whole setup. Beginning as early as the 1940's, then the '50's, **Harold I. Bowman's** outfit, began buying water rights to various places in the Sand Hills and upper House Rock Valley, then sold out in the early 1980's. In the northwest Sand Hills, which included some water rights to Two Mile Spring, **Hamblin & Maddox** sold out in 3/1957 to **David DeHaven**; after a year, DeHaven sold out to JR Jone's father **Ben Foster**, and brother Manny in 2/1958--that included shares in Two Mile water. Then **A.P. (Rawd) Sanders** had water and grazing rights between 1/1959 to 7/1978. **Jim Bryant** bought out Sanders in 7/1978, then sold out to **Vern Carner** in 6/1982. Carner bought out **Ramsey Cattle Co**. in 12/1985 from the eastern & central Sand Hills, and consolidated the entire Sand Hills range under one owner. Next change came in 8/1988 when **Stephenson & Wright** bought out Carner, then in 12/1992, **Kay Sturdevant** bought all their rights. In 10/1998, **David Gelbaum** bought everything, then sold it all to **North Rim Ranches**, a conservation group in 9/2005. In 1/2009, ownership was taken over by the **Grand Canyon Trust**. And that's how it stands as this book goes to press in the spring of 2010.

Here's what you'll find at Two Mile today--but it's private land, so there's little chance of getting official permission to see the place. That 40 acres of private land includes all the springs, but the 2 newer houses to the west appear to be on BLM land (?). At the main spring are 2 man-made tunnels with a bricked-up wall in front. Water seeps into the tunnels, then is piped down to the corral and the new houses. In May of 1937, 4 springs had been tapped and they were getting 8 gallons (about 30 liters) per/minute--a pretty good flow, but today, only one spring is producing.

About halfway between Two Mile Spring and the new houses to the west, is a well-built **red sandstone house** or cabin. Here's what Trevor Leach remembered about that place: *The Bar Z Cattle Company built that rock house, or had it built; it was Frank Rider who built it. He was Elmer Rider's dad. That's where we used to camp all the time. It must have been built in the early 1930's (?). The CCC's had their camp down a little about where the new house is now.*

Calvin C. Johnson was there as a 14-year old in June, 1937, and he had more to say: *At Two Mile Spring, they had an old rock house; it had to have been built in the late 1920's (?). It never had any doors in it, just a big rock building with big open doorways on each side and*

This is where they get water out of **Two Mile Spring**. Behind that opening & rocked-up wall are 2 tunnels which act a collectors for water to seep into, then it's piped to the corral below. **Insert Above Frank Rider**, the man who built the **old stone house** at Two Mile. (Richard & Marvin Rider foto)

This **old stone house** is located between Two Mile Spring, and the other newer houses & corral just to the left or west. People in Kanab believe this was built by **Frank Rider** in the early 1930's.

windows. Walt Hamblin and I stayed in there,....

Here's a quote from the 6/2/1939 issue from **Kane County Standard**: *The present work program of Co. 2557 [CCC spike camp out of Pipe Springs] consists of the House Rock truck trail, which is being constructed from U.S. Highway No. 89 to Sand Hill country and a division fence south of Two Mile spring. Three and one-half miles [6 kms] of the road is now completed.* This tells us that spike camp was set up in the spring of 1939.

The stone walls of the house are still in good condition, but the roof & wooden floor are rotting away. Inside is a stone fireplace, and on the east side is a later addition which was used as a storeroom or granary. Its roof was about rotted away in 2009.

Several of the old-timers the author spoke to mentioned there was an **airstrip** just west or northwest of Two Mile Spring. Melvin Mognett, one son of the late Cat skinner Jack Mognett formerly of Kanab, thought his dad had something to do with that: *At Two Mile, I think **Rawd Sanders** got that in there, and I think Dad put it in there for him [with his Cat]. From where the old ranch house was, it's kinda west, then you go down across the wash and that airport was right at the foot of the mountain. It ran north and south. It's right there by the Honeymoon Corral. Rawd sprayed all the time, he was a crop duster, and then he had all them double winged planes, and he'd come in there and land. His business was in Phoenix, he was there most of the time.*

JR Jones of Kanab added a little more to Rawd's airstrip story: *Rawd wrecked a plane out there at Two Mile and killed his sister-in-law. The end of that runway was over on the Kaibab side, and you can still go over there and find parts of that plane.*

There are 2 newer homes at Two Mile and JR remembered this: *We built the main house the first year my father-in-law Jim Bryant was there; that would have been in 1979. My brother-in-law and my wife are the ones who actually built that one. Then the other house, I had it built when Vern Carner owned it, that would have been some time in the mid-1980's* (JR Jones was Carner's ranch foreman).

One Mile Spring About a mile (1 1/2 kms) south of Two Mile, is One Mile Spring (these springs are one & 2 miles from House Rock Spring, that's how they got their names). Get to it by turning & driving southeast at the same place where you turn off the HRVR as if going to Two Mile. About halfway there, you'll come to a rough section as the road crosses a dry wash, so cars may have to be parked there. About 200m before the end of the road near the spring, is a pretty good **panel of petroglyphs**, and a good camping place. Immediately north and above the little green meadow is evidence of a former Anasazi site--but it's nothing to look at.

On the old S.M. Miera hand-drawn **Water Resources map of the 1937** survey of the Sand Hills & House Rock Valley, they have written there were 3 minor seeps at that time but they were only producing 1 1/8 gallons (4 liters) of water per/minute. Also mentioned are **2 tunnels** 65 feet (20m) long, as well as an earth tank, but it was washed out. To see these tunnels which helps collect spring water, walk down from the end of the road into the little meadow surrounded by cliffs on 3 sides. The tunnels are still there at the bottom of the southeast wall. Also, just around the corner to the south is more rock art.

There are a number of historic sites in upper House Rock Valley and One Mile appears to be one of them. Calvin C. Johnson of Kanab, who is a descendant of those who created the Johnson (Valley) community, recalls what some of his relatives were doing back in the days soon after Lee's Ferry got up and running in the last quarter century before 1900: *My grandad **Nephi Johnson, Jr.,** had the **mail contract** from **Johnson** [east of Kanab] **to Lee's Ferry.** And right close to **One Mile** there was a cave and that's where they stored their supplies. So they'd go from Johnson to One Mile and stay one night; then they rode the same horse on down to Lee's Ferry and the same horse back--all in a 4 day trip. If I remember correctly, that cave was real close to One Mile Spring and that was their overnight camp.*

They talked about this one horse; he was so good, that when they'd go over the mountain [Buckskin Mtn. just west of Wire Pass Trailhead] in winter and with heavy snow, they'd get off that mail horse and

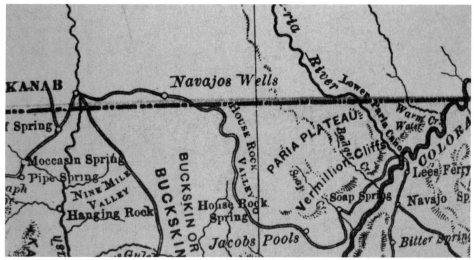

This is a copy of one of several maps from the late 1870's and beyond, which shows the **Navajo Trail**; it has been glamorized in recent years and called the **Honeymoon Trail**. This trail/route started after John D. Lee created Lee's Ferry, which allowed the Navajos to cross the Colorado and trade with the Mormons in Kanab and elsewhere in southern Utah. One of their campsites was at **Navajo Wells**; but there was water at Soap Creek, Jacobs Pools and House Rock Spring.

he'd break trail and my grandad would grab his tail and walk behind.

*The **Honeymoon Trail**; Dennis Judd was involved with that. But that's a modern-day name, they did-n't call it that back in the 1800's. In those days it was called the **Navajo Trail**; the Navajos used to camp out there at the **Navajo Wells** when they came to Kanab to trade. Then there was the **Mail Trail**. My grandad talked about the mail trail which was a little different; it come in south of the old Navajo Trail and it come down the mountain closer to House Rock Spring--the Navajo Trail come off closer to Coy-ote [to the north]. Then later on in my day, they had the old **Fuller Road**, and that was a wagon road that went down the mountain over towards Jacob Lake, and closer to where the highway is today.*

House Rock Spring One of the most important landmarks in the valley is House Rock Spring. Here's how the spring and the valley got the name. This comes from the book, ***A Mormon Chronicle: The Diaries of John D. Lee***, edited by Juanita Brooks. Brooks quotes part of Frederick Dellenbough's

The grave of **May Whiting** is just west of **House Rock Spring**. The spring is in the back end of this little indentation in the Vermilion Cliffs. From the spring, which you can reach by using the road on the left, walk west (toward this grave) on little trails at the base of the cliffs to find dozens of signa-tures of Mormon settlers who were heading south to Arizona. Many date from 1873.

Left In 2009, the Schoppmans put a door on **House Rock Spring** to keep water clean.
Top One of 2 markers on the grave of May Whiting which is just west and downhill a ways from the spring.
Above The smaller signature above is that of *JD Lee Dec 25 1871.* Lee passed by this place many times over a period of several years in the early 1870's. This signature is just west of the opening to the House Rock Spring.

story as he traveled through the region like this: *About sunset we passed two large boulders which had fallen together, forming a rude shelter, under which Riggs or someone else had slept and then had jocosely printed above with charcoal the words, 'Rock House Hotel'. Afterwards this had served as identification, and Jacob [Hamblin] and the others had spoken of House Rock Spring and House Rock Valley. We called it the same, and finally it went on the maps and is now permanent.*

Here's a little history which helps explain what **John D. Lee** and other Mormons were doing in this region just prior to Lee starting the ferry. Here's a quote from Lee's diary for Friday, April 5, 1872: *About noon reached the House Rock Spring. During the Night heavy Rain; Took shelter under a Rock. Refreshed our Selves, then commenced putting [up] a Rock House to Secure the Ranch.... Workd 1/2 day.... April 6, 1872: Finishd the House & wrote on the Door the date of location & then Rode to Jacob's Pools..... Here Jho. Mangram proposed to return home & at some future time come & Secure this & the Ranch at Soapcreek.*

The Mormons had plans to send settlers into Arizona to establish colonies, and preach to the Indians, so they were lining up & staking out water rights on all the springs they could along the way. **Jacob Hamblin** was one of the ramrods for the LDS Church at the time, and was likely the most influential person for the Mormon settlers going to Arizona. He worked with the Indians, mostly Navajo, and was an interpreter & scout. John D. Lee was also close to and worked with Hamblin. Not many years after the time Lee's Ferry was set up, 3 of Jacob Hamblin's sons got involved with grazing livestock in the Sand Hills--they were **Joe, Ben & Walt**.

At or just below House Rock Spring are a number of interesting sites. There's a **grave** of a young woman named May Whiting and a number of stone fences and signs of prior settlement. The rock house mentioned in Lee's diary is nowhere to be found today, but it was surely a flimsy structure and only meant to be a marker for water rights they were claiming. If you walk east up the drainage and into a cove in the Vermilion Cliffs about 400m from the grave site, and up against the canyon wall, you'll see a tunnel which helps collect water from House Rock Spring. From there, and all along the cliffs to the west for 300m, you'll see hundreds of signatures of some of the earliest Mormon settlers who were heading to the Arizona Territory in the very first year Lee's Ferry was in operation. Many signatures date from early June, 1873. John D. Lee's signature is there too, *December 25, 1871*.

Before you go there, keep in mind that **House Rock Spring is on private land.** It belongs to **Ira Schoppman & sons** of Cedar City, Utah. If you want to visit the place, all Ira asks is, call him at 435-586-8097 and let him know you're going there. In late spring of 2009, Schoppmans put in a new pipeline from the spring down to water troughs and the house at House Rock on Highway 89A, and according to Ira: *That water also goes to Parker east of the HRVR and to a metal trough, and it also goes to the Sand Pasture, which is to the east and the same pasture that Bonal Springs is in.* The reason they want you to call is that they're a little worried about ATV's and/or resultant vandalism at the spring (they now have a door at the tunnel entrance, but there's really nothing to vandalize beyond that).

To get there, drive north from Highway 89A on the HRVR. After 5.9 kms (3.7 miles) turn east where you see the 2 sheds and lone chimney about 150m away. After the barns, cross the dry wash and about 450m from the HRVR, turn left or north. Stop near the grave which is on the little hill to the left; that will be 2.2 kms (1.4 miles) from the HRVR. It may take a car with a little more clearance than average to get there--or walk the last part.

Another nearby place to see is just before the new gate & fence (marking the beginning of private land) as shown on the map. Park there and walk west 100m. There on a little rise, you'll see some scattered rocks and lots of pottery fragments indicating an **Anasazi pueblo** right out in the open and about 550m away from House Rock Spring. From there, walk south about another 100m and you'll see a rock foundation of what is believed to be an old stone house.

Bob Ford of Fredonia, who is an avid self-taught historian, has an idea about what may have hap-

This is the **old House Foundation** shown on **Map 41**. It's just south of the gate & Anasazi Ruins, the boundary of private land, and southwest of House Rock Spring. Bob Ford thinks there was a stone house here, then, as suggested below, it was torn down and the rocks used to build the former store & gas station on Highway 89A called **House Rock**. (Bob Ford foto)

pened at that foundation site in the past: ***Jedadiah Adair*** *had a home right there below* **House Rock Spring**. *I believe my grampa* **William Alfred (Bill) Ford** *and his brother Willard and a guy named Dave Rider tore that down, and with those stones built that House Rock store down on the highway. On the lower right-hand corner of that house on the highway, you'll see Adair's name; but Adair didn't build that one, he built the one up at House Rock Spring. The foundation of Adair's house is not on Schoppman's private land--it's just before or south of that fence & new gate. And if you look closely, that's where the Honeymoon [Navajo]Trail came through.* The place Bob is talking about (the old House Rock gas station & store) is shown on Arizona highway maps as **House Rock**.

Four Springs Just southeast of House Rock Spring is what most USGS maps call **Four Springs**. These are halfway between House Rock & Hod Brown Springs, and halfway up the cliff face, same as Hod's Spring is. On the Water Resources map drawn by S.M. Miera for the 1937 survey, it shows 6 minor seeps, 4 with names. From north to south they are; **Deer Carcass, Mackelprang**, 2 seeps with no names, then **Blue Jay & Curtis Springs**.

Mackelprang Spring surely was named after William or **Billy Mackelprang**, who was the brother of Art & Frank Mackelprang who had goats & cattle in the Sand Hills. Billy had livestock in House Rock Valley, and a few in the Sand Hills. **Curtis Spring** was named after **Earnest A. Curtis** who homesteaded the ranch that was later owned by Delwin Hamblin; that's where the lone chimney is today.

On that 1937 Water Resources map, it shows a pipeline running down to the valley south from Deer Carcass Spring and to a trough. Mackelprang Spring had a pipeline running down to the west to a another trough. Of the 2 unnamed seeps, one had been developed, but had caved in; the other was undeveloped. Blue Jay & Curtis Springs had lines running down aways, then were joined. From there the line connected to the Deer Carcass pipeline and appears to have ended in a trough.

As mentioned above, the water from House Rock Spring was piped down to **House Rock** on the highway. On that 1937 map it states that House Rock belonged to the Grand Canyon Cattle Company, but the rock house was a gas station at the time. Also listed was 4 big corrals, 6 troughs, but only one was good, and the water arrived at the rate of 3 gallons (11 1/3 liters) per/minute.

Hod Brown Spring & Ranch Now a little story of Bill & Hod Brown. Part of this information comes from the family book, ***Ebenezer Brown and his Descendants***; some comes from Hod's obituary which came out in the 1/21/1938 issue of **KCS**; and some comes from a court case regarding water rights.

These 2 men were brothers; William Manhard **(Bill) Brown** was born on 4/3/1870, while Almon Harris (Harry) **(Hod) Brown** was born on 1/15/1873. No one alive in 2009 knew how Harry got the name Hod, but it came early in life. Both brothers grew up in Kanab, but the family lived at Pipe Springs for a while. Neither one got married, so they were pretty footloose. From Hod's obituary: *In about 1900, with his brothers William and Eben Brown, went to Wyoming, where he [Hod] resided for 12 years. He returned to Kanab in 1912 and soon became engaged in the livestock business. He spent much of his time at House Rock and at the Sand Hills in northern Arizona, where his cattle ranged.*

Regarding Hod Brown being single, an interesting little article appeared in the **Kane County Independent** (a fore runner to the KC Standard in which only a few months of 1912 have been preserved) 5/7/1912 issue. It stated: *Harry [Hod] Brown and Gurn Spencer are trying to secure wives thru a matrimonial*

Far Left Bill Brown, the older of the 2 brothers.
Left Hod Brown. Both of these pictures are from the book, ***Ebenezer Brown and his Descendants.*** Both fotos were likely taken in the 1890's, and both men are buried in the Kanab City Cemetery.

agency. Kanab young ladies please take notice, they're old but not tough.

For part of that 12 years away from home, Hod was in Logan, Utah, working in the sugar industry along side Frank Little (who had Angora goats in southern Utah). After Hod came back to Kanab, he worked as a freighter for a time driving a 4-horse team & wagon.

Calvin C. Johnson remembered both men in their later years, but he knew Hod better than his brother: *Hod & Bill Brown lived together here in the north end of town [Kanab] up at their mother's home about 2 1/2 blocks from where I am now. They homesteaded the Hod Brown place which is out here about 15 miles [24 kms] right by the Utah-Arizona line. It was east of Johnsons Run a few miles--they called it Muggin's Flat. They dry farmed and homesteaded about 1200 acres [480 hectares].*

*After Hod & Bill sold their homestead out at Muggin's Flat, they come into Kanab as 2 old batches. Hod had a little acreage down below town and run a few head of sheep, and that was in the **winter of '36 & '37**--that bad winter. I remember that real well, because as a kid, I went down there and helped cut some of his sheep loose that was froze down [in the snow]. Then Hod sold that to Elmo Brown, and left the country and went to Arizona. [He died there]. When I knew them, they were older men, livin' together, and they did a little bootleggin'--home brew stuff. Both men were buried here in the cemetery.*

Most of what we know about the Hod Brown place in House Rock Valley comes from a **court case** having to do with water rights after Hod died on January 15, 1938. Three weeks after Hod died, and on **2/7/1938**, his brother Bill Brown got busy trying to make legal the fact they had occupied that land and used the water for many years. The court case involved **Delwin Hamblin**, the Plaintiff making a complaint against **Roy Woolley**, the defendant. The original complaint was filed **April 14, 1941**.

But first let's get the history part as best we can. Here's some important passages that came out in that civil case with a little editing: ***William M. [Bill] Brown** in about the year **1915** took possession of a tract of land in House Rock Valley where he established a stock raising headquarters and made improvements consisting of a residence, corrals, reservoirs, watering troughs and fencing. Adjacent to, and above, this ranch, he developed 3 small springs or seeps, known as **Hod Brown, North Cliff Dweller and South Cliff Dweller Springs**. Work consisted of tunneling, construction of intake gathering basins and laid a pipe line to his headquarters below, diverting the flow of the springs to his water troughs and reservoirs. In January, 1917, all the water developed had been put to beneficial use for domestic and stock watering purposes. Prior to the development and use, the water from these springs, after flowing for a few yards, disappeared into the sand. The total amount of water produced amounted to from 1400 to 1800 gallons per/day. Brown lived at the ranch and used the water continuously until 1919; after that date the water and ranch were used by his leasers, but he apparently knew that a half interest was owned by others.*

Another part of the court document has to do with who actually filed on the water rights for the first time. No date was given as to when that person actually filed on it. Here's more: *Water from the spring was filed on by William A. [Bill] Ford, but another document was signed by **Wm [Bill] Brown and Sixtus E. Johnson**, all from Kanab.* But Sixtus was out of the picture at that time.

Another paragraph went like this: *The grantor [Brown] claims that 1/2 the spring water and the pipeline, the 2 reservoirs together with the lumber cabin, which was used as a dwelling, 2 corrals and the fencing around the large reservoir belong to him which he made his home from **1915 until January, 1929**. Since that time, he has had renters on the property, but still claims the right to all the improvements and water.*

Since Hod wasn't around to speak for himself, it appears that his brother Bill was speaking in his behalf about one or both of them occupying the place over all those years, but no one bothered to legalize the squatting they apparently were doing. The man who first filed for water rights was **Bill Ford** but he died on 5/17/1933. It seems that since Hod, Bill Ford and Sixtus were no longer around, that left Bill Brown as the last man standing--and with all the rights. In the original complaint filed by Delwin, he is asking that Roy Woolley produce proof that he has the water rights. Woolley countered saying as of **April 21, 1938** the Arizona State Water Commission issued water rights to Bill Brown; then on **June 26, 1939**, Brown sold him the water rights and the facilities which constituted the Hod Brown Ranch.

To a make a long story short (the author didn't read the 400+ pages of the case but a court clerk mentioned the highlights) the case went to county court on **April 14, 1941** in Flagstaff before a jury which ended on July 8, 1944, but the judge ended up issuing an opinion on **July 13, 1944**. He ruled in favor of **Roy Woolley**.

But Delwin filed an appeal on **September 5, 1944**, and it went to the Supreme Court of Arizona and it ended with a final settlement on **March 13, 1946**. It was in the summary of the Supreme Court's decision that the above mentioned history was outlined--but it seems that all the documentation from the original county court filing was contradictory to evidence given to the Supreme Court. In that summery it stated that on **February 7, 1938**, Brown executed and delivered to plaintiff [Delwin Hamblin] a **quit-claim deed** with recitations as follows: Delwin paid $300 for the water rights and improvements, that Delwin was paying Bill Brown all expenses to have Brown go through official channels and have the water commission issue Brown official water rights, because it was never properly filed. It's this part, **not filing it properly**, that came to the attention of the Supreme Court. It was in the Supreme Court's summary that all the history of the Brown brothers settlement of the ranch and developing of the springs & pipeline was brought out. The Supreme Court ruled that even though the Browns had not officially filed claims on the water or the improvements at the ranch, they were still entitled to ownership, simply because they had squatted on the land. In the end, the **Supreme Court ruled in Delwin Hamblin's favor**. That judgement was issued on March 13, 1946.

Let's go back a little in time and bring in a little history leading up to Delwin buying the Curtis Ranch. As mentioned above in the history of Two Mile Spring, there was a CCC spike or side camp located there beginning in the spring & summer of 1939. They were building a road which eventually extended into the Sand Hills, plus these erected some fences. In the 9/8/1939 issue of the **KCS**, it states: *Work has started this week on the Curtis-Hamblin fence in House Rock Valley. This work is being done by the Two Mile side camp.* That fence seems to be the one you pass through on your way to Hod's Place and marked **5544T** (1690m) on **Map 41**. It appears Delwin was looking to graze some cows in that area and was hoping to use the water from Hod's Spring. This was also before the fist-a-cuffs started and the court case began--but putting in that fence may have led to the eventual court case (?).

Later that fall and in the 11/17/1939 issue of the **KCS** it talks about a preliminary engineering survey being completed for the E.A. Curtis Water Facilities Project. It was done by the St. George Soil Conservation Service (it became the BLM in 1947) office. It goes on to say: *Proposed plans call for 4635 feet [1400m] of steel pipe to bring water from the **Curtis Spring** to a cement or steel storage tank near Mr. Curtis' home. By having stock water near his barnyard, Mr. Curtis can carry approximately one hun-*

dred head of stock during the winter.... In those days, the Soil Conservation Service, or in this case the CCC's, was doing lots of such projects for ranchers, at little or no cost to the permittees.

Now on the Water Resources map of 1937, it shows a 1" (2 1/2 cm) pipe already there, coming out of a 12 foot (4m) tunnel, and running down to a trough at the base of the cliffs--but the line was broken. So it seems Curtis was looking for some help to get a new line in there.

Curtis Ranch Not a lot is known about Earnest A. Curtis, but according to Trevor Leach: *Curtis homesteaded that back in the early 1930's (?). Kid Curt we used to call him. He built that little cabin there, then Delwin had it for quite a while.*

Only problem with this info is, the name Curtis doesn't show up in the Coconino County records (it's there somewhere, this author simply didn't find it, partly because of the mess in the Coconino Courthouse records, and lack of time to search further) until he sold it to Delwin F. Hamblin. The first document this writter found was a **Grant Deed** dated **July 9, 1946**. That's when Delwin & his wife Sara paid $1600 to E. A. Curtis and his wife Francis of Jacob Lake, for the water rights to the 3 springs in Section 13, T39N, R3E (Hod Brown Spring plus the 2 Cliff Dweller seeps) and the improvements at the base of the cliffs in Section 14; that would have been the Hod & Bill Brown Ranch site.

Then on **September 4, 1946**, a **Quit-Claim Deed** was recorded stating Delwin Hamblin was buying the water rights (and 160 acres/65 hectares of private land) to the South Grass Seep, Blue Jay, Deer Carcass, Walt Hamblin and the Mackelprang Springs in Sections 11 & 14. At the same time and the same day, a **Warranty Deed** was recorded saying that Delwin also bought 640 acres (255 hectares and one full Section) of private land from Curtis (this means Curtis got it under the Desert Lands Homestead Act). He paid $1000 for all of that. All of this happened shortly after Delwin won the court case, and very likely collected all legal fees from Roy Woolley (?).

Mark Hamblin of Kanab, who comes down through the Ben Hamblin line from Jacob Hamblin, remembered a few things about the place when he visited his grandfather Delwin in the late 1950's & early 60's: *Grampa told me that Curtis moved the ranch house that was over there at Hod Browns, to where it's at right now--where the chimney is today. We always called that other place Hods.*

Regarding the pipeline that Hod & Bill Brown put in many years earlier Mark said: *It was the old* **steel pipe** *that we used to repair. We used to cut up old inner tubes and we'd have pieces strapped all over us and we'd head up there and fix it as we went--we'd patch it with rubber and lots of wire. Then sometime before he sold the place, he put in that new plastic line.*

Here's a little of what Calvin C. Johnson remembered about that confrontation between Woolley & Hamblin, and what Delwin did later: *Roy Woolley came up there and tried to run Delwin off, and they had a fist fight--but it didn't amount to a lot. Delwin didn't have many cattle there, he had just the old Curtis Ranch, that private land there, then he set up a* **deer hunting camp** *about 20 miles [32 kms] south of there at Big Saddle [Saddle Mt.?]. So that's what he run, just deer hunting camps. And he and his wife lived out there on that homestead.*

Above Delwin Hamblin's Ranch in about 1960. Notice the windmill on the far left which generated electricity and was stored in batteries for electric lights. Although the house is gone now (perhaps burned down), the chimney is still there--as is the barn on the far right.
Far Left Delwin Hamblin, sometime in the 1960's, or '70's (?).
Right Ben Hamblin, Delwins father, and full brother to Joe Hamblin (half-brother to Walt Hamblin). Joe died in 1924; Ben died in 1930; and Walt died in 1950.
(Mark Hamblin fotos)

Above A 1940's foto of the gas station-store at **House Rock** on Highway 89A.
Above Right Delwin Hamblin with their pet wolf in about 1920 (he was born in 1900 and he looks about 20 here).
Right Center Delwin's brother Ben with the same wolf. It looks like he was chained-up in the back yard.
Bottom Another dead wolf propped up for a picture with **Foot Hamblin** in the background. Foot's real name was Ferry, but he hated it, and no one seems to know how he got the name of Foot (?). He came down through **Frances Marian Hamblin** (same as Glen Hamblin?), a younger brother of Jacob Hamblin. A good guess is, all these wolves were living and roaming the wilds during the 1910's (?).
The 3 upper fotos are from Mark Hamblin, Kanab, who is Delwins grandson, and great grandson of Ben Hamblin.

This Foot Hamblin foto is from Rock Burgoyne

Trevor remembered a few more things about the time Delwin was there: *Delwin piped that water from up there [from the 4 springs mentioned above]; he had Navajos dig a trench from up there clearn down to the ranch. He was going to have me come and put it in with a Cat, but them Indians was workin' for 'im and they done it.*

Mark Hamblin spent some time with Delwin when he was growing up and he remembered some of the stories about his grandfather's younger years: *Delwin didn't get along with his dad, that was Benjamin. And Benjamin was a religious man, and Grampa didn't want to hear it. And they fought all the time, so Grampa moved to the Sand Hills with his **Uncle Joe Hamblin**. He was 11 or 12 years old when he went to the Sand Hills. I think he only went to the 6th grade--and then he was out there. Joe wasn't religious, he was a drinker! And quite often, Joe would send Grampa to town, down over the Kaibab on horseback to pick 'im up a jug. He was pretty young when he'd come to town to get that corn whiskey.*

After almost exactly 20 years in the House Rock Valley, Delwin sold out to the **Bowmans** of Salt Lake City and/or Jacob Lake. It was on **June 20, 1966** that the Warranty Deed was recorded for all the private land amounting to 800 acres (320 hectares), plus a Deed of Water Rights.... for all the springs mentioned above.

Here's a little story about a **wolf pup** raised by Delwin and his brothers. Mark Hamblin has several pictures of Delwin & brother Ben with a full grown wolf that they kept chained up in the back yard, but it must have been in Kanab, not at Delwin's Ranch. Delwin was born in 1900 and he looks like an older teenager, so the pictures must date to about 1915 to '20 (?). Mark couldn't remember much about the wolf; but Bob Ford had talked to Delwin and this is what he remembered: *Some old timer got it out of a den and gave it to those boys; that's kinda what I remember. Delwin and his brother Ben raised it.* No one alive today knows where that wolf pup came from, perhaps up on the Kaibab around Jacob Lake, or in the upper Paria River country, or even the Sand Hills (?).

When asked about wolves, Calvin C. Johnson (born in 1923) said he only heard about one wolf sighting in all his days on the range east of Kanab: *The only story I remember at all was in the 1940's; we had a guy who worked on the state road from Tropic, and his name was Garn Willis. And he trapped some too, and he claimed that there was a wolf out there right where you start to go up in the Sand Hills, and he swears the wolf run down in the Buckskin Gulch. Now those were the years I was out there get-ting my ranch, and I never saw a wolf. But he was trappin' in those days, and he tried to catch 'im, but never could.*

All this ties in with several advertisements seen in the **Kane County Independent** starting on 8/29/1912, and running into the fall months. It went like this: *$100 A REWARD OF ONE HUNDRED DOLLARS will be paid for each WOLF killed within the district bounded by Kanab Creek on the west, the Pink Cliffs and Willis Creek on the north, Pahreah Creek on the east, the drift fence and Snake Gulch on the south. The entire hide with ears and feet attached must be delivered to Mr. A. D. Findlay of Kanab. This wolf or wolves has been killing cattle recently at the Seeps, Johnson Lakes and vicin-ity. This reward holds good from August 1st to November 1st, 1912. A.D. Findlay.*

The Johnson Lakes are located just east of the lower part of Johnson Canyon; while the Seeps, or Seeps Ranch, is just southeast of the mouth of Johnson Canyon, and just south of today's Highway 89. About that same time, maybe a little later, Jet Johnson was developing the Seeps Ranch. A.D. Findlay was the father of Merle Findlay, the man who bought Joe's Ranch in March, 1945. That whole area is pretty close to the northwest corner of the Sand Hills.

Here's one little story about an interesting character who lived and worked in the Sand Hills and the House Rock Valley. Her name was **Adaline Halverson**, and she was a *pistol packin' mama*. Here's what Trevor Leach remembered about her: *Adaline Halverson lived at Poverty Ranch and Delwin's old place for a few years. She used to come here to visit my wife. She wrote her life history. She grew up in Arizona somewhere, and she broke horses when she was a kid. She got married and had 2 kids. Ray Halverson was her husband's name. One of 'um, the girl, ran off and Adaline thought she was dead, but then she came back a few years later with 4 kids. And her son, Ray Jr., married a woman twice as old as he was.*

Adaline's husband got blood poison in one of his legs; and they had to take it off--his left leg. And he rode that way--he could get on a horse and he'd ride a little. Then finally he had a heart attack and died. Then her and her boy took care of that place at Poverty; took care of Rawd Sander's place for a year or so. Now Rawd Sanders was a pilot, and he flew crop duster planes, but he got killed up on the mountain driving a water truck. He was the damndest driver I ever seen. I flew in the airplane with 'im and he was a good pilot--but he wasn't a good driver! He drove down off that mountain; I'll bet he was goin' 60 mph [100 kph] down there and he kicked that down into low gear, and I thought the motor was gonna fly right back in our faces!

After Rawd sold out in 1978, Adaline worked for Bowmans. [JR Jones adds a little here: After Jim Bryant bought out Sanders, we didn't need Adaline and her son, so Jim Glover hired 'um to work for the Bowmans and took 'um over to Big Sink. Adaline and her son lived there in that cinder block house, and they must have worked there a year or so and they kinda had a falling out--the boy got married, and Ada-line didn't get along with her boy's wife--I guess she was a little jealous of her, and they left. Then Ada-line came back a year or two later and after that she lived down there at the Hamblin place working for Bowmans again]. And she moved down into that other place that used to be Delwins.

Then later, a bull hooked her horse and she fell off and she just laid there in the valley until old Butch (Melvin) Mognett came by and seen her layin' there in the damn flat and she had a broken hip. And they got her in the hospital.... But she later wrote her life story and she was good friends with my wife. She's about like me--not too good of a writer.....

She was about 79 when she died. She was 3 years older than me so she must have been born in about 1917. She had her spot out there where she wanted to be buried under a tree; it's out there near Delwin's chimney. Then her twin sister got her to go up to Oregon and she died up there so she's buried up there somewhere. I've got a book that Dixie Northcott wrote about Adaline.

One reason for putting this story in here is that this writer met Adaline there at Delwin's old ranch in 1986 and she was limping around with that injured hip; it never did heal properly. But she was also bucking bales of hay just like a man, and had arms that looked like a man's! No flab there. And she car-ried a six-shooter on her side; and as Trevor put it: *You damn right she did, she always carried a gun! She didn't take guff from nobody!*

As of 2010, the **Rich** family still owns the old Curtis/Delwin Hamblin Ranch (as well as the Jacob Lake facilities), and the water rights to the 4-5 springs mentioned above which he still pipes down to his water trough, plus the Hod Brown Springs, but that pipeline is broken and hasn't been used in years. Read more about the Bowmans & Riches in the History of the Sand Hills, under Pine Tree Pockets.

Reestablishing California Condors to the Vermilion Cliffs

The release of 6 California Condors onto the Vermilion Cliffs on **December 12, 1996,** marked the be-ginning of the reestablishment of these rare birds into the wilds of the American Southwest. This has been a cooperative effort between the BLM, National Park Service, Arizona Game & Fish, the Pere-grine Fund at the World Center for Birds of Prey in Boise, Idaho, the San Diego Wild Animal Park and the Los Angeles Zoo.

The release site is located about 2 kms east of the House Rock Valley Road in Section 14, T39N, R3E. There's a parking place, toilet & verandah located 4.5 kms (2.8 miles) north of House Rock and Highway 89A. From there, look ENE, and you'll see white streaks of bird manure running down the highest Navajo Sandstone wall. That's the release site, plus it's a favorite roosting place for many birds. Nearby is a large cage where new birds are brought to acclimatize before actually being released.

Here are the number of condors that were released in the first few years of the program: 1996--6 birds; 1997--13; 1998--9; 1999--7; 2000--12; 2001--0; 2002--11; and for 2003--8 birds. Between 1996 & 2003, 23 birds died: 3 were shot; 5 were killed by coyotes; 1 struck a powerline; 4 died from lead poi-soning; 3 were killed by eagles; 1 starved to death; 2 were lost; 3 were captured and returned to the cap-tive breeding program; and 3 are unaccounted for. Read more updated figures on the next page. For additional or updated information, see the website **peregrinefund.org;** then click *Conservation Projects, & Condor Fact Sheet.*

California Condor Fact Sheet--May 31, 2009

Scientific Name: *Gymnogyps californianus.* **Population low:** 22 individuals in 1982. **Current World Population-Wild & Captive:** 358 individuals. **Life span:** Unknown, possibly up to 60 years. **Wingspan:** Up to 3 meters. **Weight:** Averages 7 1/4 to 10 1/2 kgs. **Body Length:** 1.2 to 1.4 meters. **Range:** Oc-curred historically from British Columbia south to northern Baja California and in other parts of the south-western United States. **Maturity:** Condors reach sexual maturity and attain adult plumage and coloration by 5-6 years of age. Breeding is likely between 6-8 years of age. **Reproduction:** One egg every other year if nesting cycle is successful. Instead of having many young and gambling that a few will survive, the condor produces very few young and provides an extensive amount of parental care. Average incubation period for a condor egg is about 56 days. **Nest Site:** Usually in a cave on a cliff or a crevice among boulders on a steep slope. **Young:** Nestlings fledge (leave nest) full grown at six months of age, however, historically, juvenile condors may be dependent on their parents for more than a year. Reintroduced condors are released on their own and must learn to forage and survive alone. **Sexes:** There is no sexual dimorphism (observable difference in size or appearance) between males and females. **Feeding:** Condors are strict scavengers. Unlike Turkey Vultures, condors do not have an exceptional sense of smell. They instead find their food visually, often by investigating the activity of ravens, coyotes, eagles, and other scavengers. Without the guidance of their parents, young inexperienced juvenile condors may also investigate the activity of humans. As young condors learn and mature this human directed curiosity diminishes. **Reasons for decline:** The main reason for the decline of the condors was an unsustainable mortality rate of free-flying birds combined with a naturally low reproductive rate. Most deaths in recent years have been directly or indirectly related to human activity. Shootings, poisoning, lead poisoning, and collisions with power lines are considered the condors' major threats. **Identification points to look for:** Numbered wing tags, white or mottled triangle under wing, no feathers on head, and head color black in juveniles or orange/pink in adults, not dark red as in Turkey Vultures.

Current Condor Numbers
May 31, 2009

Wild Population of California Condors - **189**
Arizona (Paria--Vermilion Cliffs) - - - - - - - -78   Baja California (Mexico) - - - - - - - - - - - - -15
Southern California - - - - - - - - - - - - - - - -96

Captive Population of California Condors - **169**
World Center for Birds of Prey-Boise, ID - -61   Los Angeles Zoo -22
San Diego Wild Animal Park - - - - - - - - - -36   Oregon Zoo, Portland - - - - - - - - - - - - - - - -37
Chapultepec Zoo, Mexico City - - - - - - - - - -2   Santa Barbara Zoo - - - - - - - - - - - - - - - - - - -4

TOTAL CALIFORNIA CONDOR POPULATION--358

Contacts: The Peregrine Fund---Tele. 928-355-2270; Arizona Game & Fish, Flagstaff---Tele. 928-774-5045; BLM, St. George, Utah---Tele. 435-688-3200; National Park Service---928-638-7756.
If you should observe a condor please report your sighting to The Peregrine Fund biologists at 520-355-2270 or email them at *cparish@peregrinefund.org*. Helpful information would include date, time, location, number of birds observed, and wing tag numbers if possible.

The old **Delwin Hamblin Ranch**. You can see this same chimney in the foto on page 315. Apparently the eastern part of the house burned down but everything else is rotting away. The stove is likely Delwins. The little building on the right is the top of the stairway leading down to a cellar.

Left **Elmer Rider** standing in front of the house at **Pine Tree Pockets**. In the early 1960's, he built an addition on the east end of this cabin (the other end you can't see). It was Elmer's father, **Frank Rider** who built the little stone house at Two Mile Spring. (Richard Rider foto) **Right** A picture of **Frank L. Farnsworth** in the early 1900's. He is the one who left his signature from 1911 on the base of **The Pinnacle** in the Pinnacle Valley in the Sand Hills. His signature is seen in several places on the plateau. Also seen are signatures of his son F.H. **(Hugh) Farnsworth**. Hugh left one signature (1936) on the big boulder next to where Hod Brown had his ranch below Hod Brown Spring. (Dennis Farnsworth Judd foto)

This sign is just east of the old **Curtis-Delwin Hamblin Ranch** and on the way to Hod Brown's place, or House Rock Spring. Directly above the left post is some white streaking; that's where the **condors** sometimes perch and release their droppings. Also, directly above the sign itself is the little indentation in the Vermilion Cliffs where Hod Brown Spring is located; it's just around that corner you see. And directly above the right post is the top of what the author calls the **Pottery Trail**. Look closely and you can see an area about 100+m long where you can climb up through the highest cliffs to the top of the plateau in 2 different places.

Sand Hills Cracks and Bonal Spring Indian Trail Hikes

Location & Access The **Vermilion Cliffs** is the big wall of rock rising abruptly north of Highway 89A. You'll see it as you drive between Jacob Lake in the west, and Marble Canyon/Navajo Bridge & Lee's Ferry to the east. Along this entire escarpment are only 4 easily climbable routes up through the Navajo Sandstone part of the cliffs. One route is up past Hod Brown Spring and is discussed on the previous map. On this map, one is up past 3 seep called **Bonal Spring(s)**. Because there are petroglyphs along the way, and Anasazi ruins on top, the author is calling this the **Bonal Spring Indian Trail**. To get there, drive along **Highway 89A** roughly halfway between Jacob Lake & Marble Canyon/Navajo Bridge. Between **mile posts 560 & 561**, turn north off the highway and first drive west about 100m, then go through a wire gate--please close it behind you. From that gate, head east parallel to the fence for 200m, then veer left or north for a total of 2.5 kms (1.5 miles). At that point is another road, which is also the **wilderness boundary**; it's also the old **Navajo Trail** of pioneer days, but later called the **Honeymoon Trail**. Continue west on the Navajo Trail about 200m to where the old road used to head north. You're supposed to stop & park there, but some vehicles are continuing north illegally.

The other 2 routes up through the Vermilion Cliffs are called the **Sand Hills Cracks**. There's some confusion on which route is actually called the Sand Hill Crack. The author was told by several people years ago that this name applied to the twin canyons north of the stone building at **Jacobs Pool**. However, on the *Emmett Hill 7 1/2' quad*, it's the smaller, less-conspicuous crack just to the east that's labeled **Sand Hill Crack**. This writer is now calling that the **Eastern Sand Hill Crack**; and the **Northern Crack**. To get to both of these old Indian trails, turn north from Highway 89A between **mile posts 557 & 558**. Drive through the unlocked wire gate, closing it behind you. Continue north on a good sandy road for **3.1 kms (1.9 miles)**. There you'll find the old ranch house & corrals labelled Jacobs Pool (which is on a small piece of private land). Park at the old stone building, which is on the old Navajo Trail, as well as the southern boundary of the Paria Canyon--Vermilion Cliffs Wilderness Area.

Trail/Route Bonal Spring Hike From the old Navajo Trail & wilderness boundary below **Bonal Spring,** walk north along an old sandy road to & past some livestock **water troughs**. Further along, this old track ends near the bottom of a sluffed-off section of the Vermilion Cliffs. From there, follow a trail along the plastic pipeline which brings water down from Bonal Spring to the troughs. When you come to the first steep part, veer left into a gully to avoid the first cliffs. Just above the steeper cliffs, again follow the pipeline across a flatter area, then steeper talus. From there, you can see the 3 Bonal Springs, which are about halfway up the cliff face and at the base of the Navajo Sandstone part of the wall.

There are 3 parts to Bonal Spring; the western seep has 3 cottonwood trees but no flowing water; the middle part has a man-made **square mine-like tunnel** which gathers & holds water inside; and the eastern seep which appears to be dry but the Schoppmans have captured water in a pipe and that's where the majority of their water in the valley below comes from. From the eastern-most spring with the half-buried **engine & water pump**, climb due north up the steep talus slope to the vertical Navajo wall, which has a panel of **petroglyphs**, indicating this was a route for aborigines. From there, turn left or west and make your way to another protruding wall, which is the bottom part of a **steep crack**. Scramble up that narrow defile on all-4's. At the plateau rim are some big **Anasazi ruins**, the size of a small village. The people who made this site did so because of access to the spring & valley below. There is also one long, 3-part cement watering trough. Read the history of Bonal Spring below.

Sand Hills Cracks Loop-Hike For this edition the author is adding a couple of new twists to previous hikes. One idea is to go up one of the Sand Hills Cracks, either the northern or eastern, rim walk to the other, and come down the second. You can walk in either direction, but for now, let's start by going north from **Jacobs Pool**. Walk north up an old unused track from Jacobs Pool to the base of the cliffs just below **Hancock Spring**. Once there, don't go left on the little trail with old pipe coming down from spring; instead, turn 90° east and look for some cairns marking the beginning of a big horn sheep & hiker's trail up to the top. After a short distance, you'll find what is now a pretty good trail marked with cairns most of the way. It gradually turns left and heads due north up through the various breaks in the cliff. When you reach the base of a prominent spire or **pinnacle**, look around its western base to see several panels of **petroglyphs**. Walk around this pinnacle on the left or west side, then head straight up the steep drainage behind it. As you near the top, look closely at the wall to the right or east to see more **rock art**. Because of the existence of these petroglyphs, we can surmise this is another old **Indian trail**. At the top of the cliffs is the Sand Hills or Paria Plateau. On the rim is an old sandy vehicle track you can walk on to the Jarvis Ranch & Pinnacle Valley. But for now, head southeast along the rim. Be looking for Anasazi ruins; the author didn't see any, but with water below, there could be some between the 2 old trails. The walk between the 2 cracks is easy and flat, with an occasional interesting rock to fotograph. Nice views down on Hancock Spring too.

Eastern Sand Hills Crack Let's describe this route going up as well. To reach this 4th old Indian trail or route, called here the Eastern (Sand Hills) Crack, walk northeast from **Jacobs Pool** on an old road in the direction of several springs called **Lee's Ranch** by John D. Lee in his diary; but others have called it **Rachel's Pools** or **Place**. From the clay beds below the ruins of **Rachel Lee's old stone house** (located just above the green wetter area), walk east to the **main spring** as shown on this map.

Or, you can bypass the ruins of Rachel's old house and walk east from the stone building at **Jacobs Pool** on another old road paralleling a fence. After 500m, the road turns north into a minor canyon. This old washed-out track leads directly up to the main spring. From that spring, look up to the left to see an emerging **hiker's trail** marked with a few cairns heading northeast up the steep slope. Walk up this to a bench, and head up a sandy slope a ways, then contour around to the southeast. From there, this partly-cairned trail zig zags eastward up to the bench below the obvious Navajo cliffs, then cuts back to the north. Finally, you'll reach the crack itself with signs of a constructed cattle trail. From there, head east up the steep gully. Watch closely on both sides of the crack; there are **6-7 panels of good petroglyphs on the left**, plus several etchings of early-day ranchers and/or travelers on the right. One of these reads: *G.M. Wright, 20 Apr. 1894*. From the top, you could return the same way, or head northwest and return via the Northern Sand Hills Crack & Hancock Spring. Making the loop-hike will give you a chance to see both of these old Indian trails on the same hike & day. As you hike up either of these Indian Trails, be watching for pottery fragments. The author found only a couple of potsherds on each of these trails, but the Eastern Crack was the route used by the Anasazi when they moved from the White Knolls on the plateau, down to the springs in House Rock Valley.

Sand Hills Crack, Bonal Spring and the old Navajo Trail Loop-Hike Here's an interesting and fun hike. You could start at the trailhead for Bonal Spring, but for now let's start at the old stone building called **Jacobs Pool**. Hike north up the old & now-blocked-off road toward **Hancock Spring** and

Map 42, Sand Hills Cracks and Bonal Spring Indian Trail Hikes

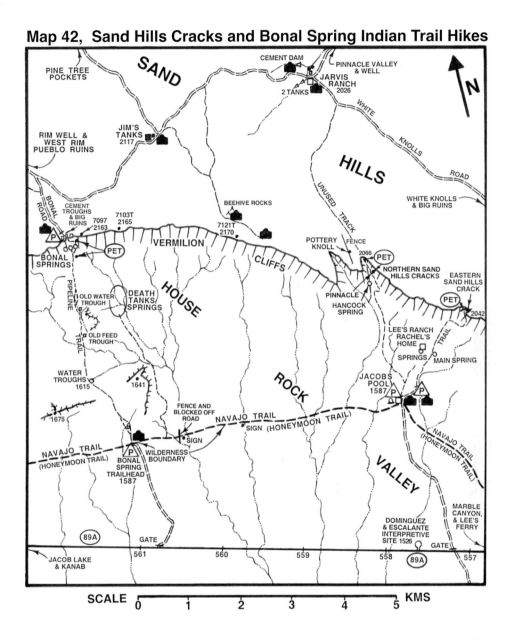

climb up the **Northern Sand Hills Crack**. Once on top with map in hand, turn left or west. Almost due west from the top of the crack, you'll come to a sandy hill with a **fence** on top running north-south. Near the top and on the east side of that hill & fence, be looking for **pottery fragments** scattered around in the sand. The author is calling this **Pottery Hill**. He never saw any ruins, but there's likely some around given the location so near Hancock Spring.

From Pottery Hill, head northwest skirting around the upper end of a 2nd canyon or crack above Hancock Spring. After that, walk west until you're on the edge of the Vermilion Cliffs, then rim-walk WNW. Along the way, you'll have some great views looking south down at **House Rock Valley** and the canyon of the Colorado River to the southeast.

Between Hancock & Bonal Springs, there are no other routes up or down the cliffs, so there are likely no ruins in that section, but in a place or two you may see some interesting rock formations similar to other parts of the Sand Hills. At a couple of places you may see other people's footprints. These would be from those who take one of 2 routes south from **Road #1104** running between the **Jarvis Ranch & Jim's Tanks**; but all vehicles must be parked at the wilderness boundary 300m or so back from the rim (all roads running toward the rim of Vermilion Cliffs--mostly ATV tracks--have been blocked off).

Finally as you near the route down to Bonal Spring, you'll come to the **big ruins** discussed earlier.

321

Above Looking north at the **Vermilion Cliffs** from the Water Troughs at 1615m. The route up to **Bonal Spring** first goes left out of the picture, then angles right up to just to the right of the **Cottonwood trees** in the upper middle part of this foto. The 2 producing springs are to the right or east of the Cottonwoods. The route to the top goes up the open slopes just right of center, then left and into the upper-most crack, thence to the top.

Right This mined-out water catchment to one of the producing **Bonal Springs** is halfway between the Cottonwood trees to the left or west, and what Ira Schoppman says is the main producing spring which is to the right or east about another 150m. You can get a drink here, but big horn sheep can get inside and may pollute it. Take your own water.

Above A closer look at the slopes leading up to **Bonal Spring** and the cliff top. See the Cottonwood trees to the left, then follow a contour line to the right or east about 100m to see the **square mine-like water catchment** for the middle spring (see it on the opposite page). From there, it's another 150m or so to the right or east again to the main spring that's now buried. The spring itself is just behind the author in the picture to the left.

Left The half-buried **water pump** that **J. F. Bonal** of Flagstaff, Arizona, carried down from the top of the Vermilion Cliffs to this main spring (behind the author and not seen). A project for the BLM, or some other volunteers, would be to shovel away the sand & rocks before it's totally buried. Ira Schoppman of Cedar City, who has the water & grazing rights to this spring and land below, says the water comes out of a perforated pipe that's now underground, then flows down to the water troughs at 1615m.

323

Above Part of the big **Anasazi ruins** on the plateau immediately above **Bonal Springs.** This might be the biggest complex of its kind in the Sand Hills.

Right From near the top of the Vermilion Cliffs looking down the steep chute or ravine heading for **Bonal Springs**. It's hard to believe Bonal put pipe down through here and pumped water up to the top for his sheep. Be watching for rock art along this route.

On USGS maps this place & building is called **Jacobs Pool**, but it had nothing to do with Jacob Hamblin, or John D. Lee. It was built in the early 1900's by the Grand Canyon Cattle Co. as part of their ranching operations. In the background are 2 steep canyons; the one on the right is what this writer calls the **Northern Sand Hills Crack**. Look closely and you can see some vegetation which is **Hancock Spring**, the water of which is still used today.

About halfway up the **Northern Sand Hills Crack**, looking down on **Hancock Spring**. Just a little ways behind the camera is the **Pinnacle** which has rock art around its base.

This is all that remains of **Rachel Lee's stone house** located near the western-most spring below the Eastern Sand Hills Crack. As you hike up to the **Eastern Crack**, and near the top, you'll see the remains of an old man-made trail. It was built by the Grand Canyon Cattle Company sometime in the early 1900's. It was never used by cattle, but only as a horse trail to get on or off the Sand Hills--according to Jay Findlay (grandson of Merle Findlay).

Left Part of one rock art panel near the top of the **Eastern Sand Hills Crack**. **Right** Looking west along the Vermilion Cliffs from about halfway between the **Northern Sand Hills Crack** and the top of the Bonal Spring Trail. In the upper left-hand corner is the **Bonal Trail** going up through the cliffs.

Left Inside the square chamber of the middle part of **Bonal Springs**. Notice the shovel in the water. **Right** These are the present-day watering troughs at the edge of the plateau above **Bonal Springs**. This was likely put in by the Bowmans because Trevor Leach can't remember this kind of trough when he was working there in the mid-1930's.

Both fotos here were taken along the **old Navajo Trail**, which during the mid-1900's gradually became known as the **Honeymoon Trail**. Calvin C. Johnson says calling it the Honeymoon Trail was a kind of promotional thing done by the tourist interests in Kanab. It's the same trail as the one which was likely pioneered, at least to some degree, by Jacob Hamblin and John D. Lee.

From there, make your way down the crack to the spring, then on down the plastic pipeline trail to the Bonal Spring Trailhead on the old **Navajo Trail**. From there, walk east along that historic trail. After about 1 km is a fence and the 4WD road to that point ends. Between that fence and Jacobs Pool, you must pay a little attention to the route as it's not perfectly clear in all places, but most of the time you'll be walking along a cow trail inside a shallow groove about 1m deep and 8-10m wide. At 2 points along the way will be a **sign** marking the route.

Elevations Trailhead for Bonal Spring, 1587m; rim of Paria Plateau, about 2163m; Jacobs Pool, 1587m; top of Northern Sand Hills Crack, 2066m; top of Eastern Crack, 2042m; Jarvis Ranch, 2026m.

Time Needed From the old **Navajo Trail** to the rim of the Sand Hills via **Bonal Spring** and back, may take roughly 4-5 hours. From **Jacobs Pool** to the top of the **Northern Crack** could take 3-5 hours, or about half a day. From Jacobs Pool to the top of the **Eastern Crack** will take 2-4 hours round-trip. To do a loop-hike doing both cracks together should take 4-5 hours, maybe longer for some. To do the loop from Jacobs Pool or Bonal Spring, should take from 7-9 hours, more for some.

Water Take your own on all hikes. But there's water in the hole in the wall which is **Bonal Spring**, lots of good water at **Hancock Spring**, and some at the main spring at Rachel's Pools (lift a lid to a covered basin or tub).

Maps USGS or BLM maps Glen Canyon Dam (1:100,000) for driving & orientation; Emmett Hill & One Toe Ridge (1:24,000--7 1/2' quads) for hiking & driving; or one of the 4 MF-1475 maps A, B, C or D (1:62,500) for hiking & driving.

Main Attractions Petroglyphs & cowboy etchings along 4 old Indian routes to the top of the Sand Hills, great views from the rim, and historic Jacobs Pool & Lee's Ranch or Rachels Place which John D. Lee helped put on the map.

Best Time to Hike Spring or fall, but you can hike year-round. Expect deep snow on top in winter.

Boots/Shoes Lightweight but rugged hiking boots or trail running shoes.

Author's Experience He's climbed to the top of the Bonal Spring Trail 3 times in 3-4 1/2 hours each, round-trip. Three trips to the top of the Northern Sand Hills Crack and back took 2-3 hours each. One trip in 1987 was to the big steel water tank east of the Jarvis Ranch; 6 1/2 hours round-trip. His 3 hikes up to the Eastern Crack took less than 2 1/2 hours each, round-trip. The loop-hike including the 2 cracks took 3 3/4 hours; and the loop from Jacobs Pool, Bonal Spring & the Navajo Trail took 7 hours.

History of the Bonal Spring Development

In previous editions of this book, this site was called **Bonal Spring**, but for this edition it's been changed to **Bonal Spring**. Dunk Findlay and others always called this Bonelli Spring (perhaps because Walt Hamblin's mother was a **Bonelli** and people got confused?), but on a BLM document dated June 24, 1940, **J. F. Bonal & wife Ubaldina** of Flagstaff, Arizona, sold their water rights of Cottonwood & Death Tank Springs and all pipelines, troughs and water pump to J. H. Jennings of Rockville, Utah.

Also, on the **Water Resources map** made by S.M. Mieda in a survey of the Sand Hills & House Rock Valley in April, May & June, 1937, it shows this spring complex with **Bonal** written across it. That map shows an upper & lower **Cottonwood Springs** (the ones that are commonly called Bonal Springs today), and 2 seeps at **Death Tanks**, below and a little east of the ones we now call Bonal. That map lists 3 earth tanks or stock ponds probably below Death Tanks.

Also described on that map is the **pump** which moves water from some of the springs up to the rim of the Sand Hills. It was described as a 300 lb. (135 kg) pressure pump, 7 horsepower, plus 2800 feet (853m) of 2" (5 cm) pipeline. Also mentioned was one trough to water sheep, and a cement cistern measuring 18'x20'x6 1/2' (6x6x2m). The map itself isn't very clear, but it seems these were the improvements & facilities to transport & handle water up on top for summer use, while the earth tanks and more pipeline below Death Tanks was perhaps used to water sheep in winter (?).

Now, some of the history in this chapter on the Sand Hills comes from the late Dunk Findlay formerly of Kanab. Here's some of what he remembered about this spring when interviewed in 1987. This site was unknown and unused by white men until the early 1900's. Sometime after about 1916, **Alex Cram**, who owned a large ranch in the lower House Rock Valley, began to develop several minor seeps. He blasted a square hole in the bottom of the Navajo Sandstone cliff in order to increase the flow and to better capture the water. Sometime later, he traded his grazing rights to a man named William J. **(Billy) Mackelprang** (the brother to Art & Frank) for 2 horses.

Later, in the early 1930's, a Basque sheepman named J. F. Bonal from Flagstaff, Arizona, came into the country and bought the water rights to the springs. Prior to that time, the lower seeps were called **Death Tanks**, because there was never much water there.

Ira Schoppman remembered this one: *There is another tank to the east maybe a mile, or 1 1/2 miles, that used to be hooked into a trough we had down almost to the highway. That's probably the one they call Lower Death Tanks. It never run enough water to fill a trough. The BLM helped us put it in, then dug it out, and it run pretty good for a year, then I think with too many dry years it just dried up. It's in them little foothills before you start up.*

Bonal brought sheep with him, but needed a better waterhole. After considering his options, he bought pumping equipment & pipe, then worked to construct a pumping station, pipeline and troughs, in order to pump water from the spring up to the plateau rim to the cement cistern mentioned above. His operation was successful, and he had water on the rim for about 4 years. His sheep were on top of the Sand Hills in the summer; down under the cliffs in House Rock Valley during the winter.

But in 1936, the newly established Grazing Service (forerunner to the BLM) ran him out. Bonal apparently had not been in the area long enough before the Taylor Grazing Act was passed in 1934, and wasn't eligible for a permit to run livestock in that part of the country. So after 4 apparently successful years, he had to abandon the operation. But his name stuck, at least on the upper seeps.

At that upper site today, you'll see a **half-buried pump & motor** and some hoses & wire at the eastern-most spring. Today, there's no visible sign of water there, but Ira Schoppman insists that's the main one they've tapped to get water down to the valley--apparently the intake pipe is buried.

The middle spring is the only one which has a large enough flow on-site to get a drink out of today; you can drink there because it's been developed. It's shaped like a square mine tunnel, which was blasted out of the lower Navajo. Inside are etchings of cowboys like *Mel & Ira Schoppman,* a mossy pool of water and a plastic pipe running down to the troughs in the valley below. Better be careful drinking this water, the author once observed hoof prints of big horn sheep inside this tomb-like tunnel that's about 3-4m deep. At the 3rd seep, or wet spot to the west, 3 cottonwood trees grow, but apparently isn't being used today. However, because of those trees, that may be the source of the name Cottonwood

Springs shown on the 1937 map mentioned above.

Above the pump and near the big wall, are scattered odds & ends of the water pumping operation. On the Navajo Sandstone wall itself are several small etchings or **petroglyphs**. On the rim of the plateau are 3 cement troughs, one after another, but according the Trevor Leach, they weren't there in the mid-1930's (he remembers some metal water troughs). They were built since Bonal left, either by Jennings, A.T. Spence or Bowmans (?). Also right on the rim and south of the troughs, are 4 or 5 structures that are the remains of a small village or perhaps a seasonal hunting camp likely built by a group of aborigines called **Virgin Anasazi**. No doubt those people established this settlement because of the existence of the springs and a route from the top of the Sand Hills to the flats below. Because of the altitude of 2163m, they probably tried growing corn--but that was likely a hit & miss proposition.

Down below in the House Rock Valley, and along your hiking route, are half a dozen water troughs and a small overflow pond. Cattle graze this area on a rotating basis. According to Ira Schoppman, the one who owns the water rights to Bonal Spring in 2010: *We rotate our cows in there every 2 years and cattle are there for 4 months. Sometimes they're there in summer, sometimes in winter.*

History of Jacobs Pool and Lee's Ranch

There have been mistakes made regarding the name of the place at the bottom of the trail going up to the Eastern Sand Hills Crack. According to one of the footnotes by Juanita Brooks in the book she and Robert Cleland edited, *A Mormon Chronicle: The Diaries of John D. Lee, 1848-1876*, mention is made that *Jacob's Pool was located on Wednesday, October 26, 1859, as Jacob Hamblin and a small party were making their second trip to the crossing of the Colorado River. They had spent a waterless day and night at the end of Buckskin Mountain, and after much wandering found a small spring. "Brs. Hamblin, Crosby, and myself dug out and walled up this spring and named it Jacob's Pool"* (from Thales Haskel's diary).

In May, 1872, Rachel Woolsey, one of John D. Lee's wives, was moved into this same area now known by various names such as The Pools, Jacob's Pool, Rachel's Pools; but in his diary, Lee calls it **Lee's Ranch** most of the time. USGS maps call another place located about 1 km southwest of Lee's Ranch, **Jacob Pool**. That's the place out in the valley a ways with the stone building and where you park if visiting this area. That old ranch house was built in the early 1900's by the Grand Canyon Cattle Company.

Lee's first shelter was a mud & willow shack, not much better than what Indians lived in. On June 2, 1872, a group of men from the Powell Survey, described as **Professor Beament & Bishop** by Lee, came through the area, and fotographed the mud hut (see the foto below).

Later in the fall of 1872, John D. started building a better house. He hired a stone mason named Elisha Everett to help, since the home was to be made of rock. Lee put the roof on, plus added 2 doors and installed temporary cupboards on Christmas Day of 1872. It measured 9x11m, had 2 doors, 2 bedrooms, a kitchen, a parlor and a wooden roof. Nearby was a cellar. The ruins of this rock house can still be seen just above the westernmost spring. In the same area, and just below the springs, are numerous rock walls, apparently used as fences or pens to hold livestock. This location is 32 kms west of Lee's Ferry, and was set up to be a way-station for Mormons who were heading south to settle in Arizona. It was one long day's travel between these 2 waterholes (Lee also made some improvements at **Soap Creek**, located about halfway between the two sites so the Mormons could have it as another rest stop if needed).

One day by wagon to the west was another site of interest, which goes back to the spring and summer of 1873. This is the resting place or way-station along the **Navajo Trail** called **House Rock Spring & Signature Rocks.** Years later, the name of this route began to be called the **Honeymoon Trail** because so many Mormons had settled in Arizona, and after the St. George Temple had opened. After that, many young Mormon couples made the trip to southern Utah along this trail or road to be married in the temple. They usually returned home in a very dreamy state, thus the name, Honeymoon Trail.

Back to Jacobs Pool. At that location are a couple of corrals and a well-built stone building. Information as to when this structure was built is scarce, but most of the old-timers around believe it was built in the early 1900's when the Grand Canyon Cattle Company ran cows throughout the entire House Rock Valley. Ira Schoppman of Cedar City who now owns the private land & water rights to House Rock Spring says: *Jacobs Pool now belongs to Grand Canyon Trust. Apparently they've piped that water*

from Hancock Spring down across the highway rather than have it at the Pools. But it was done before the Grand Canyon Trust took it over. It's piped down about a mile off the highway and it joins Mackelprang's. Donny Mackelprang still runs cows in that area, and he lives in Fredonia.

This was Rachel Lee's willow & mud shack on June 2, 1872. In the picture are Rachel, John D. Lee, 2 of his small sons and a daughter. This picture was taken near the westernmost spring at what was originally called **Jacob's Pool**, but which John D. called **Lee's Ranch** most of the time in his diary. (Arizona Historical Society)

329

The Henrieville CCC Camp

Civilian Conservation Corps (CCC's) camps were built and operated throughout the United States in the 1930's for the purpose of building roads, trails, fences, catchment basins or stock ponds and other conservation projects on public lands. Most of them were in the west. They were organized and run by the US Army in cooperation with the Forest Service, the Division of Grazing or Grazing Service (BLM after 1947) and/or the National Park Service.

The **Henrieville CCC Camp #2529, Division of Grazing #33,** was located northeast of Henrieville immediately south of present-day Highway 12, the paved road running between Bryce Canyon National Park and Escalante. It was located just below where the old Smith Ranch was originally situated. Regarding the location, Iris Smith Bushnell had this to say about the place: *The old Smith Ranch was settled by my grandfather, James Edward Smith, Sr. He was probably there in the late 1800's (?). The CCC camp was located about a quarter mile [400m] below where the Smith Ranch was. They used to live up there in the summertime; they'd raise a garden and had their cattle. I guess grandpa just abandoned the place. There wasn't anyone at the ranch when the CCC camp was built.*

Most older people in Bryce Valley know something about the camp, but maybe the best source is from one of the enrollees. Most of the story below was told to the author by Darrel Blackwell who lives in Layton, Utah:

That CCC camp was 7 miles [11 kms] up the canyon from Henrieville, and that road ended right at the camp. The road then is exactly where the paved highway is today. The next thing above the CCC camp was The Blues. In later years, they built that road and it went on up over the top into Escalante.

They had 3 or 4 barracks for the men, and there was 15 to 20 men in each barracks. Then they had the mess hall and the administration building. Now that camp was set up for the Division of Grazing [Grazing Service]. Some camps was run by the Forest Service, some by the Park Service, and the one in Henrieville was run by the Division of Grazing. And of course they had their office building, and then the army people that supervised the kids when they weren't workin', they had their own building. Then they had work shops where they kept their trucks & tools--the motorpool. They also had an infirmary or sickbay--a barracks-type place. They also had a little PX or store where you could buy candy or cigarettes. Then they had a recreational building where they had their educational programs. You see, they had educational programs for most of those kids, because most of 'um got in the CCC's before they was graduated from high school. The educational advisor that camp was from Ogden, Utah.

Then they had their wash house where they had toilets & showers. You had to go to a different building to shave & shower. The showers, toilets and wash basins was located in a buildin' just below the barracks. You had to get up and go quite a little ways from the barracks, maybe a 100 feet [30m] or so.

I don't know for sure, but I would imagine there was about 150 or 200 people in the camp at any one time. You see, the Division of Grazing, they had their own personnel, their foremen, then of course the army had their people that took care of the camp stuff.

In each barracks they had a leader and an assistant leader. I was a leader, and we slept at the head of the barracks right at the door. It was our responsibility to keep order in the barracks, and make sure it was kept clean. Then when we went out on the job in the mornin', we had a foreman that was generally an older guy that was a local person [these were called LEM's--Local Experienced Men] from some of those towns around the area. These foremen lived in the camp in barracks where the army guys lived. And each foreman was assigned a leader and an assistant leader. So it was our responsibility to watch over the men, make sure they worked, make sure everything was OK. Each foreman had, depending on the project that was goin' on, probably 15 to 20 men.

The foremen were hired by the CCC's. Most of the foremen at our camp was from over around Panguitch & Circleville. The guy who was our foreman was really old. He was a butcher who used to live in Panguitch. When we'd go out to cut posts, and when guys would get scattered out, he'd go over and lay down under a cedar tree and have a nap. He had most of us guys from Kentucky that knew how to handle an ax and knew how to cut timber.

Then we had a guy in the camp that was a night guard. It was his duty to patrol the camp at night, then he'd come into the head of the barracks ever' mornin' and wake the leader and assistant leader up, then it was their responsibility to go down through the barracks and get the guys up and washed and have them get ready for breakfast. In the CCC's, we never had guard duty like in the army.

Then we had a sergeant who had some duties over the whole camp. He was a regular CCC enrollee like the rest of us. His duties was to go with the officers and inspect the barracks, and go to town in an army truck and get the mail. He was over the clothing and PX too. We just called him Sergeant. He stayed there all the time to oversee what was goin' on around camp and in the kitchen. That camp was organized about as well as anything I've ever been in. They had everything covered, and everything worked pretty good.

There was 3 guys who were regular army in our camp. Most of the time I was there, we had an army captain, and we had a lieutenant--I think he was a 2nd lieutenant. I guess they were full-time army people, and they knew the ropes, and of course they handled all the clothing and food and stuff. Then there was a doctor. He was in charge of the clinic or sickbay. If we ever had any serious health problems, they'd send us to Fort Douglas [next to Salt Lake City]. A lot of our supplies come out of Fort Douglas too. At that time Fort Douglas was a big army post.

Don Chynoweth, grandson of Arthur Chynoweth, was a small boy when the Henrieville camp was up and running. He recalls one experience at the camp: *My grandmother Rose, Arthur Chynoweth's wife, used to do the laundry for the CCC's boys in Henrieville. And when she'd get the clothes done she'd put 'um in boxes & baskets, and take 'um back to the camp in a rubber-tired wagon with a team. On one trip, me and my cousin Wayne rode with her up to the CCC Camp. We got there about noon, took the clothes and dropped them off, and they invited us into the mess hall and said, "here, have your dinner with us". Now in them days we didn't have a lot of food--it was hard to get hold of; so I remember they were cooking these great big pork chops in metal trays. I never saw so much food! I can remember that so well.*

Now back to Darrel's story: *Some of those kids were from back east and they'd get homesick. They'd send 'um way out here and some had never been away from home before. And some of 'um had never been off concrete or blacktop--those guys from Brooklyn and Youngstown, Ohio, and those big cities, and they would get homesick and some of 'um would try to go home. They called it, "goin' over the hill". "Oh, he's gone over the hill", they'd say. And I guess they just let 'um go; we'd have a few of 'um try to go over the hill and get home, some of 'um never could make it. But if they did, they'd get a dishonor-*

able discharge just like in the military. If you got one of those dishonorable discharges, you was in pretty bad shape!

There was another camp at Bryce Canyon, but that wasn't part of ours. That Bryce Canyon camp, I think was a part of the camp from Zion [National Park]. The bigger camps would send out these people to setup temporary spike camps. The Bryce camp didn't seem to be a really big one but I remember the foreman up there was from Henrieville. Later on, when I was drivin' that mail contract I used to haul food and milk and stuff into that Bryce Canyon camp. But it wasn't a big camp like Henrievilles. They lived in buildings not tents, and they was up there quite a while. They worked on the trails in Bryce Canyon National Park.

We had a spike camp at Pipe Springs, which was in northern Arizona west of Kanab & Fredonia. Then there was one over on the Sevier River about 5 miles [8 kms] south of Panguitch on Highway 89. It was pretty close to where you turn off Highway 89 goin' east toward Bryce Canyon--about a mile or so south of there. We had quite a few guys over there. We stayed in the main camp and drove out ever' mornin' from the Henrieville Camp into Dry Valley and Butler Valley, and down into the upper part of what they called The Gut.

Afton Pollock of Tropic, son of Sam Pollock, contradicts some of this information, in part because he lived there throughout the life of the CCC camp, and Darrel didn't. Regarding spike camps, many of which were only in one spot a week or two, here's what Afton remembered: *They had a little spike camp on Watson Ridge near that CCC or BLM corral, and in the winter of 1936-37, the CCC boys brought 14 ton of cottonseed cake there for my Dad. They arrived on Christmas morning, 1936. An army cat driven by Hasle Caudill opened a road out there through snow up to my armpits! They erected a big army tent and put the cottonseed cake in it, then I'd come in from Death Valley and pickup this cottonseed cake, put it on mules and haul it down to our sheep. That spike camp was just south of where that corral is today.*

There was another little spike camp down by Round Valley [near Round Valley Neck and Round Valley or Rush Bed Seep], and another one over at the head of Cottonwood Wash by that stockade corral just south of Grosvenor Arch. It wasn't very big, they must have had 25 men there. I remember that because my brother and I came up through there with a herd of sheep in about 1936, and these boys was there workin' on that corral. They had tents for sleeping, a tent for a kitchen and a latrine. They also had a couple of spike camps out on Deer Range [along the Skutumpah Road] and in that country. They may have had one down there about halfway between Deer Creek & Crack Spring along the Paria (?).

Now back to Darrel's story again: *Then there was another big camp in Escalante just over the hill from where we were, but you couldn't go up through The Blues where the highway is today. You had to go up to Bryce, then north to Widtsoe and east clearn the hell of over Table Cliff Mountain and Barney Top in order to get to Escalante. That camp built a lot of that road goin' over to Boulder in 1937. Escalante was a big camp like ours.*

We built a corral in Butler Valley and also put a windmill in there with storage tanks for water. We done quite a lot of work out in Kodachrome Flats and Round Valley. We built that road clearn' in Butler Valley that goes down into The Gut and Wahweap country. In them days you couldn't get very far, there was washes, and it just wasn't passable. It was when they started workin' on Glen Canyon Dam that they started opening up that Cottonwood Wash road so you could drive down through there.

We built a lot of fences for the Division of Grazing to help keep cattle out of certain places. And corrals and wells. We built that catchment near the Kodachrome Turnoff, but it filled up with sediment. We built a little monument there, DG 33 is what they called it. We spelled the name out in rock on the face of it. Originally it may have covered 4 or 5 acres, then it just filled up with those floods. We also built that corral on Watson Ridge [now it's generally called the BLM Corral].

Jack Chynoweth of Tropic says: *they also had a little spike camp at Round Valley Seep, just south of the trailhead parking for Round Valley Draw. They developed that seep so water could be put into a large watering trough for cattle. They were the ones who blasted a hole in the sandstone wall nearby to keep their perishable foods in.*

Darrel again: *While in the main camp, we'd have to go out and watch the flag go up and down, and go out and do calisthenics before breakfast, and go out and stand at retreat and watch the flag go down--it was run by the army and it was strict! I'll tell you one thing, the army personnel that run our camp, the ones who took care of the boys after they'd get off work in the evening, they were 10 times stricter than the army was in World War II! I was in World War II, and the CCC camp had a lot stricter standards than the army. I mean they were more strict in the barracks on cleanliness, and more strict on everything. They held daily inspections in those barracks, and boy if they came through and flipped a quarter and if it didn't bounce up off the bed, you was in trouble! You'd be on KP [Kitchen Patrol] on the weekend when you should be in town goin' to a dance!*

In those days there wasn't no television; in fact, you'd have to have a damn good radio to get any kind of reception! You couldn't hardly get nothin'. But them little towns of Henrieville, Cannonville and Tropic, they used to have a dance ever' Friday night. They was great for us. Then a lot of times when people would get married--the locals, they'd have a wedding dance. And so the CCC camp would send a truck or two to town, and we'd always go down to those dances. Then they'd pick us up and bring us back. Goin' to dances was big in them days. Friday night was the big night down there, because they had a dance in one town one Friday night, then the next Friday it would be in the next town. And the CCC's were welcome to come and participate and dance.

We didn't have many picture shows, that recreational director was a guy named Dirk from Ogden, and he was the educational advisor. In the first camp I was in at Mammoth Cave, Kentucky, they had a rec. building where they showed movies. In our rec. hall you could play pool, or play ping pong, but mostly it was an educational-type thing, where you could go to school and learn a lot of stuff.

The pay wasn't bad for them days. One reason for setting up the CCC's was to help families who had no jobs. Most families got $25 a month, that was sent home to 'um; and their enrollee got only 5 bucks a month--$30 was your monthly pay unless you was a leader or assistant leader. A leader got $45 a month--he got $20, and the rest went home to the family. An assistant leader got $36. And they paid off in cash ever' 30 days. They'd have a big table laid out with them army blankets on it and they had the cash. All the enrollees got was the $5, and they'd send the rest to your home--but all you had to buy was toothpaste and candy and cigarettes. Ever'thing else was furnished.

The CCC's was a good organization and that's where I learnt most of the skills that I used in the contractin' business. When you'd first get to the CCC camp, the first thing you knew, they'd put you in a great big truck and put 25 men on it and send you out in the hills. Or put you up on a D-9 Cat that

331

you'd never seen before in your life and make an operator, cat-skinner, out of ya. A lot of those guys that was in the heavy equipment stuff, the ones that stayed around there, ended up workin' for the state road department.

I think the Henrieville camp was set up around **1934**; it was there when I arrived. I got there in the winter of 1936 & '37. I was there 18 months, because you could only sign up for 18 months, then you had to get out and let somebody else in. But I was around even longer than that. You see, I got married to a local girl and stayed there in Henrieville--I was there 30 years after that. I got married just a short time after I got out of the CCC's. The camp closed down in the winter of **1939-40** when the World War tactics got so bad in Europe. At that time I was drivin' the mail contract out of Henrieville to Panguitch, and I used to deliver milk and mail up to that camp. But they closed it down and then they drafted most of those people. Most of the guys went from the CCC's right into the army.

There was 7 CCC boys who married local girls. One guy lives over here in Ogden, **Hasle Caudill**, he drove a cat, a cat skinner, and he married Rhoda Chynoweth. **Hobart Feltner** of Cannonville married a Twitchell girl. He was a cook and he was there most of the time I was. Then there was **Willy Bryant** who lives down in Riverton. He was a truck driver, and he married Elma Mangum. There was another cook named **Hamby** who married another Twitchell girl. He's dead. Walter **Livinguth** was an assistant leader, and he married a Smith girl from Henrieville. **Ora Shafer** was a senior foreman. He married Rhoda Henderson and she still lives down in Cannonville. The family I married into were really strict Mormons. In fact, my father-in-law was bishop for 17 years. That was Harvey Chynoweth [**Darrel Blackwell** was the 7th].

When I got out of the CCC's, I went home first, of course--they shipped me home, then I came right back out to Henrieville. They closed all the camps just before the beginning of the war--they figured they didn't need the CCC's anymore and they needed the boys in the army instead.

Hobart Feltner of Cannonville contributed a little more information: I got there October 12, 1936, at 5 o'clock. I was in 22 months. The camp was about 2 years old when I came in [It opened in about 1934]. Darrel Blackwell came in 6 months after I arrived.

Those buildings didn't have any insulation--there was no insulation in the damn things. They was just boarded up. It was pretty cool in them buildings in winter, I can tell you that. You see, in 1936 & '37 is when that big snow storm came here, and you could walk over a fence and anything else! I told the guys, if this is the kind of stuff we're going to have around here, I'm not a goin' to be around next year!

Hasle Caudill, another enrollee and presently of Ogden, remembered a few more things. The camp had both a basketball & baseball team that went around to different towns, mostly in the summer, and played pickup games. When Hasle arrived, they had a team of work horses at the camp. In some places, they pulled fresno scrappers, but the camp's big cat put them out of work. To transport the boys around to different jobs, they used one of 8 or 10 1936 Ford 1 1/2 ton flatbed trucks equipped with wooden sides & benches (see foto).

When the big snow storm came on Christmas Day, 1936, they had to load one of the trucks with several 50 gallon barrels of water so they could get out to the cat. He then drove the cat to Watson Ridge opening a road so the CCC's could haul cottonseed cake out to Sam & Afton Pollock's sheep herds. He then broke a number of trails with the cat so feed could be spread out for the sheep. In some places, the snow was up to a man's armpits.

In 1939, just before Hasle left the CCC's, and just before the Henrieville Camp closed, he & Ora Shafer and others, built a rough road above the camp up through The Blues going in the direction of Escalante. Years later the state came in, improved it, and made it into the good paved state highway we have today.

If Rhoda Henderson Shafer's memory is correct, the camp closed down in the winter of 1939-'40, and the men & equipment were taken to Hurricane near St. George. She and her husband Ora then moved into the camp as caretakers. This was in the spring of 1940. In the fall, the Shafer's left as other people came in & started tearing the buildings down. No one knows where the lumber went to.

Willy Bryant, one of the former enrollees at the Henrieville CCC Camp, has a couple of large fotographs of the camp and men. On each of these are inscribed: **CCC Co. 2529, Camp DG [Division of Grazing]--33, Henrieville, Utah, May 20, 1938.** Also inscribed on the picture of the men is: **Lt. C. W. Callahan, Commanding; Mr. H. L. Dirks, Educational Advisor; Lt. L. J. May, Junior Officer; and Mr. Lionel Chidester, Project Superintendent.** Both pictures were taken on May 20, 1938 by Erwin Photo.

To get to this camp site, drive eastward toward Escalante from Henrieville's post office on Highway 12 for 10.2 kms (6.35 miles). Park on the highway where the valley begins to narrow and walk down a side-road toward the creek. About the only thing left to see is the rock foundation of the flagpole. This is now in a sea of tall sagebrush.

One of the trucks belonging to the **Henrieville CCC Camp** loaded with a compressor. The building behind the truck is the motorpool. That building is seen in the lower left-hand corner of the picture above on the opposite page.
(Hasle Caudill foto)

The **Henrieville CCC Camp** looking south. L to R: The motorpool, officer's quarters, infirmary, mess hall, offices for the army & Division of Grazing (DG), and on the far right are the barracks or billets which housed the enrollees. The latrines & showers are the fartherest to the right. In the center can be seen the flagpole, the base of which is the only thing that's easily visible today. (Willy Bryant foto)

This is part of the basketball team from the **Henrieville CCC Camp**, but as yet no one can identify any of the players. It seems enrollees were coming and going a lot. (Hasle Caudill foto)

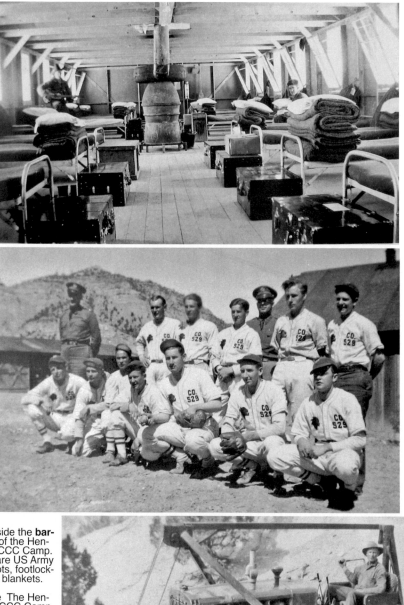

Top Inside the **barracks** of the Henrieville CCC Camp. These are US Army issue cots, footlockers & blankets.

Middle The Henrieville CCC Camp **baseball team**.

Right This is one of the **Cats** or bulldozers belonging to the **Henrieville CCC camp**. Most conservation projects in the area were done with a Cat, but some work was done with a team & fresno scrappers. (all 3 fotos are from Hasle Caudill)

334

Above Left A work crew out somewhere. Both of the above fotos are of crews belonging to the **Henrieville CCC Camp**. **Above Right** Another bunch of enrollees going somewhere. There are at least 2 cooks, and 2 guys who look as though they work for the Division of Grazing, the forerunner to todays BLM.

Below This would be late afternoon, but almost every morning & evening, the enrollees at the **Henrieville CCC Camp** would do about the same thing the army does, stand at reveille or retreat and watch the flag go up & down. Looking south towards the creek and barracks. Behind the camera is the infirmary and motorpool. (Willy Bryant fotos)

Sheep and Sheep Shearing Corrals

An interesting part of the history of Bryce Valley is the story of sheep and a couple of sheep shearing corrals. In this area, they had mostly sheep and very few Angora goats, as opposed to the Kanab and Sand Hills country, which had mostly goats. The first sheep to arrive in the Paria River Country may have been brought in by Olie Alhstrom. He brought them from Sanpete County in central Utah in about the mid-1890's (?). From that point on, and up until the mid-1940's, or at about the end of World War II, there were literally thousands of sheep roaming and overgrazing the entire country.

It seems the first corral built for the specific purpose of shearing sheep was located at the bottom of Rock Springs Bench next to Rock Springs. This may have been set up as early as the late 1890's (?). The **Rock Springs Shearing Corral** site is located about 1 1/2 kms west of Wallace Ott's Corral and along Rock Springs Creek. See **Map 15, Road Map: Rock Springs Bench Trailheads.**

In the life history of Sam Pollock (compiled by his son Afton Pollock of Tropic), he states that he first started herding sheep for R. F. Shumway in August, 1901. In his story, Sam tells of one sad experience that happened a few years later: *In the spring of 1915, I exchanged shearing dates with my father-in-law Johnny Davis. His sheep were so poor that he could not meet his date. This new date made it so I could get my fat & stronger herd to the shearing corral on the 1st & 2nd days of May [at that time, they used hand clippers to shear the sheep and the shearing corral was at Rock Springs]. On the 3rd of May, we pulled out and arrived at Little Creek [Bench] where we spent the night. It started to rain, turning to sleet and snow about 3 am. My brothers Joe and Woodruff, along with Oscar LeFevre, were with the sheep. By morning there was a foot of snow and 300 dead sheep. The sheep kept dying and by noon there were 300 more dead. I met the herders about noon and we began building fires as there was plenty of wood and timber nearby. We built 50 fires and kept them going all night. Some of the sheep crowded the fires until they were burning to death, and some were smothered. After it was all over, we had 900 dead sheep and most of them were ewes ready to lamb. Some of the sheep would freeze to death while still standing and be dead when they fell over. This together with the winter loss made 1350 sheep lost. With the loss of lambs to be born, the total loss was about 2100 head. Sheep sold for $5 per head then, which would have been around $10,650 we were in debt......*

According to Afton Pollock: *The **Rock Springs Shearing Corral** site is about 3/4's or a mile west from where Wallace Ott's Corral is. There's a spring and that's why they built the corrals there. I used to get keg water there for camp. There's still evidence of the corrals--some posts and old planks and other things, still there. This was the first shearing corral in the country, then Promise Rock Corral came after that. They had a set of troughs they watered their sheep in from this spring, and that's just below where the corral was which was on the south side of the draw [creek].*

When you go down that draw, there's some big ledges on the north and part of that ledge has caved off. Now there are 2 big boulders and a bunch of names carved on 'um. The names include George Shakespeare, Will Shakespeare, a Graf, some Littlefields, Willis' and Chynoweths--quite a few names in there. My Dad's name is there from 1936. One date is from 1904, another from 1906 and one in 1908. So that's about the time that shearin' corral was running on Rock Springs Bench.

They used to take team & wagons in there to haul things, and the route they used to get from Rock Springs to Cannonville is about the same as they use now. From the corrals, they went east then north to Watson Ridge, then the road went west across Little Dry Valley and down Road Holler [Hollow] to the Paria River then came up to the old Diamond T Ranch [the original John Wesley Mangum Ranch] and on to Cannonville. Road Holler is between Little Dry Valley and Shepherd Point.

I suppose they stopped shearing out there at Rock Springs in the late 1910's, or by about the end of World War I. Then they came up here to Promise Rock because W. J. Henderson had property there, and then they started shearin' at Promise Rock.

Just after Sam Pollock first got into the sheep herding business, a man by the name of William Jasper Henderson of Cannonville (brother of Jim Henderson who once owned the Nipple Ranch), built another shearing facility just southeast of Cannonville on some ground he owned. This became known as the **Promise Rock Shearing Corrals.** Afton Pollock made a few telefon calls around Bryce Valley to find out how this place got it's name (Lula Chynoweth Moore & Desmond Twitchell contributed information). Here's what he found--edited slightly for this book:

*William J. Henderson was part of the original group called by Brigham Young in the mid-1870's to settle Bryce Valley. While on their way, part of that group stopped in a grove of trees for a rest. One young man named John Henry laid down underneath a tree and fell asleep. A young lady named Avilda March Diana Hickman thought it would be fun to see John's reaction to a surprise shower bath and threw a bucket of water all over him. John Henry, in turn jumped up, grabbed the girl and gave her a bath in the nearby creek. This little event started a budding romance which was in full bloom by the time they reached the site that would later be called Cannonville. A short time after arriving at their new home, the young couple decided to explore the area and climbed up on top of this large flat rock. They saw the bishop working in the nearby field and soon asked him if he would come up on the rock and marry them. The bishop consented, and the marriage ceremony was performed. Ever since that day in 1877, this unusual red rock outcropping has been called **Promise Rock.***

Wallace Ott recalled the place: *They'd bring sheep out there to shear 'um so they could load the wool and take it down to the train in Marysvale.*

Afton remembered even more: *W. J. Henderson had 2 herds of sheep, and he had 2 sons who had sheep. He owned property by Promise Rock and that's why he built the shearin' corrals there. The original corral, the one where they used hand clippers, was first set up in the early 1900's (?). You notice on these pictures, they had the old hand clippers, and a grinding stone to sharpen 'um with. But the one I remember when my Dad [Sam Pollock] was shearin' sheep there, was a more modern one. After a few years, they built this other building where they had a tractor with a long belt attached, and that powered newer clippers [which ran off belts & gears]. They had 20 booths, and up to 20 shearers could work there at a time. When I was a kid about 6 years old, that would have been in about 1925, the modern corral was in good shape. I'd say that second, more modern shearing corral was built in about 1920.*

[Later on] I'd been on a mission in 1940, and I came home in 1943. Dad had me deferred [held out of the draft] because the wool was a necessary item for the troops, and they needed the wool for blankets and clothing, but I was a 23-year-old healthy young man and the war was goin' on, so I enlisted in the Air Force. I flew 75 missions over Burma and China, then when I come home in 1945, I went out with the sheep until October of 1946, then Dad sold his entire herd. He was the last one in the valley to have sheep. He sold 'um to some people down in Long Valley. The spring of 1946 was the last time

that Promise Rock Shearin' Corral was used. Just before that time, the Alhstroms went out of the sheep business, John Johnson went out of the sheep business, also Wallace Houseton and Sam Graf got out of sheep herding, and Dad was the only one left at the end of the war.

Wallace Ott and 2 other gentlemen here in Tropic had a little herd of about 800-1200 sheep, something like that, but they didn't shear'um at that shearin' corral; they brought 'um up here to Tropic and they had a little one-stall shearing place. Then they sold their sheep and went into the cow business.

There's signatures of sheepmen on all sides of Promise Rock, and on top of it. On the southeast side of Promise Rock there's a nice arch.

Promise Rock is made of the Gunsight Butte Member of the Entrada Formation, same as what you find in Kodachrome Basin just to the southeast. This large outcropping consists of several minor peaks rising above the sagebrush flats between where the upper Paria River and Henrieville Creek meet. The corrals & barn site is 300m south of the southwestern part of this big red rock outcropping. On the northwest side of this southwestern peak are lots of old sheepmen's signatures.

Promise Rock and all the land surrounding it are private, but none of the land owners are willing to allow access to the public. Check at the Cannonville visitor center for any late developments.

About the time World War II began, the sheep business in Utah started a steep decline. One reason for this was that many small-town country folk moved to the cities where they could get good paying jobs created by the war. That was a lot better work than spending months on the range herding sheep! Another reason was better roads & trucks which made it easier to haul sheep and/or supplies around. By the end of the war almost all herds in the Paria River Country were gone. Today nothing is left of these shearing facilities but a few cedar posts from the corrals themselves, and other posts which supported the roof of the shearing barn at Promise Rock.

This is what remains of the **Promise Rock Shearing Corral**. It wasn't used after 1946. Promise Rock is seen in the background to the north. On the north side of the highest point you see, is a big wall with dozens of signatures of local sheepmen. The signatures that are still visible date from just after 1900.

This picture was taken with a telefoto lens from the northern end of the **Skutumpah Road** just as it starts to drop down toward Bryce Valley and the paved road running between Kodachrome Basin and Cannonville. In the far background is the **Table Cliff Plateau and Powell Point**. The red rocks in the lower part is **Promise Rock**.

The 2 fotos above were said to be of the **Promise Rock Shearing Corrals**, but the background doesn't quite fit. But they certainly were taken in the early 1900's somewhere in the Paria River Country (?). (Cheri Schofield fotos)

Right Sam Pollock left, and his brother Lorem, packing up and moving camp somewhere in the lower **Cottonwood Wash**. Notice the sheep in the background. (Afton Pollock foto)

Hermon helped his father with the sheep between the years 1920 ~ 1937.

Afton Pollock thinks this is the shearing corral at **Rock Springs** (?). This picture would have been taken in the early 1900's. (Herman & Afton Pollock foto)

This picture shows **Sam Pollock**, 2 sheep dogs, and sheep in the background to the right. The peak to the left in the distance looks like **Castle Rock**, which is in the lower end of Cottonwood Wash. (Afton Pollock foto)

The Story of John D. Lee and the Mountain Meadows Massacre

A book on the Paria River, including Lee's Ferry, cannot be written without including the story of the life of **John D. Lee**. Nearly all Utah and Arizona residents know of him, but people from other parts of the country probably don't. This chapter is a brief summary of Lee's life, and is intended to let the reader understand events leading up to the **Mountain Meadows Massacre** and why John D. Lee was sent to the lower Paria River to establish Lee's Ferry. The author used, with permission, a book by Juanita Brooks, ***John Doyle Lee, Zealot-Pioneer Builder-Scapegoat***, as the primary source for this chapter.

John D. Lee was born on September 12, 1812, in Kaskaskia, the capital of the territory of Illinois. He lived in Illinois throughout his youth, and at age 16, left home to fend for himself. His first job was a mail rider, which lasted 6 months. He had various jobs in the several years until he got married, which was on July 24, 1833, at age 21. He married Agatha Ann Woolsey, the first of 19 women he would marry during his lifetime.

It wasn't long after this he became a convert to the **Mormon Church**. During the first 5 years of marriage, he was a missionary part of the time and had various jobs. In the period after 1838, he and the Mormons migrated to Missouri. As you might imagine, when the Mormons rode into that state proclaiming parts thereof to be their Zion, the reception wasn't too cheery. They had problems, and later had to leave, winding up in Illinois and eventually in Nauvoo where they built a temple.

Because Lee was a very religious man and totally devoted to the Church, he became one of the unofficial leaders. Because he was so good at things like farming, building homes, and working with machinery, he was called upon throughout his life to go out and help settle new colonies. He was never a high-ranking Church authority, but was a major cog in the Church's settlement program for about 30 years.

From Nauvoo, Illinois, the Mormons headed for the Missouri River in the winter of 1946-47 and the region around Council Bluffs, Iowa, and near present-day Omaha & Florence, Nebraska. Since it would take a year or two to get all the Mormons to Utah, they needed to set up several temporary encampments enroute in preparation for the long haul to the Great Basin. John D. was much involved in building these temporary settlements.

While in Iowa, the Mormons were called upon to send a battalion of soldiers to California. This they did, but church President Brigham Young asked Lee to follow the group to Santa Fe, and collect the soldiers pay and bring it back to their families who needed it a lot more than did the soldiers.

Because Lee was needed along the Missouri River area in Iowa and Nebraska, he was not chosen to accompany the first Pioneer Party to Utah in 1847. He instead followed in June of 1848. Upon arriving in Utah and the Salt Lake Valley, he immediately began to build a home for his wives. By the time he left Nauvoo, John D. Lee had 10 wives; Brigham Young 17.

In one of the church meetings on December 2, 1850, in which Lee attended, Brigham Young mentioned they were going to send a group of volunteers south to what is now Cedar City, and establish an Iron Mission. There was a group of Englishmen who had the knowledge and skills to do the iron work, but they needed support in the venture. After the meeting, Young told Lee, that when he had asked for volunteers, he meant Lee. Young said, *"If we are to establish an iron industry there, we must have a solid base of farming to help support it."*

The next thing Lee knew, he was the leader of a small group heading for southern Utah in the dead of winter. On December 11, 1850, the wagons rolled out. Lee took 2 of his wives. As one can imagine, it wasn't an easy journey. There was no road, just a trail, and snow was deep at times. They arrived at the present-day site of Parowan in February of 1851. Parowan was the first of several new settlements Lee was to set up in the next 20 years.

Things went well for Lee and the Church for several years, but in 1857 things began to change. News of an impending crisis came to the leaders of the Church on July 24, 1857. This was the 10th anniversary of the landing of the Pioneer Party in the Salt Lake Valley. They had a big celebration up Big Cottonwood Canyon southeast of Salt Lake City. During the afternoon festival, 2 men rode up the canyon with news that, *"all mail routes to the east were canceled, and an army was enroute to put down the rebellion in Utah."* According to the Mormon version of events, there was no rebellion, unless you consider it a rebellion for most of the Church authorities to have too many wives!

With this news, the church leaders and the people became a little hysterical, and there was a call to arms. Since the Mormons had been run out of several eastern states, they gradually became better prepared, in a military sense. The Church in Utah was organized not only into wards & stakes (religious groupings), but also in the event of an emergency, such as trouble with the Indians, they were organized into military companies and battalions as well. So preparations began, and in a way, Utah was almost in a state of martial law.

In many ways things went on as normal. But there began to be a very deep distrust for all non-Mormons. There were wagon trains crossing Utah all summer long, most of which were heading for northern California. But those who came late in the season usually went to California via the southern route. This route ran close to present-day Highway 91 and Interstate I5.

Since Salt Lake City was at about the halfway point between the populated eastern states and the coast, it was an important place to stop, rest and restock supplies. However, because of the impending arrival of Johnston's Army, the leadership of the Church issued orders to all settlements not to sell food stuffs to any gentiles (non-Mormons). The Church leaders also went to great pains to convince the various Indian leaders to join the Mormons to help repel the US Army. The Indians were told to join the Mormons and help fight Johnston's Army, or the army would kill all the Indians.

One can imagine the hardships this must have created for those unlucky travelers who were caught up in the middle of this Utah problem. One of these groups of wagons was called the **Fancher Party or Train**. It was a loosely knit group of several independent elements who had joined forces in Utah to travel in greater safety. The leader was **Charles Fancher**. He had crossed the country in 1855, selected and made arrangements to buy a large tract of land, and returned east in 1856 to bring his family and friends to join him to settle in California. They had a reported $4000 in gold coins, a large herd of cattle & horses and 11 well-stocked wagons. There were 11 families, with 29 children; a total of 65 people. Traveling with the Fancher Train was a group of horsemen with their supply wagons. They called themselves the **Missouri Wildcats**.

Quoting now from Juanita Brooks' book on John D. Lee: *"This group all arrived in Salt Lake City on*

Map 43, John D. Lee's Country

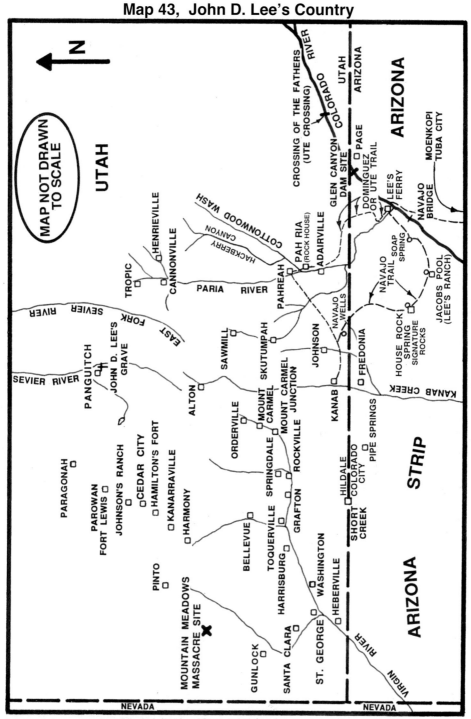

Adapted from Juanita Brooks' book, *JOHN DOYLE LEE--Zealot, Pioneer Builder, Scapegoat*

John D. Lee, age unknown.
(Utah State Historical Society foto)

August 3 & 4, and mindful of the fate of the Donner Party in 1846, decided to take the southern route. They followed a few days behind President George A. Smith on his journey south ordering the people to keep their grain and not to sell a kernel to any gentile. The Fancher Train was well-to-do; they had cash to pay or goods to trade, but no one would sell. The attitude of the Mormons all along the way was one of belligerence and hostility, aggravated by the attitude of the group of "Missouri Wildcats", who spoke of the Mormon leaders with scorn, and boasted of what they had done in Missouri." This was the way things shaped up in Utah in the late summer and early fall of 1857.

As the Fancher Train moved south through the state, one thing after another aggravated the situation. The Mormons wouldn't sell them anything, and the emigrant train, especially the Missouri Wildcats, did or said things to upset the Mormons. Finally the emigrants arrived in Cedar City, the last place on the road to California to get provisions. Since the locals wouldn't sell them anything, it's been said some of the Missourians helped themselves to some of the gardens. The local Mormon police tried to arrest some members of the party, but were just laughed at. So things continued to get worse.

"In the Sunday service at Cedar City on September 6, 1857, Stake President Isaac C. Haight spoke with bitterness of the coming of Johnston's Army, which he called an armed mob, and made pointed reference to the Fancher Train which had left only the day before. Following the regular service, a special priesthood meeting [men only] was called at which time the problems connected with the Fancher Train were discussed. Were they mice or men that they should take such treatment? Should they let such braggarts come into their midst and boast of the indignities they had heaped upon them in Missouri and Nauvoo? Should a man who would boast that he had the gun that 'shot the guts out of Old Joe Smith' go unpunished?" Such were the feelings of the people in Cedar City.

Finally at the meeting, a resolution was passed to the effect that "We will deal with this situation now, so that our hands will be free to meet the army when it comes." But then there was more discussion. Some wanted to do away with the emigrants who were the chief offenders; others preferring to let them all go and prepare themselves for the real war with Johnston's Army. Another resolution was presented to the effect that they should send a rider to Brigham Young in Salt Lake City seeking his council. It was passed, and they sent a rider (who returned late, and after the big event was over).

Still later a third resolution was passed, that of sending a messenger to John D. Lee at Harmony asking him to come and manage the Indians. At that time, Lee was an "Indian Farmer", or agent, and was second in command. Jacob Hamblin was the agent, but since he was in Salt Lake City, it was Lee who was called upon for advice. Lee had gotten on well with the Indians, and it's been said he spoke at least a few words of their language.

In the meantime, the Fancher Train had proceeded to a high meadow in the northern part of the **Pine Valley Mountains**. This was barely one day's drive from Cedar City. This place was called, and would always be known as, **Mountain Meadows.** They made camp near a spring and had plans to stay awhile to let their cattle recuperate, and until the weather got cooler, so they could cross the desert in more comfort.

Meanwhile back in Cedar City, things were happening at a rapid pace, with horsemen hurrying back and forth between Cedar City and Parowan, and between Mountains Meadows and Cedar City. At that time, there were 3 men who were the most important leaders in the area: **William H. Dame** from Parowan was appointed colonel commanding all the Iron County military. **Isaac C. Haight** was the Stake President who lived in Cedar City, and **John D. Lee**, who was the acting Indian agent, in the absence of **Jacob Hamblin**.

The Mormons were successful in getting the Indians on their side at this time. It seems both groups had no need for these emigrants, but for different reasons. A band of Indians had followed the Fancher Train south from Holden in central Utah, and had hoped the Mormons would help them attack the wagon train, and steal the cattle and other needed items. This same band of Indians joined others in the area of Cedar City, and had asked Lee to join them for an attack at Mountain Meadows. It seems that Lee had gone back home to Harmony to set things in order, and promised the Indians he would return on Tuesday, September 8.

But the Indians were ready for action, and knowing they and the Mormons were on the same side, made a predawn attack on the emigrant camp on the morning of September 8. The emigrants were caught by surprise, but were well-equipped and repulsed the attack. Later, Lee stated that 7 white men were killed, along with several Indians. When Lee joined the Indians on Wednesday the 9th, they were upset and excited. They insisted the Mormons join them to make another attack immediately. Lee wanted to go south and get help from the Santa Clara and Washington settlements, but about that time a group of settlers from those communities came, and they decided to send a messenger to Haight in Cedar City. Lee left at 2 pm.

In Cedar City, the bell rang out for the militia to gather. A statement was read that some of the emigrants had been killed, and they wanted volunteers to help bury them. But according to Brooks' story, a Nephi Johnson indicated a deception on the part of Isaac C. Haight. Johnson later suggested that Haight had said something to the effect that, *"Lee had suggested that they withdraw and let the emigrants go, and Haight sent word to Lee to clean up the dirty job he had started, and that he had sent out a company of men with shovels to bury the dead, but they would find something else to do when they got there."*

During the night of Wednesday the 9th of September, the military unit from Cedar City arrived at the Fancher camp. But at the same time, 3 emigrants had left camp under the cover of darkness and had gone to Cedar City to ask for help from the Mormons. As they neared their destination, and while watering their horses in a small stream, they were attacked by members of the Mormon Militia. One man was killed, and the other 2 scattered. It was later learned the remaining 2 men were killed by Indians at the Santa Clara crossing, down the Virgin River a ways. Again in Cedar City, the Mormon leaders gathered for council. It was decided to send John M. Higbee to Parowan in the night for advice from William. H. Dame.

Higbee returned the next day, Thursday the 10th, and delivered the message from Colonel Dame to Lee near the emigrant camp. The message indicated he should compromise with the Indians, allowing them to take all the cattle, then allow the emigrants to go. But then in the same message, Dame indicated if things couldn't be worked out, *"save women and children at all hazards"*. Lee was in a predicament, and with conflicting orders. What to do? Years later Lee insisted, *"that he had written orders to the effect that the emigrants must be decoyed from their shelter and all who were old enough to testify slain"*. Later in court, a man named Klingensmith testified that *"Lee's instructions came through Higbee from Dame at Parowan"*. Klingensmith must have overheard the conversation between Higbee and Lee, *"Orders is from me to you that they are to be decoyed out and disarmed, in any manner, the best way you can."*

So there Lee was faced with a decision. The Indians and Mormons both wanted revenge. The Mormons felt they had rights to some kind of blood atonement for the way the Missourians had treated them back in Far West and Nauvoo. The Indians also wanted some of the cattle; and the Mormons knew the Fancher Party was a wealthy group and had all those wagons and household goods. Greed must have been a factor in what was to be the final decision.

Lee along with a William Bateman, carried a white flag into the emigrant camp and negotiations began. Lee told them that if those guilty men would come back to Cedar City and face charges, they would all be given protection. But to do this, they would all have to show good faith and give up their arms. This the emigrants did, but ever since, people have wondered why they would give up their weapons (?). The day was **Friday, September 11, 1857.**

After the agreement was reached, all rifles and other weapons of the emigrants, were loaded into one wagon, along with all the children under the age of about 10 years (17 in all). This wagon moved out in front. Then a second wagon was loaded up with the emigrants who had been wounded in the previous Indian attack. Some said there were 2 men and a woman; others stated there were some older children as well.

Following the second wagon were the women and older children walking in an unorganized group. Following them were the emigrant men, walking in single file, each escorted by an armed member of the Mormon Militia.

The idea was to save the small children, but have no witnesses. The first wagon went way out in front, so they couldn't see anything. Lee walked just in front of the second wagon, which was at least 500m behind the first. When the first wagon was just out of sight, somewhere near the marching men, the signal was given, *"Do your duty. Instantly all the guns were fired, and at the same moment the Indians leaped from their ambush and fell upon the women and [older] children. The teamsters with Lee, and their assistants killed the ones in the second wagon and threw the bodies out into the brush beside the road."* The plan was carried out to perfection, and it was over in a hurry. It was estimated 120 people were murdered.

Just after the massacre, the Indians stripped the bodies for clothing and valuables. Then Lee issued the order to let the Indians have what they had, but take no more. They were to return to their camp where some beef was ready for supper. The men of the Mormon Militia then heard several speeches by Higbee, Lee and others, to the effect that they had defended Zion and their families well, and that they had carried out *"God's wishes"*. The men were then ordered to stay the night and bury the bodies before leaving for home the next morning.

The wagon with the rifles and children moved on up the valley to the Hamblin Ranch where Rachel Hamblin was living. She cared for the children and put them to bed. Lee came later, and during the night, Haight & Dame came to the ranch. The next morning, they all went back to Mountain Meadows and saw the ghastly site. The bodies were still being buried, and in the same holes the emigrants had dug previously to protect themselves from the Indians.

Then there was an argument between Haight and Dame about the orders given. The orders were confusing alright! This is the way Juanita Brooks stated part of the argument in her book.
"We must report this to President Young," Dame was saying.
"How will you report it?" Haight wanted to know.
"I will report it just as it is, a full report of everything."
"And will you say that it was done under your orders?"
"No"
Haight was furious with rage.
"You know that you issued the orders to wipe out this company, and you cannot deny it! You had better not try to deny it! If you think you can shift the blame for this onto me, you're fooled! You'll stand up to your orders like a man, or I'll send you to Hell Cross Lots."

About this time Lee interrupted to tell them it was done now and that they should go on from there. When the men finished with the burial, they gathered at the nearby spring and washed up. Then they all gathered around and Isaac C. Haight addressed the men. They were to say nothing to anyone and block it from their minds. Then they gathered in a circle, with Dame, Haight, Lee and Higbee at the 4 corners, and pledged they would never discuss it with anyone. Finally everybody left, including Lee, who wouldn't return to Mountain Meadows until the day he died.

A few days later they all met in Cedar City, and since John D. Lee was closest to Brigham Young, he was assigned to travel to Salt Lake City with the news of the killings. He left September 20, and arrived on the 29th. He reported the event to Brigham Young, which was written down by Wilford Woodruff. At that time, John D. reported it as a job done by Indians.

The emigrant children were put into different homes and cared for. As far as they were concerned, it was Lee and the other Mormons who had saved them from the Indians--the Indians being the ones who killed their parents. The wagons and other contraband were placed in the Bishop's Warehouse to be given out to needy Mormon families.

In the months and years after the massacre everything went about as normal, given the circumstances. Lee took wife No. 17, a 22-year-old girl from England, on January 7, 1858, when he was age 46. This was Emma Batchelor, the one who would accompany John D. to the lower end of the Paria River in 1871, to set up a home at Lonely Dell, later to be known as Lee's Ferry.

After the massacre, Lee was involved in setting up the Cotton Mission on the Santa Clara River, near present-day St. George. While in the area, John D. stopped in Washington (just east of St. George), and bought some land, including a house in town, where he soon had 2 of his wives. And speaking of wives, still later in 1858, Lee seemed to be courting a young girl named Mary Ann. He apparently proposed to her, but she refused. She even wrote 2 letters of protest to Brigham Young. In January of 1859, he mentions in his diary that she wanted instead to marry John D's oldest son, which she did.

It was in August of 1858, after peace had finally been arranged between the Mormons, and Johnston's Army & the Federal Government, that a George A. Smith and James McKnight, both Church officials, went to southern Utah, and made out 2 reports on the massacre. The reports didn't amount to a hill of beans, because everyone remained silent.

In the meantime, Lee lived at the fort in Harmony most of the time, where he had about 4 of his wives. Since there were lots of travelers passing through Utah at that time, he took advantage of the situation and set up a caravansary or way-station, to accommodate the wagon trains. Harmony was in the right place. They got most of their business in the fall and early winter. For a couple of years after the massacre, things went well for John D., but then things gradually changed.

According to Juanita Brooks, in *"April [1859] word came that Judge Cradlebaugh was on his way to investigate the Mountain Meadows Massacre, accompanied by a force of two hundred soldiers. Jacob Forney, the new Indian agent, came ahead to gather up the surviving children that they might be returned to their relatives in the east. They took Charley Fancher from the Lee household, although he was reluctant to go, and in line with the policy followed by all who had kept any of the children, Lee made out a bill to the government for his care."* With this, the beginning of the federal investigation, John D. Lee went into hiding, and was on the run for the next 15 1/2 years.

Judge Cradlebaugh and his party arrived at Cedar City in May of 1859, and set up camp in a big field about 2 1/2 kms from town. His assignment was to *"collect and bury the bones of the slain emigrants, and to arrest as many participants in the massacre as he could catch.*

The judge brought warrants for the arrest of a half-dozen of the leaders, and he wanted information concerning others who were involved. He found the local people reluctant to talk, for none knew anything for a certainty, and if they did, they would not betray their brethren into the hands of the enemies of the church. A few did want to talk, but feared the consequences. At least one participant came to the judge secretly late at night and told the story of that tragic day, giving some names and details, and begging for protection and anonymity. The burden of the crime was more than he could bear."

Because many of the participants were either in hiding or had gone to different states, the judge was unable to make a single arrest. There was eventually a reward of $5000 offered for the arrests of Dame, Haight, Higbee, Klingensmith and Lee. But no one ever turned any of them in. After spending a month in the area, the judge gave up and returned to Salt Lake City.

In the years 1860 & '61, things went quite well for John D., considering. He had 2 homes; one in Harmony, the other in Washington, and nearly all the wives he wanted. Both places were opened as caravansaries & taverns, and business was good.

Right at the end of 1861, there was a stormy period which lasted from December 25 until the beginning of February, 1862. This was a disaster for everyone in the region, and especially for John D. Lee and his families. The fort they had been living in at Harmony was made of mud bricks, and it literally melted away. During the first part of February, they were all trying to move out of the Harmony Fort and into some new dwellings at nearby New Harmony. But before they could all get moved, the roof of part of the building caved in, killing 2 of Lee's children.

Down at Washington, things were just as bad. John D. had just recently erected a molasses mill, which had earned him good money the previous fall. It had been swept away in the flood, and the machinery buried in sand & mud. Because of this 40-day storm, it took Lee about 4 full years to get back to the financial position he had been in before the floods.

In 1866, John D. finally was on his feet again and doing better. In that year he took his last wife, Ann Gordge, who was from Australia and just 18 years of age. Later in the same year, he lost his first bride, Agatha, who died of a lingering illness. This was a sad occasion for Lee, and seemed to be a sort of beginning of the end for him.

It was about this time that the people of Harmony began giving him untold misery. *"Whisperings about the massacre continued; the stories became more numerous and highly colored. In many ways his neighbors showed their disapproval--by turning their cattle into his grain fields, interfering with his water ditches, and making snide remarks to his wives or children. He always attended church, he was first to fill the assignment made by Brigham Young to get out poles for the new telegraph line, he was prompt in paying his tithes. At Parowan and Cedar City, he was often called upon to speak at church, and at Kanarra he was held in high esteem. Perhaps his very industry, his driving use of his family and hired help, his shrewd trading, his ability to amass property and to live well made his neighbors all the more critical of him."*

In the fall of 1867, he made a trip to Salt Lake City with a herd of goats belonging to Brigham Young, his adopted father. When he returned in December, he found his estate falling apart. Without Agatha, and his 2 oldest sons away on missions, there had not been the same enthusiasm as had been the case earlier.

It was also in the late 1860's that trouble began to brew for Brigham Young and the Church leadership, and since John D. was always a strong supporter of the President, he began to feel the pinch as well. In 1868, there appeared in Salt Lake City a new publication, the **Utah Magazine.** This, as it turned out, was a voice for those who were becoming discontented with the Church leaders and their policies. Some of the unrest resulted in a number of excommunications in the northern part of the state. Many of these people wanted to be members of the Church, but were simply critical of the leaders; thus they were booted out of the Church.

The original complaint against Young was, he got too involved with their financial dealings; but later they condemned Young for condoning murder. During this period, there were some mysterious deaths in Salt Lake City. Dr. K. Robinson was assassinated in 1866; John V. Long, former secretary of Brigham

Young, was found dead in a ditch in April, 1869; and Newton Brassfield was murdered on one of the main streets of Salt Lake in April, 1866. These men were part of the group generally known as the **God-beites**, after it's chief spokesman, W. S. Godbe. Some historians have wondered if Brigham Young's body guard Orrin Porter Rockwell had a hand in these killings.

One of their worst complaints about Brigham Young was that he gave public recognition to men who had participated in the Mountain Meadows Massacre. The **Utah Reporter**, published in Corrine (in the middle of northern Utah's gentile country), *"ran a series of open letters addressed to Brigham Young, demanding that those guilty of that outrage be brought to justice. The articles were signed by 'Argus,' who claimed to have lived in Southern Utah and learned the facts from some of the participants."*

During the winter of 1869-70, Lee defended Brigham Young by visiting many communities in southern Utah, to as far north as Fillmore, and by making speeches in Young's behalf.

In **September of 1870**, Brigham Young led a small group of men to explore areas east of the southern Utah settlements. Lee joined this group, and was assigned the job of locating the best route (as they were heading into new country without roads), and making camps along the way. William H. Dame was in charge of preparing meals.

Their route went through Panguitch, south to Roundy's Station (now called Alton), then down Johnson Canyon. At some point along the way, Brigham Young had a private talk with John D. He was urging Lee to move. Quoting again from Juanita Brook's book, Young said, *"I should like to see you enjoy peace for your remaining years. Gather your wives and children around you, select some fertile valley, and settle out here."*

Along the way they met, and were joined by John W. Powell. The party traveled east from the bottom of Johnson Canyon to the Paria River. They got as far as the **Peter Shirts' (Shurtz) farm at Rock House**, which at that time was called Pah Ria on Utah state maps, and found a small patch of green corn and some squash. Lee was not impressed and made the statement, *"I wouldn't bring a wife of mine to such a place as this."* After the visit to the Paria River, they came to the conclusion there was little there to attract future settlements, and left. On their return, the party surveyed and laid out the site of Kanab, to be settled by some of those same men (one group had already tried to settle Kanab in about 1865, but had left on account of the Black Hawk War). After the lots were numbered, the settlers each drew a number from a hat to select their home site.

Brigham Young wanted Levi Stewart to set up a sawmill to make lumber to build Kanab. Levi stated he had worked with Lee before and would like to have him as a partner again. John D. reluctantly said yes, out of sheer obedience to the Church leader. The group then returned to the southwest Utah settlements via Pipe Springs.

Lee immediately set to work to sell his property and settle accounts. He put up for sale and sold his holdings in Harmony, but kept the Washington property, leaving several of his wives there until he could get back later. He started the trip to Kanab with wife Rachel and her children, 4 wagons, and 60 head of stock. It took 10 days to travel the very rough 150 kms.

From Kanab, they went east to what is today Johnson, about 16 kms east of Kanab. They then went north up Johnson Canyon to a moderately high grassy valley now called Skutumpah. This was to be their new home, but they were to live temporarily a little above Skutumpah where the sawmill was to be located. It was about 15 kms to a site on Mill Creek where they built a camp. It was in late October, 1870, that he first built a cabin for Rachel.

When the engineer and surveyor arrived, they quickly set up the sawmill, but almost immediately it broke down. Someone would have to return to Parowan for a new part. With Rachel safe in the new cabin, Lee left to get other members of his family. He met a second family group at Pipe Springs--it was one of his sons-in-laws and several children, along with 3 wagons and 40 head of cattle. At that time, mid-November, 1870, he was handed a letter which had to do with his excommunication from the Mormon Church! It was dated **October 8, 1870**. At that time he mentioned it to no one.

The group went straight for Skutumpah, set up a tent for a temporary home, and went upcanyon to Rachel's cabin. Help from Kanab finally came in early December, and they worked fast and furious, because of the coming winter. The work at the sawmill was so fast, the wagons coming and going from Kanab, couldn't keep up. On December 13, news came of a disastrous fire in Kanab; the fort had burned to the ground, and 6 members of the bishop's family were killed. That ended the winter logging operation in the upper Skutumpah area.

John D. left Rachel and the others, and made a trip back to Washington, where he had a cold reception from his other wives and children. The next morning he went to St. George to speak to Brigham Young, who was in his winter home, about his excommunication. He pleaded his case saying that he had been loyal to him and the Church, and that now he was being singled out to bear the guilt of the massacre. He also stated that the decision to attack the Fancher Train was a mutual agreement between the highest Church leaders in the area. After the meeting, Lee left and returned to Harmony, where he was invited to speak in church on Christmas Day, 1870.

Upon his return to Washington, he received a note from a high Church official, stating, *"If you will consult your own safety & that of others, you will not press yourself nor an investigation on others at this time lest you cause others to become accessory with you & thereby force them to inform upon you or to suffer. Our advice is, trust no one. Make yourself scarce & keep out of the way."*

After these kind words, and on January 2, 1871, John D. set out once again for Skutumpah, this time with Caroline (Mrs. Lee No. 4), and her 8 children. It took them 15 days to reach Skutumpah this time, because of the heavy snows and poor travel conditions. Upon arriving, the whole family set to work cutting trees and sawing lumber in order to build and finish a large home for Caroline. When that was completed, they dismantled Rachel's cabin, and reconstructed it again down at Skutumpah. By the first of March, they began the third house, but about that time, Emma, wife No. 17, came up in an empty wagon. She was distressed, trying to decide which way to go--whether to stay with John D. or leave him for someone else. She decided to stay with her husband.

Soon after this, and as the sawmill was roaring full blast, Lee sold his interest in the site. With all the lumber he needed, he continued to work at Skutumpah until he had finished 4 homes, each with wood floors, shingle roofs, and glass windows. In June, 1871, he made another quick trip back to St. George to attend to business. While there he worked to sell out his Washington property, and bring the rest of his family to Skutumpah.

Enroute, and in Johnson Canyon, he met Isaac C. Haight, who was also in hiding and laying low. Together they went to Kanab, but waited outside town while Jacob Hamblin and John Mangum brought them food, and more importantly, news. The news this time was that the federal authorities were clamping down on polygamists, and they were advised to transfer all their property to their wives. Lee set out to do this at once, naming Rachel Woolsey, Polly Young, Lavina Young, Sarah Caroline Williams, and Emma Batchelor as recipients. All of his other wives had deserted him by that time. But the real heart-breaking news was that he was ordered by the Church to take one or 2 of his wives, and move down to the Colorado River at the mouth of the Paria River. That was in **August of 1871**.

This was John D. Lee's greatest decision. But he would obey. He had 5 wives; which 2 would he take? He was heading for some wild country, and would end up in the middle of the desert and be in country controlled by Navajos. Problems would be immense, but even though he had been excommunicated, he still had the secret backing of Brigham Young. After all, it was Young who had ordered him to go.

The first wagons rolled out of Skutumpah in November of 1871. It consisted of 3 wagons, 57 head of livestock of various kinds, and Caroline and her family. At their first camp in lower Johnson Canyon, Jacob Hamblin joined them. He knew the country better than anyone, and he and Lee had a long discussion on the best route to take. It was decided to have the wagons head down what was called in those days the Navajo Trail while John D. and 14-year old son Ralph would take the cattle to the new settlement of Pah Ria, and drive them straight down the canyon.

At the Paria River, which maps of that era labelled **Pah Ria River**, he met Tom Adair and John Mangum, and was happy to have these men join him. The going downriver was more difficult than anyone had anticipated. *"They spent 8 days on the trail, much of the time in water. Two days and one night they traveled without stopping because there was no place to camp. When their provisions were gone, they shot a cow that had become hopelessly mired in quicksand and cut steaks from her, living for the next few days on a meat diet."*

Upon arriving at the mouth of the Paria, they found no wagons. Brigham Young had sent out a work crew to build a road, but neither the work crew nor Caroline had reached the Paria. Adair and Mangum returned to Pah Ria via the **Dominguez or Ute Trail**, while Lee and Ralph headed around the Vermilion Cliffs hoping to meet their wagons enroute. Because it was unfamiliar country, John D. got lost, and ended up returning all the way to Skutumpah.

The next day John D. and wives Emma & Rachel, and several wagons, headed out to find Caroline. Below Johnson, they found one broken-down wagon, and knew she had gone to Kanab instead. She had changed her mind, and had decided to go and stay there the winter and to give birth to another child, rather than go into the wilderness alone.

Back on the road again, the new contingent made it to the Colorado River on December 23, 1871. (At Signature Rocks next to House Rock Spring, John D. left his signature, **J.D. Lee Dec 25 1871.** In this time period, 5 pages, and from December 4th through the 26th, are missing from John D.'s diary. Someone else's diary must have been used to get the date of Dec. 23--or the date on the rock is something else--it is hard to read now). The next morning, when they all had a chance to look around, Emma said,*"oh what a lonely dell"*. And forever more the name of the small settlement or ranch at the mouth of the Paria River has been called **Lonely Dell**.

The first thing they did at the lower Paria River was build a house. The first shelter was a dugout built against the hill and lined with rock. It would later be a cellar. The second was a rock building with a door and 2 windows. When the 2 shelters were finished, John D. rode upcanyon a ways to check on his cows. When he returned, he found Emma with a new baby, which was born on January 17, 1872. They named her Francis Dell Lee.

The very next day, **January 18**, they saw Navajos across the river. The Indians wanted Lee to help them across. John D. and Rachel first had to work on one of John W. Powell's boats, which had been left there in 1869 on his first Colorado River trip. After repairs, Lee & Rachel made the first ferry crossings. It took 3 trips to get all the Navajos across. They later made some trades, Lee and his families ended up with blankets, cloth for making clothing, and other needed items. The Navajos got 2 horses, a mule and a colt.

In April, 1872, a group of miners came into camp, and the Lee family helped accommodate them. Emma cooked, in exchange for their help in building up the place, and for some needed tools. It was at about this time it was decided they would build 2 places; one at Lonely Dell, the other at the springs known as **Jacobs Pool**; in Lee's diary, he called it **Lee's Ranch** most of the time. The 2 places were 32 kms apart, but Jacobs Pool would be a welcome stop for travelers who were making the long journey from Utah to Arizona. It must be remembered that Lee was sent there to set up a ferry and provide food, shelter and accommodations for travelers, many of whom would be Mormons. The church at that time was expanding into Arizona, and Lee, although officially excommunicated, was instrumental in this expansion, along with **Jacob Hamblin**.

By early May 1872, Rachel moved. The first shelter at Jacobs Pool was made with mud & willows, and didn't give much shelter. On June 2, a group of engineers of the Powell Survey, passed through the area and fotographed Rachel's first little willow shack (see the picture on page 329). This was a different group than Powell's river expedition.

In was on July 13, that Major Powell and his survey crew landed at Lonely Dell with the boat Cañonita, and were out of about everything except coffee & flour. Emma cooked for them and both groups shared what they had; the expedition members enjoying Emma's vegetables.

John D. was in and out of Lonely Dell and Jacobs Pool. He had to help build shelters and go north & west to get supplies from the settlements. This was all fine, because as long as he was on the move, it would be difficult for the authorities to track him down. At that time the federal people were always after the *"cohabs"*, or polygamists, and a bit later they were after Lee for his involvement in the Mountain Meadows Massacre.

In October 1872, a small military group out to explore & survey the Colorado River made it to Lonely Dell and met Mrs. Lee No. 17, but no John D. They explored up the Paria River, but one of their group drowned. That full story is told in the hiking section in the Lower Paria River Gorge, page 182.

On December 16, 1872, a man named Heath came with a load of lumber for the purpose of building a ferry. While he and a crew were in the process of building a boat, John D. was at Rachel's place making a fine home. He had hired Elisha Everett to help do the rock work, for there was no other material there with which to build. This new home was mostly completed on Christmas Day, 1872. It measured about 9x11 meters, had 2 doors, 2 bedrooms, a kitchen, a parlor and was covered with a wooden roof. Nearby was a cellar. If you're there today, you can still see the remains of this 1872 dwelling, just above the western-most spring which is northeast of the ranch building called Jacobs Pool on the USGS maps. See the hiking section and **Map 42** (page 231), for the location.

The ferry boat was completed by January 11, 1873. Counting the Lee family and work crews, there were 22 people in all at the ferry site, and they all took a ride in the new boat, which they called *"The*

Colorado." A little later, on February 1, 1873, a group of 12 men used the ferry for the first time. They were heading south to explore the Little Colorado River country for the Church. From February 1873 until about November 1874, John D. Lee was the ferryman at what then and now is called **Lee's Ferry.** The first company of settlers on their way south arrived in April, 1873. They were charged $3.00 a wagon, and $.75 a horse for the service. For those who didn't have the money, payment could be made in food or supplies, so things worked well for the new ferryman.

In the summer of 1873, a message came from Kanab that a unit of 600 soldiers were on their way to Lee's Ferry to set up a permanent camp. This spooked Lee pretty bad, so he swam a horse across the Colorado River, and headed south to Moenkopi. While at Moenkopi, John D. met Jacob Hamblin and later they made a deal for a swap. They agreed to trade places; Lee's or rather, Rachel's home and holdings at Jacobs Pool, for Jacob's claim at Moenave, near Moenkopi. In the fall, Jacob would help Rachel make the move down into Arizona. As it turned out, the story of the soldiers coming to Lee's Ferry wasn't true.

For about a year, things went well and uneventful. Then came the fall of 1874. A Sheriff named Stokes had warrants for the arrest of eight men who were the leaders of, and had participated in, the Mountain Meadows Massacre. By then the name of John D. Lee was at the top of the list. The Sheriff was partly familiar with Lee's habits, and was aware of where his wives lived. At the time, Caroline lived in **Panguitch.** It was on a visit to this wife that Lee was captured. This was in early **November of 1874.** They took John D. to **Beaver** in a wagon. He was there in jail from November 10, until **July 23, 1875,** when the trial for the massacre at Mountain Meadows began.

At the trial, the indictment included William H. Dame, Isaac C. Haight, John D. Lee, John M. Higbee, George Adair Jr., Elliot Wilden, Samuel Jukes, P.K. Smith, and William Stewart. Because everybody involved had sworn secrecy, no one would testify except Philip Klingensmith. As it turned out Klingensmith's testimony was rather accurate and precise. The defense made the point, *"that while Lee was present and might have participated, he was there by command of his superiors, both military and ecclesiastical, whose orders in this time of military rule would be death to disobey. While they admitted the facts of the massacre and all its unbelievable horror, they placed the responsibility upon the Mormon Church and its doctrine that men were justified in 'avenging the blood of the Prophets' as a part of their duty to God."*

In the end it was a hung jury. The 8 Mormon members of the jury were for acquittal, the 4 gentiles for conviction. This meant another trial. This time Lee would be held in Salt Lake City. But this meant hardship for his families. Rachel left Moenkopi for the Utah settlements; Caroline was in Panguitch; Lavina and Polly remained at Skutumpah; and Emma stayed on at Lonely Dell. As for the ferry, the church sent Warren Johnson and his family to Lonely Dell to take charge of that operation.

John D. Lee left Beaver on August 9, 1875, and was taken to Salt Lake City. He was kept in the state penitentiary, which at that time was in the area of present-day Trolley Square. As one might expect, Lee was a model prisoner, and ended up with many privileges. At various times he taught other inmates how to read, was a kind of doctor, and was even entrusted with some keys to the place. For some reason, he was released on May 11, 1876, on $15,000 bail. He was to appear in Beaver 4 months later for the trial.

In the period before the second trial, John D. traveled around visiting his various wives and families. He was at Lonely Dell in August. His sons had tried to talk him into going to Mexico to escape, but he insisted that by doing so, he would be admitting guilt. In late August of 1876, he left Lee's Ferry and headed for Skutumpah via the Dominguez Trail. Just after he left, a messenger came via the Navajo Trail, with word from the Church authorities counseling Lee to jump bond and leave the country. The Church would assume the full responsibility to the bondsman. But he missed the message.

In Beaver, the second trial began in **September, 1876.** For some reason the atmosphere of this trial was totally different. Twelve jurors were selected, all in good standing in the Mormon Church. During the trial, 7 witnesses were called, again all good members. They were all now willing to talk about the whole thing. The witnesses told of John D. Lee's participation, and that of Klingensmith's, but he had immunity since he had turned state's evidence. They also spoke of how Haight and Higbee were involved, but they were both dead at the time of the 2nd trial. It was very clear that something had been worked out so that everyone pointed the finger at John D. Lee. To resolve the issue, it seems clear that it was necessary to have a scapegoat, so that life for the Church could go on as normal. Lee never did take the stand or defend himself. He sat through the trial in silence.

At the end and when the jury came back, the statement read, *"Guilty of murder in the first degree."* Lee immediately wrote to Emma for more money, to take the case to a higher court. His attorney, W. W. Bishop felt he had been sold out. Meanwhile 2 petitions were circulated in southern Utah, asking that the Governor give him clemency. The Governor said he would consider the move if Lee would speak up and tell all, and make an attempt to implicate those above him. But Lee remained silent, and there was no clemency.

So on **March 23, 1877,** John D. Lee was taken back to Mountain Meadows, the scene of the crime. There were a number of people there, including James Fennimore, the photographer who Lee had known and made friends with at Lonely Dell. A foto of the place shows John D. sitting on his coffin. Lee was blindfolded, but his hands were free when the 5 shots were fired. He fell back in the coffin and it was closed and loaded into a wagon. He was then carried to Panguitch and buried in the cemetery just east of town and south of the Highway 89.

To get to Mountain Meadows today, drive west out of Cedar City toward Beryl Junction and Enterprise, then turn south on State Highway 18 running toward St. George. About halfway between Enterprise & Central, between mile post 31 & 32, is the turnoff to the west and Mountain Meadows. From St. George, drive north toward Veyo & Central and in the direction of Enterprise. Just off the paved road to the west is a new memorial built on a hill overlooking the valley. This was built in 1990. From this hillside overlook, drive west down a good gravel road to a new monument where a number of those killed were buried. The original plaque placed there in 1932 read:

MOUNTAIN MEADOWS
A FAVORITE RECRUITING PLACE ON THE OLD SPANISH TRAIL
In this vicinity, September 7-11, 1857, occurred one of the most lamentable tragedies in the annals of the West. A company of about 140 Arkansas and Missouri emigrants led by Captain Charles Fancher, enroute to California, was attacked by white men and Indians. All but 17, being small children, were killed. John D. Lee, who confessed participation as leader, was legally executed here March 23, 1877. Most of the emigrants were buried in their own defense pits.

The **first monument** at Mountain Meadows was erected in **May, 1859** by Brevet Major James H. Carleton and 80 soldiers of the first Dragoons from Fort Tejon, California. Assisting were Captains Reuben P. Campbell and Charles Brewer, with 270 men from Camp Floyd, Utah. The bones of about 34 of the emigrants were buried where the monument is now. The remains of others were buried 2 1/2 kms north near the place of the actual massacre.

The original monument, consisting of a stone cairn topped with a cedar cross and a small granite marker set against the north side of the cairn, was not maintained. The Utah Trails & Landmarks Association built a protective wall around what remained of the 1859 monument and, on **September 10, 1932,** installed a bronze marker. That marker was replaced with another one on **September 15, 1990**.

In 1990, there was a new memorial erected on a hill overlooking Mountain Meadows with the names of those who died in the massacre. Along the paved path to this monument are several plaques recounting the story of the massacre, plus a map showing all the historic sites. During that dedication ceremony for the new plaque, no apologies were given and it seemed everyone, especially the Mormons, were trying to put this one behind them as far as possible. It also seems that whoever made the new plaque was trying to put the blame for the massacre as far behind them as possible too.

On **September 11, 1999**, another ceremony took place at the grave site, this time dedicating a new monument which replaced the one built in 1932. Located there today is a large parking lot, a cement sidewalk/trail across a small stream, a memorial structure with several plaques (see foto below and on next page), and a toilet. This is the last of the monuments commemorating the site.

On **March 25, 2004**, Washington City (immediately east of St. George) officials announced they would honor several of the city's founding fathers by placing statues of them in front of the city museum. One of the 5 was John D. Lee. However, there were loud protests from a number of people and organizations, among them the Arkansas-based **Mountain Meadows Monument Foundation**. So the city backed off, and later Jerry Anderson of Leeds, Utah (east of St. George and just off I-15), the man who made the statue, ended up selling it to a woman in California. As of 2/24/2010, Jerry had no idea where the statue was, or what might be the intended purpose of that purchase. No doubt about it, John D. Lee is a collector's item and the statue could be worth a small fortune in the future.

In **June, 2007**, the Mountain Meadows Monument Foundation tried for the 2nd time to have the LDS Church turn the ownership of the monument over to the Federal Government, but Church leaders turned down the request. Stay tuned.

This is the latest monument to the massacre at **Mountain Meadows.**

Mountain Meadows, March 23, 1877. John D. Lee sits on his coffin (far left) awaiting execution by a firing squad. At his left, the Deputy U.S. Marshal reads the death warrant. On horseback in the background are some of Lee's sons. They were kept at a distance as it was feared they would attempt a last minute rescue. The firing squad is hidden under the canvas, far right. (Library of Congress foto)

The **tombstone** of **John D. Lee** which is in the northeast corner of the cemetery in Panguitch, Utah. To get there, drive along Highway 89 immediately east of Panguitch. Between mile posts 130 & 131, turn south at the cemetery sign, and drive a short distance.

The latest monument at **Mountain Meadows**. Across the little stream is the monument at the main burial site. On the hill behind the camera is another memorial with signs & maps showing the layout of all historical sites in the valley.

History of Ghost Towns along the Paria River

Bryce Valley Ghost Towns

One of the best sources for the history of the first settlements in the upper Paria River drainage, known today as Bryce Valley, is *The Geology and Geography of the Paunsaugunt Region-Utah*, by Herbert E. Gregory. Most of the following account is adapted from his early geologic explorations and travels throughout the region.

In the 1860's & 70's, there were surveying parties traveling across parts of the upper Paria and Escalante Rivers, and they noted several large valleys which looked promising for settlement. One of the surveyors was A. H. Thompson, who said the upper valley of the Paria River was well-watered, had good soil, and a good climate. He also noted there were coal beds close by and good range for grazing livestock.

Because of such reports, the first pioneer white settlers in the upper Paria Valley were the families of David O. Littlefield and Orley D. Bliss, who on December 24, 1874, laid out farms near the junction of the Paria River and Henrieville Creek. With the arrival of eight additional families in 1875, the original cluster of log houses at the base of the red cliffs grew into a small settlement called **Cliff Town**. Since those earliest days, the name gradually changed to **Clifton**. The old Clifton townsite is located about 3 kms due south of Cannonville.

One of the new settlers, **Ebenezer Bryce**, who is said to have come to Clifton in 1875 or '76, decided they needed more room and looked for another location to farm. He selected a site farther upstream in what was known then as Henderson Valley. This new settlement was first called **New Clifton.** Bryce, in association with Daniel Goulding and others (1878-80), constructed an irrigation canal 11 kms long, planted orchards, and took up livestock raising.

It was during this time, when Eb Bryce ran cattle into the canyons to the west, that Bryce Canyon received it's name. An early-day saying around the region, which Bryce is given credit for, makes a statement about herding cattle into the area which is now called Bryce Canyon National Park. That statement was, *It's a hell of a place to lose a cow!*

Bryce left New Clifton in 1880, while Goulding left in 1883. They sold their holdings to Isaac H. Losee, Orville S. Cox, and Ephriam Cottall. They renamed the site **Losee** or **Loseeville.** The Losee townsite is located about 3 kms due east of present-day Tropic, in what is now called **East Valley**.

Now back to Clifton. About 2 years after settlement, the people in the tiny rural village of Clifton found themselves too closely hemmed in between the cliffs and the bank of the Paria, and their farmland in the process of being carried away by flood waters. So in 1877 Clifton was mostly abandoned, with most of its settlers going to a new site about 3 kms north. This new town was named **Cannonville**, after a high-ranking dignitary of the Mormon Church, George Q. Cannon.

While some of those who abandoned Clifton went to and settled Cannonville, 3 families headed east instead, and settled on Henrie Creek, about 8 kms east of Cannonville. This is present-day **Henrieville** and **Henrieville Creek**, named in honor of James Henrie, then-president of the Panguitch Stake of the LDS Church. An interesting side note; the first time any of these towns were named on a map of the state of Utah was in 1884. Cannonville & Henrieville were both on that map. The first time the name Losee appeared on any state map was in 1893.

In 1886, Seth Johnson, Joseph & Eleazer Asay, Richard C. Pinney, and other stockmen took up lands on lower Yellow Creek about 5 kms southwest of Cannonville and thus became the pioneer set-

This is the monument about **Losee or Loseeville**. It's located next to the main road in East Valley east of Tropic, and near the Losee Cemetery (the cemetery is about 200m north of this monument and in the middle of a field).

Map 44, Bryce Valley Ghost Towns and Coal Mines:
Georgetown, Clifton and Losee

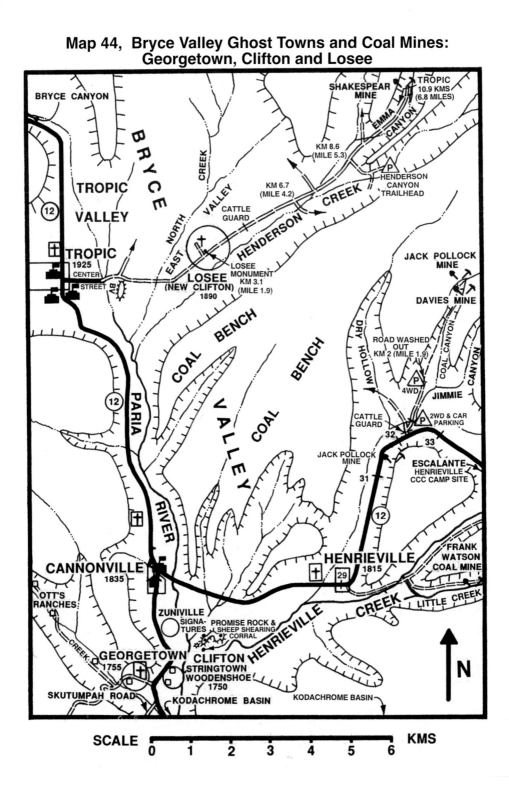

tlers of **Georgetown.** Like Cannonville, this new ranching community was named after George Q. Cannon.

It was during the early 1880's, Cannonville became the center of prosperity for the entire valley. That's where a Mormon Church was built, and where the most prosperous cattlemen lived. Later on, in the early 1890's, people were beginning to move out of Georgetown on account of the lack of water. Shortly after 1894, the town was so small, it became part of the Cannonville Ward of the LDS Church. A year or two later, it was all but deserted except for a ranch or two.

About the same time Georgetown was thriving, there were some families who moved back into the areas left abandoned in the former Clifton settlement. Perhaps it wasn't totally deserted in the first place (?). In the late 1880's and/or early 1890's, this small area received the nickname of **Stringtown.** It seems there were a number of separate ranches strung out along the road between Cannonville & Georgetown; thus the name Stringtown. It was never incorporated into a town or an organized LDS ward or congregation.

If you talk to old-timers in the Bryce Valley about early-day settlements, they will always mention the name **Woodenshoe.** The man who knew a little more about it than anyone else was the late Kay Clark of Henrieville. He recalled stories and history of his grandfather, Owen W. Clark. After the Clarks moved into, then out of, the Clark (or White House) Cabin on the lower Paria, they attempted to resettle Adairville, but that didn't work, so they moved north again to Pahreah for several years. That place wasn't as promising as they had hoped, so again they moved, this time north to what was then Stringtown, which was actually part of Cannonville at the time. They lived there until 1896, then sold the farm to some Dutch people. This family was poor and often wore wooden shoes; thus the name Woodenshoe was attached to the area of the original settlement of Clifton.

Another interesting story about an early Bryce Valley settlement comes from Wallace Ott of Tropic. When he was just a wee small boy of 3 or 4 years of age, he remembered an event and place just south of Cannonville, in the same general area as Clifton, Stringtown and Woodenshoe. It seems that in about 1914 or '15, there came into the valley a wagon train of Mormons who had fled Mexico. It was in August of 1912, that the Mormons of Chihuahua and Sonora had to leave, because of the Mexican Revolution and Poncho Villa. It must have taken them a couple of years to make it north to the Paria Valley, otherwise Wallace, who was born in 1911, wouldn't have remembered the event.

They came in the late summer or early fall and asked if it was OK to make a temporary camp about 1 km south of Cannonville. Permission was granted and they simply made a half circle with their wagons and camped for the winter. They were the poorest people Wallace had ever seen. Many were of large polygamist families and the Church had to help out for a time. In the spring, they all set out in different directions looking for new homes. In the meantime, their camp had gotten the local nickname of **Zuniville.**

Going back in history for a moment. By 1886, the increasing population of the valley was using about all the land the available water would irrigate, but north of Cannonville there remained a large fertile valley of unirrigated land that was otherwise suitable for cultivation. To increase farmland, in 1889 the people of Cannonville revived an old scheme outlined by Ebenezer Bryce back in 1880. That plan was to divert water from the East Fork of the Sevier River on top of the Paunsaugunt Plateau (the high country just west of Bryce Canyon National Park) through a ditch or canal that would pass over the Pink Cliffs to the land in the upper Bryce Valley.

At the instigation of William Lewman, the locally financed **Cannonville & East Fork Irrigation Company** was organized. A reservoir site was selected and a survey made for a feeder canal about 16 kms long. Maurice Cope was made boss of the project, and work began **May 15, 1890.** Anticipating the successful completion of the project, James Ahlstrom, C.W. Snyder and others, began building houses on land that the proposed ditch was intended to water. In 1891, a townsite was laid out which was later

Near the northern end of the Skutumpah Road looking northeast toward **Table Cliff Plateau. Promise Rock** is the big red rock in the middle; while **Clifton** occupied all the flatland in the middle of the picture. Cannonville is to the left just out of sight; Henrieville is to the right just out of sight.

called **Tropic**, allegedly after its fine climate. On **May 23, 1892**, the new-found water was flowing through the townsite and onto the adjoining fields. This date marks more than a century of continuous habitation of Tropic, which is truly a man-made oasis.

The first time the name Tropic was displayed on any state map of Utah was in 1902. However, that name was placed where Losee was situated out in what is now Easy Valley, and the name Losee was placed where Tropic is today.

The canal from the East Fork, known locally as the **Tropic Ditch,** is still used today, as it's the lifeblood of Tropic. It took 2 years of voluntary labor and hard work by 50 men, women and boys from Cannonville and the neighboring communities to finish the project. It was mostly hand work with pick & shovel, or with team & fresno scrappers. The only payment received was a reliable water supply and a better place to make a home. On the plateau, the canal can be seen about 100m south of Ruby's Inn as you drive toward the entrance to Bryce Canyon National Park; or in the lower end of Tropic Canyon, as water comes out of Water Canyon and along the Mossy Cave Trail. The water is put into a pipe somewhere near the parking lot next to the highway at the end of **Water Canyon.**

Today in the area of Georgetown, you'll find the cemetery just north of the road. It's still used today by some people who reside in Cannonville. It has some old graves dating from the late 1800's. A little further down the road to the west, you'll see the remains of an old ranch, but this one dates from the early 1900's, and isn't that historic. However there used to be a couple of old 1920's cars hidden in the sagebrush out back. Just across the road from this old homestead (to the northwest) are the foundations of an even older home, complete with the remains of a wooden pipeline.

There's nothing remaining of anything historic in the area of Clifton, Stringtown or Woodenshoe, however there are 2 very old cabins east of the paved road as you drive south out of Cannonville. They are out in the fields a ways and are clearly visible from the road. These may date from the later days of the Woodenshoe era, and are still used today as barns for livestock and storage.

If you drive due east out of Tropic and past the *"BV"* on the hillside, you'll be in the general area of New Clifton or Losee. There's nothing there today except the old **Losee Cemetery**. The author counted 7 tombstones, only 3 of which could still be read. Two belonged to young children, the other an older woman. They all had died in 1889 or 1890.

To get to the cemetery, drive east out of Tropic on **Center Street**, over a low hill and to about the middle of East Valley. Once there, locate a narrow lane running north from the main graveled road. That lane takes off 3.3 kms (1.95 miles) from the main highway in Tropic. At the beginning of that lane is a monument to the early settlement of New Clifton & Losee. About 250m north of the main road and to the right 100m in the middle of a field, is the small cemetery site with a meter-high fence around it. If you park on the road, then walk to the site and disturb nothing, no one should care if you cross that private land. Local farmers occasionally find stones or other old debris in the Losee area, but this graveyard is really the only thing to see.

Middle Paria River Ghost Towns

What is believed to be the very first white settler to make a home anywhere in the Paria River drainage was a man named **Peter Shirts** (sometimes spelled Shurtz). His homestead has always been known as **Rock House**, but later this same area was called **Pah Ria** on some older maps of the state of Utah. Today, most people believe the location of his home was in or near what is now called **Rock House Cove**. More below. Most of this information about Shirts comes from an unpublished family document, *History of Peter Shirts and his Descendants,* by his grandson Ambrose Shurtz.

The entrance to **Georgetown's Cemetery**, which is south of Cannonville

Peter was born in 1808 in St. Claire, Ohio. He married for the first time in 1831, then became a Mormon convert in 1832. In 1835, he worked on the Mormon Temple in Kirkland, Ohio, and became a high ranking church leader in 1844. Later he lived in Nauvoo, Illinois, where he worked on the temple there. He came to Utah in 1849, and became part of a group to settle in Parowan in 1851. In 1852, he helped build Shirts Fort just south of Cedar City. With John D. Lee, Shirts helped settle the area around what is now known as St. George, then helped survey the site for the future Las Vegas in 1855. He was apparently not part of the Mountain Meadows Massacre and was not a polygamist. Peter had 4 wives altogether, but only one at a time.

Shirts migrated to the Paria River in the spring of 1865 with his family--a wife and 2 children. The presumed site is about 8-9 kms downstream from what would later be known as the second **Pahreah** townsite, and on the east side of the river. In the back side of a cove, it's been said, he built his home up against a cliff, behind which was a cave. He walled up the front part with rocks, partly because rocks were so abundant, and logs weren't; and partly it's been said, so the Indians couldn't smoke him out. The roof of the home was covered with flat slabs of rock, called flagstone, of which there is an abundant supply in the area. He enlarged the rear end of his cave to store grain & produce. This is how the place got the name Rock House.

One story says he built his house right over a ditch, so he could have water if under attack. But in the story told by Ambrose, Peter dug a hole down to the water table right in the floor of his home. After he raised a good crop that first year, the Black Hawk War broke out, and hostilities erupted between the Indians and Mormon white settlers all over Utah.

On November 12, 1865, Erastus Snow, one of the leaders of the Mormon Church, wrote to all settlers in the region reminding them of the impending crisis and to obey their Church military leaders. One of the main events signaling the beginning of the Black Hawk War was the killing of a Dr. Whitmore and Robert McIntyre by Indians at Pipe Springs, located west of Kanab, Utah & Fredonia, Arizona. This happened in January of 1866. At the time of that attack, Peter Shirts was already besieged by Piute Indians, who killed or ran off all of his livestock. A militia force stationed in St. George, under the command of Col. MacArthur, attempted to rescue Shirts, but deep snows prevented a speedy march.

The military didn't get to the region until later, but in the meantime Shirts had outlasted the Indians, and by winter's end, was apparently in better condition than his attackers, who were half starved. He talked to the Indians, explaining that since they had run off and/or killed his oxen, he could no longer plow his ground. When the militia finally arrived, they found Shirts behind a plow pulled by 6 Piutes. Shirts and his family returned with the militia, or were removed unwillingly, to Toquerville. On March 10, 1866, he gave a report of his adventures to Erastus Snow.

According to one story (2 or 3 versions exist) of the history of Rock House, March 1866 was the last time anyone lived at the Shirts Homestead. Later, on December 7, 1869, Jacob Hamblin guided a small group of settlers to explore possible sites for a settlement of some kind on the Paria River. It seems that some of that group stayed there in the area of Rock House. About a year later, Brigham Young, John D. Lee and others, returned to find someone raising a garden (see page 345 in John D. Lee's story).

However, there's a little different story about Rock House, as told by Herbert E. Gregory, the geologist who did a lot of exploring in that part of the country in the 1920's. He claims that Shirts stayed right there on the land for 3 full years, instead of being marched off by the Mormon Military in March of 1866 (perhaps he went back after reporting to Snow in Toquerville?). He then packed up and high-tailed-it for the San Juan River. Gregory also states that Rock House was relocated in 1871 (perhaps late 1869 or early 1870?) by 6 families, who did well for a short time. In 1872, 11 more families came in and grew corn & sorghum. Gregory quoted someone as stating: *In 1874, trouble with the ditches, [no doubt caused by floods] caused the 15 families at Rock House to relocate above the hogsback [The Box], at*

Left Samuel Chynoweth moved to Pahreah in the fall of 1892 and lived there for 15-20 years with his 4 sons; Will, Sam, Arthur and Harvey. Since 1892, they have been one of the most important families in the history of Pahreah and Bryce Valley. (Mary Jane Chynoweth Fuller foto). **Right Thomas Washington Smith Jr.** the son of the second & last bishop of Pahreah. (Thayne Smith foto)

Map 45, Middle Paria River Mines and Ghost Towns: Pahreah, Rock House, Pah Ria and Adairville

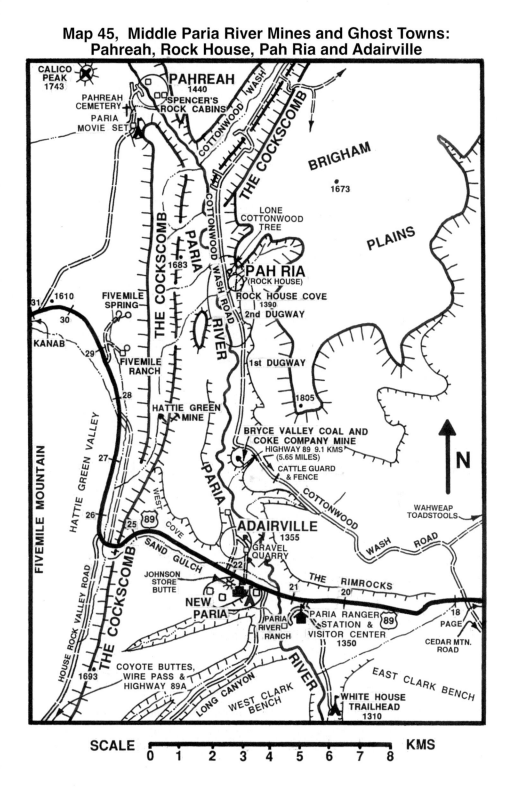

SCALE

0 1 2 3 4 5 6 7 8 KMS

the present site of **Pahreah**.

To finish the story of Peter Shirts, he apparently was in the Cedar City area in the late 1860's, then by 1877, was wandering alone around the Four Corners area. He attempted to settle on lower Montezuma Creek near the San Juan River. According to the *Reeves Survey* (**Utah Historical Quarterly, Spring, 1998**), he was at the Mitchell Ranch on September 4, 1878, and ended up guiding the Reeves crew for 2 weeks. Also, some of the Hole-in-the-Rock Expedition members met him in the same place during the winter of 1879-80, then he was with his son Don Carlos in Escalante in 1882. In the spring of that year he left with his burro packed with supplies and headed for Fruitland, New Mexico. Later that same year he got sick and died. He apparently is buried in the Fruitland cemetery.

Now going back to that first settlement on the Paria as told by various sources. It was in December of 1869, when Jacob Hamblin was sent by the Mormon Church to guide a group of settlers in organizing an Indian farm on the Paria River. According to a family history written by Thomas W. Smith, Jr. (the father of Thayne Smith of Kanab) in 1948, the group was headed by his father Thomas W. Smith, Sr. This history was told to him by Elizabeth J. Smith who was born in 1861. Her story is very similar to that told by Gregory, the geologist.

Elizabeth contends that Peter Shirts came there with Ezra Meeks, both of whom were interested in mining, and may have been the first to locate what later became known as the Hattie Green Copper Mine not far west of Rock House.

Hamblin's or Smith's group (?) included John Mangum and his son Joseph; Jacob, James, Joseph, and J. H. Heath; Allen F. Smithson, Thomas W. Smith, Sr; and James O. Wilkins who was a son-in-law to John Mangum (from **Red Hills of November**, p131). Thomas Adair was there, but may have come in with a 2nd group (?). At first this group did well. They built homes, a rock guard house, where men could cook and have safe lodging, and corrals. By March, 1870, they had 2 1/2 kms of ditches and 800m of fence built, and had 8 Indians there helping and learning about agriculture. Some of the first information about this settlement comes in the form of a letter from Jacob Hamblin to Erastus Snow of the LDS Church. It was dated March 27, 1870.

The location where this group settled was at or near the place where Peter Shurtz had his farm or camp. This was 8-9 kms below the later settlement which is called Old Pahreah today. On an 1871 map of Utah, it shows a place called & spelled **Paria** located near the Utah-Arizona state line and on the west side of the creek about where Adairville would later be situated. But that is not a good map! However, on an 1874 map of Utah, and one of better all around quality, it shows **Pah Ria** several kms below The Box, where the Paria cuts through The Cockscomb, and on the east side of the river. This would be the approximate location of Peter Shirts' place.

In the story of John D. Lee, Juanita Brooks mentions a trip to the Paria River in September of 1870 by John D. and Brigham Young. Along the Paria near Peter Shirts settlement, they found some green corn and squash, but Lee didn't like the looks of the place and refused to take any of his wives there to live. The people there at that time must have been part of the Hamblin-Smith group.

In **A Mormon Chronicle: The Diaries of John D. Lee,** he mentions he was in the Pahreah settlement on Sunday, March 3, 1872. In an evening meeting led by Jacob Hamblin, a branch of the Church was organized with Allen F. Smithson to preside, and John Mangum as his 1st councilor. Throughout that time period, Lee was calling the place the **Pahreah settlements**. He often passed through Pahreah on his way to Skutumpah and his Lonely Dell Ranch at Lee's Ferry via the Dominguez Trail.

Herbert E. Gregory thinks that after about 3 years, they were driven out by floods, and couldn't get water in their ditches and onto their fields. At that time, about 1873 or '74, they relocated; some went downstream as did Tom Adair, to settle at what would later be known as **Adairville,** while others went north through The Box of the Paria and founded another settlement site.

An interesting side-note, the 1874 map of Utah also shows **Molly's Nipple, Lake Adair and Swallow Park** for the first time. The 1875 map looks the same as in 1874, but the 1879 version shows Adairville on the east side of the river (people today think it was mostly on the west side), and **Pahreah** above The Box in it's present location. An 1893 map shows Pahreah and Adamsville (a typo error?). Other maps up through 1915 show Pahreah & Adairville (or Adamsville), but on the 1922 version, both are missing. On a 1930 map, both are shown again, but not on later maps.

The second townsite of **Pahreah** did very well at first. They grew fruit & nut orchards, vineyards, vegetable farms, sorghum and raised cattle & sheep. In 1877, Pahreah was large enough to have an organized LDS (Mormon) ward by itself, and was part of the Kanab Stake (a group of regional wards of the LDS Church). According to Thomas W. Smith's family story: *Allen F. Smithson was appointed as the [Pahreah] ward's first bishop. He was the father of Elizabeth J. Smith, mother of the writer of this story. Thomas W. Smith, Sr. was the ward's second and last bishop.*

Pah Ria/Pahreah seems to have been organized as a branch of the Kanab Ward in March of 1872, then later, and at the second townsite with lots more settlers, it became a full ward of the Church.

According to most accounts, by the spring of 1884, the number of people living at Pahreah reached an all-time high. At that time, there were 47 families including 107 members of the Mormon Church, plus a number of other cattlemen and about 20 Piute Indians living there.

But then came a series of floods, the first of which was in 1883. It was followed by the severe winter of 1883-84, then more flooding in the summer of 1884, which washed away farm houses and fields and converted the shallow stream channel into a wash that extended in places from wall to wall across the valley. This spelled doom for Pahreah and people started leaving. By September of 1884, only 48 people remained. The next year, 1885, the Church ward was disbanded. By 1892, only 8 families remained. Incidentally, *Pahreah* is a Piute word meaning *muddy water*.

We know that John W. Mangum, the son of John Mangum, was there from the late 1870's through the mid-1890's with a short stay in Arizona during the mid-1880's. The original Smith family of Thomas W. Smith, Sr. was there into the 1890's, as he was buried there in the cemetery in 1892. Susan R. Smith stayed on and was buried there in September, 1897. See the picture of the memorial in the Pahreah Cemetery. It lists the graves of 13 people buried there. They were Smiths, Smithsons, Twitchells and one Mangum.

The Chynoweths were an important family in Pahreah during its waning years. According to Will Chynoweth's daughter, Mary Jane C. Fuller, Sampson Chynoweth left England in late 1870, and settled at the mining town of Junction south of Marysvale, Utah. Between 1887 & 1892, they were in Antimony and in the cattle business. In the fall of 1892, they moved to Pahreah with a herd of cattle. That fall, Will Chynoweth left his signature in the year 1892 at the bottom of the Lower Trail in Hackberry Canyon. Harvey Chynoweth was born in Pahreah in 1893, and we know at least some of the family was there in 1901. By 1916, Will Chynoweth was there, and that's when he met his wife, who was just passing

Above **Pahreah** in the early 1900's, likely in 1912, when Spencer was mining gold there. Looking south toward The Box of the Paria on the left. To the right of the highest peak is the location of the former Paria Movie Set. Notice the **rip gut or stake & rider** fence in the foreground. (John H. Johnson & Ferrell Brinkerhoff foto)

Above Left John W. Mangum, the son of John Mangum, one of the original setters at Pahreah. J.W.M. lived at Pahreah from 1870-'76, and from 1891-'95. Six of his 13 children were born in Pahreah during those 2 time periods. He died in Cannonville in 1920. (Twila Mangum Irwin foto)
Right Sam Chynoweth and his young wife **Edith** in Lethbridge, Alberta. Sam got into some kind of trouble (he was accused of stealing horses, or something?) and lived in Canada--British Columbia and Alberta--for about 35 years before returning to Henrieville in about 1934. No one around Bryce Valley admits to knowing anything about that part of Sam's life. (Lula Chynoweth Moore foto)

through. Sampson Chynoweth died in Henrieville in 1920.

In Sam Pollock's unpublished life story, he states that in August of 1901, and as a boy of 16, he and a fellow by the name of Butler, were returning from wrangling cows in the House Rock Valley with only the clothes on their backs and a couple of tired, lame horses. They walked into Pahreah barefoot leading their steeds, and were helped by some of the folks. Sam recalled the Chynoweths, Twitchells, and his uncle Seth Johnson as living there at the time. Not far north of Pahreah at the Dugout Ranch, William Swapp was living. Further along, they left one poor horse at the John W. Mangum Ranch, which at that time was just west of Shepherd Point, about 3 kms south of Cannonville. Tommy Richards later bought it and called it the Diamond T Ranch.

In the years following the original exodus, people came and went, but mostly left for greener pastures. However, even in its declining years, Pahreah received a **post office on July 26, 1893**, and Emily P. Adair was the first postmaster. As time went on, things got even worse, and the post office closed on **March 1, 1915**.

In 1912, promoter **Charles H. Spencer** brought his miners up from Lee's Ferry, and tried unsuccessfully to extract gold from the colorful Chinle clay beds. This was after the gold mining failure at Lee's Ferry. In 1921, Spencer once again returned to Pahreah, this time to do some surveys for a pro-

Top Unidentified people and house in **Pahreah** in the early 1900's. (John H. Johnson & Ferrell Brinkerhoff foto) **Above Arthur Chynoweth**, his wife **Roselia** (Rose) holding baby Rhoda, and Hazel (3 years old) at Pahreah in 1922. (Don Chynoweth foto)

posed dam to be located in The Box of the Paria River just downstream from the Pahreah townsite. Add this to the long list of failures for Spencer.

Throughout the early 1900's, there were only one or 2 families living in or around Pahreah at any one time. Their sources of income were from farming & ranching, and supplying sheepmen or goat herders who had large flocks in the region during the winter months.

In the *History of Marian Mangum*, a chapter written by himself and documented in the Mangum family history book, ***John Mangum: Revolutionary War Soldier***, he tells a story of his life in Pahreah beginning in about 1914, after he and the family had been wandering around Idaho and other places:

My father [John Wesley Mangum], John [Long John William Mangum] and I bought the ranch that was once the town of Pahreah in Kane County, where I grew up. The old town had been abandoned several years before and there were only 3 of the old houses remaining. The floods that came down the Pahreah Creek had washed away the land that once was building lots and left high banks.

We 3 farmed together and could raise about anything we wished to plant. We raised molasses cane and made molasses. My father always did the boiling of the molasses in a large vat which was set over a fire in a rock pit. One had to know his business to make good molasses, and Father really did know how. When it was time to cut the cane and make it into molasses, we all worked, children and all. Father always cooked the last batch of molasses into candy. Then we would all get together and have a candy pulling party under the big mulberry trees. One summer we made eight hundred gallons of mo-

lasses.

We raised wagon loads of melons, both watermelons and cantaloupes or muskmelons. Some of the watermelons grew so large a man could hardly lift them. We had a black cow that loved the melons. Every night the children would cut a tub full of melons and feed them to the cow. She would eat all the melons, letting the juice run back into the tub, then she would drink the juice. In 1924 we went to Oregon.....

Marian never states exactly who went to Oregon, but it seems it was just himself. It seems the father, John Wesley Mangum, went to Cannonville, but his brother, known to most people in the area as Long John (because he as so tall and lanky), may have stayed on at Pahreah, living there either full or part-time.

John (Long John) William Mangum and his only son, Herman, lived in the Pahreah area, including the Dugout and Fivemile Ranches, until the mid-1930's, then left for Idaho. In about the same time period as Long John, Jack Seaton was around and he ranched and was the sheepman supplier for awhile. According to Leola Scheonfeld of Kanab, Jack lived in a dugout just southwest of Pahreah for several years. Then on April 2, 1932, Jack Seaton traded his holdings at Pahreah for a home & land in Horse Valley southeast of Henrieville. This trade was with Jim Ed Smith. For 3 full years, Jim Ed Smith, along with his son Layton, lived in Pahreah.

Iris Smith Bushnell of Henrieville, one daughter of Jim Ed Smith, lived at Pahreah part of the time in the early & mid-1930's as a young girl. Here's some of what she remembered:

I was about 10 or 11 years old when Dad & Mother bought that place and we moved down there. Pahreah was a kind of stopping-off place for the stockmen around there. There was a lot of old rock houses and sheds that was left after the floods came and most people moved away. We lived in one of the places. It was a little old log cabin with a room on the back made of lumber. That was the kitchen. The kitchen must have been built with that lumber Dad brought down from the old oil well in the upper Rush Beds.

Dad and Layton, who was my oldest brother, lived there the year-round. They had cattle and a farm, and they raised quite a lot of alfalfa. Dad also went around to the old homes that belonged to the people who left, and fixed 'um up. He had about 10 or 11 of those old log & rock houses fixed up for the stockmen to store their food & supplies in. He charged a little for rent, and he took care of everything for 'um. He made a little money on that.

The rest of the family lived here in Henrieville and we'd go to school here in the winter time. When school was out in the spring, which was usually in April, Dad would come up the creek in a wagon and get us and take us down there. We'd stay down there in the summer and in September he'd bring us back up here to go to school.

At Pahreah, there were lots of fruit trees, including a big mulberry next to the house, but it was nectarines that I remember most. In the summer they raised beautiful melons. We fattened pigs on watermelons. We also had some grape vines, and they did real good too. We were there for several years, then Dad traded Pahreah for a ranch that's down here just south of Cannonville on the Paria Creek.

Layton Smith recalled the family sold [perhaps traded?] their holdings at Pahreah to Roy Twitchell in March of 1935, after living there only 3 years. Roy was old then and most of the work was done by his son Cecil, and a couple of stepsons. The Twitchells stayed on for about 4 years, but it was a tough life. Finally, after the long winter of 1938 & '39 (this may have been the winter of **1936-37** (?), which was the worst in history for that area), the Twitchells apparently just walked off the land and left the country.

Charley Francisco, presently of Tropic, along with his father Charles Edward Francisco, then went down to Pahreah in the spring of 1939 and started planting crops and cleaning ditches. In the meantime, it seems that a man named Burge bought the land for back taxes (?). Burge was from somewhere in the east and never lived at Pahreah. Instead, he collected some rent money from the Franciscos.

Charles E. Francisco and his boy Charley were in & out of Pahreah in the 1930's and knew the country. Charley remembered Charles H. Spencer coming back to Pahreah (with a daughter in her 20's) in

The **Jim Ed Smith family** at **Pahreah**, 1933. From L to R: Marjorie, Flora, Jim Ed, Deward (small boy), Nellie (mother), Alta Rea (little girl), Doris, Laura and baby Ronald, and Iris Smith (Bushnell). The cabin to the right was the last place to be lived in at Pahreah. It had an extensions on the back made with lumber brought down from the old 1930 Rush Beds Oil Well in the Upper or Northern Rush Beds. The cabin to the left is where the girls slept in summer. (Iris Smith Bushnell foto)

the early 1930's (Wallace Ott says Spencer was there in 1932, the year the Lindbergh baby was kidnapped) and was again working on a scheme of some kind. Spencer was old then and was perhaps dreaming of ways to lose more money with another of his gold mining adventures.

Charley Francisco remembered Spencer and Old Pahreah: *We lived up here in Henrieville, and the first time I went down there, they had big vats of mercury--we called it quicksilver then--and that quicksilver got away from 'um and nobody knows where it went. It was a semi-truck load, and that cost a lot of money! They was tryin' to collect gold & silver from them clay beds.*

Jim Ed Smith had built granaries, and stables big enough for 20 head of horses. He had a wonderful place there at Piaria [Pahreah]. All the cowboys & sheepmen left their supplies right there in them big cellars--there was 6 or 8 of 'um. The CCC boys made some of them cellars at Piaria, and the sheepmen used them for their warehouses. That's where the sheepmen headquartered in winter. From Piaria, they went in every direction--but they'd come back once in a while for their supplies--and Jim Ed Smith supplied feed for all their horses. They'd have a big string of pack mules they packed all their supplies back out to their camps with. They only had to come in there every 3 weeks or so and they'd stay over night.

Dad was down there all the time for about 3 years. At that time our family lived up here in Henrieville, and went down to Piaria in summer, but we had to come back to go to school in winter. We raised everything--we had alfalfa, a lot of corn, we raised everything to feed other people's livestock in winter. That country was their winter range. If those cattle would get snowed-in and weak, they'd die before spring, so those guys would gather all the weak ones and herd 'um to Piaria and my Dad would feed 'um. Dad fed a lot of cows for the Kanab ranchers the same way. He'd feed 4 or 5 cows, and they'd give him one. Otherwise the cows would have died.

That cabin Jim Ed Smith lived in and the one the BLM tore down piece by piece and moved back from the river [it burned down in the winter of 1994-'95, but the chimney is still there] was the one we lived in. I graduated from the 8th grade while I was there at Piaria in the summer of 1939. I had to leave school early that spring and go down there with my father and didn't graduate, so they sent me school material and I done it that summer so's I could graduate. At that time I was goin' to school in Cannonville. I was about 17 years old when we finally left Piaria. Me and my father were the last ones to farm there. Everybody had gone, and the mining had gone. If I'm not mistaken, I think we finally left Piaria after the summer of 1941. When the war started, then everybody left the country to get work.

Calvin C. Johnson of Kanab, mentions an interesting event at Pahreah during the summer of 1943. Movie makers went there and filmed a picture about Buffalo Bill and Geronimo. They had 300 Navajos, plus Joel McCrae, Anthony Quinn and Maureen O'Hare. They built a little dam across the Paria inside The Box to back water up during the shooting. You may still see parts of that dam.

The hills around Old Pahreah are very colorful, mostly due to the Chinle clay beds, and because of that, the place became a favorite for movie makers during the 1950's & '60's. For one movie, *Sergeants Three*, they built a model town which later became known as the **Paria Movie Set.** This was in 1962. That fake town was built in a little valley about 1 1/2 kms south of the site of Old Pahreah. The last movie to be made there was in 1973. In 1998, a big flood came down the valley and damaged the set, so between 2000 & 2002 someone partially built another one in the same place. It was rebuilt because this is on the tourist circuit for which Kanab & Kane County depend. But, bad news for everybody, especially western movie lovers, on **August 25, 2006,** somebody set fire to the place and burned it down. As of 2009, there were no plans, or more importantly money, for rebuilding the Paria Movie Set.

At Old Pahreah today, is part of a corral, some fence posts, the chimney of the old cabin that was the last to be lived in, evidence of old ditches & canals and a couple of rock cellars. About 400m southeast of the chimney of the cabin the Smith's lived in, are several rock structures and some remains of the sluicing operation dating from Spencer's time in 1912, 1920 and evidently in 1932. One of these rock buildings is in relatively good condition.

To get to **Old Pahreah,** drive along Highway 89 about halfway between Kanab & Page. Between mile posts 30 & 31, turn north and drive 7.6 kms (4.7 miles) to the site of the Paria Movie Set, and a small campground with toilets & picnic tables (but no water). Just up the road to the north at Km 8.4/Mile 5.2, is the **Pahreah Cemetery** on the left. In 2003, descendants of the original Smith family who settled Pahreah, erected a new iron fence & gate, plus new tombstones. The original grave markers were unreadable and removed. The one large tombstone monument lists 13 people buried there. If you drive beyond the cemetery and about 9.5 kms (5.9 miles) from the highway, is the end of the road at the edge of the river. Park at or near the sign, and walk east across the river to the sites mentioned above. Wear an old pair of shoes, or remove shoes, to wade in the usually ankle-deep water of the Paria River.

To reach the original settlement site on the Paria River which was first called **Rock House,** and/or **Pah Ria** or **Pahreah**; or **Rock House Cove** as it's now called on some maps, drive along Highway 89 about halfway between Page & Kanab. Between mile posts 17 & 18, turn north onto the Cottonwood Wash Road. Drive 15.1 kms (9.4 miles). There you'll see a lone cottonwood tree on the right next to the road. Just east of that is Rock House Cove. It's in the western part of Section 4, T42S, R1W, on any USGS map.

That cottonwood tree is near the north end of a 200m-long line of tamaracks. They're so large, they're almost like trees, but someone set fire to them in about 2000 (?), and what you see today is a lot of younger growth. No one can say for sure if this is the Peter Shirts Homestead, or if it's part of the settlement of Pah Ria, but those tamaracks are (were) the biggest this author has seen, and in a line too straight to have occurred by accident. The author has never found any sign of the rock house, but most people who have seen the cove are convinced this is indeed part of somebody's early homestead dating back to the 1860's or '70's. However, it's very possible the tamaracks got there a little later, because they were first known to exist in St. George only after 1880 (?). The late Kay Clark, formerly of Henrieville, once stated he remembered a pile of rocks towards the south end of that line of tamaracks, but they're not visible today.

As for the people who farmed this part of the Paria shortly after Shirts, all of their farms, ditches, barns and homes, have all been washed away by floods. In fact, that entire valley, which ranges in width from 600-800m, is a virtual river flood plain today. See the aerial foto on page 365.

Adairville is another of the tiny farming & ranching settlements along the middle Paria River. The site of this little cluster of ranches is just north of mile post 22 on present-day Highway 89, about halfway between Page & Kanab. This place is just east of The Cockscomb, whereas Old Pahreah is just to the west of this same cockscomb ridge.

All sources seem to agree that Adairville was first settled in 1873 or '74, by a group of cattlemen, led by Tom Adair. Some of these settlers came down from Rock House/Pah Ria, where Adair had originally

360

settled. In the beginning, Adairville was prosperous, as they farmed the land, planted gardens and raised livestock. According to Gregory, there were 8 families at Adairville in 1878, but they had some of the same problems as the earlier settlers had upstream at Rock House/Pah Ria, and later at Pahreah. They had some floods, which lowered the creek bed, and they couldn't get water to their fields. Also, water in the river in the heat of summer didn't always reach their settlement. Water in the Paria is reliable down to where it crosses The Cockscomb, but below The Box, it gradually seeps into the sands and disappears during early summer. So in 1878, those 8 families left, most of whom went upstream to resettle at what is today Old Pahreah.

In the years after 1878, there was nearly always a rancher or two in the area. The late Kay Clark, said his grandfather Owen Washington Clark, built the cabin, which was later known as the **White House**, in 1887. This is downstream 1 km from where the trailhead to the Lower Paria River is today (all that's left of that homestead is a pile of rocks that appear to be the remains of a chimney on a bench on the east side of the river). After a year or so there, they moved upstream to the area of Adairville and lived there for a couple of years. After that, the family moved upstream to Pahreah for a while, then on up to Bryce Valley in the early 1890's. Read more about the history of the White House in the hiking section under, **Map 29, Buckskin Gulch & Paria River Loop Hike.**

After the Clarks left Adairville, it's not certain just what happened to the place for a number of years, but the late Elbert (Farmer) Swapp of Kanab, remembered some of the later history. Elbert believed the land around Adairville was abandoned from the 1890's until the 1930's. However, the Cross Bar Land & Cattle Company filed on water rights in the area in 1912, according to courthouse records.

Finally the Adairville area was homesteaded by Charley Cram & Charley Mace in the 1930's, but they sold out to Elbert & Orson Swapp in the early 1940's. For many years, the Swapps owned most of the land south of Highway 89. The Swapps built the brick & cement ranch house just southwest of the Paria Ranger Station in the 1940's. Most people refer to this as the **Paria River Ranch.**

Some of the land just north of the highway, and right where Adairville was founded, was homesteaded in the late 1930's by Sandal Findlay. He later sold out to Fay Hamblin and Floyd Maddox. Here's what **Charley Hepworth** of Page told the author in 2009: *Ina Fae Hamblin Frost, who is Fay Hamblin's daughter, she owned it and I bought it from her. MacDonald leased it from her.* Ina Fae's husband was Denzel Frost. The Frosts leased it to the MacDonald family in the 1980's. After Merrill MacDonald passed away, his sons got out of the ranching business. In the late 1980's, Hepworth started buying up the various small parcels of private land that formerly made up old Adairville. As of 2009, Hepworth owns all of what was Adairville, but he leases the eastern part to Western Rock, a big nation-wide outfit; they dug out part of the land as a gravel pit and use the gravel for cement and road base. At the north end of Hepworth's place, they have a new well, a center pivot irrigation system and raise some crops.

Today, there's nothing left to see of old Adairville, except for some of the old trees, ditches, fences and a shed or two (from the early or mid-1900's) near the new gravel pits. In there someplace is one *grave of a Mrs. Goodrich who died in childbirth,* according to Sam Pollock's story, but it's all private land, and permission would have to be granted before entering.

South of Highway 89 and Johnson Store Butte, are now 6-8 new homes forming a rural settlement generally called **New Paria**. Those people commute to Page or Kanab to work each day, or are retired. Halfway between mile posts 21 & 22, and on the south side of Highway 89, is the **Paria River Guest Resort**. They have a small campground, a hostel (including one dorm room with 14 beds, internet connections, hot showers, etc.) restaurant and horseback riding; Tele. 928-660-2674. Also, where you turn south from the highway going up to the West Clark Bench, is the **Paria Outpost & Outfitters**, which has a restaurant (Friday & Saturday night BBQ's) and guided scenic tours (with 4WD's going into the Sand Hills & White Pockets, etc), Tele. 928-691-1047.

The **last cabin** to be lived in at **Pahreah**. The part of this cabin made of lumber was the kitchen, shown here. The lumber was brought down from the old 1930 Rush Beds Oil Well by Jim Ed Smith and Long John Mangum in about 1932. Some of that oil well lumber was also used to build the house at the Fivemile Ranch near the Hattie Green Mine. (Iris Smith Bushnell foto)

IN MEMORY OF

	BORN	DIED
THOMAS W. SMITH	DEC. 23 1815	DEC. 28 1892
SUSAN R. SMITH	SEPT. 2 1813	SEPT. 10 1897
MARY L. SMITH	AUG. 11 1866	SEPT. 10 1880
ELLEN SMITH	DEC. 23 1882	DEC. 26 1882
TABITHA S. SMITH	MAR. 8 1871	JAN. 22 1883
WILLIAM W. SMITH	OCT. 18 1819	DEC. 7 1884
MARTHA A. R. MANGUM	JAN. 26 1849	JULY 4 1890
RUPERTA A. TWITCHELL	JAN. 10 1877	FEB. 15 1879
JOHN S. TWITCHELL	APRIL 1 1891	SEPT. 10 1891
DENNIS A. SMITHSON	MAR. 2 1878	SEPT. 2 1879
ALLEN R SMITHSON	FEB. 11 1816	SEPT. 27 1877
MARGARET L. SMITHSON	MAY 20 1866	MAY 10 1883
SUSAN E. R. SMITHSON	SEPT. 16 1865	JAN. 24 1883

The memorial plaque at the **Pahreah Cemetery** not far north of the site of the former Paria Movie Set. The death dates on this plague gives a short history of the town of Pahreah.

Left Harvey Chynoweth was born in 10/1893 at Pahreah. That was one year after the Samuel Chynoweth family moved there. This picture was taken in about 1915. **Right** Will Chynoweth in what looks like a foto studio setting in 1903. Will was born in 4/1876 in Junction, Utah, making him 27 when this foto was taken. (Lula Chynoweth Moore fotos)

Arthur Chynoweth and his 2 sons on a wagon in 1924. Art was born in Junction, Utah, in 1/1884, and died only 2 years after this foto was taken, in 1926. Lloyd is on the left, with Lawrence on the right. This foto was taken in Henrieville. (Don Chynoweth foto)

Far Left Elije Moore, a long time resident of Henrieville. He ran cattle in the Wahweap Country to as far as Lone Rock and the Colorado River. (Lula Chynoweth Moore foto)

Left Herm Pollock was from Tropic. He found these Anasazi pots in some ruins on West Clark Bench in 1937 while herding sheep. (Afton Pollock foto)

Below Left Harvey Chynoweth, early 1900's. (Iris Smith Bushnell foto)

Below Sam Chynoweth, maybe in Canada (?). (Mary Jane Chynoweth Fuller foto)

The very colorful clay beds of the Chinle Formation. This is the parking place for the **Paria Movie Set**, but the buildings were burned down by vandals in 8/2006.

The same colorful Chinle clay beds as seen above, but this is the **cemetery** for **Old Pahreah**.

This fire place is all that remains of the last cabin to be lived in at **Old Pahreah**. It had been moved back from Paria River flood waters, but was later torched by some vandals back in the 1990's (?).

Looking down onto the rounded **Rock House Cove**--lower half of foto--located 8-9 kms downstream from Old Pahreah. See the main road, and the Y-shaped line of tamaracks; they could only have been planted by a farmer. It's in this area that the settlement of **Pah Rea** was first laid out in about 1870, and first appeared on Utah state maps in 1874.

Geology of the Paria River Drainage

While most people aren't really interested in geology, it's only a matter of time and one or more trips to the Colorado Plateau, before many get hooked. All you have to do is look at a map of the lower 48 states, and you'll see that many of our national parks and monuments are found on the Plateau.

The Colorado Plateau is a vast physiographic region covering the southeastern half of Utah, the northern half of Arizona, the northwestern corner of New Mexico, and the western fifth of Colorado. In other words, it covers the middle third of the Colorado River drainage system.

What makes the Colorado Plateau so unique are the flat-lying rocks. During millions of years while the sediments were being laid down, the land remained relatively flat. Sometimes it was below sea level or was under the waters of a freshwater sea or lake. But always it remained relatively flat, even during this last time period when the entire region was uplifted to create what we have today. And what we have is a colorful and majestic canyon country unequaled anywhere.

Because much of the Plateau is dry and has very little vegetation, the rocks are laid bare, and can be examined by all. This is why so many people become interested in geology when visiting this part of the world.

The Paria River drainage is near the middle of the Colorado Plateau, and has at least its share of unique geologic wonders. The Paria begins at Bryce Canyon National Park and Table Cliff Plateau, and ends at Lee's Ferry on the Colorado River. In between are canyons like Bull Valley Gorge, Deer Creek, Round Valley Draw, the Buckskin Gulch, and the Lower Paria River Gorge. Perhaps the most interesting geologic feature of all is The Cockscomb. All these areas combine to make a fascinating geology field trip.

Geologic Formations and Where They're Exposed

If we follow a line from the top of the Table Cliff Plateau & Powell Point, south to Lee's Ferry on the Colorado River, we'll pass along all, or most, of the formations which are exposed in the drainage. Let's begin at the top of the Table Cliff and run down through the different formations, and where they're most prominently seen. At the end of this list are 3 formations which are exposed in Kaibab Gulch, just west of the Buckskin Trailhead. Two of these are not exposed along the lower Paria River.

Tuff of Osiris It's found only on top of Table Cliff Plateau just north of Powell Point. It's of volcanic origin, as is the top of the Aquarius Plateau, located further north and east.

Variegated Sandstone Member--Claron (formerly the Wasatch) Formation This is usually considered the top of the Claron Formation, and seen only in a few places on the rim of Bryce Canyon N.P. and on top of Table Cliff Plateau. It's more weather resistant, therefore it's a kind of capstone.

White Limestone Member--Claron Formation This is prominently seen all along the rim of the Pink Cliffs in Bryce Canyon, the Sunset Cliffs on the west side of the Paunsaugunt Plateau, and the upper part of Table Cliff Plateau. This and the Pink Limestone below, look nothing like ordinary limestone.

Pink Limestone Member--Claron Formation Seen on the lower slopes of Table Cliff and on Canaan Peak, as well as in Bryce Canyon. In this member are found **Hoodoos** for which Bryce Canyon is famous. It's the same member as is seen in all the Pink Cliffs, the Sunset Cliffs, and in Cedar Breaks National Monument. This crumbly limestone formation is full of iron, which gives it its color.

Pine Hollow Formation An indistinct mudstone strata immediately below the Pink Cliffs of Bryce Canyon and Table Cliff Plateau.

Canaan Peak Formation Another indistinct formation below the Pinks at the bottom of the Table Cliff Plateau. Made up of cobble, pebble, and sandstone conglomerate.

Kaiparowits Formation A slope-maker, made of sandstone, limestone, siltstone and clays, and is seen most prominently east of The Cockscomb, or between Henrieville and the pass between Table Cliff Plateau and Canaan Peak.

Wahweap Formation This is a cliff-making formation, most prominently exposed as the east-side ridge of Cads Crotch, one of the features of the upper end of The Cockscomb. It's a brownish-yellowish sandstone, mudstone, siltstone and shale.

Straight Cliffs Formation This formation is another cliff-maker. It's best seen as the highest ridge of The Cockscomb east of Cottonwood Wash. It also forms the western ridge of Cads Crotch, which is the eastern of the 2 valleys within the larger structure called The Cockscomb.

Tropic Shale The name tells the tale; it's mostly the blueish gray clay beds you see around the town of Tropic, the type location. It's also the grays you see above Henrieville on the way to Escalante. That area is called **The Blues.** Another location is in the lower end of the main valley of The Cockscomb, the Cottonwood Wash. You'll be driving along this gray clay area in the lower 16-18 kms of the Cottonwood Wash Road. It begins just north of Highway 89, and is slick as hell when wet.

Dakota Sandstone This is mostly a light brown sandstone, which makes a prominent cliff, but it also has siltstone and some shale. You'll see this as one of the prominent and intermediate ridges within The Cockscomb Valley which in this case is called Cottonwood Wash. It's the first prominent ridge just west of the gray Tropic Shale.

Henrieville Sandstone The type location for this is near the town of Henrieville. It's seen in only a few areas, from the head or northern end of The Cockscomb, up through Butler Valley and at the head of Round Valley Draw. It's a yellow cliff-making massive sandstone. It's best seen at the Butler Valley Arch, more commonly known as **Grosvenor Arch**. It's that part of the wall from the top of the arch down to ground level. The Dakota Sandstone is immediately above the top of the arch.

There's a question on whether or not the **Morrison Formation** is exposed in this area, especially along The Cockscomb. In the lower end of The Cockscomb, the author sees no gap between the Dakota and the top of the Entrada, but there may be a thin layer of Morrison in there somewhere. Some reports place it there, but those are not detailed reports. Thompson & Stokes leave it out in their studies.

Escalante Member--Entrada Sandstone An indistinct and mostly white sandstone member of the Entrada Formation seen in the upper slopes of Kodachrome Basin, and west of Cannonville.

Cannonville Member--Entrada Sandstone This is a mostly fine-grain reddish-brown to buff-colored sandstone. Its type location are the slopes around Cannonville, but it's also prominently exposed in Kodachrome Basin. It's the white upper slopes and cliffs you see above the more scenic red sandstone in the park, and west of Cannonville.

Gunsight Butte Member--Entrada Sandstone This is the reddish brown sandstone layer you see in the Cannonville Slots southwest of Cannonville and in Kodachrome Basin. In this member, are found

Geology Cross-Section
Table Cliff Plateau to Lee's Ferry

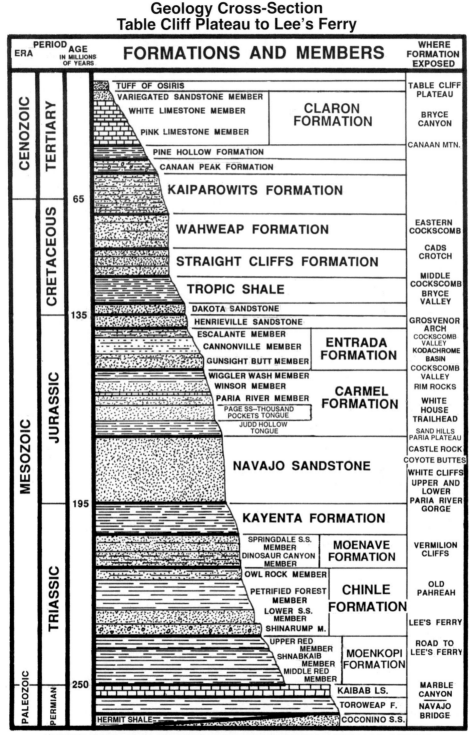

ERA	PERIOD	AGE IN MILLIONS OF YEARS	FORMATIONS AND MEMBERS		WHERE FORMATION EXPOSED
CENOZOIC	TERTIARY		TUFF OF OSIRIS		TABLE CLIFF PLATEAU
			VARIEGATED SANDSTONE MEMBER	CLARON FORMATION	
			WHITE LIMESTONE MEMBER		BRYCE CANYON
			PINK LIMESTONE MEMBER		
			PINE HOLLOW FORMATION		CANAAN MTN.
			CANAAN PEAK FORMATION		
		65	KAIPAROWITS FORMATION		
MESOZOIC	CRETACEOUS		WAHWEAP FORMATION		EASTERN COCKSCOMB
			STRAIGHT CLIFFS FORMATION		CADS CROTCH
			TROPIC SHALE		MIDDLE COCKSCOMB BRYCE VALLEY
		135	DAKOTA SANDSTONE		
			HENRIEVILLE SANDSTONE		GROSVENOR ARCH
	JURASSIC		ESCALANTE MEMBER	ENTRADA FORMATION	COCKSCOMB VALLEY
			CANNONVILLE MEMBER		KODACHROME BASIN
			GUNSIGHT BUTT MEMBER		COCKSCOMB VALLEY
			WIGGLER WASH MEMBER	CARMEL FORMATION	RIM ROCKS
			WINSOR MEMBER		WHITE HOUSE TRAILHEAD
			PARIA RIVER MEMBER		
			PAGE SS--THOUSAND POCKETS TONGUE		SAND HILLS PARIA PLATEAU
			JUDD HOLLOW TONGUE		CASTLE ROCK COYOTE BUTTES
			NAVAJO SANDSTONE		WHITE CLIFFS UPPER AND LOWER PARIA RIVER GORGE
		195	KAYENTA FORMATION		
	TRIASSIC		SPRINGDALE S.S. MEMBER	MOENAVE FORMATION	VERMILION CLIFFS
			DINOSAUR CANYON MEMBER		
			OWL ROCK MEMBER	CHINLE FORMATION	OLD PAHREAH
			PETRIFIED FOREST MEMBER		
			LOWER S.S. MEMBER		LEE'S FERRY
			SHINARUMP M.		
			UPPER RED MEMBER	MOENKOPI FORMATION	ROAD TO LEE'S FERRY
			SHNABKAIB MEMBER		
			MIDDLE RED MEMBER		
PALEOZOIC	PERMIAN	250		KAIBAB LS.	MARBLE CANYON
				TOROWEAP F.	NAVAJO BRIDGE
			HERMIT SHALE	COCONINO S.S.	

ADOPTED FROM: BUSH--GEOLOGY MAP OF THE VERMILION CLIFFS-PARIA CANYON
SCALE 1:62,500, MAPS USGS MF-1475 A, B, C, & D

most of the **sand pipes** in Kodachrome Basin. Another good place to see this one is in The Rimrocks, which is just north of Highway 89 and Paria Ranger Station & Visitor Center. There it's the white cliffs which form the bulk of The Rimrocks. This is just above the colorful Winsor Member of the Carmel Formation. In this location it's mostly white with some reds at the bottom. You can also see this member in the lower end of Cottonwood Wash immediately east of the road. It's the white sandstone monoliths you see standing up alone like icebergs. The **pedestal** parts of the **toadstools** you see in The Rimrocks and along Wahweap Creek are made of this fine-grained white sandstone.

Wiggler Wash Member--Carmel Formation The type location for this strata is in the southern part of Kodachrome Basin where it's a thin gypsum layer just below the red Gunsight Butte Member.

Winsor Member--Carmel Formation This is a mostly sandstone layer you can see just north of the Cottonwood Wash Road in the southern part of Kodachrome Basin. It's largely indistinct there, but the author believes this is the very colorful beds of clayish-looking deposits you see just north of Highway 89, between the eastern side of The Cockscomb to just east of the Paria Ranger Station & Visitor Center (?). These are the purple and white banded layers forming the layer under The Rimrocks Toadstools.

Paria River Member--Carmel Formation These are indistinct beds of mostly sandstone, mixed with thin layers of siltstone, as well as some limestone & gypsum. This one may be seen between the Paria Ranger Station & Visitor Center, and the White House Trailhead.

Thousand Pockets Tongue--Page Sandstone This is a massive sandstone layer, once considered the top of the Navajo. It's type location is in the area just east of the top of the Dominguez Trail & Pass, in the lower end of the Paria. It's the smooth white sandstone you see at the White House Trailhead and around the town of Page, Arizona. White House Spring comes out of the bottom of this tongue. (On the BLM map-guide-booklet, *Hiker's Guide to Paria Canyon*, it shows a geology cross section on page 31. It shows the Temple Cap Sandstone immediately above the Navajo. However, in the source they used, the USGS Bulletin 124, 1989, it states, the Temple Cap Sandstone exists only to the west of Johnson Canyon, which is a few kms east of Kanab.)

Judd Hollow Tongue--Carmel Formation This tongue separates the Page Sandstone from the Navajo below, and is easily seen all along the Cottonwood Wash. It's the first layer above the massive white and yellowish Navajo Sandstone on the west side of the road. You'll also see it as you walk downstream from the White House Trailhead and into the Lower Paria River Gorge. The type location for this member is in Judd Hollow, which is just above where the old Adams Pump still sits in the middle part of the Lower Paria River Gorge.

Navajo Sandstone This formation is probably the most famous and most prominent of any formation on the Colorado Plateau. This is the one in which many of the fantastically narrow slot canyons are made. It is a massive sandstone, up to 600m thick, and is considered by many to be one large fossil sandune. It was created by wind-blown sand, therefore it has lots of crossbedding. The Navajo is seen as the **White Cliffs** between Highway 89 and Cannonville, and in the narrows of Bull Valley Gorge, Round Valley Draw, upper Deer Creek, Castle Rock & Yellow Rock, the Buckskin Gulch, and the Lower Paria River Gorge. It's the Navajo Sandstone which forms the fantastic slopes and colors of the **Teepees** and **The Wave** in the **Coyote Buttes & White Pockets**. It's also seen as the top-most part of the big cliffs making up the **Vermilion Cliffs** exposed on the south side of the Sand Hills/Paria Plateau. Elsewhere, you see the Navajo in the big walls of Zion National Park, all the canyons of the Escalante, throughout the San Rafael Swell, Robbers Roost Country, in the Moab area, and all across the Navajo Nation, which is the type location.

Kayenta Formation Wherever you see the Navajo, you'll see this one just below. Frankly, the author can't remember seeing a geology cross section without these 2 together. The Kayenta is usually a deep reddish brown formation made of mudstone, sandstone and siltstone layers. It normally forms the series of benches just below the Navajo.

Moenave Formation This is the red cliff-maker just below the Kayenta, and above the Chinle clay beds. To the east of the Echo Cliffs Monocline (just east of Lee's Ferry and running south), this one phases into, and is called the Wingate Sandstone. But between the Paria and Zion National Park, it's the Moenave filling the same or similar slot. This formation forms the lower cliffs just above the talus slopes along the Vermilion Cliffs and in the bottom end of the Lower Paria River Gorge.

Owl Rock Member--Chinle Formation An indistinct mostly sandstone layer just below the Moenave cliffs along the base of the Vermilion Cliffs and just above the varicolored banded slopes around Old Pahreah, the site of the former Paria Movie Set and in lower Hackberry Canyon.

Petrified Forest Member--Chinle Formation This is the same formation where all the petrified wood is found in northern Arizona. It's also full of petrified wood along the Paria in Utah. This is the very colorful and fotogenic banded layers of clay you see around the site of Old Pahreah and the former Paria Movie Set. It's this red, purple, green, pink and white layered formation which has attracted movie makers to Old Pahreah throughout the years. It's also seen in lower Hackberry Canyon behind the Frank Watson cabin, and just east of Coyote Wash & north of Coyote Spring along the House Rock Valley Road. It's this bentonite clay that Trevor Leach used to line the bottom of reservoirs with in the Sand Hills so they would hold water.

Lower Sandstone Member--Chinle Formation Another indistinct sandstone bed in the lower part of the Chinle. Probably best seen in the lower end of the Paria around Lee's Ferry and just above the prominent Shinarump Bench.

Shinarump Conglomerate Member--Chinle Formation A white and very course sandstone and pebblestone conglomerate, which forms a very prominent ridge, cliff or bench throughout Utah and northern Arizona. It's white only when disturbed, otherwise it's normally covered with desert varnish and very dark colored (**desert varnish** covers many smooth vertical canyon walls such as those made from Navajo or Wingate Sandstone. It occurs when rain washes minerals from other formations down on some walls. After evaporation, all that's left is a coating of iron-rich minerals that resembles black varnish). In other parts it's called the Black Ledge; because of desert varnish. It's best seen around Lee's Ferry, where it forms what is called Lee's Backbone, which is on the south side of the Colorado River. This member is also full of petrified wood and in some places, uranium. All the uranium mines in the area of Lee's Ferry are in this member of the Chinle.

Moenkopi Formation This is the chocolate brown-colored strata you'll see all across Utah and Arizona, wherever the Chinle's Shinarump Member is found. It makes up the slope below the Shinarump and is composed of clay beds along with sandstone and siltstones. You drive on it as you make the side-trip to Old Pahreah. It's also seen along the road running between the Navajo Bridge/Marble Canyon, and Lee's Ferry.

Kaibab Limestone This formation is seen at the land surface just west of the Buckskin and Wire Pass

Trailheads, and on Buckskin and Fivemile Mountains. It's the capstone along the rim of Kaibab Gulch (that part of the gulch, wash or canyon just above the Buckskin Trailhead). It's this limestone which forms the top layer throughout the House Rock Valley. You are driving atop the Kaibab as you approach Marble Canyon and Lee's Ferry along Highway 89A from either direction. It forms the top layer in Marble Canyon, as seen at the rest stop & visitor center at Navajo Bridge. You can also see the Toroweap and Coconino Formations in Marble Canyon if you stop at the Navajo Bridge on your way to Lee's Ferry.

Toroweap Formation In the Paria drainage, this formation is only seen in Kaibab Gulch, just upcanyon from the Buckskin Trailhead, where the channel cuts deep into Buckskin Mountain.

Hermit Shale This is the lowest or oldest of all formations found in the Paria River system. It's the red rock seen only in the very bottom of the Kaibab Gulch, just upcanyon above the Buckskin Trailhead. Normally the Coconino Sandstone is in that slot, but it's missing in Kaibab Gulch. However, the Coconino is seen just emerging in Marble Canyon below the bridge.

Above Looking southeast toward the **Upper Ferry Terminal**. This is one of 2 old boilers used by Charles H. Spencer during his mining activities at **Lee's Ferry** between 1910 & 1912. This one seems to be the same as the one shown in the mining chapter of this book; a 2nd boiler is half buried in sand closer to the river. The Spencer Trail is to the left just out of sight. The Lee's Ferry Fort and other buildings are within 100m of this boiler.

Left This picture was taken at **Old Pahreah** sometime after Charles H. Spencer was involved with trying to separate gold from the Chinle clay beds starting in 1912. Sitting on top of some of the mining equipment is Rose Chynoweth, wife of Arthur on the right; and Laura Moore Babb on the left. **Arthur and Rose Chynoweth** lived there until about 1922. (Iris Smith Bushnell foto)

369

Mining History: The Paria River Drainage

Coal

Not a lot of mining has occurred in the drainage of the Paria, but in the early days of settlement, coal was mined in various places and used mostly in the blacksmith trade. If you look at **Map 44, Bryce Valley Ghost Towns and Coal Mines**, page 351, and **Map 45, Middle Paria River Mines and Ghosts Towns**, page 355, you'll see coal mines near each of the former or present townsites. Most of the coal mining has occurred in the upper reaches of the Paria northeast of Tropic and north of Henrieville.

The coal mined in Bryce Valley comes from the bottom part of the Straight Cliffs Formation, while that coming from the mine above Adairville comes from the Dakota Sandstone. There are also coal beds in the Tropic Shale, but they're so thin it has always been uneconomical to mine.

The most northerly coal mine in the valley is usually called the **Shakespeare Mine,** but sometimes it's referred to as the **Emma Canyon Mine**. It's located about 11 kms northeast of Tropic, in a little side-drainage of Henderson Valley, called **Emma Canyon.**

The late Herm Pollock believed it was his grandfather William W. Pollock and his brother Jack, who may have been the first to dig coal out of this mine. They were among the earliest settlers to the valley and both were blacksmiths. They needed coal to do their work; on the other hand, Obe Shakespeare, longtime Tropic resident, told the author he never knew coal in his life, until an uncle started mining it not too many years ago. Many Bryce Valley families used cedar (piñon/juniper) wood in their stoves, even though coal was there for the taking.

After the earlier blacksmith days, nothing happened in the coal mining business until the late 1930's. This is when Lewis and Vern Ray (father & son) came into the valley from Orderville, and filed on the mineral rights to the coal in Emma Canyon. They mined coal for 5-6 years, until about the mid-1940's, then sold it to Alton and Vernal Shakespeare. They were the ones who did more mining than anyone. They shipped it to as far away as St. George and Panguitch, but most of it stayed in the valley. The mine was active until perhaps the late 1950's, then business slowed down and it was not used after about 1960. One person thought the state closed it down because of water and safety problems (?).

Finally in 1964, Alton Shakespeare sold the mine for a reported $75,000 to a man from Denver. This new owner was hoping to invest more money in the business and make big profits, but nothing ever happened to the scheme, and coal hasn't been mined there since.

The Shakespeare Mine is located in the bottom part of the Straight Cliffs Formation where there's a total of nearly 4 meters of coal in 4 separate seams. To get to this site (in the NW corner of Section 22, T36S, R2W), drive east out of Tropic on Center Street toward the old townsite of Losee in East Valley. There are several side roads, so follow this map in a northeast direction and straight into Emma Canyon. Stay on this main road, which is generally good for any car. From the main highway in Tropic to the mine is 10.9 kms (6.8 miles). See **Map 44, page 351**.

In the area north of Henrieville are the **Pollock & Davies Mines.** These are both in the Straight Cliffs Formation, and presumably across the narrow canyon from each other (?). Old timers in Henrieville called the one place the **Jack Pollock Mine.** He was one of the earliest settlers in Henrieville and he used the coal for blacksmithing. Today there is little or no evidence this old mine ever existed, but the one just across the canyon did operate for a while and is clearly visible. This was the **Davies Mine.** The author was told of these 2 separate mines, across the canyon from each other, but has only seen the mine on the east side of the canyon. Maybe there was only one mine that had 2 names (?).

Left The hole (dark place below the bright sandstone) seen in the lower right is a shallow adit in **Emma Canyon** and is likely part of the **Shakespear Mine**. Another adit is to the lower left in the shadows. **Right** The remains of a chute at the mine in **Coal Canyon** north of Henrieville.

Map 46, Mine Locations in the Paria River Drainage

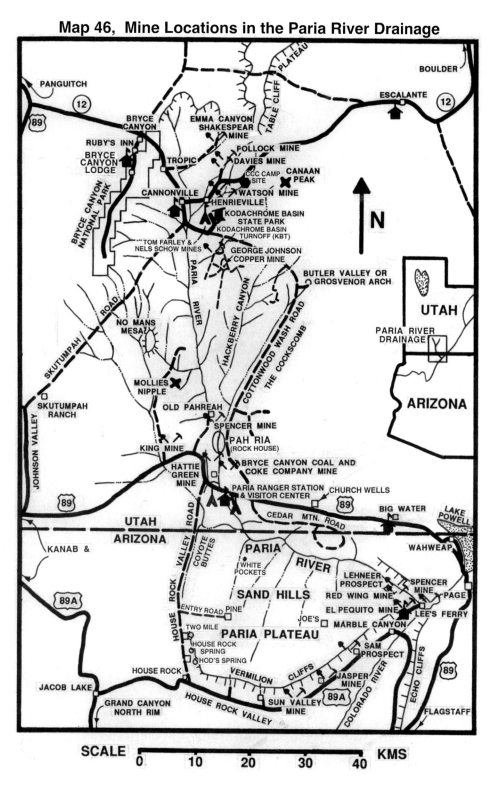

Wallace Ott of Tropic recalled a time he took Byron Davies up **Coal Canyon** and showed him the veins of coal. That was in the early 1940's and after Davies had tried, apparently unsuccessfully, to mine coal from a mine down around Adairville. It was Davies who did some mining in Coal Canyon in the 1940's. He ran a shaft into the beds from 30-50m, but didn't have the money to go into mining big time. The Davies Mine has one vein nearly 3m in thickness; another about 2m thick. The mining that was done was more for a promotional scheme than anything else. Davies, Ott and others, including Alfred Foster, organized the Garfield Coal Company in about 1960, but nothing has happened since.

To get to these old mines, which are supposed to be nearly side by side, drive north out of Henrieville on Highway 12 in the direction of Escalante. After about 5 kms, and between mile posts 32 & 33, turn left, or northwest. The mines are almost due north of that point in Coal Canyon, which is between Jimmie Canyon & Dry Hollow. See **Map 44, Bryce Valley Coal Mines and Ghost Towns**, page 351. From the highway drive west only about 30m on a graded road while crossing a cattle guard, then turn right or north onto a rough dirt track. From there continue north crossing a dry wash for which you may need at least a HCV (cars should be parked there at the dry wash). Continue north for a total of 2 kms (1.2 miles) to where the road is washed out. Stop and park there--don't attempt to go further as there are nearly a dozen washouts between there and the mines. From there it's about 2 kms to the site (located in the north half of Section 36, T36S, R2W). The Davies Mine is on the south side of the canyon, and there is still a pile of coal and a chute at the site. Across the canyon, you can just barely make out a faint line indicating the possible location of the Pollock Mine (?).

Not far south of the mines in Coal Canyon is another old coal mine one old-timer called the **Jack Pollock Mine** (?). It appears Jack Pollock had several mines (?). It's immediately east of Highway 12 between mile post 31 & 32, north of Henrieville. No one alive in Henrieville today knows much about the history of this mine, except that one cold winter day, 2 boys from Henrieville went into the mine and started a fire to get warm. When they left, they failed to put out the fire properly and it started the coal burning. Later the state of Utah had to send men and equipment down to cover the shaft and smother the fire. If you know where to look, you can still see some of the coal from the highway.

There's supposed to be another old coal mine not far east of Henrieville. If you hike on some old roads about 5 kms east of town and into Little Creek, you may see the **Frank Watson Mine**. This is the same man who built the cabin in the lower end of Hackberry Canyon. After he left the Hackberry country, he went to Henrieville for a while, then ran a small store out on Watson Ridge just south of Kodachrome Basin. His hottest seller was rot-gut whiskey known locally as *Jamaica Ginger*. After he left the store, he started working a coal mine in Little Creek, but he apparently only worked that for one winter. The author walked up Little Creek in December of 2003 but never saw anything resembling a mine. And no one in Henrieville today seems to know anything about it or whether or not it exists (?). It's possible a cave-in has occurred hiding the entrance (?).

In the Adairville area, and not far north of Highway 89 & the Paria Ranger Station & Visitor Center, is another old abandoned coal mine. About 2 1/2 kms due north of the site of Adairville, and in a small side-canyon just east of the Paria River, is the site of the **Bryce Canyon Coal and Coke Company Mine**. This old mine is located in the center of Section 21, T42S, R1W, and in the Dakota Sandstone. See **Map 45, Middle Paria River Mines and Ghost Towns**, page 355.

This mine was first opened in the late 1930's by Byron Davies of Cannonville. It's been said he took some good coal out by truck in the direction of Kanab, but apparently he couldn't find a market for it. They mined it for just a couple of years, then sold it to David Quilter in about 1940. No mining ever took

Left Looking down on the **Bryce Canyon Coal and Coke Company Mine**, which is less than 150m from the Cottonwood Wash Road. **Right** Just above the mine you see on the left, and on the rim of the little canyon, are billions of **fossil sea shells** of some kind.

place after that and it was abandoned.

To get there, drive along Highway 89 to between mile posts 17 & 18, about 5 kms east of the Paria Ranger Station, then turn north onto the Cottonwood Wash Road and drive 9.1 kms (5.65 miles). At that point you'll be about 600m west of the only fence & cattle guard around. Park right on the road at or next to a dry creek bed. From where you park, walk southwest about 100m and look right down on the mine, which has one collapsed shaft and a tumbled-down loading chute. Continue south along the east side of the drainage, which by then is a small canyon, and locate a route down the steep slope to the mine. While on the rim, notice what you're walking on. At that point is a broken-up shaley limestone bed which has literally billions of fossil shells roughly 140 million years old. These clam-like shells range in size from your fist down to marble-size.

Copper

Prospecting for copper has been carried on at a number of places in the Paria River drainage, but only a small amount of low-grade copper ore was ever shipped from the **Hattie Green Mine.** The history of this mine goes back to the late 1800's. It was March 8, 1893, that George J. Simonds filed a claim or notice of location on what was called the Hattie Green. Just a few days later, there were several other locations registered in the area just to the north. They were the Silver Queen and Gold King claims which are about 1 km north of the Hattie Green and evidently on top of The Cockscomb (?). These were filed by several members of the Ahlstrom family. In the same time period, Tom Levy, Oren Twitchell and Murphy Alexander filed on what was called the Red Bird Claim. This was just south of The Box of the Paria. Of all these claims, only the Hattie Green saw any mining activity.

According to the late Kay Clark of Henrieville, 2 brothers named Clint & Pat Willis, worked this mine in the late 1910's and early 1920's. They are the ones who did most of the work on the tunnels and adits (test pits) you see, and who lugged out most of the copper ore. Kay Clark did some poking around the place and filed on the old claims in the 1960's, but nothing came of that.

To get to the Hattie Green, located in Section 18, T42S, R1W, turn east from Highway 89 just south of mile post 28. Go through a gate (close it behind you), then cross a sandy wash going south. After a ways, you'll east, then south, then north inside a minor draw within The Cockscomb. From where you park under a big piñon tree, it's about 1 km to the mine, which sits atop The Cockscomb Ridge on the right. If you see any signs along the way indicating **No Trespassing--then stop!** There is some private land to cross before reaching the mine, but heretofore, the owners seem to care less (?). Read more on route details in the hiking section under **Map 27, The Hattie Green Mine Trail & Fivemile Ranch.**

At the mine there are 2 tunnels, one coming in from the east side, the other from the west. **In about 2008, both tunnels were closed** for safety reasons--but here's what you used to be able to see. The west-side tunnel has wooden tracks which small ore cars rolled on within the mine. Deep inside are branch tunnels running left & right. Inside the east-side tunnel is a wooden doorway, a shaft going down to a lower tunnel, and an old hand-cranked wooden hoist. Too bad both of these interesting places have been blocked off. Right on top of the ridge is an ore heap with the turquoise-colored stained rocks still lying there. There are also 3 other adits or test prospects in the area.

There was another attempt to mine copper about halfway up **Rock Springs Bench,** which is south and a little east of Kodachrome Basin. This mine is located in the SE1/4 of the NW1/4 of Section 35, T38S, R2W. A rough track leading to 2 shafts leaves the main road next to a 5m-tall rock pinnacle, as shown on **Maps 15 & 22.** It was called the **George Johnson Mine** and about the only guy around in 2004 who knew much about it was Wallace Ott of Tropic. Here's some of what he remembered:

Left One of 2 shafts at the **George Johnson Copper Mine** on Rock Springs Bench. Sitting is Afton Pollock, and his son Steve. This shaft has a ladder going down but only a fool would use it. **Right** The squy or arasta just downhill to the east from the **Tom Farley & Nels Schow Mines**. Far right is Wallace Ott; next is Afton Pollock, 2 of Bryce Valley's oldest. Picture was taken 3/9/2004.

One of those guys who started that mine was named George Johnson. He had a store in Tropic. and he opened up the first mine back before the turn of the century--in the 1890's sometime. George's brother Sixtus Johnson was there too, along with John Johnson who was their younger relative. George hired some guys to dig a shaft 100 feet [30m] deep and that shaft has still got water in it [it was dry in 2004]. They were after copper and lead--mostly copper, and a little silver. This was called the George Johnson Mine. He's the one that put up the money, but he never actually did any of the digging.

The last time anyone worked out there was in about 1935. I was there part of the time they was diggin' it. They done all their drilling by hand; of course that was Navajo Sandstone and it wasn't all that hard. The guy who done the drilling was Byron Davies, and he had done mining up at Eureka. [Mining and following those veins wasn't easy]. You would start down on a vein and get down maybe 10 or 15 feet [3m to 5m], then it would go off in a different direction.

Byron would go down in the shaft, then they had a pulley-like thing fixed so they could send a 25 gallon bucket down on a cable, then he'd load the rock and a horse would pull it up and dump it. The one that run the horse and pulled the rock out was Clyde Johnson; he was my cousin. They'd a gone down to 100 feet [30m], but they didn't quite make it that far because the water got the best of 'um.

When Byron would blast, he always blasted a kind of a shelf out of the way so that when the bucket was goin' up, he's sit back in this little hole, so if that bucket or cable broke loose, or a rock fell, it wouldn't hit 'im. Then he'd drill again and blast, and of course he'd have to put a long fuse on it--they didn't have electric caps then--so he could get in the bucket and they'd pull 'im out, then the blast would go off. Then they'd have to wait till the smoke and dust got out of there. The smoke from the fuse and dynamite was poison, so they had to wait awhile before he'd go back to work. They put that 2nd shaft down in about 2 weeks. Those shafts are still there, open and dangerous!

The only money I know of that was made from that mine, and I don't know if they paid their expenses or not, was by 2 guys from Cannonville who had a big truck. They went out on that bench and gathered up a lot of ore that was layin' around, with lead and copper, and loaded it up. They loaded that truck several times and took it up to the mill in Midvale, and put it through that mill and they got a little money out of it. But the people that run the mill said it wasn't quite high enough grade, so they quit. They hauled quite a little ore up there, but there wasn't any real money made on it. Loren Twitchell was the one who owned the big White truck. He was in this country truckin' for quite a few years haulin' posts and wood and stuff. And the guy that helped him was Mayben Johnson. Clyde Johnson and Byron Davies were workin' for George Johnson.

Lead

There were 2 small insignificant lead mines in the upper part of the Paria drainage. The site is at the southern end of Watson Ridge, just west of Ott's Corral & Rock Springs Creek, and in the NW1/4 of the SE1/4 of Section 22, T38S, R2W. The mine entrances are 75m apart and 200m west of the Rock Springs Bench Road; while the squy or arasta is 15m west of the same road. **See Maps 15 & 22.** Wallace Ott described the mines as we walked around the place:

They tried to mine it just after the turn of the century. It was a lead mine. Nels Peter Schow was the first one. He dug that tunnel that goes in on the south. Nels told me, he took some powder and another man out there, and after mining awhile, Nels reached down to pick up a rock or something and that other guy who had a pick, run that pick right through Nel's hand. And of course, they was here with only a wagon and they took him to town in that. This would have been in the early 1900's and a little before

Left That part of the **King Mine** that's about 700m east of the Nipple Ranch Road. **Right** The open shaft to the Tom Farley/Wilford Clark Lead Mine. Afton Pollock is on the left.

I was born in 1911.

Then in about 1945, Tom Farley came into this country from Arizona and from near the Mexican border and camped near that mine for one summer. Wilford Clark and his son Kay was grubstakin' 'im. I think they had a claim on it. They was a feedin' Tom while he was workin' at the mine. Tom was tellin' me about the vegetables they brought out here. He had a new .22 rifle and he was always out huntin' rabbits; there used to be quite a lot of rabbits out here. He was eatin' rabbits and that garden stuff the Clarks brought out.

Tom brought the ore down from the shaft on top of the hill to this squy [arasta] which is this round cemented place where he ground up the ore. He had a little motor here to run the squy to drag a big rock around in a circle to grind the ore into a powder, and another little motor to pump water up from Rock Springs Wash. After he'd grind a while, he'd wash the ore out with his hose and down into a chute made with big planks. The chute was lined with burlap and that burlap would catch that heavier metal, then when he figured it was loaded with metal, he's stop the water and let it drain and take up the burlap and wash it out in water and he got quite a lot of pure lead. He had a seamless sack and was going to take that lead up to the mill in Murray [near Salt Lake City] to have it tested.

I'd call the mine on the south side of the hill the **Nels Schow Mine**, *that's the tunnel. And the shaft on top is the* **Tom Farley/Wilford Clark Mine**.

Manganese

Another mining operation took place not far south of Kitchen Corral Point and along the Nipple Ranch Road. This was the **King Mine** and its primary mineral was manganese. See **Map 9**, page 53.

According to Calvin C. Johnson of Kanab, this operation first began sometime in the late 1930's. It was on November 15, 1939, that John H. Brown filed a claim and started mining. It was soon found they couldn't separate the manganese from the bentonite clays of the Petrified Forest Member of the Chinle Formation. After Brown gave up, several Johnson brothers from Short Creek, Arizona (this place is now called Colorado City, Arizona & Hildale, Utah), worked it for 6-8 months. This was in the early 1940's. Then it was abandoned for about a decade.

In 1954 or '55, a bigger outfit came in with a man named Bennett in charge. In the year or two they worked the area, they spent upwards of $250,000 to develop it. They made five small dams in the one little canyon where most of the mining took place. They then built another dam across Kitchen Corral Wash and caught flood waters; plus they used water from some nearby springs. They then pumped this water up the canyon to the five reservoirs, and used the water in the attempt to separate manganese from the clays. At the height of the operation, 20-25 local men worked there. But they also had trouble with separation, and soon closed down.

To see this old abandoned mine, drive along Highway 89 about halfway between Page & Kanab. Just east of mile post 37, turn north onto the Nipple Ranch Road and drive 5.5 kms (3.4 miles). At that point a road runs northeast into a minor canyon. Drive about half a km from the main road and park under a large cedar tree. From there, you can walk upcanyon on an old & partly washed out road about 200m to the old ponds, one mine tunnel, and some loading chutes (it's in the middle of Section 2, T42S, R3W). When you return to the Nipple Ranch Road, turn northwest and drive to Km 7/Mile 4.4 (from Highway 89), and on your right or east about 100m, you'll see some mining scars and an old loading chute on the nearest hillside.

Uranium

In the very bottom end of the Paria River Canyon in the vicinity of Lee's Ferry, and along Highway 89A just under the Vermilion Cliffs, are a number of uranium mines & prospects. These all go back to the 1950's uranium boom days.

If you're coming downcanyon out of the Lower Paria River Gorge, you'll pass the **Red Wing Mine** about 6 1/2 kms up from Lee's Ferry, and about half a km south of the Wilson Ranch site (in the north half of Section 3, T40N, R7E). This mine has 2 tunnels, 13m & 17m long. The adits were tunneled into the Shinarump Member of the Chinle Formation, but the vegetal trash heaps (derived from vegetation such as logs) where the uranium is concentrated, are right at the contact point of the Shinarump above and the Moenkopi below. About half a km upcanyon from the Wilson Ranch is another adit, called the **Lehneer Prospect**. Not much happened there.

Near Lee's Ferry is the **El Pequito Mine**. It's found about 2 kms west of the Lonely Dell Ranch, at the head of a minor canyon just north of Johnson Point. El Pequito is in the Shinarump, but at the contact point of the Moenkopi. Mineralization occurs in an old stream channel in the Shinarump. This mine is found in the northwest corner of Section 14, T40N, R7E.

Going southwest from Lee's Ferry, you'll find the **Sam Prospect** in the southeast corner of Section 2, T39N, R6E. It's about 3 kms west of Vermilion Cliffs Lodge, along Highway 89A, and on the south side of Badger Creek. This adit is in the upper part of the Petrified Forest Member of the Chinle Formation. Not much went on there.

Further along to the southwest is the **Jasper Mine** in the southwest corner of Section 27, T39N, R6E. It's about half a km northeast of Cliff Dwellers Lodge and about 100m from the highway. It too was located at or near the contact point of the Shinarump and Moenkopi. They found small amounts of many minerals, including copper staining, but not much else.

The only real uranium mine in these parts was the **Sun Valley Mine**. It's 5 kms southwest of Cliff Dwellers Lodge, and in the south half of Section 6, T38N, R6E. At the time it was studied by Lane & Bush, this mine was owned and operated by Intermountain Exploration Co. The mine was started in 1954 during a period of intense uranium exploration in the area. An inclined shaft was sunk on a Shinarump outcropping, with the ore being on the contact with the Moenkopi. Several hundred tons of high grade uranium ore was shipped before the shaft was filled with mud from a flash flood. Later, a vertical shaft was sunk, and a drift was driven to connect with the old, sand-filled workings, but there was no further production. The Sun Valley Mine has been worked in recent years on a sporadic basis. Today most of these old mines and prospects are included in the new Vermilion Cliffs National Monument.

Gold

The story of gold mining along the Paria River is also the story of **Charles H. Spencer**. As one writer put it, *"he seemed to enjoy the pursuit more than the gold itself, especially when it meant spending other peoples money looking for it."*

Spencer first arrived in the Colorado River country in 1909, where he set up an operation on the lower San Juan River far upstream from Lee's Ferry on the Colorado. There he was trying to separate gold from the Wingate Sandstone. While there, a couple of prospectors told him about the possibilities of finding gold in the Chinle Formation at Lee's Ferry, and that coal existed north of the Colorado River a ways. With that tip, he made tracks for Lee's Ferry, arriving there in April, 1910.

On arriving at the Ferry, Spencer looked things over and decided the Chinle clays 300m from the river could be a possibility. He speculated that a boiler could power a high pressure hose, which could wash the clays & shales down to the river where gold could then be recovered with the help of an amalgamator. But his first job was to send his men out to look for the promised coal field. It was found in a side-drainage of Warm Creek called **Crosby Canyon**, about 45 kms upstream in Glen Canyon.

While the hunt for coal went on, Spencer began experimenting with power dredging at Lee's Ferry. At first he used wood to power the boiler. He then set up power hoses to wash the gold-bearing clays down to a sluice and amalgamator at the river. Gold is indeed in the Chinle, but it's in the form of very fine dust. The method used to separate the gold from the clay, was to run the muddy water over the amalgamator which had mercury in the bottom. The mercury was supposed to absorb and trap the gold, allowing other materials to pass over. But instead, the operation merely clogged the amalgamator, and the mercury did not absorb the gold. While chemists worked on the problem, Spencer was thinking about how to get the coal from Warm Creek to Lee's Ferry.

At first it was thought coal could be brought in by mule, using an old trail called the **Dominguez or Ute Trail**, which entered the canyon about 5 kms above the Ferry. Because of the extra distance, it was decided to make a shortcut route directly above the operation on the Colorado. So in the fall of 1910, Spencer and his men constructed the **Spencer Trail** from the river to the top of the cliffs. From there it was hoped they could head northeast with mules for the Warm Creek coal fields. But the trail was never used to bring in coal; instead, it was more of an promotional scheme than anything else. Spencer finally decided to bring coal downriver in a boat.

The next job was to build a wagon road right down the dry stream bed of Warm Creek to the Colorado River. While workers were building the road, others were building a barge on the banks of the river. This all went well; they brought coal down the canyon, loaded it onto the barge, then floated it down to Lee's Ferry. But then the problem was to get the barge back upstream.

This problem, it was thought, could be solved by a tugboat of some kind. So with more investors money, a 9m-long tug boat called the **Violet Louise,** was purchased and brought to Lee's Ferry. As it turned out, it was far too underpowered to push a large barge upstream against the current. The current wasn't that fast, but pushing a barge wasn't easy.

While Spencer worked on problems at the Ferry, the managers of the Chicago company he worked for, ordered a steam-powered boat from San Francisco. The boat was built in 1911, dismantled, and shipped by train to Marysvale, Utah, the end of the railway line at the time. It was then put onto large wagons for the remainder of the 320 km trip to the mouth of Warm Creek. There it was reassembled in the spring of 1912 and it was the biggest thing to ever sail the Colorado River above the Grand Canyon. It measured 28m x 8m, was powered by a coal boiler, and had a 4m-wide stern paddle wheel. Even though this part of the project wasn't one of Spencer's ideas, the boat was named the **Charles H. Spencer.**

The next problem was to find a crew for the boat. This wasn't easy in the middle of the desert, but they found a crew anyway, with a fellow by the name of Pete Hanna at the helm, the only crew member who had any experience with boats. They loaded the deck full of coal for the trial run. But almost immediately, they hit a sandbar. Then another. Finally Hanna turned the boat around and allowed it to sail down the river backwards, which gave it better maneuverability. They spent one night in the canyon, then finished the 45 km run to Lee's Ferry the next morning.

They then had to figure out how to get the steamer back upstream against the current, which was stronger than anyone had expected. Hanna decided to keep most of the coal which had been brought down on board, to ensure passage back up to Warm Creek. This was a good move, because they barely made it back to Warm Creek. They again loaded the boat as full as possible, and returned to Lee's Ferry, where it sat for a couple of months. All this, while the chemists and the workers figured out what to do about separating the gold from the Chinle clays.

Finally it was decided to try something different. They ended up towing the original barge upstream with the Spencer. This worked fine. They then loaded both the barge and the steamer with coal. The barge was then allowed to drift downstream with several workers guiding it around the sandbars, with the Spencer following. This worked fine too, and it appeared they had this part of the gold mining problem solved. The only thing left to do was find a successful way to get the gold out of the clay. This Spencer was never able to do, and the steamboat had made its last run.

Spencer left Lee's Ferry later in 1912, bound for the nearly abandoned settlement of Pahreah. Meanwhile, the steamship *Charles H. Spencer* sat on the river tied to the bank. In 1915, the combination of high water and piles of driftwood, put the boat on its side and it sank in one meter of water. Later, parts were stripped off and taken away, and some of the lumber from its decks was used for various projects. Today, you can just barely see the sunken remains of the boat and its boiler just upstream from Lee's Fort, at the bottom end of the Spencer Trail. Nearby are 2 boilers used for mining, and parts of the stern paddle wheel. Just north of the boiler one can still see scars where they operated the power sluicing machinery. The best sources of information about the history of Lee's Ferry is found in the books, **Desert River Crossing** and **Lee's Ferry.** See **Further Reading** in the back of this book for more.

From Lee's Ferry, Spencer moved his operations to Pahreah. He was accompanied by Herbert A. Parkyn. The new dream was to extract gold from the same Chinle clays at Pahreah, but they failed at that too. They did however set up some stone buildings at Pahreah, and tried some sluicing. These sites are still there at Old Pahreah today. Several attempts were made to refinance new schemes, including building a dam across The Box of the Paria River just below the Old Pahreah townsite, but that too failed to bring in more money. That was in 1921. In 1932, he again returned to Pahreah to look things over, this time with his daughter, but nothing came of that.

Charles H. Spencer was in and out of Pahreah and Lee's Ferry all his life, but he never made a dime from any of his big-time mining schemes.

This unusual monument is located on Highway 89 at the **turnoff to Old Pahreah**. The plaque tells a little history of the town. In the far background to the left is Mollies Nipple.

Top These are workmen starting to build the **Charles H. Spence steamboat** at Lee's Ferry. Trevor Leach has this high quality foto, and he says one of the men you can barely see in the background is his father, **Albert or Bert Leach**. The picture was taken in 1912.

Below Left This boiler, belonging to Charles H. Spencer's mining operation, is heading for either Lee's Ferry or Pahreah (?). It appears there are several ox teams pulling wagon loads of supplies coming down a narrow canyon. (John H. Johnson & Ferrell Brinkerhoff foto)

377

Above Charles H. Spencer right (facing camera) working with vats of mercury trying to extract gold from the Chinle clays at **Pahreah**. Charles Edward Francisco is in the middle with his back to the camera.
Right Spencer's mining operation at Pahreah. Some of this stuff is still there and visible today.
Below Ox teams pulling wagons with mining supplies, apparently from Lee's Ferry to Pahreah. All fotos were taken at **Pahreah** in 1912. (John H. Johnson & Ferrell Brinkerhoff fotos)

This stone cabin & cellar at **Old Pahreah** were built by Charles H. Spencer in 1912. He was trying to extract gold from the Chinle clay beds behind the camera. These are located on the east side of the Paria River and in the southeastern part of what was the farming community of Pahreah.

This is the boiler Charles H. Spencer used while at **Lee's Ferry**. This foto was taken in 1911 or 1912 when mining was in full operation. This boiler is still at Lee's Ferry near the bottom of the Spencer Trail, and where the steamship *Charles H. Spencer* is sitting in the waters of the Colorado. (This picture was taken from an information board at Lee's Ferry--National Park Service foto)

This is all that's left of the steamship *Charles H. Spencer*. This sign and the remains are immediately below the trail that runs upriver to the Upper Ferry Terminal at **Lee's Ferry**.

The steamship *Charles H. Spencer* as it appeared in August, 1915. Today, all you'll see is the half-submerged boiler and other parts in the cold, clear waters of the Colorado River. There's a sign marking the place just below the beginning of the Spencer Trail, and along the path to the Upper Ferry Terminal. See picture above. (E.C. La Rue & USGS foto)

Map 47, Bryce Valley and Skutumpah Road Ranches

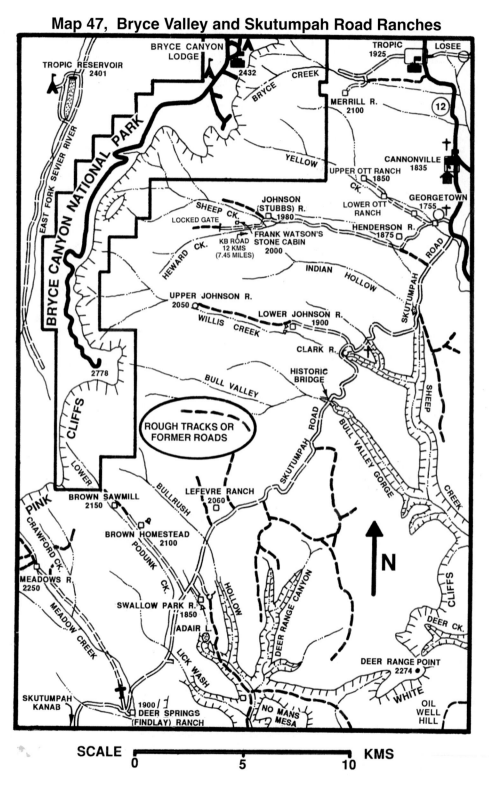

TROPIC RESERVOIR 2401

BRYCE CANYON LODGE

TROPIC 1925

LOSEE

2432

BRYCE CREEK

MERRILL R. 2100

(12)

EAST FORK SEVIER RIVER

BRYCE CANYON NATIONAL PARK

YELLOW

CANNONVILLE 1835

UPPER OTT RANCH 1850

CK.

SHEEP CK.

JOHNSON (STUBBS) R. 1980

LOWER OTT RANCH

GEORGETOWN 1755

LOCKED GATE

FRANK WATSON'S STONE CABIN 2000

HENDERSON R. 1875

HEWARD CK.

KB ROAD 12 KMS (7.45 MILES)

INDIAN HOLLOW

SKUTUMPAH ROAD

UPPER JOHNSON R. 2050

LOWER JOHNSON R. 1900

WILLIS CREEK

CLARK R.

2778

BULL VALLEY

HISTORIC BRIDGE

SHEEP

CLIFFS

LOWER

ROUGH TRACKS OR FORMER ROADS

SKUTUMPAH ROAD

BULL VALLEY GORGE

CREEK

PINK

BROWN SAWMILL 2150

BULLRUSH

LEFEVRE RANCH 2060

N

CRAWFORD CK.

BROWN HOMESTEAD 2100

PODUNK CK.

DEER RANGE CANYON

CLIFFS

MEADOWS R. 2250

MEADOW CREEK

SWALLOW PARK R. 1850

HOLLOW

DEER CK.

ADAIR L.

SKUTUMPAH KANAB

LICK WASH

DEER RANGE POINT 2274

1900 /1

DEER SPRINGS (FINDLAY) RANCH

NO MANS MESA

WHITE

OIL WELL HILL

SCALE

0   5   10

KMS

Further Reading

History Books
A Mormon Chronicle: The Diaries of John D. Lee--1848-1876, Edited and Annotated by Robert G. Cleland and Juanita Brooks, University of Utah Press, Salt Lake City, Utah
Desert River Crossing, Historic Lee's Ferry on the Colorado River, 3rd Edition, Rusho-Crampton, Tower Productions, Salt Lake City & St. George, Utah.
Ebenezer Brown and his Descendants, Jennie Brown Hollist, 1979, Bob Davis Publishing Company.
Emma Lee, Juanita Brooks, Utah State University Press, Logan, Utah.
Golden Nuggets of Pioneer Days--A History of Garfield County, Daughters of Utah Pioneers, Panguitch, Utah.
History of Kane County, Daughters of Utah Pioneers, Kanab, Utah.
John Doyle Lee, Zealot-Pioneer Builder-Scapegoat, Juanita Brooks, A.H. Clark Co.
John Mangum: Revolutionary War Soldier, Mangum Family History Compiled by Dallas Mangum.
Lee's Ferry, A Crossing of the Colorado River, Measeles, Pruett Publishing.
Lee's Ferry and Lonely Dell Ranch Historic Districts, (a booklet) Grand Canyon Natural History Association, South Rim-Grand Canyon, Arizona.
Lee's Ferry: From Mormon Crossing to National Park, P. T. Reilly, Utah State University Press, Logan, Utah.
Mountain Meadows Massacre, Juanita Brooks, University of Oklahoma Press.
Some Dreams Die, Utah's Ghost Towns, George A. Thompson, Dream Garden Press.
The Red Hills of November: A Pioneer Biography of Utah's Cotton Town, Andrew Karl Larson, The Deseret News Press, Salt Lake City, Utah.
Utah Ghost Towns, Stephen L. Carr, Western Epics.
Utah--Since Statehood, *Historical & Biographical,* Volume IV, The S.J. Clarke Publishing Co., 1920.

Geology
Chinle Formation of the Paria Plateau, J. P. Akers, Masters Thesis, University of Arizona, 1960.
Geology of Bryce Canyon National Park, Lindquist, Bryce Canyon Natural History Association.
Geology of Kane County, Utah, Doelling, Davis & Brandt, USGS Bulletin 124, 1989.
Geology of Table Cliff Region, Utah, Bowers, Bulletin 1331-B, USGS, 1972.
Geology of Utah's Parks and Monuments, Sprinkel, Chidsey & Anderson, Utah Geological Association, Salt Lake City, Utah.
Mine and Prospect Map, Vermilion Cliffs, USGS Map MF-1475-D, Miscellaneous Field Studies (also contains maps A, B & C).
Map-Geology of the Kaiparowits Plateau, Carter & Sargent, USGS Map I-1033-K.
Sandstone and Conglomerate-Breccia Pipes and Dikes of the Kodachrome Basin Area, Kane County, Utah, Cheryl Hannum, Masters Thesis, Brigham Young University, 1979.
Stratigraphy of the Dakota and Tropic Formations, Lawrence, Bulletin 19, Utah Geological Survey, 1965.
Stratigraphy of the San Rafael Group, Southwest and South Central Utah, Thompson & Stokes, Bulletin 87, USGS, October 1970.
The Geology and Geography of the Paunsaugunt Region, Utah, Gregory, Professional Paper 226, USGS.
The Kaiparowits Region, Gregory & Moore, Professional Paper 164, USGS.

Magazines and Unpublished Manuscripts & Family Histories
A Brief History of Early Pahreah Settlements, Thomas W. Smith (Thayne Smith of Kanab, Utah).
An Episode of Military Exploration and Surveys (A survey party's account of riding up the Paria River Gorge), The United Service, Vol. 5, Number 119, October 1881.
Biography of John G. Kitchen, J. G. Kitchen Jr., Kanab, Utah, 1964.
California Condors, Updates on restocking public lands with condors: from Arizona Desert Digest, Arizona Game & Fish Department, and The Peregrine Fund.
Desert Bighorn Sheep Restocking, Arizona Game & Fish Department, Wildlife Surveys & Investigations, 1984.
First Motor Sortie into Escalante Land, Breed, National Geographic Magazine, September, 1949.
History of Deer Spring Ranch, Graden Robinson, Kanab, Utah.
History of Peter Shirts [Shurtz] and his Descendants, Ambrose Shurtz, 1963, unpublished family history, but available at Special Collections, BYU Library, Provo, Utah. (Soon a real book may be published?)
Historic Utilization of Paria River, P. T. Reilly, Utah Historical Quarterly, Vol. 45, Number 2, 1977.
Lee's Ferry at Lonely Dell, Juanita Brooks, Utah Historical Quarterly, Vol. 25, 1957.
Samuel & Emily Pollock, compiled by Afton Pollock, Tropic, Utah.
Things That Remind me of my Brother: Herman Pollock, compiled by Afton Pollock, Tropic, Utah.
Vegetation and Soils of No Man's Mesa, Utah, Mason & others, Journal of Range Management, January, 1967.
William Chynoweth: An American Cowboy, Mary Jane Chynoweth Fuller, Orem, Utah

Other Guidebooks by the Author

Books listed in the order they were first published. Some are momentarily out-of-print; others may never be reprinted. (Prices as of May, 2010, and may change without notice)

Climber's and Hiker's Guide to the World's Mountains (4th Edition), Kelsey, 1248 pages, 584 maps, 652 fotos, ISBN 0-944510-18-3. US$36.95 (Mail Orders US$40.00).

Utah Mountaineering Guide (3rd Edition), Kelsey, 208 pages, 143 fotos, 54 hikes, ISBN 0-944510-14-0. US$10.95 (Mail Orders US$13.00).

China on Your Own: and *Guide to China's Nine Sacred Mountains*, Kelsey, **Out of Print.**

Non-Technical Canyon Hiking Guide to the Colorado Plateau (5th Edition), Kelsey, 384 pages, 120+ hiking maps, **285 color fotos**, new ISBN 978-0-944510-22-3. US $19.95 (Mail Orders US$22.00).

Hiking and Exploring Utah's San Rafael Swell (3rd Edition), Kelsey, 224 pages, 32 mapped hikes, plus History & Geology, 198 fotos, ISBN 0-944510-17-5. US$12.95 (Mail Orders US$15.00).

Hiking and Exploring Utah's Henry Mountains and Robbers Roost, *Including The Life and Legend of Butch Cassidy,* (3rd Edition), Kelsey, 288 pages, 38 hikes or climbs, **311 mostly color fotos**, ISBN 978-0-944510-25-4. US$15.95 (Mail Orders US$18.00).

Hiking and Exploring the Paria River, *Including: The Story of John D. Lee & the Mountain Meadows Massacre,* (5th Edition), Kelsey, 384 pages, 41 mapped hiking areas from Bryce Canyon to Lee's Ferry, **523 mostly color fotos**, ISBN 978-0-944510-26-1. US$19.95 (Mail Orders US$22.00).

Hiking and Climbing in the Great Basin National Park--*A Guide to Nevada's Wheeler Peak, Mt. Moriah, and the Snake Range,* Kelsey, **Out of Print.**

Boater's Guide to Lake Powell (5th Edition), *Featuring: Hiking, Camping, Geology, History & Archaeology,* Kelsey, 288 pages, **263 color fotos**, new ISBN 978-0-944510-24-7. US$19.95 (Mail Orders US$22.00).

Climbing and Exploring Utah's Mt. Timpanogos, Kelsey, 208 pages, 170 fotos, ISBN 0-944510-00-0. US$9.95 (Mail Orders US$12.00). **Out of Print, but will be updated in a few years.**

River Guide to Canyonlands National Park & Vicinity, Kelsey, 256 pages, 151 fotos, ISBN 0-944510-07-8. US$11.95 (Mail Orders US$14.00). **Out of Print for a few years.**

Hiking, Biking and Exploring Canyonlands National Park & Vicinity, Kelsey, 320 pages, 227 fotos, ISBN 0-944510-08-6. US$14.95 (Mail Orders US$17.00). **Out of Print for a few years.**

Life on the Black Rock Desert: A History of Clear Lake, Utah, Venetta B. Kelsey, 192 pages, 123 fotos, ISBN 0-944510-03-5. **Out of Print for a few years.**

The Story of Black Rock, Utah, Kelsey, 160 pages, 142 fotos, ISBN 0-944510-12-4. US$9.95 (Mail Orders US$12.00).

Hiking, Climbing & Exploring Western Utah's Jack Watson's Ibex Country, Kelsey, 272 pages, 224 fotos, ISBN 0-944510-13-2. US$9.95 (Mail Orders US$12.00).

Technical Slot Canyon Guide to the Colorado Plateau, 2nd Edition, Kelsey, new ISBN 978-0-944510-23-0, 336 pages, **341 color fotos**. US$19.95 (Mail Orders US$22).

Here are 2 of the later historical structures at **Lee's Ferry**. The one on the right is the **Spencer Bunkhouse**, apparently built to house Charles H. Spencer's crew while he was there in the gold mining business from 1910 to 1912. The other building on the left is the **USGS residence**.

Distributors for Kelsey Publishing

Primary Distributor All of Michael R. Kelsey's books are sold by this distributor. A list of Kelsey's titles is shown on the previous page.
Brigham Distribution, 110 South, 800 West, Brigham City, Utah, 84302, Tele. 435-723-6611, Fax 435-723-6644, Email brigdist@sisna.com.

Most of Kelsey's books are sold by these distributors.

Alpenbooks, 4206 Chennault Beach Road, Suite B1, Mukilteo, Washington, USA, 98275, Website *alpenbooks.com*, Email cserve@alpenbooks.com, Tele. 425-493-6380, or 800-290-9898.
Books West, 11111 East, 53rd Avenue, Suite A, Denver, Colorado, USA, 80239-2133, Tele. 303-449-5995, or 800-378-4188, Fax 303-449-5951, Website *bookswest.net*.
Liberty Mountain, 4375 West 1980 South, Suite 100, Salt Lake City, Utah, 84104, Tele. 800-578-2705 or 801-954-0741, Fax 801-954-0766, Website *libertymountain.com*, Email sales@libertymountain.com.
Treasure Chest Books, 451 North, Bonita Avenue, Tucson, Arizona, USA, 85745, Tele. 520-623-9558, or 800-969-9558, Website *treasurechestbooks.com*, Email info@rionuevo.com.

Some of Kelsey's books are sold by the following distributors.

Canyonlands Publications, 4860 North, Ken Morey Drive, Bellemont, Arizona, USA, 86015, Tele. 928-779-3888, or 800-283-1983, Fax 928-779-3778, Email info@clpbooks.net.
High Peak Books, Box 703, Wilson, Wyoming, USA, 83014, Tele. 307-739-0147.
Rincon Publishing, 1913 North Skyline Drive, Orem, Utah, 84097, Tele. 801-377-7657, Fax 801-356-2733, Website *RinconPub@UtahTrails.com*.
Recreational Equipment, Inc. (R.E.I.), 1700 45th Street East, Sumner, Washington, USA, 98390, Website *rei.com*, Mail Orders Tele. 800-426-4840 (or check at any of their local stores).
Online--Internet: *amazon.com; adventuroustravelers.com; btol.com* (Baker-Taylor); *Ingrams.com; Bdaltons.com; borders.com* (teamed with amazon.com).

For the **UK and Europe**, and the rest of the world contact: **Cordee**, 3a De Montfort Street, Leicester, England, UK, LE1 7HD, Website *cordee.co.uk*, Tele. Inter+44-116-254-3579, Fax Inter+44-116-247-1176.

This building is known as **Lee's Fort**, and is situated at Lee's Ferry. Just to the left and out of sight is the American Placer Corp. Office. The plaque you see at the bottom of this picture was put there by the Daughter's of the Utah Pioneers in 1968. It reads:

LEE'S FERRY
John D. Lee settled here in Dec. 1871 and established ferry service thirteen months later [January, 1872]. After her husband's death, Warren M. Johnson ran the oar-driven ferry for Emma Lee, 1875 to 1879, when the Church of Jesus Christ of Latter-day Saints purchased her interest. Johnson served until 1895. He was followed by James S. Emett who sold to the Grand Canyon Cattle Company in 1909. Coconino Country operated the ferry from 1910 to 1928.